P9-CLU-660

AROUND MEXICO CITY
Pages 130–57

THE GULF COAST
Pages 238–55

THE YUCATÁN PENINSULA
Pages 256–87

• Monterrey

• Zacatecas

THE COLONIAL HEARTLAND

Guanajuato •
• Querétaro

Morelia •

MEXICO CITY
Puebla • • Xalapa
Taxco • AROUND MEXICO CITY

SOUTHERN MEXICO
Pages 212–37

• Mérida
THE YUCATÁN PENINSULA
• Campeche

Chetumal •

THE GULF COAST

SOUTHERN MEXICO
• Acapulco
Oaxaca • • Tuxtla Gutiérrez

0 kilometers   250

0 miles   250

MEXICO

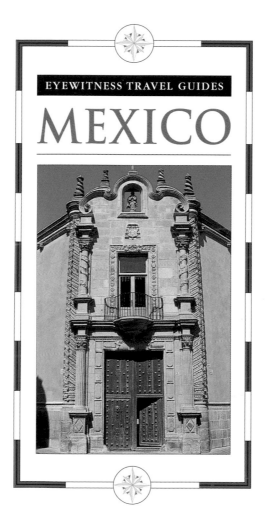

EYEWITNESS TRAVEL GUIDES

MEXICO

DK

LONDON, NEW YORK,
MELBOURNE, MUNICH AND DELHI
www.dk.com

PROJECT EDITOR Nick Inman
ART EDITORS Stephen Bere, Marisa Renzullo
EDITORS Elizabeth Atherton, Claire Folkard, Emily Green,
Freddy Hamilton, Jane Oliver, Sophie Warne, Lynda Warrington
US EDITOR Mary Sutherland
DESIGNERS Gillian Andrews, Jo Doran, Paul Jackson,
Tim Mann, Nicola Rodway
MAP CO-ORDINATOR David Pugh
RESEARCHER Eva Gleason
PICTURE RESEARCHERS Monica Allende, Ellen Root
DTP DESIGNER Maite Lantaron, Pamela Shiels

MAIN CONTRIBUTORS
Nick Caistor, Maria Doulton, Petra Fischer, Eduardo Gleason, Phil Gunson,
Alan Knight, Felicity Laughton, Richard Nichols, Chloë Sayer

CONSULTANTS
Antonio Benavides, Simon Martin, Lourdes Nichols

MAPS
Michael Bassett, Sharon O'Reilly, Richard Toomey (ERA-Maptec Ltd)
(BIMSA Cartosistemas, S.A. de C.V.)

Reproduced by Colourscan (Singapore)
Printed and bound by South China Printing Co. Ltd.

First American Edition, 1999
03 04 05 10 9 8 7 6 5 4 3

Published in the United States by Dorling Kindersley Publishing, Inc.,
375 Hudson Street, New York, New York 10014

Reprinted with revisions 2001, 2002, 2003
Copyright © 1999, 2003 Dorling Kindersley Limited, London

ALL RIGHTS RESERVED UNDER INTERNATIONAL AND PAN-AMERICAN
COPYRIGHT CONVENTIONS. NO PART OF THIS PUBLICATION MAY BE REPRODUCED,
STORED IN A RETRIEVAL SYSTEM, OR TRANSMITTED IN ANY FORM OR BY ANY MEANS,
ELECTRONIC, MECHANICAL, PHOTOCOPYING, RECORDING, OR OTHERWISE,
WITHOUT PRIOR WRITTEN PERMISSION OF THE COPYRIGHT OWNER.
PUBLISHED IN GREAT BRITAIN BY DORLING KINDERSLEY LIMITED.

ISSN 1542-1554
ISBN 0-7894-9720-4

THROUGHOUT THIS BOOK, FLOORS ARE REFERRED TO IN ACCORDANCE WITH EUROPEAN
USAGE, I.E., THE "FIRST FLOOR" IS THE FLOOR ABOVE GROUND LEVEL

**The information in this
Eyewitness Travel Guide is checked regularly.**
Every effort has been made to ensure that this book is as up-to-date
as possible at the time of going to press. Some details, however,
such as telephone numbers, opening hours, prices, gallery hanging
arrangements and travel information are liable to change. The
publishers cannot accept responsibility for any consequences arising
from the use of this book, nor for any material on third party
websites, and cannot guarantee that any website address in this
book will be a suitable source of travel information. We value the
views and suggestions of our readers very highly. Please write to:
Publisher, DK Eyewitness Travel Guides,
Dorling Kindersley, 80 Strand, London WC2R 0RL, Great Britain.

Produced with the generous help of the Proyecto México, Dirección
de Divulgación, Coordinación Nacional de Difusión, Instituto Nacional
de Antropología e Historia, Córdoba 45, Col. Roma, Delegación
Cuauhtémoc, CP 06700, Mexico

◁ The Maya site of Tulum in the Yucatán Peninsula

Plaza Santo Domingo in Oaxaca

CONTENTS

HOW TO USE
THIS GUIDE 6

INTRODUCING
MEXICO

PUTTING MEXICO
ON THE MAP 10

Mural on the Teatro de los
Insurgentes in Mexico City

A PORTRAIT OF
MEXICO 12

MEXICO THROUGH
THE YEAR 30

THE HISTORY OF
MEXICO 38

MEXICO REGION BY REGION

INTRODUCING MEXICO
128

AROUND MEXICO CITY
130

NORTHERN MEXICO 158

THE COLONIAL HEARTLAND 180

SOUTHERN MEXICO 212

TRAVELERS' NEEDS

WHERE TO STAY 290

WHERE TO EAT 306

A selection of Mexico's wide variety of delicious seafood

SHOPPING IN MEXICO 328

SURVIVAL GUIDE

PRACTICAL INFORMATION 336

TRAVEL INFORMATION 348

GENERAL INDEX 358

PHRASEBOOK 381

MEXICO CITY

INTRODUCING MEXICO CITY 58

THE HISTORIC CENTER 60

REFORMA AND CHAPULTEPEC 82

SAN ÁNGEL AND COYOACÁN 96

FARTHER AFIELD 106

SHOPPING IN MEXICO CITY 114

ENTERTAINMENT IN MEXICO CITY 116

MEXICO CITY STREET FINDER 118

Maya village in Xcaret theme park on the Yucatán Peninsula coast

THE GULF COAST 238

THE YUCATÁN PENINSULA 256

Street performers in Plaza Cívica, Tuxtla Gutiérrez

Statue of Tlaloc in Xalapa Museo de Antropología

Temple of the Inscriptions at the ancient Maya site of Palenque

HOW TO USE THIS GUIDE

THIS GUIDE helps you to get the most from your visit to Mexico. It provides detailed practical information and expert recommendations. *Introducing Mexico* maps the country and sets it in its historical and cultural context. The six regional sections, plus *Mexico City*, describe important sights,

using maps, photographs, and illustrations. Features cover topics from food and wine to fiestas and native wildlife. Restaurant and hotel recommendations can be found in *Travelers' Needs*. The *Survival Guide* has tips on everything from making a telephone call to using local transportation.

MEXICO CITY
This is divided into three areas, each with its own chapter. A final chapter, *Farther Afield*, covers peripheral sights. All sights are numbered and plotted on the chapter's area map. Information on each sight is easy to locate as it follows the numerical order on the map.

A locator map shows where you are in relation to other areas of the city center.

All pages relating to Mexico City have red thumb tabs.

Sights at a Glance lists the chapter's sights by category: Churches and Cathedrals, Museums and Galleries, Streets and Squares, Historic Buildings, Parks and Gardens.

1 Area Map
For easy reference, sights are numbered and located on a map. City center sights are also marked on the Mexico City Street Finder (pages 118–25).

2 Street-by-Street Map
This gives a bird's-eye view of the key areas in each chapter.

Stars indicate the sights that no visitor should miss.

A suggested route for a walk is shown in red.

3 Detailed information
The sights in Mexico City are described individually. Addresses, telephone numbers, and opening hours are provided along with information about admission charges, photography, guided tours, wheelchair access, and public transportation.

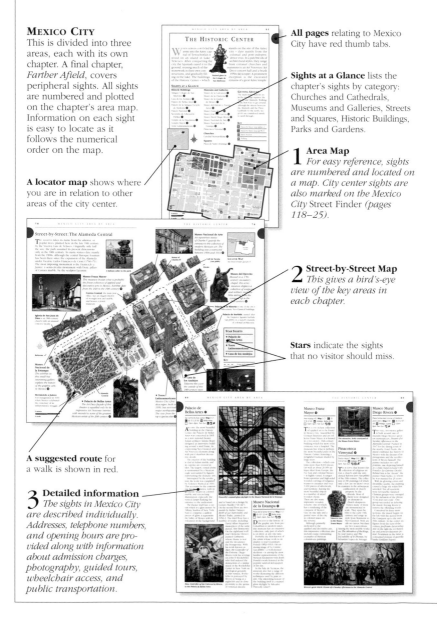

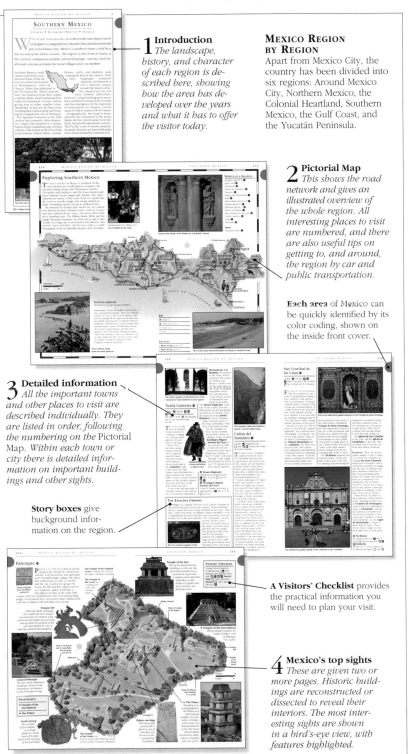

1 Introduction
The landscape, history, and character of each region is described here, showing how the area has developed over the years and what it has to offer the visitor today.

MEXICO REGION BY REGION
Apart from Mexico City, the country has been divided into six regions: Around Mexico City, Northern Mexico, the Colonial Heartland, Southern Mexico, the Gulf Coast, and the Yucatán Peninsula.

2 Pictorial Map
This shows the road network and gives an illustrated overview of the whole region. All interesting places to visit are numbered, and there are also useful tips on getting to, and around, the region by car and public transportation.

Each area of Mexico can be quickly identified by its color coding, shown on the inside front cover.

3 Detailed information
All the important towns and other places to visit are described individually. They are listed in order, following the numbering on the Pictorial Map. Within each town or city there is detailed information on important buildings and other sights.

Story boxes give background information on the region.

A Visitors' Checklist provides the practical information you will need to plan your visit.

4 Mexico's top sights
These are given two or more pages. Historic buildings are reconstructed or dissected to reveal their interiors. The most interesting sights are shown in a bird's-eye view, with features highlighted.

INTRODUCING MEXICO

PUTTING MEXICO ON THE MAP 10-11
A PORTRAIT OF MEXICO 12-29
MEXICO THROUGH THE YEAR 30-37
THE HISTORY OF MEXICO 38-55

Putting Mexico on the Map

Geographically, mexico is considered to be part of North, rather than Central, America. It covers an area of almost 2 million square kilometers (760,000 square miles) and has a population of 91 million. Administratively, the country is divided into 31 states and a Federal District, in which stands the vast, sprawling capital, Mexico City.

COLORADO

UNITED

OF AM

ARIZONA

NEW MEXICO

TEXAS

San Diego
Tijuana
Mexicali
Ensenada
San Felipe
Puerto Peñasco
Tucson
Sonoyta
Nogales
Agua Prieta
El Paso
Ciudad Juárez

BAJA CALIFORNIA NORTE

SONORA

Bahía Kino
Hermosillo
Ojinaga
Chihuahua
CHIHUAHUA
Chihuahua
Ciudad Acuña
Piedras Negras

Gulf

Guaymas
Santa Rosalía
Mulegé
Loreto

Guerrero Negro

of

California

Hidalgo Del Parral
Jiménez
COAHUILA
Monclova

MEXICO

BAJA CALIFORNIA SUR

Isla Magdalena

La Paz

San José del Cabo
Cabo San Lucas

SINALOA
Los Mochis
Culiacán

DURANGO
Torreón
Saltillo

Durango
ZACATECAS

PACIFIC

OCEAN

Mazatlán
Fresnillo
SAN LUIS POTOSÍ
Zacatecas
San Luis Potosí
AGUASCALIENTES

NAYARIT
Tepic
GUANAJUATO
Guanajuato

Puerto Vallarta
Guadalajara

JALISCO
Laguna de Chapala
Morelia

Manzanillo
Colima
MICHOACÁN
COLIMA

Zihuatanejo

Río Grande
Río Bravo

GREATER MEXICO CITY

Nicolás Romero
Coacalco
San Cristóbal Ecatepec
Chiluca
Tlalnepantla
Lago de Texcoco
Naucalpan
Texcoco
Ciudad de Mexico
Ciudad Nezahualcoyotl
Tlalpan
Chalco

0 kilometers 15
0 miles 10

◁ Detail of Diego Rivera's mosaic façade on the Teatro de los Insurgentes in Mexico City

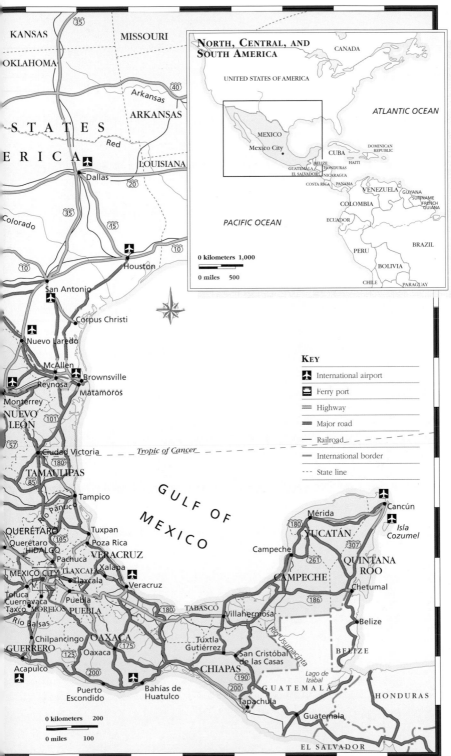

NORTH, CENTRAL, AND SOUTH AMERICA

CANADA

UNITED STATES OF AMERICA

ATLANTIC OCEAN

MEXICO

Mexico City

CUBA

DOMINICAN REPUBLIC

HAITI

BELIZE
GUATEMALA   HONDURAS
EL SALVADOR   NICARAGUA

COSTA RICA   PANAMA

VENEZUELA   GUYANA
SURINAME
FRENCH
GUIANA

COLOMBIA

PACIFIC OCEAN

ECUADOR

BRAZIL

PERU

BOLIVIA

CHILE

PARAGUAY

0 kilometers 1,000

0 miles   500

KANSAS

MISSOURI

OKLAHOMA

Arkansas

ARKANSAS

35

40

S T A T E S

Red

LOUISIANA

E R I C A

Dallas

20

Colorado

35

15

10

Houston

10

San Antonio

Corpus Christi

Nuevo Laredo

McAllen

Brownsville

Reynosa

Matamoros

Monterrey

NUEVO
LEON

101

57

Ciudad Victoria

Tropic of Cancer

TAMAULIPAS

85

180

Tampico

Río Pánuco

GULF OF

QUERÉTARO

105

Querétaro

HIDALGO

Tuxpan

Poza Rica

MEXICO

Pachuca

VERACRUZ

Xalapa

MEXICO CITY   TLAXCALA

Toluca

Tlaxcala

Veracruz

Cuernavaca

Puebla

Taxco   MORELOS

PUEBLA

Río Balsas

180

TABASCO

Chilpancingo

OAXACA

Villahermosa

GUERRERO

125

175

Acapulco

Oaxaca

200

Tuxtla
Gutiérrez

San Cristóbal
de las Casas

CHIAPAS

190

Puerto
Escondido

Bahías de
Huatulco

200

GUATEMALA

Tapachula

Guatemala

EL SALVADOR

Mérida

180

Cancún

Isla
Cozumel

YUCATÁN

307

Campeche

261

QUINTANA
ROO

CAMPECHE

Chetumal

186

Belize

Río Usumacinta

BELIZE

Lago de
Izabal

HONDURAS

KEY

✈ International airport

⛴ Ferry port

▬ Highway

▬ Major road

Railroad

International border

State line

0 kilometers   200

0 miles   100

A PORTRAIT OF MEXICO

*A*T ONCE ORDERLY AND CHAOTIC, *Mexico assaults the senses with the sights and sounds, tastes and smells of a unique mix of cultures and landscapes. Nowhere else in the Americas are ancient history and magic rituals so inextricably entwined with the routines of modern daily life.*

Mexico's arid north abuts the US along a 3,140-km (1,950-mile) border. This frontier is the only place on the planet where the so-called "first" and "third" worlds come face-to-face. To the south, Mexican territory ends amid tropical forest on the banks of the Usumacinta river, the border with Guatemala. North and south Mexico are starkly different. The northern states are wealthier, whiter, more urban, and industrialized. Although there are indigenous communities in the north, the southern states are home to the vast majority of the country's Indians, most of whom remain peasant farmers.

La Catrina, a Days of the Dead figure

Between these extremes there are many Mexicos to be seen. Modern agribusiness exists alongside pre-Columbian farming techniques. Rural Indian groups maintain their ancestral rites while the urban middle classes worship Western consumerism.

This is also a populous country. Of a total population of almost 100 million, one fifth is crammed into the Valley of Mexico, around 2,100 m (7,000 ft) above sea-level. The country is dominated by Mexico City. The vast, sprawling capital is one of the biggest cities in the world and its growth shows no sign of slowing down.

Fishermen preparing their nets on a beach in the Yucatán

◁ The hilltop archaeological site of Monte Albán near Oaxaca

Decorative tiles in the city of Puebla

THE MEXICAN WAY OF LIFE

The traditional Mexican view of the world can be thought of in terms of concentric circles. First comes the family, at the center of which is the venerated matriarch. Mother's Day is one of the most important dates in the Mexican calendar, and it is no coincidence that some of the harshest slang words and insults in Mexican Spanish incorporate variations on the word *madre*. Yet with the family under assault, as elsewhere in the world, from the forces of modernity, today this social fabric is being subjected to

Cycling, an inexpensive way of getting around town

unprecedented strain. Loyalties outside the family are traditionally confined to an immediate circle of friends, who may be *compadres* or *comadres* (godparents to one's children), or simply *cuates* ("pals").

Wider society, as well as authority figures, tend to be regarded with suspicion, and although confrontations are usually avoided, compliance is often no more than lip service. Mexicans have a tendency (particularly in the south) to say "yes" even when they mean "no," and to regard rules as an unwarranted constraint. Yet Mexican society is far from homogeneous.

Despite centuries of interbreeding between European settlers and native Mexican "Indians," 20 percent of Mexicans still consider themselves to be purely indigenous. The common culture of Mexico, as can be seen in the national cuisine, fiestas, and the arts and crafts, blends contributions from all quarters. Even so, many pre-Columbian traditions, untouched by European influences, survive to this day.

Stalls in the market of San Cristóbal de las Casas

The Convento de la Santa Cruz in Querétaro

RELIGION

Almost nine out of ten Mexicans regard themselves as Catholic, but Mexican Catholicism has incorporated many elements of pre-Christian religion. The most venerated figure, especially among the poor, is the Virgin of Guadalupe, the country's patron saint. Said to be one of the three "untouchable" institutions (the others are the army and the presidency), the dark-skinned Virgin appeared, according to legend, in 1531 on a site once dedicated to the pagan mother-goddess Tonantzin. Shrines to the Virgin are to be found all over Mexico, even in remote places.

The state has had an uncomfortable relationship with the Catholic Church, as a result of the latter's support first for the Spanish colonial authorities and later for the Emperor Maximilian. Until the Salinas reforms of the 1990s, priests were forbidden to appear in public in their vestments and

Mexico had no diplomatic relations with the Vatican. Paradoxically, the two great heroes of Mexican independence, Hidalgo and Morelos, were both priests.

In opposition to the Catholics, the influence of evangelical protestants is growing rapidly in Mexico. Unlike most Catholics, the evangelicals tend to be enthusiastic and regular practitioners of their religion.

THE ARTS AND SPORTS

Mexico has a rich artistic tradition and in the 20th century, in particular, has made outstanding contributions in the fields of painting, architecture, literature, and film.

Many of the murals of Diego Rivera, José Clemente Orozco, and David Alfaro Siqueiros and the canvases of Frida Kahlo and Rufino Tamayo are acknowledged masterpieces. Octavio Paz, the great contemporary interpreter of *mexicanidad* ("Mexican-ness") won a Nobel prize for literature, and the novelist Carlos Fuentes is world renowned. Mexican film's heyday was the 1940–50s, although every so often the country can still release an international hit, such as the 1992 *Like Water for Chocolate*.

Traditional mask

Festival in honor of the Virgin of Guadalupe, December 12

Charrería, a popular spectator sport, particularly in the north

Almost more interesting than formal works of art are the expressions of folk art for which Mexico can be justifiably proud. Mariachi music has gained adherents as far away as Belgium and Japan. Mexican crafts, meanwhile, are testament to a limitless creativity.

Mexicans are sports mad. The most popular sports – soccer, boxing, bullfighting, and baseball – have been imported from other countries. Wrestling, *lucha libre*, is also an import but with a distinctive Mexican stamp on it, in the form of masks worn by the combatants. A uniquely Mexican sport is *charrería*, which is somewhat akin to rodeo. It centers on competitions to test skills of horsemanship but has a whole culture of bright costume and festivity surrounding it.

Masked wrestlers in *lucha libre*

POLITICS AND ECONOMICS

Since the upheaval of the Revolution between 1910 and 1920, Mexico has been the most politically stable country in Latin America. With the collapse of the Soviet Union, the Institutional Revolutionary Party (PRI) inherited the title of the world's oldest political regime. Peruvian novelist Mario Vargas Llosa once described Mexico's system as "the perfect dictatorship" for its ability to change presidents – and even modify its ideology – every six years, while retaining an iron grip on power. The government of Carlos Salinas de Gortari (1988–94) swept away much of the economic control the PRI had formerly championed. His successor, Ernesto Zedillo, pursued the neoliberal recipe with equal enthusiasm. The cost, however, was a widening gap between rich and poor. As a consequence, challenges to the regime, both from within the PRI and from an increasingly active opposition, grew steadily, leading to PRI's defeat in the 2000 elections, the first time it has been out of power since 1929. Changes are expected under the government of Vicente Fox and the National Action Party (PAN). So

Mariachis performing in Zacatecas

far, however, political competition has done little to eradicate the endemic corruption for which Mexico, sadly, has a deserved reputation. With roots at least as old as the Spanish colonial era, corruption flourished during the PRI's bureaucratic monopoly. It was further boosted by the 1970s oil boom and the growth of crime syndicates who were able to buy political and police protection.

In 1994 the Zapatista National Liberation Army (EZLN) burst onto the scene with the seizure of six towns in the state of Chiapas. Although formal hostilities lasted less than two weeks, negotiations failed to

Mexico City's futuristic stock exchange building

prosper, and tension has remained high. Other small guerrilla groups have emerged, with more radical agendas.

The EZLN's uprising coincided with

Cadets at the military medical school on parade

Mexico's entry into the North American Free Trade Agreement (NAFTA) with the US and Canada, a treaty the guerrillas – almost all of them Maya peasants – saw as inimical to their interests. NAFTA was a bold attempt to overcome almost two centuries of suspicion between Mexico and its northern neighbor. But while the two economies are increasingly interlinked, the relationship remains delicate. The thousands of undocumented migrants who annually cross the border in search of a better life – and the drug traffickers who exploit the same routes – are major sources of friction. Mexico's rapid transformation from an

agricultural to an industrial economy has failed to resolve the employment problems of its growing population: one million jobs per year are needed to keep pace with the new entrants to the market, with the shortfall is provided by the precarious "informal" economy.

Partly as a legacy of the struggle for independence and the Revolution, and partly as a result of living next door to a super-power, Mexicans are enthusiastically patriotic. Their nationalism reaches its height each September 15. On this date Father Hidalgo's call or cry ("*El Grito*") for Mexican independence is repeated everywhere, from the Palacio Nacional in Mexico City to the humblest town hall. Nonetheless, tradition is under threat. Younger Mexicans are as likely to celebrate Hallowe'en (a European/US festival) as they are to honor their ancestors on the Days of the Dead at the same time of year.

A political rally in the capital

The Landscape and Wildlife of Mexico

Resplendent quetzal

DESPITE SERIOUS THREATS to its environment, Mexico remains one of the three richest nations on earth in terms of the variety of its flora and fauna. With more than 30,000 plant species, almost 450 different mammals, and over 1,000 types of bird – many of which are unique to Mexico – it is a naturalist's paradise. The reason for this natural wealth is the range of habitats, from snow-capped volcanoes to mangroves, deserts, and tropical forests, not to mention part of the world's second-longest barrier reef.

The volcano Pico de Orizaba, Mexico's highest mountain

DESERTS AND SCRUBLANDS

Over half of Mexico's land is classified as arid, and another 30 percent as "semi-arid." The only true desert – where the annual rainfall is less than 25 cm (10 inches) – is the Desierto de Altar in northwest Sonora. The dry scrublands that cover much of northern Mexico, particularly Chihuahua, Sonora, and Baja California, conceal a surprising abundance of wildlife.

The desert tortoise is threatened with extinction because of the trade in wild animals. A recovery program has begun in Mapimí in northern Mexico (see p173).

Cactuses (see p171) *have adapted to the harsh conditions of life in deserts.*

Rattlesnakes *of several different species are among the many reptiles found in Mexico. They are typical of arid zones.*

WETLANDS

These habitats, which range from ponds to mangrove swamps and coastal lagoons, are fast disappearing through land reclamation, pollution, and urbanization. They are home to wading birds such as herons or egrets. The saline lagoons of the Yucatán Peninsula support colonies of flamingos *(see p272).*

The leopard frog *and its innumerable relatives fill the air of the wetlands with their chorus of croaking.*

The sora, *a member of the rail family, is a winter visitor found in reed beds across the country.*

Mangroves *grow along tropical coastlines in brackish water. They provide a habitat for wading birds and other fauna.*

COASTS

Mexico's coastline totals over 10,000 km (6,250 miles) in length. On the Pacific, promontories and islets are common, while on the Atlantic side the coastline is sandy. A magnificent coral reef lies off the coast of Quintana Roo. Isolated beaches provide nesting grounds for species of sea turtle.

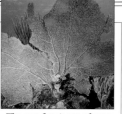

The sea fan is one of many fascinating species found on the coral reef (see p283).

Whales, including the world's biggest, the blue whale, are seen off Baja California (see p164).

MOUNTAINS AND CANYONS

Mexico is a land of mountains: more than half the country is over 1000 m (3,200 ft) above sea level. Mountainsides are typically clad in pine or pine-oak forest. There are also arid mountains in the North, including the haunt of the endangered Mexican bighorn sheep, and areas of cloud forest and montane rainforest in the south.

Bighorn sheep, sacred to some pre-Columbian people, roam the remote, arid northwest mountains.

The bobcat is a medium-sized feline, sometimes glimpsed amid the thornscrub of northern Mexico.

Yellow-eyed junco is one of the most familiar birds of the Mexican mountains.

TROPICAL FORESTS

Rainforest is the earth's richest habitat in terms of the number of species it supports. Mexico's rainforest is on the Atlantic slope south of the isthmus of Tehuantepec, with isolated remnants in northern Oaxaca and southern Veracruz. These areas' rich wildlife includes jaguars, parrots, and the extraordinary quetzal, a bird sacred to the Maya *(see pp46–7)*.

The jaguar is Mexico's biggest cat, but it has suffered from the loss of its jungle habitat in the south and west.

The keel-billed toucan is unmistakable because of its huge, multicolored bill.

Armadillos defend themselves from predators by rolling into a ball.

The Indigenous Peoples of Mexico

MEXICO'S INDIGENOUS inhabitants are probably more numerous today than at the time of the Spanish Conquest. However, the precise definition of "indigenous" is debatable. Official statistics show that more than one in ten of the population of 93 million belongs to one of the 56 Indian language groups. Some, like the Tarahumara, Huichol, and Lacandón *(see p232)*, retain much of their pre-Columbian way of life. Most, however, have abandoned traditional dress (at least in public) and ways of life, and are often indistinguishable from mixed-race Mexicans.

The Yaqui of Sonora perform their evocative Danza del Venado (Deer Dance) during Easter Week and on the Day of the Dead.

The Trique of Oaxaca are among the less numerous indigenous peoples. Here a woman is using a traditional loom, one end of which is fastened to a tree while the other is tied around her back to maintain the tension.

A string of shamans' baskets form the tail of the serpent.

Eight ancestors inhabit the second level of creation. They have no legs and cannot speak.

A creator god in the form of a serpent is at the heart of creation.

The Maya civilization (see pp46–7) went into decline before the arrival of the Spanish. The descendants of the Maya, who inhabit the state of Chiapas and the Yucatán Peninsula, speak a large number of mutually unintelligible languages. These women belong to the Tzotzil Maya.

The mockingbird carries people's memories from the past to the present.

The Tarahumara (see p174), who live in the area around Copper Canyon in Chihuahua state, play a tough endurance game called rarajipari, in which two opposing teams kick wooden balls around an improvised mountain course. The game can last for several days.

The Huichol (see p184) are known in Mexico for their dazzlingly colored handicrafts, especially beadwork. They cling precariously to the lands of their ancestors on the border of Jalisco and Nayarit states.

WHERE MEXICO'S INDIGENOUS PEOPLE LIVE

The indigenous population is concentrated mainly in the south, although some large groups – the Yaqui, Mayo and Tarahumara – are in the north. The states of Oaxaca and Chiapas have the largest proportion of indigenous inhabitants. The five most widely spoken indigenous languages are Nahuatl (the language of the Aztecs), peninsular Maya, Zapotec, Mixtec, and Otomí.

The third or outer level of creation is the realm of plants, animals, and all other natural phenomena.

An open flower symbolizes life rising from the earth.

The Shaman is a cross between a priest and a healer, with a vast knowledge of medicinal plants. There is no easy dividing line between magic, ritual, and traditional medicine in indigenous culture. However, all are rapidly being supplanted by "western" science and medicine.

HUICHOL YARN PAINTING

Mexico's indigenous people make an extraordinary variety of crafts *(see pp330–33)*, usually in bright colors and based on striking, symbolic designs. This painting depicts the Huichol view of creation as divided into three phases or levels, each inhabited by different beings.

Catholicism in Mexico is a mixture of Christianity, brought by the Spanish, and lingering beliefs from ancient Mexico. The indigenous inhabitants of Mexico merely adapted their religion to that of their rulers without abandoning belief in their ancient gods.

The sun is shown with a snake beneath it, which symbolizes its path across the sky.

An earth mother has a seed of corn in her chest and ears of corn to either side.

The tortilla (see p308), a flat corn (maize) pancake, is the staple food of both indigenous and mixed-race Mexicans. Here an Indian woman prepares tortillas the way it has been done for generations.

Corn (maize) was unknown to Europeans before the conquest of the Americas. Along with beans, it is still the essential crop grown by Mexican peasants, although the agricultural way of life is increasingly threatened by the globalization of the world economy.

Architecture in Mexico

Waterspout on Casa de los Muñecos, Puebla

MOST COLONIAL HOUSES in Mexico were highly functional, with an interior courtyard for privacy and wrought-iron grilles to protect the windows. The Baroque age introduced flamboyance, while local materials, such as Puebla tiles, led to the growth of regional styles. Neo-Classicism, fashionable after 1785, favored austerity, but French influence in the 1800s brought a return to ornamentation. In the 20th century, Modernism was embraced with enthusiasm.

Façade tiles on the Casa del Alfeñique, Puebla (see p150)

EARLY COLONIAL (1521–c.1620)

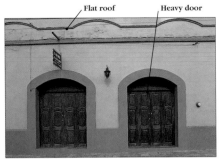

Flat roof   Heavy door

These houses in San Cristóbal de las Casas (see p231) have courtyards, flat roofs, and simple doorways.

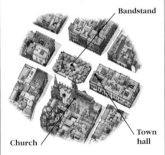

Casa de Montejo (1543–9) in Mérida (see p270) has a Plateresque façade showing two conquistadors in full armor.

THE PLAZA MAYOR

Mexican town-dwellers take pride in their *plaza mayor* (main square). Under Spanish rule, urban planning was strictly controlled, and towns were modeled on the capital. Straight streets led to a large plaza with civic and religious buildings, plus *portales* (arcades) for the merchants. Urban renewal in the late 1800s equipped the squares with statues, bandstands, and cast-iron lamps and benches.

Bandstand

Church   Town hall

BAROQUE (c.1630–c.1800)

Wrought-iron balcony

Ornamental details carved in limestone include the coat of arms of the Marqués de Jaral de Berrio.

Palacio de Iturbide in Mexico City (see p79) was designed in about 1780 by Francisco Guerrero y Torres. The sumptuous former residence has an exuberant façade.

These figures are thought to depict inhabitants of nearby Tlaxcala.

Figures from classical mythology

Outer wall of red stone

Finely carved pilasters flank the high doorway, which admitted carriages to the central patio.

Casa de los Muñecos (House of the Figures; late 18th century), in Puebla (see p150), has a façade adorned with locally made azulejos (glazed tiles).

NEO-CLASSICAL (1785–c.1880)

Stone statues portray eight of the nine Muses.

Upper balustrade

The portico has two rows of fluted columns.

Teatro Juárez in Guanajuato (see p203) was commissioned in 1873 and built by Antonio Rivas Mercado. It combines Neo-Classicism with lavish French styles of decoration.

PORFIRIAN (1876–1911)

This late 19th-century stained-glass window showing a coat of arms is from the Museo Bello in Puebla (see p152).

French-influenced ornamental stonework

Islamic-style window

This eclectic mansion in Guadalajara was completed in 1908. The era (see p53) freely combined Rococo, Neo-Classical, Neo-Baroque, and other styles.

RURAL ARCHITECTURE

Many Indian populations use local materials to build houses in styles particular to their region. Depending on geography and climate, houses may be square, rectangular, apsidal, or round. In regions with heavy rainfall, roofs are steep and often thatched with palm or grass, while overhanging eaves protect walls of poles or wattle-and-daub. Where trees are plentiful, wooden houses are common. In areas with low rainfall, builders use stone, bricks, or adobe (mud bricks).

Nahua house in Hidalgo, with log walls and a roof of *zacate* (grass)

Thatched Maya house of rubble masonry and plaster, in the Yucatán

MODERN (c.1920–PRESENT)

The outline emulates New York skyscrapers on a smaller scale.

Luis Barragán's Casa Gilardi, in Mexico City, has a ground floor characterized by broad, intersecting planes of color. The 1970s design incorporates water as an architectural element.

Innovative vertical windows

Indoor pool

Imposing angular doorway

Yellow-painted glass panes admit shafts of light.

The Loteria Nacional (see p85) was built around 1936 by José A. Cuevas. Formality and symmetry give it an Art Deco appearance.

Church Architecture

Figure in Santo Domingo, Oaxaca

AFTER THE CONQUEST, new towns were dominated by churches and cathedrals. Throughout the 16th century, missionary friars acted as architects, using Renaissance, Plateresque, and Mudejar styles. Native carvers added details, and the result was *tequitqui*, a blend of Indian and European elements. The Baroque style of the 1600s became even more ornamented after 1750, with the Ultra-Baroque, or Churrigueresque.

Domes of Mitla church (see pp226–7)

EARLY MONASTERIES

As Spanish friars took their conversion work into remote territories, they established a network of missions. Each colonial monastery, with its church, was virtually self-sufficient, incorporating living quarters for the friars, a school, hospital, library, wells, and orchards. Crenellated stone walls and other defensive characteristics gave many missions a fortress-like appearance.

The Plateresque portal of San Agustín Acolman (see p138), *finished in 1560, contrasts with the monastery's overall severity. Beside the door are two pairs of garlanded columns on angel pedestals, with a saint set between each pair.*

The mission church at Mulegé in Baja California (see p168) *was built by the Jesuits in the 18th century. The simple, functional design is characteristic of remote missions.*

Atrium

Izamal's Convento de San Antonio de Padua (see p273) *was built on the site of a Maya religious center by the Franciscans between 1553 and 1561. The colonnade enclosing the large atrium was added in about 1618, the wall belfry in the 1800s.*

The façade *has detailed, exuberant carving. This scene shows the Baptism of Christ, surrounded by cherubs, spirals, and foliage. It is flanked by statues of St. Sebastian and St. Prisca.*

The dome is covered with glazed tiles, probably from Puebla, and inset with eight rectangular windows. The dome's frieze reads "Gloria a Dios en las alturas" ("Glory to God in the Highest"). External ribs lead to a tile-domed lantern, surmounted by a cross.

Richly decorated **retablos (altarpieces)** line the nave, adding to the cumulative splendor. This *retablo*, dedicated to St. Joseph, is adorned with cherubs, ears of corn, shells, and fruit.

The sacristy is reached by a door beside the high altar.

Finials

The main retablo, conceived in high Churrigueresque style by Isidoro Vicente de Balbás, depicts the glory of the Christian Church. Heavily gilded, the carved wood conveys richness and splendor. Estípite (inverted) pilasters (see p143) replace the Classical columns of earlier times.

South entrance

Baptistery

IGLESIA DE SANTA PRISCA, TAXCO

Begun in 1751, and finished in just seven years, the parish church of Taxco *(see pp146–7)* exemplifies the Churrigueresque style of Mexican architecture. The style is characterized by dazzling surface ornament that conveys flowing movement and obscures the form beneath. The huge costs of this church were borne by wealthy silver magnate José de la Borda.

San Francisco Acatapec *(see p149)*

POPULAR BAROQUE

Rural churches of the Baroque period often display enormous exuberance and charm. These eclectic, imaginative creations are aptly classified as *barroco popular*. In Puebla, the popular passion for ornamentation found expression in the glistening tiles that cover church façades with vivid patterning. Interiors exhibit a profusion of plaster figures, such as clusters of angels, cherubs, saints, animals, flowers, and fruit. These were accentuated with brilliant gold leaf and color.

Mexican Muralists

Emiliano Zapata, by Posada

THE MEXICAN MURAL MOVEMENT, lasting from the 1920s to the 1970s, produced some of the greatest public revolutionary art of the 20th century. The initial motivation was provided by José Vasconcelos, Minister for Education, whose mural program sought to develop a national art and cultural identity for Mexico. Several artists joined the movement, but Diego Rivera, David Alfaro Siqueiros, and José Clemente Orozco are regarded as the masters. By painting the walls of public buildings, they upheld the socialist ideal of accessible art for all. The muralists accorded special status to José Guadalupe Posada (1852–1913), whose engravings had chronicled an earlier age.

This mosaic decoration *(1956) on a house in Acapulco (see p218) was created when Rivera was staying in the city toward the end of his life.*

DAVID ALFARO SIQUEIROS (1898–1974)

Revolutionary politics shaped the life and work of Siqueiros and fired the revolutionary aesthetic behind his ambitious projects. His mural style, flamboyant and experimental, conveyed a dramatic sense of movement.

Patriots and Parricides *(1945) decorates a staircase in part of the Secretaría de Educación Pública in Mexico City (see p72). Here, a detail shows Mexico's betrayers descending into hell. Siqueiros used this mural project to forge a dynamic relationship between painting and architecture.*

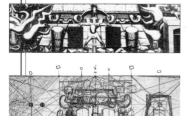

These preparatory pieces *were for* Tropical America *(1932), a vast fresco in Los Angeles. In preparing and executing his murals Siqueiros made innovative use of photographic projection, airbrushing, and industrial paints.*

The figures hold symbols of science and learning.

The People for the University, the University for the People *(1952–6) is a relief mosaic at Mexico City's main university (see p111). This powerful panel with protruding forms was described by Siqueiros as "sculptured painting." With his concept of Plastic Integration, he advocated a synthesis of painting, architecture, and sculpture.*

DIEGO RIVERA (1886–1957)

Rivera's panoramic images of Mexico combine social criticism with a faith in human progress. Inspired by early Italian fresco painting and pre-Columbian iconography, his intricate visual narratives incorporate allegory and symbolism.

The Zapotec Civilization *(1942), part of a series of murals in the Palacio Nacional* (see pp66–7), *celebrates the achievements of pre-Columbian cultures.*

A Popular History of Mexico *(1953), shown here in detail, is a mosaic façade on the Teatro de los Insurgentes* (see p110).

La Calavera Catrina, from an engraving by Posada

Diego Rivera age 10

Frida Kahlo in traditional dress

José Guadalupe Posada

DREAM OF A SUNDAY AFTERNOON IN THE ALAMEDA CENTRAL

This vast painting (1947–8), now displayed in the Museo Mural Diego Rivera *(see p81)*, combines autobiography, history, and fantasy. This detail is from the central section.

JOSÉ CLEMENTE OROZCO (1883–1949)

Orozco's murals, expressionist in spirit, movingly challenged the mythologizing of Mexican history. The bold forms and use of visual metaphor owed much to his early experience as a caricaturist.

The Family *(1926), at the Antiguo Colegio de San Ildefonso in Mexico City* (see p71), *is one of a series of large murals devoted to agrarian revolt. Dramatic composition, broad strokes, and harsh coloring evoke the tragic struggle of the oppressed.*

Omniscience *(1925), on the main staircase of the Casa de los Azulejos* (see p75), *is metaphysical rather than political. The figures represent inspiration, force, and intelligence.*

Music and Dance

Across Mexico, celebrations are accompanied by music that owes its variety to a fusion of musical traditions. Pre-Conquest musicians played wind and percussion instruments. Today the reed-flute, conch shell, and *huehuetl* drum evoke the sounds of ancient Mexico. The Spanish introduced stringed instruments. Over time, Mexican music evolved into the *sones* (strains) of Jalisco, Veracruz, and other states. Mexico has also absorbed influences from the rest of Europe, and Africa, Cuba, and the US.

Man with accordion

MARIACHIS

Mariachi music originated in the state of Jalisco during the 19th century, when *mariachi* musicians (from the French word *mariage*) played music for weddings and balls. Suitors still often engage *mariachi* bands to serenade their girlfriends at home.

A *mariachi* **band** can consist of between seven and 15 musicians.

The violin leads the *mariachi* melody.

Trumpets are a recent addition to *mariachi* music.

The guitar was introduced to Mexico by the Spanish.

Mariachi musician in traditional costume

Mariachi *bands* *can be seen in the Plaza Garibaldi in Mexico City, playing songs about love, betrayal, and revolutionary heroes.*

TRADITIONAL DANCES

Mexico has a vast range of regional dances performed only in their specific areas. During religious celebrations, they take place in squares and in front of churches. Dancers, who are usually male, communicate the storyline through dance steps, sign language, and sometimes words. Some dances hark back to pre-Columbian times and ancient rituals; others were introduced by Spanish friars and show European influence.

Tlaxcala Carnival dancers *wear elaborate garments embroidered with sequins, and carved wooden masks with pale skin tones. Carnival is a time for revelry when dancers parody their ancient oppressors.*

Quetzal dancers *in Cuetzalan wear headdresses of reeds and colored paper, tipped with feathers. The steps of this Nahua dance relate to the passage of the sun.*

VOLADORES

During this ancient Nahua and Totonac ritual, five men climb to the top of a pole often reaching as high as 30 m (100 ft) While one plays a drum and a reed-pipe on a tiny platform at the top, the other four "fly" to the ground, suspended on ropes.

Each volador circles the pole 13 times before reaching the ground, making a total of 52 turns. This symbolizes the 52-year cycles of the Mesoamerican calendar (see p47). The central pole represents a vertical connection between the Earth, the heavens above, and the underworld below.

Totonac voladores wear velvet panels decorated with sequins and beads.

Headdresses are adorned with mirrors and plastic flowers.

Voladores *can be seen performing regularly at El Tajín (see pp242–3) and outside the National Anthropology Museum in Mexico City (see pp90–95).*

Tiger dancers perform during festivals in the state of Guerrero. These ancient dances reflect the preoccupations of farming communities and once featured jaguars or ocelots.

A conchero dancer performs for the Virgin of Guadalupe in Mexico City. Traditional instruments are used by concheros. Dance steps are also accompanied by the rattle of seed pods worn on the ankles.

Devil Mask with real horns from Michoacán

Male Mask from Puebla

Tiger Mask with animal teeth from Guerrero

MASKS

Masks were worn for a range of dances in ancient Mexico and Spain. Today, Mexican masks represent men and women, supernatural beings, and birds and animals, and can be realistic or stylized. Wood is the most common material, but some mask-makers rely on leather, clay, paper, cloth, gourds, and even wax. Dancers look through slits above or below the painted eyes.

Dancehalls in the capital and Mexico's other major cities attract devotees of danzón, merengue, mambo, cumbia, salsa, rock, and other musical styles. Events in Salón México (1995), a remake of a classic movie, took place at the famous dancehall of the same name in Mexico City (see p117).

MEXICO THROUGH THE YEAR

Radishes sculpted for Oaxaca's *Noche de los Rábanos*

IN THE WORDS of Mexican poet Octavio Paz, "Fiestas are our only luxury." Indeed, every day is a saint's day or other cause for celebration somewhere in Mexico, with fireworks exploding, a band playing, and the population dancing. Some traditional fiestas derive from indigenous celebrations, while others were brought by the Christian Spanish conquistadors. Many now blend the two influences.

Most events are localized, but a few occasions are celebrated throughout the country – particularly Independence Day, the Day of the Dead, and the day honoring the Virgin of Guadalupe *(see p109)*. Visitors should be warned that many fiestas include cockfights, but these take place in separate arenas and are visible only to those who choose to enter.

The weather is an important factor determining when to visit. For combining a beach and inland vacation consider autumn; the weather is glorious, but cooler for visiting archaeological sites. There are also fewer tourists at this time of year. Winter is a good time to see wildlife.

Indigenous and Christian traditions mixed in an Easter procession

SPRING

THE TEMPERATE weather conditions of spring, just before the start of the rainy season, make this a perfect time to visit the coast. However, Easter Week is one of the busiest times, and transportation gets booked up in advance. At this time of year jacaranda and flame trees blossom in a riot of color in town squares all over the country. In late spring the weather is hot, and fruits such as mangos, mameys, pineapples, and papayas fill the markets. Migratory birds, particularly birds of prey, can be seen on the Gulf Coast as they fly along it when making their way north to their summer habitats.

Easter Week *(Semana Santa; Mar/Apr)* is celebrated all over Mexico but is particularly beautiful in the southern states and in the Colonial Heartland. Passion plays are performed in most regions, notably in Taxco (Guerrero), Pátzcuaro (Michoacán), San Cristóbal de las Casas (Chiapas), Ixtapalapa in greater Mexico City, and throughout Oaxaca state.

On Palm Sunday there are processions, and palm crosses are sold outside churches. Good Friday sees parades of women swinging incense holders and carrying flowers in front of images of Christ and the Virgin Mary. They are accompanied by solemn singing, torchbearers, and hooded penitents. On this day the steps of Christ along the route to his crucifixion are re-enacted. Participants include self-flagellating sinners, robed children, and Roman soldiers. Realistic re-enactments of the whipping and crucifixion of Christ may also be staged. In the evening and on Easter Saturday cardboard "Judases" are burned and fireworks let off. On the Saturday, it is also customary in some towns to throw water at passers-by.

The Tarahumara Indians *(see p20)* have evolved their own version of the Easter story featuring an annual running battle between wicked "pharisees" and "soldiers" guarding the Virgin.

Natalicio de Benito Juárez *(Mar 21)*. Wreaths are laid at monuments to the reforming president on his birthday, notably in Guelatao, near Oaxaca, where he was born.

A Cinco de Mayo parade, which celebrates the Battle of Puebla

One of the *voladores* taking part in a Corpus Christi display

Sol a Sol Regatta *(mid-Apr)*, Isla Mujeres (Quintana Roo). Fireworks, a basketball match, and parties mark the end of a boat race from St. Petersburg, Florida to the island.

Feria de San Marcos *(Apr/May)*, Aguascalientes. Cultural, sporting, and other events combine at this important fair *(see p185)*.

Labor Day *(Día del Trabajo; May 1)*. Marches organized by trade unions and political parties culminate with speeches in town squares.

Cinco de Mayo *(May 5)*. The commemoration of the Battle of Puebla, a Mexican victory over the invading French army in 1862, is celebrated with particular enthusiasm in Puebla state *(see p153)*.

Mother's Day *(Día de la Madre; May 10)*. Every *mamacita* in Mexico is honored on this day and, finances permitting, taken out to lunch, regaled with flowers, or serenaded by mariachis *(see p28)*.

St. Isidore's Day *(May 15)*. Seeds, agricultural implements, ox yokes, and animals are blessed before planting begins in rural Mexico.

Corpus Christi *(May/Jun)*. Church services and parades take place all over Mexico. In Papantla (Veracruz), there is a special performance by the *voladores*, or "flyers" *(see p29)*, whose ritual invokes fertility, communicating with the heavens, and honoring the sun.

SUMMER

WITH THE ARRIVAL of the rains, summer is usually considered the off season in Mexico. However, the rain tends to fall in the afternoon, and the mornings are bright and clear. The high precipitation ensures the countryside is verdant making this a good time to tour inland. At this time of the year, the air in Mexico City is also at its cleanest. Markets everywhere are bursting with flowers, fruit, and vegetables; and only in these months can visitors taste fresh *cuitlacoche* corn fungus *(see p311)*, Mexico's answer to truffles, and the elaborate *chiles en nogada (see p309)*.

Horseman competing in the Lienzo Charro

Navy Day *(Día de la Marina; Jun 1)*. Port towns organize events to honor the navy. Official festivities take place in Guaymas (Sonora) and include uniformed processions, regattas, and fleet parades.

Lienzo Charro *(Jun)*, Mexico City. There are displays of horsemanship *(charrería, see p74)* by riders in costumes and huge sombreros on most Sundays at the Lienzo Charro in the third section of Chapultepec Park *(see p88–9)*. The main event is in June, when a national *charro* exhibition is held .

Guelaguetza *(late Jul)*, Oaxaca. Regional dances are performed in a variety of costumes in the beautiful main fiesta of Oaxaca state *(see p225)*.

Feast of the Assumption *(Día de la Asunción; Aug 15)*. Church services and processions take place everywhere. In many towns, the streets are decorated with carpets of flowers, over which the procession of the statue of the Virgin passes. The most lively celebrations take place in Huamantla (Tlaxcala), where the Fiesta de la Virgen de la Caridad *(see p139)* lasts for nearly two weeks and ends with bulls being let loose in the streets of the town.

PUBLIC HOLIDAYS

Año Nuevo (New Year's Day; Jan 1)
Día de la Constitución (Constitution Day; Feb 5)
Natalicio de Benito Juárez (Birthday of Benito Juárez; Mar 21)
Jueves Santo (Easter Thursday)
Viernes Santo (Good Friday)
Día del Trabajo (Labor Day; May 1)
Cinco de Mayo (May 5)
Día de la Independencia (Independence Day; Sep 16)
Descubrimiento de América (Columbus Day; Oct 12)
Día de la Revolución (Revolution Day; Nov 20)
Día de la Virgen de Guadalupe (Festivity of the Virgin of Guadalupe; Dec 12)
Noche Buena (Christmas Eve)
Navidad (Christmas Day)

Costumed dancer at the Guelaguetza

Costumed horsemen in an Independence Day celebration

AUTUMN

As THE RAINY SEASON ends, the countryside is still green, the weather is warm, and days are long. Rivers are full, so the white-water rafting season begins in Veracruz and San Luis Potosí. Autumn is a good time to travel in-land, especially with the added attraction of cultural events during the Festival Internacional Cervantino. The luxuriant vegetation of the Gulf Coast and Chiapas can also best be appreciated at this time of year, without heavy rains. In early and late autumn respectively, Mexico celebrates its two principal fiestas, Independence Day and the Days of the Dead.

Presidential Address (Sep 1). During the afternoon on this day people watch the pre-sident's speech on television or listen to it on the radio.
El Grito/Independence Day (Día de la Independencia; Sep 15–16). Father Miguel Hidalgo's "cry" to arms (Grito) to free Mexico of Spanish rule in 1810 (see p49) is commemorated all over Mexico, particularly in

A packed crowd witnesses a bullfight at Plaza México in Mexico City (see p110)

Hidalgo, Morelia, and Mexico City. Fiestas take place in every town square on the evening of September 15, including fireworks, music, and the throwing of eggshells filled with confetti. Later, local officials repeat Hidalgo's shout, while in Mexico City the president himself makes the cry from the balcony of the Palacio Nacional (see pp66–7). The next day is an occasion for parades. Child-ren in particular dress in national costume or as Inde-pendence heroes.
Descubrimiento de América (Oct 12). Originally the celebration of the discovery of the Americas, this day is now more of a hom-age to the peoples of ancient Mexico.
Festival Internacional Cervantino (Oct), Guanajuato. Music, dance, and theater groups from all over the world gather in Guanajuato (see pp202–5) for the highlight of Mexico's cultural calendar. The festival is dedicated to the Spanish writer Miguel Cervantes, crea-tor of Don Quixote. It began in the 1950s when Cervantes-inspired one-act plays staged by students here. Col-onial buildings blend into stage settings for performances which may feature period costumes and even horses.

Bisbee International Marlin Fishing Tournament (last week of Oct), Cabo San Lucas (Baja California Sur). A large cash prize for the biggest catch is on offer at this international event.
Tecate Mexicali Surf Festival (Oct), Ensenada (Baja California Norte). The surfing fraternity hits Mexico for wave-riding competitions.
Days of the Dead (Días de Todos Santos; Oct 31– Nov 2). Mexico's most colorful fiesta (see pp34–5).
Baja Mil Off Road Race (1st week of Nov), Baja California, from Ensenada to La Paz or vice-versa depending on the year. Hundreds of motor-cycles, beach buggies, and pickups from around the world take up the challenge of this grueling off-road race.
Bull-fighting season (Nov– Mar). The grandest bullrings include those in Mexico City, Aguascalientes, San Luis Potosí, and Zacatecas.
International Silver Fair (Feria de la Plata; Nov/ Dec), Taxco (see pp146–7). Stun-ning displays of silverwork can be admired, and prizes are awarded to the best silversmiths.

Days of the Dead decoration

Revolution Day (Día de la Revolu-ción; Nov 20). Small boys have black moustaches painted on them and wear red kerchiefs and boots. The girls are decked out as lupitas (female revolutionaries) in frilly skirts and loop earrings. There are also parades by sportsmen and women.
Día de Santa Cecilia (Nov 22). The patron saint of musicians is feted with much gusto. There are celebrations in the Plaza Garibaldi in Mexico City, Querétaro, and Pátzcuaro (Michoacán).
Puerto Escondido Inter-national Surf Tournament (last week of Nov), Puerto Escondido (Oaxaca). Surfers from all over Mexico and the US congregate in the sun to compete on Oaxaca's waves.

WINTER

IN ALL AREAS, temperatures drop at night in December, but, with the exception of Northern Mexico, the weather is still good enough for beach vacations. Over Christmas and the New Year, Mexicans and foreigners alike flock to the coastal resorts. In Mexico City, December brings the extravagant celebrations for Mexico's patron saint, the Virgin of Guadalupe. This is also the season when the first whales (see p164) reach Baja California and migratory monarch butterflies (see p211) arrive in Michoacán. In the markets, citrus fruit is in plentiful supply.

Día de la Virgen de Guadalupe

(Dec 12). The appearance of Mexico's patron saint in 1531 on the Cerro del Tepeyac hill is remembered in every town and village. Thousands of pilgrims flock to her shrine in Mexico City (see p109) to view her from a crowded moving walkway. In the rest of the country las mañanitas (an early-morning birthday song) is sung at dawn, and special church services are attended. Boys dress up as Juan Diego, the Indian who encountered the Virgin's apparition.

A piñata, filled with a mixture of sweets and fruit

Posadas (Dec 16–24). These parties re-enact the nativity story of Mary and Joseph seeking lodging, and take place over the course of nine nights in all parts of Mexico. The participants carry candles and lanterns and sing the posadas song. Each night culminates in a party at a different house. An essential part of any posada is the piñata, a clay pot filled with mandarin oranges, sugar cane, and candy and decorated with crepe paper, sometimes in the shape of comic heroes or animals. This is suspended overhead on a rope, and blindfolded children take turns swinging at it with a stick. In the end they crack it open and unleash a shower of candy and fruit.

Day of the Holy Innocents (Día de los Inocentes; Dec 28). A day for practical jokes.

Epiphany (Día de los Santos Reyes; Jan 6). Mexican children receive their Christmas presents from the Three Kings in the morning and eat the traditional rosca de reyes, a ring-shaped cake filled with dried fruits and containing a hidden image of the baby Jesus. Most cities have processions to celebrate the arrival of the Kings. There are spectacular ones on Avenida Juárez and Xochimilco in Mexico City, in Querétaro, and in Campeche,

An Indian in a headdress for the Día de la Virgen de Guadalupe

Mérida, and Tizimín in the Yucatán Peninsula.

The Night of the Radishes
(Noche de los Rábanos; Feb 24), Oaxaca. Radishes carved into fantastic shapes, including nativity figures, are put on display and offered for sale amid general festivities in the zócalo (see p222).

Candlemas (Día de la Candelaria; Feb 2). Baby Jesus is lifted out of the nativity scenes. Streets are decorated with paper lanterns; in some villages there are bull runs and bullfights. Most towns have an outdoor fiesta in the main square with music, sideshows, fireworks, and dancing.

Feria Artesanal del Mundo Maya (Feb), Mérida (Yucatán). This fair offers a good opportunity to see a variety of Maya handicrafts.

Flag Day (Día de la Bandera; Feb 24). School children parade and pay homage to the flag. There are official ceremonies in the main squares of most towns.

Carnival (Feb/Mar). The days preceding the rigors of Lent are celebrated nationally with extravagant parades, floats, confetti, dancing, and the burning of effigies. The most spectacular partying takes place in port towns such as La Paz and Ensenada in Baja California, Acapulco, Mazatlán (Sinaloa), Campeche in the Yucatán, and, most famously, in El Puerto de Veracruz on the Gulf Coast.

A colorful carnival parade in the Yucatán Peninsula

The Days of the Dead

ACCORDING TO popular belief, the dead have divine permission to visit friends and relatives on Earth once a year. During the Days of the Dead, the living welcome the souls of the departed with offerings of flowers, specially prepared foods, candles, and incense. This is not a morbid occasion, but one of peace and happiness. Celebrations vary from region to region but in general the souls of children are thought to visit on November 1, in the evening, and those of adults on November 2, before departing for another year.

Skeleton candle-holder

Skull masks and clothing painted with bones are sometimes worn by city children during the Days of the Dead. Carnival dancers may also take the role of Death, a familiar presence during Mexican festivals.

A photo of the dead person is a common focal point for Days of the Dead altars.

Candle sticks and incense burners

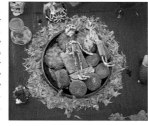

Sugar figures, bread, and other foodstuffs are temptingly displayed. The dead are believed to take the essence or the aroma of the offerings, which are themselves later consumed by the living.

ALTARS FOR THE DEAD

Many families keep holy pictures and images of saints on a shelf or table. For All Saints' and All Souls' Days (November 1 and 2) these home altars carry offerings for the dead. In towns and cities, offerings may also be displayed in public places. Shown here is an altar in the Museo del Anahuacalli (see p111), evoking the life and work of muralist Diego Rivera (see p104).

The marigold (cempasúchil), often referred to in Mexico as "the flower of the dead," is used in profusion. Here Diego's name is spelled out among scattered marigold petals.

WHERE TO SEE THE DAYS OF THE DEAD

Celebrations occur virtually everywhere in central and southern Mexico. Before the festival, market stalls sell an abundance of sugar figures, pottery, flowers, and skeleton toys. In Toluca (see p144) trestle tables are piled high with sweets. Most Mexicans visit cemeteries during the morning of November 2, but Purépecha villagers living around Lake Pátzcuaro hold a vigil on the night of November 1 (see p207). In Tzintzuntzán (see p206), masked villagers perform dances.

Isla Janitzio, an island in Lake Pátzcuaro, where the celebrations are particularly colorful

Personalized altars are set up in homes and adorned with the dead person's favorite foods and drinks, and other objects, such as children's toys.

Hand-made paper cuts, with the delicacy of lace, decorate many altars.

Papier-mâché skeletons *are often displayed in public places. Like Posada's skeletons, they perform everyday activities.*

Portrait of José Guadalupe Posada, from a mural by Diego Rivera *(see p81).*

Fine textiles and articles of new clothing are sometimes set out on altars.

Calla lilies, which feature in many of Rivera's paintings, are included here among the offerings.

This child's grave in San Pablito, Puebla, with brightly colored flowers among the images painted on it, is typical of the highly personal style of decoration often used. Before the Days of the Dead, cemeteries throughout Mexico are tidied and graves repainted.

ARTS AND CRAFTS FOR THE DAYS OF THE DEAD

Death is portrayed with humor and even affection by craftspeople and artists. Skulls and skeletons are fashioned from sugar, tin, wood, paper, clay, and bone. Skeletons shown as bishops and shoe-cleaners participate side by side in the modern equivalent of the medieval dance of death. In the words of poet and essayist Octavio Paz, "The Mexican is familiar with death, jokes about it, caresses it, sleeps with it, celebrates it …" Many objects are made especially for the Days of the Dead; others are sold year round in galleries and craft shops.

This papier-mâché and wire skull, sporting skeletons and angels, was created by Saulo Moreno. The green growths of the apple tree stress the idea of regeneration.

Sugar skulls may be inscribed with the name of a person living or dead or, as here, with a fitting sentiment: "Amor Eterno" ("Everlasting Love").

Humorous miniature scenes, peopled with spectral figures, are made for the occasion. In this example skeleton gamblers of painted clay are depicted playing poker in a wooden, mirror-lined room.

La Catrina, by the engraver José Guadalupe Posada (see p80), is widely associated with the Days of the Dead, and her image often appears in works by craftspeople.

The Climate of Mexico

COASTAL INFLUENCES and sharp variations in altitude both have an impact on Mexico's climate. The cold Californian current lowers temperatures and rainfall on the Pacific coast, and, along with the North Pacific anticyclone, contributes to the arid nature of northwestern Mexico. In sharp contrast, the Caribbean coast in the southeast, which faces warm waters, has a tropical climate. Inland, temperatures are much cooler in the central mountains.

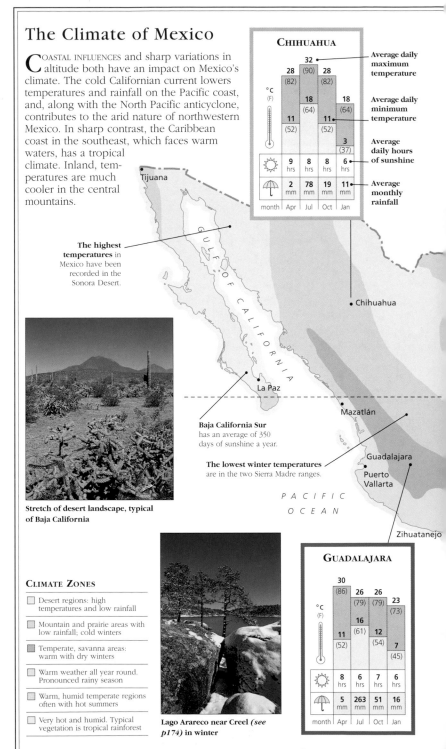

CHIHUAHUA

Average daily maximum temperature

Average daily minimum temperature

Average daily hours of sunshine

Average monthly rainfall

°C (F)				
	32 (90)			
	28 (82)		28 (82)	
		18 (64)	18 (64)	
	11 (52)	11 (52)		
				3 (37)
☼	9 hrs	8 hrs	8 hrs	6 hrs
☂	2 mm	78 mm	19 mm	11 mm
month	Apr	Jul	Oct	Jan

Tijuana

The highest temperatures in Mexico have been recorded in the Sonora Desert.

GULF OF CALIFORNIA

• Chihuahua

La Paz

Mazatlán

Baja California Sur has an average of 350 days of sunshine a year.

The lowest winter temperatures are in the two Sierra Madre ranges.

Guadalajara

Puerto Vallarta

PACIFIC OCEAN

Stretch of desert landscape, typical of Baja California

Zihuatanejo

CLIMATE ZONES

☐ Desert regions: high temperatures and low rainfall

☐ Mountain and prairie areas with low rainfall; cold winters

☐ Temperate, savanna areas: warm with dry winters

☐ Warm weather all year round. Pronounced rainy season

☐ Warm, humid temperate regions often with hot summers

☐ Very hot and humid. Typical vegetation is tropical rainforest

Lago Arareco near Creel (see p174) in winter

GUADALAJARA

°C (F)				
	30 (86)	26 (79)	26 (79)	23 (73)
		16 (61)		
	11 (52)		12 (54)	7 (45)
☼	8 hrs	6 hrs	7 hrs	6 hrs
☂	5 mm	263 mm	51 mm	16 mm
month	Apr	Jul	Oct	Jan

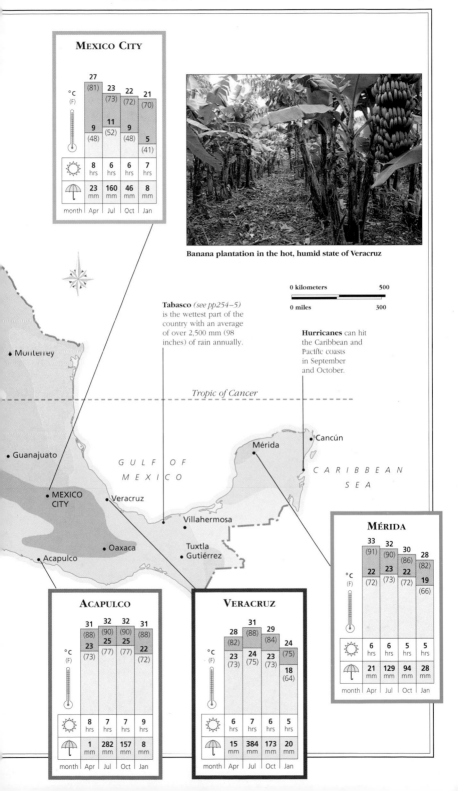

MEXICO CITY

°C (F)				
	27 (81)	23 (73)	22 (72)	21 (70)
	9 (48)	11 (52)	9 (48)	5 (41)
☀	8 hrs	6 hrs	6 hrs	7 hrs
☂	23 mm	160 mm	46 mm	8 mm
month	Apr	Jul	Oct	Jan

Banana plantation in the hot, humid state of Veracruz

0 kilometers 500

0 miles 300

Tabasco *(see pp254–5)* is the wettest part of the country with an average of over 2,500 mm (98 inches) of rain annually.

Hurricanes can hit the Caribbean and Pacific coasts in September and October.

Tropic of Cancer

• Monterrey

• Guanajuato

• MEXICO CITY

• Veracruz

Mérida

• Cancún

GULF OF MEXICO

CARIBBEAN SEA

• Villahermosa

• Oaxaca

Tuxtla • Gutiérrez

• Acapulco

MÉRIDA

°C (F)				
	33 (91)	32 (90)	30 (86)	28 (82)
	22 (72)	23 (73)	22 (72)	19 (66)
☀	6 hrs	6 hrs	5 hrs	5 hrs
☂	21 mm	129 mm	94 mm	28 mm
month	Apr	Jul	Oct	Jan

ACAPULCO

°C (F)				
	31 (88)	32 (90)	32 (90)	31 (88)
	23 (73)	25 (77)	25 (77)	22 (72)
☀	8 hrs	7 hrs	7 hrs	9 hrs
☂	1 mm	282 mm	157 mm	8 mm
month	Apr	Jul	Oct	Jan

VERACRUZ

°C (F)				
	28 (82)	31 (88)	29 (84)	24 (75)
	23 (73)	24 (75)	23 (73)	18 (64)
☀	6 hrs	7 hrs	6 hrs	5 hrs
☂	15 mm	384 mm	173 mm	20 mm
month	Apr	Jul	Oct	Jan

THE HISTORY OF MEXICO

MODERN MEXICO IS THE PRODUCT *of a collision of two cultures that occurred when the Spanish conquistadors defeated the Aztecs in 1521. In the following centuries, the ancient civilizations of Mexico fused with the Catholic European culture of Spain. After gaining its independence in the 19th century, Mexico set about forging its own identity, a process that continues today.*

Mesoamerica, a region of which ancient Mexico formed a large part, had a history stretching back three millennia by the time the Spanish arrived. Although powerful imperial states – especially that of the Aztecs – had developed, they were no match for the superior arms of the Spanish conquistadors, who overran the country and imposed their rule and religion on the indigenous population.

Statue of Benito Juárez

For the next 300 years Mexico was a colony of Spain. Hungry for silver, the Spaniards pushed into the arid north, founding new cities. In central and southern Mexico they lorded it over a subjugated Indian population, who worked on Spanish estates, paid tribute to the Crown, and worshiped the Christian God – albeit without completely abandoning old religious beliefs and practices. During the 18th century, however, Spain's grip on its colony weakened as it confronted rival imperial powers in the Americas and disgruntled colonial subjects in Mexico itself.

The Napoleonic Wars in Europe triggered a struggle for independence in Mexico that was finally accomplished in 1821. In the mid-19th century, however, the US expanded its territory southward, squeezing Mexico into its present-day borders.

Not until the mid-20th century, following the Revolution launched in 1910, did the country at last achieve stability and sustained economic growth. Nevertheless, social problems, some of them deriving from the colonial past, remain serious.

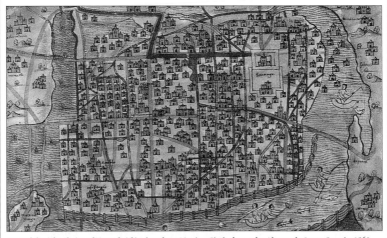

Map of the island city of Tenochtitlán (modern Mexico City), drawn by Alonso de Santa Cruz in 1560

◁ The Totonac civilization as seen by Diego Rivera in his mural in the Palacio Nacional *(see pp66–7)*

THE OLMECS

Settlers arrived in Mexico having crossed the Bering landbridge from Asia to Alaska some 20 millennia ago. By the second millennium BC farming villages were springing up. Sometime around 1500 BC the first notable culture, that of the Olmecs, was established on the hot and humid Gulf coast, principally at San Lorenzo *(see p253)* and later at La Venta *(see p254)*. The Olmecs built ceremonial centers rather than cities, and their earthen pyramids suggest that they were governed by a central authority capable of mobilizing extensive manpower. They rafted heavy basalt blocks downriver and carved them into massive heads and other sculptures with stylized or feline ("were-jaguar") features. They also produced ceramics and exquisite jade figurines. During the first millennium BC, however, the Olmec centers declined. San Lorenzo was the scene of systematic destruction and desecration in around 900 BC – although by whom is uncertain – and Olmec civilization faded into obscurity.

Olmec stone figure

THE CLASSIC MAYA

The Olmec "mother culture" inspired a series of successor cultures in the lowlands to the east and the highlands to the west. In the lowlands dense Maya settlements, grouped around massive ceremonial centers, began to form in the Mexico-Guatemala border region by about 500 BC. Maya civilization reached its greatest flowering in the "Classic Period" of AD 200–900. Numerous cities developed in which elaborate temples were surrounded by elite residential quarters, and cultivated fields. The Classic Maya pursued a vigorous ritual life and practiced sophisticated art *(see p233)*. They also acquired remarkable mathematical and astronomical knowledge. This made it possible for them to do the elaborate calculations needed for the "Long Count" of their calendar, which spanned millennia *(see p47)*.

Once thought of as pacific, the Maya actually engaged in regular and ruthless intercity warfare. Glyphs *(see pp46–7)* on their stelae – carved stone obelisks – record the victories of great rulers, who warred, allied, intermarried, and patronized the arts in the same way as the princely families of

Carving in the palace of Palenque, one of the greatest cities of the Classic Maya

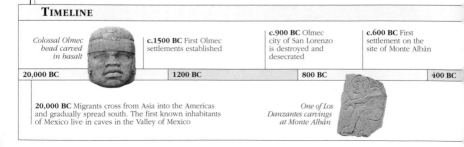

TIMELINE

Colossal Olmec head carved in basalt

c.1500 BC First Olmec settlements established

c.900 BC Olmec city of San Lorenzo is destroyed and desecrated

c.600 BC First settlement on the site of Monte Albán

20,000 BC	1200 BC	800 BC	400 BC

20,000 BC Migrants cross from Asia into the Americas and gradually spread south. The first known inhabitants of Mexico live in caves in the Valley of Mexico

One of Los Danzantes carvings at Monte Albán

Wall painting in Tomb 105 at Monte Albán, the center of Zapotec civilization

Renaissance Italy. By around AD 800, however, the Classic Maya faced crisis: the population had outstripped available resources, and several centers were destroyed and abandoned, the victims, perhaps, of epidemics or peasant revolt.

THE RISE AND FALL OF TEOTIHUACÁN
In the central highlands, meanwhile, other cities flourished. The population of the hilltop Monte Albán *(see pp220–21)*, for instance, climbed from 5,000 in 500 BC to around 25,000 in AD 700. When the city declined, Mitla *(see p226)* and other lesser towns sprang up to contest its power in the area around Oaxaca.

All these cities were overshadowed, however, by the great Classic metropolis of Teotihuacán *(see pp134–7)*, built on an imposing site in an open valley to the north of what is now Mexico City.

Funerary mask from Teotihuacán

Teotihuacán rose to prominence around 200 BC and reached the height of its power in AD 400–500, when it dominated the valley and a wider hinterland beyond. Its influence stretched far to the south, into the Maya region. By this time it had become a vast city of some 125,000 inhabitants, making it one of the largest cities in the world.

During the 7th century disaster struck. Like the cities of the Classic Maya, Teotihuacán may have overstretched its resources. Poverty and discontent appear to have increased, and nomads from the arid north began to threaten the city. Around 650 the city was attacked and partially burned by these northern invaders, or local rebels, or both. It did not disappear suddenly but entered a long decline, as its population was leached away. The fall of Teotihuacán sent shockwaves throughout Mesoamerica.

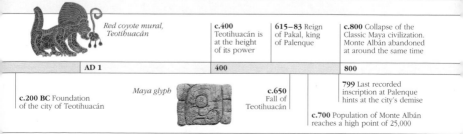

Red coyote mural, Teotihuacán	**c.400** Teotihuacán is at the height of its power	**615–83** Reign of Pakal, king of Palenque	**c.800** Collapse of the Classic Maya civilization. Monte Albán abandoned at around the same time	
AD 1		**400**		**800**
c.200 BC Foundation of the city of Teotihuacán	*Maya glyph*	**c.650** Fall of Teotihuacán	**799** Last recorded inscription at Palenque hints at the city's demise **c.700** Population of Monte Albán reaches a high point of 25,000	

THE TOLTECS

The collapse of Teotihuacán and decline of Monte Albán resulted in a phase of fragmentation and militarization in central Mexico. A series of successor states such as Cacaxtla *(see p156)*, and Xochicalco *(see p145)* carved out local fiefs. One, the Toltec state, built a loose hegemony between about 900 and 1100. Probably northern migrants, the Toltecs settled in the north of the Valley of Mexico. Here they built the city of Tula *(see p144)*, which may have had a population of 40,000. The Toltecs, who were keen traders dealing especially in obsidian, exacted tribute from dependent communities. They also developed a militarist culture, evident in the serried ranks of their Atlantes (stone warriors), gruesome

Atlante statue at Tula

friezes depicting war and sacrifice, skull racks, *chacmools* (reclining sacrificial statues), and military orders such as the Eagle and Jaguar Knights.

Tula collapsed and was torched and desecrated around AD 1100, but its influence lived on. Some Toltecs are thought to have migrated to the Yucatán in the 10th century, where their influence is evident. Among them may have been a prince or leader called Quetzalcoatl (meaning the "Feathered Serpent"), who was later transformed into a god. Since the collapse of the Classic Maya cities, power had shifted to the northern part of the Yucatán Peninsula, especially Uxmal and the other cities of the Puuc hills. Around AD 1000 Toltec motifs – feathered serpents, Atlantes, and *chacmools* – began to appear, notably at Chichén Itzá. This city headed a regional confederacy until, in about 1200, it was overthrown by the nearby Mayapán, and Izamal, and by other rivals on the coasts of the Yucatán Peninsula.

THE AZTEC EMPIRE

The last great Mesoamerican empire, that of the Aztecs (often called the Mexica), also arose in the Valley of Mexico, from where it went on to dominate much of the Mexican heartland. The Aztecs arrived as a poor, ill-equipped band, who had trekked overland from their distant northern homeland, Aztlán (the location of

The Aztec legend of the eagle perching on a prickly pear cactus, illustrated in the Codex Mendoza

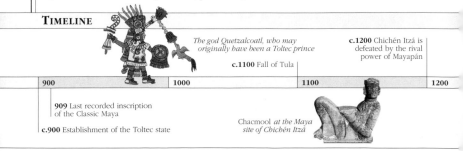

TIMELINE

The god Quetzalcoatl, who may originally have been a Toltec prince

c.1200 Chichén Itzá is defeated by the rival power of Mayapán

c.1100 Fall of Tula

900   1000   1100   1200

909 Last recorded inscription of the Classic Maya

Chacmool at the Maya site of Chichén Itzá

c.900 Establishment of the Toltec state

which is unknown). They initially served as the menials and mercenaries of established cities. In around 1325, however, they were advised by their tribal god, Huitzilopochtli, to pitch their tents where they saw an eagle perched on a cactus, devouring a snake. This omen (depicted on Mexico's national flag) was seen on a lake-island, which thus became the site of the city of Tenochtitlán. Ruthless fighters with a sense of providential mission, the Aztecs gradually expanded their territory. At the same time they boosted agriculture by creating fertile *chinampas*, irrigated fields, to feed the urban population.

By the 1420s they had emerged as the dominant power in the Valley of Mexico. Their loose tribal organization gave way to an imperial system based on strict hierarchy, a warrior ethic, and a despotic emperor. Soon, their conquests spread to the rich lowlands of the south and east. Tribute poured in. At the same time, constant warfare provided prisoners, feeding the demand for human sacrifice to appease their gods – for only by feeding palpitating hearts to the gods could the fragile cosmos be maintained in place. Mass sacrifices – like that which took place to mark the dedication of the rebuilt Templo Mayor *(see pp68–70)* in 1487, when 20,000 prisoners were said to have been immolated – served to terrorize enemies and bolster the empire.

The Meeting of Cortés and Moctezuma, attributed to Juan Correa (c.1645–1716)

ARRIVAL OF THE SPANISH

When the first Spanish voyagers made contact with Mesoamerica in the 1500s, the Aztec Empire was huge, populous, and dynamic. But it faced population pressures, internal dissidence, and resistance from outlying states: the Tarascan empire in present-day Michoacán, and the tough highland principality of Tlaxcala *(see p156)*, to the east.

Hernán Cortés landed on the coast of what is now Veracruz in 1519 and marched to Tenochtitlán. But first he defeated, then joined forces with, the Tlaxcalans who proved invaluable allies in the Spaniards' destruction of Aztec power. By means of such alliances, Cortés was able to confront and finally defeat the Aztec empire of Moctezuma II (1502–20). After a bloody and destructive siege, Tenochtitlán was conquered.

The Conquest of Mexico as depicted in a mural by Juan O'Gorman (1905–82)

Carving of the Aztec goddess Coyolxauhqui in the Templo Mayor, in Mexico City

1300	1400	1500
c.1325 The Aztecs found Tenochtitlán (modern Mexico City) on a lake-island	**1426–40** The Aztecs take control of the Valley of Mexico under Emperor Itzcoatl	**1502** Accession of Moctezuma II as Aztec emperor

1500s Aztec wars with Tlaxcala, to the east, which later becomes a Spanish ally

1520 On July 1, the so-called Noche Triste ("Sad Night"), the Spanish are defeated by the Aztecs

1519 Cortés lands on the coast of Veracruz

1521 The Spanish capture Tenochtitlán and the Aztec Empire falls

Mesoamerica

THE TERM MESOAMERICA refers to a geographical region whose people shared a broadly similar culture before the arrival of the Spanish (see p43). It covers what is now central and southern Mexico, Belize, Guatemala, and parts of Honduras and El Salvador. The people of Mesoamerica had many things in common, including gods, a calendar, and building practices, but had different languages and customs. The civilizations are normally divided into "highland" (especially the Valley of Mexico) and "lowland," such as the Maya.

Chacmool
These carved reclining figures can be seen at central Mexican and Maya archaeological sites. The stone dishes often found on their stomachs are said to have held sacrificial offerings, but there is no evidence for this.

Ballgame
The ballgame, played with a rubber ball (see p277), was a feature of most civilizations of Mesoamerica. This stone disk shows a Maya player.

MAP OF MESOAMERICA
The civilizations shown on the map did not always exist at the same time. Often, as in the case of the Mixtecs and the Zapotecs, one group would take over the territories of its predecessors.

Pyramids
Mesoamerican pyramids are stepped and, like this one at Edzná (see p261), crowned with a temple. The Aztecs used them for human sacrifices, while for the Maya they were usually funerary buildings. They were often built on top of earlier pyramids.

Human Sacrifice
The need to appease gods with human blood was a strong belief in ancient Mexico, particularly to the Aztecs. This codex illustration shows Aztec priests killing victims, whose bodies are then thrown down the steps of the temple.

Obsidian
A hard, glassy volcanic stone, obsidian was fashioned into domestic items, weapons, and sacrificial knives such as this one. Metals were not used until the late Classic period and never for functional objects.

Jade
This green stone was more highly prized than gold in Mesoamerica. The Zapotecs, in particular, used it to make objects such as this fearsome-looking bat-god pendant.

Food
Many foods now eaten all over the world originated in Mesoamerica. They include tomatoes, chilies, chocolate, and corn (maize). This scene from an Aztec codex shows a granary being filled with corn.

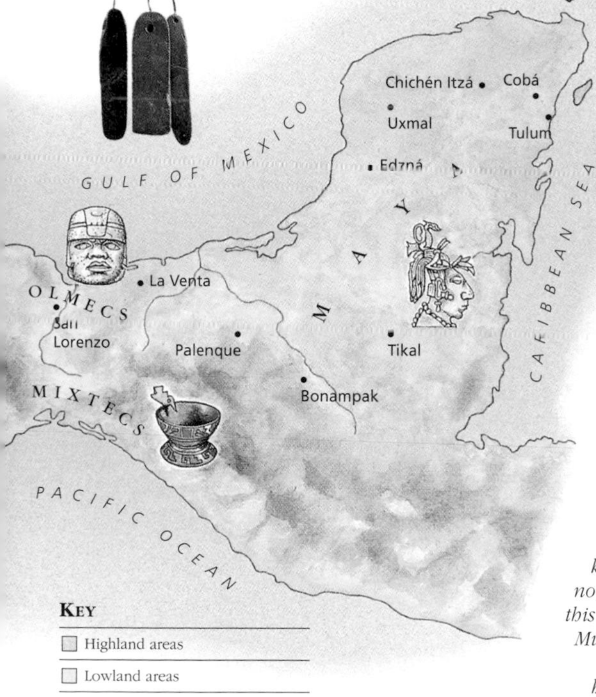

Technology
Although the wheel was known, it was used only for nonfunctional objects such as this Huastec toy dog in Xalapa Museum (see pp248–9). Most burdens were carried by human porters or by canoe.

GULF OF MEXICO

Chichén Itzá • Cobá
Uxmal
• Edzná
Tulum

M A Y A

CARIBBEAN SEA

O L M E C S
San Lorenzo
• La Venta
Palenque
Tikal
Bonampak

M I X T E C S

PACIFIC OCEAN

KEY
☐ Highland areas
☐ Lowland areas

PERIODS OF MESOAMERICA

PRECLASSIC						CLASSIC		POSTCLASSIC		
Olmecs						Classic Veracruz		Totonacs		
					Maya					
							Tarascans			
				Teotihuacán			Toltecs	Aztecs		
			Zapotecs					Mixtecs		
1500 BC	1200 BC	900 BC	600 BC	300 BC	0	AD 300	AD 600	AD 900	AD 1200	AD 1500

The Maya

U NLIKE THE OTHER PEOPLES of Mesoamerica, the Maya did not develop a large, centralized empire. Instead they lived in independent city-states. This did not impede them in acquiring advanced knowledge of astronomy and developing sophisticated systems of writing, counting, and recording the passing of time. The Maya were once thought to have been a peaceful people, but they are now known to have shared the lust for war and human sacrifice of other pre-Columbian civilizations.

LOCATOR MAP

☐ Extent of Maya Territory

Mural from Bonampak
*The Maya were the finest artists of Mesoamerica
(see p232). Their talent for portraiture can be
seen especially in the extraordinary series of
murals painted in a temple at Bonampak.*

In the Tzolkin or Sacred Round
20 day names were combined
with 13 numbers to give a
year of 260 individually
named days.

Architecture
*Pyramids, palaces, and other
great works of Maya architecture can be seen at such sites
as Palenque (see pp234–7),
Chichén Itzá (see pp274–6),
Cobá (see p284), and Tulum
(see pp284–5). This detail is
from Uxmal (see pp262–4).*

20 named days

GLYPHS
Other Mesoamerican civilizations developed writing systems, but none was as complete or sophisti-cated as that of the Maya. They used about 800 different hieroglyphs (or simply "glyphs"), some representing whole words, others phonetic sounds. Some glyphs were under-stood as early as the 1820s, but the major advances in decipherment really began in the 1950s.

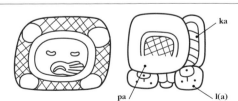

A Maya glyph can represent either a whole word, or the sounds of which it is composed. Some words were written in several ways. Above are two ways of writing the name Pakal, the ruler of Palenque. Pakal means "shield," depicted by the left glyph.

ASTRONOMY
The Maya had a knowledge of astronomy that was very advanced for their time. They observed and predicted the phases of the moon, equinoxes and solstices, and solar and lunar eclipses. They knew that the Morning and Evening Star were the same planet, Venus, and calculated its "year" to 584 days, within a fraction of the true figure (583.92 days). It is almost certain that they calculated the orbit of Mars as well. Remarkably, they achieved all this without the use of lenses for observing distant objects, instruments for calculating angles, or clocks to measure the passing of seconds, minutes, and hours.

The Observatory at Chichén Itzá

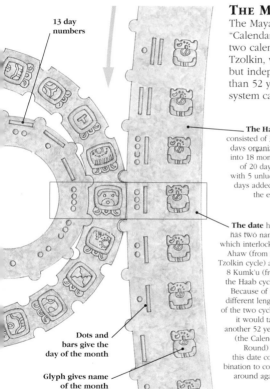

13 day numbers

THE MAYA CALENDAR
The Maya observed the 52-year "Calendar Round." This resulted from two calendar cycles, the Haab and the Tzolkin, which acted simultaneously but independently. For periods longer than 52 years the Maya used a separate system called the Long Count.

The Haab consisted of 365 days organized into 18 months of 20 days – with 5 unlucky days added at the end.

The date here has two names which interlock: 4 Ahaw (from the Tzolkin cycle) and 8 Kumk'u (from the Haab cycle). Because of the different lengths of the two cycles, it would take another 52 years (the Calendar Round) for this date combination to come around again.

Dots and bars give the day of the month

Glyph gives name of the month

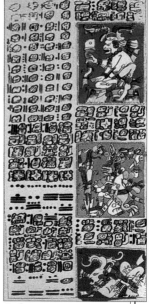

Codex
Maya books, codices, were created by writing on both sides of a thin sheet of bark, which was then folded like a concertina. Only four have survived, including the Dresden Codex, a replica of which is shown above.

NUMBERS
Mesoamerica used a vigesimal counting system, that is they worked to base 20 rather than base 10. The Maya represented numbers with dots (units) and bars (fives).

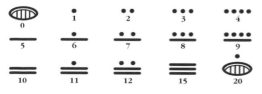

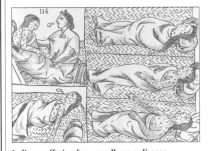

Indians suffering from smallpox, a disease
introduced to Mexico by the Spaniards

COLONIAL MEXICO

Following their defeat of the Aztecs,
the conquistadors entrusted the Indian
population to Spanish *encomenderos.*
These quasi-feudal seigneurs were
expected to protect and convert their
charges, who, in return paid them tribute. Spanish expeditions probed the
outer reaches of Mesoamerica –
Oaxaca, Chiapas, and the Yucatán
Peninsula. Lured by the promise of silver, they also penetrated the Gran
Chichimec, the region to the north,
beyond the boundaries of Aztec and
Tarascan domains, to reach distant
Zacatecas and beyond. Hand in hand
with this military conquest in search
of booty went a spiritual conquest.
Franciscan and Dominican friars tire-
lessly preached to, converted, whipped,
and baptized the Indians.European diseases such as smallpox produced
massive Indian mortality.

MEXICO IN THE 17TH CENTURY

During the 17th century, the institution
of the hacienda *(see pp50–51)* was
established by rich Spaniards looking
for the good life of the hidalgo in the
colonies. The distant Crown, represented by the Viceroy, managed to
exert only a loose control over these

settlers who came to farm and mine,
and the colony enjoyed a measure of
independence. Nevertheless, "New
Spain" remitted huge quantities of bullion to its European overlord.

As the colonial economy matured,
the settlers produced a Mexican-born,
Creole elite, proud of their new homeland. Indians, whose numbers had
begun to recover, learned how to cul-
tivate European crops and raise cattle.
The mixing of Spanish-born settlers
with Indians created intermediate
castes. The wealthy white elite
financed grandiose haciendas, great
town residences, and lavish churches
(see pp24–5). Creole accomplishments
were also evident in Mexico City's
flourishing University (the oldest in
the Americas) and the literary output
of the Baroque age, notably the plays
and poems of Sor (Sister) Juana Inés

Diego Rivera mural depicting the harsh treatment
of Indian laborers by their European masters

TIMELINE

The Virgin of Guadalupe

1531 An apparition initiates the cult
of the Virgin of Guadalupe *(see p108)*

1629 A major flood hits
Mexico City and takes
five years to subside

1651 Birth of
Sor Juana Inés
de la Cruz

1550   **1600**   **1650**

1546 Zacatecas
(see p192)
founded following
the discovery of
silver deposits

1571 The Spanish Inquisition
arrives in Mexico. The first auto-
da-fé is held three years later

*Sor Juana
Inés de la
Cruz*

de la Cruz. Compared to Europe, 17th-century Mexico was a tranquil place. The authority of the Church, combined with the lack of a regular army, created an underlying stability for the colony.

THE COMING OF INDEPENDENCE

In the 18th century, however, the new Bourbon dynasty in Spain sought to emulate French colonialism in clawing back Mexico's partial autonomy, centralizing royal power, weakening the Church, creating a regular army, boosting bullion remittances, and extracting more taxes. Relations between Spain and Mexico worsened as Creoles increasingly resented the interference of Spanish officials. Indians and lower castes suffered from higher taxes and – as the population grew and shortages of basic goods recurred – lower living standards. The old alliance between Crown and Church weakened: in 1767 the Jesuits were expelled.

International events compounded these tensions. Repeatedly involved in European wars, Spain was short of cash and incapable of controlling the sea-lanes to Mexico. To the north, the French and British threatened the colony's far-flung frontiers, which embraced the present southern United States, from Florida to California. The American Revolution of 1776 afforded an example of colonial rebellion, and Napoleon's overthrow of the Bourbon monarchy in 1808 provoked a crisis in the colonial government. On September 16, 1810, a parish priest, Miguel Hidalgo, gave his famous call to arms in the cause of independence,

Hidalgo shown in a mural by Juan O'Gorman in Castillo de Chapultepec *(see p88)*

Independence leader José María Morelos (1765–1815)

El Grito ("The Cry"). The revolt failed, however, and Hidalgo was executed. A second revolt four years later, lead by another priest, José María Morelos, was similarly crushed. But repression could not shore up a tottering empire. Guerrilla resistance continued. In 1821, shortly after the army had seized power in Spain, Mexico's Creole elite proclaimed the country's independence. Spain lacked the will or ability to fight on, and its principal American colony became the independent nation of Mexico.

1692 Riots in Mexico City caused by food shortages and ethnic tensions

King Charles III of Spain

1810 On Sep 16 Miguel Hidalgo launches a popular revolt against Spanish rule. The rebels are defeated. Hidalgo is executed the following year

1820 Liberal military coup takes place in Spain

1700	1750	1800

1700 The Bourbon dynasty ascends the throne of Spain

1759–88 Reign of the reformist King Charles III

1767 Expulsion of the Jesuits from Mexico

1765 Bourbon "reforms" tighten Spain's hold on Mexico

1814 José María Morelos leads a second attempt at Mexican independence. He is captured and executed in 1815

The Hacienda

MEXICO'S HACIENDAS, or country estates, evolved during the colonial and post-colonial era. Production was determined by what the land and climate could offer. Some estates were given over to cattle, or to corn and wheat; others grew sugar cane or agave for making the alcoholic drink *pulque*. Landowners in the Yucatán grew rich cultivating henequen (sisal), whereas those in mountainous areas, such as Zacatecas, often ran silver mines. The 1910 Revolution brought about the destruction of many haciendas, but some have been preserved or recently restored, and a few now serve as hotels *(see p290)*.

Laborers on a Porfirian hacienda where, by 1910, many rural Mexicans lived and worked

A TYPICAL HACIENDA

This illustration shows an idealized 19th-century hacienda. Under Porfirio Díaz, many estates experienced their most prosperous phase. To make up for their isola-tion, haciendas were often self-sufficient, with dairies, brick-kilns, orchards, and other facilities.

Lookout and defensive tower

Gardens offered an escape for the landowner from the working life of the hacienda.

Casa Grande (Main House)
This spacious and comfortably fur-nished building lay at the heart of the hacienda. During the Porfirian era, houses were often remodeled to resemble European castles or English stately homes. Landowners rarely lived on their estates, preferring to make brief visits from the city.

Worksheds
Each hacienda incorporated special buildings and work areas. The men shown above are breaking ore at a mining estate in Guanajuato.

Stable for horses and mules
The art of horsemanship (charrería, see p74) was crucial to life on the hacienda. Horses were needed for agriculture, for transporting produce, and to aid the laborers on mining estates.

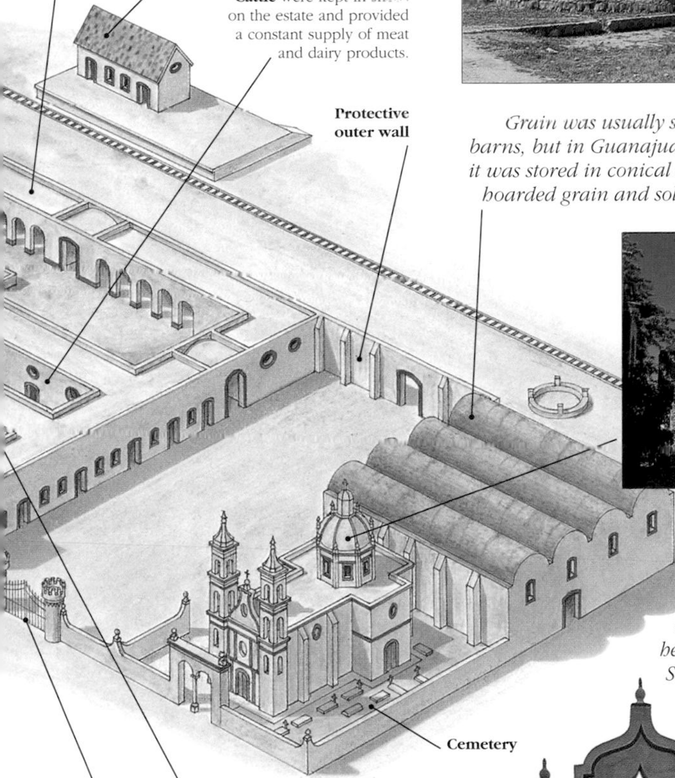

A private railroad station allowed landowners to transport their produce rapidly through difficult terrain.

Cattle were kept in sheds on the estate and provided a constant supply of meat and dairy products.

Protective outer wall

Granaries
Grain was usually stored in immense barns, but in Guanajuato and Zacatecas it was stored in conical silos. Landowners hoarded grain and sold it in lean times.

Church
Landowners were responsible for the spiritual welfare of their workforce. Shown here is the church at Santa María Regla, near Huasca (see p139).

Cemetery

Servants' quarters were usually in a poor condition. Laborers lived with their families in a single, cramped room.

Entrance gate
Some haciendas resembled fortresses, with high walls and lookout towers. This Moorish-style double archway is from the sisal hacienda at Yaxcopoil in the Yucatán (see p271).

THE NEW NATION

Mexico achieved its independence at great cost. The economy was ravaged, and Spanish capital fled the country. After a brief imperial interlude – when Agustín de Iturbide made himself Emperor Agustín I (1821–3) – Mexico became a republic. But political consensus proved elusive. Mexico's elites were roughly divided into liberals, who favored a progressive, republican, free-trading secular society, and conservatives, who preferred a centralized, hierarchical state, backed by Church and army, possibly capped by a monarchy. Administrations came and went: 30 presidents governed in the 50 years after 1821. The army absorbed the bulk of revenue and generated a host of *caudillos* who built up their retinues and contested for power, often without principle or ideology. Prominent among them was Antonio López de Santa Anna, whose slippery opportunism and shifting alliances with Church, army, and financiers enabled him to attain the presidency no fewer than 11 times.

Monumento a los Niños Héroes *(see p89)*

WAR WITH TEXAS

Texas broke away from the rest of Mexico in 1836. Victorious at the Alamo, Santa Anna's forces were crushed by the Texans a month later at San Jacinto. Ten years after this, Texas' decision to join the US sparked a war in which the US invaded Mexico by land and sea. Mexican resistance, though dogged, was ill-coordinated. The capital fell after fierce fighting, during which a group of cadets (the Niños Héroes – Boy Heroes) died defending Chapultepec Castle rather than surrender. The war ended with the Treaty of Guadalupe Hidalgo (1848), in which Mexico lost nearly half its territory – the vast area stretching from Texas to California – to the US.

LOCATOR MAP

▨ *Mexican territory before 1848*

☐ *Modern Mexico*

THE REFORM

Defeat in the war against the US provoked political reassessment and polarization. A new generation of liberals, led by the Indian lawyer Benito Juárez, advocated radical reforms to modernize the country. In 1854 they ousted Santa Anna and embarked on a radical

Benito Juárez, the popular leader who steered Mexico through the period of the Reform

TIMELINE

1824 Federal republic created

General Antonio López de Santa Anna

1840–46 War of the Castes: Maya revolt in the Yucatán

1846–8 Mexican-American War

1862 May 5: Mexican forces defeat French invaders at Puebla

1860 Reform laws

1820	1830	1840	1850	1860

1821 Mexican independence declared under Agustín de Iturbide

1836 Rebellion of Texas. Santa Anna victorious at the Alamo but defeated at San Jacinto

1848 In the Treaty of Guadalupe Hidalgo, Mexico loses nearly half its territory, and the present-day border along Río Grande to the north is established

1857 Liberal democratic constitution

1858–61 War of the Reform: liberal victory under Juárez

The Execution of Emperor Maximilian by the French painter Édouard Manet

PORFIRIO DÍAZ

After Juárez's death in 1872 the liberal leaders jockeyed for succession. A young general, Porfirio Díaz, hero of the war against the French, seized power in 1876. A canny politician, Díaz placated the Church and marginalized or eliminated his rivals. Consolidating his hold on government in the 1880s, he ruled as an authoritarian president until 1911. During the so-called *porfiriato*, Mexico prospered and became more centralized than ever before. Communications improved; cities expanded. But by the 1900s the elderly dictator had alienated the peasantry, who had lost their fields to commercial haciendas. The middle class, meanwhile, chafed under the political restrictions of the regime and yearned for genuine democracy. The scene was set for the Revolution of 1910.

program, known as La Reforma (The Reform). In the 1857 democratic constitution they separated Church and state; sold off Church and other corporate-owned lands; and made all citizens equal before the law.

The Church and the army resisted these measures, but in the ensuing War of the Reform (1858–61) the liberals were victorious. In 1864, however, the conservatives struck a deal with Maximilian of Hapsburg, who assumed the Mexican throne, backed by the French bayonets of Napoleon III. Maximilian, a liberal, humane, but naive ruler, found himself depending on repression to maintain his crown. The liberals wore down the French and their conservative allies in a guerrilla struggle. In 1866 Napoleon III withdrew his troops and a year later, Maximilian was cornered at Querétaro, captured, and executed by a firing squad. Mexico's last monarchy had fallen; the republic under the national hero, Juárez, was restored.

Detail of a mural by Juan O'Gorman showing Porfirio Díaz (seated) and some of his ministers

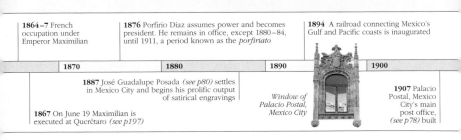

1864–7 French occupation under Emperor Maximilian

1876 Porfirio Díaz assumes power and becomes president. He remains in office, except 1880–84, until 1911, a period known as the *porfiriato*

1894 A railroad connecting Mexico's Gulf and Pacific coasts is inaugurated

| 1870 | 1880 | 1890 | 1900 |

1887 José Guadalupe Posada *(see p80)* settles in Mexico City and begins his prolific output of satirical engravings

Window of Palacio Postal, Mexico City

1907 Palacio Postal, Mexico City's main post office, *(see p78)* built

1867 On June 19 Maximilian is executed at Querétaro *(see p197)*

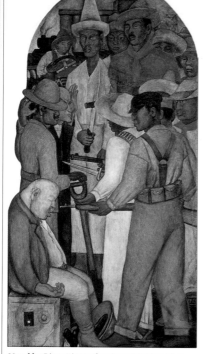

Mural by Diego Rivera showing reprisals against the rich during the Mexican Revolution

THE REVOLUTION

In 1910 Francisco I. Madero, an idealistic young landlord, opposed Díaz's seventh reelection to the presidency. When the regime rigged the election Madero called for a national uprising. The ensuing revolution, which brought together disaffected peasants and urban middle-class progressives, induced the aged dictator to negotiate and resign. Madero was elected president, but he could not meet popular demands for agrarian reform and greater democratization and at the same time satisfy conservatives who preferred the authoritarian stability of Díaz to democracy. In Morelos, south of Mexico City, Emiliano Zapata led a fresh rebellion, championing the cause of villagers who – like his own family – had lost land to the sugar plantations. Madero, however, was not ousted by such popular movements but by the military, who assassinated him in February 1913. The ruthless Victoriano Huerta formed a new regime so unpopular that the opposition united against it. Zapata allied with the great northern revolutionary leader, Pancho Villa (see p173), who had built up a formidable army on the prairies of Chihuahua, and in a second period of civil war (1913–14), these and other supporters of the constitution defeated Huerta and destroyed the regular army.

Villa and Zapata could not stomach the authority of their nominal chief, the dour provincial landlord Venustiano Carranza. A revolutionary convention, at Aguascalientes, failed to broker a peace. In a third and final bout of civil war, in 1915, Carranza's leading general, Álvaro Obregón, defeated Villa, reducing him to an outlaw. Zapata and others fought on, but it was clear that Carranza's faction had won, and in 1917 they promulgated a radical new constitution.

AFTERMATH OF REVOLUTION

Mexico was exhausted after the Revolution. Over a million people had died during it, or emigrated because of it. The currency had collapsed, and the country's infrastructure was in tatters. Carranza's

Poster of the revolutionary leader Emiliano Zapata

TIMELINE

1923 Pancho Villa is assassinated

1928 Assassination of Obregón

1929 Partido Nacional Revolucionario formed

1938 Nationalization of the oil industry

1917 Mexico's current liberal, revolutionary constitution is passed

1940 Assassination of Trotsky in Mexico City (see p103)

1910

1930

1950

1910 Mexican Revolution is launched by Madero

1919 Assassination of Zapata

1920 Military revolt ousts and kills Carranza

1934 Cárdenas becomes president

1941–5 Mexico allies with the US during World War II

1911 Madero becomes president but is assassinated in 1913

Venustiano Carranza

1956 The Torre Latinoamericana is built in Mexico City (see p75)

coalition, dominated by reformers such as Obregón and Plutarco Elías Calles, was shaky. Carranza was ousted and killed in 1920. In the following years, the infant revolutionary regime battled to survive against pressures from the Church, fearful of its anticlericalism, and from the US, which disapproved of such a radical constitution. In 1928, Obregón was assassinated. Calles responded to the crisis this

Union poster in support of the reforms instituted by President Cárdenas

caused by organizing a new national party, the Partido Nacional Revolucionario (PNR), the forerunner of the party which, under different names (PRM, PRI), governed Mexico until ousted in the 2000 elections.

MODERN MEXICO
President Cárdenas (1934–40), confronting the depression, implemented a sweeping agrarian reform, boosted the rights of organized labor, and, in 1938, nationalized the foreign-owned oil industry. Subsequent political leaders, typified by President Alemán (1946–52), favored industry and the private sector, which became the motor of an "economic miracle" – the sustained, low-inflation growth of the 1950s and 60s.

The miracle eventually ended. In 1968, on the eve of the Mexico City Olympics, student protests were bloodily repressed, tarnishing the regime's legitimacy. Seeking to recoup prestige, while reorienting the economy, the gov-

ernments of the 1970s borrowed and spent, partly on the basis of Mexico's second oil boom. Inflation quickened and, in 1982, the economy slumped. President Salinas (1988–94) opted for "neo-liberal" reform, privatizing state enterprises, cutting protective tariffs, and concluding the North American Free Trade Agreement with the US and Canada. Shortly after Salinas left office at the end of his six-year term, Mexico suffered devaluation and recession. Mexico's problems in the 1990s were compounded by an armed rebellion in the poor state of Chiapas *(see p230)*. Despite intermittent government repression and negotiation, the situation in Chiapas remains unsettled. Economic woes combined with social unrest led to victory for the center-right Partido Acción Nacional (PAN) in the 2000 elections, raising hopes for change under president Vicente Fox.

Parade during the opening ceremony of the 1968 Olympic Games, staged in Mexico City

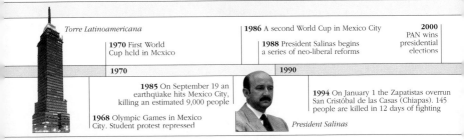

Torre Latinoamericana

1970 First World Cup held in Mexico

1970

1968 Olympic Games in Mexico City. Student protest repressed

1985 On September 19 an earthquake hits Mexico City, killing an estimated 9,000 people

President Salinas

1986 A second World Cup in Mexico City

1988 President Salinas begins a series of neo-liberal reforms

1990

1994 On January 1 the Zapatistas overrun San Cristóbal de las Casas (Chiapas). 145 people are killed in 12 days of fighting

2000 PAN wins presidential elections

INTRODUCING
MEXICO CITY

MEXICO CITY AT A GLANCE 58-59
THE HISTORIC CENTER 60-81
REFORMA AND CHAPULTEPEC 82-95
SAN ÁNGEL AND COYOACÁN 96-105
FARTHER AFIELD 106-113
SHOPPING IN MEXICO CITY 114-115
ENTERTAINMENT IN MEXICO CITY 116-117
STREET FINDER 118-125

Mexico City at a Glance

MEXICO CITY is a huge, hectic, overpopulated, and often smog-ridden metropolis, as well as the center of commerce and government for the country. Yet despite the problems of modern city life, the oldest capital of the New World is rich in both indigenous and colonial history. The aptly named Historic Center was the site of the Aztec capital, while the elegant Reforma district mixes colonial architecture with striking contemporary buildings. Allow at least two or three days to explore the city in full.

LOCATOR MAP

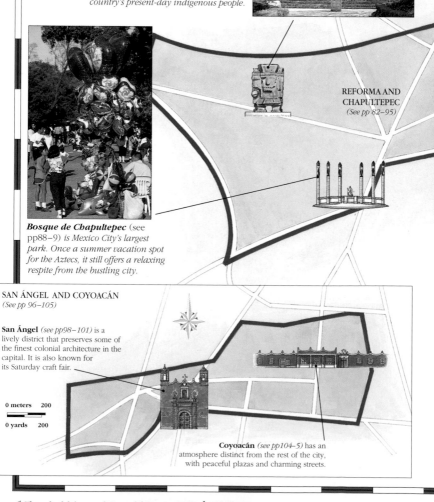

The National Anthropology Museum (see pp90–95) *is considered one of the finest museums of its kind in the world. It explores Mexico's prehistory; the lives and beliefs of the Maya, Aztecs, and other great civilizations; and the ways of life of the country's present-day indigenous people.*

REFORMA AND CHAPULTEPEC
(See pp 82–95)

Bosque de Chapultepec (see pp88–9) *is Mexico City's largest park. Once a summer vacation spot for the Aztecs, it still offers a relaxing respite from the bustling city.*

SAN ÁNGEL AND COYOACÁN
(See pp 96–105)

San Ángel *(see pp98–101)* is a lively district that preserves some of the finest colonial architecture in the capital. It is also known for its Saturday craft fair.

0 meters   200

0 yards   200

Coyoacán *(see pp104–5)* has an atmosphere distinct from the rest of the city, with peaceful plazas and charming streets.

◁ **The colorful domes of Museo del Carmen in San Ángel district**

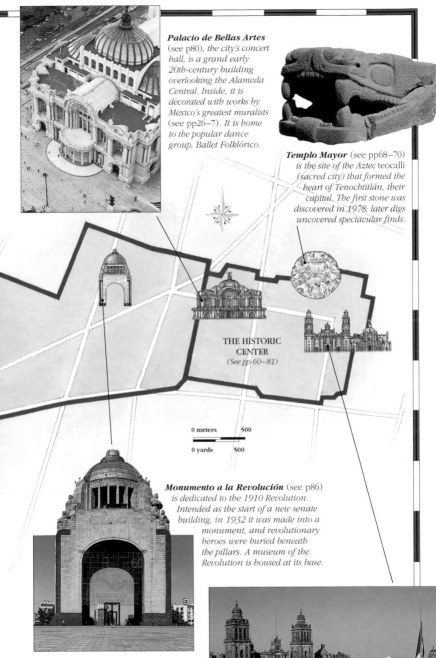

Palacio de Bellas Artes (see p80), *the city's concert hall, is a grand early 20th-century building overlooking the Alameda Central. Inside, it is decorated with works by Mexico's greatest muralists (see pp26–7). It is home to the popular dance group, Ballet Folklórico.*

Templo Mayor (see pp68–70) *is the site of the Aztec teocalli (sacred city) that formed the heart of Tenochtitlán, their capital. The first stone was discovered in 1978; later digs uncovered spectacular finds.*

THE HISTORIC CENTER
(See pp 60–81)

0 meters   500
0 yards   500

Monumento a la Revolución (see p86) *is dedicated to the 1910 Revolution. Intended as the start of a new senate building, in 1932 it was made into a monument, and revolutionary heroes were buried beneath the pillars. A museum of the Revolution is housed at its base.*

Catedral Metropolitana (see pp64–5) *was completed in 1813 after almost 300 years construction. Latin America's largest church, it dominates the main square of the city. Its Baroque altars and side chapels are magnificently ornate.*

The Historic Center

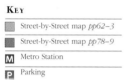

When Hernán Cortés led his army into the Aztec capital of Tenochtitlán it stood on an island in Lake Texcoco. After conquering the city the Spanish razed it to the ground, reusing much of the stonework in their own constructions, and gradually filling in the lake. The buildings of the Historic Center – which stands on the site of the Aztec city – date mainly from the colonial and post-independence eras. In a patchwork of architectural styles, they range from colonial churches and mansions to an Art Nouveau/Art Deco theatre-cum-gallery and a 1950s skyscraper. A prominent exception is the excavated remains of the great Aztec temple.

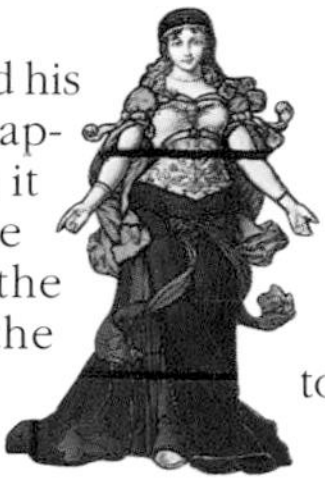

Stained glass in the Colegio de San Ildefonso

Sights at a Glance

Historic Buildings

- Antiguo Colegio de San Ildefonso 4
- Casa de los Azulejos 15
- Palacio de Bellas Artes 17
- Palacio de la Antigua Escuela de Medicina 9
- Palacio Nacional 2
- Secretaría de Educación Pública 7
- Templo Mayor 3
- Torre Latinoamericana 16

Museums and Galleries

- Laboratorio Arte Alameda 20
- Museo de la Caricatura 5
- Museo de la Charrería 12
- Museo de la Ciudad de México 11
- Museo del Ejército y Fuerza Aérea 13
- Museo Franz Mayer 19
- Museo José Luis Cuevas 10
- Museo Mural Diego Rivera 21
- Museo Nacional de Arte 14
- Museo Nacional de la Estampa 18

Churches

- Catedral Metropolitana 1
- Templo de la Enseñanza 6

Squares

- Plaza de Santo Domingo 8

Getting Around

The main metro stations are in the two large squares, the Zócalo and Alameda. Walking is the best way to get around, although the streets between the Alameda and the Plaza Garibaldi (to the north, *see p109*) are considered unsafe to stroll through.

Key

- [ ] Street-by-Street map *pp62–3*
- [ ] Street-by-Street map *pp78–9*
- [M] Metro Station
- [P] Parking

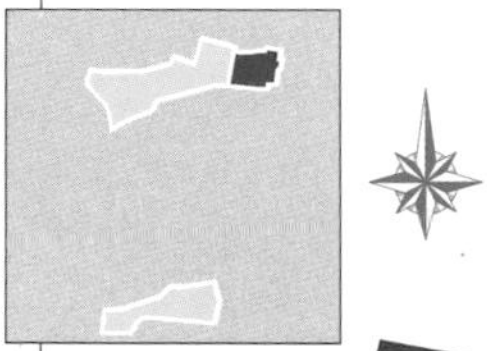

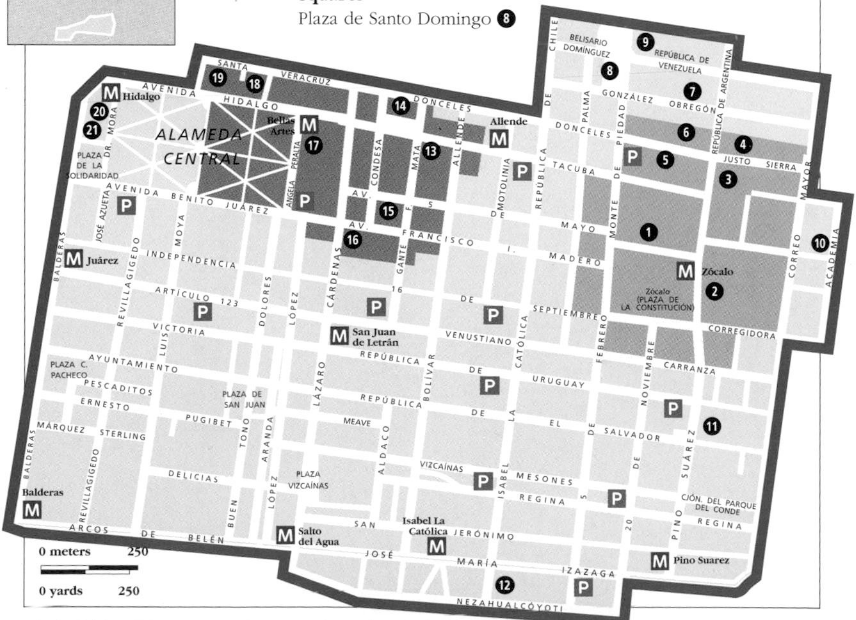

The lobby of the Gran Hotel *(see p292)*, on the Zócalo

Street-by-Street: Zócalo

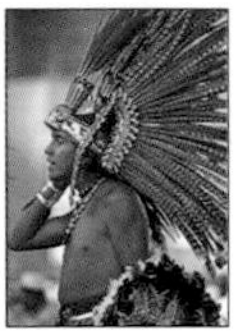

Indian dancer performing in the Zócalo

THE PLAZA de la Constitución, invariably known as the Zócalo, is one of the biggest public squares in the world. A giant national flag flies in the middle of this vast paved space, which is dominated by two buildings, the cathedral and the Palacio Nacional. On the square stand other public buildings, restaurants, shops, and hotels. At one corner are the sunken remains of the Aztecs' principal temple complex. A good view of the Zócalo can be had from the terrace of the Hotel Majestic.

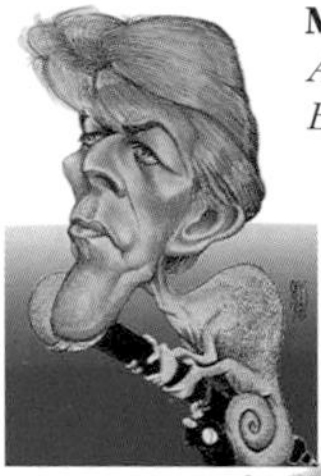

Museo de la Caricatura
A caricature of singer David Bowie is among the works of cartoon art housed in this 18th-century building 5

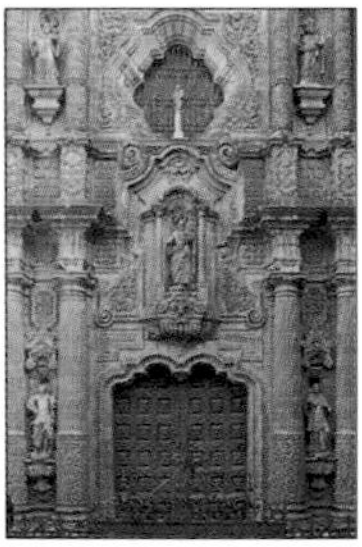

Templo de la Enseñanza
A dazzling gold altarpiece is the main feature of this late 18th-century Baroque church, which was built as a convent chapel 6

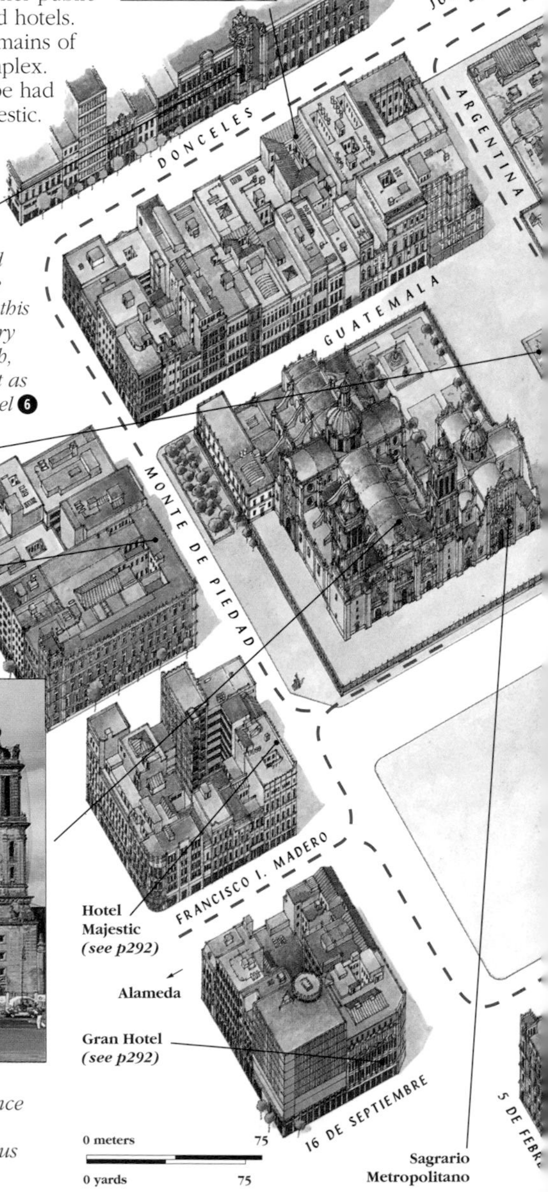

JUSTO SIERRA
ARGENTINA
DONCELES
GUATEMALA
MONTE DE PIEDAD
FRANCISCO I. MADERO
16 DE SEPTIEMBRE
5 DE FEBRE
Hotel Majestic (see p292)
Alameda
Gran Hotel (see p292)
0 meters 75
0 yards 75
Sagrario Metropolitano

Fuente de la Zona Lacustre is a water monument that incorporates a relief map of the Aztec city of Tenochtitlán.

Nacional Monte de Piedad, a government-run pawn shop, occupies a historic building dating from the 16th century.

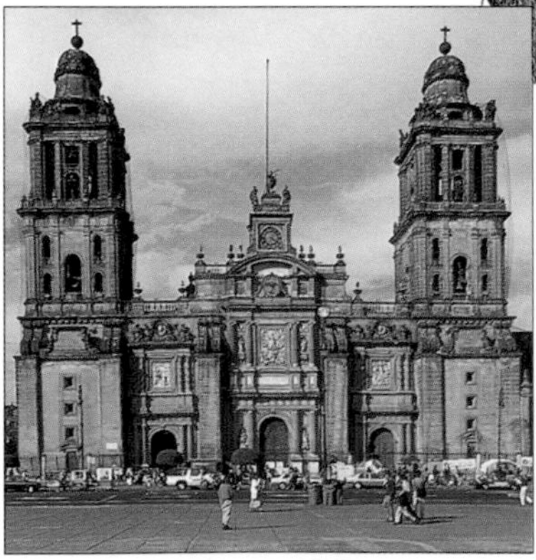

★ Catedral Metropolitana
Although damaged by the subsidence affecting the center of Mexico City, this is still one of the greatest religious buildings in Latin America 1

Colegio de San Ildefonso
Great murals, stained glass, and other decorative details can be seen in this former seminary ❹

★ Templo Mayor
Pathways lead through the excavated remains of this Aztec temple unearthed in the 1970s ❸

REFORMA AND CHAPULTEPEC
HISTORIC CENTER

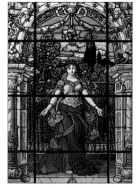

LOCATOR MAP
See Street Finder map pp124–5

SEMINARIO
ZÓCALO (PLAZA DE LA CONSTITUCIÓN)
PINO SUÁREZ
20 DE NOVIEMBRE

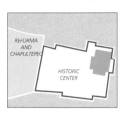

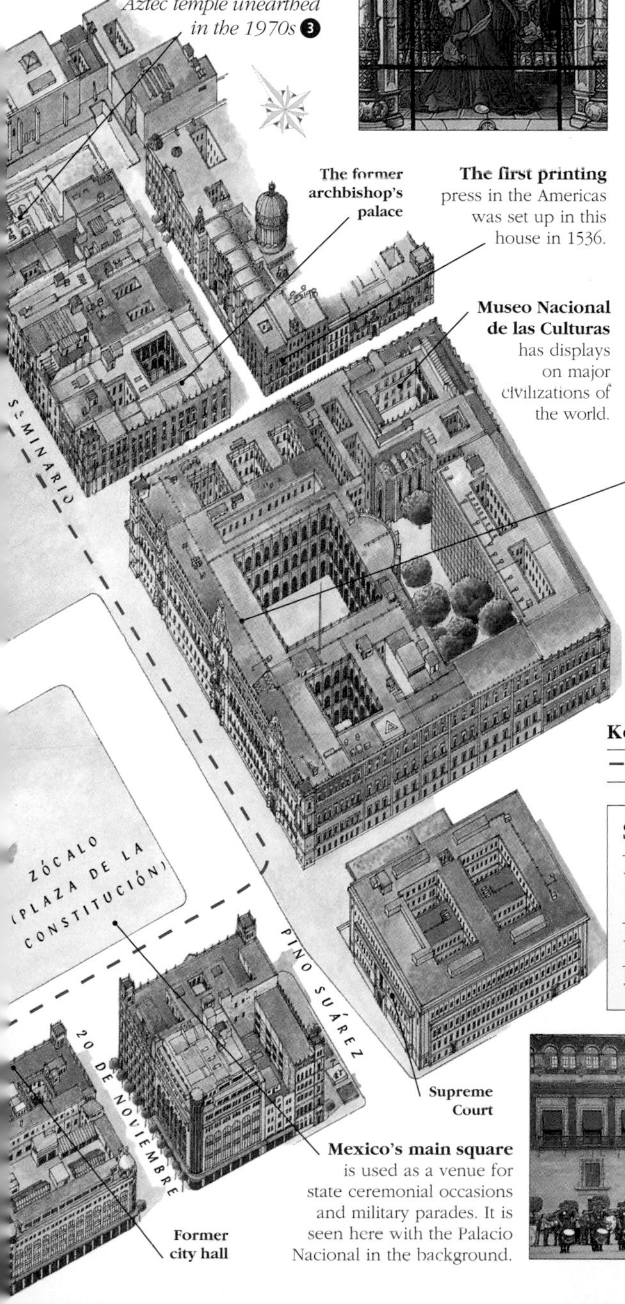

The former archbishop's palace

The first printing press in the Americas was set up in this house in 1536.

Museo Nacional de las Culturas has displays on major civilizations of the world.

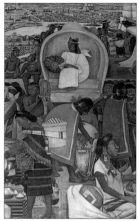

★ Palacio Nacional
Murals above the stairs and along two walls of the courtyard of this palace illustrate Diego Rivera's view of the history of Mexico ❷

Key

– – – Suggested route

STAR SIGHTS

- **★ Catedral Metropolitana**
- **★ Templo Mayor**
- **★ Palacio Nacional**

Supreme Court

Former city hall

Mexico's main square is used as a venue for state ceremonial occasions and military parades. It is seen here with the Palacio Nacional in the background.

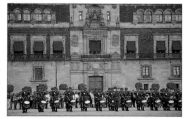

Catedral Metropolitana ❶

Hymn book on view in the choir

THE BIGGEST CHURCH in Latin America, Mexico City's cathedral is also at the heart of the world's largest Catholic diocese. Its towers rise 67 m (220 ft) above the Zócalo, and it took almost three centuries – from 1525 to 1813 – to complete. This extraordinarily long period is reflected in the multiple styles of its architecture and internal decoration, ranging from Classical through Baroque and Churrigueresque to Neo-Classical. It has five principal altars, and 16 side chapels containing a valuable collection of paintings, sculpture, and church furniture.

Sacristy
The sacristy contains 17th-century paintings and items of carved furniture such as this decorated cabinet.

Kings and Queens
The sculptures adorning the Altar de los Reyes are of kings and queens who have been canonized.

The high altar is a block of white marble carved with images of saints.

Side entrance

★ **Altar de los Reyes**
The two oil paintings on this Baroque masterpiece are the Adoration of the Kings *and the* Assumption of the Virgin, *both by Juan Rodríguez Juárez.*

STAR SIGHTS
★ Altar de los Reyes
★ Choir

Capilla de San José
This side chapel is one of 16 dedicated to saints and manifestations of the Virgin, all exquisitely decorated with statues and oil paintings.

The Sinking Cathedral
The cathedral is sinking into the soft clay of what was once the bed of Lake Texcoco. Scaffolding has been installed in the interior in an attempt to stabilize the building.

Sagrario Metropolitano
Built in the mid-18th century as the parish church attached to the cathedral, the Sagrario has a sumptuous high Baroque façade adorned with sculpted saints.

The clocktower
is decorated with statues of Faith, Hope, and Charity.

The façade is divided into three and flanked by monumental bell towers.

Main entrance

★ Choir
With its gold-alloy choir-rail imported from Macao, superbly carved stalls, and two magnificent organs, the choir is a highlight of the cathedral.

Palacio Nacional ❷

THE NATIONAL PALACE stands on the site of Moctezuma's palace which became the residence of Hernán Cortés after his conquest of Mexico *(see p43)*. Today it houses the offices of the President. The most interesting feature of this Renaissance building is the great mural above its main staircase, painted by Diego Rivera between 1929 and 1935 in the aftermath of the Revolution. This, along with the accompanying series of panels that Rivera painted on the first floor walls of the courtyard, depict the artist's personal view of the country's turbulent history *(see pp39–55)*.

Main courtyard of the Palacio Nacional

Álvaro Obregón and Plutarco Elías Calles steered Mexico through the difficult years after the Revolution.

The History of Mexico

The mural gives a partisan view of the history of Mexico as a struggle between "heroes" (pre-Columbian peoples, independence leaders, and revolutionaries) and "villains" (colonialists, conservatives, and capitalists).

Aztecs and Tlaxcalans
This panel in the courtyard shows the Tlaxcalans – who allied with Cortés – fighting their rivals the Aztecs.

Porfirio Díaz and Francisco I. Madero, who put an end to Díaz's dictatorship, are among the figures in the left-hand arch.

Cortés' mistress, "La Malinche," and their son

The Inquisition was charged with trying heretics until its abolition in 1813.

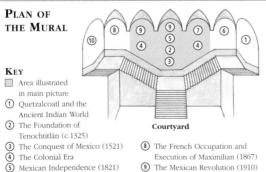

Plan of the Mural

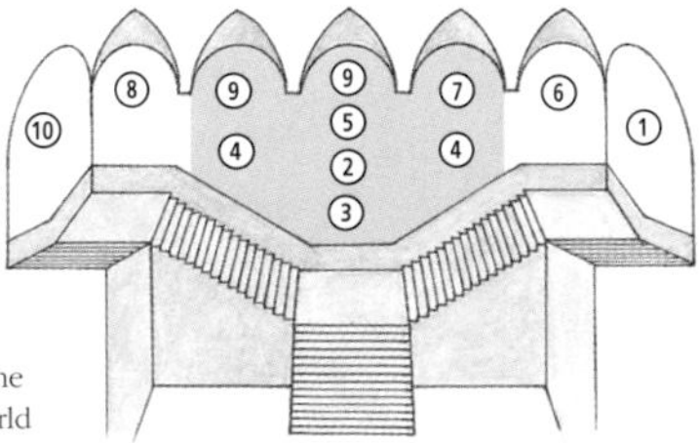

Key

- ☐ Area illustrated in main picture
- 1 Quetzalcoatl and the Ancient Indian World
- 2 The Foundation of Tenochtitlán (c.1325)
- 3 The Conquest of Mexico (1521)
- 4 The Colonial Era
- 5 Mexican Independence (1821)
- 6 The US Invasion of Mexico (1847)
- 7 The Reform Laws (1857–60)
- 8 The French Occupation and Execution of Maximilian (1867)
- 9 The Mexican Revolution (1910)
- 10 Modern Mexico: The Struggle of the Classes

Eagle on a Cactus
The eagle, with a serpent in its beak, depicts the legend of the founding of Tenochtitlán (see p43).

Revolutionary Leaders
Emiliano Zapata is one of the men standing behind the banner inscribed with the Zapatista rallying cry, "Land and Freedom."

Arrival of Cortés
Hernán Cortés is shown arriving in Veracruz in 1519 in this panel on the courtyard wall.

Miguel Hidalgo

Benito Juárez holds a scroll representing the 1857 constitution and the Reform Laws.

General Antonio López de Santa Anna

A fat monk symbolizes the wealth and power of the Church before the Reform Laws of the 19th century.

Franciscan missionaries baptize Indian converts after the Conquest.

Skulls symbolize the Aztec practice of human sacrifice.

Cuauhtémoc, the last Aztec emperor, is taken captive by the Spanish.

The Tarascans
This panel in the courtyard shows the craft skills of the Purépechas – whom the Spanish called the Tarascans.

Tenochtitlán (detail)
The largest courtyard mural shows Aztec market traders selling a variety of wares.

The Conquest of the Mexico
Across the bottom of the mural rages the battle between the Spanish and the Aztecs. This detail shows an Aztec warrior in an animal costume killing a mounted conquistador.

Templo Mayor ❸

THIS GREAT TEMPLE, built by the Aztecs in the 14th and 15th centuries, stood at the heart of Tenochtitlán. The temple complex was almost completely destroyed by the Spaniards after their conquest of the Aztec capital. The chance discovery of the extraordinary Coyolxauhqui carving in 1978 prompted excavations that uncovered the remains of superimposed temples denoted by the stage of construction to which they belong. Stage I is not visible as it is buried beneath Stage II.

View of the Templo Mayor archaeological site

Chacmool
This reclining figure may have been an intermediary between god and man. Offerings were placed in the bowl it holds.

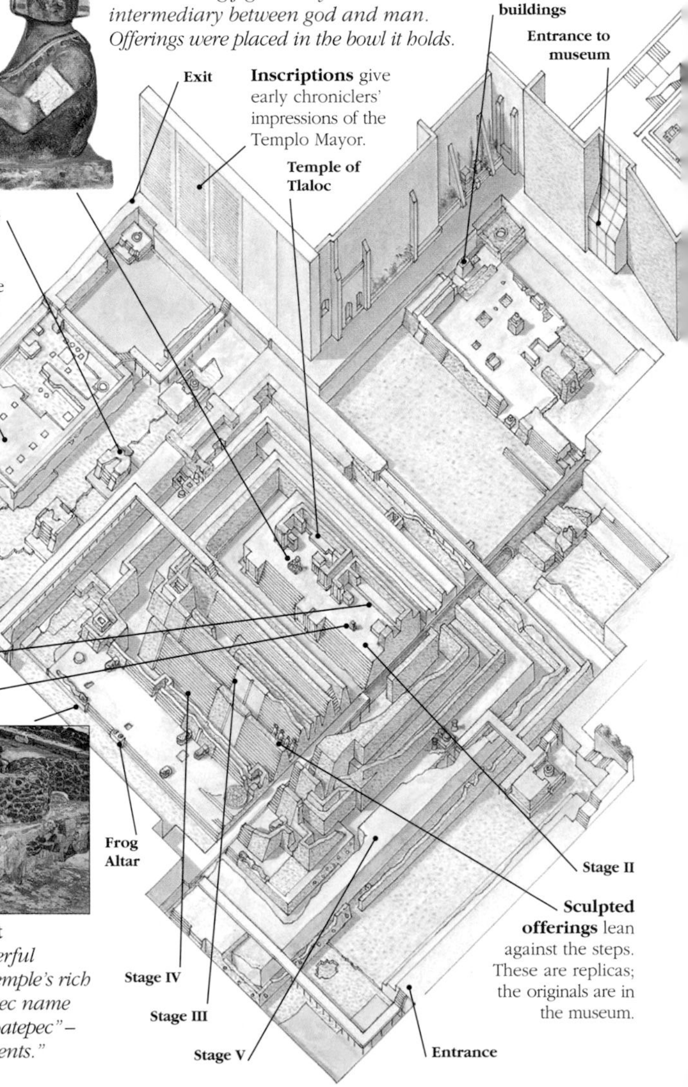

Ruins of colonial buildings

Entrance to museum

Exit

Inscriptions give early chroniclers' impressions of the Templo Mayor.

Temple of Tlaloc

Tzompantli-shrine

The Eagle Knights (now displayed in the museum) were found in this temple.

North Court

Stage VI

Temple of Huitzilopochtli

Sacrificial Stone

Frog Altar

Stage II

Sculpted offerings lean against the steps. These are replicas; the originals are in the museum.

Writing Serpent
The snake is a powerful component of the temple's rich symbolism. The Aztec name for the temple – "Coatepec" – means "Hill of Serpents."

Stage IV

Stage III

Stage V

Entrance

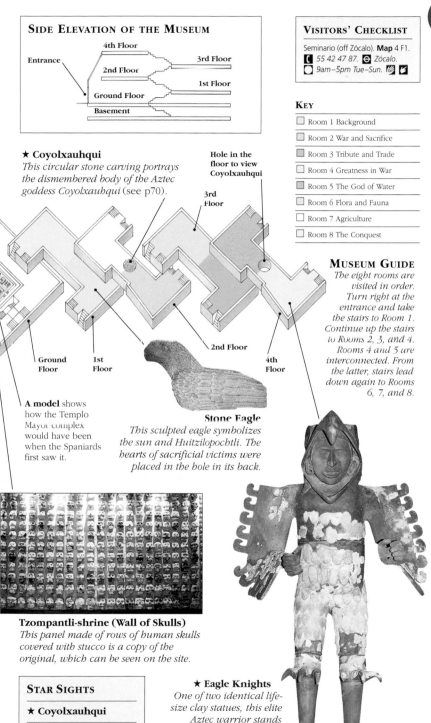

SIDE ELEVATION OF THE MUSEUM

Entrance

4th Floor
3rd Floor
2nd Floor
1st Floor
Ground Floor
Basement

VISITORS' CHECKLIST

Seminario (off Zócalo). **Map** 4 F1.
📞 55 42 47 87. ⊜ Zócalo.
🕐 9am–5pm Tue–Sun. 🅰 🅱

KEY

☐ Room 1 Background
☐ Room 2 War and Sacrifice
☐ Room 3 Tribute and Trade
☐ Room 4 Greatness in War
☐ Room 5 The God of Water
☐ Room 6 Flora and Fauna
☐ Room 7 Agriculture
☐ Room 8 The Conquest

★ Coyolxauhqui
This circular stone carving portrays the dismembered body of the Aztec goddess Coyolxauhqui (see p70).

Hole in the floor to view Coyolxauhqui

3rd Floor

MUSEUM GUIDE
The eight rooms are visited in order. Turn right at the entrance and take the stairs to Room 1. Continue up the stairs to Rooms 2, 3, and 4. Rooms 4 and 5 are interconnected. From the latter, stairs lead down again to Rooms 6, 7, and 8.

Ground Floor
1st Floor
2nd Floor
4th Floor

A model shows how the Templo Mayor complex would have been when the Spaniards first saw it.

Stone Eagle
This sculpted eagle symbolizes the sun and Huitzilopochtli. The hearts of sacrificial victims were placed in the hole in its back.

Tzompantli-shrine (Wall of Skulls)
This panel made of rows of human skulls covered with stucco is a copy of the original, which can be seen on the site.

STAR SIGHTS

★ **Coyolxauhqui**

★ **Eagle Knights**

★ Eagle Knights
One of two identical life-size clay statues, this elite Aztec warrior stands proudly in his eagle feather costume.

The Building of the Templo Mayor

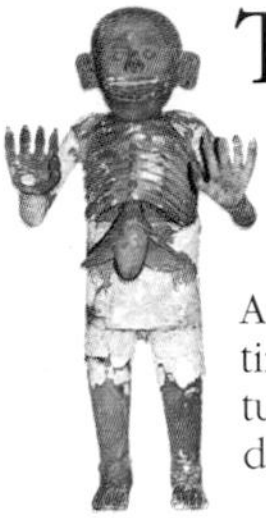

THE AZTECS ERECTED their most important religious building on the spot where – in fulfilment of a prophecy *(see p43)* – they had seen an eagle perched on a cactus devouring a snake. The first temple was built some time after 1325, according to Aztec sources, but it was enlarged many times over the course of the next two centuries. The twin temples on its summit were dedicated to the god of war, Huitzilopochtli, and the god of rain and water, Tlaloc. Aztec chronicles tell that both deities were frequently appeased with human sacrifices.

Statue of Mictlantecuhtli *(see p265)*

The ruins of the temples today

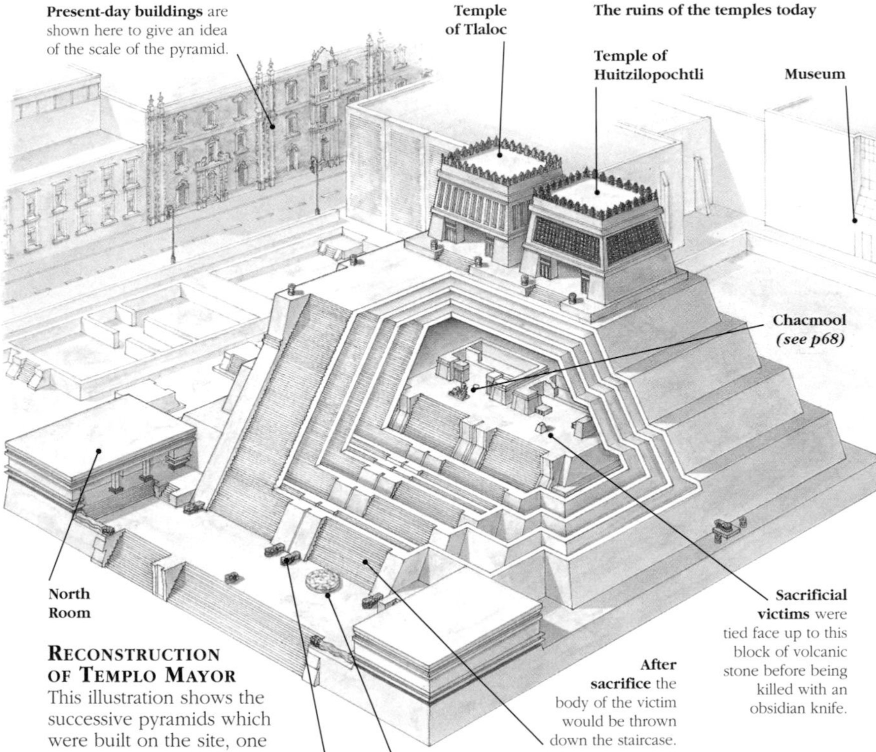

Present-day buildings are shown here to give an idea of the scale of the pyramid.

Temple of Tlaloc

Temple of Huitzilopochtli

Museum

Chacmool *(see p68)*

North Room

RECONSTRUCTION OF TEMPLO MAYOR
This illustration shows the successive pyramids which were built on the site, one on top of the other.

After sacrifice the body of the victim would be thrown down the staircase.

Sacrificial victims were tied face up to this block of volcanic stone before being killed with an obsidian knife.

Two snake heads guard the foot of the main staircase. They indicate that the temple was built as a symbolic re-creation of Coatepec – "the Hill of the Serpent" – a sacred place in Aztec mythology.

A carved round stone shows the separated head, limbs, and torso of the Aztec goddess Coyolxauhqui. According to legend she was slain and dismembered by Huitzilopochtli, her brother, because she had killed their mother, Coatlicue. The stone is now in the museum (see p69).

The Creation, a mural painted by Diego Rivera in 1922 in the Antiguo Colegio de San Ildefonso

Antiguo Colegio de San Ildefonso ❹

Justo Sierra 16. **Map** 4 F1.
📞 5 702 63 78. Ⓜ Zócalo, Allende.
🕐 10am–5;30pm Tue–Sun. 🎦 Tue free. 🈳

THIS 16TH-CENTURY building, originally a Jesuit seminary, is an outstanding example of Mexican civil architecture from the colonial era. It was remodeled during the 18th century, and the greater part of the present-day building dates from 1770–80. The façade on Calle San Ildefonso, however, which combines Baroque and Neo-Classical styles, is original.

Today the building belongs to the national university and serves as a museum. Its star attraction is the collection of murals from the earliest years of the Mexican muralist movement – including master-ful works by Rivera, Siqueiros, and Orozco (*see pp26–7*). In fact, San Ildefonso is regarded as the birthplace of the move-ment. The first murals com-missioned included those of David Alfaro Siqueiros, who in 1922–4 painted four works around the stairwell of the Colegio Chico, the oldest of the three patios which make up the San Ildefonso complex. Perhaps the best-known of these is *The Funeral of the Sacrificed Worker*. At around the same time, José Clemente Orozco was painting a series of murals on the north wall of the Patio Grande with equally universal themes – among them motherhood, freedom, and justice and the law. These include *Revolutionary Trinity* and *The Strike*. Arguably the most dramatic piece, however, is *The Trench*. The Orozco works to be found on the staircase – including a nude study of Cortés and his indig-enous mistress La Malinche – relate mostly to the theme of *mestizaje*, or the mixing of the races that formed the Mexican nation. The Anfiteatro Simón Bolívar contains an early work by Diego Rivera, *The Creation*. The other murals in this hall were painted by Fernando Leal between 1930 and 1942. The conference room to the north of the Patio Grande, known as El Generalito, is furnished with 17th-century carved wooden choir stalls.

Museo de la Caricatura ❺

Donceles 99. **Map** 4 E1. 📞 5 704 04 59. Ⓜ Zócalo. 🕐 11am–6pm daily (5pm Sat, Sun). 🎦 🈳 reserve in advance.

WITH ITS intricately adorned and finely preserved Baroque façade, the former Colegio de Cristo is one of the best examples in Mexico City of an upper-class 18th-century dwelling. Originally conceived in 1610 as an educational foundation for poor students, it was rebuilt in the 1740s, and later became a private house. The tiny patio and the broad staircase with its low, stone archway are among the highlights. In the 1980s, the build-ing was restored to house the collection of the Mexican Society of Cartoonists. This in-cludes contemporary cartoons and works by the influential early 20th-century artist, José Guadalupe Posada.

Courtyard of the Museo de la Caricatura, formerly the Colegio de Cristo

The gold main altarpiece of the Templo de la Enseñanza

Templo de la Enseñanza ❻

Donceles 104. **Map** 4 E1.
Ⓜ *Allende.* ⭕ *7:30am–8pm Mon–Sat, 10am–2pm Sun.*

ONE OF THE MOST remarkable churches in Mexico City, the Templo de la Enseñanza has an extremely narrow and ornate façade sloping backward slightly from ground level. The atrium is tiny and the interior decoration the height of late 18th-century "ultra-Baroque."

Built as a convent church, La Enseñanza was vacated by the nuns as a result of the 19th-century anti-clerical Reform Laws. It was later used by government bodies, including the Ministry of Education.

The dazzling gold main altarpiece is studded with the sculpted figures of saints. It rises up to the roof of the church, its height enhancing its vertical dimensions, and it is flanked by huge paintings. The vault above is adorned with a fresco of the Virgin of El Pilar, to whom the church is dedicated. In the lower choir, which is situated to either side of the altar, are lattice-work screens intended to hide the nuns from the gaze of other worshipers.

Secretaría de Educación Pública ❼

República de Argentina 28. **Map** 4 E1. Ⓒ *55 12 17 07.* Ⓜ *Zócalo, Allende.* ⭕ *9am–6pm Mon–Fri.*

THIS FORMER convent building, dating from 1639, is renowned for its large series of murals by Diego Rivera *(see p27)*. Painted between 1923 and 1928, they reflect Rivera's diverse influences: Italian frescoes, French cubists, and pre-Columbian Mexico.

The ground floor of the first patio is dedicated to the glorification of labor, a highlight being a mural showing a country schoolmistress giving a lesson. On the staircase is a series of landscapes from regions of Mexico, while on the third floor, in a panel called *The Painter, The Sculptor and the Architect*, is a well-known self-portrait. The first floor walls contain monochrome *grisailles* depicting scientific, artistic, and intellectual labor, and on the top floor are portraits of workers' heroes, such as Zapata. The second patio, on the ground floor, features a series of panels depicting popular fiestas, of which *The Day of the Dead* is particularly noteworthy. The third floor draws on revolutionary songs (*corridos*) for its

subject matter and includes a panel, *The Arsenal*, in which the artist Frida Kahlo hands out guns to revolutionaries.

In stark contrast to the style of Rivera is a striking mural by David Alfaro Siqueiros, *Patriots and Parricides*. This is located on the staircase in a part of the building which used to be a customs house (the Ex-Aduana), near the República de Brasil entrance.

Plaza de Santo Domingo ❽

Map 4 E1. Ⓜ *Allende.*

Tower of the church of Santo Domingo

SECOND ONLY in importance to the Zócalo itself, the Plaza de Santo Domingo (officially called Plaza 23 de Mayo) is steeped in history. The Dominicans built a convent here – the first in New Spain – in 1527, of which all that remains today is a restored chapel, the Capilla de la Expiación. Most of the other buildings that flank the square date from the 18th century. The church of Santo Domingo, with its sober façade partly covered in red volcanic *tezontle* stone, was erected between 1717 and 1737. Its tower is capped by a pyramidal pinnacle covered with Talavera tiles. The interior of the church contains statues of saints thought to date from

Siqueiros mural of *Patriots and Parricides* in the Secretaría de Educación Pública

Façade of the Capilla de la Expiación in the Plaza de Santo Domingo

Statue of *The Giantess* in the patio of the Museo José Luis Cuevas

building in which the Holy Inquisition carried out its fearsome interrogations from the late 16th century onward. The building today dates from the 18th century and underwent restoration in the 1970s. It is notable for its Baroque façade – unusually set on the corner of the building – and for its graceful main courtyard. There are "hanging" arches in each corner of the courtyard, with the supporting pillars set into the wall behind. A typical 19th-century apothecary's store, transferred in its entirety from Oaxaca, is one of the museum's more unusual features. It has displays on the history of Mexican medicine from pre-Columbian times, including sacred and medicinal plants and details of their traditional uses.

the 16th century, as well as oil paintings by Juan Correa and Alonso López de Herrera. The antique organ and the 18th-century cedar-wood choir stalls with carved images of the saints are among the treasures. The side altars are impressive for their gold embellishments.

The uneven subsidence that led to the demolition of previous churches on this site is widely evident in the square. From the door of the church, the undulation of the Tuscan-style *portales*, or arcade, which runs down the west side of the square, is noticeable. Under the arcade sit scribes, who, for a small fee, will fill out official documents using old manual typewriters.

Palacio de la Antigua Escuela de Medicina ❾

Brasil 33, cnr of Venezuela. **Map** 4 E1.
📞 55 29 75 42. Ⓜ *Zócalo, Allende.*
🕐 *9am–6pm daily.*

N OW HOME to the Museum of Medicine of the National University (UNAM), the Palacio de la Inquisición stands on the site of the

Museo José Luis Cuevas ❿

Academia 13. **Map** 4 F2. 📞 55 42 61 98. Ⓜ *Zócalo.* 🕐 *10am–6pm Tue–Sun.* 🈳 🎫 *reserve in advance.*
📷

F ORMERLY THE cloisters of the Santa Inés convent, this 17th-century jewel was converted to private dwellings in the 19th century and declared a national monument in 1932. Since 1988 it has housed an art gallery reflecting the personal tastes of Mexican painter and sculptor José Luis Cuevas.

The exquisite patio is dominated by the massive bronze sculpture of *La Giganta* (*The Giantess*), which Cuevas created specifically for this space. A number of smaller bronzes by the artist are dotted around the ground floor. The galleries contain paintings by Cuevas and other Mexican artists, including a number of portraits of him and his wife Bertha. There are also temporary

exhibits by foreign artists. At the entrance to a small "dark room" dedicated to Cuevas' works of erotica, visitors are warned, tongue-in-cheek, of the dangers they pose to those of a puritan upbringing.

The doors of the ex-convent church of Santa Inés, next door to the museum, are carved with reliefs showing scenes from the life of the saint (including her beheading) and portraits of the founders of the convent kneeling in prayer.

Nearby, on the corner of La Santísima and Moneda, is the Iglesia de la Santísima Trinidad (Church of the Holy Trinity), built in the 18th century. Worth noting here are the oval paintings of the martyrs in the nave, two wooden sculptures representing the Trinity, and a crucifix inlaid with bone and precious woods.

Doorway of the Iglesia de la Santísima Trinidad

Façade of the Museo de la Ciudad de México

Museo de la Ciudad de México ⓫

Pino Suárez 30, cnr of República del Salvador. **Map** 4 E3. **(** 55 42 00 83. **M** Zócalo. ⏰ 10am–6pm, Tue–Sun. 🎟 🚻 ♿

THE PALACE of the counts of Santiago de Calimaya, long renowned for their ostentatious lifestyle, is regarded as one of the most outstanding 18th-century buildings in the city. Built in 1781, the palace is faced with red volcanic *tezontle* stone. Its Baroque portal and magnificent carved wooden doors convey the social standing of its former inhabitants. At the foot of the southwest corner, the builders incorporated a stone serpent's head, which was taken from a wall made up of similar heads that surrounded the Aztecs' ceremonial center.

The first courtyard is noteworthy for the fountain with its carving of a mermaid holding a guitar, and for the trilobate arches near the staircase. Also outstanding is the richly carved stone doorway to the first-floor chapel.

In the early 20th century, the painter Joaquín Clausell lived in the building. The walls of his studio, on the third floor, are covered with an unusual mural, consisting of a collage-like set of scenes influenced by the Impressionists that Clausell met when he was in France.

The building has been occupied by the Museum of Mexico City since 1960. However, at present the collection is limited mostly to furniture and carriages associated with the house.

Museo de la Charrería ⓬

Isabel la Católica 108 (corner of José María Izazaga). **Map** 4 D3. **(** 57 09 50 32. **M** Isabel la Católica. ⏰ 10am–6pm Mon–Fri. 🎟 reserve in advance.

DEDICATED TO the Mexican art of horsemanship, this museum is located in what was once a Benedictine chapel dedicated to the Virgin of Monserrat. The remains of the chapel date from the 18th century, and its façade is still intact.

Inside, the museum displays the fancy, silver-trimmed costumes of the *charro* and his female equivalent, along with a wide variety of artifacts associated with the culture of *charrería*. Included in the collection are ornate saddles, spurs, and guns, as well as several of the impressive competition trophies awarded to the most successful *charros*. Watercolors of *charrería* events, a model of a *charro* stadium *(lienzo)*, and brief historical descriptions of the development of the art help to put the collection in context.

Museo del Ejército y Fuerza Aérea ⓭

Filomeno Mata 6, cnr Tacuba. **Map** 4 D1. **(** 55 12 32 15. **M** Allende, Bellas Artes. ⏰ 10am–6pm Tue–Sat, 10am–4pm Sun. ♿ 🎟 reserve in advance. 🚻 🚻 ♿

HOUSED IN what was once the chapel of a 17th-century Betlemitas hospital, this museum is notable for the three dramatic relief sculptures in metal on the wall facing Calle Filomeno Mata. They were created for the Paris Exposition of 1889 by Jesús F. Contreras and represent the indigenous chieftains Izcóatl, Nezahualcóyotl, and Totoquihuatzin.

Inside the museum is another statue worthy of note, depicting the last Aztec emperor, Cuauhtémoc. The museum itself is dedicated to the long and eventful history of the Mexican armed forces from the Conquest to the 20th century. Exhibits include chain mail, horse armor, and a fascinating array of weapons ranging from swords to rifles.

Nearby, on Calle Tacuba, is the Café Tacuba (see p314), a restaurant renowned for its excellent Mexican cuisine.

CHARRERÍA

Charrería is the Mexican art of horsemanship and the culture associated with it. The *charro* is akin to a US cowboy. He dresses in traditional costume and proves his skill and daring in the saddle at *charreadas* (rodeos), wielding a lasso on horseback. But *charros* are seldom working cowboys. More often they are well-off landowners who can afford their fancy costumes. *Charrería* is more than a display of equestrian talent, however, and a *charro* event is a social occasion in which food, drink, and music also play an important role.

Saddle in Museo de la Charrería

Museo Nacional de Arte ❶

Tacuba 8. **Map** 4 D1. 🔲 51 30 34 00.
Ⓜ Allende. 🔲 10:30am–5:30pm
Tue–Sun. 🔳 Sun free ⬛ ☑ ⬛ ⬛

CREATED IN 1982, the Museo Nacional de Arte is worth a visit for the building alone. An imposing, Neo-Classical piece of architecture, it was completed in 1911 as the Ministry of Communications and Public Works. Its double staircase, in bronze and marble, is enclosed by a semi-circular window three stories high. The interior, with its intricate ironwork and many candelabra, is sumptuous.

The museum's galleries encompass Mexican art from the 16th century to 1954. The collection includes commercial engravings, political cartoons, and folk art, as well as paintings. Much of the collection of religious art from the 16th to early 19th century resulted from confiscations following anti-clerical reform laws in the 19th century (see p53). As well as works by the great muralists – Rivera, Siqueiros, and Orozco (see pp26–7) – the outstanding pieces include a series of landscapes by 19th-century painter José María Velasco. One room is devoted to portraits by different artists, including a depiction of the art-lover María Asúnsolo by David Alfaro Siqueiros.

Right in front of the museum is the Plaza Manuel Tolsá, centering on one of the city's favorite monuments. Known as El Caballito (The Little Horse), it is in reality a massive equestrian statue of Charles IV of Spain by Manuel Tolsá (1802).

Casa de los Azulejos ❶

Francisco Madero 4. **Map** 4 D2.
🔲 55 18 01 52. Ⓜ Bellas Artes, Allende. 🔲 7am 1am daily. 🔳

THE 16TH-CENTURY "House of Tiles" was originally the palace of the counts of Orizaba. The blue-and-white tiled exterior is attributed to a 1737 remodeling by the 5th countess, who is said to have imported the style from the city of Puebla, where she had been living previously. Now occupied by the Sanborn's store (see p114) and restaurant (see p314) chain, the lovingly restored building conserves much of its original Mudéjar interior. The main staircase is decorated with waist-high tiling, and there is a mural on the first floor landing by José Clemente Orozco, entitled Omniscience, which was painted in 1925 (see p27). On the upper floor it is worth taking note of the mirrors surrounded by

Window of Casa de los Azulejos

elaborate gold frames containing the figures of angels and cherubs.

Across the street is the Iglesia de San Francisco, once part of the largest convent in New Spain, which had been built on the site of the Aztec Emperor Moctezuma's zoo. The church is entered via the Capilla de Balvanera, a chapel with a Churrigueresque façade and a decorated interior, but there is little left of interest inside.

Torre Latinoamericana at dusk

Torre Latinoamericana ❶

Eje Central Lázaro Cárdenas and Francisco I. Madero. **Map** 4 D2.
🔲 55 21 08 44. Ⓜ Bellas Artes.
🔲 9:30am–11pm daily. 🔳 🔳

THIS SKYSCRAPER rises 44 floors and its 182-m (600-ft) height boasts the best view of Mexico City – smog permitting. Completed in 1956, the steel-framed structure has survived a number of earthquakes, notably that of 1985. In 30 seconds, its express elevators whisk visitors to the 37th floor. On the 38th floor is an aquarium claiming to be the highest in the world. A second elevator rises to a 42nd-floor viewing platform and a cafeteria. From here a spiral staircase leads to the open-air cage below the TV mast.

Staircase in the Museo Nacional de Arte

Street-by-Street: The Alameda Central

THE ALAMEDA takes its name from the *álamos*, or poplar trees, planted here in the late 16th century by the Viceroy Luis de Velasco. Originally only half the size, the park assumed its present dimensions only in the 18th century. Its many statues date mainly from the 1900s, although the central Baroque fountain has been there since the expansion of the Alameda under Viceroy Carlos Francisco de Croix (1766–71). The most imposing monument is the Hemiciclo a Juárez, a semi-circular monument with Doric pillars of Carrara marble, by the sculptor Lazanini.

A balloon seller in the park

Museo Franz Mayer
This museum houses what is probably the finest collection of applied and decorative arts in Mexico. Exhibits date from the 16th to the 19th century **19**

Palacio Postal, the main post office, has an elegant interior of wrought iron and marble, and houses a postal museum.

Iglesia de San Juan de Dios is an 18th-century church with an unusual concave façade.

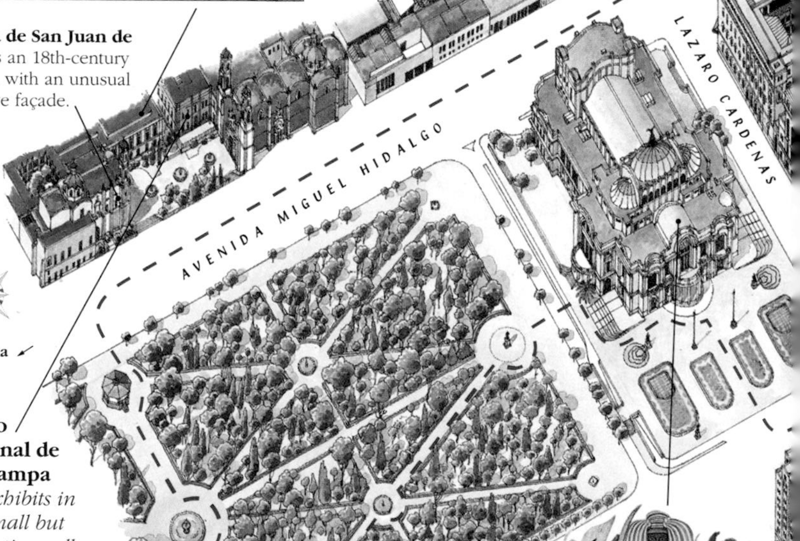

Reforma

Museo Nacional de la Estampa
The exhibits in this small but interesting gallery explain the history of the graphic arts in Mexico **18**

Hemiciclo a Juárez
was inaugurated in 1910 when Mexico celebrated the centenary of its independence struggle.

Alameda Central

AVENIDA MIGUEL HIDALGO

LAZARO CARDENAS

AVENIDA JUÁREZ

★ Palacio de Bellas Artes
The Art Nouveau façade of this theater is equalled only by its impressive Art Deco interior, with murals by some of the greatest Mexican artists of the 20th century **17**

0 meters 100
0 yards 100

◁ Façade of the Palacio de Bellas Artes

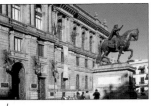

Museo Nacional de Arte
An equestrian statue of Charles IV guards the entrance to this collection of modern Mexican art. The building was constructed between 1904 and 1911 ⓮

REFORMA AND CHAPULTEPEC PARK
HISTORIC CENTER

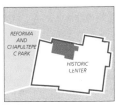

LOCATOR MAP
See Street Finder pp124–5

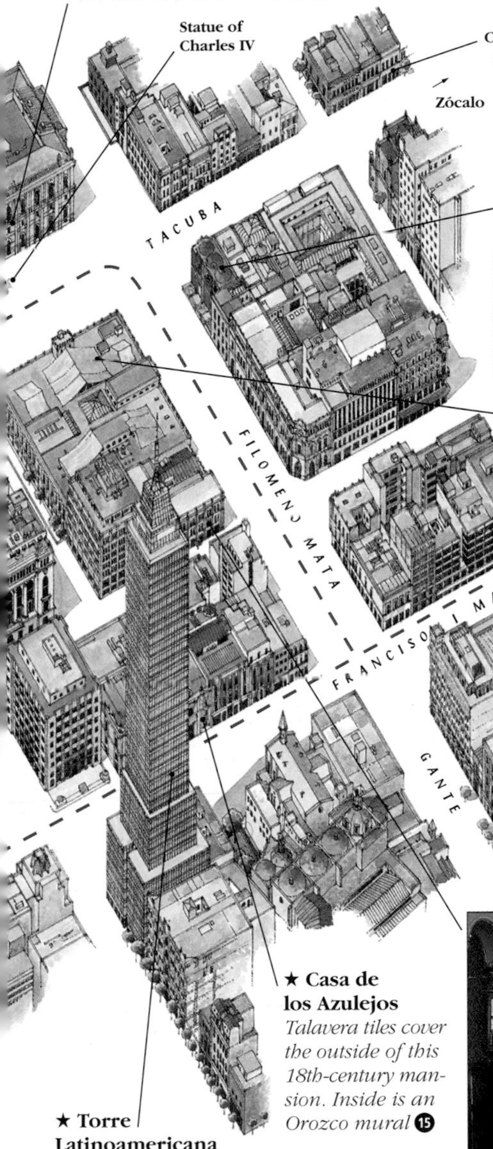

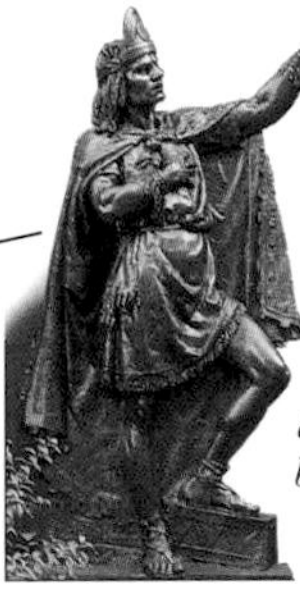

Statue of Charles IV
Café Tacuba (see p314)
Zócalo
TACUBA
FILOMENO MATA
FRANCISCO I MADERO
GANTE

Museo del Ejército
Housed in a 17th-century monastery chapel, this army museum displays a collection of weaponry and military memorabilia dating from the conquest up to the 20th century ⓭

Palacio de Minería is one of the city's finest 19th-century Neo-Classical buildings.

Palacio de Iturbide, named after the Emperor Agustín de Iturbide *(see p52)*, is a superb example of colonial architecture.

STAR SIGHTS

- ★ **Palacio de Bellas Artes**
- ★ **Torre Latinoamericana**
- ★ **Casa de los Azulejos**

KEY

— — — Suggested route

★ Casa de los Azulejos
Talavera tiles cover the outside of this 18th-century mansion. Inside is an Orozco mural ⓯

★ Torre Latinoamericana
Mexico City's first skyscraper was built in the 1950s and has survived many major earthquakes ⓰

Bar La Ópera is an old-fashioned restaurant on 5 de Mayo. A legend says that a bullet hole in the ceiling was made by Pancho Villa *(see p54)*.

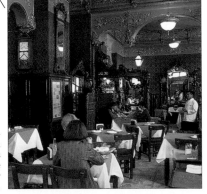

Palacio de Bellas Artes ⓱

Eje Central & Ave Juárez. **Map** 3 C1.
☎ *55 12 25 93.* Ⓜ *Bellas Artes.*
🕙 *10am–5:45pm, Tue–Sun.* ♿
🎟 *reserve in advance.* ▣ 🎁 ∅
ⓦ *www.cnca.gob.mx.*

Arguably the most beautiful building in the Historic Center, the Palacio de Bellas Artes was conceived in 1905 as a new national theater. Italian architect Adamo Boari designed an innovative building around a steel frame, incorporating Neo-Classical and Art Nouveau elements together with pre-Columbian decorative details.

The exterior of the building is clad in Italian marble and its cupolas are covered in tiles. The largest, central dome is surmounted by a Mexican eagle surrounded by figures representing the dramatic arts.

Interrupted by the revolution, the work was completed by Federico Mariscal in 1934. This accounts for the contrasting Art Deco interior, with its geometric shapes in colored marble and eyecatching illumination, especially the vertical lamps flanking the entrance to the auditorium.

The theater itself has a curtain which is a glass mosaic by Tiffany Studios of New York. Said to comprise a million pieces of glass, it represents

Pinoncelly's stained glass skylight in the Museo Nacional de la Estampa

the Valley of Mexico with its volcanoes in the background and is based on a design by Gerardo Murillo ("Dr Atl"). On the second floor are two murals by Rufino Tamayo: *Birth of our Nationality* and *Mexico Today*, painted in 1952–3. The third floor includes David Alfaro Siqueiros' masterpiece of the same period, *New Democracy.* On the righthand wall José Clemente Orozco painted *Catharsis*, whose theme is war and bourgeois decadence. With his work known as *Man, the Controller of the Universe*, Diego Rivera took his revenge on John D. Rockefeller, who had ordered the destruction of a similar mural at the Rockefeller Center in New York on ideological grounds. He portrays Rockefeller among the debauched rich at a nightclub, with the germs of venereal disease above them.

Man, the Controller of the Universe by Rivera, in the Palacio de Bellas Artes

Museo Nacional de la Estampa ⓲

Av Hidalgo 39. **Map** 3 C1.
☎ *55 21 22 44.* Ⓜ *Bellas Artes.*
🕙 *10am–6pm, Tue–Sun.* 🎟 *Sun free.* 🎟 *reserve in advance.*

Dedicated to the history of the graphic arts, from pre-Columbian to modern times, this museum has an extensive collection, only part of which is on show at any one time.

Probably the best-known of the artists whose work is on display is José Guadalupe Posada (1852–1913). His enduring image of *La Calavera Catrina (see p27)* – a well-dressed skeleton – is among the most familiar representations of the Mexican fascination with death. Posada's work featured in the popular satirical newspapers of his day.

In the Sala de Técnicas is a range of works illustrating the different techniques used by print artists. The building itself has a 1986 stained-glass skylight by Salvador Pinoncelly.

Museo Franz Mayer ⑲

Av Hidalgo 45. **Map** 3 C1. 🎔 *55 18 22 65.* Ⓜ *Hidalgo, Bellas Artes.* ◯ *10am–5pm, Tue–Sun.* 🎫 *Tue free.* 🎫 *reserve in advance.* ▣ ❒

THIS IS THE richest collection of applied art to be found in Mexico City. Assembled by German financier and art collector Franz Mayer, it is housed in a two-storey, 16th-century building which for most of its existence was a hospital. The museum has what is perhaps the most beautiful courtyard in the Historic Center, featuring a delightful fountain shaded by large trees.

The collection – which contains more than 8,000 pieces (as well as about 20,000 antique tiles) from Europe, the Far East and colonial Mexico – is highly varied. Exhibits include tapestries, high-relief wooden carvings of religious scenes, ceramics, and over 1,000 pieces of silverwork, and furniture. Among the most beautiful objects are a number of inlaid wooden chests. There are also some impressive wooden screens, one of which has a rendering of the conquest of Mexico City on one side and a partial view of the city in the colonial period on the reverse.

Talavera vase in the Museo Franz Mayer

This impressive collection of applied and decorative arts also has a number of outstanding examples of Mexican colonial-era paintings.

The attractive, leafy courtyard of the Museo Franz Mayer

Laboratorio Arte Alameda ⑳

Doctor Mora 7. **Map** 3 B1. 🎔 *55 10 27 93.* Ⓜ *Hidalgo.* ◯ *10am–5pm, Tue–Sun.* 🎫 *Sun free* 🎫 *reserve in advance.* ⌀

THIS MUSEUM of contemporary art is located in the former convent and church of San Diego de Alcalá, built in the 16th century. From 1964 to 1999, the building housed the Pinacoteca Virreinal, a collection of religious art now displayed in the Museo Nacional de Arte *(see p75)*. In 2000 the doors opened to Mexico City's newest museum, the Laboratorio Arte Alameda. This art space is dedicated to showing major works by key Mexican and international artists, and focusing on transdisciplinary, temporary exhibits and events. With its cutting-edge shows, it hopes to interest new audiences in contemporary art and to raise the profile of Mexican artists.

Museo Mural Diego Rivera ㉑

Corner of Colón and Plaza Solidaridad. **Map** 3 B1. 🎔 *55 12 07 54.* Ⓜ *Hidalgo, Juárez.* ◯ *10am–6pm Tue–Sun.* 🎫 *Sun free.*

THIS SMALL, two-story gallery is built around one of muralist Diego Rivera's greatest masterpieces, *Dream of a Sunday Afternoon in the Alameda Central*. Painted in 1947 for the dining room of the nearby Hotel Prado, the mural combines the history of Mexico with the dreams of its protagonists and the recollections of Rivera himself. The painter includes two self-portraits, one depicting himself as a child, hand-in-hand with Posada's *La Calavera Catrina*. Behind him is his "dream," the painter Frida Kahlo, to whom he was married for 25 years.

With its glowing colors and dreamlike quality, the painting caused a huge stir when first unveiled. Not all reactions were favorable: Christian groups were outraged by the inclusion of the phrase "God does not exist." One group succeeded in defacing the mural, forcing Rivera to remove the offending words.

Conceived in three sections, the mural begins on the left with the era from the Conquest up to the mid-19th century. In the center are figures from the turn-of-the-century *porfiriato* dictatorship *(see p53)* and on the right the revolutionary and post-revolutionary period. Prominent in the latter is a mounted portrait of guerrilla leader Emiliano Zapata.

Rivera's great mural, *Dream of a Sunday Afternoon in the Alameda Central*

PASEO DE LA REFORMA AND BOSQUE DE CHAPULTEPEC

IN THE 1860s, during the short-lived reign of the Emperor Maximilian *(see p53)*, a grand avenue was laid out between the city of Mexico and the Bosque de Chapultepec. This broad, elegant, tree-lined boulevard, the Paseo de la Reforma, is now flanked by tall modern office buildings. Little evidence remains of the mansions with which it was lined at the turn of the century. But the statues and fountains that adorn Reforma, including the golden Angel of Independence that is the city's symbol, maintain a link with the glories of the past. South of the Paseo is the triangle of streets called

El Caballito, a sculpture on the Paseo de la Reforma

the Zona Rosa, which is filled with shops, hotels, restaurants, and cafés. Beyond this are Roma, a district of offices and shops, and La Condesa, popular for its many informal restaurants. The Bosque de Chapultepec, at the western end of the avenue, was a sacred site in pre-Columbian times. Once the residence of the Aztec emperors, it has been a public park since 1530. The castle on the top of the steep hill at its northeastern end was also Maximilian's home. Today, with its boating lakes, zoo, and cafés, the Bosque de Chapultepec is a very pleasant place to escape the hustle and bustle of the city.

SIGHTS AT A GLANCE

Historic Buildings
Castillo de Chapultepec **8**
Monumento a la Revolución **3**

Museums and Galleries
Museo de Arte Moderno **7**
Museo de Cera **4**

Museo Nacional de Antropología **10**
Museo Nacional de San Carlos **2**
Museo Rufino Tamayo **6**
Sala de Arte Siqueiros **5**

Parks
Bosque de Chapultepec **9**

Streets
Paseo de la Reforma **1**

GETTING AROUND
Auditorio, Chapultepec, and Constituyentes are the best metro stations for the Bosque de Chapultepec. Hidalgo station is situated at the opposite end of Reforma from Chapultepec.

KEY

M	Metro station
i	Tourist information
P	Parking

◁ **A bar in the Zona Rosa, south of the Paseo de la Reforma**

Paseo de la Reforma ❶

Bronze statue of couple

THE CENTRAL 3.5-KM (2-MILE) stretch of Reforma, which links the center of the city with Chapultepec, was once lined with beautiful houses. These have now given way to less stately hotels and office blocks, but Paseo de la Reforma nevertheless remains one of the outstanding city streets of Latin America. The monuments that adorn its *glorietas*, or traffic circles, have a special place in the affection of Mexico City's residents. Between the Caballito and the Angel is a series of smaller statues, commissioned in the 19th century, which commemorate prominent Mexicans from each state. The road continues to the southwest across the Bosque de Chapultepec.

Monumento a la Independencia
Popularly known as the Angel of Independence, this figure was created by Antonio Rivas Mercado. and was erected in 1910. It commemorates the heroes of the struggle against Spanish colonial rule (see p49).

Diana Cazadora
The bronze figure of Diana the huntress, by Juan Fernando Olaguíbel (1896–1971), was once thought to offend public decency. At the request of the city authorities she was covered up. but only temporarily.

Hotel Sheraton

RÍO PÁNUCO
RÍO SENA
RÍO TÍBER
RÍO GUADALQUIVIR
RÍO VOLGA
RÍO NILO
RÍO MISSISSIPPI
RÍO ATOYAC
PASEO DE LA REFORMA
NIZA
GENOVA
AMBERES
HAMBURGO
LONDRES
GENOVA
FLORENCIA
OXFORD
PRAGA
HAMBURGO
LONDRES
TOKIO
LIVERPOOL
SEVILLA
TOKIO
HAMBURGO
LIEJA
MARIANO ESCOBEDO
JOSÉ VASCONCELOS

US Embassy

Monumento a los Niños Héroes & Chapultepec Park

Japanese Embassy

Bolsa de Valores
Mexico City's stock exchange is in a futuristic building which has a glass-domed dealing floor. This is flanked by a pencil-slim glass tower which houses offices.

0 meters		250
0 yards		250

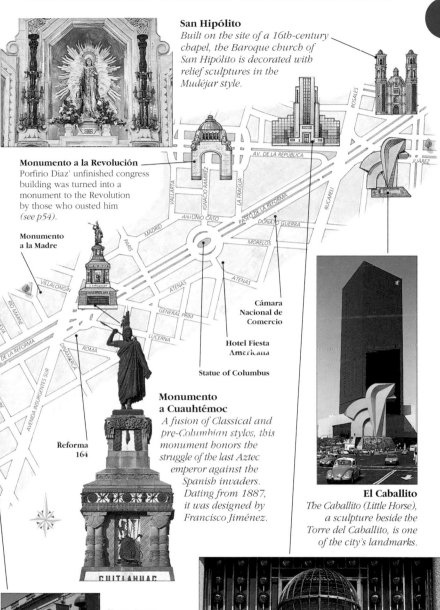

San Hipólito

Built on the site of a 16th-century chapel, the Baroque church of San Hipólito is decorated with relief sculptures in the Mudéjar style.

Monumento a la Revolución
Porfirio Diaz' unfinished congress building was turned into a monument to the Revolution by those who ousted him *(see p54).*

Monumento a la Madre

Cámara Nacional de Comercio

Hotel Fiesta Americana

Statue of Columbus

Monumento a Cuauhtémoc

A fusion of Classical and pre-Columbian styles, this monument honors the struggle of the last Aztec emperor against the Spanish invaders. Dating from 1887, it was designed by Francisco Jiménez.

Reforma 164

El Caballito
The Caballito (Little Horse), a sculpture beside the Torre del Caballito, is one of the city's landmarks.

Zona Rosa
The "Pink Zone" is a triangle of partly pedestrianized streets to the south of Reforma, with shops and cafés. Sadly, the area is not what it was and is not considered to be completely safe.

Lotería Nacional
The National Lottery building, designed by José A. Cuevas and completed around 1936, includes details of Art Deco craftsmanship (see p23).

Museo Nacional de San Carlos ❷

Puente de Alvarado 50. **Map** 3 A1. 🄲
55 66 83 42. Ⓜ *Hidalgo, Revolución.*
◯ *10am–6pm Wed–Mon.* 🈺
🈺 *Mon free.* 🚫

OCCUPYING an imposing
Neo-Classical edifice
completed in the early 19th
century, the San Carlos museum has the largest collection
of European art in Mexico. The
bulk of the collection consists
of paintings spanning the 14th
to the early 20th century,
including notable examples of
the Flemish, French, Italian,
and Spanish schools. Among
the highlights are engravings
by Goya and sculptures by
Rodin. The origin of these
riches is to be found in the
collections assembled by the
San Carlos Academy of Mexico,
established by the Spanish
King Charles III in 1783.

Seven galleries on the upper
floor house the permanent
collection. Pride of place at
the entrance is given to *La
Encarnación,* a stunning
gilded altarpiece dating from
1465, by Pere Espallargues.

At one time the building
was home to a "museum of
strange objects," but this collection was later moved to the
nearby Museo del Chopo, a
twin-towered Art Nouveau
structure. Built between 1903
and 1905, toward the end of
the dictatorship of Porfirio
Díaz *(see p53),* this steel-

The impressive Monumento a la Revolución
in the Plaza de la República

framed museum was known
for many years as the "crystal
palace," because of its resemblance to the famous London
building of that name.

Monumento a la Revolución ❸

Plaza de la República. **Map** 3 A1.
🄲 *55 46 21 15.* Ⓜ *Revolución.*
◯ *9am–5pm Tue–Fri; 9am–6pm Sat,
Sun.* ♿ 🈺 *Sun free.*

THE STRIKING dome-topped
cube that is the Monu-
mento a la Revolución was
originally designed as part of
a new parliament
building under the
dictator Porfirio Díaz.
Due to unanticipated
problems with the
marshy ground, it was
never completed.
Then, in 1932, as an
alternative to demo-
lishing it, the architect
Carlos Obregón
Santacilia proposed
that it be converted
into a monument
celebrating the 1910
revolution that put an
end to the *porfiriato.*
Stone cladding and
sculptures were added,
and the remains of
revolutionary heroes
such as Francisco Villa
were interred at the
base of the columns.
The austerity of the
monument's func-
tional and Art Deco styling is
relieved by details in bronze.
The statues, sculpted by
Oliverio Martínez de Hoyos,
represent independence, the
19th-century liberal reform,
and the post-revolutionary
agrarian and labor laws.

At the base of the monu-
ment is a museum dedicated
to the 50-year period from
the expulsion of the French
in 1867 to the 1917 revolutionary constitution. The exhibits on display range from
photographs, documents, and
reproductions of period newspapers to carriages, clothing,
and contemporary artifacts.

Rear façade and gardens of the Museo Nacional de San Carlos

Museo de Cera and Museo Ripley ❹

Londres 4. **Map** 2 F3. 📞 *55 46 37 84*. Ⓜ *Insurgentes, Cuauhtémoc.* ◯ *11am–7pm Mon–Fri; 10am–7pm Sat & Sun.* 🖼 ◻ ◻ 🚫

HOUSED IN a striking Art Nouveau mansion that was designed by architect Antonio Rivas Mercado, the Museo de Cera (wax museum) is an entertaining trip through Mexican history and culture. One room contains effigies of every Mexican president since 1920. Other rooms feature personalities as diverse as Emiliano Zapata, the comedian Mario Moreno (Cantinflas), and soap opera star Verónica Castro. A robot of tenor Plácido Domingo sings an operatic aria, while in the dungeons below the torture victims groan and scream.

Adjacent is the Ripley's Believe it or Not! museum of the bizarre, containing everything from a copy of the Mona Lisa made from pieces of toast to the ever-popular calf-with-two-heads. Those of a delicate disposition should avoid the tunnel that imitates the physical effects of an earthquake.

A sports car covered in coins and flag in the Museo Ripley

Sala de Arte Siqueiros ❺

Tres Picos 29. **Map** 1 A3. 📞 *55 31 33 94*. Ⓜ *Auditorio, Polanco.* ◯ *10am–6pm Tue–Sun.* 🖼 *Sun free.* 📷 *reserve in advance.* 🚫

THIS WAS THE home and studio of the celebrated Mexican muralist David Alfaro Siqueiros. Just weeks before his death in 1973 he bequeathed it, with all its contents, to the nation. The painter's life and work are represented here by a collection that includes finished works as well as drawings, plans, models, and photo-montages of his many murals. There is also a selection of photographs and documents charting the events of Siqueiros' life, which was singularly eventful. It included two prison terms, one of which was for his part in a plot to kill León Trotsky *(see p103)* – Siqueiros had been a supporter of Stalin. In spite of this, his painting was popular, and in the 1940s and 1950s the state commissioned him to produce several works.

The ground-floor gallery is the site of the 1970's mural entitled *Maternity*, which was originally designed for a school. A ramp leads to the upper floor and the galleries which contain paintings by Siqueiros. The gallery situated on the second floor is devoted solely to the work of other artists, both foreign and contemporary Mexican.

Modern interior of the Museo Rufino Tamayo

Façade of the Sala de Arte Siqueiros, the artist's former home

Museo Rufino Tamayo ❻

Cnr of Paseo de la Reforma & Gandhi. **Map** 1 B4. 📞 *52 86 65 19*. Ⓜ *Chapultepec.* ◯ *10am–5:40pm Tue–Sun.* 🖼 *Sun free.* ♿ 📷 *reserve in advance.*

THE OUTSTANDING collection of modern painting and sculpture assembled by one of Mexico's foremost 20th-century artists, Rufino Tamayo, and his wife Olga, occupies a futuristic, concrete-and-glass museum set among the trees of Chapultepec park *(see pp88–9)*. The building was designed by architects Teodoro González de León and Abraham Zabludovsky, and was awarded the national prize for architecture in 1981.

Sculpture at the Museo Rufino Tamayo

Housed within this light and airy gallery are some 800 paintings in all, as well as drawings, sculptures, and graphic art. There are also a number of paintings by Rufino Tamayo himself. Among the many other modern artists represented in the gallery are Pablo Picasso, Joan Miró, Mark Rothko, Colombian artist Fernando Botero, and Francis Bacon, whose *Two Figures with a Monkey* (1973) is one of the most outstanding pieces in the museum.

Museo de Arte Moderno ❼

Cnr of Paseo de la Reforma & Gandhi.
Map 1 B4. 🎫 *52 11 87 29.*
Ⓜ *Chapultepec.* ⭘ *10am–5:30pm
Tue–Sun.* 🎟 *Sun free.* ▧

A WIDE RANGE of 20th-century
Mexican painting and
sculpture is housed in this
gallery of modern art. The
collection includes works by
all the well-known figures –
Rufino Tamayo, Diego Rivera,
David Alfaro Siqueiros *(see
pp26–7)*, and Frida Kahlo – as
well as artists who do not
belong to the mainstream established by the muralists and
others since the Revolution.

Foreign artists, such as Leonora
Carrington, who have worked
in Mexico, are also represented.
   The museum has a fine array
of oils by Tamayo and several
works by Francisco Toledo,
his fellow Oaxacan. Among
the other highlights are Frida
Kahlo's *The Two Fridas*, Diego
Rivera's portrait of Lupe Marín,
and *Las Soldaderas* by José
Clemente Orozco. Contemp-
orary artists in the collection
include Alberto Castro Leñero,
Irma Palacios, and Emilio Ortiz.
   Sculptures are exhibited in
the museum's gardens, and
the adjacent circular gallery
houses temporary exhibitions
of modern Mexican and international art.

Castillo de Chapultepec ❽

Bosque de Chapultepec. **Map** 1 A5.
🎫 *55 53 62 68.* Ⓜ *Chapultepec.*
⭘ *9am–5pm Tue–Sun.*
🎟 *Sun free.* ▧ 🚫

T HE HILL which forms the
highest point of the Bosque
de Chapultepec once stood
on the lake shore across the
water from Tenochtitlán *(see
p94)*. On its summit stands
this 18th-century castle, now
housing the Museo Nacional
de Historia. A crucial battle
was fought here in 1847,
when army cadets died trying
to defend the fortress against
invading US troops. In the

Bosque de Chapultepec ❾

A FAVORITE WEEKEND recreational spot for
residents of Mexico City, Chapultepec
has been a public park since the 16th
century. Its tree-shaded paths are lined with
vendors selling everything from Mexican snacks
to balloons and cotton candy for children. Its
attractions include a zoo, a boating lake, a
number of museums and galleries, and often,
live, open-air entertainment. There is also a
botanical garden that dates from the earliest
days of the republic. It is well worth making
the climb up to the castle terrace, from which
the view across the city is stunning.

***Auditorio
Nacional*** ①
*Mexico's national concert
hall is a favored venue
for arts events. In front
of it stands this
contemporary
sculpture by
Juan Soriano.*

Boaters on Lago Chapultepec

"Papalote" Museo del Niño ⑨
Opened in 1993, this children's museum has
over 400 interactive exhibits, organized into
five themes: the human body, expression, the
world, "Con-science," and communication.
A giant video screen shows educational
movies. There is also an internet room.

0 meters   500
0 yards   500

Fuente de Tláloc ⑧
*This fountain was designed by
muralist Diego Rivera. Tlaloc was
the central Mexican rain deity
(see p265), and one of the most
important gods in the pantheon.*

*Fuente de
Petróleos*

BOULEVARD PRESIDENT

*Fuente de
Física Nuclear*

*Lago
Mayor*

*Fuente de
la Juventud*

*Fuente
de Tláloc*

*Lago
Menor*

*Monumento a
Nicolás Copérnico*

*Museo
Nacional de
Historia Natural*
⑨

View from the castle of Monumento a los Niños Héroes and Reforma

1860s, the castle became the palace of Emperor Maximilian *(see p53)*. Subsequently it served as an official residence for presidents of the republic. The museum covers Mexican history from the Conquest to the Revolution. Exhibits include period artifacts and paintings, and items relating to historical figures. A tailcoat that once belonged to Francisco I. Madero, the eyeglasses of Benito Juárez, and the rifles used in the execution of Maximilian are all on display.

The walls of the museum are decorated with large murals showing historical events. The most striking of these is Siqueiros' *From the Porfiriato to the Revolution.*

In the castle's grounds is the Galería de Historia, known as the Museo del Caracol (the "Snail Museum") because of its shape. In it, the visitor is guided through a series of dioramas illustrating scenes from the struggle for independence up to the Revolution.

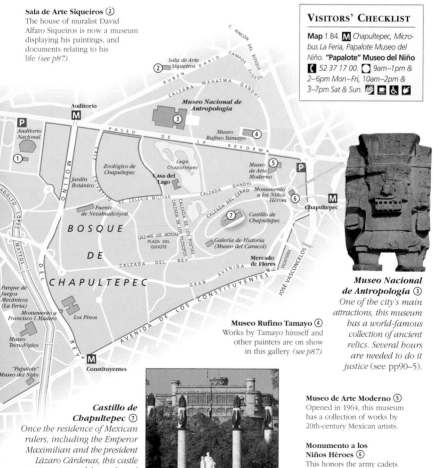

Sala de Arte Siqueiros ②
The house of muralist David Alfaro Siqueiros is now a museum displaying his paintings, and documents relating to his life *(see p87)*.

VISITORS' CHECKLIST

Map 1 B4. [M] *Chapultepec, Microbus La Feria, Papalote Museo del Niño.* **"Papalote" Museo del Niño** ☎ *52 37 17 00.* 🕐 *9am–1pm & 2–6pm Mon–Fri, 10am–2pm & 3–7pm Sat & Sun.*

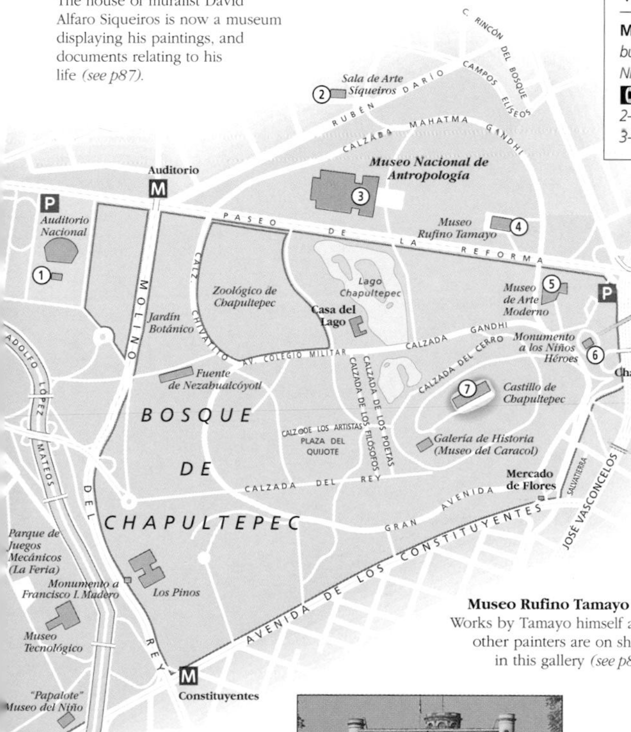

Museo Nacional de Antropología ③
One of the city's main attractions, this museum has a world-famous collection of ancient relics. Several hours are needed to do it justice (see pp90–5).

Museo Rufino Tamayo ④
Works by Tamayo himself and other painters are on show in this gallery *(see p87)*.

Castillo de Chapultepec ⑦
Once the residence of Mexican rulers, including the Emperor Maximilian and the president Lázaro Cárdenas, this castle enjoys views of the park and of the Paseo de la Reforma.

Museo de Arte Moderno ⑤
Opened in 1964, this museum has a collection of works by 20th-century Mexican artists.

Monumento a los Niños Héroes ⑥
This honors the army cadets ("boy heroes") who died defending the castle in 1847 *(see p52)*.

Museo Nacional de Antropología ❿

Stucco head from Palenque

INAUGURATED IN 1964, the vast and airy National Museum of Anthropology by Pedro Ramírez Vázquez is a just setting for a world-renowned collection of finds from Mexico's pre-Columbian cultures. The museum's large, central patio is almost entirely covered by an 84-meter (275-ft) long canopy which is balanced on an 11-meter (36-ft) pillar. This canopy is thought to be the largest concrete structure in the world to be supported by a single pillar.

The courtyard with bronze conch shell sculpture beside the pond

★ **Olmec Heads**
Two of the massive, basalt heads for which the Olmecs (see p254) are best known stand close together in the Gulf Coast gallery. Found at San Lorenzo (see p253), they may be portraits of high-ranking people.

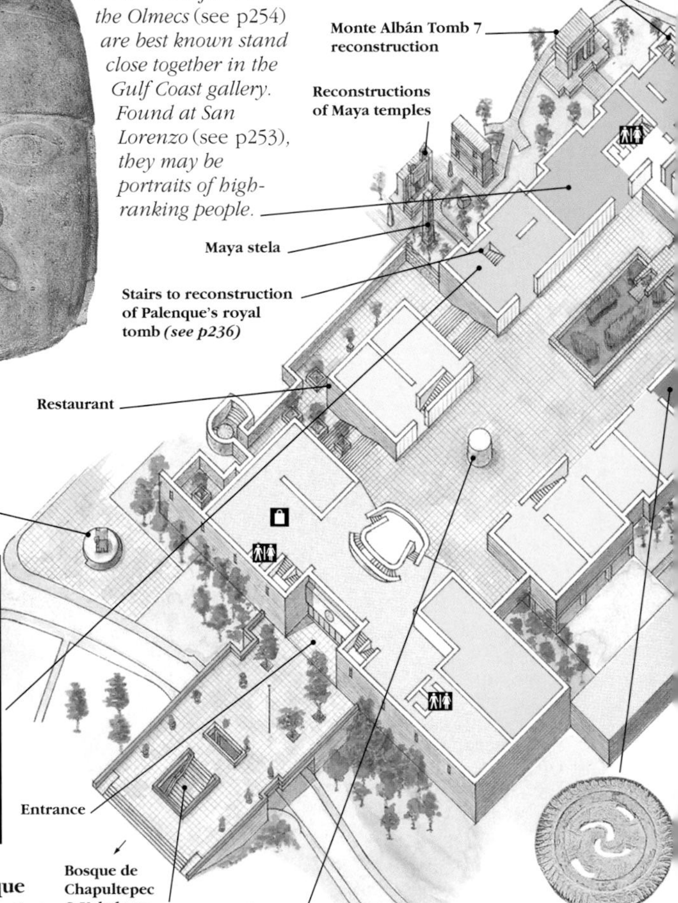

Stairs to reconstruction of Tomb 104 at Monte Albán (see pp220–1).

Monte Albán Tomb 7 reconstruction

Reconstructions of Maya temples

Maya stela

Stairs to reconstruction of Palenque's royal tomb (see p236)

A giant statue of a rain deity, either Chalchiuhtlicue or Tlaloc *(see p264),* stands near the museum's entrance.

Restaurant

Head of a young man from Palenque
This distinctive, life-size carved head was found among offerings in the tomb at the base of the Temple of the Inscriptions at the Classic Maya site of Palenque.

Entrance

Bosque de Chapultepec & Voladores

Steps to taxis and bus stop

The pillar supporting the canopy is decorated with bas reliefs of European and ancient Mexican civilizations.

Stela de la Ventilla
This carved pillar from Teotihuacán served as a movable marker in the ballgame (see p276).

★ Sun Stone
This intricately carved stone is the highlight of the Aztec room. The earth or sun god at the center is surrounded by signs for the 20 days of the Aztec ritual calendar.

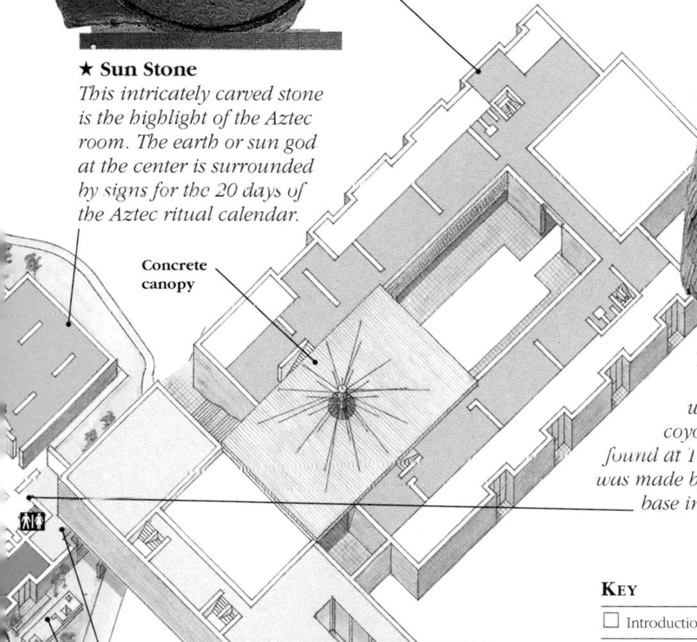

The Ethnology collections on the upper floor of the museum show aspects of the traditional lifestyle of the major indigenous groups of Mexico *(see pp20–1)*.

VISITORS' CHECKLIST

Cnr of Gandhi and Paseo de la Reforma. **Map** 1 A3. 55 53 63 81. Chapultepec. 9am–7pm Tue–Sun.

Toltec Coyote-Headed Warrior
This head of a warrior wearing a coyote headdress was found at Tula (see p144). It was made by covering a clay base in mother-of-pearl.

Concrete canopy

Giant Atlante sculpture from Tula *(see p144)*

Model of Teotihuacán

Tarascan house

KEY

- ☐ Introduction and Prehistory
- ☐ Preclassic Era
- ■ Teotihuacán
- ☐ Toltecs
- ☐ Aztecs *(see pp94–5)*
- ☐ Oaxaca
- ■ Gulf Coast
- ☐ The Maya
- ☐ Northern and Western Mexico
- ■ Ethnology collection
- ☐ Temporary exhibitions
- ☐ Nonexhibition space

★ Funerary Mask
This stone mask, encrusted with shell, turquoise, pyrite, and jade, is among the finest of the many priceless pre-Columbian treasures that the museum contains.

STAR EXHIBITS

★ Sun Stone

★ Olmec Heads

★ Western Funerary Mask

GALLERY GUIDE
The ground floor is dedicated to archaeological finds from ancient Mexico, each room dealing with a particular civilization or region of the country. Doors lead out to structures built within the grounds of the museum. The upper floor displays ethnology collections.

Exploring the Museo Nacional de Antropología

THE TWELVE GALLERIES on the ground floor are all accessible from the central patio, so that a tour can begin wherever the visitor likes. Although the first seven galleries are in chronological order, covering the history of the central plateau, the following five galleries visit the various regions of Mexico, including one dedicated to the great civilization of the Maya. The upper floor is devoted to a collection of costumes, houses, and artifacts of the 56 surviving indigenous cultures in Mexico as well as exploring aspects of their religion, social organization, and festivals.

Totonac stone carving

Detail from the reconstruction of the Temple of Quetzalcoatl façade

INTRODUCTORY GALLERIES

THE FIRST THREE galleries present an introduction to the study of anthropology, and an outline of the historical development of Mesoamerica *(see pp44–5)*, which ran from what is now northern Mexico down to western Honduras and El Salvador. An account of the prehistoric origins of the indigenous Mesoamerican cultures helps set the rest of the museum in context.

PRECLASSIC ERA

BEGINNING with the earliest agricultural settlements in the central plateau around 1700 BC, the Preclassic gallery illustrates the rise of more complex cultures, shown in particular detail through the development of the ceramic arts. Outstanding among the collection are a number of figures influenced by the Olmecs *(see p254)* from the Gulf of Mexico, including the "jaguar-boy" found at Tlapacoya in Mexico state. There is also a reconstruction of an intact burial site from Tlatilco in Mexico state, in which the skulls exhibit the cranial deformation and filed teeth that are typical of that period.

TEOTIHUACÁN

CENTERED ON the mysterious, ancient city that the Aztecs dubbed "the place where men became gods," the culture of Teotihuacán *(see*

Geometric sculpture of the water-goddess Chalchiuhtlicue

pp134–6) was among the most important of the Classic era in Mesoamerica. The gallery is dominated by the huge stone statue of the water-goddess, Chalchiuhtlicue. Along one wall a reconstruction of the façade of the Temple of Quetzalcoatl, reproduces the original blues and reds with which it was painted. Colorful murals of Teotihuacán life adorn the gallery's side walls.

Some of the finest pieces are less monumental. They include a wide variety of pottery vessels for domestic use, such as grain and water storage urns, figurines, and funerary masks showing a talent for lapidary, and obsidian carvings. The inhabitants of Teotihuacán, whose culture reached its height between 100 BC and AD 800, were experts in fashioning shiny

black obsidian knives. There are also statues that illustrate aspects of the religious way of life in Teotihuacán.

TOLTECS

AS TEOTIHUACÁN declined, other cities of the central plateau, Tula in particular, rose to prominence. The founders of Tula *(see p144)* were the Chichimecas from the north, who adopted the name Toltecs, meaning "artists." They soon acquired a reputation as specialists in the military arts.

The most noticeable exhibit is a gigantic stone warrior figure known as an Atlante, with which the Toltecs are most commonly associated. These figures were used as pillars in their temples.

The Toltec gallery also includes items from other cities of the Postclassic period, including Xochicalco in

One of the original Atlantes sculptures from Tula *(see p144)*

**Crude Toltec
pottery work**

Morelos, which more properly belong to the Teotihuacán tradition. Notable among them are stone carvings dedicated to the god Quetzalcoatl, and the stylized head of a macaw, which was perhaps used as a ball-court marker. Xochicalco's most famous monument, the serpent frieze around the base of the temple of Quetzalcoatl, is illustrated with a photographic mural.

OAXACA

FOLLOWING ON FROM the Aztec Hall *(see pp94–5)*, this is the first gallery dedicated to the regions of Mexico. It presents the artifacts of the two great peoples of Oaxaca: the Zapotecs, builders of the hilltop city of Monte Albán, and their neighbors and successors the Mixtecs, who created Mitla, with its stone friezes.

On display are polychrome ceramic pieces from both cultures. In the garden is a reconstruction of a Monte Albán tomb. Both peoples were skilled in the art of jewelry, and there are many examples here.

GULF OF MEXICO

AMONG THE MOST spectacular, and the best-known of all the museum's exhibits are the extraordinary colossal stone heads from the Preclassic Olmec culture, which flourished from 1200 to 600 BC. The Olmecs also produced smaller, but equally remarkable, sculptures of heads and figures in a variety of types of stone, most of them with the characteristic Olmec features of

**Huastec sculpture
of the god Xilonen**

broad, flat-nosed faces and thick lips, curled downward.

The Olmecs share this gallery with the Totonacs from central Veracruz and the Huastecs from the northern shores of the Gulf. The best-known creations of the Totonacs are the carved stone "yokes," the purpose of which is still not fully understood. The Huastecs were some of the finest artists of Mesoamerica, particularly in their use of clay, bone, and shell.

**Stela from Yaxchilán showing
a Maya ruler, circa AD 800**

THE MAYA

THERE IS NO DOUBTING the special hold of the Maya on the imagination of visitors to Mexico, whether because of the intricate beauty of their great stone cities in the jungle, such as Palenque in Chiapas *(see pp234–7)*, or the continuing mystery of their sudden decline, before the arrival of the Spanish conquistadors.

Among the highlights of the Maya gallery are carved stelae, such as the one from Yaxchilán, lintels from the Classic period, and a particularly outstanding carved head of a young man, found at Palenque. A small, underground gallery contains a reconstruction of the royal tomb of Pakal found beneath Palenque's Temple of the Inscriptions. It also displays artifacts from the site, including

high-quality stucco heads. The outside garden features several reconstructions of Maya ceremonial buildings, together with a group of other sculptures and stelae.

NORTHERN AND WESTERN MEXICO

THE SPARSELY INHABITED northern deserts never produced the great civilizations characteristic of central and southern Mexico. Nonetheless, the ceramic art from Paquimé *(see p170)* – the most notable of the so-called Oasis cultures – has a distinctive elegance, with its geometric patterns, smooth-polished surfaces and adornments such as copper or turquoise. The gallery also contains examples of metalwork, and models of the unique multi-story adobe houses of Casas Grandes.

At the height of the Aztec (Mexica) empire, the Tarascans (Purépechas), the dominant culture of the Pacific coast, retained their independence, and with it a distinctive artistic tradition. This gallery provides evidence of their skill in metalworking (they were among the first in the region to use gold, silver, and copper for jewelry and utensils), and in pottery.

Other items of particular note include the polished earthenware from Classic-era Colima, and the ceramics of the cloisonné technique using different colored clays, which is thought to have originated there.

**Colima
earthenware**

ETHNOLOGY COLLECTION

THE ELEVEN interconnected galleries on the top floor of the museum, beginning with Gallery 13, are devoted to all aspects of Mexican ethnology, including housing, costumes, artifacts, religions, social structures, and the festivals of the 56 surviving indigenous cultures of Mexico.

The Aztec Hall

Model of the Templo Mayor (see pp68–70)

THE LARGEST GALLERY in the museum displays the treasures of the Mexica culture – better known as the Aztecs. When Hernán Cortés and his conquistadors arrived in 1519 *(see p49)*, the Aztecs ruled most of what is now Mexico, either directly or indirectly. This gallery gives the visitor a strong sense of the everyday culture of the Aztec people, the power and wealth of their theocratic rulers, and their enormous appetite for blood, sacrifice, war, and conquest.

Realistic stone head, possibly representing the common man

LARGE SCULPTURES

THE ENTRANCE LANDING and central section of the gallery are devoted to large stone sculptures. Near the entrance is the Ocelotl-Cuauhxicalli, a 94-cm (3-ft) high stone vessel in the form of a jaguar-eagle. It was used as a receptacle to hold the hearts of human sacrificial victims. A statue of Coatlicue, the mother of Coyolxauhqui and later of Huitzilopochtli *(see p70)*, is one of the few representations of the goddess in Aztec art. This statue shows her with eagle's claws, a dress made of snakes, and a necklace of hearts and hands. She has been decapitated, and two serpents emanate from her neck to symbolize blood. Other large sculptures here are the goddesses Coyolxauhqui and Cihuateteo, a small-scale representation of a *teocalli* or temple, and a *tzompantli*, an altar of skulls from the Templo Mayor. On the wall opposite the door, dominating the gallery, is the Sun Stone.

THE AZTEC PEOPLE AND THEIR HISTORY

THE SECTION to the right of the entrance describes the Aztec people, their physical appearance and their history. The most conspicuous piece here is a carved round stone, known as the Stone of Tizoc, which records the victories of Tizoc, the seventh ruler

THE LAKE CITY OF TENOCHTITLÁN

The Aztecs' capital city, Tenochtitlán, was built on an island in a shallow lake. Stone causeways connected the city to the shore of the lake, and an aqueduct brought fresh water. Temples and other civic and ceremonial buildings stood at the center of the city (sacred precinct), around what is now the Zócalo *(see pp62–3)*. This area was surrounded by a great wall.

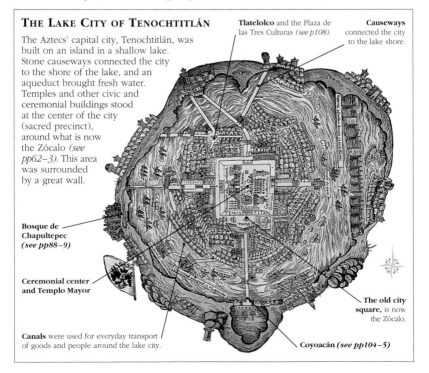

Tlatelolco and the Plaza de las Tres Culturas *(see p108)*.

Causeways connected the city to the lake shore.

Bosque de Chapultepec *(see pp88–9)*

Ceremonial center and Templo Mayor

Canals were used for everyday transport of goods and people around the lake city.

The old city square, is now the Zócalo.

Coyoacán *(see pp104–5)*

of the Aztecs (1481–6). This trachyte stone was found in the Zócalo. Another object of interest is a stone head with inset teeth and eyes to add to its realism. It is thought to represent the common man. Other sculptures represent everyday Aztec people, including a statue of a Mexica noble dressed in robes appropriate to his rank.

This part of the museum includes a model of the temple complex that stood at the center of Tenochtitlán. Surrounded by a wall, the complex focused upon the Templo Mayor topped by its twin shrines. The rounded temple in front of the Templo Mayor was dedicated to the god Quetzalcoatl. Above the model hangs a large painting by Luis Covarrubias showing the city as it may have looked when first seen by the Spanish.

Polished obsidian statue of a monkey god

SACRED OBJECTS

THE DISPLAY cases to the left of the entrance show items used for religious purposes by the Aztecs. One of the most interesting pieces is a vase in the form of a pregnant monkey, carved out of obsidian, a hard black, volcanic stone akin to glass. This vase symbolizes the wind loaded with black rain clouds which will engender growth and fertility. Also on display here is the stone altar on which human sacrificial victims were stretched in order to remove their hearts. Other items include solar disks, sacrificial knives, and representations of various deities.

THE SUN STONE

Often mistakenly referred to as the Calendar Stone, this basaltic disk was unearthed in the Zócalo in 1790. The carvings describe the beginning of the Aztec world and foretell its end. The Aztecs believed they were living in the fifth and final "creation" of the world. Each creation was called a sun. The stone is 3.6 m (12 ft) in diameter and weighs 24 tonnes.

The central god could be the sun god Tonatiuh or the earth god Tlaltecuhtli.

The 20 days of the Aztec month are shown on the inner band.

Two fire serpents run around the rim of the stone, their tails meeting at the date of creation.

Four square panels around the center indicate that the previous suns (creations) were destroyed by jaguars, wind, rain, and water

OTHER EXHIBITS

ASPECTS OF Aztec daily life are described in other parts of the hall. There are notable collections of craft objects. The ceramics section shows plates, vases, masks, and other items, many with decorative work. Pieces of Aztec jewelry made out of bone, gold, wood, crystal, and shells are displayed, while their clothing includes animal skins and feathers. The musicality of the Aztecs is shown with a range of instruments, such as flutes and whistles. A wooden drum *(huehuetl)* is finely carved with a warring eagle and vulture.

Along the back wall are documents and drawings explaining the system of tribute that sustained the Aztec economy. Here there is also a diorama of the market in Tlatelolco, part of Tenochtitlán, showing a scene of pots, food, and other goods being bought and sold.

Aztec shield made out of animal hide and feathers

SAN ÁNGEL AND COYOACÁN

AT THE TIME of the Spanish conquest, Coyoacán ("place of the coyotes") was a small town on the shore of Lake Texcoco. It was connected to the Aztec capital of Tenochtitlán, an island in the lake, by a causeway. After conquering Tenochtitlán, Hernán Cortés set up his headquarters here in 1521 while the city was rebuilt along Spanish lines.

Nearby San Ángel was then a village called Tenanitla, where Dominican and Carmelite friars chose to settle after the conquest. It became known as San Ángel in the 17th century, after the foundation of the convent-school of San Angelo Mártir. Its official name today is Villa Álvaro Obregón, but this is rarely used.

Until this century both San Ángel and Coyoacán were rural communities well outside Mexico City. The growth of the metropolis has since

Monumento a Álvaro Obregón, San Ángel

swallowed them up, but both retain a good deal of their original colonial architecture. Much favored as a place of residence by artists and writers, many of whom prefer the relative tranquillity of San Ángel and Coyoacán to the bustle nearer the city center, they are also popular with families for weekend day trips.

Some of the area's famous inhabitants in the past have included Diego Rivera, Frida Kahlo, and Russian revolutionary León Trotsky. The latter was assassinated in Coyoacán in August, 1940. The former homes of all three are among the area's attractions, along with a number of museums and art galleries. Restaurants and specialty shops abound, and there are popular weekend craft markets in the Jardín Centenario (in Coyoacán) and the Plaza San Jacinto (in San Ángel).

SIGHTS AT A GLANCE

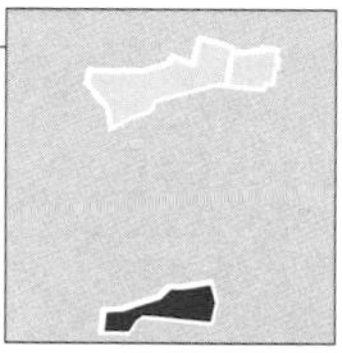

Museums and Galleries
Casa/Museo León Trotsky ❿
Museo de la Acuarela ❽
Museo de Arte Carrillo-Gil ❺
Museo del Carmen ❸
Museo Estudio Diego Rivera ❹
Museo Frida Kahlo ❾

Churches
Iglesia de San Antonio
  Panzacola ❻

Streets and Squares
Avenida Francisco Sosa ❼
Coyoacán see pp104–105 ⓫
Plaza San Jacinto ❷

Walks
*San Ángel to Coyoacán
  see pp98–9* ❶

GETTING AROUND
The streets of San Ángel and Coyoacán are ideal for a peaceful stroll. The metro is the best way to get there from the city center. The closest stations are at Viveros and Miguel Ángel de Quevedo, both in Coyoacán, and General Anaya (to the east).

KEY
▬ Walk route
▦ Street-by-Street map *pp104–5*
Ⓜ Metro station
🛈 Tourist information
🅿 Parking

◁ **Tree sculpture in Plaza Hidalgo, Coyoacán**

A Walk from San Ángel to Coyoacán ❶

FEW PARTS OF MEXICO CITY can boast a domestic architecture of the colonial and pre-revolutionary eras as well-preserved as that of Coyoacán and San Ángel. This walk connects the two squares at the heart of these districts, both of which are well-known in the city for their weekend craft fairs. The walk often follows tree-lined, cobbled streets. Along the way are churches, museums, art galleries, and monuments, as well as some picturesque places to stop for a meal.

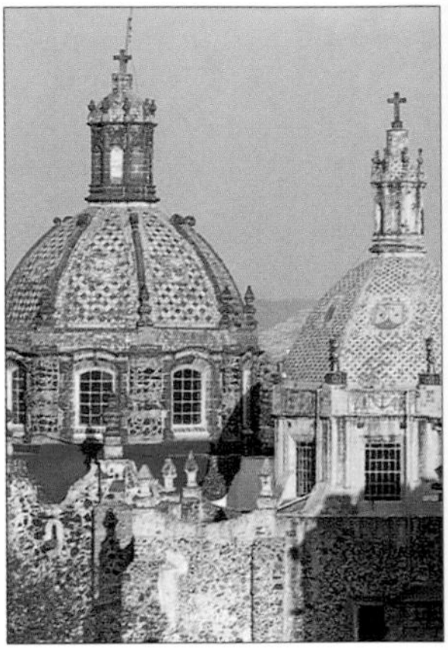

The domes of the Museo del Carmen in San Ángel

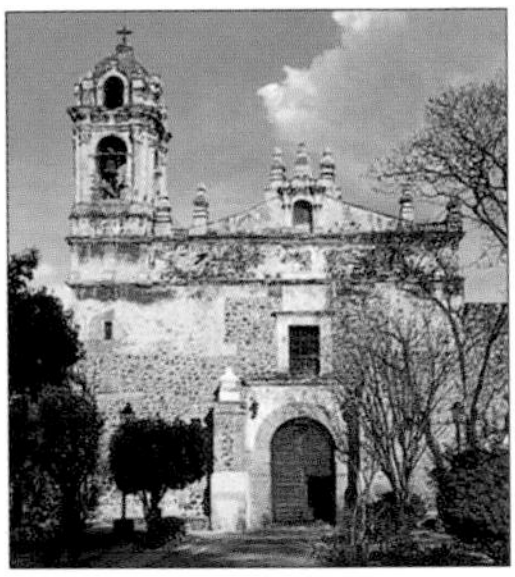

Iglesia de San Jacinto, on the main square of San Ángel

Sights on Walk

Plaza San Jacinto ①
Museo del Carmen ②
General Álvaro Obregón ③
Plaza Federico Gamboa ④
San Antonio Panzacola ⑤
Avenida Francisco Sosa ⑥
Museo Nacional de la Acuarela ⑦
Plaza Santa Catarina ⑧
Jardín Centenario ⑨

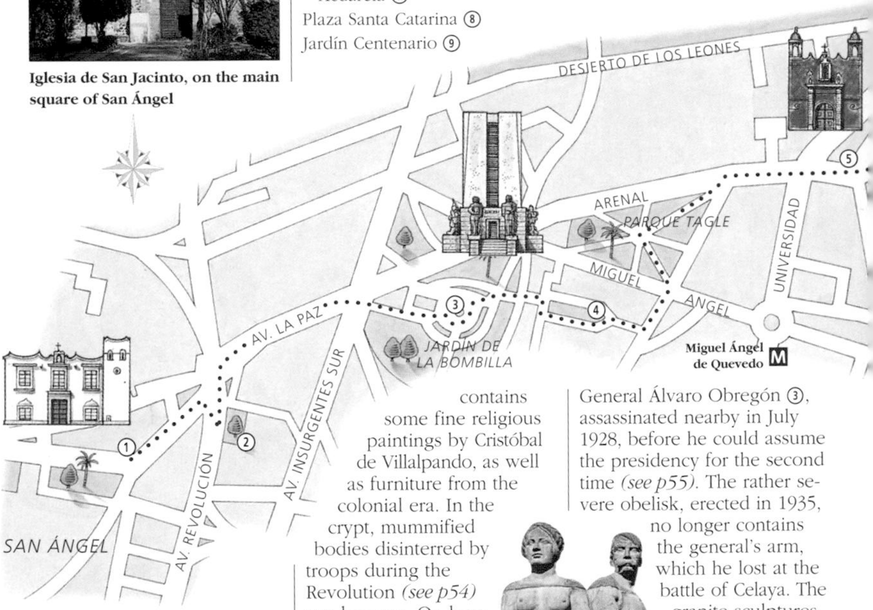

San Ángel
Leave Plaza San Jacinto ① *(see p100)*, a pleasant square with numerous restaurants, by Calle Madero. At the end of this road you will pass the Centro Cultural de San Ángel on your right. On reaching Avenida Revolución, turn right and cross over to reach the Museo del Carmen ② *(see p100)*. The church of this former monastery has three tiled domes that are the symbol of San Ángel. The museum contains some fine religious paintings by Cristóbal de Villalpando, as well as furniture from the colonial era. In the crypt, mummified bodies disinterred by troops during the Revolution *(see p54)* can be seen. On leaving the church, turn right and walk along Revolución then right again into the cobbled street of Avenida La Paz where there are some good but pricey restaurants *(see p316)*.

Chimalistac
Cross Avenida Insurgentes and will you come to the Jardín de la Bombilla, the small, wooded park that surrounds the monument to General Álvaro Obregón ③, assassinated nearby in July 1928, before he could assume the presidency for the second time *(see p55)*. The rather severe obelisk, erected in 1935, no longer contains the general's arm, which he lost at the battle of Celaya. The granite sculptures that flank the monument are the work of Ignacio Asúnsolo (1890–1965). Cross Calle Chimalistac and walk along a lane to Plaza Federico Gamboa ④. This square (which is also known as Plaza Chimalistac) is named after a writer and politician of the *porfiriato (see p53)*. The chapel of San Sebastián

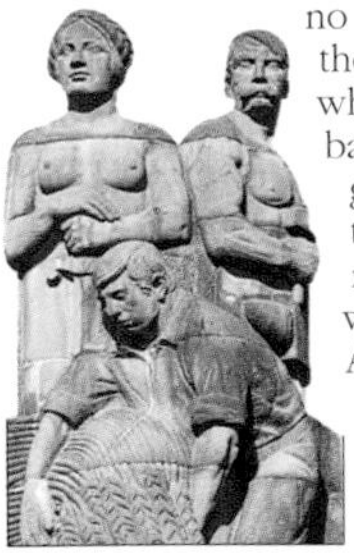

Detail of Monumento a Álvaro Obregón

Chimalistac, dating from the 17th century, sits crosswise in the square. It is notable, among other things, for a stunning Baroque altarpiece with 18th-century religious paintings. San Sebastián was one of the few open chapels in Mexico City. The atrial cross which stands in front of it is a relic of the days when mass was celebrated in the outdoors.

On leaving the square, turn left and walk along Ignacio Allende, a narrow street, until you reach Miguel Ángel de Quevedo. Cross this to stroll in Parque Tagle. Once through the park, bear right into Calle Arenal. Walk along this quiet street until you reach the bustling Avenida Universidad.

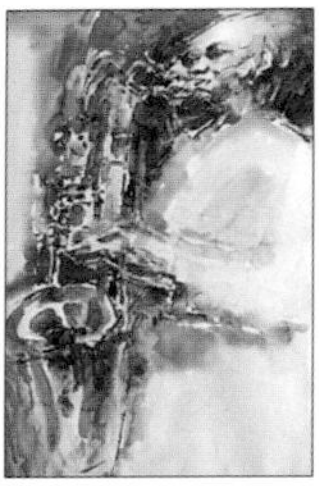

Jazz **by Angel Mauro Rodríguez in Museo de la Acuarela**

Avenida Francisco Sosa

Directly across Universidad stands the chapel of San Antonio Panzacola [5] *(see p101)*, a tiny jewel of a church dating from the 17th century. Next to the chapel is an old stone bridge over a tributary of the Río Magdalena. Cross this and you come to one of the prettiest streets in the city. Avenida Francisco Sosa [6] *(see p102)* is also one of the oldest colonial streets in Latin America. Take the first turn on the right down Calle Salvador Novo for a short detour to visit a gallery of watercolor paintings, the Museo Nacional de la Acuarela [7] *(see p102)*. Halfway along Francisco Sosa you come to the enchanting Plaza Santa Catarina [8] where story-tellers gather on Sunday lunchtimes. The main building on the square is a lovely yellow church with a triple-arched façade. Opposite the chapel is the Casa de la Cultura Jesús Reyes Heroles, a university arts center with a beautiful, leafy garden. At the end of Francisco Sosa you arrive at the twin arches of what was once the gateway into the convent of San Juan Bautista. This then leads into the pleasant quare of Jardín Centenario at the heart of Coyoacán [9] *(see pp104–5)*.

Tips for Walkers

Starting point: *Plaza San Jacinto, San Ángel.* ***Length***: *3.5 km (2 miles).* ***Places to eat***: *Plaza San Jacinto, Avenida La Paz, Plaza Santa Catarina, Jardín Centenario.* ***Metro station***: *Miguel Ángel de Quevedo.*

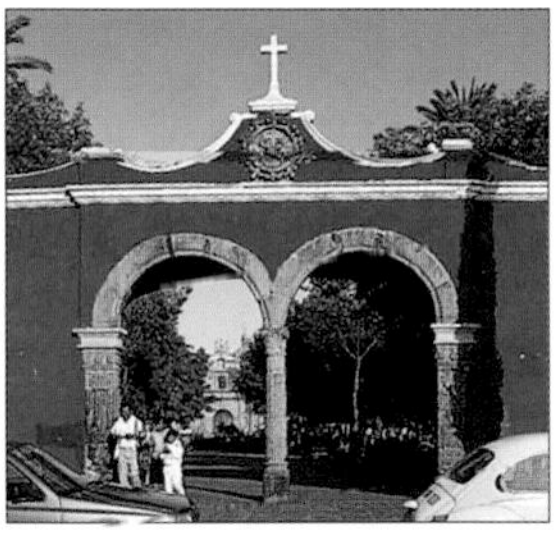

Archway on Jardín Centenario, in the center of Coyoacán

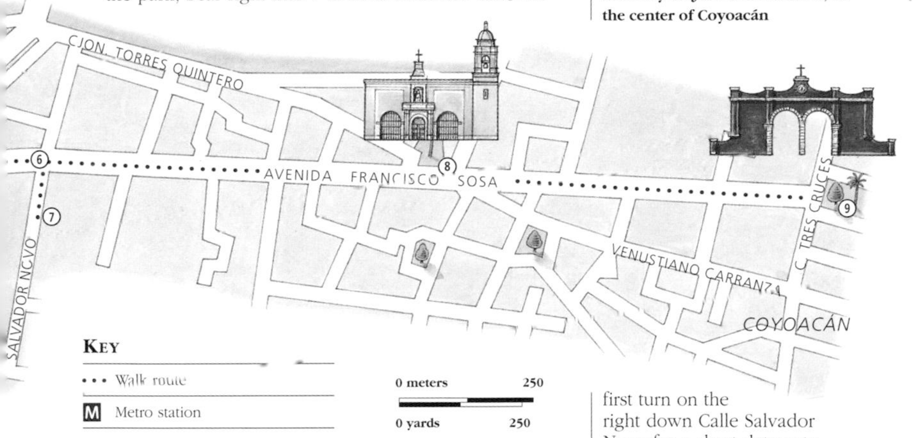
CJON. TORRES QUINTERO
AVENIDA FRANCISCO SOSA
SALVADOR NOVO
TRES CRUCES
VENUSTIANO CARRANZA
COYOACÁN
6
7
8
9
KEY
Walk route
M Metro station
0 meters 250
0 yards 250

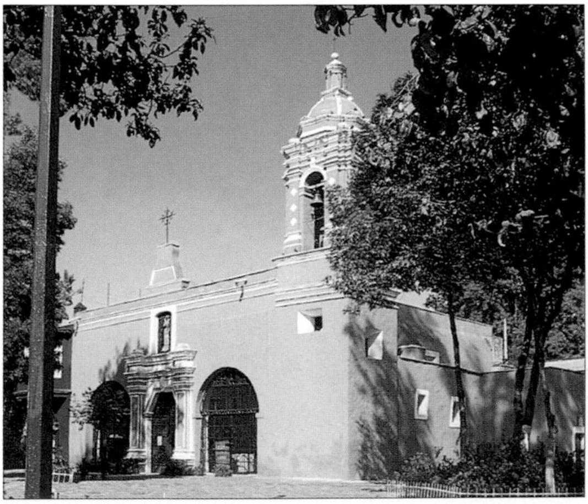

The charming Iglesia de Santa Catarina on the square of the same name

Plaza de San Jacinto ❷

San Ángel. **M** *Miguel Ángel de Quevedo.*

O**N SATURDAYS** this square, which forms the center of San Ángel, is an excellent place to shop for Mexican handicrafts, either at the outdoor stalls or in the Bazar del Sábado, which is located in a 17th-century house in the northwest corner.

The 16th-century Iglesia de San Jacinto, just off the square, was originally annexed to a Dominican monastery of the same name. The church has a fine dome. In the interior, the carved wooden screen, and the onyx font in the nave are both worth seeing.

The most impressive building on the north side of the square is the Casa del Risco, also known as the Casa del Mirador, a well-preserved, 18th-century house built for the Marqués de San Miguel de Aguayo and donated to the nation in 1963. Constructed around an interior courtyard with an extravagant fountain, the house contains a wealth of colonial furniture and decor.

On the square's west side is a plaque commemorating the soldiers of the Irish-American San Patricio batallion who died fighting for Mexico against the United States in 1846–7.

Dazzling main altarpiece in the church of the Museo del Carmen in San Ángel

Courtyard of the Museo del Carmen

Museo del Carmen ❸

Avenida Revolución 4. **C** *56 16 15 04.* **M** *Miguel Ángel de Quevedo.* ○ *10am–5pm Tue–Sun.* 🗓 *Sun free.* 🚫

T**HE CARMELITE** monastery-school of San Angelo Mártir, built in the early 17th century, gave its name to the San Ángel district. The three beautiful domes that rise above it, elaborately decorated with colorful tiles, are still a symbol of the area. Later the monastery and its church became known as El Carmen. Today it serves as a museum of furniture, paintings, and other artistic and historical objects from the colonial period. Much of the original interior is preserved, including the monks' cells. In the crypt a dozen mummified bodies, which were disinterred by troops during the Revolution *(see p49)*, are displayed in glass-topped coffins. Decorative details include Talavera tiles from Puebla and carved, painted ceilings. The chapel on the first floor contains an 18th-century gold-painted altarpiece inset with oil paintings of

saints. Other highlights to look out for in the museum are a series of religious paintings by the 18th-century master Cristóbal de Villalpando and a richly carved door with symbols representing the Virgin Mary.

Diego Rivera's workshop, surrounded by a cactus hedge

Museo Estudio Diego Rivera ❹

Corner of Calle Diego Rivera and Altavista. **C** *55 50 15 18.* **M** *Viveros, Barranca del Muerto.* ○ *10am–6pm Tue–Sun.* 🗓 *Sun free.* 🚫

O**NE OF MEXICO'S** most outstanding 20th-century architects, Juan O'Gorman, built these twin houses in 1931–2 for two of the country's most distinguished painters, Diego Rivera and Frida Kahlo. Surrounded by a cactus hedge, the houses are connected by a rooftop bridge, over which Frida used to take Diego his meals. *The Two Fridas* and several other of her most well-known works were painted here. Behind her house is a building her father used as a photographic studio.

The large living room/studio in Rivera's house contains an assortment of his personal belongings, from paintbrushes to huge, papier-mâché skeletons and pre-Columbian pottery. Other rooms are devoted to temporary exhibitions of the artists' work.

Across the street is the San Ángel Inn *(see p316)*, an elegant restaurant, with a beautiful garden popular with Mexico's elite. Built in 1692, it was originally a Carmelite monastery. After 1915 it was turned into a restaurant and today it is known for its excellent cuisine and its string of famous patrons, among them Brigitte Bardot, Henry Kissinger, and Richard Nixon.

Museo de Arte Carrillo-Gil ❺

Avenida Revolución 1608. 📞 55 50 62 89. Ⓜ *Miguel Ángel de Quevedo.* 🕐 *10am–6pm Tue–Sun.* 🎫 *Sun free* ♿ 📷 *reserve in advance.* 🚫 🌐 *www.macg.inba.gob.mx*

THIS LIGHT and airy gallery on three floors holds a permanent collection of art that embraces some of the finest 20th-century Mexican artists. Founded in 1974, the collection was assembled by Dr. Alvar Carrillo and his wife and includes works by Diego Rivera, José Clemente Orozco, and David Alfaro Siqueiros. Among the Rivera canvases are a number of works from the artist's Cubist period. Less well-known, but equally interesting, are paintings by Austrian Wolfgang Paalen (1905–1959) and German Gunther Gerzso, a contemporary artist.

Dr. Carrillo, who studied medicine in Paris, began supporting avant-garde artists in his native Mexico from the late 1930s onward, by purchasing their works and through published criticism. He was himself a

The red façade of the Capilla de San Antonio Panzacola

painter of some note, and a close friend of Orozco.

Not far from the museum, near the corner of Revolución and La Paz, is the well-known San Ángel flower market. You can pick up anything here, from an extravagant arrangement to a single rose at any time of the day or night. It is an especially fine sight at night, when the rich colors of the flowers glow under the artificial lights.

Colorful display of blooms on a stall in the San Ángel flower market

Capilla de San Antonio Panzacola ❻

Corner of Avenida Universidad and Avenida Francisco Sosa. Ⓜ *Miguel Ángel de Quevedo, Viveros.*

THIS TINY 17th-century chapel originally belonged to the nearby parish church of San Sebastián Chimalistac *(see p99)*. It sits next to a miniature stone bridge over a stream at the end of Avenida Francisco Sosa *(see p102)*. Painted a striking dark red color, with reliefwork in a contrasting creamy white, its façade includes a niche containing a statue of St. Anthony. Above the arched entrance is a relief sculpture of St. Sebastian the martyr. The arch is flanked by pilasters supporting a molded entablature. The undulating roofline ends in twin towers and has a cross in its center.

The frontage of Casa Alvarado, one of the residences on Avenida Francisco Sosa

Avenida Francisco Sosa ❼

Between San Ángel and Coyoacán.
Ⓜ Miguel Ángel de Quevedo.

MEXICO CITY'S most attractive street is also one of the oldest colonial streets in Latin America. Running approximately 1.5 km (just under a mile) between Avenida Universidad and the Jardín Centenario in Coyoacán (see pp104–105), it is lined with handsome residences.

At the beginning of it stands the quaint, 17th-century chapel of San Antonio Panzacola (see p101). A short way farther along the avenue, soldiers stand guard outside the imposing city residence of the former Mexican president, Miguel de la Madrid. Continuing down the street there are a number of very attractive residences including the Casa de la Campana (No. 303) and No. 319, which has a replica Atlante (see p144) outside it. No. 383 is another interesting colonial house, thought to have been constructed in the 18th century by Pedro de Alvarado, the Spanish conqueror of Mexico and Guatemala. The house next door belonged to his son. About halfway along the avenue is the pleasant Plaza Santa Catarina. On this square stand a church and the Casa de la Cultura Jesús Reyes Heroles, an arts center. A short way farther along is the cultural department of the Italian embassy. At the end of the street, on the corner of Jardín Centenario in Coyoacán, is the 18th-century Casa de Diego de Ordaz.

Museo Nacional de la Acuarela ❽

Salvador Novo 88. ☎ 55 54 18 01
Ⓜ Miguel Ángel de Quevedo.
🕙 11am–6pm Tue–Sun. ⃠
📷 reserve in advance.

DEDICATED primarily to some of the finest works by Mexican watercolor artists from the 19th century to the present day, this museum is located in a small, two-story house set in a pretty garden.

The larger part of the collection consists of works by contemporary artists, including many winners of the Salón Nacional de la Acuarela annual prize for watercolors. Embracing a wide range of styles and subject matter, it may surprise those who think of watercolors primarily in terms of delicate landscapes. Two outstanding canvases are La Carrera del Fuego and Jazz, both by Ángel Mauro Rodríguez, which can be seen on display on the ground floor of the museum.

There is an international room containing a selection of paintings by artists from all over the Americas, as well as Spain and Italy, including US artists Robert Wade and Janet Walsh. A separate gallery in the garden outside houses temporary exhibitions.

The Museo Nacional de la Acuarela, home to a collection of watercolors

FRIDA KAHLO (1907–54)

Arguably Mexico's most original painter, Frida Kahlo led a troubled life. A childhood bout of polio left her right leg slightly withered. Then, when she was 18, she broke her back in a traffic accident which rendered her incapable of having children. The pain she suffered for much of her life is reflected in many of her often violent and disturbing paintings, particularly her self-portraits. In 1929 she married the muralist Diego Rivera. Rivera was a notorious womanizer but Frida too had affairs, with both women and men – including León Trotsky. She and Rivera divorced in 1939, remarried the following year but thereafter lived separately.

Bronze statue of Frida Kahlo

Museo Frida Kahlo 🟒

Londres 247. 📞 55 54 59 99.
Ⓜ Coyoacán. 🕐 10am–5.45pm
Tue–Sun. 📷 🚫 🚭

THIS IS THE HOUSE where the painter Frida Kahlo was born, lived for much of her life, and eventually died. She painted some of her famous works here, many of them inspired by the pain she suffered as a result of breaking her back. This house is a treasure trove, not only of Frida's paintings, but also of innumerable artifacts associated with her life and that of her lover Diego Rivera, with whom she shared the house. Donated to the nation by Rivera in 1955, not long after Frida's death, it is preserved much as it was when they lived there.

On display are letters and diaries as well as ceramics and other everyday items. A handwritten accounts book shows the couple's earnings and outgoings for March/April 1947, including the fee earned by Frida Kahlo for the famous painting *The Two Fridas*. One wall is covered with Rivera's collection of "*retablos*": small paintings created as religious offerings in gratitude for prayers answered. There are also giant paper "Judas" figures, burned on Easter Saturday as a symbolic destruction of evil forces *(see p30)*, as well as pre-Columbian art collected by Rivera. Frida's wheelchair

THE ASSASSINATION OF TROTSKY

The intellectual, León Trotsky, was born Lev Davidovitch Bronstein, in Russia, in 1879. He played a leading role in the Bolshevik seizing of power in 1917 and in forming the Red Army to fight the Russian Civil War of 1918–20. But Lenin's death in 1924 led to a power struggle within the ranks of the victorious revolutionaries, and in 1927 Trotsky was forced into exile by his rival, Joseph Stalin. He was granted asylum in Mexico in 1937 but even across the Atlantic he was not safe from Stalin's purge of all his opponents. His house was assaulted in May 1940 by Mexican Stalinists led by the muralist David Alfaro Siqueiros *(see p26)* and machine-gunned for 20 minutes. Then on August 20, 1940, he was fatally wounded by another assassin, Ramón Mercader, who pierced

León Trotsky

his skull with an icepick.

and one of the stiff corsets she was obliged to wear constantly because of her disability are also on display here.

Casa/Museo León Trotsky 🟟

Avenida Rio Churubusco 410. 📞 56 58 87 32. Ⓜ Coyoacán. 🕐 10am–5pm, Tue–Sun. 📷 🎥 🚫

LEÓN TROTSKY, the Russian revolutionary, lived in this house from 1939 until his assassination in 1940. Before moving here he lived with the muralists Diego Rivera and Frida Kahlo.

To frustrate would-be assassins, Trotsky fitted the windows and doors with armor-plating, raised the height of the sur-

rounding wall, and blocked off most of the windows that overlooked the street, among other things. All this foiled one attempt on his life: about 80 bullet holes can still be seen in the outer walls.

However, these precautions did not stop Ramón Mercader, a regular visitor to the house, who had won his victim's confidence. The room where the murder took place is just as it was, complete with the chair and table where Trotsky was sitting when he died.

Trotsky's typewriter, books, and other possessions can be seen where he left them. One of the photographs on display shows him on his arrival in Mexico in 1937, standing on the quay in Tampico with his wife Natalia and Frida Kahlo.

Frida Kahlo's brightly colored kitchen with pottery on display

Street-by-Street: Coyoacán ⓫

Once the haunt of conquistador Hernán Cortés and his Indian mistress "La Malinche," the atmospheric suburb of Coyoacán is an ideal place for a stroll, especially on the weekend, when a lively craft fair operates in its two main squares, Jardín Centenario and Plaza Hidalgo. Packed with cafés, restaurants, and cantinas, its narrow streets retain much of their colonial-era charm. Calle Felipe Carrillo Puerto, heading south out of the plaza, is a good place to shop for curios. Coyoacán is also known in Mexico City for its delicious ice cream.

Casa de Cortés
The north side of Plaza Hidalgo is taken up by this distinctive 15th-century building, now used as government offices.

Indoor craft bazaar (open at weekends)

Cantina La Guadalupana *(see p116)*

Avenida Francisco Sosa
This narrow, pretty street (see p102) leading to nearby San Ángel is a delight to stroll along. It is lined with handsome, well-maintained mansions which were built by wealthy families in colonial times.

Gateway of former monastery

Casa de Diego de Ordaz
While named after the conquistador Diego de Ordaz, the house dates only from the 18th century. At one corner is this ornate niche with a statue of the Virgin Mary.

Jardín Centenario
was once the atrium of the monastery of San Juan Bautista, of which only the church remains.

Plaza Hidalgo
The Casa de Cortés faces the church of San Juan Bautista across this spacious square centering on a bandstand.

Iglesia de San Juan Bautista
Once part of a convent dedicated to St. John the Baptist, this church was originally built in the 16th century. Though much altered, it still has a number of interesting relief sculptures on its façade.

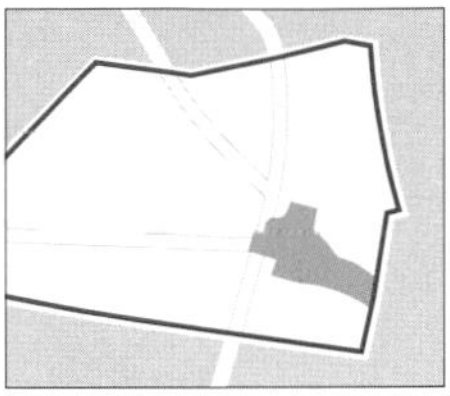

Plaza de la Conchita
This quiet colonial square shaded by trees, and with a stone cross in the middle, is the prettiest spot in Coyoacán.

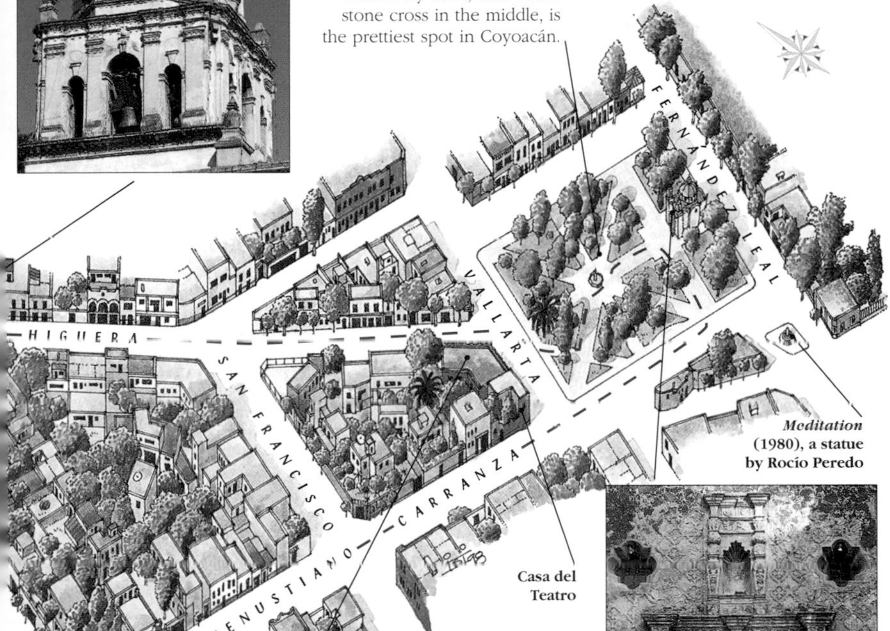

LOCATOR MAP

Meditation (1980), a statue by Rocío Peredo

Casa del Teatro

0 meters 50

0 yards 50

Iglesia de la Conchita
This tiny church, officially the Capilla de la Concepción, has an intricately carved, Mudejar-style façade. The interior contains a Baroque altarpiece and some outstanding colonial paintings.

Casa de la Malinche
Traditionally associated with Cortés' mistress "La Malinche," this 16th-century house was probably built for Ixtolinque, a local chieftain. Today it is the home of two well-known Mexican artists, Rina Lazo and Arturo García Bustos.

KEY

- – – – Suggested route

FARTHER AFIELD

There is plenty worth discovering in this massive, sprawling city beyond the Historic Center. Head north to the Plaza Garibaldi and you can be serenaded by mariachis or explore the nearby ruins of Tlatelolco, Tenochtitlán's twin city. The Basílica de Guadalupe, the largest shrine to the Virgin Mary in all of the Americas, is even farther north, on the site where legend says she appeared in 1531. In the south, Xochimilco preserves the only remnant of Lake Texcoco and its pre-Columbian floating gardens. Boatmen will ferry you around its tree-lined canals. The 2,500-year-old pyramid of Cuicuilco, meanwhile, is thought to be the oldest structure in the city.

SIGHTS AT A GLANCE

Museums and Galleries
Museo Anahuacalli ❼
Museo Dolores Olmedo
    Patiño ⓬
Museo Nacional de las
    Intervenciones ❻

Public buildings
Universidad Nacional
    Autónoma de Mexico ❽

Squares and Markets
Mercado de La Merced ❹
Plaza Garibaldi ❸

Churches
Basílica de Guadalupe ❶

Historic Sites
Pirámide de Cuicuilco ❾
Tlatclolco and Plaza de las
    Tres Culturas ❷

Suburbs
Tlalpan ❿
Xochimilco ⓫

Streets
Avenida Insurgentes Sur ❺

Key
	Main sightseeing areas
	Parks and open spaces
	Greater Mexico City
✈	Airport
🚉	Train station
🚌	Bus station
	Highway
	Major road
	Minor road

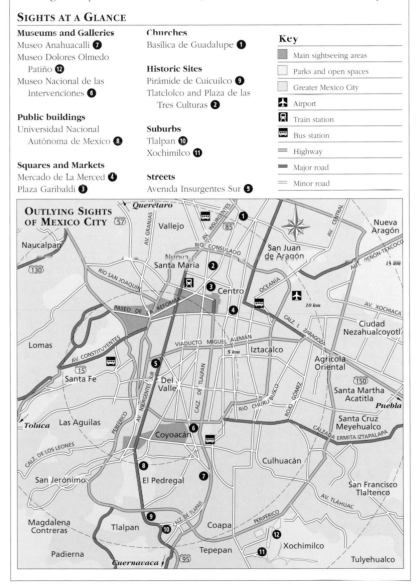

◁ Colorfully decorated punts in the floating gardens of Xochimilco

The Antigua Basílica de Guadalupe

Basílica de Guadalupe ❶

Plaza de las Americas 1. **[** 55 77 60 22. **M** La Villa. **◯** 6am–8pm daily. **♿**

THE RICHEST AND most visited Catholic shrine in all the Americas is a complex of buildings at the foot of a hill, the Cerro del Tepeyac. According to legend it was here in 1531 that a brown-skinned Virgin Mary miraculously appeared to the Indian Juan Diego in 1531. She is named after the Virgin of Guadalupe in Extremadura, Spain.

The Antigua Basílica was built in the early 18th century. Twin towers flank its Baroque façade, which features relief carvings of the Virgin. It is overshadowed by the circular, modern church that now stands beside it, which can accommodate up to 10,000 worshipers. An object of veneration inside it is Diego's tunic on which the image of the Virgin was supposedly imprinted as proof of the miracle he witnessed. There is also an interesting museum.

The impressive Capilla del Pocito is a late 18th-century chapel regarded as one of the finest achievements of Mexican Baroque architecture. The Virgin is supposed to have appeared four times in all. This chapel was constructed on the site of her fourth appearance. It is roughly elliptical in shape and its domed roof is faced with dazzling blue and white Talavera tiles *(see p153)*.

Next door to another chapel, the Capilla de Indios, is a house in which Juan Diego is said to have lived after the Virgin's first appearance until his death in 1548.

Each year on December 12 an estimated 50,000 people assemble at the shrine to celebrate the anniversary of the appearance of the Virgin.

Tiles on the Capilla del Pocito, near the Basílica de Guadalupe

Plaza de las Tres Culturas ❷

Eje Central & Ricardo Flores Magón. **M** Tlatelolco, Garibaldi. **◯** 9am– 6pm Tue–Sun. **♿**

THE REMAINS of the ceremonial center of Tlatelolco form a major part of the Plaza de las Tres Culturas. The square gets its name ("The Three Cultures") from the mix of modern, colonial, and pre-Columbian architecture that have developed around it

Tlatelolco, the "twin city" of the Aztec capital, Tenochtitlán, was the most important commercial center of its day. The site here has a "templo mayor" similar to that of Tenochtitlán *(see pp68–9)*. There are also smaller temples including the "calendar temple", dedicated to the god of the wind. It owes its name to the glyphs adorning three of its sides, which represent dates in the Aztecs' ritual calendar. In the northwest corner of the archaeological zone, the remains of the carved "wall of serpents" can be seen, which marked the boundary of the ceremonial center.

The Spanish erected their own temples on the site, particularly the Templo de Santiago, a Catholic church in a severe, almost militaristic, style. Built by the Franciscan order, and finished in 1610, the church has twin towers flanking the main door. Over the side door are statues of the apostles. The original font, in the form of a shell, can still be seen inside. It is said that Juan Diego, who witnessed the appearance of the Virgin of Guadalupe, was baptized here. Beside the church is a Franciscan monastery, built in 1660.

The modern era is conspicuously represented by several buildings, particularly the concrete-and-glass foreign ministry tower. Scattered around the plaza are sculptures by Federico Silva. Between the monastery and the nearby residential tower block is a 1944 mural by David Alfaro Siqueiros (see p26). Entitled *Cuauhtémoc Against the Myth*, it combines sculpture with alfresco painting. Cuauhtémoc was the last Aztec emperor, killed by the Spanish under Hernán Cortés. In front of the Templo de Santiago is a plaque that reads: "On 13 August 1521, heroically defended by Cuauhtémoc, Tlatelolco fell into the hands of Cortés. It was neither triumph nor defeat, but the painful birth of the *mestizo* nation that is Mexico today."

In October, 1968, the Plaza de las Tres Culturas was the scene of another painful moment in Mexican history, when the military opened fire on student protesters, killing several hundred.

The entrance of the Templo de Santiago in the Plaza de las Tres Culturas

Plaza Garibaldi ❸

N of the Alameda, off Lázaro Cárdenas.

THE PLAZA GARIBALDI is the home of mariachi music. Dressed in their tight-trousered costumes, mariachi musicians can be seen scouting for work among the heavy traffic of the nearby Eje Central at most times of the day and night. Mariachi music was born in Jalisco on the Pacific Coast. In the first two decades of the 20th century there was heavy migration from Jalisco to the capital, and the Plaza del Borrego (later renamed the Plaza Garibaldi) became the mariachis' home from around 1920 onward. Today the area abounds with bars and restaurants serving a staple fare of tacos and tequila.

Mariachi statue in the Plaza Garibaldi

A mariachi (the term refers to the band, not the individual musician) can be hired per song or per hour. Rates vary, according to the number of musicians and their ability.

Visitors are warned that the streets between the Alameda and the Plaza Garibaldi can be dangerous to walk through and are advised to reach the square by taxi.

Mercado de La Merced ❹

Anillo de Circunvalación & Calle Callejón de Carretones. **M** *Merced.* ☐ *daily.* ♿

SAID TO BE the biggest market in the Americas, La Merced is certainly the largest in Mexico City, with 5,514 separate stalls. It occupies the spot on which an Aztec market stood prior to the conquest by the Spanish.

La Merced is divided into seven sections, six of which specialize in different types of merchandise, while the seventh is a traditional market. The market is particularly good for food, especially chilies, fruits, and fresh vegetables.

The northern section of the market used to be occupied by the Convento de la Merced. The restored 17th-century Moorish-style cloister of the monastery can still be seen on the other side of the Anillo de Circunvalación at República de Uruguay 170. It is noted for the richness of its carved stonework.

THE VIRGIN OF GUADALUPE

On December 12 each year, thousands of pilgrims flock to the Basílica de Guadalupe to commemorate the apparition of Mexico's patron saint on the Cerro del Tepeyac. Acts of veneration also take place in every town and village throughout the country. Birthday songs, *las mañanitas*, are sung at dawn. Special services are then held, followed by dancing and music in town squares, with children dressed in local costumes. As often in Mexico, a Catholic tradition has merged with pre-Columbian influence: the cult of the Virgin of Guadalupe has distinct parallels with that of Tonantzin, a Mesoamerican mother-goddess.

The Virgin of Guadalupe, patron saint of Mexico

Façade of the Teatro de los Insurgentes on Avenida Insurgentes Sur

Avenida Insurgentes Sur ❺

South from Glorieta de Insurgentes.
Ⓜ *San Antonio, Barranca del Muerto.*

THE AVENIDA de los Insurgentes runs just over 30 km (18 miles) from the capital's border with Mexico State in the north to the start of the highway to Cuernavaca in the south, and is said to be the longest street in Latin America.

Its southern (Sur) stretch has several sights of interest. Just a few blocks south of its junction with the Viaducto Miguel Alemán stands the World Trade Center, formerly the Hotel de México. This is without doubt one of the most prominent buildings on the Avenida. Its slim, glass tower is surmounted by a huge circular section that has a revolving floor.

The Polyforum Siqueiros, one of Mexico City's most audacious works of modern architecture, is next door to the World Trade Center. Its upper floor, which is reached by twin, circular staircases, is topped by an octagonal dome. This is decorated by one of David Alfaro Siqueiros' *(see p26)* finest works, *March of Humanity*, one of the largest murals in the world.

At Eje 6 Sur and Insurgentes is the Ciudad de los Deportes, which includes a football stadium and the Plaza México, reputedly the world's largest bullring. It seats up to 60,000 people and is surrounded by statues commemorating the great bull-

fighters, including Manuel Rodríguez ("Manolete"), who was in the arena's inaugural program in 1946.

Just before the junction with Barranca del Muerto is the Teatro de los Insurgentes, built in the early 1950s by architect Alejandro Prieto. The curved façade is adorned with an allegorical mural by Diego Rivera on the theme of theater in Mexico. Completed in 1953, the mural centers on a huge pair of hands holding a mask, around which are gathered significant revolutionary and independence heroes.

Museo de las Intervenciones ❻

Cnr of General Anaya & Calle 20 de Agosto. Ⓒ 56 04 06 99. Ⓜ *General Anaya.* ◯ *9am–6pm, Tue–Sun.* ▨ *Sun free.*

THIS FORMER CONVENT still bears the bullet holes from a battle that took place here between US and Mexican forces in 1847. Today it is a museum dedicated to the foreign invasions of Mexico since its independence in 1821. The collection consists

Cloister in the Museo de las Intervenciones

The carriage of Benito Juárez in the Museo de las Intervenciones

of weapons, flags, and other artifacts, including a throne and saber belonging to Agustín de Iturbide *(see p52)* and a death mask of the Emperor Maximilian *(see p53)*, as well as paintings, maps, and models.

Adjoining the museum is the former convent church, which has some superb gilded altarpieces, as well as religious paintings from the 16th to the 18th century. These include *La Asunción* by the 16th-century painter Luis Juárez and the 17th-century work *La Virgen y San Ildefonso* by Manuel de Echave.

Rear façade of the unusual Museo del Anahuacalli

Museo del Anahuacalli ❼

Museo 150. ☎ 56 17 43 10.
◯ 10am–6pm Tue–Sun. ⬤ public
hols. 📷 ♿ ground floor. 🎫 reserve
in advance. 📷

THIS UNIQUE museum was conceived and created by muralist Diego Rivera to house his collection of pre-Columbian art. It was completed after his death by architects Juan O'Gorman, and Heriberto Pagelson, and

Rivera's own daughter, Ruth. Built of black volcanic stone, it takes the form of a pyramid. The collection consists of some 2,000 pieces, representing most of the indigenous civilizations of Mexico. There are funerary urns, masks, and sculptures from the ancient culture of Teotihuacán. The studio, although never actually used by Rivera, has been set up as if it were, with his materials and half-finished works on display. A smaller gallery next to the pyramid contains an exhibition of papier mâché sculpture relating to the Days of the Dead, celebrated from October 31 through November 2 *(see pp34–5)*.

Image of the Goddess of Maize in the Museo del Anahuacalli

Universidad Nacional Autónoma de México (UNAM) ❽

Ciudad Universitaria ☎ 56 22 64 70.
Ⓜ Universidad, Ciudad Universitaria.
◯ 8am–9:30pm daily. ⬤ public
hols. ♿ Ⓦ www.unam.com

LATIN AMERICA's largest university occupies a vast campus in the south of the city. Many of the most interesting buildings are concentrated in a relatively small area close to Avenida Insurgentes. To the west of the avenue is the striking Olympic stadium, which became the symbol of the 1968 Mexico Olympics. Over the main entrance is a high-relief painting by Diego Rivera. Facing the stadium, on the east side of Insurgentes, is the rectory tower, adorned with dramatic murals by David Alfaro Siqueiros. The theme of the

mural on the south wall is the recurring struggle of the Mexican people to forge an independent identity, while on the north wall is a mural of glass mosaic tiles depicting the functions of the university *(see p27)*. The adjacent Museo Universitario has changing exhibitions of contemporary art. Nearby is the Biblioteca Central, one of the university's most spectacular buildings. Its tower is covered with mosaics by Juan O'Gorman. Each wall illustrates a period of Mexican history and the scientific achievements it produced.

A separate complex of buildings farther south on Insurgentes includes one of the city's major centers for performance arts, the Sala Nezahualcóyotl *(see p117)* and the Hemeroteca (a newspaper library). The Espacio Escultórico, a huge concrete circle, contains some modern sculpture. However the remarkable natural sculpture of the twisted volcanic rock on which the campus is built is even more impressive.

Close to the Olympic stadium is the university's Jardín Botánico. As well as its cactus collection, the garden has an arboretum and a section devoted to jungle plants. Located in the Pedregal ecological reserve, home to a unique volcanic ecosystem, the garden is also noted for its collection of Mexican medicinal plants.

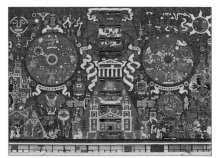

Mosaic on the Biblioteca in the University, depicting the scientific achievements of Mexican history

Unusual remains of the circular
Pirámide de Cuicuilco

Pirámide de Cuicuilco ➒

Av Insurgentes Sur & Periférico.
☎ 56 06 97 58. ◯ 9am–4:45pm
daily. 🖼

THIS PYRAMID belongs to
the earliest known urban
civilization in the Valley of
Mexico, founded around 600
BC. It is all that is left of the
ceremonial center of a settlement thought to have com-
prised as many as 20,000
inhabitants at its peak. The
surviving structure is a
truncated, layered cone, just
25 m (82 ft) high but 100 m
(328 ft) across. The eruption of
a nearby volcano, Xitle,
forced the inhabitants of the
area to flee around 100 AD.
The solidified lava, which can
be as much as 8 m (26 ft)
deep, makes excavation of
the area difficult. However, a
museum on the site exhibits
the pottery, tools, and spear-
heads that have been found.

Another pre-Columbian ceremonial site within the urban
area is the Cerro de la Estrella
(southeast of the city), which
was inhabited from AD 1000
until the arrival of the Spanish.

Tlalpan ➓

Mex 95. 25 km south of city center.

IN THE AGE of the Spanish
viceroys, Tlalpan was a
favorite country retreat both
for ordinary Mexicans and the
nobility. As a result, a large
number of elegant mansions
and haciendas were built
here from the early 18th
century onward.

Visitors to the old town,
now the seat of Mexico City's
largest *delegación* (suburban
area), can stroll along narrow
streets and admire the beautiful architecture, which dates
from the 17th to the 20th century. The 18th-century Casa
Chata, the Casa del Marqués
de Vivanco, and the Casa del
Conde de Regla are among
some of the
outstanding
buildings here.

In the central
Plaza de la
Constitución, with
its *porfiriato*-era
bandstand and
busts of national
heroes scattered
around, is the
Capilla del
Rosario, a 17th-
century chapel
with a Baroque
façade. Nearby is
the 16th-century
Dominican church
of San Agustín,
which has a large
courtyard. In the same square
stands the tree from which 11
patriots, who rebelled against
the French occupation under

Carved wooden doorway
of the Casa Chata

The garden of the Hacienda
de Tlalpan, now a restaurant

the Emperor Maximilian, were
hanged in 1866. Maximilian's
wife, the Empress Carlota,
occupied the Casa de Moneda
(on the corner of Juaréz and
Moneda), which was later
used as a military barracks.

On Avenida San Fernando,
the church of Santa Inés has a
plaque commem-
orating the brief
detention of inde-
pendence hero
José María Morelos
here in 1815.

The former
country house of
General Antonio
López de Santa
Anna, the hero of
the Alamo, stands
at the corner of
San Fernando and
Madero. He was
elected president
of Mexico 11
times. On the
Calzada de
Tlalpan, what was
once the old Hacienda de
Tlalpan is now an elegant
restaurant *(see p316),* with
restful fountains and colorful
peacocks in its garden.

Xochimilco ⓫

Prolongación División del Norte. 20
km SE of city center. Ⓜ *Embarcadero.*

KNOWN AS "the place of the
flower fields" in Nahuatl,
the language spoken by the
Aztecs, Xochimilco was once
a lakeside village connected
to Tenochtitlán by a causeway.
Today it is the only part of
Mexico City still to have the
canals and semi-floating flower
and vegetable gardens, or
chinampas, built by the
Aztecs. Originally created

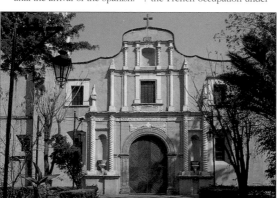

The yellow façade of the church of San Agustín in Tlalpan

The Iglesia de San Bernardino in the main square of Xochimilco

on a base of aquatic roots that were then covered with soil, the *chinampas* remain an important source of flowers and vegetables to Mexico City even today.

A favorite weekend pastime, popular with tourists as well as *chilangos* (the city's inhabitants), is to rent one of the many flower-decked punts, which have roofs and a table down the middle. A local boatman poles the punt along between banks shaded by willows. Waterborne mariachis will provide entertainment while smaller boats sell typical Mexican snacks. An optional stop provides an opportunity to haggle for rugs or other handicrafts at a local craft market.

On land, Xochimilco has a village-like atmosphere that is far removed from the bustle of the historic center of Mexico City. One of the architectural highlights in the main square is the Iglesia de San Bernardino. A fortified monastery built by the Franciscans in the late 16th century, it has a Classical-style façade with some

hints of early Baroque. The magnificent main altarpiece contains paintings and sculptures of the apostles and other saints. Other altarpieces contain beautiful paintings by colonial-era masters such as Cristóbal de Villalpando and Juan Correa.

Near San Bernardino is the Capilla del Rosario, a pretty chapel built in 1768. It is completely covered in a profusion of high-relief mortar-work and Puebla-style tiles.

A row of colorful boats in Xochimilco

Museo Dolores Olmedo Patiño ⓬

Av México 5843. 🚾 56 76 10 55. Ⓜ La Noria. ⏰ 10am–6pm, Tue–Sun. ▢ ▢ Ⓦ www.arts-history.mx/ mdop.html

THIS IS THE LARGEST private collection of works by muralist Diego Rivera. It is housed in a beautiful 17th-century mansion in Xochimilco known as the Finca Noria, which was donated to the nation in 1994 by the wealthy collector and friend of Rivera, Dolores Olmedo.

As well as 137 works by Rivera, there are also 25 by Frida Kahlo and more than 600 pre-Columbian artifacts. The Rivera collection spans many periods of the artist's life. It includes several self-portraits as well as studies for large works. The excellent portrait, *The Mathematician*, was painted in 1919. Among the best-known of the Kahlo works here are *Self-Portrait with a Monkey*, *The Broken Column*, and *The Deceased Dimas*. There are also some pieces on display by Angelina Beloff, Rivera's first wife. A separate part of the collection is dedicated to Mexican popular culture.

The landscaped grounds of the mansion contain animals and plants native to Mexico, including the Mexican hairless dog, or *xoloitzcuintle*.

SHOPPING IN MEXICO CITY

THE BEAUTY of shopping in Mexico City is the vast range and accessibility of goods. Strolling around the city, visitors will stumble upon a dizzying number of vibrant street markets, selling anything from quality crafts and fresh flowers to rice-grain sculptures and witchcraft accessories. Those looking for elegant fashions and classy

Handmade wall hanging in the Plaza de San Jacinto

boutiques should head to Avenida Masarik in Polanco, or the touristic outlets of the Zona Rosa. Visitors in search of everyday essentials, as opposed to a hectic shopping experience, will fare better with neighborhood markets and grocery stores, or the ultimate convenience of one of the city's many comprehensive department stores.

A stall in the Plaza de San Jacinto, part of the lively Saturday morning market

CRAFTS AND GIFTS

THE MOST complete selection of Mexican crafts *(see pp330–33)* can be found at **Fonart**, a state-run chain. Prices here may be above average, but all items are genuine crafts. The staff know the origins of every piece and can arrange international shipping.

A pleasant place to shop for unusual and original handicrafts is the **Bazar del Sábado** (Saturday Market) in the Plaza San Jacinto in San Ángel *(see p100)*. Stalls are open only on Saturdays between 10am and 2pm. The heart of the market is the cluster of stalls around the fountain of an indoor patio belonging to a colonial building. The stalls sell a wide variety of crafts and gift items, including jewelry, clothing, Tiffany lampshades, gilt work, embroidered pillows, rice-grain sculptures, candles, wall hangings, and paper flowers. Shoppers can also enjoy a buffet breakfast to the accompaniment of *marimba* players.

The **Mercado de Londres** (or Mercado de Insurgentes) in the Zona Rosa specializes in silver jewelry, sold by weight, painted papier-mâché

trays and picture frames, and also finely embroidered shawls and waistcoats. There is a large selection of crafts from all over the country in the **Mercado de la Ciudadela**. Prices are very reasonable here, although this is often reflected in the fact that many of the articles are not of the finest quality. The **Centro Artesanal de Buenavista**, advertised as Mexico's largest crafts market, is in actual fact a very large and usefully positioned shop selling the usual choice of handicrafts.

ART AND ANTIQUES

ART AND ANTIQUE outlets in Mexico City tend to be concentrated in Polanco, the Zona Rosa, San Ángel, and more recently in Roma as well. In Polanco, **Oscar Román** and the **Galería Misrachi** specialize in contemporary Mexican art. The antique shops in the Zona Rosa, including **Coloniart**, are concentrated around the **Plaza del Ángel**, where an antique market is also held on Saturday mornings. Some of the best known galleries in Roma include **Galería OMR** and **Casa Lamm**. In San Ángel, the **Galería**

Kin is a must for lovers of contemporary art. Downtown, the **Monte de Piedad** *(see p62)* is a pawnshop that sells second-hand jewelry.

BOOKS AND NEWSPAPERS

LOCAL NEWSPAPERS can be purchased from street vendors, whereas international papers, magazines, guidebooks, and novels are all sold at **Sanborn's**, the department store, and in top hotels. Two famous bookstores, **Librería Gandhi** and **El Parnaso**, are found in the south of the city.

SWEETS

MEXICANS tend to have a very sweet tooth. The city's many quality candy stores include downtown's **Dulcería de Celaya**. The popular **La Flor de Lis** chain is also well known for its tasty sweets *(see p308)*.

The Dulcería de Celaya candy store, which attracts business from all over the city

A stall selling fresh produce in the Mercado de la Merced

CIGARS

FOR CIGAR aficionados the best specialty shops are **La Casa del Habano** and **La Casa del Fumador**, which both stock a wide range of national and imported cigars, as well as pipe tobaccos. Genuine *Habanos* (Havanas) can be bought here quite reasonably.

MARKETS

EACH NEIGHBORHOOD has its local market, and there are also several larger and more specialized markets. All of these are regular shopping places for Mexico City's residents, and give an insight into their daily life. Beware of pickpockets in all markets.

The **Mercado de Sonora** is a sprawling covered market specializing in seasonal wares, such as Christmas decorations and Easter candy. It also has permanent sections selling herbs, toys, and witchcraft accessories. It makes a heady combination of the kitsch and the occult for the few tourists who come here.

Close by is the huge **Mercado de La Merced** *(see p109)*, Mexico City's largest market, which operates daily. Of the thousands of stalls, the greatest proportion are devoted to fruit, vegetables, and flowers. The remainder sell a variety of other items.

DEPARTMENT STORES

THE TWO largest department store chains in Mexico are **El Palacio de Hierro** and **Liverpool**, both of which have branches in most of the city's American-style shopping malls. Here shoppers can find anything and everything they might need. Each branch has large collections of international designer fashions, alongside local designs and the store's own brands. For English-language books, reasonably priced souvenirs, photographic equipment, and toiletries, any branch of **Sanborn's** is a good bet. In addition, these stores provide a choice of restaurants. Though influenced by Mexican cuisine, they also serve international "fast food" to suit all tastes *(see p306)*.

A modern-looking branch of the Liverpool chain store

CRAFTS AND GIFTS

Bazar del Sábado
San Jacinto 11,
San Ángel.
(56 16 00 82.

Centro Artesanal de Buenavista
Aldama 187,
Colonia Guerrero.
(55 26 03 15.

Fonart
Patriotismo 691,
Colonia Mixcoac.
(55 63 03 06.

Mercado de la Ciudadela
Balderas, cnr of Emilio Dondé. **Map** 3 B2.

Mercado de Londres
Londres 154,
Zona Rosa.
Map 2 E4.
(55 33 25 44.

ART AND ANTIQUES

Casa Lamm
Álvaro Obregón 99A.
Map 2 F5.
(55 11 08 99.

Coloniart
Estocolmo 37, Zona Rosa.
Map 2 E3.
(55 14 47 99.

Galería Misrachi
Lafontaine 243.
(52 50 41 05.

Galería Kin
Altavista 92, San Ángel.
(55 50 89 10.

Galería OMR
Plaza Río de Janeiro 54,
Colonia Roma. **Map** 2 F4.
(55 11 11 79.

Monte de Piedad
Monte de Piedad 7.
Map 4 E2.
(55 18 20 06.

Oscar Román
Julio Verne 14, Polanco.
(52 80 04 36.

Plaza del Ángel
Londres 161, Zona Rosa.
Map 2 E4.
(32 08 90 20.

BOOKS AND NEWSPAPERS

Librería Gandhi
Miguel Ángel de Quevedo
134, Chimalistac.
(56 61 09 11.

El Parnaso
Carrillo Puerto 2,
Coyoacán.
(56 58 31 75.

Sanborn's
Francisco I. Madero 4.
Map 4 D2.
(55 18 01 52.

SWEETS

Dulcería de Celaya
Cinco de Mayo 39. **Map** 4
D2 **(** 55 21 17 87.

La Flor de Lis
Huicapan 17,
Colonia Condesa.
(52 86 22 29.

CIGARS

La Casa del Fumador
Moliere 222, Polanco.
(52 81 16 18.

La Casa del Habano
Av Presidente Masarik 393,
Polanco. **Map** 1 A2.
(52 82 10 46.

MARKETS

Mercado de La Merced
Anillo de Circunvalación
& Callejón de Carretones.

Mercado de Sonora
Av Fray Servando Teresa de
Mier, cnr of Circunvalación.

DEPARTMENT STORES

Liverpool
Venustiano Carranza 92.
Map 4 D2.
(51 33 28 00.

El Palacio de Hierro
Av 20 de Noviembre 3.
(57 28 99 05.

ENTERTAINMENT IN MEXICO CITY

MEXICO CITY offers a wide variety of entertainment. In the evenings you can choose between salsa music joints or traditional *cantinas*. On a Sunday, you can experience folk ballet at the Palacio de Bellas Artes, watch the *charros* (*see p346*) in their dazzling costumes on horseback, or attend

Window detail from Salón México

a bullfight in the world's largest bullring. There is also always an excellent range of dance, classical music, and opera. There is a full cultural calendar year round in the city, but the main annual event is the Festival del Centro Histórico, which is usually held before Easter, in March or April.

The Palacio de Bellas Artes, home of the Mexican National Symphony Orchestra

ENTERTAINMENT GUIDES AND TICKETS

FOR INFORMATION in English on events, *The News* has a "What's on" section on Fridays and Saturdays, and the local paper *Reforma* has daily listings. The weekly Spanish guides, *Laberinto, Tiempo Libre*, and *Dónde Ir* have complete information including a restaurant guide, sports events, and activities for children.

Tickets for almost all events can be bought through **Ticketmaster**, which charges a commission as well as a delivery charge. Sanborn's (*see p115*) have Ticketmaster counters where charges are lower. Most theaters and sports stadiums also sell tickets directly. The **Instituto Nacional de Bellas Artes** (INBA) operates several theaters and auditoriums, and has its own ticket booths and information service.

CLASSICAL MUSIC, DANCE, AND THEATER

THE NATIONAL Opera and the National Symphony Orchestra perform alternate seasons at the **Palacio de Bellas Artes**. The building is also host to a wide range of other music and dance events, including the Amalia Hernández Ballet Folklórico. Large scale classical and contemporary music events are held at the **Auditorio Nacional**. The **Sala Ollin Yoliztli** and the **Sala Nezahualtcóyotl** in the UNAM university complex also play host to a range of events.

At the Consejo Nacional de Artes (CNA), an arts complex, the **Auditorio Blas Galindo** is fast becoming an important concert hall for the city.

Contemporary and classical dance programs are held at the **Teatro de la Danza**. The National Dance School performs at the **Teatro Raúl Flores Canelo** at the CNA.

The **Insurgentes**, **Hidalgo**, and **Centro Cultural Telmex** theaters feature national and international companies.

CANTINAS

MEXICO'S ANSWER to the local bar is the *cantina*, which is both a simple lunchtime restaurant and a meeting place in the evenings. *Cantinas* were originally frequented

exclusively by men, and some still display the sign outside that bans women, children, and men in uniform. *Cantinas* close around midnight, and on Saturdays and Sundays open only at lunchtime.

El Nivel, near the Zócalo, is the oldest *cantina* in the city and houses an interesting art collection. **La Guadalupana**, in Coyoacán (*see p104*), is also worth visiting.

BARS, CLUBS, AND ROCK MUSIC

MANY NEW bars are currently reviving the downtown area of Mexico City. The bars around the Juárez and Condesa neighborhoods are popular with the young crowd. Nightclubs range from the trendy to the glamorous. Rock concerts are held at the **Auditorio Nacional** or at various smaller venues around the city.

LATIN AMERICAN MUSIC AND MARIACHIS

ONE OF MEXICO'S most famous bars for *cumbia*, merengue, *danzón*, and salsa music is **Bar León**, favored

Dancing to authentic Latin American music in Salón México

by lovers of Latin American music who appreciate the loud, authentic sounds. The **Salón Tropicana** has three dance floors and its own bands, as well as visiting performers. **Mama Rumba** is favored by a younger, hipper crowd who come for the potent Caribbean cocktails and Cuban music. **Salón México** is a recreation of the legendary venue of the same name *(see p29)*. Plaza Garibaldi *(see p109)* is a traditional last stop for a night out, where mariachi musicians compete to be

Mariachis playing in a café on Plaza Garibaldi

heard above each other. In the bars around the square, such as **Tenampa**, you can listen to the music in comfort.

ENTERTAINMENT FOR CHILDREN

Bosque de Chapultepec *(see pp88–9)* has a number of attractions that will keep children of all ages entertained, especially **La Feria** (an amusement park) and the **Zoo**.

SPECTATOR SPORTS

Mexicans are avid sports fans, and soccer is a national passion. Matches can be seen at the **Estadio Azteca**. Baseball, played at the **Foro Sol**, also has a large following. Boxing matches are held at the **Arena Coliseo**. Typical Mexican masked wrestling can be experienced at the **Arena México** or the **Toreo de**

Footballers in action in Mexico City's Estadio Azteca

Cuatro Caminos. Bullfights take place at the **Plaza Monumental de Toros México** on Sunday afternoons. *Charreadas*, trials of traditional equestrian skills *(see p74)*, are held at the **Rancho del Charro**. For more information on spectator sports, see page 346.

DIRECTORY

TICKET SALES

Instituto Nacional de Bellas Artes
Information
[52 80 87 71.

Ticketmaster
[53 25 90 00.
[W] www.ticketmaster.com.mx

CLASSICAL MUSIC, DANCE, AND THEATER

Auditorio Blas Galindo
CNA, corner of Calzada de Tlalpan & Río Churubusco.
[54 20 44 00.

Auditorio Nacional
Paseo de la Reforma 50.
[52 80 92 50.

Centro Cultural Telmex
Av Cuauhtémoc 19.
[55 14 23 00.

Palacio de Bellas Artes
Corner of Avenida Juárez and Lázaro Cárdenas.
[55 21 92 51.

Sala Nezahualtcóyotl
Centro Cultural Universitario,
Insurgentes Sur 3000,
UNAM.
[56 22 71 28.

Sala Ollin Yoliztli
Periférico Sur 5141.
[56 06 49 58.

Teatro de la Danza
Campo Marte,
Paseo de la Reforma.
[52 80 87 71.

Teatro Hidalgo
Av Hidalgo 23. **Map** 3 C1.
[55 21 58 59.

Teatro Insurgentes
Av Insurgentes Sur 1587.
[56 11 42 53.

Teatro Raúl Flores Canelo
CNA, corner of Calzada de Tlalpan & Río Churubusco.
[54 20 44 00.

CANTINAS

La Guadalupana
Higuera 14,
Coyoacán.
[55 54 62 53.

El Nivel
Corner of Moneda and Seminario. **Map** 4 E2.
[55 22 61 84.

LATIN AMERICAN MUSIC AND MARIACHIS

Bar León
Brasil 5. [55 10 30 93.

Mama Rumba
Querétaro 230.
[55 64 69 20.

Salón México
Callejón de San Juan de Dios 25.
[55 10 99 15.

Salón Tropicana
Lázaro Cárdenas 43.
[55 29 73 16.

Tenampa
Plaza Garibaldi 12.
[55 26 61 76.

ENTERTAINMENT FOR CHILDREN

Chapultepec Zoo
Bosque de Chapultepec, First Section.
[55 53 62 29.

La Feria
Bosque de Chapultepec, Second Section.
[52 30 21 21.

SPECTATOR SPORTS

Arena Coliseo
Perú 77.
[55 26 16 87.

Arena México
Dr. Lavista 189.
Map 3 A4.
[56 06 85 58 ext. 122.

Estadio Azteca
Calzada de Tlalpan 3465.
[56 17 80 80.

Foro Sol
Magdalena Michuca.
[57 64 84 46.

Plaza Monumental de Toros México
Augusto Rodin 241.
[55 63 39 61.

Rancho del Charro
Av Constituyentes 500
[52 77 87 10.

Toreo de Cuatro Caminos
Anillo Periférico Norte
[55 80 07 44.

MEXICO CITY STREET FINDER

HE MAP BELOW shows the area covered by the city center street map on the following pages. The map references given in the text for centrally located places of interest, hotels, restaurants, shops, and entertainment venues refer to these maps. Sights in San Ángel and Coyoacán are

Visitor to Mexico City

located on the map on page 97, and more distant attractions in Mexico City can be found on the Farther Afield map on page 107. Opposite is a map showing the main highways used for crossing, or getting around, the vast and potentially confusing area that is greater Mexico City.

KEY

▢ Major sight	🔳 Police station
▢ Place of interest	✝ Church
▢ Other building	☒ Post office
M Metro station	— One way street
P Parking	▬ Pedestrian street
🛈 Tourist information	
✚ Hospital	

SCALE OF MAPS 1–4

0 meters   300

0 yards   300

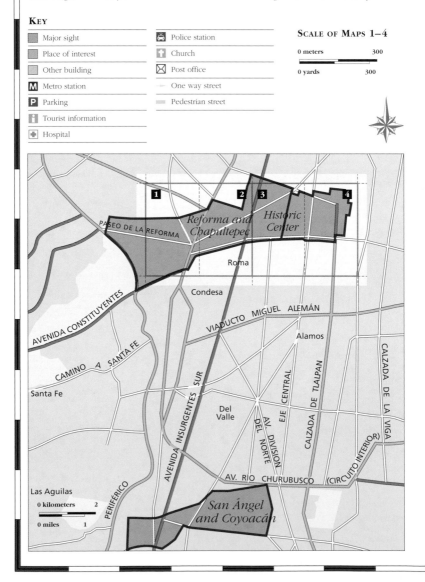

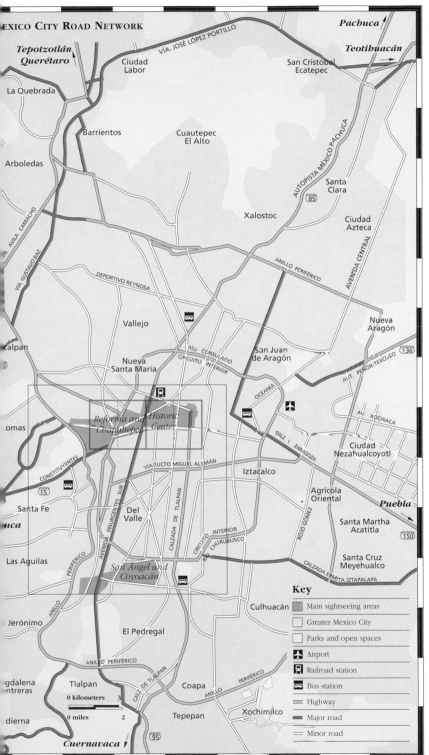

MEXICO CITY ROAD NETWORK

Tepotzotlán Querétaro

Pachuca

Teotihuacán

La Quebrada

Ciudad Labor

VÍA JOSÉ LÓPEZ PORTILLO

San Cristóbal Ecatepec

Barrientos

Cuautepec El Alto

AUTOPISTA MÉXICO PACHUCA

Santa Clara

85

Arboledas

Xalostoc

Ciudad Azteca

DR. ÁVILA CAMACHO

VÍA GUSTAVO BAZ

DEPORTIVO REYNOSA

ANILLO PERIFÉRICO

AVENIDA CENTRAL

calpan

Vallejo

Nueva Santa María

RÍO CONSULADO
CIRCUITO INTERIOR

San Juan de Aragón

Nueva Aragón

136

omas

Reforma and Chapultepec

Historic Center

OCEANÍA

AUT. PEÑÓN-TEXCOCO

AV. XOCHIACA

CONSTITUYENTES

VIADUCTO MIGUEL ALEMÁN

CALZ L ZARAGOZA

Ciudad Nezahualcoyotl

15

Iztacalco

Puebla

Santa Fe

AVENIDA INSURGENTES SUR

Del Valle

CALZADA DE TLALPAN

Agrícola Oriental

uca

CIRCUITO INTERIOR
RÍO CHURUBUSCO

ROJO GÓMEZ

Santa Martha Acatitla

150

Las Aguilas

PERIFÉRICO

San Angel and Coyoacán

CALZADA ERMITA IZTAPALAPA

Santa Cruz Meyehualco

Jerónimo

ANILLO

El Pedregal

Culhuacán

ANILLO PERIFÉRICO

PERIFÉRICO

gdalena ntreras

dierna

Tlalpan

CALZ. DE TLALPAN

Coapa

ANILLO

PERIFÉRICO

Tepepan

Xochimilco

95

Cuernavaca

0 kilometers 3

0 miles 2

Key

Main sightseeing areas

Greater Mexico City

Parks and open spaces

✈ Airport

🚉 Railroad station

🚌 Bus station

— Highway

— Major road

— Minor road

Mexico City Street Finder Index

A

Abril, 2 de	3C1
Academía	4F2
Acapulco	1C5
Agreda y Sánches, José María	4E4
Alcázar	3A1
Aldaco	4D3
Aldama	3A1
Alemán, Lucas	4D4
Alhóndiga	4F3
Allende	4D1
Altamirano, Ignacio	2E1
Amberes	2E3
Aranda	3C3
Arcos de Belén	3B3
Arenal	4F5
Argáez, Joaquín	1B5
Arriaga, Joaquín	4F5
Arriaga, José Joaquín	4D5
Arriaga, Ponciano	3A1
Artículo 123	3C2
Artistas, Calzada de los	1A5
Atenas	3A2
Avenida 5 de Mayo	4D2
Avenida Benito Juárez	3B1
Avenida Chapultepec	1C4
Avenida Constituyentes	1A5
Avenida Cuauhtémoc	3A5
Avenida de la República	3A1
Avenida Francisco I. Madero	4D2
Avenida Hidalgo	3C1
Avenida Insurgentes Centro	2F2
Avenida Insurgentes Sur	2E5
Avenida Marina Nacional	1C1
Avenida Mazatlán	1C5
Avenida Morelos	3A2
Avenida Oaxaca	2D5
Avenida Parque Vía	2D2
Avenida Presidente Masarik	1A2
Avenida Río San Joaquin	1B1
Avenida Sonora	1C5
Avenida Yucatán	2E5
Axayácatl	2D1
Ayuntamiento	3B2
Azueta, José	3B2

B

Bahía Ascención	1C1
Bahía de Ballenas	1B1
Bahía de Banderas	1C1
Bahía de Caracas	1C2
Bahía de Chachalacas	1C1
Bahía de Coquí	1C2
Bahía de Corrientes	1C2
Bahía de Descanso	1B1
Bahía de Guantánamo	1B2
Bahía de la Concepción	1C2
Bahía de Las Palmas	1C2
Bahia de Mangueiras	1B2
Bahía de Morlaco	1B1
Bahía de Pérula	1C1
Bahía de Pescadores	1C1
Bahía de Todos los Santos	1B1
Bahía del Espíritu Santo	1B1
Bahía Magdalena	1B1
Bahía Montejo	1B2
Bahía San Hipólito	1B1
Bahía Santa Bárbara	1B1

Balderas	3B3
Baranda, P.	3A1
Barcelona	3A3
Barreda, Gabino	2E1
Barrera, Juan de la	1B5
Bécquer	1C2
Belgrado	2E3
Berlin	2F3
Berna	2D3
Biarritz	2D4
Bolívar	4D5
Boturini, Lorenzo	4D5
Bradley	1B2
Bruselas	3A3
Bucareli	3A3
Buen Tono	3C3
Buffon	1B2
Burdeos	1C4

C

Cacahuamilpa	2D5
Cadena, Longinós	4D4
Cadetes del 47	1B5
Campos Elíseos	1A3
Canal, Callejón	4F4
Candelarita, Callejón	3B3
Cantú	1B3
Cárdenas, Lázaro	3C5
Carmen	4F1
Carranza, Venustiano	4D2
Carretones	4F3
Caso, Antonio Maestro	3A2
Castellanos, Erasmo	4F2
Cerrada del 57	4D1
Cerrada G. Prieto	2D1
Cerro, Calzada del	1A5
Chavero, Alfredo	4D5
Chihuahua	2E5
Chimalpopoca	4D4
Chimalpopoca, 1a. Cerrada	3C4
Chimalpopoca, 2a. Cerrada	3C4
Circular de Morelia	3A4
Clavijero	4F5
Colima	2D5
Colima, Cerrada	2F4
Colón	3B1
Comte	1C2
Condesa	4D2
Contreras, Manuel María	2E1
Copenhague	2E3
Copérnico	1B3
Córdoba	2F4
Corregidora	4F2
Correo Mayor	4F2
Covarrubias, Francisco Díaz	2D1
Cozumel	2D4
Cozumel, 2a Cerrada	2D4
Cruces, Las	4F3
Cuenca, Laura M. de	3C4
Cuitláhuac	4F5
Cuitláhuac, Callejón	4F5
Curie	1B3
Cuvier	1B2

D

Dante	1B3
Darwin	1B3
Delgado, Agustín Callejón de	4E4
Delicias	3C3
Descartes	1B3

Dinamarca	2F3
Doctor Andrade	3B5
Doctor Barragán	3C5
Doctor Carmona y Valle	3A5
Doctor Claudio Bernard	3A4
Doctor Daniel Ruiz	3C4
Doctor Erazo	3A5
Doctor J. Terres	3B5
Doctor J. Velasco	3A5
Doctor Jiménez	3B5
Doctor José Ramos	3A5
Doctor Juan Navarro	3A4
Doctor Lavista	3A4
Doctor Liceaga	3A4
Doctor Manuel Gutiérrez Zavala	3B3
Doctor Martínez del Río	3A5
Doctor Mora	3B1
Doctor Olvera	3A5
Doctor Pascua	3C4
Doctor Pasteur	3B5
Doctor Rafael Lucío	3A5
Doctor Río de la Loza	3B3
Doctor Salvador Garciadiego	3A5
Doctor Valenzuela	3C3
Doctor Vértiz	3B5
Dolores	3C2
Domínguez, Belisario	4D1
Donceles	4D1
Dondé, Emilio	3B2
Dresde	2D4
Dublin	1C4
Durango	1C5
Durango, Privada	3A4

E

Echeveste	4D3
Edison, Privada	3A1
Emparán, J.	3A1
Escobedo, General Mariano, Calzada	1A2
Escuela Médico Militar	4F4
Escutia, Juan	1B5
Esmeralda, Callejón	3B1
Esperanza, Callejón	4D3
Estocolmo	2E3
Estrasburgo	2E3
Eucken	1A2
Euclides	1A2
Euler	1A2

F

Farías, Gómez	2F1
Febrero, 5 de	4D5
FF. CC. Nacionales	1B1
Filósofos, Calzada de los	1A4
Flamencos, Callejón	4E3
Flammarion	1B2
Florencia	2D3
Flores, Manuel M.	4D5
Fray Servando Teresa de Mier	4E4
Frontera	3A5
Fuente, Juan de la	3C4

G

Galeria Plaza	2D4
Gandhi, Calzada	1A4
Gandhi, Mahatma, Calzada	1A3
Gante F. Mata	4D2
Garay, Francisco de	3A3

Gardenia	3A3
Gastillo, Antonio del	2F1
Gauss	1A1
General M. Alemán	4F1
General P. A. de los Santos	1B5
General Prim	3A2
Génova	2E3
Girón, Callejón	4F1
Goethe	1C2
González, Abraham	3A3
González Obregón	4E1
Gran Avenida	1A5
Guadalajara	1C4
Guanajuato	2E5
Guaymas, Cerrada	3A3
Guerra, Donato	3A2
Guttenberg	1B2

H

Halley	1B2
Hamburgo	1C4
Hamburgo, Cerrada	2E3
Havre	2E3
Hernández, Gabriel	3B3
Herodoto	1C2
Héroes	3B1
Herrera, Alfonso	2E1
Herschel	1B2
Homero	1A2
Horacio	1A2
Hormiguero, Callejón	4F4
Huichapan	2D5
Humboldt	3B2

I

Icaza, Francisco Alvarez de	3C5
Ideal	3A3
Iglesias, José María	3A1
Igualdad, Callejón	4D3
Independencia	3C2
Isabel la Católica	4D5
Iturbide	3B2
Itzcoatl	2D1
Ixtlilxóchitl, F. Alva	4D4
Ixtlilxóchitl, F. Alva, Cerrada	4D5
Izazaga, José Maria	4D3

J

Jalapa	2E4
Janeiro, Cerrada Río de	2F4
Jesús María	4F3
Jiménez	4D3

K

Kant, Emmanuel	1B3
Kelvin	1A2
Kepler	1B1

L

Lafayette	1B2
Lafragua, Jose María	3A2
Lago Alberto	1A1
Lago Ilmen	1A1
Lago Iseo	1A1
Lago Mask	1A1
Lago Muritz	1B1
Lago Patzcuaro	1C1
Lago Xochimilco	1B1
Lago Zirahuén	1C1
Laguna de Mayrán	1C1
Lancaster	2D3

Lanz, José 4F5
Laplace 1B2
Lassaga, Juan Lucas 4E4
Leibniz 1B2
León y Gama, Antonio 4D5
Leyva, Gabriel 4D1
Lisboa 3A3
Liverpool 2E4
Londres 2D4
López 3C3
Lorenzana, Francisco 2D1
Loreto 4F2
Lotería 3B1
Lucerna 3A3

M

Madrid 2F2
Manzanares 4F2
Manzanares, 2ª Callejón 4F2
Marconi 4D1
Mariscal, Ignacio 3B1
Márquez Sterling 3B3
Marroquí, J. María 3C2
Marsella 2F3
Martínez, Enrico 3B3
Mascota 3A3
Matehuala 1C5
Mayas 4D5
Mazatlán, Cerrada 1C5
Meave 4D3
Medellín 2D4
Melgar, Agustín 1B5
Mérida 2F4
Mesones 4E3
Mexicanos 4D4
Michelet 1C2
Milán 2F3
Milton 1C2
Moneda 4F2
Monte de Piedad 4E2
Monterrey 2E4
Montes, Ezequiel 2F2
Montiel, Julián 4D5
Morelia 3A4
Moroleón, Cerrada 3A5
Motolinia 4D1
Moya, Luis 3C2

N

Nájera, Manuel Gutiérrez 4D5
Nápoles 2F3
Newton 1A1
Nezahualcóyotl 4D3
Niños Héroes 3B5
Niza 2E3
Noviembre, 20 de 4E3
Noviembre,
　Diagonal 20 de 4D4

O

Obregón, Álvaro 2D5
Ocampo, Melchor,
　Calzada 1B4
Ocotlán 2D4
Orizaba 2F4
Oro 2E5
Orozco y Berra 3B1
Otomies 4D5
Oxford 2D3

P

Pachuca 1C5
Pachuca, Cerrada 1C5
Palma 4E1
París 2F2
Parra, Porfirio 3C5

Paseo de la Reforma 1A4
Peña, Rafael Ángel de la,
　Prolongación 4F5
Peñafiel, Guadalupe 4D5
Pensador Mexicano 3C1
Peralta, Angela 3C2
Pescaditos 3B2
Petrarca, Francisco 1A2
Pimentel, Francisco 2D1
Pino Suárez 4E3
Plaza 2 de Abril 3C1
Plaza Adolf
　López Mateos 3C3
Plaza C. Pacheco 3B2
Plaza Capitán Malpica 3C3
Plaza Ciudadela 3B2
Plaza Comercio 3B3
Plaza Concepción 4D1
Plaza de la Constitución 4F2
Plaza de la República 3A1
Plaza de la Solidaridad 3B1
Plaza de San Juan 3C2
Plaza Florencia 2E4
Plaza Galerias 2D1
Plaza Grijalva 2D2
Plaza Loreto 4F1
Plaza Luis Cabrera 2F5
Plaza Madrid 2E5
Plaza Melchor Ocampo 1C3
Plaza Morelia 3A4
Plaza Río de Janeiro 2F4
Plaza San Fernando 3B1
Plaza San Pablo 4F3
Plaza San Salvador
　El Seco 4D3
Plaza San Salvador
　El Verde 4E4
Plaza Santa Cruz 4E4
Plaza Santo Domingo 4E1
Plaza Tlaxcoaque 4E4
Plaza Vizcaínas 3C3
Plaza Vizcaya 2D1
Poe, Edgar Allan 1B3
Poetas, Calzada de los 1A4
Pomona 2E4
Praga 2D4
Prieto, Guillermo 2D1
Puebla 1C5
Puente de Alvarado 3A1
Puente de Peredo 3C2
Puente Santo Tomás 4F4
Pugibet, Cerrada 3C3
Pugibet, Ernesto 3B2

Q

Querétaro 2F5
Quetzalcóatl 2D1

R

Ramírez, Ignacio 3A2
Ramos, Arizpe M. 3A1
Real de Romita 3A4
Regina 4D3
Renan 1C2
Rendón, Serapio 2F2
República de Argentina 4E1
República de Bolivia 4F1
República de Brasil 4E1
República de Chile 4E2
República de Colombia 4E1
República de Cuba 4D1
República de El Salvador 4F3
República de Guatemala 4F1
República de Uruguay 4D2
República de Venezuela 4E1
Revillagigedo 3B3

Rey, Calzada del 1A5
Rincón del Bosque 1B3
Rinconada de los Reyes,
　Callejón 4E3
Rinconada Zoquipa 4F5
Río Amazonas 2E2
Río Amoy 2D2
Río Amur 2D2
Río Angel de la Peña 4D5
Río Atoyac 1C4
Río Balsas 2D2
Río Barragán de Toscano 4D5
Río Danubio 2D2
Río de la Plata 1C3
Río Duero 1C3
Río Ebro 2D2
Río Elba 1C4
Río Eufrates 2D2
Río Ganges 1C3
Río Grijalva 2D2
Río Guadalquivir 2D3
Río Guadiana 2E2
Río Hudson 1C3
Río Lerma 1C4
Río Marne 2E2
Río Misisipí 1C3
Río Nazas 1C3
Río Neva 2E2
Río Niágara 2D3
Río Nilo 2D3
Río Panuco 1C3
Río Papaloapan 2D3
Río Po 2D2
Río Rhin 2E2
Río Sena 2D2
Río Tamesis 2F2
Río Tíber 2D2
Río Tigris 2D2
Río Ussuri 2D2
Río Usumacinta 2E2
Río Volga 2D3
Río Yang Tse 2D2
Río, Cerrada Río de 3A4
Rivas, Francisco 3C5
Rodano 1C4
Rodriguez del
　Toro, L. M. 4D1
Rodríguez Puebla 4F1
Roldán 4F3
Roma 2F3
Rosales 3B1
Rosas Moreno 2E1
Rousseau 1B2
Rubén Darío 1A3

S

Sadi Carno 2F2
Salamanca 2D4
Salvatierra 1B5
San Antonio Abad,
　Callejón 4E4
San Fernando 3B1
San Ildefonso 4F1
San Jerónimo 4D3
San Miguel, Callejón 4E4
San Pablo 4F3
San Salvador El Verde 4D4
Santa Veracruz 3C1
Santísima 4F2
Schiller 1A3
Schultz, Miguel E. 2E1
Seco 4D3
Seminario 4E1
Septiembre, 13 de 1B5
Septiembre, 16 de 4D2
Sevilla 2D4

Shakespeare 1B2
Sierra, Justo 4F1
Sinaloa 1C5
Solá, Antonio 1C5
Soledad 4F2
Spencer 1A3
Sudermann 1A2
Sullivan 2E2

T

Tabaqueros 4E2
Tabasco 2D5
Tacuba 4E1
Taine 1A2
Talavera 4F3
Tampico 1C5
Tasso, Torcuato 1A2
Terán, J. 3B1
Thiers 1B2
Tizapán 4D3
Tizoc 2D1
Tláloc 2D1
Tlaxcoaque 4E4
Tokio 1C4
Toledo 1C4
Tolsá 3A3
Tolstoi 1B4
Tonalá 2E5
Tonatzin 1C1
Topacio 4F5
Torres, José Antonio 4E5
Tres Estrellas 4E5
Tres Picos 1A3
Tresguerras 3B3
Turín 3A3

U-V-W

Uruapan 2E4
Vadillo, Basilio 3B1
Valerio Trujano 3C1
Valladolid 2D4
Vallarino, Juan 4F5
Vallarta, Cerrada 3A2
Vallarta, Ignacio L. 3A2
Valle, Leandro 4E1
Varsovia 2D3
Varsovia, Privada 2D3
Vasconcelos, José 1B5
Velázquez de León,
　Joaquin 2D1
Venecia 2F3
Veracruz 1C5
Versalles 3A3
Vicario, Leona 4F1
Victor Hugo 1B3
Victoria 3C2
Viena 2F3
Viga, Calzada de la 4F5
Villalongín, Manuel 2D2
Ville Salado Alvarez 4D4
Vizcaínas 4D3
Wallon, Enrique 1A2

X-Y

Xicotencatl 4D1
Xocongo 4E5
Yucatán 4F2

Z

Zacatecas 2F5
Zamora 1B5
Zapotecos 4D4
Zaragoza 3B1
Zaragoza, Privada 3A1
Zarco 3B1

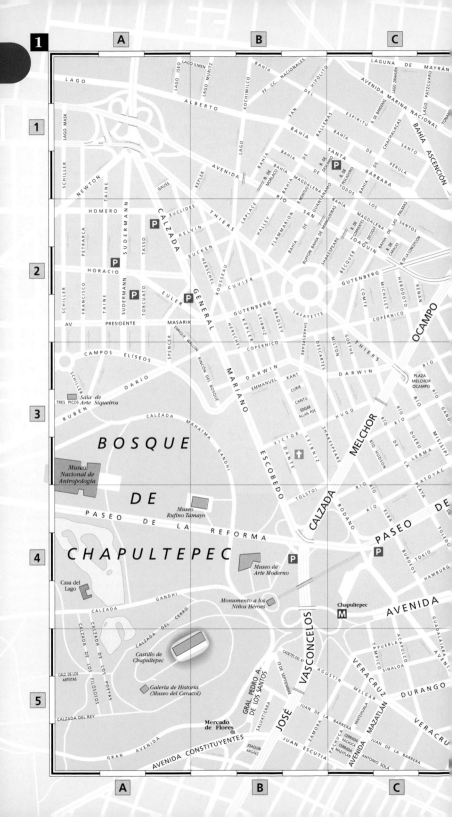

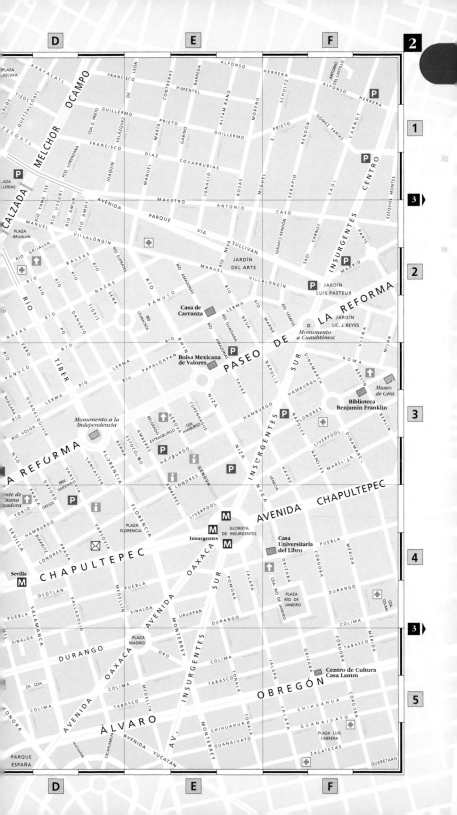

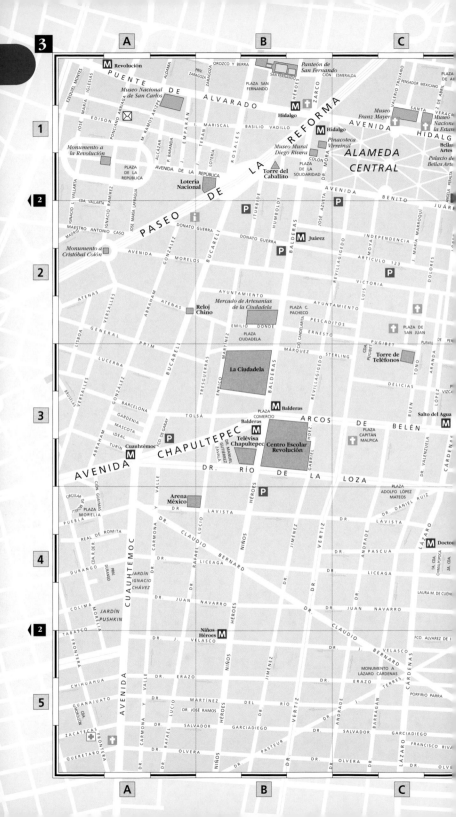

MEXICO
REGION BY
REGION

MEXICO AT A GLANCE 128-129
AROUND MEXICO CITY 130-157
NORTHERN MEXICO 158-179
THE COLONIAL HEARTLAND 180-211
SOUTHERN MEXICO 212-237
THE GULF COAST 238-255
THE YUCATÁN PENINSULA 256-287

Mexico at a Glance

MEXICO IS AN ENORMOUSLY varied country, and traveling from one part to another can seem like crossing between different worlds. The north is characterized by its deserts, and great mountains and canyons, with the Baja California peninsula as a place apart. The area northwest of the capital has the country's finest colonial architecture. Central and Southern Mexico, and the Gulf Coast region, are most visited for their pre-Columbian ruins.

Cañón del Cobre (see pp176–7), *a spectacularly deep and scenic canyon, can be viewed from one of the world's most extraordinary railroads.*

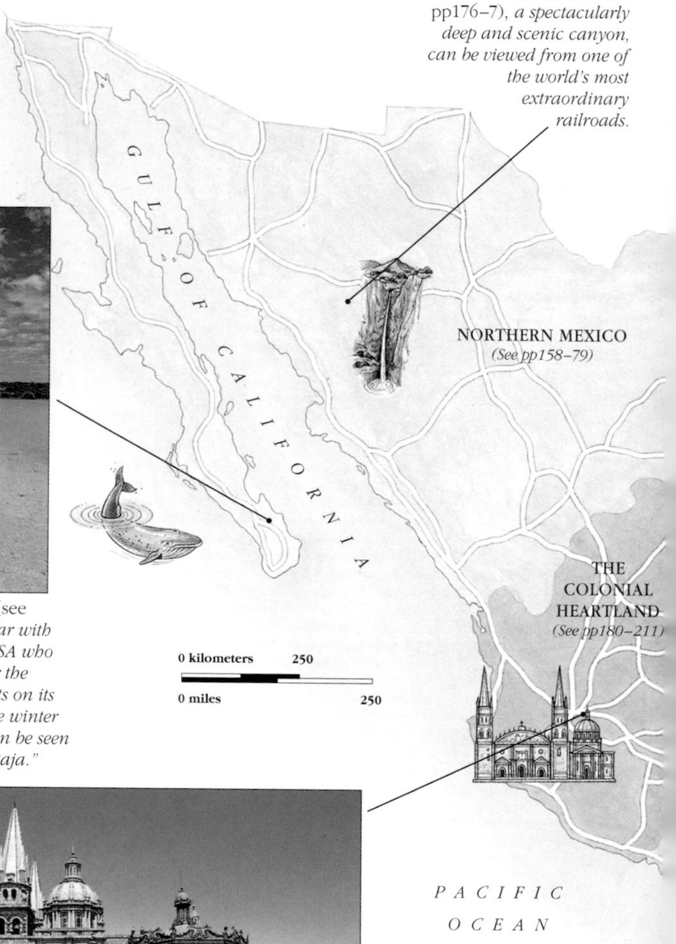

NORTHERN MEXICO
(See pp158–79)

THE COLONIAL HEARTLAND
(See pp180–211)

Baja California (see pp162–5) *is popular with visitors from the USA who head especially for the beaches and resorts on its southern tip. In the winter months, whales can be seen off the shores of "Baja."*

0 kilometers   250

0 miles   250

PACIFIC
OCEAN

Guadalajara (see pp188–9) *is dominated by its 16th-century cathedral. It is the largest of the colonial cities to the northwest of Mexico City. Also worth visiting are San Miguel de Allende, Morelia, and Guanajuato.*

◁ **Ocher-colored houses in Campeche, on the Yucatán Peninsula**

El Tajín (see pp242–3) was home to the Totonac civilization between AD 700 and 900. It is one of the best places in Mexico to see voladores dancers perform (see p29).

Palenque (see pp234–7) is notable for its fine stucco carvings. Beneath its main temple, the Temple of Inscriptions, is the only known Maya crypt, which was created for Pakal, the ruler of Palenque.

Teotihuacán (see pp134–7) was once the most powerful city of the New World. Its people left behind a fascinating legacy, including the towering Pyramids of the Sun and the Moon.

GULF OF MEXICO

THE YUCATÁN PENINSULA (See pp256–87)

MEXICO CITY

AROUND MEXICO CITY (See pp130–57)

THE GULF COAST (See pp238–55)

SOUTHERN MEXICO (See pp212–37)

Oaxaca (see pp222–5) is an elegant colonial city with a number of churches and museums, and two lively markets. This relief of the Virgin is found over the main door to the cathedral.

Chichén Itzá (see pp274–6) is the best preserved of Mexico's Maya ruins, with temples, an observatory, and the largest ball-court in Mexico. It flourished from the 11th to the 13th century.

AROUND MEXICO CITY

GUERRERO (NORTH) • HIDALGO • MEXICO STATE
MORELOS • PUEBLA • TLAXCALA

S NOWCAPPED VOLCANOES, *among them Mexico's highest peaks, tower over the country's central plateau – a series of vast plains and broad valleys at altitudes of around 2,000 m (6,550 ft). Centered on the Valley of Mexico, the country's heart for over two millennia, this region has an unparalleled collection of stunning pre-Columbian and colonial monuments, set against dramatic natural backdrops.*

These highlands were densely populated even before the arrival of the Spanish in 1519. Great civilizations flourished here and built extensive cities and awesome ceremonial sites such as Tula and Teotihuacán. Spanish missionaries fanned out from here to explore and pacify the vast territories later consolidated as New Spain. They dotted the region with fortress-like convents and opulent churches such as San Francisco Javier in Tepotzotlán. Puebla, the provincial capital east of Mexico City, with its exuberant ecclesiastical and secular architecture, was one of the colony's most important cities. Meanwhile, the discovery of precious metals sparked the development of mining towns, most notably the picturesque Taxco.

Today, busy highways radiate from Mexico City to burgeoning cities in the neighboring states. So far, however, the incursions of modern Mexico into the region have not significantly disturbed the area's natural beauty, protected in part by a series of national parks.

A rich volcanic soil accounts for the region's endless fields of crops – rice and sugar cane at lower altitudes in the south, grain and vegetables elsewhere. The land once belonged to huge estates, run from imposing haciendas. After the Revolution, much of it became communal, and it remains the principal means of subsistence for the region's rural population, many of whom are Nahua and Otomí Indians, the two largest of Mexico's indigenous groups.

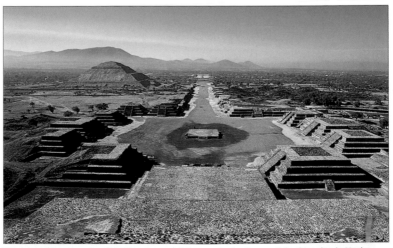

The ruins of the great city of Teotihuacán, one of the most fascinating pre-Columbian sites in Mexico

◁ Crafts on display in a market in the colonial town of Taxco

Exploring Around Mexico City

T HE ROUTES NORTH of Mexico City lead to a colonial treasure trove at the Museo Nacional del Virreinato, and to the pyramids of Tula and Teotihuacán, the latter Mexico's most visited pre-Columbian site. To the east, beyond Popocatépetl and Iztaccíhuatl volcanoes, is the splendid colonial city of Puebla, a good base for visiting isolated Cantona and the ancient murals at Cacaxtla. The western part of the region has cool forests and scenic lakes, while to the south warmer weather attracts visitors to busy Cuernavaca and beautiful Taxco, famed for its silversmiths and Churrigueresque church.

Dome of the Iglesia
de la Compañía
in Puebla

SIGHTS AT A GLANCE

Cacaxtla **19**
Cantona **21**
Cholula **17**
Convento de Actopan **6**
Cuernavaca **14**
Huasca **5**
Malinalco **11**
MEXICO CITY pp56–125
Mineral del Monte **4**
Museo Nacional del Virreinato pp140–43 **7**
Pachuca **3**
Popocatépetl and Iztaccíhuatl **16**
Puebla pp150–53 **18**
San Agustín Acolman **2**
Taxco pp146–7 **12**
Teotihuacán pp134–7 **1**
Tepoztlán **15**
Tlaxcala **20**
Toluca **10**
Tula **8**
Valle de Bravo **9**
Xochicalco **13**

Querétaro

Guadalajara

ATLACOMULCO

MUSEO NACIONAL DEL VIRREINATO

Morelia

VALLE DE BRAVO

IXMIQUILPAN

TULA

TOLUCA

MEXICO CITY

TEPOZTLÁN

MALINALCO

CUERNAVACA

IXTAPAN DE LA SAL

XOCHICALCO

BEJUCOS

Ixtapa

TAXCO

IGUALA

Acapulco

The Pyramid of the Sun, the largest structure at Teotihuacán

GETTING AROUND

Modern toll highways lead out of Mexico City in all directions, and signs indicating them are being improved. Two highways, the Periférico and Circuito Interior, partially circle the capital, while the Viaducto cuts across it from west to east. A network of mostly paved roads connects the outlying towns and cities. Frequent express buses serve the cities, and bus services from here to smaller towns are highly efficient. However, a car or taxi is needed for remote sights such as Cantona. The few trains still running no longer take passengers.

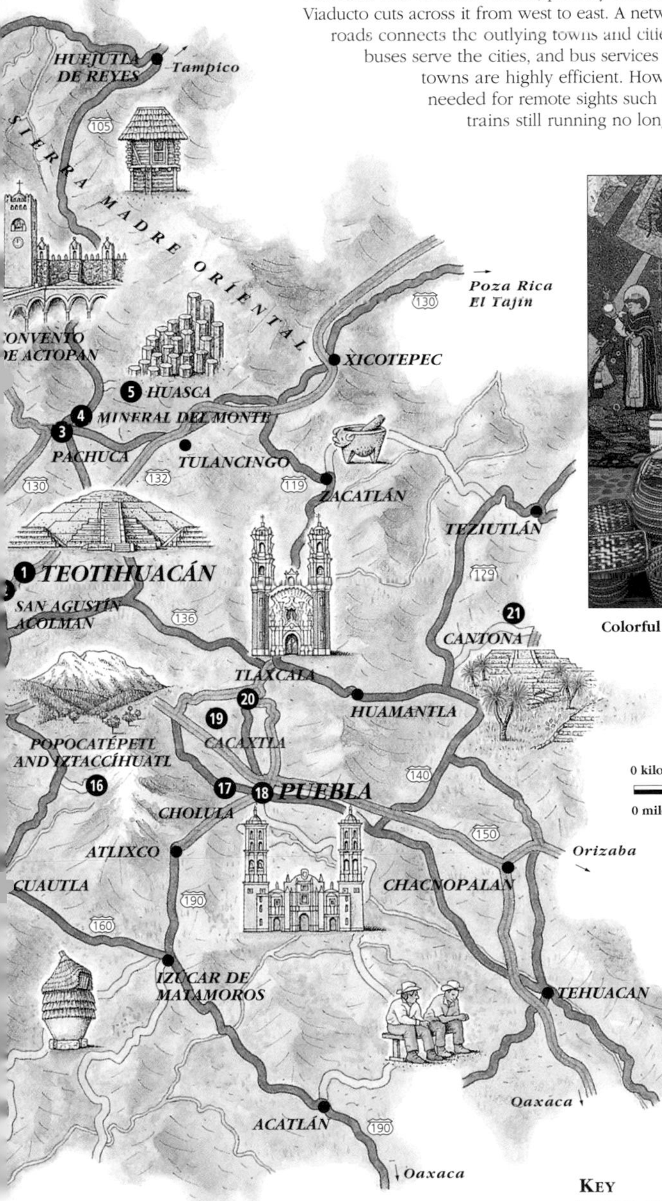

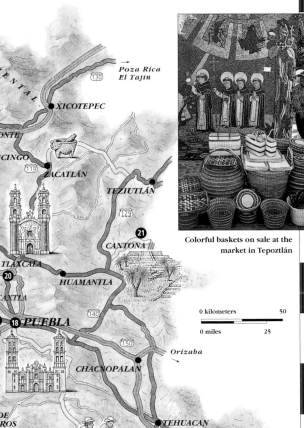

Colorful baskets on sale at the market in Tepoztlán

HUEJUTLA DE REYES
Tampico
105

SIERRA MADRE ORIENTAL

CONVENTO DE ACTOPAN

Poza Rica
El Tajín
130

XICOTEPEC

5 HUASCA
4 MINERAL DEL MONTE
3 PACHUCA
130
132
TULANCINGO
119
ZACATLÁN
TEZIUTLÁN
129

1 TEOTIHUACÁN
SAN AGUSTÍN ACOLMAN
136

21 CANTONA

TLAXCALA
HUAMANTLA
20
19 CACAXTLA

POPOCATÉPETL AND IZTACCÍHUATL
16
140

17 **18** PUEBLA
CHOLULA
150

ATLIXCO
Orizaba

CUAUTLA
190
CHACNOPALAN
160

IZÚCAR DE MATAMOROS
TEHUACÁN

ACATLÁN
190
Oaxaca

Oaxaca

0 kilometers   50
0 miles   25

KEY

≡ Highway
≡ Other major road
≡ Minor road
≈ River

SEE ALSO

• *Where to Stay* pp294–6
• *Where to Eat* pp317–19

Teotihuacán ❶

ITS NAME MEANING "the place where men become gods," Teotihuacán is one of the most impressive cities of the ancient world. Founded before the Christian era, this colossal urban center once housed up to 125,000 people and covered over 20 sq km (8 sq miles). It dominated life in the region for 500 years before being destroyed (possibly by its own people) and abandoned, around AD 650. Later, the site was held sacred by the Aztecs, who believed it had been built by giants. The ceremonial center, with its temples, palaces, and pyramids, bears witness to the city's splendor but has revealed little about its creators and inhabitants. Their origin, way of life, and even demise remain a mystery.

Mask on Temple of Quetzalcoatl

The Temple of Quetzalcoatl with the Pyramid of the Sun behind

Avenue of the Dead
This wide avenue runs the length of the present site but once stretched much farther toward the south. It was named by the Aztecs who mistakenly believed that the buildings lining it were royal tombs.

Palaces of Tetitla, Atetelco, Zacuala, and Yayahuala *(see p137)*

Entrance 1

Mexico City

Entrance 2

The Superimposed Buildings (*Edificios Superpuestos*)

Restaurant

The Citadel

★ Temple of Quetzalcoatl
Masks of the plumed serpent Quetzalcoatl and a god sometimes identified as rain god Tlaloc decorate this temple. Built around AD 200, it was later covered by a pyramid, which has now been partially removed.

Living quarters for the ruling classes were probably situated here.

0 meters	250
0 yards	250

★ Pyramid of the Moon
Although smaller than the Pyramid of the Sun, this four-tiered structure rises just as high, due to a difference in ground level. It offers the best view of the site.

VISITORS' CHECKLIST

Mexico State. Mex 132, 47 km (29 miles) NE of Mexico City. (594) 56 00 52. from Central Camionera del Norte, Mexico City. 7am–6pm daily (last adm: 5pm). Parking at entrances. **Museum** 8am–5pm.

★ Quetzalpapalotl Palace Complex
This group of buildings has fine carvings and murals (see p136).

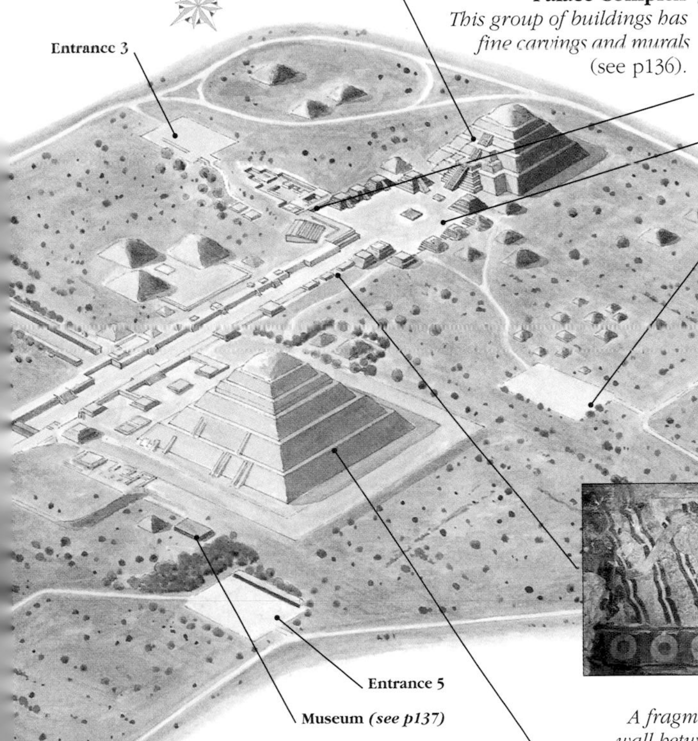

Entrance 3

Plaza of the Moon

Entrance 4

Palace of Tepantitla *(see p137)*

Jaguar Mural
A fragment of mural on a wall between two staircases depicts a colossal jaguar set against water motifs.

Entrance 5

Museum *(see p137)*

★ Pyramid of the Sun
This immense pyramid ranks among the biggest in the world (see p137). Probably completed during the 2nd century AD, it is made of adobe bricks and earth, covered with gravel and stone. This would have been coated with brightly painted stucco. Chambers and a tunnel have been found beneath the structure.

STAR FEATURES

★ Temple of Quetzalcoatl

★ Pyramid of the Moon

★ Quetzalpapalotl Palace Complex

★ Pyramid of the Sun

Quetzalpapalotl Palace Complex

THIS MAZE OF residential and temple structures grew slowly over several centuries. The last part to be built was probably the elegant Palace of Quetzalpapalotl, uncovered in 1962 and reconstructed with mostly original materials. It sits atop the now buried Temple of the Feathered Conches (2nd–3rd century AD). The Jaguar Palace, just to the west, has a large courtyard faced by a portico and a stepped temple base.

The Palace of Quetzalpapalotl is named for the mythological creatures (bird-butterflies) carved into its courtyard pillars. They have obsidian eyes and are surrounded by water and fire symbols.

Murals in the Jaguar Palace show plumed jaguars playing musical instruments made from feathered shells.

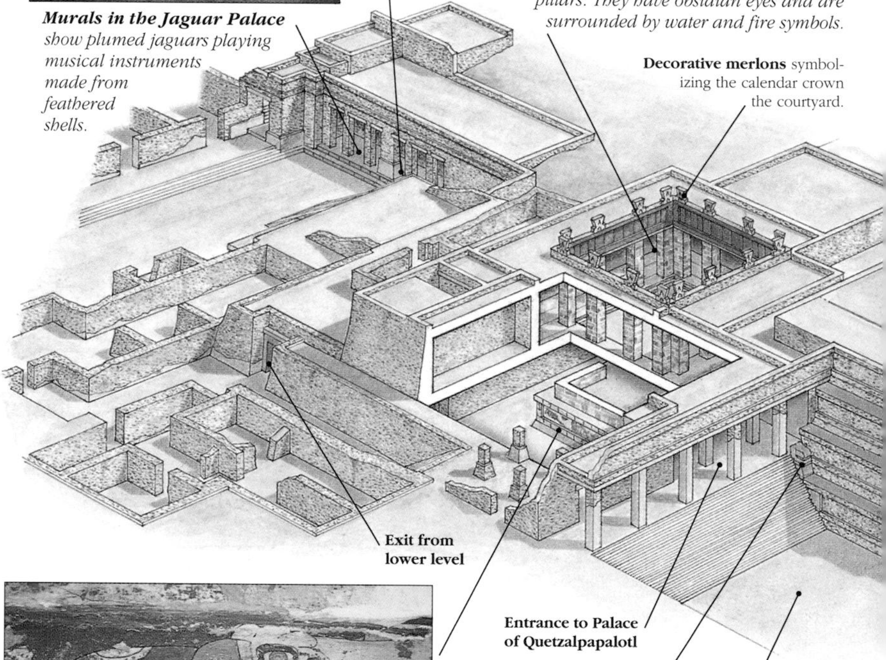

Entrance to lower level

Decorative merlons symbolizing the calendar crown the courtyard.

Exit from lower level

Entrance to Palace of Quetzalpapalotl

Plaza of the Moon

The Temple of the Feathered Conches is an older structure that archaeologists discovered buried beneath the Palace of Quetzalpapalotl. It sits on a platform adorned with brilliantly colored murals such as this one, which depict green parrot-like birds spewing water from their beaks. Reliefs of feathered conches and four-petaled flowers decorate the temple façade.

A stone serpent's head of enormous proportions juts out from the top of a steep staircase and guards the porticoed entrance to the Palace of Quetzalpapalotl.

Exploring Teotihuacán

IN ORDER TO APPRECIATE the grandeur and colossal scale of this awesome site, visitors should be prepared for long walks over uneven ground and stiff climbs up steep stairways – all at an altitude of 2,300 m (7,550 ft) and often under a hot tropical sun. Comfortable shoes, a hat, and sunblock are a must, plus basic rain gear in summer.

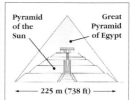

TWO PYRAMIDS

The Pyramid of the Sun stands on a base of very similar dimensions to that of the Great Pyramid of Egypt, but it is only half the height – 65 m (213 ft), as against 144 m (472 ft). It consists of about 2.5 million tonnes of stone and earth, compared with the Great Pyramid's 6.5 million.

Partially restored mural depicting feathered coyotes, at Atetelco

The Museum

The on-site museum is located just south of the Pyramid of the Sun. It displays artifacts found at Teotihuacán, explanatory maps and diagrams, and, beneath the glass floor of its main hall, a scale model of the city. The shady gardens outside are a good place to rest during a tour of the site. They are planted with botanical species native to the area and decorated with original Teotihuacán sculptures.

Outlying Palaces

Several ancient dwelling complexes are situated beyond the fence and road that ring the site. Some 500 m (0.3 miles) east of the Pyramid of the Sun lies the **Palace of Tepantitla**, which contains the most important and colorful murals discovered so far at Teotihuacán. These include representations of elaborately dressed priests, the rain god Tlaloc, and his carefree paradise, Tlalocan, where miniature human figures frolic in an Eden-like setting.

Bird spewing water, in the museum

Just west of the site, and best reached by car, are four other palaces: Tetitla, Atetelco, Zacuala, and Yayahuala. **Tetitla** is a maze-like complex of more than 120 walls, showing remnants of refined frescoes depicting birds, jaguars, priests, and various deities. **Atetelco** is distinguished by a miniature altar in one courtyard and, in another, stunning red murals of jaguars and coyotes with feathered headdresses. **Zacuala** and **Yayahuala** are extensive complexes with sophisticated drainage systems, and vestiges of wall paintings in their many rooms, corridors, courtyards, and porticoes.

THE UNEARTHING OF TEOTIHUACÁN

For more than 1,000 years after its decline, the crumbled ruins of Teotihuacán remained hidden below a thick layer of earth and vegetation. Despite being venerated by the Aztecs, the site was never noticed by Cortés and his men when they passed by during their retreat from Tenochtitlán in 1520. The structures visible today, a mere tenth of the city, were excavated at digs that began in 1864 and continue to this day. Early 20th-century reconstructions partially destroyed and distorted some of the principal edifices, but since then more systematic explorations have resulted in the unearthing of the Temple of Quetzalcoatl in the 1920s and the Palace of Quetzalpapalotl 40 years later. Chambers were discovered under the Pyramid of the Sun in 1971, and in 1998 archaeologists found human remains and offerings inside the Pyramid of the Moon.

Bones found on the site

Bird fresco at Tetitla, excavated in the 1950s

The Plateresque façade of the church of San Agustín Acolman

San Agustín Acolman ❷

Mexico State. Acolman, off Mex 85, 38 km (24 miles) NE of Mexico City. 🚌 Acolman. ⬜ Tue–Sun. 📷

ONE OF Mexico's oldest monasteries, San Agustín Acolman was founded in 1536 by Augustinian monks sent here to convert the local Indians. It is notable for its atrium, a Christian version of the pre-Columbian ceremonial plaza, where crowds of Indian disciples would gather to hear the new religion preached from a chapel balcony above. The fortress-like building, now housing colonial paintings and sculptures, is typical of New Spain's early monasteries.

The forbidding aspect of the monastery is softened, however, by the adjoining church's beautiful Plateresque façade, which is characterized by classic Italian Renaissance columns, richly decorated door arches, and a choir window replicating the portal below. The sparse interior of the 57-m (187-ft) nave is notable only for its apse, which boasts Gothic fan vaulting and is adorned with rich frescoes.

Detail on façade of San Agustín Acolman

Pachuca ❸

Hidalgo. 🏛 245,000. 🚌 ℹ️ Plaza Independencia, (771) 715 14 11. 📷 Feria Regional de Pachuca (Oct).

PACHUCA, capital of Hidalgo state, lies in the heart of one of Mexico's richest mining areas. The center of town, with its steep, narrow lanes and small squares, retains some buildings from the two mining booms of the 16th and 18th centuries.

Undoubtedly, the most significant colonial complex is the late 16th-century **Ex-Convento de San Francisco** and its adjoining church. The church contains the remains of the 3rd-century martyr St. Columba, whose mummified body was brought here in the 18th century. Part of the massive monastery building houses the **Fototeca Nacional** (National Photographic Archive) and the **Museo de Fotografía**. The latter has exhibits on the history of photography and shows selections from the 1 million photos on file. One section is dedicated to the Casasola Archive, an outstanding chronicle of the Mexican Revolution and post-Revolutionary daily life. It is also worth seeing the photographs and mining equipment at the **Museo de Minería** and the mineral samples at the **Museo de Mineralogía**. The tower in the main plaza, the 40-m

(130-ft) Neo-Classical **Reloj Monumental** (Monumental Clock), has an eight-bell carillon made by the creators of Big Ben in London.

ENVIRONS: The hills of **El Chico**, a vast national park north of Pachuca, are very popular with hikers, fishermen, and rock climbers.

🏛 **Fototeca Nacional and Museo de Fotografía**
Casasola. ☎ (771) 714 36 53. ⬜ Tue–Sun.
🏛 **Museo de Minería**
Mina 110. ☎ (771) 715 09 76. ⬜ Tue–Sun. 📷
🏛 **Museo de Mineralogía**
Abasolo 600. ☎ (771) 717 20 00, ext. 1302. ⬜ daily.

Mineral del Monte ❹

Hidalgo. 🏛 11,000. 🚌 ℹ️ Rubén Licona Ruiz 1, (771) 797 05 10, ext. 1302. 📷 Día del Rosario (Jan 1).

ALSO KNOWN AS Real del Monte, this mining town, at an altitude of 2,700 m (8,800 ft), used to be the richest in the area. Gold and silver were discovered here before the Conquest (see p43), and the Spanish started mining in the mid-1500s. The mines were later abandoned, but reopened in the late 1730s under Pedro Romero de Terreros.

The town's steep streets, stairways, and small squares are lined with low buildings, some dating back to colonial times. The houses with high

The charming colors of houses on the central plaza in Mineral del Monte

Symmetrically patterned fresco at the Convento de Actopan

sloping roofs and chimneys indicate a Cornish influence, the legacy left by the 350 Cornishmen employed by the English company that ran the mines between 1824 and 1848. They are also responsible for *pastes*, a local specialty based on the Cornish pasty, as well as for introducing soccer to Mexico.

Huasca ❺

Hidalgo. 🏠 600. 🚌 to Pachuca.
ℹ️ *Plaza Principal, (771) 792 02 53.*
🎭 *San Sebastián (Jan 20).*

THE PICTURESQUE village of Huasca is best known for its *haciendas de beneficio*, haciendas where mineral ores were refined. One of the most visited is **San Miguel Regla**, 3 km (2 miles) northeast of town. It is now a hotel *(see p294)* and offers guided tours of its *beneficio* installations. More impressive is **Santa María Regla**, a little farther away, which has vaulted cellars, and patios with stone drag mills and melting ovens. From here visitors can access the spectacular 15-km (9-mile) canyon **Prismas Basálticos**, whose walls are made up of red and ocher basalt hexagons.

Adam and Eve fresco, Convento de Actopan

🏛️ **Santa María Regla**
7 km (4.5 miles) NE of Huasca.
⭘ *daily.* 🖼️ 🚻

Convento de Actopan ❻

Hidalgo. Actopan, 36 km (22 miles) NW of Pachuca. 🚌 *Actopan.* ⭘ *daily.* 🖼️ 🎫 *reserve in advance.* 🚻

THIS IMPOSING structure, built in the 1550s, is one of Mexico's most remarkable and best preserved 16th-century fortress-monasteries. Even more spectacular than its Plateresque church façade, square Moorish tower, and vaulted open chapel are its frescoes, which are considered the most beautiful and extensive from this era in Mexico.

The finest include the portraits of saints on the main stairs and the depiction of hermits in the De Profundis hall, which is in a style reminiscent of native codices. Perhaps most impressive of all are the naïve scenes of heaven and hell in the open chapel.

ENVIRONS: In Ixmiquilpan, 40 km (25 miles) farther north, stands the **Ex-Convento de San Miguel Arcángel**. Now a museum, it displays some fine frescoes that incorporate a range of subjects, including Indian warriors, Biblical scenes, and pre-Columbian figures.

🏛️ **Ex-Convento de San Miguel Arcángel**
Av Angeles, Ixmiquilpan. ⭘ *daily.*

FIESTAS AROUND MEXICO CITY

Chalma Pilgrimages
(Jan 6, Easter week, May 3, Jul 1), Chalma *(see p145).* Hordes of pilgrims, laden with colorful flowers, can be seen making their way to the shrine of El Señor de Chalma – by foot, on their knees, by car, bicycle, or bus. Pentecost celebrations on May 3 include traditional dances by the splendidly attired Concheros dancers.

Chalma pilgrims armed with bunches of flowers

Fiesta de los Tiznados
(Jan 21), Tepoztlán *(see p148).* Revelers smear themselves with ash in remembrance of the ancient Tepoztec king, who fled his enemies disguised as a peasant.
Battle of Puebla *(May 5),* Puebla *(see pp150–53).* The 1862 Mexican victory over the French *(see p52)* is re-enacted, with military parades and fireworks.
Fiesta de la Virgen de la Caridad *(mid Aug),* Huamantla *(see p157).* On the first Sunday of the fiesta the image of the Virgin is carried over 5 km (3 miles) of sawdust carpet, and her church is decorated. The following Sunday, bulls run through the streets as part of the *Huamantlada*.
Reto al Tepozteco *(Sep 8),* Tepoztlán *(see p148).* Following tradition, local villagers race one another up Tepozteco Hill, before consuming copious quantities of *pulque (see p313).*

Museo Nacional del Virreinato ⓐ

The country's most complete collection of colonial art and artifacts, one of its finest Baroque churches, and a splendid former Jesuit college built in the 17th and 18th centuries together make up this stunning museum covering Mexico's viceregal era. The church and college buildings, a vast complex with courtyards and gardens in the quaint village of Tepotzotlán, were nearly complete when the Jesuits were expelled from New Spain in 1767. They were extensively restored and opened as a museum in 1964. Exhibits include treasures preserved in situ as well as pieces brought here from other collections around the country.

Gardens
Formerly an orchard, the peaceful gardens have a chapel and an aqueduct.

Claustro de los Naranjos
This courtyard, once a place of meditation for novices, is filled with orange trees.

Ivory Statues
These figures of the Virgin Mary and Christ show the Asian features characteristic of religious carvings created in the Orient. They were probably brought to New Spain from the Philippines.

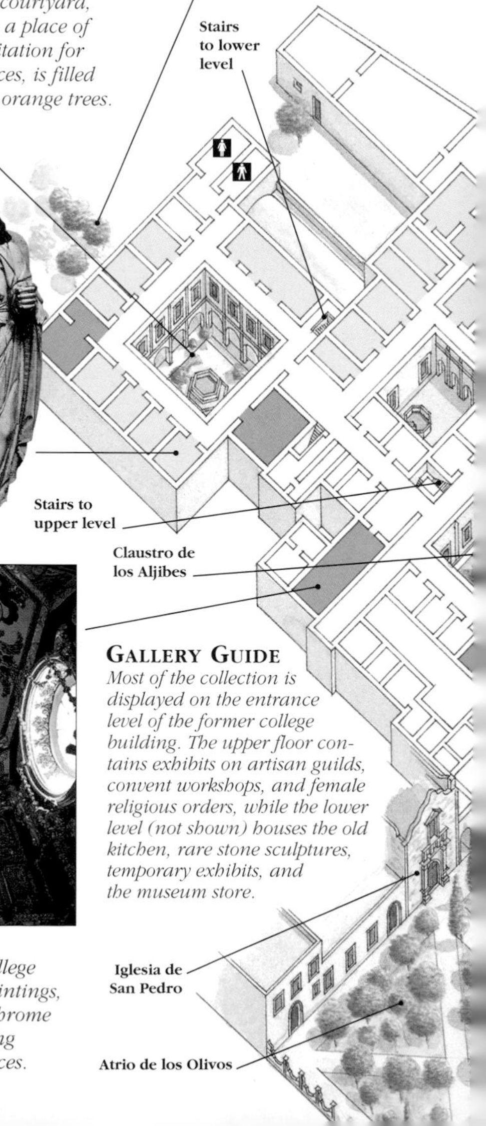

Stairs to lower level

Stairs to upper level

Claustro de los Aljibes

GALLERY GUIDE
Most of the collection is displayed on the entrance level of the former college building. The upper floor contains exhibits on artisan guilds, convent workshops, and female religious orders, while the lower level (not shown) houses the old kitchen, rare stone sculptures, temporary exhibits, and the museum store.

★ Capilla Doméstica
The chapel was for the exclusive use of college residents. Profuse decorations include paintings, statuettes, reliquaries, mirrors, and polychrome plasterwork, all effective means of inspiring religious awe in the students during services.

Iglesia de San Pedro

Atrio de los Olivos

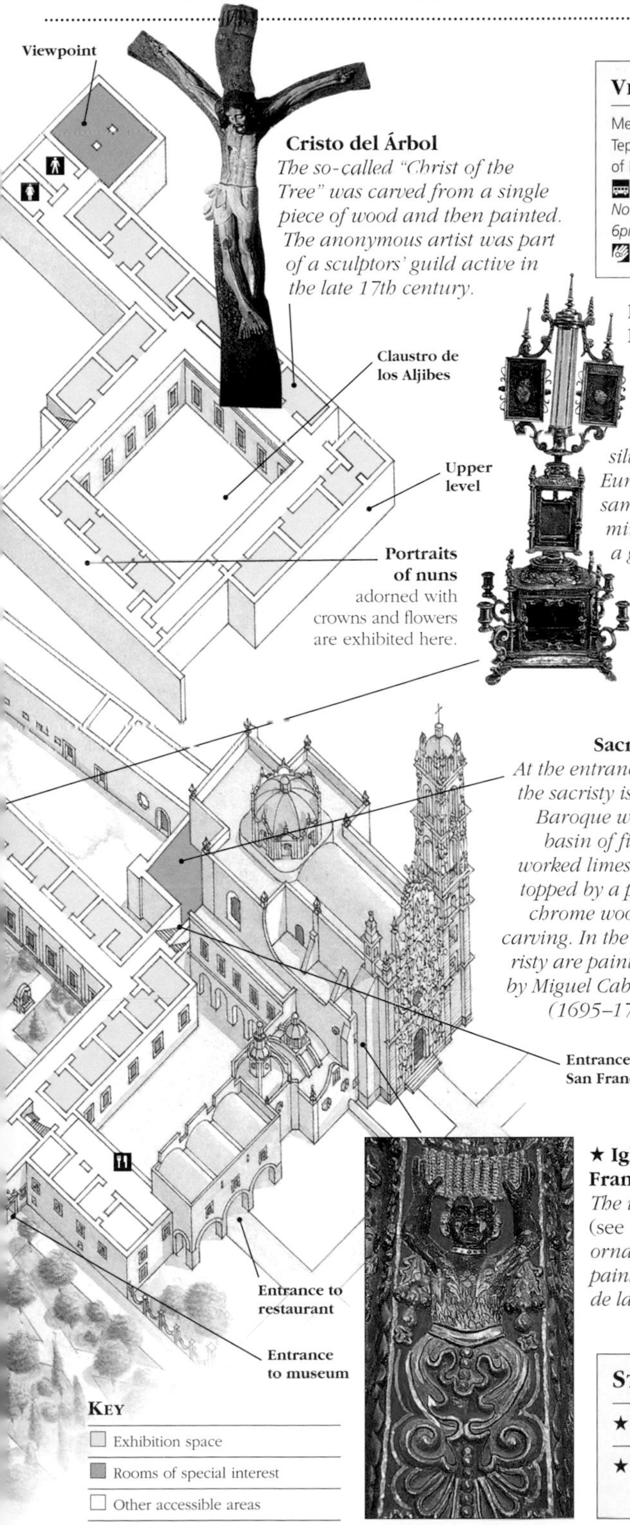

Viewpoint

Cristo del Árbol
The so-called "Christ of the Tree" was carved from a single piece of wood and then painted. The anonymous artist was part of a sculptors' guild active in the late 17th century.

VISITORS' CHECKLIST

Mexico State. Plaza Hidalgo, Tepotzotlán, 44 km (27 miles) N of Mexico City. 58 76 03 32. from Central Camionera del Norte, Mexico City. 9am–6pm Tue–Sun (last adm: 5:30pm).

Relicario de San Pedro y San Pablo
This late 16th-century reliquary of St. Peter and St. Paul is made of embossed gold-plated silver and compares with European examples of the same period. A wealthy miner commissioned it as a gift to the Jesuit order.

Claustro de los Aljibes

Upper level

Portraits of nuns
adorned with crowns and flowers are exhibited here.

Sacristy
At the entrance to the sacristy is this Baroque washbasin of finely worked limestone topped by a polychrome wooden carving. In the sacristy are paintings by Miguel Cabrera (1695–1768).

Entrance to Iglesia de San Francisco Javier

★ Iglesia de San Francisco Javier
The interior of the church (see pp142–3) is awash with ornate detail, such as this painted figure in the Camarín de la Virgen, a side chapel.

Entrance to restaurant

Entrance to museum

STAR FEATURES

★ Capilla Doméstica

★ Iglesia de San Francisco Javier

KEY

☐ Exhibition space

☐ Rooms of special interest

☐ Other accessible areas

Iglesia de San Francisco Javier

Carved angel, Camarín de la Virgen

CONSTRUCTED IN THE late 1600s, this majestic Baroque church is famous for its splendid 18th-century additions: the richly decorated Churrigueresque façade and tower, the exuberant gold altars, a trio of unusual chapels on one side, and the Miguel Cabrera murals in the chancel and cross vaults. The façade and interior are both prime examples of Mexican High Baroque. Together they form a harmonious whole equaled only by Santa Prisca in Taxco *(see p147)* and San Cayetano near Guanajuato *(see p205).*

The altar to St. Stanislaus Kostka honors a Polish Jesuit who served as a model to the novices and students of the institution.

★ **Main Altar**
The most imposing of the altars in the church is dedicated to St. Francis Xavier, patron saint of the Jesuit college.

Entrance from museum

The altar to the Virgin of Guadalupe centers on a Miguel Cabrera painting of the patron saint of Mexico.

The Casa de Loreto is said to be a replica of the Virgin Mary's Nazareth home, which angels moved to Loreto in Italy when the Muslims invaded the Holy Land. A 17th-century image of the Virgin of Loreto adorns the gold altar in the otherwise sober interior.

Corridor

Corridor

★ **Camarín de la Virgen**
This profusely decorated octagonal chamber once served as a dressing room for the Virgin of Loreto – the statue's vestments and jewels were changed regularly. The beautiful dome is shaped like a papal tiara.

★ **Relicario de San José**
Built to house relics revered by the Jesuits, this chapel resembles the inside of a treasure chest.

Dome
The dome rising above the intersection of the Latin Cross nave is best seen from a viewpoint in the museum (see pp140–41).

The altar to St. Ignatius Loyola shows the founder of the Jesuits holding a book displaying the order's crest and motto.

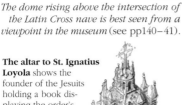

Pulpit

The bell tower has 13 bells hanging on three levels under a tiled dome topped by a filigreed iron cross.

Altar to the Virgen de la Luz
A multitude of cherubs and angels surrounds the central image of the Virgin and Child; one proffers a basket containing souls from purgatory. The pulpit (beside the altar) is from a church in Mexico City.

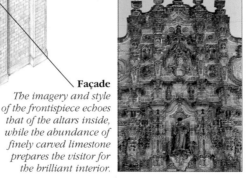

Façade
The imagery and style of the frontispiece echoes that of the altars inside, while the abundance of finely carved limestone prepares the visitor for the brilliant interior.

Estípite Pilasters
So-called estípite *pilasters form the verticals of the altars. Inspired by the proportions of the human figure,* estípites *taper off at the base, thus appearing to be upside down. Many are decorated with faces.*

STAR FEATURES

★ **Main Altar**

★ **Camarín de la Virgen**

★ **Relicario de San José**

The towering Atlantes, standing guard on the Pyramid of the Morning Star at Tula

Tula ❽

Hidalgo. Off Mex 57, 85 km (53 miles) N of Mexico City. 🚌 *Tula de Allende* then taxi. ◯ *daily.* 🌐

THE MOST IMPORTANT Toltec site in Mexico, Tula flourished as a great urban center from AD 900–1200, after the decline of Teotihuacán *(see pp134–7)* and prior to the rise of Tenochtitlán *(see pp41–2).* At its peak, the city covered up to 16 sq km (6 sq miles) and had an estimated population of 40,000. Then inner strife, invasions, and fire destroyed the Toltec empire and this, its capital. Only remnants of the main palaces, temples, and ballcourts survive on a windswept hill overlooking the small town of Tula de Allende.

The site is most famous for its giant stone sculptures, the Atlantes. At a height of 4.6 m (15 ft), these four warrior figures in battle gear crown the Pyramid of Tlahuizcalpantecuhtli, or the Morning Star. Together with a massive serpent and other pillars, they probably once supported an ornately carved roof. (Note that parts of the sculptures are reproductions.) The base of the temple and the Coatepantli, or Serpent Wall, on its northern flank, are decorated with carved friezes of serpents, eagles, and jaguars, some devouring human hearts.

Certain stylistic elements at Tula – such as the column-filled Palacio Quemado (Burnt Palace), the *chacmool* sculptures, and the huge size of Ballcourt No. 2 – underline the site's similarity to the Maya city of Chichén Itzá *(see pp274–6).* Legend tells that Toltec king Topiltzín was driven out of Tula and fled to the Yucatán Peninsula where he ushered in a cultural renaissance. Recent theories dispute this, however, suggesting that the similarities are a result of Maya influence on Tula, not vice versa.

Valle de Bravo ❾

Mexico State. 🏠 21,500. 🚌 ℹ Cnr. Porfirio Diaz and Ignacio Zaragoza, (726) 262 16 78. 🎭 Santa Cruz (May 3), San Francisco (Oct 4).

SET AMONG pine-covered volcanic mountains, the beautiful colonial town of Valle de Bravo can trace its origins back to the earliest days of Spanish rule. It achieved its current popularity after the construction of an artificial lake in the 1950s. "Valle" offers an equable climate, a wide variety of sports (especially hang gliding, horseback riding, and waterskiing), and stunning scenery. The landscape around the town and lake is perfect for hiking, and trails wind past mountain streams, cornfields, and patches of wildflowers.

Easy access from Mexico City and a lively nightlife make the town a favorite weekend destination for the capital's élite, but during the week peace returns to the cobbled streets.

The pastel tones of Templo de la Santa Veracruz in Toluca

Toluca ❿

Mexico State. 🏠 665,600. ✈ 🚌 ℹ Av Urawa 100, (722) 219 61 58. 🎭 Virgen del Carmen (Jul 16).

THE CAPITAL CITY of Mexico State is, at 2,680 m (8,790 ft) above sea level, the highest state capital in the country.

Founded by the Spaniards in the late 17th century, Toluca is full of fine buildings. In the city center, near Plaza de los Mártires, are the 18th-century **Templo de la Santa Veracruz** and the 19th-century **Portales**, a series of arched walkways lined with cafés and shops. To the north is the **Museo de Bellas Artes**, which exhibits Mexican art from the last four centuries. Nearby, the **Cosmo Vitral Jardín Botánico** shows botanical specimens in the beautiful old market, its walls and ceiling ablaze with colorful stained glass. Every Friday, Toluca plays host to what is thought to be the country's largest market, which offers a huge diversity of products.

The lake at Valle de Bravo, popular with watersports enthusiasts

To the southeast, the suburb of **Metepec** is famous for its brightly colored, ceramic *árboles de la vida* (trees of life; *see pp330–31*), loosely based on the story of Adam and Eve; examples can be purchased.

ENVIRONS: Just 8 km (5 miles) west of Toluca is the **Centro Cultural Mexiquense**, a large complex of museums devoted to modern art, local history, and regional crafts.

The extinct, snow-capped **Nevado de Toluca** volcano, Mexico's fourth highest mountain at 4,690 m (15,387 ft), is a 45-km (28-mile) drive southwest. A dirt road leads to the top, and hikers can descend into the crater. On clear days the views are spectacular.

The hilltop ceremonial center of **Teotenango** is 25 km (16 miles) south of Toluca. Dating from AD 900, the extensive site features several restored pyramids, plazas, a ballcourt, and a museum.

🏛 **Museo de Bellas Artes**
102 Santos Degollado Poniente.
📞 *(722) 215 53 29.* ◯ *Tue–Sun.*
🖾 *Wed free.*
🌵 **Cosmo Vitral Jardín Botánico**
Plaza Garibay. 📞 *(722) 214 67 85.*
◯ *Tue–Sun.* 🖾 🛇 🛇
🏛 **Centro Cultural Mexiquense**
Av Morelos Oriente 302. 📞 *(722) 274 14 00.* ◯ *Mon–Fri.* 🖾 *Tue, Sun free.*

View of the town below from the lofty ruins of Malinalco

Malinalco ⓫

Mexico State. Off Mex 55, 70 km (43 miles) SE of Toluca. 🚌 *Malinalco town.* ◯ *Tue–Sun.* 🖾

HEWN FROM a steep volcanic mountainside, this Aztec ceremonial center sits on a narrow ledge 20-minutes' climb above the town of Malinalco. Begun in 1501, it was still unfinished at the time of the Spanish conquest.

Its main structure, the House of the Eagle, is carved entirely out of the rock, including the wide staircase in front. The doorway represents the fanged mouth of a serpent, and the circular chamber inside has integrated sculptures of jaguars and eagles. The building is thought to have been used for initiation ceremonies of high-ranking Aztec knights. Behind it stand the remains of the Temple of the Sun and the Tzinacalli Edifice, where the bodies of knights killed in combat were burned and deified.

ENVIRONS: Chalma, a small village in a deep gorge 12 km (7 miles) east of Malinalco, attracts crowds of pilgrims all year *(see p139)*. They venerate an image of Christ that is said to have miraculously replaced a pagan statue in 1533.

Taxco ⓬

See pp146–7.

Pyramid of the Plumed Serpent at Xochicalco

Xochicalco ⓭

Morelos. Off Mex 95, 40 km (25 miles) SW of Cuernavaca. 🚌 *Alpuyeca then taxi.* ◯ *daily.* 🖾

THE EXTENSIVE ruins of Xochicalco, an important city-state in pre-Columbian times, spread across a plateau offering splendid views. The city rose to prominence after the decline of Teotihuacán and flourished from AD 700 to 900, before being eclipsed by the rise of the Toltecs in the region.

About 30 per cent of the site has so far been unearthed and partially restored, including three ballcourts and the remains of several pyramidal structures. An on-site museum displays ceramics and sculptures found during archaeological work.

The Pyramid of the Plumed Serpent, excavated in 1777, is considered one of the most beautiful monuments in the country. It shows remarkably well-preserved bas-reliefs featuring serpents, figures carved in a distinctly Maya style, and glyphs. One theory suggests that the pyramid commemorates a meeting of astronomers from throughout Mesoamerica.

Another highlight is the Observatory, a large underground cave with a narrow shaft bored 8 m (26 ft) through the rock. Twice a year, on May 14–15 and July 28–29, the sun casts the hexagonal image of the shaft on the chamber floor.

The stained-glass ceiling of Cosmo Vitral Jardín Botánico in Toluca

Street-by-Street: Taxco ⑫

Image of the Virgin, Santa Prisca

S ET AGAINST a spectacular rugged mountainside, 1,800 m (6,000 ft) above sea level, Taxco is one of the least spoiled colonial towns in Mexico. The Spaniards were drawn to the area in 1522 by Aztec tales of rich mineral deposits, and the subsequent silver boom lasted for 100 years. The town's fortunes have been revived twice since, with the discovery of new lodes by José de la Borda in the 18th century, and the arrival of William Spratling in 1932, who established it as a center for silversmiths. There are fine views of the town from the *teleférico* (cable car).

View across the tiled roofs of Taxco

Casa Borda
Overlooking the main square, this house was built by the Borda family in 1759 for the parish priest. Today, it holds exhibitions by local artists.

The Museo de la Platería Antonio Pineda charts the history of Taxco silver-mining, and displays exquisitely designed silverwork, some by William Spratling.

The Casa de Figueroa was built for the Count of Cadena. It has a dark and interesting history involving subterfuge and murder.

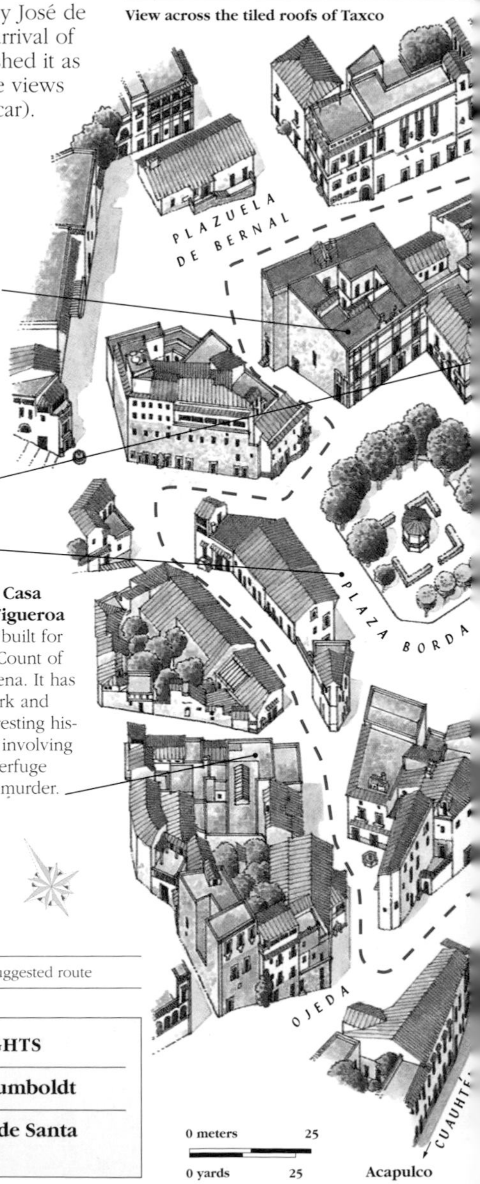

PLAZUELA DE BERNAL

PLAZA BORDA

OJEDA

CUAUHTÉ

Plaza Borda
This intimate and lively square is lined with charming old buildings. There are numerous restaurants and bars nearby. In addition, the area abounds with silver shops, filled with the high-quality pieces for which Taxco's many silversmiths are famous.

KEY

– – –   Suggested route

STAR SIGHTS

★ **Casa Humboldt**

★ **Iglesia de Santa Prisca**

0 meters   25
0 yards   25

Acapulco

★ Casa Humboldt
Formerly an inn, this beautifully maintained building is named after Baron von Humboldt, the German naturalist, who spent a night here in 1803. It contains a well-organized regional and historical museum.

VISITORS' CHECKLIST

Guerrero. 48,000. Av de los Plateros 104, (762) 622 01 31. Av de los Plateros 126, (762) 622 07 98. Santa Prisca y San Sebastián (Jan), Feria Nacional de la Plata (Nov/Dec).
Museo de la Platería (762) 622 06 58. Thu–Tue. **Casa Humboldt** (762) 622 55 01. Tue–Sun. **Museo Guillermo Spratling** (762) 622 16 60. Tue–Sun. Sun free.

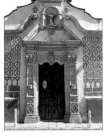

Cable car
Mexico City
ALLE JUAN RUIZ DE ALARCON
DELGADO
CALLE DE LA VERACRUZ
EL ARCO

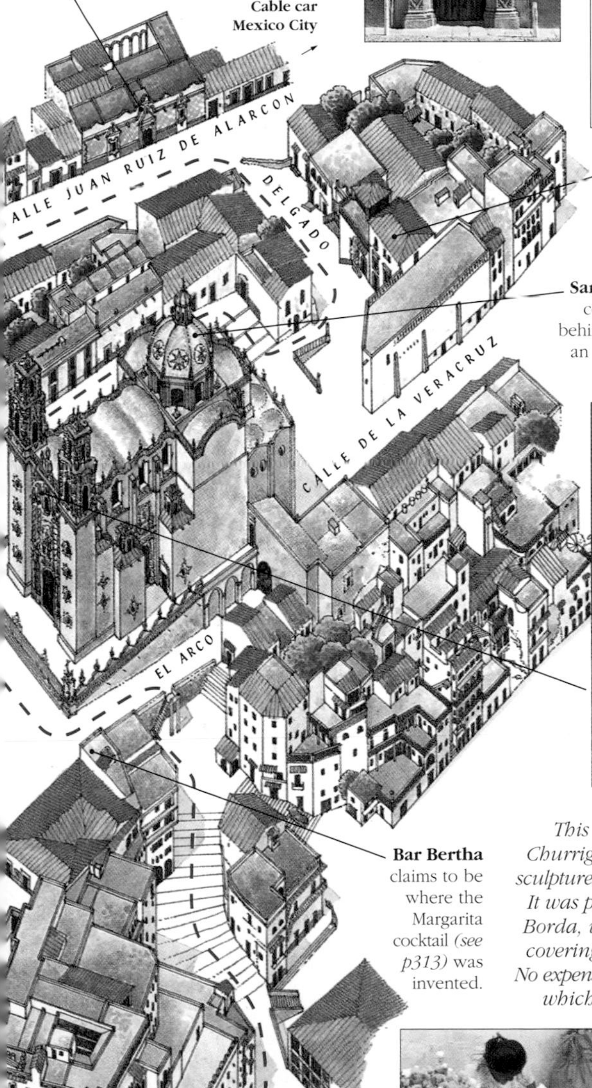

Museo Guillermo Spratling contains William Spratling's collection of pre-Columbian artifacts and works of art from around the world.

Santa Prisca's octagonal dome is covered with colorful tiles. Rising behind the church's twin towers, it is an unmistakable landmark that can be seen from all over the city.

★ Iglesia de Santa Prisca
This magnificent church, with its Churrigueresque façade and ornate sculptures, dominates the Plaza Borda. It was paid for by José (Joseph) de la Borda, who made his fortune by discovering important deposits of silver. No expense was spared in construction, which took seven years (1751–58).

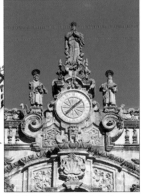

Bar Bertha claims to be where the Margarita cocktail *(see p313)* was invented.

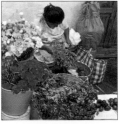

Local Market
Off the south side of the Plaza Borda is Taxco's bustling market. Stalls laden with fresh produce, basketware, and local crafts crowd the narrow steps.

The imposing façade of the
Catedral de la Asunción

Cuernavaca ⓮

Morelos. 🏛 338,000. 🚌
ℹ Av Morelos Sur 187, (777) 314 38
72. 🎭 Feria de la Flor (Easter), Feria
de Tlaltenango (Sep 8).
🌐 www.morelostravel.com

CUERNAVACA, inhabited since
1200 BC, is one of the
oldest cities in the country.
Originally called Cuauhnáhuac
("Place of the Whispering
Trees"), it was renamed Cuernavaca ("Cow's Horn") by the
Spanish. Today it is a popular
weekend destination for
visitors from Mexico City.

The **Palacio de Cortés** was
built by the Spanish on the site
of the Aztec pyramids they had
destroyed. It served as Cortés's
residence until his return to
Spain in 1540. Known for a
series of 1930 Diego Rivera
murals depicting Mexico's history, it also contains the
Museo Regional
Cuauhnáhuac, a
fine collection of
archaeological and
historical artifacts.

The fortress-like
**Catedral de la
Asunción**, dating
from the 1520s, has
refurbished murals
thought to have
been painted by
artists brought over
from China or the
Philippines in the
early days of Span-
ish trade. The
**Museo Robert
Brady**, situated in a
former cloister of
the cathedral, holds

the extensive art and craft collection of this American artist.

The well laid-out **Jardín
Borda**, created by the former
silver magnate José de la
Borda (see pp146–7) in the
18th century, became a popular retreat for the Emperor
Maximilian and his young
wife (see p53). The garden
includes a small museum.

To the east is the **Taller
Siqueiros**, which is dedicated
to the work of the
great Mexican
muralist (see p26).

ENVIRONS: About
25 km (16 miles)
northwest of the
town is the beau-
tiful **Lagunas de
Zempoala Park**,
with its six lakes
fringed by dense
forests. Only 10 km
(6 miles) of the 70
km **Cacahuamilpa
Caverns** have been
explored. Around
20 of the majestic
chambers, many
more than 40 meters (120 ft)
high, are illuminated.

Section from a Diego
Rivera mural in the
Palacio de Cortés

🏛 **Palacio de Cortés**
Avenida Leyva. 📞 (777) 312 81 71.
🔵 Tue–Sun. 🎟 Sun free. 📷
🏛 **Museo Robert Brady**
Netzahualcóyotl 4. 📞 (777) 318 85
54. 🔵 Tue–Sun. 🎟
♣ **Jardín Borda**
Av Morelos 271. 📞 (777) 312 92 37.
🔵 Tue–Sun. 🎟 Sun free. 📷 📷
🏛 **Taller Siqueiros**
Venus 7, Jardín de Cuernavaca.
📞 (777) 315 11 15. 🔵 daily. 📷

Tepoztlán ⓯

Morelos. 🏛 33,000. 🚌 🎭 Los
Tiznados (Jan 20 & 21), Carnival
(Feb/Mar), Reto al Tepozteco (Sep 8).

LYING IN A LUSH green valley,
Tepoztlán is surrounded
by spectacular volcanic rock
formations. A tiring but worth-
while climb above the town
stands the **Santuario del
Cerro Tepozteco**, a shrine
dedicated to
Tepoztecatl, the
ancient god of
pulque (see p313).
The dominant
building in the
town itself is the
massive, fortified
16th-century
**Ex-Convento
Dominico de la
Natividad**, whose
austere cloister still
has delightful mural
fragments. For lovers
of pre-Columbian
art, the **Museo de
Arte Prehispánico**
holds a small but
interesting collection, the
legacy of the poet Carlos
Pellicer (see p255).

ENVIRONS: The town of
Cuautla, 27 km (17 miles) to
the southeast, is the site of the
last resting place of Emiliano
Zapata, one of the heroes of
the Revolution (see p54).

🏛 **Museo de Arte
Prehispánico**
González. 📞 (739) 395 10 98.
🔵 Tue–Sun. 🎟

Surviving murals in the Ex-Convento Dominico de la Natividad, Tepoztlán

Popocatépetl and Iztaccíhuatl ⑯

Mexico State. Off Mex 115, 14 km
(9 miles) E of Amecameca.
(52 05 10 36 (updated reports).
🚌 Amecameca then taxi.

THE SNOW-CAPPED volcanoes of Popocatépetl, or "Popo," ("Smoking Mountain") and Iztaccíhuatl ("Sleeping Lady") are the second and third highest peaks in Mexico, standing at 5,465 m (17,930 ft) and 5,230 m (17,160 ft) respectively. On occasion, strong winds manage to blow the smog away, revealing these mountains as two of the country's most awesome sights.

According to legend, the warrior Popocatépetl fell in love with Iztaccíhuatl, an Aztec princess. To win her hand, he defeated a great rival in battle. Wrongly believing him to be dead, the princess herself then died of a broken heart. Legend has it that, in his grief, Popocatépetl turned himself and his princess into these two adjacent mountains. The outline of Iztaccíhuatl bears an uncanny resemblance to that of a sleeping woman.

The **Paso de Cortés**, a saddle between the two peaks accessible by car, is an ideal base for walks on Iztaccíhuatl, but ascents of the peak itself should be left to the experts. Access to Popocatépetl is currently not permitted due to the threat of volcanic activity.

Nuestra Señora de los Remedios, with Popocatépetl behind

The arcade on the western flank of Cholula's *zócalo*

Cholula ⑰

Puebla. 🏛 1,350,000. 🚌 ℹ 12 Orientecorner, 4 Norte, (222) 261 23 93. 📅 Carnival (Feb/Mar), Virgen de los Remedios (1st week of Sep).

BEFORE SUBJECTING it to one of the bloodiest massacres of the Conquest, Cortés described Cholula as "the most beautiful city outside Spain." In pre-Columbian times it had been a sacred city – a place of pilgrimage – and a large and important commercial center.

The arcade on the west side of Cholula's large *zócalo* (main square) shelters restaurants and cafés. Opposite is the fortified, Franciscan **Convento de San Gabriel**. Founded in 1529 on the site of a temple to Quetzalcoatl (see p265), the main church has a single nave with rib vaulting and Gothic tracery. Visitors can tour the monastic kitchen, dining rooms, cloisters, and sleeping areas. On the left of the atrium is the **Capilla Real**, built for Indian converts. It acquired its 49 mosque-like domes in the early part of the 18th century.

To the east is the **Zona Arqueológica**, a site which is dominated by the remains of the largest pyramid ever built in Mesoamerica, at 65 m (213 ft) high. Since the 1930s, archaeologists have dug 8 km (5 miles) of tunnels through this Great Pyramid, identifying at least four stages of

The impressive double gateway of San Gabriel, Cholula

construction between 200 BC and AD 800. Visitors enter the tunnels on the north side, and emerge several hundred meters later on the east.

Opposite the entrance to the tunnel is a museum with a large cut-away model of the pyramid and artifacts from the site. Digs on the south side have revealed the **Patio de los Altares**, an area of astounding acoustics, used for public ceremonies and probably the sacrifice of children. On top of the pyramid sits the 1874 church of **Nuestra Señora de los Remedios**. The wonderful view from the atrium takes in Puebla (see pp150–53), the volcanoes, and Cholula's many other churches.

ENVIRONS: The extraordinary folk-Baroque church of **Santa María Tonantzintla**, 5 km (3 miles) south of Cholula, has an interior that is bursting with colorful saints, fruit, angels, and cherubs. Begun in the 16th century, it took its Indian craftsmen 200 years to complete. The church of **San Francisco Acatepec** (see p25), 1.5 km (1 mile) farther south, has a façade entirely covered in typically colorful, handmade Talavera tiles (see p153).

🏛 **Convento de San Gabriel**
Corner of Calle 2 Sur & Av Morelos.
◻ daily. 🅰
🅰 **Zona Arqueólogica**
Av Morelos. ◻ Tue–Sun. 📷

Street-by-Street: Puebla ⑱

MEXICO'S FOURTH LARGEST CITY, Puebla is best known for the beautiful Talavera tiles that adorn its walls, domes, and interiors; for *mole poblano (see p308)*, Mexico's national dish, which originated here; and for being the site of an important battle on May 5, 1862 *(see p52)*.

The streets of the compact city center are lined with churches, mansions, and other handsome old buildings and are a delight to stroll around.

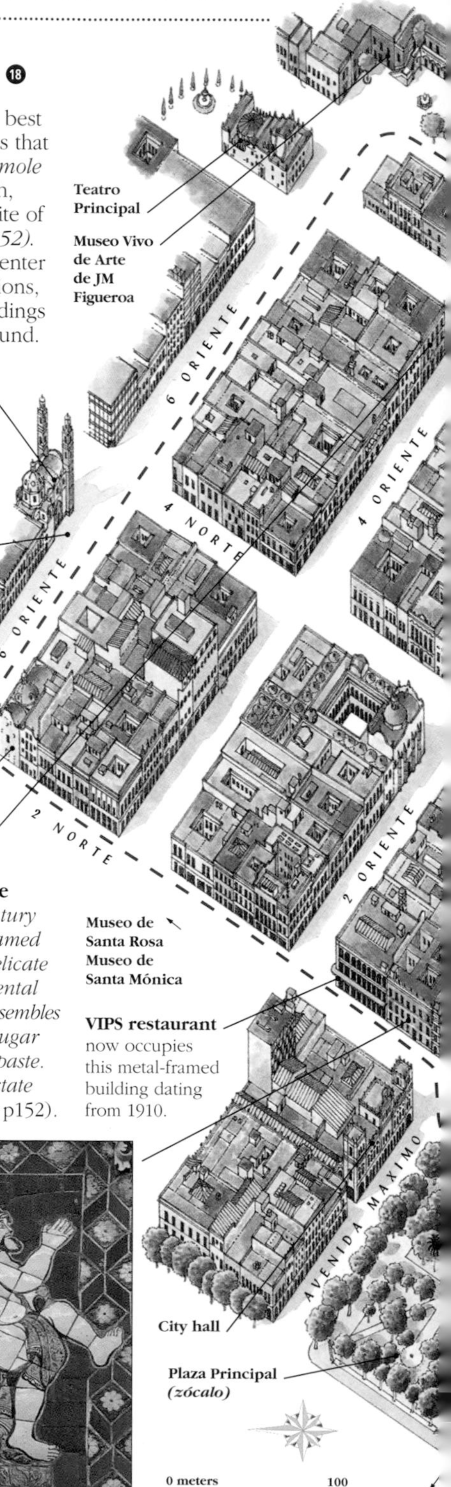

Teatro Principal

Museo Vivo de Arte de JM Figueroa

Templo de San Cristóbal
Built in the 17th century as part of an orphanage, this church is noted for its collection of colonial sculptures.

Calle 6 Oriente is known for its shops selling handmade candies, crystallized fruits, and *rompope (eggnog, see p312)*.

Museo de la Revolución
The Revolution of 1910 supposedly began in this house, which is now a museum (see p152).

Iglesia de Santa Clara

★ Casa del Alfeñique
This 18th-century house is so named because its delicate white ornamental plasterwork resembles alfeñique, a sugar and almond paste. It houses the state museum (see p152).

Museo de Santa Rosa
Museo de Santa Mónica

VIPS restaurant now occupies this metal-framed building dating from 1910.

Casa de los Muñecos
The façade of this house, built for an 18th-century mayor, is covered with decorative red tiles. Several panels show dancing figures.

City hall

Plaza Principal (zócalo)

STAR SIGHTS

★ **Casa del Alfeñique**

★ **Cathedral**

0 meters 100
0 yards 100

Museo Bello

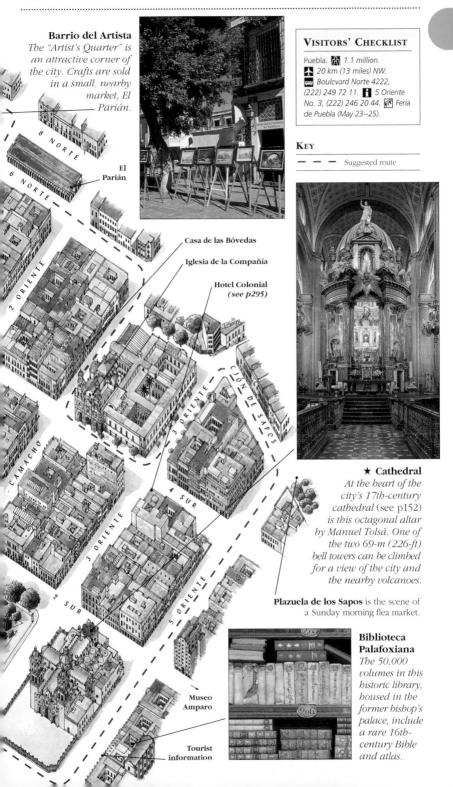

Barrio del Artista
The "Artist's Quarter" is an attractive corner of the city. Crafts are sold in a small, nearby market, El Parián.

El Parián

VISITORS' CHECKLIST

Puebla. 1.1 million.
20 km (13 miles) NW.
Boulevard Norte 4222,
(222) 249 72 11. 5 Oriente
No. 3, (222) 246 20 44. Feria
de Puebla (May 23–25).

KEY

‒ ‒ ‒ Suggested route

Casa de las Bóvedas

Iglesia de la Compañía

Hotel Colonial
(see p295)

★ Cathedral
At the heart of the city's 17th-century cathedral (see p152) is this octagonal altar by Manuel Tolsá. One of the two 69-m (226-ft) bell towers can be climbed for a view of the city and the nearby volcanoes.

Plazuela de los Sapos is the scene of a Sunday morning flea market.

Museo Amparo

Tourist information

Biblioteca Palafoxiana
The 50,000 volumes in this historic library, housed in the former bishop's palace, include a rare 16th-century Bible and atlas.

Exploring Puebla

FOUNDED IN 1531, Puebla was the first settlement in Mexico to be laid out on a grid pattern by Spanish colonialists, rather than elaborating on an existing settlement. Modern Puebla is a state capital and university city that has preserved its rich heritage of colonial architecture. In recent decades many of its finest buildings have been transformed into museums displaying collections of colonial art and regional crafts, as well as historical and archaeological finds from all over Mexico.

Ornate onyx washbasin situated in the sacristy of the city's cathedral

🛡 Cathedral

Juan de Palafox, Bishop of Puebla, consecrated the city's cathedral (the second largest in Mexico after the one in the capital) in April 1649. It is built in a combination of Renaissance and Baroque styles.

The pillars around the large atrium – the plaza in front of the building – are surmounted by statues of angels, symbols of the town whose full name is Puebla de los Angeles ("People of the Angels").

Inside there are five naves and 14 side chapels. The main altar, known as the *ciprés*, was designed by Manuel Tolsá in 1797. Standing on an octagonal base, it consists of two superimposed "temples" supported by eight pairs of Corinthian columns, crowned by a tiled dome in imitation of that of St. Peter's in Rome. Behind the *ciprés* is the Altar de los Reyes whose dome was painted in 1688 by Cristóbal de Villalpando.

🏛 Museo Regional de la Revolución Mexicana

6 Oriente No. 206. 📞 *(222) 242 10 76.* ⏰ *Tue–Sun.* 📷 *Tue free.*
The conflict that supposedly sparked the Mexican Revolution in 1910 took place in this house. Aquiles Serdán, his family, and about 17 others, all liberal activists who opposed Porfirio Díaz's dictatorship *(see p53)*, resisted arrest and were killed by soldiers after a long gun battle. The house is now a museum of revolutionary memorabilia.

🏛 Casa del Alfeñique

4 Oriente No. 416. 📞 *(222) 232 42 96.* ⏰ *Tue–Sat.* 📷 ♿
Puebla's state museum now occupies this Baroque mansion, with its ornate red and white façade. Exhibits include carriages, paintings, costumes, and ornately furnished rooms.

🏛 Museo Amparo

2 Sur No. 708. 📞 *(222) 229 38 50.* ⏰ *Wed–Mon.* 📷 *except Mon.* ♿
Occupying a restored 18th-century hospital, this museum houses one of the finest collections of pre-Columbian and colonial art in the country.

The first section is divided into eight rooms devoted to pre-Columbian art. An introductory room includes a timeline comparing Mesoamerican cultures *(see pp44–5)* with contemporary cultures from around the world. A multilingual audiovisual system gives information on the artistic techniques employed, and the significance of the pieces in these rooms. The first section ends in an area dedicated to the collection's finest pieces, such as a Huasteca necklace of 17 tiny skulls carved out of bone, an Olmec statue known as *The Thinker*, and a Maya altar from Palenque.

Stone statue on display in Museo Amparo

In the second section, the rooms are filled with colonial pieces, starting with a painting of the Virgin of Guadalupe in a silver frame. Other exhibits here include Manuel Tolsá's model for the altar in the cathedral, and an unusual 18th-century statue of St. Anthony of Padua. A tradition in Puebla is for girls searching for a partner to turn the statue on its head; when they get married, they turn him back on his feet.

🏛 Museo Bello

Zetina Gonzalez y 5 de Mayo. 📞 *(222) 232 47 20.* ⏰ *Tue–Sun.*
Without ever leaving his beloved city of Puebla, for fear he would not return, 19th-century industrialist José Luis Bello, owner of cigar and textile factories, managed to assemble this eclectic collection. There are some 2,500 pieces, and the emphasis is very much on variety rather than a particular theme. Exhibits include a collection of locks and keys; Chinese porcelain and ivory; gold and silver pocket watches; European furniture; and 16th- to 18th-century Talavera pottery in colorful, earthy designs.

One of the exquisitely ornate rooms in the Museo Bello

⊞ Taller Uriarte Talavera
4 Poniente No. 911. ☎ *(222) 242 54 07.* ◯ *Mon–Fri.* ▢ ▣
This Talavera pottery work-shop offers guided tours to visitors. The production process can be seen through from the early purifying of the clay, to the painting, glazing, and final firing of the piece.

⛪ Iglesia de Santo Domingo
Corner of 5 de Mayo and 4 Poniente. ☎ *(222) 242 36 43.* ◯ *daily.*
One of the most elaborately decorated chapels in Mexico is contained in this Baroque church. Built in the second half of the 17th century, the **Capilla del Rosario** is a riot of gilt carving. Along the walls, grotesque heads spew golden vines whose tendrils twist and twine to form the frames of six paintings depicting the mysteries of the rosary. The dome is no less ornate with saints, cherubs, dancing angels, and a heavenly choir. The main church has a fine onyx pulpit.

Highly decorated dome of the Capilla del Rosario

⛫ Museo de Santa Rosa
14 Poniente No. 305. ☎ *(222) 232 92 40.* ◯ *Tue–Sun.* ▨ *Tue free.*
Six blocks north of the city center, in Puebla's market area, is the 17th-century convent of Santa Rosa. The building has served at different times as an Augustinian nunnery, hospital for the mentally ill, and tenement for more than 1,500 people. It was salvaged in 1968 and converted into a museum to display crafts produced in the state of Puebla.
Worth seeing in particular among the exhibits is the huge tree of life *(see pp330–31)* from Izúcar de Matamoros, which represents an Indian interpretation of the story of Adam and Eve. There are also

Kitchen of the former convent of Santa Rosa, now a museum

brightly colored embroideries, carnival masks, and furniture finely inlaid with mother-of-pearl, malachite, and bone.
The highlight of the Santa Rosa museum, however, is the vaulted kitchen, which is entirely covered with tiles. Tradition has it that the famous *mole poblano (see p308)* was invented by the Augustinian nuns in this atmospheric room.

⛫ Museo de Santa Mónica
18 Poniente No. 103. ☎ *(222) 232 01 78.* ◯ *Tue–Sun.* ▨ *Sun free.*
Built around an attractively decorated tile-and-brick cloister, the 17th-century Convento de Santa Mónica was used to hide nuns during the years of clerical persecution after the 1857 Reform Laws. With the help of hidden doors and concealed passages, the nuns lived here

in secret until 1933, when they were finally evicted. The building is now the Museum of Religious Art. As well as paintings, sculptures, and ecclesiastical artifacts, there is a macabre collection of instruments and clothing that were used by the nuns for the purpose of self-mortification.

♣ Cerro de Guadalupe
2 km (1.5 miles) NE of city center.
This large park, which contains two forts and several museums, marks the site of the historic Battle of Puebla. On May 5, 1862 a small Mexican army under General Ignacio Zaragoza defeated a much larger French army that had invaded Mexico. The victory proved short-lived, but the day has still become one of national celebration.

TALAVERA POTTERY

The colorful, glazed pottery so characteristic of Puebla is a fusion of Arabic, Spanish, Italian, and Chinese influences. The earliest pieces, with cobalt blue designs on a white background, are typically Moorish. The technique was brought to Mexico in the 16th century by Dominican monks from Talavera de la Reina, Spain. New colors, such as green, black, and yellow, were introduced from Italy in the 17th century, while pieces imported from China and the Philippines inspired floral and animal designs. It takes six months to produce an authentic piece of Talavera pottery.

Talavera jars for sale in Puebla

Cacaxtla ⓭

Tlaxcala. Off Mex 119, 30 km (19 miles) NW of Puebla. 🚍 *(246) 416 00 00.*
🚌 *from Tlaxcala.* 🕐 *daily.* 🎫 *Sun free.* 📷 *reserve in advance.* ♿
🌐 *www.inah.gob.mx*

MEANING "the place where rain dies in the earth," Cacaxtla was the capital of the Olmeca-Xicalanca, a Gulf Coast group who dominated this area from the 7th–10th centuries AD. Some of Mexico's best preserved murals, probably painted by Maya artists, were discovered here in 1974.

The 22-m (72-ft) *Mural de la Batalla* depicts a violent battle between jaguar and eagle warriors, with no fewer than 48 human figures in vibrant colors. Glyphs *(see pp46–7)* are inserted among the characters.

Two other extraordinary murals are in Edificio A. The *Hombre-jaguar* represents a lord dressed in a jaguar skin standing on a "jaguar-snake." Surrounding him is a border of sea creatures. Also in Edificio A, the *Hombre-ave* is a "bird-man" painted in black with an eagle headdress. He holds a blue serpent staff and stands on a plumed snake. Heads of corn around the edge have small human faces.

ENVIRONS: Just 2 km (1 mile) away is another Olmeca-Xicalanca site, **Xochitécatl**, whose platforms and pyramids date from about 1000 BC.

The vivid and well-preserved
Hombre-ave **mural at Cacaxtla**

The richly gilded interior of the Basílica de Ocotlán, near Tlaxcala

Tlaxcala ⓴

Tlaxcala. 🔢 *73,000.* 🚍 ℹ️ *Cnr of Av Juárez & Lardizábal, (246) 465 09 60.* 🎭 *Carnival (Feb/Mar), Virgen de Ocotlán (3rd Mon of May).*

OFTEN SEEN AS a provincial backwater, the city of Tlaxcala is, in fact, one of the country's colonial treasures. Its seclusion is partly due to the historical independence of the local people, the Tlaxcaltecas. During the Conquest they took up arms against their old enemy, the Aztecs, joining Cortés to conquer Tenochtitlán.

The so-called Ciudad Roja (Red City) is dominated by earthy tones of terracotta and ocher. In the center is the spacious tree-filled *zócalo* (main plaza) with its bandstand and fountain, the latter given by King Philip IV of Spain in 1646.

The colorful and richly decorated brick, tile, and stucco façade of the **Parroquia de San José** dominates the northwest corner of the square. At the entrance to this church two fonts have pedestals depicting Camaxtli, the ancient Tlaxcalan god of war and hunting, and the Spanish imperial coat of arms. Beside the altar is a 17th-century painting showing the baptism of a Tlaxcalan chief, watched by Cortés and his mistress, La Malinche.

The 16th-century **Palacio de Gobierno** flanks the north side of the *zócalo*. Exterior details include the French-style stucco added at the start of the 20th century. Inside, murals by artist Desiderio Hernández relate the history of Tlaxcala.

Across Plaza Xicoténcatl to the south, a path leads uphill to the **cathedral**, which has a stunning Moorish-style coffered ceiling and contains the font used to baptize the four local chiefs who allied with Cortés. The **Museo Regional**, in the cloisters next door, has a collection of pre-Columbian

The ornate bandstand in Tlaxcala's shady and peaceful *zócalo*

◁ **Rich stuccowork in the dome of the** *camarín* **at Basílica de Ocotlán**

Decoration in Basílica de Ocotlán

pieces, including a large stone figure of Camaxtli, the god of war. The two rooms upstairs are dedicated to colonial art.

The **Museo de Artes y Tradiciones Populares** (west of the *zócalo*) is described as a living museum. Here craftspeople demonstrate techniques involved in their work.

Environs: On a hill above the city, the twin-towered **Basílica de Ocotlán** is one of the most lavish Churrigueresque churches in Mexico, comparable with those in Tepotzotlán *(see pp140–3)* and Taxco *(see pp146–7)*. The 18th-century façade combines hexagonal brick and white-stucco decoration. The interior and adjoining *camarín* are an explosion of Baroque giltwork. Pilgrims flock here in May for the procession of the Virgin.

Nearby villages include **Santa Ana Chiauhtempan**, known for its embroidery and weaving, and **Tizatlán**, where a 16th-century chapel with frescoes stands beside the remains of a pre-Columbian palace.

In **Huamantla**, 45 km (28 miles) east of Tlaxcala, the 16th-century Convento de San Francisco has a polychrome Churrigueresque altarpiece dedicated to the Virgin of Charity. The Virgin is celebrated at a popular fiesta held here in August *(see p31)*.

🏛 **Museo Regional**
Ex-Convento de San Francisco, off Plaza Xicoténcatl. ☎ *(246) 462 02 62.* 🕒 *Tue–Sun.* 🎟 *Sun free.*

🏛 **Museo de Artes y Tradiciones Populares**
Boulevard Emilio Sánchez Piedras 1. ☎ *(246) 462 23 37.* 🕒 *Tue–Sun.* 🎟 ✋ *reserve in advance.* 🛍

Cantona ㉑

Puebla. 30 km (19 miles) NE of Oriental via 4 km (2.5 miles) of unpaved road from Tepeyahualco. 🚌 *tours from Puebla.* 🕒 *Tue–Sun.* 🎟
[W] www.inah.gob.mx

The remains of what was once a major city occupy a vast area of low hills beside a lava field. Only ten percent of the well-maintained site, which is dotted with yuccas and pine trees, can be visited.

Little is known about the history of Cantona but it was probably inhabited from about AD 700–950. One of the most built-up of all Mesoamerican cities, it may have supported a population of 80,000.

A full visit will take at least two hours. A signposted route from the parking lot sets off on one of the ***calzadas***, or cobbled streets, which connect the various parts of Cantona. This leads past the ruins of houses and patios before climbing to the **Acrópolis**, the cluster of public buildings at the heart of the city. Soon the route reaches the first of 24 **ballcourts** excavated here – more than at any other site in Mexico. Of these, 12 are unusual in that they form parts of complexes with a pyramid at one end and the playing area at the other.

The path reaches the **Plaza Oriente** and then loops back to **El Palacio** and the **Plaza Central**. The return to the parking lot is along a second *calzada*.

Platforms and a pyramid at Cantona, interspersed with yucca plants

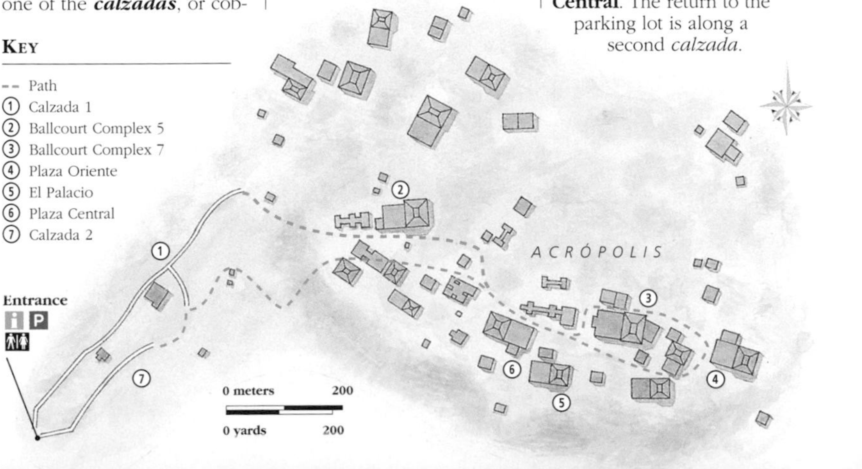
Key
Path
1 Calzada 1
2 Ballcourt Complex 5
3 Ballcourt Complex 7
4 Plaza Oriente
5 El Palacio
6 Plaza Central
7 Calzada 2
Entrance
ACRÓPOLIS
0 meters 200
0 yards 200

NORTHERN MEXICO

Baja California Norte • Baja California Sur
Chihuahua • Coahuila • Durango • Nuevo León
Sinaloa • Sonora • Tamaulipas

With its stark mountains *and arid plains, giant cactuses and men on horseback, the North is the Mexico of popular imagination. Sparsely populated and occupying over half the country's landmass, it stretches from the magical beaches of Baja California to the marshes and islands of the Gulf of Mexico.*

Two mountain ranges, the eastern and western Sierra Madre, cross this great territory from north to south. Between them lies the vast Chihuahuan Desert, the largest in North America. To the northwest is the Sonoran Desert, which extends down the beautiful 1,300-km (800-mile) long peninsula of Baja California. It is here that the North's best beaches are located.

Although often austere, the mountains conceal beautiful places where cool pine forests, placid lakes, and thunderous waterfalls can be found. The Sierra Tarahumara holds forested ravines, deeper than the Grand Canyon, which are traversed by one of the world's most spectacular railroads.

Though no great pre-Columbian civilization ever developed in this region, the superb pottery and unique architecture of the Paquimé culture and the mysterious cave paintings of Baja California hold their own fascination. Present-day indigenous survivors, like the Tarahumara people of the Sierra Madre Occidental, cling to a traditional way of life quite apart from modern Mexican society.

The region is delimited to the north by the 1,950-mile (3,140-km) border with the United States, which for much of its length follows the Río Grande (known as the Río Bravo in Mexico). Receiving influences from the cultures on either side of it, the border region is almost a third country, defined by its unique blend of languages, music, and food.

Even as far south as Monterrey, Mexico's industrial heartland, the influence of the gringo is still strongly felt. But here the accumulated wealth and economic power – enshrined in the glass and concrete of bold modern architecture – are purely and soberly Mexican in character.

Local men in the town of Hidalgo del Parral

◁ Desert landscape in flower near Bahía de los Ángeles in Baja California

Exploring Northern Mexico

DISTANCES INVOLVED when traveling between sights in the region should not be underestimated. Sun worshipers will find some of Mexico's finest beaches on the 800-mile (1,300-km) peninsula of Baja California, which also has spectacular desert scenery and varied wildlife, including the gray whale. On the mainland, Mazatlán is the closest major beach resort to the US border and a popular retreat from northern winters. Inland, the vertiginous gorges of the Copper Canyon are great for hiking. Elsewhere, you can walk the streets of western film sets near Durango or take in the culture and nightlife of modern cities such as Tijuana and Monterrey.

Wildflowers and cactuses, common in Northern Mexico

SAN DIEGO
TIJUANA
MEXICALI
1
ENSENADA
2
SAN LUIS RÍO COLORADO
5
PUERTO PEÑASCO
Tucson
TRANSPENINSULAR HIGHWAY
3
NOGALES
DOUGLAS
15
7
AGUA PRIETA
2
CABORCA
PAQUIMÉ
15
12
10
BUENAVENTURA
BAHÍA DE LOS ÁNGELES
4
HERMOSILLO
14
16
BAHÍA KINO
YÉCORA
GUERRERO NEGRO
5
GUAYMAS
15
VIZCAÍNO BIOSPHERE RESERVE
6
SAN IGNACIO
7
8
SANTA ROSALÍA
CREEL
19
COPPER CANYON
21
MULEGÉ
9
22
ÁLAMOS
20
BATOPILAS
LOS MOCHIS
10
LORETO
VILLA INSURGENTES
15
CULIACÁN
LA PAZ
11
SAN JOSÉ DEL CABO
12
13
CABO SAN LUCAS

PACIFIC OCEAN

BAJA CALIFORNIA

GULF OF CALIFORNIA (SEA OF CORTÉS)

SEE ALSO
- *Where to Stay* pp296–8
- *Where to Eat* pp319–20

Lovers' Beach at Cabo San Lucas, cut off by rocks and accessible only by boat

0 kilometers 200

0 miles 100

SIGHTS AT A GLANCE

Alamos **22**
Bahía de los Angeles **4**
Batopilas **20**
Cabo San Lucas **13**
Chihuahua **16**
Ciudad Cuauhtémoc **17**
Cañón del Cobre *pp176–7* **21**
Creel **19**
Durango **24**

Ensenada **2**
Guerrero Negro **5**
Hermosillo **14**
Hidalgo del Parral **18**
Loreto **10**
Mazatlán **23**
Monterrey **26**
Mulegé **9**
Paquimé **15**

La Paz **11**
Saltillo **25**
San Ignacio **7**
San José del Cabo **12**
Santa Rosalía **8**
Tijuana **1**
Transpeninsular Highway **3**
Vizcaíno Biosphere
Reserve **6**

GETTING AROUND

The region's road network is generally good, but distances can be huge and toll roads expensive. Avoid nighttime driving and beware of deteriorations in the road surface and *vados* (fords), which – even when dry – require a slower speed. Buses offer an alternative to pricey air travel and are usually comfortable. One of the few passenger train services still running is the spectacular Chihuahua-al-Pacífico (*see p176*). Several car-ferry services link mainland Mexico with Baja California.

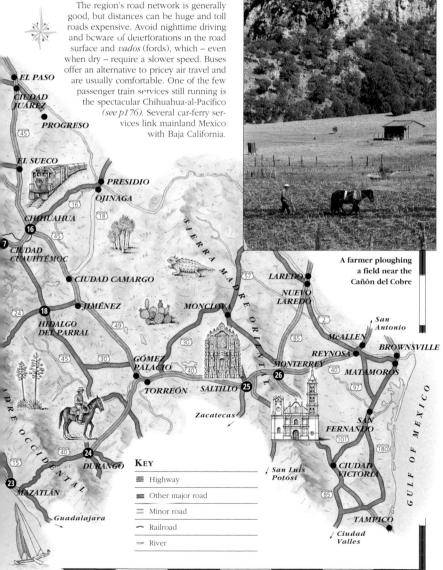

A farmer ploughing a field near the Cañón del Cobre

KEY

- Highway
- Other major road
- Minor road
- Railroad
- River

The OMNIMAX theater at the Centro Cultural Tijuana

Tijuana ❶

Baja California Norte. 👥 *1,212,000.*
✈ 🚌 🚇 *Paseo de los Héroes
10289, (664) 634 63 30.*
🎭 *Aniversario de Tijuana (Jul).*

JUST OVER THE BORDER from San
Diego (California), Tijuana is
the quintessential border city
and claims to be the world's
busiest crossing, with up to
35 million visitors a year.

Towering skyscrapers and
massive shopping malls are a
measure of its modernity. Most
people come here to shop or
party. The best shopping is in
the quiet bazaars on either side
of Avenida Revolución. Painted
pottery, leather boots, silver

jewelry, mezcal, and tequila
are the most popular buys.
Customers are encouraged to
barter with the stallholders. The
vibrant nightlife is also centered on Avenida Revolución,
where there are plenty of
restaurants and cafés.

Tijuana also has a few cultural attractions, the main one
being the futuristic **Centro
Cultural Tijuana** beside the
river. Concerts and art exhibitions are held here, and there
is an OMNIMAX theater that
shows movies about Mexico.

🏛 **Centro Cultural Tijuana**
Cnr of Paseo de los Héroes and Mina.
📞 *(664) 687 96 00.* ⏰ *Tue–Sun.* 🔒
reserve in advance. 💿 🅿 🎬 *movies.*

THE MEXICO-US BORDER

The US and Mexico are
separated by a land
border that runs for
3,140 km (1,950 miles)
between the Pacific
Ocean and the Gulf of
Mexico. There are 23
crossings between
Tijuana in the west
and Matamoros in the
east. Most US citizens
who cross the border
are on day-trips for a

Signs and a souvenir stall mark the
Mexico-US border crossing at Tijuana

taste of the exotic, to
shop, or to enjoy themselves in a country where their dollar
goes further. For Mexicans, however, the border is the gateway to "El Norte," the promised land of high salaries and
consumer goods. The meeting of the two worlds creates a
vibrant mix of cultures, but it has its down-side – most visible
in the steadily lengthening and constantly patrolled "wall"
– the barrier erected by the US to deter illegal immigrants.

Ensenada ❷

Baja California Norte. 👥 *370,000.*
✈ 🚌 🛈 *Blvd Lázaro Cárdenas 1477,
(646) 172 30 22.* 🎭 *Carnival (Feb/
Mar), Vendimia Wine Festival (Aug).*

THIS BUSY PORT and cruise-
ship destination is popular
with fishermen, surfers, and
divers. The scenic drive from
Tijuana takes just 90 minutes,
past curving bays and red
bluffs that hint at the spectacular desert landscape farther
south. A lookout just before
the city offers a view over the
bay with its flocks of seabirds.

City sights include the twin-
towered church of **Nuestra
Señora de Guadalupe** and
the giant sculpted heads of
three national heroes – Juárez,
Hidalgo, and Carranza – on
the Plaza Cívica. The **Riviera
del Pacífico**, near the waterfront, was a hotel in the 1930s
but now houses exhibitions.
In the lobby is a remarkable
3-D mural showing the 18th-
century Jesuit missions of
the Californias. **Bodegas de
Santo Tomás**, which makes
some of Baja's finest wine
from grapes grown in vineyards south of town, offers
daily tours and wine tasting.

Ensenada's small but lively
"party district" clusters around
the old-fashioned **Hussong's
Cantina** on Avenida López
Mateos. This bar was founded
in the 19th century by the
German Hussong family, still a
powerful force in the city.
Visitors can buy a Hussong's
T-shirt in the Hussong mall.

ENVIRONS: The beaches in
town are not recommended,
but a few miles south are the
clean and pleasant **Playa El
Faro** and **Playa Estero**, both
of which have superb sunsets.
Farther south is **La Bufadora**,
where a cleft in the rock produces a spout of sea foam,
especially when the waves
swell in windy weather. The
best diving in the area is here.

About 90 km (56 miles)
inland of Ensenada is **Parque
Nacional Constitución de
1857**, reached by a winding
road among hills made of huge
boulders. Here, surrounded by
pine trees, is tranquil **Laguna
Hanson**, a haven for birds.

The heads of three national heroes on Plaza Cívica in Ensenada

🏛 **Riviera del Pacífico**
Corner of Blvd Costera and Av Riviera.
【 *(646) 176 43 10.* ◯ *Mon–Sat.* ♿
🍷 **Bodegas de Santo Tomás**
Av Miramar 666. 【 *(646) 178 25 09.* ◯ *Mon–Sat.* 📷 📹 📱

Transpeninsular Highway ❾

Baja California Norte and Sur. Mex 1, Tijuana to Cabo San Lucas. 🚌 *serving the whole highway.*

THE TWO EXTREMES of Baja California are linked by one highway, the two-lane Mex 1, which runs 1,700 km (1,060 miles) from Tijuana to Cabo San Lucas (*see p169*). There are few places worth stopping for on the long drive, but the desert landscapes of the north

do have an austere beauty. The **Parque Nacional San Pedro Mártir**, reached via a side road 140 km (87 miles) south of Ensenada, includes the 3,095-m (10,154-ft) snowcapped peak, Picacho del Diablo. Farther south, near the truck stop of Cataviña, is the so-called **Rocky Desert**, with its jumble of massive boulders and wide variety of cactus species.

Bahía de los Angeles ❹

Baja California Norte. 🏛 *450.*

LOCATED ON THE beautiful bay of the same name, and reached by a paved, if rather rutted, 68-km (42-mile) spur road off Mex 1, Bahía de los Angeles is a peaceful spot even by Baja standards. Popular with sportfishing enthusiasts, it also offers opportunities for diving and kayaking around the numerous islands in the bay. Other attractions include a sea turtle conservation project and trips across a spectacular desert landscape to see Indian rock paintings and the well-preserved San Borja mission. Boats are available to visit various offshore islands.

Desert scenery beside the Transpeninsular Highway south of Cataviña

FIESTAS OF NORTHERN MEXICO

Easter *(Mar/Apr)*, Cusarare and Norogachi (Chihuahua). The most important ceremony of the Tarahumara Indians re-enacts the Crucifixion story as a battle between "soldiers" and evil "pharisees," the latters' bodies often painted with white clay. It is accompanied by singing and dancing.

Tarahumara Indians, taking part in Easter celebrations

Carnival *(Feb/Mar)*, La Paz. Thought by some to be the best in Mexico, the carnival at La Paz consists of six days of parades, feasting, music, and cockfights. Mazatlán also hosts a spectacular party.
Fiesta de las Flores *(1st week of May)*, Nogales (Sonora). As this festival coincides with the anniversary of the Battle of Puebla (May 5), floats display both flowers and battle motifs.
Día de la Marina *(Jun 1)*, Guaymas (Sonora). Mock naval battles and spectacular fireworks commemorate the Mexican marines.
Nuestra Señora del Refugio *(Jul 4)*, Durango. The highlight here is the fascinating Matachines dance, performed by men wearing long animal-skin tunics, feathers in their hair, and wooden-soled sandals.
Vendimia Wine Festival *(Aug)*, Ensenada. Growers and producers show off their wares in Mexico's principal wine region.

Guerrero Negro ❺

Baja California Sur. 🏃 10,000. ✈ 🚌

GUERRERO NEGRO, "Black Warrior," is named after a whaling ship that ran aground in a lagoon near the town in the middle of the 19th century. The lagoon is the main breeding ground of the California gray whale – which most visitors come here to see. It also provides the raw material for the world's largest sea-salt operation, which environmentalists say may threaten the long-term future of the whales, only recently brought back from the brink of extinction. Seven million tons of salt per year is produced from

Sea salt leaving the evaporation works south of Guerrero Negro

thousands of evaporation ponds south of the town, and barges take the washed salt to the island of Isla Cedros, where it is transferred to ocean-going ships. The island itself remains almost unspoiled and supports unusual plant species and the endangered Cedros mule deer. Isla Cedros can be reached from Guerrero Negro by a light aircraft that makes the crossing twice a week.

Vizcaíno Biosphere Reserve ❻

Baja California Sur. Mex 1, S of Guerrero Negro. 🚌 Guerrero Negro.

COVERING 25,000 sq km (9,600 sq miles), this preserve is claimed to be the largest protected natural area in Latin America. It stretches from the Peninsula de Vizcaíno across Baja California to the east coast. The whale

Horse and rider, Sierra de San Francisco

sanctuaries of Laguna Ojo de Liebre and Laguna San Ignacio fall within its boundaries, as do the islands of Natividad, Asunción, and San Roque, part of the Sierra de San Francisco, and – in the east – the triple volcano of Las Tres Vírgenes.

Ranging from coastal mangroves and sand dunes to arid upland plateaus and the occasional fresh-water oasis, the preserve's ecosystems harbor a wide variety of species. Apart from the whales, other interesting animals are the endangered bighorn sheep (*borrego cimarrón*), the pronghorn

WHALE-WATCHING IN GUERRERO NEGRO

Two dozen species of cetaceans are found off the coasts of Baja California, from the small, endangered *vaquita*, confined to the northern reaches of the Sea of Cortés, to the world's largest animal, the blue whale. The best place to see these magnificent creatures is at Guerrero Negro, where the most common species, the California gray whale, can be seen in February and March, either from the shore or, better still, from a small boat.

A curious whale approaching two boatloads of enthusiasts, Guerrero Negro

The California gray whale (Eschrichtius robustus), *makes one of the longest migrations of any mammal. After a 9,500-km (6,000-mile) trip from Alaska, it calves in the warm lagoons of Mexico's Pacific coast. Once almost extinct, the species has recovered, and its numbers are now rising.*

How to See the Whales
The whales can be viewed with binoculars from several vantage points on the shore, such as the one reached by a dirt road from Mex 1 approximately 8 km (5 miles) south of Guerrero Negro. A better option is to go on an organized dinghy trip lasting 2–3 hours. Choose a reputable company that will not approach the whales too closely.

One such is Malarrimo, which has an office next to its restaurant (*see p319*) on the same side of the road as Vanessa's Store. An alternative is to strike a deal with a local fisherman to take you out in his boat. Farther south in Baja California you can often see whales at Laguna San Ignacio, Bahía de Magdalena, on the eastern side of the peninsula between Loreto and La Paz, and at Cabo San Lucas.

ANCIENT CAVE PAINTINGS OF BAJA CALIFORNIA

The cave paintings of Baja California have been compared with the aboriginal art of Australia and prehistoric paintings in the caves of France and Spain. When 18th-century Jesuit missionaries asked about the origin of the paintings, the local Cochimí Indians attributed them to a race of giants who had come from the north. It is now thought that ancestors of the Cochimí themselves painted the images. Their exact age is unknown, but some may date from 1200 BC. The complexity of the beliefs suggested by the paintings has led to a reassessment of the supposedly "primitive" hunter-gatherer society encountered by the Spanish on their arrival.

Cave Paintings
The images, usually in black and red, depict human figures with their arms raised, various animals, and abstract designs of unknown significance.

Painting of hunters and prey in a cave near San Ignacio

antelope, elephant seals, and several kinds of sea turtle. The Laguna San Ignacio (reached from the town of San Ignacio) holds what is believed to be the densest breeding colony of ospreys in the world. Herons, egrets, brown pelicans, and various other seabirds can also be spotted here.

Much of the interior of the preserve, with its strangely-shaped *cirio* (or "boojum") trees and giant Mexican cereus *(see p171)*, is practically inaccessible, but a passable road leads up the Peninsula de Vizcaíno to Bahía Tortugas.

San Ignacio ⓻

Baja California Sur, 🏛 750 🚌

STANDING AMONG thousands of date palms, the church at San Ignacio is one of the most imposing and best-preserved missions in Baja California. Although originally founded by Jesuits in 1728, before their expulsion from Spanish America, the church seen today was actually built in 1786 by Dominicans, with money from the queen of Spain. Its whitewashed Baroque façade, with masonry details in reddish lava stone, holds four polygonal windows and four niches containing carvings of saints. St. Peter and St. Paul flank the main door, with its intricately carved lintel. The interior has original furniture and altar-pieces, as well as a beautiful main altar decorated with 18th-century oil paintings.

In the canyons near San Ignacio are the ancient Indian cave paintings. The **Cueva del Ratón** (Cave of the Mouse) is the easiest to reach, via a turnoff to San Francisco de la Sierra, 45 km (28 miles) north on the Transpeninsular *(see p163)*. However, the most spectacular and best-preserved paintings are to be found in the **Cueva de las Flechas** (Cave of the Arrows) and the **Cueva Pintada** (Painted Cave). You must be accompanied by an approved guide – a visit to the last-named sites in the San Pablo canyon involves a two- or three-day camping trip with mules. A small **museum** in San Ignacio has exhibits on the cave paintings.

🏛 **San Ignacio Museum**
Prof. Gilberto Valdivia Péna. 📞 *(615) 154 02 22.* 🕐 *Nov–Apr: daily; May–Oct: Tue–Sat.*

The 18th-century mission church at San Ignacio

The arid landscape of the Sierra de San Francisco, north of San Ignacio ▷

Santa Rosalía ❽

Baja California Sur. 🔊 *10,500*. 🚌
🚢 📷 *Santa Rosalía (Sep 4)*.

THIS SMALL TOWN was founded
by a French copper-mining
company in the 1880s. The
copper ran out, and the company moved on in the 1950s,
but engines and rolling stock
from the mine railroad, along
with some of the mine installations, can still be seen.

Many of Santa Rosalía's
buildings are two-story, timber
structures with verandas, which
give the town a strangely
Caribbean look. Another curi-
osity is the **Iglesia de Santa
Bárbara**, a prefabricated,
metal-framed church designed
by Gustave Eiffel, of Eiffel
Tower fame, and shipped
here in 1895. The waterfront
walk, the Andador Costero, is
a pleasant place for a stroll.

Overlooking the town is a
small mining museum, the
Museo Histórico Minero.

🏛 **Museo Histórico Minero**
Jean-Michel Cousteau.
🕐 *Mon–Sat*. 📷

**Santa Rosalía's Iglesia de Santa
Bárbara, designed by Gustave Eiffel**

Mulegé ❾

Baja California Sur. 🔊 *46,000*. 🚌
📷 *Santa Rosalía (Sep 4)*.

THIS ATTRACTIVE town has a
lovely church, founded by
Jesuit missionaries. Set on a
bluff, it has superb views of
the Santa Rosalía River below.
Not far away is the **Museo
Mulegé**, which has displays
on the town's history. It is
housed in an old whitewashed
prison building, complete
with tiny, crenellated towers.
Mulegé is popular with scuba
divers, but for some of the
best beaches in Mexico take

A view across to the Bahía Concepción, the bay to the south of Mulegé

the road south out of Mulegé,
past the **Bahía Concepción**.
The color of the water here
changes dramatically from
deep blue to an intense green.

🏛 **Museo Mulegé**
Cananea. 🕐 *Mon–Sat*. 📷 ♿

Loreto ❿

Baja California Sur. 🔊 *11,800*. ✈ 🚌
🛈 *Corner of Francisco Madero and
Salvatierra, (613) 135 00 36.* 📷 *Virgen
de Loreto (Sep 8), San Javier (Dec 3).*

ONCE THE CAPITAL of the
Californias (made up of
present-day California and
Baja California), Loreto is now
better known as a magnet for
the sportfishing fraternity. The
heart of the town is the
area around Plaza Cívica
and the superbly restored
**Misión Nuestra Señora
de Loreto**. The mission,
the first in the Californias,
was badly damaged by a
hurricane and earthquake
in the 19th century. The
original stone building
(1699) survives as a side
chapel to the main church.
From here, 18th-century
Jesuit missionaries em-
barked on a campaign to
evangelize (and hence

peacefully subdue) the indigenous population. The **Museo
de las Misiones** in the mission explains how this was
accomplished and displays
period artifacts, including huge
cooking pots that the priests
used in their attempts – initially
more successful – to influence
the Indians by way of their
stomachs. In the museum
courtyard is a colonial, horse-
driven *trapiche* (sugar mill).

In addition to fishing, there
is good diving, kayaking, and
snorkeling, especially around
the offshore islands of **Isla
del Carmen** and **Coronado**.

🏛 **Museo de las Misiones**
Corner of Loreto and Misioneros.
📞 *(613) 135 04 41.* 🕐 *Tue–Sun.*
📷 *Sun free.*

**Fishing boats moored at the small
marina near the center of Loreto**

La Paz ⓫

Baja California Sur. 🏢 197,000. 🛬
🚆 🚢 🚌 Carretera Transpeninsular,
km 5.5, (612) 124 01 99.
🎭 Carnival (Feb/Mar), Fundación
de La Paz (May 2–7).
🖥 www.gbcs.gob.mx

THE CAPITAL of the state of Baja California Sur, La Paz sits beside the largest bay on the Sea of Cortés, at the foot of a peninsula endowed with some excellent, and often half-deserted, beaches. Its curving, 5-km (3-mile) malecón (waterfront promenade) is lined with palm trees, hotels, and restaurants and is a lovely place for a stroll. Sit on a bench and enjoy the sunset, or walk along the dilapidated pier. A few blocks farther south is the main square, Plaza Constitución.

La Paz owes its foundation, by the conquistador Hernán Cortés, to the abundance of pearls in nearby waters, and its fortunes have often risen and fallen with those of the pearl industry. It dominated the international market in the 19th century, but in the 1940s a combination of disease and over-exploitation wiped out the oyster beds. Nowadays, in addition to its government offices and port facilities, its economy increasingly relies on tourism and on its status as one of the premier sportfishing destinations in the world.

La Paz's well laid-out **Museo Regional de Antropología** has interesting displays on pre-Columbian rock paintings and other aspects of Baja's indigenous heritage, as well as on its struggle for independence.

The nearby islands are popular with divers for their reefs, caves, and shipwrecks, and many also have fine beaches. **Isla Espíritu Santo** offers fantastic sailing opportunities and the chance to swim with wild sea lions.

🏛 **Museo Regional de Antropología**
Corner of 5 de Mayo and Altamirano. 📞 (612) 125 64 24. ⏰ Mon–Sat.
📷 Sun free.

The spectacular rock archway at Lovers' Beach, Cabo San Lucas

San José del Cabo ⓬

Baja California Sur. 🏢 22,000. 🛬
🚆 🚢 🚌 Carretera Peninsular ed.
Pedrin, (624) 142 33 10. 🎭 San
José (Mar 13–21).

SITUATED AT THE TIP of the Baja peninsula, the pleasant town of San José del Cabo is centered around the shady Plaza Mijares. On weekends there is an arts and crafts market. Farther inland is the old town, while to the south of Plaza Mijares, the streets slope downward to the beachfront boulevard with its modern tourist hotels, resort complexes, and condominiums. On the east side of the town is a palm-fringed estuary, said to be home to over 200 different species of birds, including flocks of migrant ducks, which find refuge here from the northern winter.

Pelicans at Cabo San Lucas

A few kilometers farther east is the village of **Pueblo la Playa**, which has beautiful white-sand beaches, often deserted.

Cabo San Lucas ⓭

Baja California Sur. 🏢 28,500. 🚌
🎭 Día de San Lucas (Oct 18).

A MINIATURE Acapulco, where it often seems that the official language is English, Cabo San Lucas is famous for its romantic "Lovers' Beach." Accessible only by boat, the beach is set among the jagged rocks known as Los Frailes (The Friars), which seem to form the tip of the peninsula. The beach is framed by a rock archway considered to link the waters of the Pacific with those of the Sea of Cortés.

One of the world's best game-fishing locations, the town has a sizable marina and a waterfront strip crowded with bars, discos, and restaurants. Farther inland, much of the old town remains intact.

Beach activities are concentrated on the long **Playa El Médano**, where the swimming is safest and jet-skis can be rented. The diving is excellent around Los Frailes, where there is an immense underwater canyon.

Between Cabo San Lucas and San José del Cabo are several top-class golf courses and some stunning beaches.

A colorful building on one of the streets around Plaza Constitución in La Paz

Ruins of the ancient adobe buildings at Paquimé, northern Mexico's most interesting archaeological site

Hermosillo

Sonora. 🏔 *609,000*. ✈ 🚌 ℹ *Calle Comonfort, (662) 217 00 44.* 🎫 *Wine Festival (Jun), San Francisco (Oct 4).* 🅦 *www.sonora.gob.mx/turismo*

Sonora's busy, thriving capital city – where cattle ranchers rub shoulders with car workers – has a quieter, prettier side too. Centered on the **Plaza Zaragoza**, with its lacy white bandstand, its outstanding feature is the 19th-century **cathedral** with its twin towers and pale yellow dome, each surmounted by a cross. The cathedral's dazzling white façade is a blend of architectural styles, with Neo-Classical predominating. It is remarkably harmonious considering it took over a century to build.

The more severely Neo-Classical **Palacio de Gobierno** contains frescoes painted in the 1980s by three artists whose inspiration ranged from indigenous creation myths to the Mexican Revolution. In a

The brilliant white façade of Hermosillo cathedral

beautifully restored building, that was once the state penitentiary, is the **Museo de Sonora**, with galleries on the geology and ecology of the state and its development from prehistoric times to the present.

🏛 **Palacio de Gobierno**
Doctor Paliza. 🕻 *(662) 212 00 02.* ◻ *Mon–Sat.* 🎫 *reserve in advance.*
🏛 **Museo de Sonora**
Jesus García Final. 🕻 *(662) 217 25 80.* ◻ *Tue–Sun.* 🎫 *reserve in advance.* 🚻

Paquimé

Chihuahua. 8 km (5 miles) SW of Casas Grandes. 🚌 *from Chihuahua.* ◻ *daily.* 🎫

The most important archaeological site in northern Mexico, Paquimé is an extraordinary complex of adobe buildings, quite unlike central and southern Mexican sites. Set on a plateau overlooking the Casas Grandes river, it flourished between the 10th and 14th centuries and probably housed over 3,000 people. Its partial destruction by fire in about 1340 and the disappearance of its inhabitants before the arrival of the Spanish have yet to be fully explained.

Walls of packed earth, up to 1.5 m (5 ft) thick, a mazelike construction, and "apartment buildings" as much as five floors high with internal staircases are among the site's characteristic features. The

Modern Paquimé pot

houses also contain stoves for heating and beds in the form of alcoves. Low doorways in the shape of a thick "T" may have been partly for defence purposes. An impressive network of channels brought spring water from 8 km (5 miles) away for filtration and storage in deep wells. From here it was channeled to domestic and agricultural users, while another system of conduits drained away the waste. The inhabitants of Paquimé, whose language and ethnic origin are unknown, raised macaws for ceremonial purposes. The low, adobe pens with circular entrances, in which the birds were kept, remain intact. Other architectural elements seen here, including ballcourts, suggest cultural influence from Mesoamerican societies farther south.

Unique to Paquimé, however, is a particularly fine type of pottery, distinguished by a high polish and geometric or anthropomorphic designs. The most typical colors are black and reddish brown on a buff background. The style has been revived by local potters, some of whom command high prices for a single piece. More modestly priced examples can be bought in the nearby town of Casas Grandes Viejo. The site museum contains original ceramics as well as a model of the city as it would have looked in its heyday.

The Cactuses of Northern Mexico

THE LANDSCAPES of Northern Mexico are characterized by the extraordinary variety of cactuses that grow there. About 300 species of cactus exist in the Sonoran Desert, the most diverse desert in the world. They are superbly adapted to retain water and withstand fierce climatic extremes. Their fleshy stems, often protected by spines, are filled with water-storing tissue and surrounded by a thick, waxy layer to help retain moisture. Cactuses can remain dormant for long periods and then burst into bloom after a brief downpour. In Mexico, cactuses are used for food and drink, for roof coverings, and to make fish hooks and pot scourers.

Flowers from a pincushion cactus

Prickly pears (Opuntia species), *the largest cactus group, are also called Indian figs. Many have edible red, green, or purple fruits.*

The desert landscapes of the North have a certain stark beauty.

Boojum tree

Prickly pear

Barrel cactus

Agave

The giant Mexican cereus (Pachycereus pringlei) *is a tall, treelike cactus. They are often planted close together in rows to form fences.*

The saguaro (Carnegiea gigantea) *can grow to 16 m (52 ft) tall, taking nearly 150 years to reach its full height. Large specimens can hold several tons of water.*

The boojum tree (Idria columnaris) *is an extraordinary sight. It is seen mainly in the deserts of Baja California.*

Agaves *are used to make tequila (see p313) and henequen (see p273). Some species take up to 50 years to flower.*

SUCCULENTS

Most cactuses store water in fleshy stems, but many other succulents, such as the agaves, store moisture in their leaves. Succulents grow very slowly to reduce their need for water, and many have shallow, but very extensive, root systems.

The barrel cactus (Ferocactus) *derives its name from its rounded shape. Mexico has nine species of barrel cactus.*

Chihuahua ⑯

Chihuahua. 🏘 *670,000.* ✈ 🚇 🚌
ℹ️ *Palacio de Gobierno, (614) 429 34
21.* 🎭 *Santa Rita (May 22).*

THE GHOSTS OF TWO Mexican
heroes, Pancho Villa and
Father Miguel Hidalgo *(see
p49)*, seem to haunt the
streets of Chihuahua. Set
among rugged hills in a semidesert landscape, it owes its
foundation to the rich veins
of silver discovered nearby in
the colonial period. The city's
aqueduct, referred to by
locals as "los arquitos" (the
arches), dates from that era.
Its best-preserved section is
at the intersection of Calle 56
and Calle Allende. Today
Chihuahua relies mostly on
automobile manufacturing
and cattle-ranching.

The Plaza de Armas, the
main square of Chihuahua, is
dominated by the **cathedral**.
This impressive, twin-towered
building in rose-colored stone
dates from the 18th century. Its
1920s altar of Italian marble is
particularly fine. A side chapel
contains a museum of religious
art, open on weekdays.

The **Palacio de Gobierno**
on Plaza Hidalgo (to the
northeast of the main square)
is a late 19th-century building.
Its courtyard features striking
murals by Aarón Piña Mora
that illustrate episodes from
Chihuahuan history. There is
also an eternal flame commemorating Independence hero
Father Hidalgo – it marks the
spot where he was executed
by firing squad in 1811 after
leading a rebellion against the
Spanish crown. Two blocks
away, on Avenida Juárez, the
Palacio Federal preserves
within its walls the remains of
the church tower that served

The Art Nouveau Quinta Carolina, on the outskirts of Chihuahua

as Hidalgo's cell. It contains
a few poignant reminders of
the priest's incarceration and
fate, including a tiny lantern
with which he illuminated the
last few nights of his life.

Undoubtedly the best-known
Chihuahuan resident was
Francisco "Pancho" Villa,
the mustachioed hero of
the 1910–20 revolu-
tionary war *(see p54)*.
The **Museo Histórico
de la Revolución**
features the bullet-
riddled Dodge at
whose wheel he met
his end in 1923. The
museum is situated in
his former house,
and much of his
furniture and other
household goods
are still here. The
galleries behind the house
recount the story of the
Revolution. There is also a
death mask of Villa, taken just
hours after his assassination.

Perhaps the finest house in
the city is the Quinta Gameros,
to the southeast of the Plaza de
Armas, which now houses the
**Centro Cultural Universita-
rio Quinta Gameros**. It is
worth paying the admission
price to this
exquisite Art
Nouveau mansion
just to see the
dining room with
its fantastic wood
carvings. The
rooms upstairs
house permanent
exhibitions, inclu-
ding paintings
and sculptures by
Mexican artist
Luis Aragón.

Statue on the façade of
Chihuahua cathedral

ENVIRONS: Around 20 km
(12 miles) to the southeast of
Chihuahua is the picturesque
mining town of **Santa Eulalia**.
A stroll through its cobbled
streets is enjoyable, particularly
on a Sunday, when bands
play in the town plaza.

The **Cumbres de
Majalca National Park**,
situated about 70 km
(43 miles) to the
northwest of
Chihuahua, offers
opportunities for
hiking, rock-
climbing, and
wilderness camping
among forested
canyons and peaks.

🏛 **Museo
Histórico de la
Revolución**
Decima 3014. 📞 *(614) 416 29 58.*
🕐 *Tue–Sun.* 🎟 ♿ &. *ground floor.*

🏛 **Centro Cultural
Universitario**
Paseo Bolívar 401. 📞 *(614) 416 66 84.*
🕐 *Tue–Sun.* 🎟 ☑ &. *ground floor.*

Ciudad
Cuauhtémoc ⑰

Chihuahua. 🏘 *124,000.* 🚌 ℹ️ *Cnr
of Allende and Agustín Melgar, (625)
581 22 66.* 🎭 *San Antonio (Jun).*

THE INDUSTRIOUS Mennonite
farmers who have made
Cuauhtémoc what it is today
arrived in 1921 at the invitation
of President Obregón. Originally from the Netherlands,
these fundamentalist Christians
had settled in Canada but came
into conflict with the authorities there when they resisted
the draft for World War I.

**A beautifully preserved section of Chihuahua's
aqueduct, which dates from colonial times**

PANCHO VILLA (C.1878–1923)

A member of a bandit group as a young man, Francisco "Pancho" Villa became an influential leader of the Revolution after joining the campaign to depose Porfirio Díaz in 1910 (*see p54*). His excellent military strategies and charismatic leadership inspired great loyalty in his División del Norte army and made him a folk hero, particularly around Chihuahua where he had his headquarters. In 1920

The death mask of Pancho Villa

Álvaro Obregón took power and encouraged Villa to retire to a hacienda in Canutillo (Durango). Three years later, on a trip into Hidalgo del Parral, he was assassinated. About 30,000 people attended his funeral.

dry arroyo), is the **Museo Francisco Villa**. It is housed in the building from which Villa's assassins fired the fatal shots, and a bronze starburst on the pavement outside marks the place where he died. The building is now a library, with the Villa museum on the first floor. It includes photos taken after the murder, as well as a model of the scene.

ENVIRONS: Parral can be used as a southern gateway to the rugged landscape of the Sierra Tarahumara, which stretches away to the northwest, while 15 minutes' drive east of town are the hot mineral springs of **El Ojo de Talamantes**, in the lush Valle de Allende.

Farther to the east is a stark, inhospitable desert region, the **Bolsón de Mapimí**, which encloses a remote area called the "Zone of Silence." Rumored to be a landing site for UFOs or a kind of Mexican Bermuda Triangle, it gets its name from the popular theory that radio waves cannot enter or leave it. A few kilometers east is the massive **Mapimí Biosphere Reserve**, home to a fascinating variety of rare desert plants and animals.

🏛 **Museo Francisco Villa**
Corner of Barreda & Juárez. **(** (614) 416 29 58. **◯** Tue–Sun. 🚫 **&** ground floor. 📷 reserve in advance.

This is the largest Mennonite group in Latin America. Their self-sufficient farms, known as camps, stretch north and south from Cuauhtémoc. Often blond and blue-eyed, the Mennonites stand out from their Mexican neighbors and have remained culturally distinct. Although they have embraced some modern technology, they still have a very traditional way of life. Their pitched-roofed, woodframe houses and barns give this part of Mexico a strangely European aspect.

Mennonite men, with their trademark denim overalls, usually speak Spanish, but many of the women speak only the Low German dialect of their ancestors. The easiest way to meet them is to buy some of the excellent cheese, which is their best-known product. The cheese factory at Camp 6½ (all the camps are numbered, not named) is open to visitors, except on Sundays, when everything apart from the churches closes down.

Hidalgo del Parral ⑱

Chihuahua. 🏘 *101,000.* 🚌 ℹ *Cnr of Miranda & República de Cuba, (636) 522 52 82.* 🎉 *Francisco Villa (Jul 20).*

MOST FAMOUS as the site of Pancho Villa's murder, Parral (as it is usually known) was founded in 1631. It owes its existence to the gold and silver mines, and at the end of the 19th century it was one

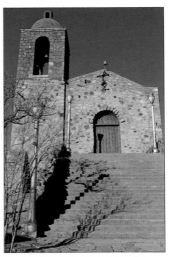

of the most opulent cities in Mexico. Its churches are noted for the chunks of ore that went into their construction.

The La Prieta minehead still overlooks the town. Nearby is the **Templo de la Virgen de Fátima**, the church dedicated to the miners' patron saint. Built at the end of the 19th century, it has small pieces of metal from the mines, including silver and gold, set into its walls. In place of traditional pews are stools shaped like claim markers.

Another outstanding building is a 19th-century church, **Parroquia de San José**. Situated on the town's main square, it has an unusual diamond pattern on its walls.

Farther to the west, at the corner of Calle Primo de Verdad and Riva Palacio, is the splendid **Casa de Alvarado**. It was built at the start of the 20th century for the Alvarado family, whose fortune came from La Palmilla – believed at the time to be the richest silver mine in the Americas. Notice the anguished face over the main door, which is said to be that of an Indian mine worker. Nearby, over one of the bridges that span the Parral River (in winter just a

A Mennonite man in traditional dress

The Templo de la Virgen de Fátima, the miners' church in Hidalgo del Parral

The beautiful Lago Arareco, high in the mountains of the Sierra Madre Occidental

Creel 🄆

Chihuahua. 🏘 *4,000.* 🚉 🚌
🏨 *López Mateos, (635) 456 01 26.*
🎭 *Carnival (Feb/Mar).*

R EDOLENT OF WOOD smoke and fresh mountain air, the small logging town of Creel is the main road and rail gateway to the largely unspoiled Sierra Tarahumara and the Copper Canyon *(see pp176–7)*. It is an excellent place to join the spectacular Chihuahua-al-Pacífico railroad, or to disembark and spend a few days exploring the pine-clad mountains.

Near the railroad station are the town plaza and Creel's main street, Calle López Mateos. Two churches stand on the square along with the Tarahumara Mission shop, which gives informal advice to visitors as well as selling Indian artifacts and books about the surrounding sierra. On the other side of the railroad tracks is the **Casa de las Artesanías**, a government-run museum and craft shop. It tells the story of railway tycoon Enrique Creel (after whom the town is named) and includes exhibits about the numerous Jesuit missions in the area and the culture of the

Tarahumara Indians. One glass case contains mummified bodies found in the nearby hills.

The best spot around the town for a gentle stroll or a picnic is at **Lago Arareco**, just 5 km (3 miles) to the south. The U-shaped lake is surrounded by unusual rock formations and a fragrant pine forest. A few kilometers farther along the same road is the start of a 4-km (2.5-mile) trail that winds through a scenic canyon to

Cascada Cusárare, a 30-m (100-ft) waterfall. Other attractions within easy reach of Creel include the hot springs at **Recohuata**, the weird, mushroom-shaped rocks of the **Valle de los Hongos**, and **El Divisadero**, the viewpoint over the breathtaking Copper Canyon. Chihuahua-al-Pacífico trains stop here briefly, but there are also minibus tours to the viewpoint for those who wish to spend longer contemplating the magnificent view. Tours to various sights, including helicopter trips over the canyons, are available in town.

ENVIRONS: A three- or four-hour drive northwest of Creel is the dramatic **Cascada de Basaseáchic**. At almost 300 m (1,000 ft) high, this is the third highest waterfall in North America. The towering falls are surrounded by 57 sq km (22 sq miles) of national park, with excellent walking trails and campgrounds. The park also contains several other waterfalls.

🏛 **Casa de las Artesanías**
Av Ferrocarril 178. 📞 *(635) 456 00 80.* ⭘ *Tue–Sun.* 🎫

THE TARAHUMARA INDIANS

A very private people, the Tarahumara Indians moved up into the mountains of the Sierra Madre Occidental about 400 years ago to avoid the Spanish missionaries. Since then, they have kept themselves very much apart from the rest of Mexico, preferring to live in small self-sufficient farming communities. They call themselves the Raramuri (Runners) and are superb long-distance athletes. The traditional tribal sport, *rarajipari (see p20)* involves teams of runners kicking a wooden ball for huge distances across rugged mountain slopes. Participants wear sandals on their feet, and matches can last for several days.

A Tarahumara Indian woman and her children in traditional dress

The Hacienda Batopilas, built by a wealthy silver baron

Batopilas ⑳

Chihuahua. 👥 *12,400.* 🚌

BARELY MORE than a single street wide, and clinging to the riverbank at the bottom of a 1.5-km (1-mile) deep canyon, Batopilas is one of Mexico's hidden treasures. And it was treasure, in the form of silver, that brought the Spanish, and later the noted US politician Alexander Shepherd, to this remote spot. Not the least remarkable fact about this extraordinary place is that it was built when the only way in and out was by mule train over the mountains. Today, it can still take three hours to traverse the 60 km (37 miles) of dirt road that link Batopilas with the Creel-to-Guachochi highway. As it descends, the road drops over 2,100 m (7,000 ft) down the canyon wall via a hair-raising sequence of bends.

Batopilas was the birthplace of Manuel Gómez Morín, who formed PAN (Partido de Acción Nacional), the main opposition party to the long-running PRI *(see p55)*. There is little more than a plaque and a bust to mark the fact, but monuments to another former resident, Alexander Shepherd, abound. Shepherd, the last governor of Washington DC, created the Batopilas Mining Company in the 1890s. The ruins of his home, the **Hacienda San Miguel**, now romantically overgrown with wild fig and bougainvillea, lie just across the river from the town entrance. Much of the aqueduct he built is still intact, and his hydroelectric plant, which made Batopilas the second electrified town in Mexico, is once again working. The **Hacienda Batopilas**, now a hotel, is another noteworthy edifice. It has fantastic domes and arches.

ENVIRONS: Farther down the canyon, remote **Satevó** has a domed church, a testament to the zeal of the Jesuits who brought the Gospel here.

Cañón del Cobre ㉑

See pp176–7.

Decorative wall tiles in Alamos

Alamos ㉒

Sonora. 👥 *25,000.* 🚌 ℹ️ *Juárez 6, (647) 428 04 50.* 🎭 *Virgen de Concepción (1st Sun of Dec).*

A COLONIAL JEWEL, set on the western edge of the Sierra Madre Occidental, Alamos owed its fame and fortune to the silver discovered here in the 17th century. However, its restoration is largely due to the community of people who have moved here from the US.

On the main plaza is the Baroque **Parroquia de la Purísima Concepción**, built between 1783 and 1804. It has an ornate bell tower with china plates, allegedly donated by the women of Alamos, embedded in its walls. Sadly, most of the plates were broken in the Revolution. Also on the square is the **Palacio Municipal** (1899), which has a square tower and iron balconies. Nearby, the **Museo Costumbrista** charts the local history.

However, it is the restored Sonoran mansions, with their interior patios and large windows with wrought-iron grilles, that give the town its flavor. Tours of some of these homes take place every Saturday.

🏛 **Museo Costumbrista**
Guadalupe Victoria 1. 📞 *(647) 428 00 53.* 🕐 *Wed–Sun.* 🈺 ♿ 📷 *reserve in advance.*

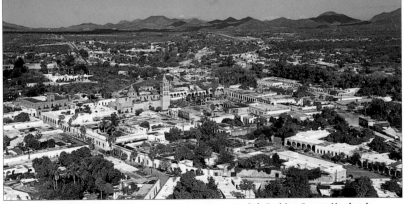

The attractive colonial town of Alamos, centered on the Parroquia de la Purísima Concepción church

Cañón del Cobre (Copper Canyon) ㉑

Bigger by far than the Grand Canyon, yet nowhere near as well known, Mexico's Copper Canyon region is one of the great undiscovered wonders of North America. Here, rivers have carved half-a-dozen canyons into the volcanic rock of the Sierra Madre Occidental. Amid the pine forests are spectacular waterfalls, weird rock formations, and tranquil lakes, some of which can be seen from the awe-inspiring railroad that winds across the northern part of the region. Thinly populated, the canyons are home to the Tarahumara Indians (see p174) and also contain evocative relics of past mining booms.

The spectacular Cañón del Cobre, over 1.5 km (1 mile) deep and 50 km (31 miles) in length

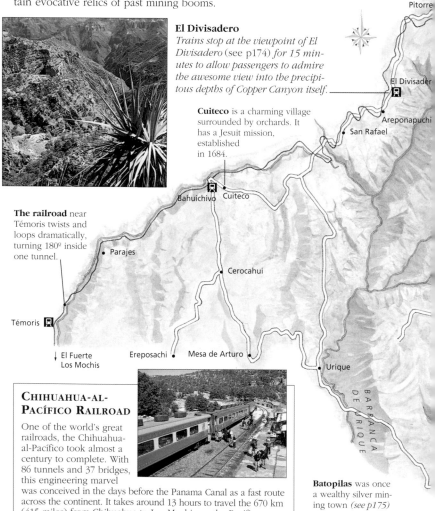

El Divisadero
Trains stop at the viewpoint of El Divisadero (see p174) for 15 minutes to allow passengers to admire the awesome view into the precipitous depths of Copper Canyon itself.

Cuiteco is a charming village surrounded by orchards. It has a Jesuit mission, established in 1684.

The railroad near Témoris twists and loops dramatically, turning 180° inside one tunnel.

Pitorre

El Divisader

Areponapuchi

San Rafael

Bahuichivo   Cuiteco

Parajes

Cerocahui

Témoris

El Fuerte
Los Mochis

Ereposachi   Mesa de Arturo

Urique

B A R R A N C A   D E   U R I Q U E

CHIHUAHUA-AL-PACÍFICO RAILROAD

One of the world's great railroads, the Chihuahua-al-Pacífico took almost a century to complete. With 86 tunnels and 37 bridges, this engineering marvel was conceived in the days before the Panama Canal as a fast route across the continent. It takes around 13 hours to travel the 670 km (415 miles) from Chihuahua to Los Mochis on the Pacific coast. The most spectacular scenery is to be found between Creel and El Fuerte, a stretch that drops more than 2,000 m (6,550 ft).

Batopilas was once a wealthy silver mining town (see p175) and now makes an excellent base for hiking excursions in the canyons.

Batop

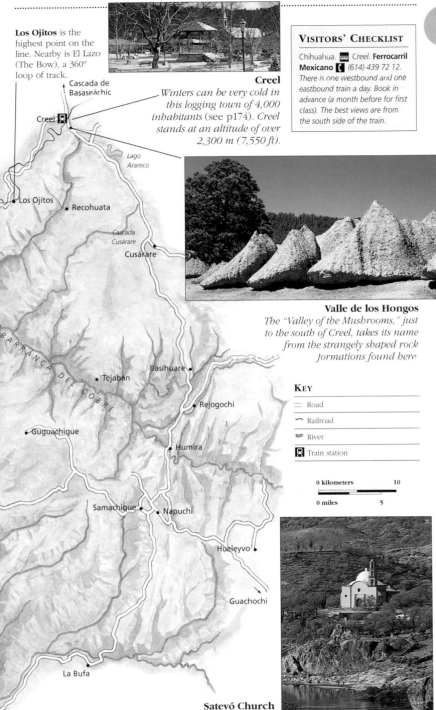

Los Ojitos is the highest point on the line. Nearby is El Lazo (The Bow), a 360° loop of track.

Creel
Winters can be very cold in this logging town of 4,000 inhabitants (see p174). Creel stands at an altitude of over 2,300 m (7,550 ft).

VISITORS' CHECKLIST

Chihuahua. 🚌 *Creel.* **Ferrocarril Mexicano** 📞 *(614) 439 72 12. There is one westbound and one eastbound train a day. Book in advance (a month before for first class). The best views are from the south side of the train.*

Cascada de Basaseáchic

Creel 🚉

Lago Areco

Los Ojitos · Recohuata

Cascada Cusárare

Cusárare

Valle de los Hongos
The "Valley of the Mushrooms," just to the south of Creel, takes its name from the strangely shaped rock formations found here

BARRANCA DEL COBRE

· Tejabán   Basíhuare ·

· Rejogochi

· Guguachique

Humíra ·

KEY

═ Road
⌒ Railroad
▬ River
🚉 Train station

0 kilometers — 10
0 miles — 5

Samachique · · Napuchi

Hueleyvo ·

Guachochi

La Bufa

Satevó Church
Known as the "lost cathedral," this remote church was probably built by Jesuit missionaries in the 17th century, long before the first road penetrated the canyon. No record of its construction exists.

· Satevó

Fishing boats on Mazatlán's peaceful beachfront, the Playa del Norte

Mazatlán ❷

Sinaloa. 🏙 60,000. ✈ 🚌 🚢
🅸 Cnr of Tiburón & Camarón Sábalo,
(669) 916 51 60. 🎭 Carnival (Feb/Mar).

SITUATED JUST SOUTH of the Tropic of Cancer, Mazatlán is the most northerly of all Mexico's major resorts. An agreeable climate and almost 20 km (12 miles) of beaches make it extremely popular. Another attraction is the Mazatlán carnival, which is claimed to be the third largest in the world, after those of Rio and New Orleans.

A waterfront boulevard connects the narrow streets and 19th-century architecture of the old town with the expensive beach hotels of the touristic Zona Dorada (Golden Zone). Of the offshore islands, **Venados, Lobos,** and **Pájaros** all offer an enticing combination of wildlife and uncrowded, sandy beaches, and are easily and cheaply reached by small boats. The misleadingly named **Isla de la Piedra,** however, is not actually an island but a peninsula across the estuary. Famous for its sandy beaches fringed with coconut palms, it is the site of one of Mexico's largest tourist developments, the Estrella de Mar.

Historic Mazatlán is worth visiting for its beautifully restored, Italianate **Teatro Ángela Peralta,** named after a famous Mazatlán-born opera singer, and its intriguing **cathedral** – Neo-Gothic on the outside, exuberantly Baroque on the inside, and noted for its gilded altar. Both buildings date from the late 19th century. However, Mazatlán's oldest church is

the **Iglesia de San José,** built in 1842 on the slopes of the Cerro de la Nevería (Icebox Hill). The Cerro, which offers a spectacular view of the city by day or night, acquired its name from the 19th-century practice of storing imported ice in a tunnel carved into the hillside. The country's biggest aquarium, the **Acuario Mazatlán,** has more than 250 species of fish and other marine creatures from around the world.

ENVIRONS: Sinaloa is one of the few areas where the pre-Columbian ball-game known as *hulama* is still played (*see p277*). The town of **El Quelite,** 50 km (31 miles) north of Mazatlán along Mex 15, holds matches on Sundays.

🦎 Acuario Mazatlán
Av Deportes 111. 🅲 (669) 981 78 15. 🕐 daily. 🚫 🅿 🅷

Durango's Baroque cathedral, with its impressive twin towers

Durango ❷

Durango. 🏙 491,000. ✈ 🚌 🅸
Florida 100, Barrio del Calvario, (618) 811 21 39. 🎭 Feria Nacional (Jul 8).

THIS CITY'S main attraction is its association with the movie industry, particularly Westerns. Many restaurants and shops with cowboy themes trade on Durango's cinematographic past.

There are also several important buildings. On the north flank of the Plaza de Armas stands the impressive **cathedral.** Begun in 1695, it has a Baroque façade and a fine choir with gilded stalls featuring figures of saints. A few blocks west of the plaza is the **Palacio de Gobierno,** the seat of the state government, known for

Detail of a mural at Durango's Palacio de Gobierno

its striking set of 20th-century murals painted by Francisco Montoya de la Cruz, Guillermo Bravo, and Guillermo de Lourdes. The **Casa del Conde de Suchil,** a late 18th-century mansion east of the plaza, now houses shops and a bank. In the bank, the original interior can still be seen. The exquisite Art Nouveau **Teatro Ricardo Castro,** built in 1900, holds what is reputedly the country's largest hand-carved relief made from a single piece of wood.

ENVIRONS: There are a number of movie locations outside the city, most notably the **Villa del Oeste** set. Nearby is the village of **Chupaderos,** which was probably Durango's most used Hollywood location.

For superb views of mountains and canyons, head west on Mex 40, which reaches around 2,600 m (8,530 ft) above sea level. The highlight is the **Espinazo del Diablo** (Devil's Backbone), a winding 9-km (6-mile) stretch along a narrow ridge about 130 km (81 miles) west of Durango.

🏛 Villa del Oeste
Mex 45, 12 km (7 miles) N of Durango. 🕐 daily. 🚫 🅷

Saltillo cathedral's pulpit, with its gold-leaf decoration and saintly figurines

Saltillo 🟠

Coahuila. 🏛 *580,000.* ✈ ☐
🛈 *Blvd de Carranza 3206, (844) 439 27 45.* 🛈 *Ferias (Jul–Aug).*

DUBBED "the city of columns" because of the number of buildings characterized by Neo-Classical colonnades, Saltillo is also famous for what is probably the most beautiful **cathedral** in northeast Mexico. Dominating the old Plaza de Armas, the Churrigueresque façade of this 18th-century building has six columns richly embellished with carved flowers, fruit, and shells.

Inside, visitors can climb the smaller of the two towers, and view the Spanish 16th-century wooden cross in the Capilla del Santo Cristo, which is located in the main body of the church. The cathedral also holds a large collection of colonial oil paintings, but its principal treasure is the remarkable silver front of the side altar dedicated to San José. So fine is the silverwork, in fact, that the piece is often exhibited elsewhere and replaced in the cathedral by a photograph.

On the opposite side of the plaza is the state government headquarters, the **Palacio de Gobierno**, which contains a mural charting the history of Coahuila. The other building of note in the center, which stands out both for its history and for its attractive,

tiled cupola, is the **Templo de San Esteban**. This church served as a hospital for injured Mexican troops during the US invasion of Mexico *(see p52)*.

Saltillo also has a unique museum dedicated to the birds of Mexico. The **Museo de las Aves de México** contains an outstanding collection of stuffed birds, covering over 670 different species, donated by ornithologist Aldegundo Garza de León. The skillfully designed displays, which incorporate bird skeletons, eggs, and fossils, explain many of the most interesting aspects of avian ecology and behavior.

🏛 Museo de las Aves de México
Corner of Hidalgo & Bolivar. 📞 *(844) 414 01 67.* ☐ *Tue–Sun.* 🎦 ♿ 🔲

Monterrey 🟠

Nuevo León. 🏛 *1.1 million.* ✈ ☐
🛈 *Hidalgo 441 Oriente, (81) 8345 09 02.* 🛈 *Virgen de Guadalupe (Dec 12).*

MEXICO'S third-largest city is a thriving industrial center with some of the most striking 20th-century architecture in the country. Perhaps the best examples are the **Planetario**, which houses science exhibitions and a planetarium, and the **Basílica**

de la Purísima, finished in 1946 and a very influential piece of church architecture. In the Gran Plaza, claimed locally to be the largest civic square in the world, the **Museo de Arte Contemporáneo** (MARCO) houses an important collection of Latin American modern art. A monumental but featureless sculpture, the **Faro del Comercio**, towers above Monterrey's cathedral.

ENVIRONS: Occupying an area of mountainous semidesert west of Monterrey is one of the largest national parks in Mexico, the **Parque Nacional las Cumbres de Monterrey**. Two of the most accessible sights within the park are the dramatic 25-m (82-ft) Cola de Caballo falls and the spectacular Grutas de García caves.

🏛 Planetario
Ave Gómez Morín 1100. 📞 *(81) 8303 00 03.* ☐ *Tue–Sun.* 🎦 🔲 🔲
🏛 MARCO
Cnr Zuazua & Jardon. 📞 *(81) 8342 48 20.* ☐ *Tue–Sun.* 🎦 *Wed free.* ♿ 🔲 *in advance.* 🔲 🔲

Monterrey's massive cultural complex, the Planetario

HOLLYWOOD IN MEXICO

Clear blue skies and magical, semidesert landscapes made Durango for many years a favorite location for the movie industry, especially for Westerns. The stars who have filmed here range from John Wayne and Kirk Douglas to Anthony Quinn and Jack Nicholson. Some of the best-known movies shot near Durango include John Huston's *The Unforgiven* and Sam Peckinpah's *The Wild Bunch* and *Pat Garrett and Billy the Kid*. A few Hollywood locations can be visited, including the Villa del Oeste (officially called Condado Chávez) and Chupaderos.

The dusty village of Chupaderos, one of Durango's Wild West movie locations

THE COLONIAL HEARTLAND

AGUASCALIENTES • COLIMA • GUANAJUATO
JALISCO • MICHOACÁN • NAYARIT • QUERÉTARO
SAN LUIS POTOSÍ • ZACATECAS

*C*HARMING, WELL-PRESERVED *towns built during colonial times
characterize the states to the north of Mexico City, where
sun-drenched coastlines and humid jungles adjoin cactus-
strewn mesas and snow-capped volcanoes. Indian villages, bustling
cities, and beach resorts also form part of this vast and varied territory.*

Following the fall of the Aztec empire *(see p43)*, Spanish soldiers marched north to conquer the nomadic Indian tribes of this region. Missionaries also came, to spread the Gospel, and adventurers to seek their fortune, some exploiting the veins of precious metal in the area's arid hills, others its fertile plains.

Soon opulent, Spanish-style cities, brimming with palaces, churches, and convents, were founded in the area. Zacatecas, Guanajuato, and San Luis Potosí boomed as a result of being the principal suppliers of silver and gold to the Spanish royal family. Aguascalientes, San Miguel de Allende, and Querétaro were all important stopovers on the silver route to the capital. The city of Morelia established itself as the cultural and social hub of New Spain's western province, and Guadalajara rose to prominence as the gateway to the Pacific ports of Manzanillo and San Blas.

In the early 19th century, general discontent with Spanish rule began to simmer in Querétaro, and nearby colonial strongholds. The plotting, and first armed uprising, by rebels here earned the region the title "the Cradle of Independence." Ferocious battles were fought in the cities of Guanajuato, Zacatecas, and Morelia, until Mexico declared its independence from Spain in 1821 *(see p49)*.

Today, the Colonial Heartland of Mexico remains a relatively prosperous region, thanks to its rich agricultural lands, thriving industry (which includes the production of tequila), and increasingly popular tourist attractions.

A volcano rises above fertile plains in Nayarit state, where agriculture is the main source of income

◁ The elaborate, polychromatic interior of the Santuario de Nuestra Señora de Guadalupe in Morelia

Exploring the Colonial Heartland

Beaches and colonial cities are the tourist magnets of this region. Big, booming Puerto Vallarta and the smaller, less hectic Manzanillo are resort cities on the long, beautiful Pacific coastline. Inland, Guadalajara is a modern metropolis notable for its majestic colonial core. The old towns of Zacatecas, San Luis Potosí, Aguascalientes, Guanajuato, San Miguel de Allende, and Querétaro were constructed with fortunes amassed from silver and gold. Pátzcuaro and Morelia are colonial jewels in Michoacán. Off the beaten track are Huichol and Cora Indian villages in the Sierra Madre Occidental, the ghost town of Real de Catorce, isolated missions in the untamed Sierra Gorda, and the majestic waterfalls of the lush Huasteca Potosina.

Indian pottery on sale at a market in Pátzcuaro

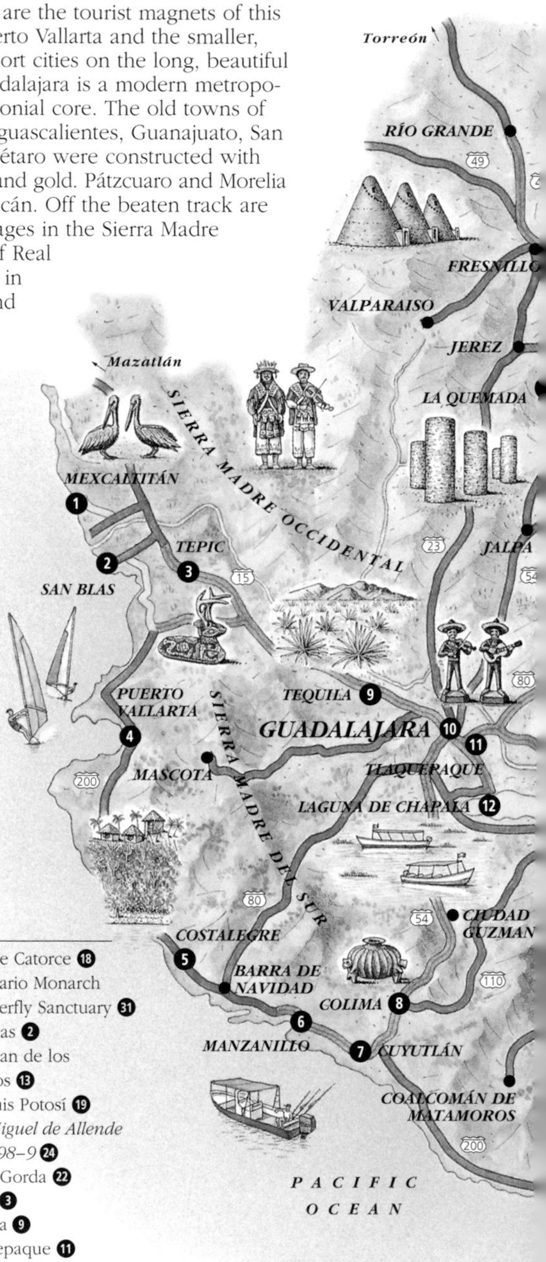

SIGHTS AT A GLANCE

Aguascalientes ⑮
Colima ❽
Costalegre ❺
Cuyutlán ❼
Guadalajara pp188–9 ❿
Guanajuato pp202–5 ㉕
Huasteca Potosina ⑳
Lagos de Moreno ⑭
Laguna de Chapala ⑫
Manzanillo ❻
Mexcaltitán ❶
Morelia pp208–11 ㉚
Paricutín ㉖
Pátzcuaro ㉙
Las Pozas ㉑
Puerto Vallarta ❹
La Quemada ⑯
Querétaro pp196–7 ㉓

Real de Catorce ⑱
El Rosario Monarch
  Butterfly Sanctuary ㉛
San Blas ❷
San Juan de los
  Lagos ⑬
San Luis Potosí ⑲
*San Miguel de Allende
  pp198–9* ㉔
Sierra Gorda ㉒
Tepic ❸
Tequila ❾
Tlaquepaque ⑪
Uruapan ㉗
Zacatecas ⑰

Tours
Lake Pátzcuaro ㉘

Torreón
RÍO GRANDE (49)
FRESNILLO
VALPARAISO
JEREZ
LA QUEMADA
Mazatlán
MEXCALTITÁN ❶
SIERRA MADRE OCCIDENTAL
TEPIC ❸ (15)
SAN BLAS ❷
JALPA (23)
PUERTO VALLARTA ❹
TEQUILA ❾
GUADALAJARA ❿ ⑪
TLAQUEPAQUE
MASCOTA (200)
LAGUNA DE CHAPALA ⑫
SIERRA MADRE DEL SUR
COSTALEGRE ❺ (80) (54)
CIUDAD GUZMAN
BARRA DE NAVIDAD
COLIMA ❽ (110)
MANZANILLO ❻ CUYUTLÁN ❼
COALCOMÁN DE MATAMOROS (200)
PACIFIC OCEAN

SEE ALSO
• *Where to Stay* pp298–301
• *Where to Eat* pp320–23

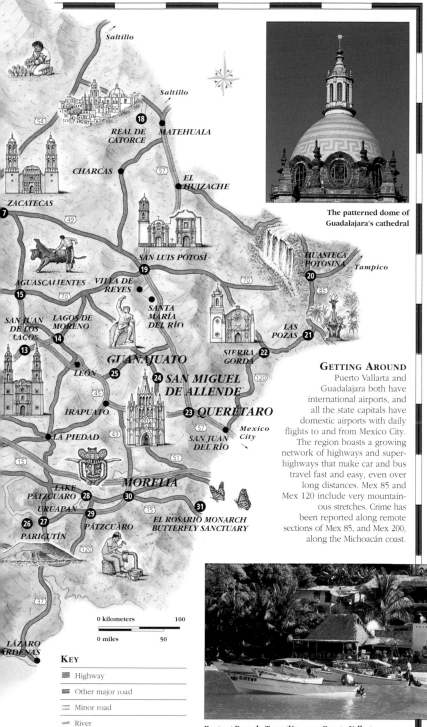

Saltillo

Saltillo

ZACATECAS

⑦

54

REAL DE
CATORCE

CHARCAS

49

18

MATEHUALA

EL
HUIZACHE

57

The patterned dome of
Guadalajara's cathedral

SAN LUIS POTOSÍ

19

HUASTECA
POTOSINA

Tampico

20

70

85

AGUASCALIENTES

15

70

VILLA DE
REYES

SANTA
MARÍA
DEL RÍO

SAN JUAN
DE LOS
LAGOS

13

LAGOS DE
MORENO

14

LEÓN

25

IRAPUATO

45

LA PIEDAD

43

15

GUANAJUATO

SAN MIGUEL
DE ALLENDE

24

23

QUERÉTARO

57

SIERRA
GORDA

22

LAS
POZAS

21

120

Mexico
City

SAN JUAN
DEL RÍO

51

LAKE
PÁTZCUARO

28

URUAPAN

26   27

PARICUTÍN

120

29

MORELIA

30

15

PÁTZCUARO

31

EL ROSARIO MONARCH
BUTTERFLY SANCTUARY

GETTING AROUND

Puerto Vallarta and
Guadalajara both have
international airports, and
all the state capitals have
domestic airports with daily
flights to and from Mexico City.
The region boasts a growing
network of highways and superhighways that make car and bus
travel fast and easy, even over
long distances. Mex 85 and
Mex 120 include very mountainous stretches. Crime has
been reported along remote
sections of Mex 85, and Mex 200,
along the Michoacán coast.

37

0 kilometers   100

0 miles   50

LÁZARO
CÁRDENAS

KEY

▦ Highway

▬ Other major road

═ Minor road

≈ River

Boats at Boca de Tomatlán, near Puerto Vallarta

Mexcaltitán ❶

Nayarit. 🏘 *1,000.* 🚤 📷 *Fiesta de San Pedro y San Pablo (Jun 28–9).*

T HIS TINY ISLAND, its name meaning "Place of the Moon Temple," is no more than 400 m (1,310 ft) across. It sits in a lagoon in Mexico's largest mangrove swamp area, and in the rains of August and September the streets become canals. According to legend the Aztecs slept here on the way to their promised land.

Although no Aztec artifacts have been found here, the archaeological pieces on display in the **Museo del Orígen**, located in the former town hall, nonetheless emphasize the importance of the island of Mexcaltitán as "The Cradle of Mexicanism."

🏛 **Museo del Orígen**
Plaza Principal. 📞 *no phone.*
🚪 *Tue–Sun.* 📷 ♿

San Blas ❷

Nayarit. 🏘 *43,000.* 🚌 ℹ *José María Mercado 29.* 📷 *Día de San Blas (Feb 2), Carnival (Feb/Mar), Día de la Marina (Jun 1).*

L ITTLE REMAINS from San Blas' colonial heyday, when it was a thriving seaport, an important shipbuilding center, and a garrison for the Spanish Armada. The only visible legacies are the ruins of an 18th-century Spanish fort and church, and a large, crumbling 19th-century customs house.

The panoramic view of the serene Bay of Matanchén near San Blas

---

THE HUICHOL INDIANS

There are still some 50,000 Huichol Indians living in Mexico, mostly in villages in the Sierra Madre Occidental mountains. They are known for their secret religious rites. An indispensable ingredient in these ceremonies is the hallucinogenic

peyote cactus, which grows miles away in the state of San Luis Potosí. Every September, Huicholes go to their sacred mountain near Real de Catorce *(see p193)* to gather the plant. Huichol traders are known for their colorful *nierika* yarn paintings and *chaquira* beadwork.

Part of a brilliantly colored yarn painting by the Huichol Indians

---

Today San Blas is a sleepy fishing village of palm groves and mangrove-fringed estuaries. It is the state's oldest developed resort, with a few hotels and palm-thatched restaurants catering to the swimmers and surfers attracted by the 19 km (12 miles) of golden beaches around the Bay of Matanchén. Beware of the mosquitoes that descend at sunset.

ENVIRONS: For boat trips through the lush jungle estuaries teeming with wildlife, head to the jetties east of town, on the road to Matanchén.

Boats awaiting intrepid jungle adventurers

The most popular destination is **La Tovara**, a freshwater spring and swimming hole adjacent to a crocodile farm.

Tepic ❸

Nayarit. 🏘 *305,000.* ✈ 🚌 ℹ *Cnr of Av México and Calzada del Ejército Nacional, (311) 214 80 71.* 📷 *Feria Nacional de Tepic (Feb 25–Mar 21).*

A PROVINCIAL town with an agreeable climate, Tepic was founded in the foothills of an extinct volcano in the 16th century. Not far from the Plaza Principal and the **cathedral** is the **Museo Regional de Nayarit**. Here, finds from shaft-tombs and displays about the Cora and Huichol Indians can be seen. The **Casa de los Cuatro Pueblos** (House of the Four Peoples) is a museum devoted to the Coras, Huicholes, Tepehuanos, and Mexicaneros. These people flock to Tepic on May 3 to visit the grass cross at the **Templo y Ex-Convento de la Cruz de Zacate**.

ENVIRONS: In the verdant hills 30 km (19 miles) southeast of Tepic is the picturesque **Santa María del Oro** lake, popular with hikers and birdwatchers.

🏛 **Museo Regional de Nayarit**
Av México 91 Norte. 📞 *(311) 212 19 00.* 🚪 *daily.* 📷 🎟 *in advance.*
🏛 **Casa de los Cuatro Pueblos**
Hidalgo 60 Oriente. 📞 *(311) 212 17 05.* 🚪 *Mon–Sat.*

Puerto Vallarta ❹

Jalisco. 🚗 184,000. ✈ 🚌
🛈 Plaza Marina 144–6, (322) 221 26
76. 🎭 Día de Guadalupe (Dec 12).

HOLLYWOOD stars discovered the tropical paradise of Banderas Bay in the 1960s. Since then, Puerto Vallarta has become one of Mexico's top Pacific resorts. Now 1.5 million tourists flock here annually to savor the beautiful beaches, the year-round pleasant climate, amazing aquatic sports, and the vibrant nightlife.

The resort stretches for more than 40 km (25 miles) around the bay, but its heart is Puerto Vallarta's old town, **Viejo Vallarta**. This area has managed to conserve some of the quaintness of a Mexican village, with its white-washed, tile-roofed houses and stone-paved streets stretching toward the jungle-clad mountains. The small **Isla Río Cuale**, an island in the river dividing the town, is the location for boutiques, cafés, and a botanical garden.

Head to the *malecón*, the waterfront boardwalk, for water taxis serving other parts of the bay, such as the Zona Hotelera, the main hotel strip which extends to the seaport in the north. Farther north is Marina Vallarta, Mexico's largest marina, surrounded by luxury hotels, shopping malls, and a golf course. Beside the marina, although in another state (Nayarit) and even another time zone, is **Nuevo Vallarta**. This is the most recent development on the bay, and its miles of beach, river, and estuary frontage reach as far as the town of **Bucerías**. The tourist infrastructure then peters out, leaving a string of small, pristine beaches that stretch to the bay's northernmost point, **Punta Mita**.

The southern, more scenic arc of Banderas Bay begins with **Playa de los Muertos** (Dead Men's Beach), the old town's most popular section of coastline. From here, the road winds past villa-dotted cliffs and sparkling blue coves to **Mismaloya**, before turning inland. Beyond this point, the exotic coves and superb swimming and snorkeling beaches are accessible only by boat.

ENVIRONS: To the north of Puerto Vallarta are some of the area's most famous diving sites, including **Las Marietas**, **Corbeteña**, and **El Morro**. Trips to the forests, canyons, and villages of the hinterland are also easily arranged.

Sailboats moored in the calm waters of Puerto Vallarta's marina

FIESTAS IN THE COLONIAL HEARTLAND

Fiesta de Año Nuevo *(Jan 1)*, Ihuatzio (Michoacán). Purépecha Indians perform traditional masked dances to music and Pirecua songs. For the dance of "Los Viejitos" (The Old Men), originally dedicated to the elderly pre-Columbian god Huehuetéotl, dancers hobble around wearing masks and woollen shawls.

Masked Indian dancing at the Fiesta de Año Nuevo

Easter Week *(Mar/Apr)*, Tzintzuntzan and Tarímbaro (Michoacán). A realistic crucifixion of Christ is re-enacted by a volunteer, who is flogged and carries his own wooden cross. Traditional processions also take place in San Miguel de Allende and Guanajuato.
Feria de San Marcos *(Apr/May)*, Aguascalientes. Crowds of up to 100,000 jam the town and fairground around the clock, to see exhibitions, parades, and fireworks, listen to concerts, and cheer at bullfights, cockfights, and *charreadas*, the riding and rodeo shows.
Day of the Dead *(Nov 1–2)*, Pátzcuaro and Isla Janitzio (Michoacán; *see p207*). Dead relatives and ancient gods are remembered, and traditional masked dances are performed, including "The Fish," in which fishing nets symbolically haul in a fish-masked dancer.

A sheltered, tranquil bay at the northern end of the Costalegre

Costalegre ❺

Jalisco. 🚌 Chamela, Barra de Navidad, Cihuatlán. 🛈 Jalisco 67, Barra de Navidad, (315) 355 51 00.

JALISCO's beautiful "Happy Coast" stretches for more than 200 km (125 miles), south from Puerto Vallarta (see p185) to the border with Colima state. The Mex 200 highway runs parallel with the coastline but mostly inland, taking in lush green mountain ranges and the occasional banana plantation. Most of Costalegre's white-sand beaches are accessible only to hotel guests or from the ocean. The luxury resorts – some with golf courses, polo fields, and airstrips – are shielded by gates and guards and can be reached only by private roads.

Set on a beautiful bay 165 km (102 miles) south of Puerto Vallarta, the resort of **Careyes** was developed in the late 1960s by an Italian entrepreneur. The resulting colorful mix of Mediterranean and Mexican architecture, featuring open living areas and enormous palm-thatched roofs, or *palapas*, has become known as the "Careyes Style." If money is no object, some of the dream houses perched on the soaring cliffs can be rented.

Somewhat more affordable are the lodgings found on the bays of Chamela, Tenacatita, and Cuastecomate. Swimming here is much safer than on the open-ocean beaches, which are subject to both dangerous waves and treacherous currents. The southernmost of the bays on the coast is **Bahía de Navidad**, where the family resort of **Melaque** and the fishing village of **Barra de Navidad** are found. Most of Barra's small restaurants and modest hotels are squeezed onto a narrow sandbar, which enjoys sunsets over the Pacific Ocean and views of a peaceful lagoon to the east. Small boats from Barra ferry customers to the rustic eateries of **Colimilla**, a lagoon-side hamlet at the foot of a towering wooded peninsula. The peninsula is now dominated by the massive Isla Navidad resort, which has an ecological preserve and a 27-hole golf course with superb views.

Manzanillo ❻

Colima. 🏘 124,000. ✈ 🚌 🛈 Blvd Miguel de la Madrid 1033, (314) 333 22 77. 🎉 Fiestas de Mayo (May 1–10), International Sailfish Fishing Tournament (1st week of Nov).

MEXICO's MOST important west coast shipping center, Manzanillo is also Colima state's foremost beach resort and calls itself "The Sailfish Capital of the World." The colorful houses of the old port cling to a hill overlooking the main harbor, while the newer part of town covers a sandbar separating the lagoon from the ocean. Most of Manzanillo's restaurants and hotels are located along the white sands of **Las Brisas** and **Playa Azul**.

Separating the Bahía de Manzanillo from the Bahía de Santiago is a peninsula, site of **Las Hadas** ("The Fairies"), a luxury Moorish-style hotel with a golf course which opened in the 1970s. Hotels now line most of the Bahía de Santiago, from La Audiencia to Playa Miramar. To see an outstanding collection of pre-Columbian artifacts from the region, head to the **Museo Universitario de Arqueología**.

🏛 **Museo Universitario de Arqueología**
Glorieta San Pedrito. 📞 (314) 332 22 56. 🕐 Tue–Sat. 🎫 Sun free. 🎦 reserve in advance. ⚟

Cuyutlán ❼

Colima. 🏘 940. 🚌 🎫 Fiesta de la Santa Cruz (May 2–3).

CUYUTLÁN is a traditional resort on the central part of Colima's coast. It is characterized by black volcanic sand, pounding surf, and the Mexican tourists that descend on the town on weekends. It is at the tip of the immense Cuyutlán Lagoon, which extends south for 32 km (20 miles) from Manzanillo.

Salt from the area provided an essential ingredient for ore processing in colonial times. The tiny **Museo de la Sal** gives an insight into the salt economy, its workers, and its harvesting methods. A spectacular springtime phenomenon seen on the coast here is the

Manzanillo's grand Las Hadas resort

Volcán de Fuego, seen from the road heading out of Colima toward Guadalajara

ola verde, when glassy green waves up to 10 m (33 ft) in height gleam with phosphorescent marine organisms.

🏛 **Museo de la Sal**

Juárez. ○ *Peak season: daily; low season: Fri–Sun.* ♿

Bandstand in the tropical Jardín de Libertad, Colima

Colima ❽

Colima. ⚐ *130,000.* ✈ 🚌
ℹ *Hidalgo 96, (312) 312 83 60.*
🎉 *San Felipe de Jesús (Feb), Feria de Todos los Santos (Oct 27– Nov 11).*

THE GRACEFUL provincial town of Colima, capital of one of Mexico's smallest states, was the first Spanish city on the west coast. It has been rebuilt several times since 1522 because of earthquakes, but the center still boasts Neo-Classical buildings, several museums, and tropical parks, such as the **Jardín de Libertad**.

La Campana archaeological site on the outskirts of town was an important pre-Columbian settlement between AD 700 and 900, with the earliest remains dating back as far as 1500 BC. Major exploration in the mid-1990s unearthed several monumental plazas and structures. Ceramic vessels and human and animal figurines from early shaft-tombs

can be seen in the **Museo de las Culturas de Occidente**. The **Museo Universitario de Artes Populares** exhibits regional and national folk art, covering both pre-Columbian and more recent Indian masks and costumes.

ENVIRONS: The route heading north out of the city offers impressive views of the active **Volcán de Fuego** and the taller, dormant **El Nevado de Colima** behind. The foothills of both provide wonderful hiking opportunities.

🏛 **Museo de las Culturas de Occidente**
Corner of Galván & Ejército Nacional. 📞 *(312) 312 31 55.* ○ *Tue–Sun.* 📷
🏛 **Museo Universitario de Artes Populares**
Gabino Barreda & Manuel Gallardo. 📞 *(312) 312 68 69.* ○ *daily.*
📷 *Sun free.* 🚻 ♿

Tequila ❾

Jalisco. ⚐ *35,500.* 🚌 ℹ *Jose Cuervo 33, (33) 3668 16 47.* 🎉 *Fiesta Septembrina (Sep 16), Feria Nacional del Tequila (Dec 1–12).*

EVERYTHING in Tequila reminds the visitor of Mexico's most famous drink *(see p313)*, especially the heavy scent from more than a dozen distilleries. Plantations of *Agave tequilana weber* surround the town, the cores, or *piñas*, of which have been used to make the precious liquid since the 16th century. The town remains the country's largest producer and now exports to nearly 100 countries. A must is a distillery tour followed by a tasting session. The biggest and oldest factories include La Perseverancia and La Rojeña, where original equipment and a cooking pit can be seen.

Harvesting the *Agave tequilana weber*, in fields near Tequila

Guadalajara ⑩

UNTIL JUST A FEW DECADES AGO, the capital of the state of Jalisco was a placid provincial town. Then an industrial boom swiftly transformed Guadalajara into a modern metropolis second only to Mexico City. A broad industrial belt and sprawling suburbs now ring the historic center. However, the traditional flavor of the "Pearl of the West" or "City of Roses" lingers on in the vast series of squares, lined with majestic colonial buildings, that make up the core of the city. Distinctive and once separate communities such as Zapopan, with its sacred basilica, and Tlaquepaque *(see p190)* have their own attractions and are now suburbs of the city.

Guadalajara's imposing cathedral, seen from the Plaza de Armas

⛪ Cathedral

Construction of this monumental cathedral began shortly after Guadalajara was founded in 1542. However, it was not finished until the early 18th century, and then in a medley of styles. Two earthquakes, in 1750 and 1818, destroyed the original façade and towers. They were replaced in the mid-19th century by the present yellow-tiled twin spires, which soon became the recognized symbol of the city.

More than a dozen mostly Neo-Classical altars grace the otherwise somber interior. Among the 18th- and 19th-century paintings in the sacristy is one, *The Assumption of the Virgin,* which may have been painted by the Spanish artist Bartolomé Esteban Murillo.

🏛 Museo Regional de Guadalajara

Corner of Av Hidalgo and Liceo. 【 *(33) 3614 99 57.* ◯ *Tue–Sun.* 🎟 *Sun, Tue free.* ◻

A lovely, 18th-century former seminary is now the home of the Museo Regional de Guadalajara. The ground-floor galleries have displays on palaeontology, prehistory, and archaeology. Among exhibits here are a complete mammoth skeleton found in the state, and a replica of a shaft tomb discovered in Zapopan. Upstairs there are ethnographic displays about Indian tribes, a gallery focusing on local history since the Conquest, and paintings by both colonial and contemporary Jalisco artists.

Open, horse-drawn carriages can be hired at the museum entrance for a ride through the city's historic center.

🎭 Palacio de Gobierno

Cnr of Moreno & Av Corona. 【 *(33) 3668 18 02.* ◯ *daily.*

Finished in the Baroque style in 1774, the Palacio de Gobierno is today the seat of the Jalisco state government. Murals by José Clemente Orozco adorn the main staircase, the dome of the former chapel, and the upstairs congress chambers. They celebrate Independence hero Miguel Hidalgo, who proclaimed the abolition of slavery in Mexico here in 1810. The wooden main door is intricately carved with nude female busts. Originally made for the cathedral, the door was deemed inappropriate and later installed here.

The Plaza de Armas, outside the building, has an ornate bandstand where concerts are staged on Thursday and Sunday evenings.

Sculpture on Plaza de Armas

🎭 Teatro Degollado

Plaza de la Liberación. 【 *(33) 3613 11 15.* ◯ *daily.*

A row of eight Corinthian columns, topped by a triangular frieze depicting Apollo and the nine Muses, makes up the portico of the 1,400-seat Teatro Degollado. Performances take place in the red and gold five-tier interior, under sparkling chandeliers and a dome with a fresco showing scenes from Dante's *Divine Comedy.* The Neo-Classical theater has been remodeled several times since its 1866 inauguration.

🏛 Instituto Cultural Cabañas

Cabañas 8. 【 *(33) 3617 43 22.* ◯ *Tue–Sun.* 🎟 *Sun free.* ♿ ◻ ◻ ◻

Founded by Bishop Juan Cruz Ruiz de Cabañas in 1805, this former hospice is the largest colonial edifice in the Americas and one of Mexico's finest Neo-Classical buildings. The structure, with its massive central dome and 23 courtyards, was the work of Manuel Tolsá.

For most of its history, until 1979, the building served as an orphanage, at times housing up to 3,000 children. It was then restored and turned into an exhibition center, with permanent and temporary displays, and a school for the performing and fine arts.

Mural of Miguel Hidalgo, painted by José Clemente Orozco, in the Palacio de Gobierno

Frog-shaped fountains in the pedestrianized Plaza Tapatía

Frescoes by José Clemente Orozco, executed in the late 1930s, cover the interior of the former chapel, with the central *Man in Flames* in the dome. These masterworks take as their themes the Conquest, political terror, and the de-humanization of modern man.

The Plaza Tapatía, fronting the building, marks the end of a nine-block pedestrian zone extending from the cathedral.

✝ Churches

There are many fine colonial churches within easy walking distance of the cathedral. The **Templo de San Juan de Dios**, with its vivid gold, white, and blue interior, backs onto a square where mariachi musicians and fans congregate.

To the south is the **Templo de San Francisco Neri**, which has a beautiful Plateresque façade. This church and the **Capilla de Aranzazú**, across the street, used to be part of a Franciscan monastery. The chapel contains three ornate Churrigueresque altars.

The lateral façade of the **Templo de Santa Mónica**, to the northwest, is an excellent example of Baroque styling.

✝ Basílica de Zapopan

Zapopan, 7 km (4 miles) NW of center. ☎ *(33) 3633 66 14.* 🕒 *daily.* 📷 ♿

The early 18th-century Basílica de Zapopan is home to one of the most revered religious relics in Mexico, the Virgen de Zapopan. The small corn-paste statue was presented to the Indians of the region by a Franciscan friar in the 16th century and is believed to bring relief from natural catastrophes. To the right of the basilica's entrance is a small museum displaying Huichol Indian crafts *(see p184)*.

VISITORS' CHECKLIST

Jalisco. 👥 *1.6 million.* ✈ *17 km (11 miles) S.* 🚌 *Calle Salvador Hinojosa, (33) 3600 03 91.* [i] *Morelos 102, (33) 3668 16 00.* 🎉 *Virgen de Zapopan (Oct 12).*

An ornate Baroque side entrance to the Templo de Santa Mónica

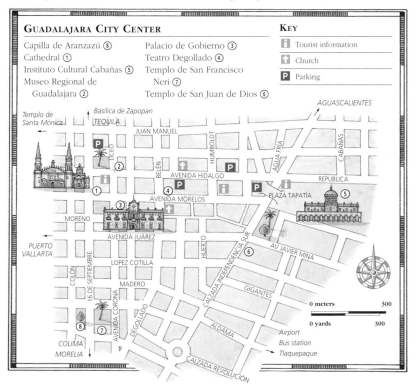

GUADALAJARA CITY CENTER

Capilla de Aranzazú 8
Cathedral 1
Instituto Cultural Cabañas 5
Museo Regional de Guadalajara 2
Palacio de Gobierno 3
Teatro Degollado 4
Templo de San Francisco Neri 7
Templo de San Juan de Dios 6

KEY

[i] Tourist information

✝ Church

[P] Parking

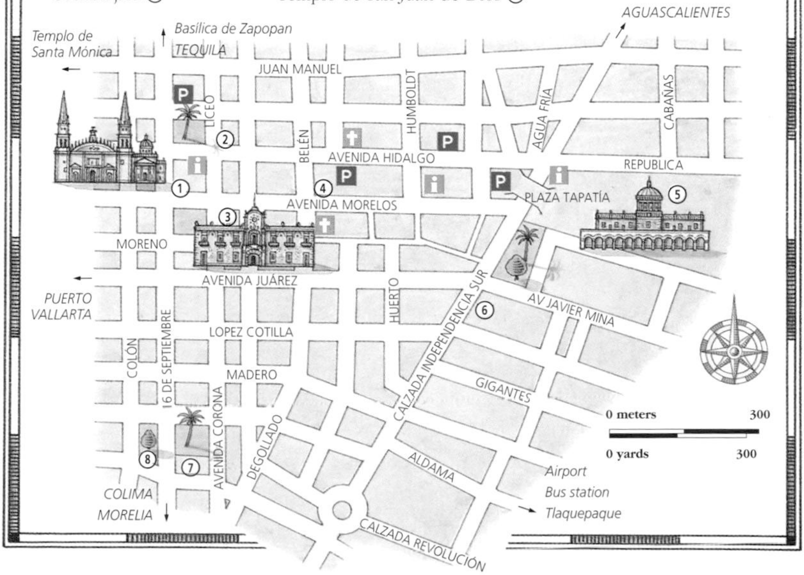

AGUASCALIENTES
Templo de Santa Mónica
Basílica de Zapopan
TEQUILA
JUAN MANUEL
HUMBOLDT
LICEO
BELÉN
AGUA FRÍA
CABAÑAS
AVENIDA HIDALGO
REPUBLICA
PLAZA TAPATÍA
AVENIDA MORELOS
MORENO
AVENIDA JUÁREZ
PUERTO VALLARTA
HUERTO
CALZADA INDEPENDENCIA SUR
AV JAVIER MINA
LOPEZ COTILLA
COLÓN
16 DE SEPTIEMBRE
MADERO
GIGANTES
AVENIDA CORONA
DEGOLLADO
ALDAMA
COLIMA
MORELIA
CALZADA REVOLUCIÓN
Airport
Bus station
Tlaquepaque
0 meters 300
0 yards 300

Tlaquepaque ⓫

Jalisco. 🚆 *Guadalajara.* ℹ️ *Morelos 288, (33) 3635 57 56.* 🎭 *Fiestas de Tlaquepaque (Jun).*

Once a separate potters' village and stylish weekend retreat for the residents of Guadalajara (*see pp188–9*), Tlaquepaque is now effectively a suburb of the city. However, it retains a village atmosphere.

The overwhelming selection of pottery, blown glass, textiles, metal, wood, and papier-mâché items cluttering the crafts shops is the main factor that attracts large numbers of visitors to come here.

There are also many restaurants. A favorite meeting spot off the appealing, flower-filled central square is El Parián. Hailed as the world's biggest cantina, it gathers a total of 34 eating and drinking establishments around its giant courtyard. In the center of the courtyard is a bandstand where mariachi musicians often play.

The best ceramics pieces from Tlaquepaque and the surrounding region can be appreciated at the **Museo Regional de la Cerámica**. Located in a beautiful old mansion, the museum counts a 16th-century kitchen among its most interesting exhibits.

Mariachi statuettes in a shop in Tlaquepaque

Many of the items sold in Tlaquepaque are in fact made in workshops in the neighboring suburb of Tonalá. Like Tlaquepaque, this was once a village outside Guadalajara, and was originally an Indian settlement. Its streets become an open-air craft market on Thursdays and Sundays.

🏛 **Museo Regional de la Cerámica**
Independencia 237. 📞 *(3) 635 54 04.* 🕐 *Tue–Sun.* ✅ 🚻

Laguna de Chapala ⓬

Jalisco. 🚆 *Chapala, Ajijic.* ℹ️ *Madero 407 Altos, Chapala, (376) 5 31 41.*

Mexico's largest natural lake, the Laguna de Chapala, supports a popular resort area, the Ribera, along its northwestern shore. However, the lake is drying up, mainly

A view of the Laguna de Chapala, Mexico's largest lake

because of the increasing water needs of the burgeoning population and industry of nearby Guadalajara.

The built-up Ribera has a near-perfect climate, and its proximity to Mexico's second city has for decades resulted in streams of foreign visitors. It stretches for 21 km (13 miles) from the old-fashioned resort of **Chapala**, where writer D.H. Lawrence stayed, to the village of Jocotepec at the western end of the lake. **Ajijic**, an artists' colony with cobblestone streets, crafts shops, galleries, and a 16th-century chapel, is the most picturesque village of the Ribera. Farther west, the spa resort of **San Juan Cosalá** offers the attractions of public swimming pools and a natural geyser.

Boat trips from Chapala head for two islands: the tree-covered **Isla de los Alacranes**, with its fish restaurants; and **Mezcala**, with the ruins of a 19th-century fort where independence fighters held out for four years before surrendering to the Spanish in 1816.

The scenic road along the mostly undeveloped southern shore opens up splendid views of the lake.

San Juan de los Lagos ⓭

Jalisco. 👥 *50,000.* 🚆 ℹ️ *Fray Antonio de Segovia 10, (395) 785 09 79.* 🎭 *La Candelaria (Jan 25–Feb 2), Fiesta de la Primavera (late May).*

The imposing 18th-century cathedral in San Juan de los Lagos is one the most important Catholic sanctuaries in Mexico. An estimated nine million pilgrims travel here every year to venerate the Virgen de San Juan de los Lagos, a small 16th-century corn-paste statue enshrined

A candy stall on Calle de Independencia, Tlaquepaque

in an altar originally made for the church of Santa Maria degli Angeli in Rome.

The cathedral, which reaches a height of 68 m (223 ft), has a sumptuous interior. In its vast sacristy is a group of large 17th- and 18th-century paintings, six of which have been attributed to Rubens. Touching votive pictures, expressing gratitude to the Virgin for favors granted, line the walls of a room beside the sacristy.

Many colonial buildings have been lost from the town's narrow streets, but the **Capilla de los Milagros** and **Casa de la Cultura**, both dating from the 17th century, are fine examples that have survived.

A colorful mural depicting life in Mexico, San Juan de los Lagos

Lagos de Moreno **⑭**

Jalisco. 🏠 *130,000.* 🚌 🛈 *Jvarez 426 Centro, (474) 742 24 66.* 🎭 *Feria de Agosto (late Jul–early Aug).*

Tourists rarely stray into this architectural jewel, which boasts many 18th- and 19th-century buildings and is known as the "Athens of Jalisco."

In colonial times, Lagos de Moreno was on the silver road between Zacatecas and Mexico City. The magnificent Baroque **parish church**, the more sober **Templo y Ex-Convento de Capuchinas**, and a bridge with Neo-Classical decoration all date from this era. The town peaked as a prosperous cattle-ranching center in the late 1800s, when it was enhanced by the charming **Teatro Rosas Moreno**. Two stately Neo-Classical residences from the same time are still here and look out onto the central park. These buildings now house the **Palacio Municipal** and the **Hotel de París**.

The arcaded main courtyard of the Palacio de Gobierno, Aguascalientes

Aguascalientes **⑮**

Aguascalientes. 🏠 *640,000.* 🚂 🚌 🛈 *Plaza de la Patria, (449) 915 11 55.* 🎭 *Feria de San Marcos (mid-Apr–mid-May), Las Calaveras (early Nov).*

Named after its hot springs, Aguascalientes still attracts visitors to its thermal baths but is today best known for its popular spring fair, the Feria de San Marcos (*see p185*).

The colonial red and pink **Palacio de Gobierno** has a spectacular maze of arches, pillars, and staircases around its main courtyard. An entertaining series of murals inside were painted by Oswaldo Barra Cunningham, a pupil of Diego Rivera. Across the Plaza de la Patria is the 18th-century **cathedral**, with a gallery of colonial paintings, and the Neo-Classical **Teatro Morelos**.

The **Museo de Arte Contemporáneo** displays prize-winning contemporary works, and the **Museo José Guadalupe Posada** has

The 18th-century cathedral on Plaza de la Patria in Aguascalientes

engravings by Mexico's best known satirical cartoonist. In contrast, **Museo Descubre** is an up-to-date interactive science museum.

🏛 **Museo de Arte Contemporáneo**
Juan de Montoro 222. 📞 *(449) 918 69 01.* ◌ *Tue–Sun.* 🎟 *Sun free.*
🏛 **Museo José Guadalupe Posada**
Diaz de León. 📞 *(449) 915 45 56.* ◌ *Tue–Sun.* 🎟 *Sun free.* ♿
🎫 *reserve in advance.*
🏛 **Museo Descubre**
Avenida San Miguel. 📞 *(449) 978 03 38.* ◌ *daily.* 🎟 ♿ 🎫 🖥 🖨

La Quemada **⑯**

Zacatecas. Mex 54, 57 km (35 miles) SE of Zacatecas. 🚌 *from Zacatecas.* ◌ *daily.* 🎟

The archaeological site at La Quemada stretches over a steep hill rising from a wide, arid valley. From around AD 350, La Quemada was an important religious and political center and the focal point for trade between the area and Teotihuacán (*see pp134–7*). After AD 700, La Quemada seems to have substituted trade with more bellicose activities. In around 1100, it apparently suffered a violent end, despite an 800-m (2,600-ft) long and 4-m (13-ft) tall defensive wall on its northern slope.

It takes about two hours to explore the site by following the steep, rocky path that leads from the lower Main Causeway and Hall of Columns all the way up to the Citadel.

The Churrigueresque façade of the cathedral in Zacatecas

Zacatecas ⓱

Zacatecas. 🏘 124,000. ✈ 🚌
ℹ Av Hidalgo 403, (492) 922 34 26.
📷 La Morisma (Aug), Feria de
Zacatecas (1st two weeks of Sep).

FOUNDED in 1546, shortly
after the discovery of metal
deposits in the area, Zacatecas
was soon supplying silver to
the Spanish crown. The city is
remarkable for its Baroque
limestone buildings that fill a
narrow valley between steep,
arid hills. Aristocratic patrons
lined the small squares and
streets with stately mansions,
convents, and churches.

🔒 Cathedral

The profuse decoration on
the three-tiered façade of the
city's cathedral is considered
one of the prime examples of
the Churrigueresque style (see
pp24–5) in Mexico. Apostles,
angels, flowers, and fruit
adorn the pillars, pedestals,
columns, and niches in dizzying excess. This exuberant
exterior contrasts strangely
with an interior whose treasures were lost in the turmoils
of the Reform (see p52) and,
later, the Revolution (see p54).
Most of the building was
constructed between 1730
and 1775, but the northernmost of the two towers was
not completed until 1904.

The cathedral's two lateral
façades are both compara-
tively sober. A crucified Christ
adorns the one that faces north
toward the Plaza de Armas
and its 18th-century palaces.
On the east side of the plaza is
the most striking of these palaces, the Palacio de Gobierno,
which now contains offices.

🔒 Ex-Templo de San Agustín

Plazuela de Miguel Auza. 📞 (492)
922 80 63. ⏰ Tue–Sun.
This large Augustinian church
and its adjoining convent
were tragically sacked during
the Reform years (see p52).
Their Baroque splendor suffered further when they were
later turned into a hotel and
casino. Presbyterian missionaries from the US purchased
the church in the 1880s and
proceeded to strip it of its
Catholic decoration, tearing
down the tower and ripping
out the main façade. Only
the splendid Plateresque side
entrance was spared. Ornate
blocks from the exterior are
now piled up like giant jigsaw
pieces inside, a stark reminder
of the former grandeur that is
now a blank, white wall.

These days the church is
used as an exhibition and
convention center, while the
former convent is now the seat
of the Zacatecas bishopric.

🏛 Museo Pedro Coronel

Plaza de Santo Domingo. 📞 (492)
922 80 21. ⏰ Fri–Wed. 📷
The Zacatecan painter and
sculptor, Pedro Coronel, is
responsible for this
unique art collection
spanning a number of
civilizations and conti-
nents, from Egyptian
mummy cases to
works by Goya and
Hogarth. All this
is housed on the
labyrinthine upper
floors of a former
Jesuit college and
seminary. There is
also a beautiful library
of 25,000 volumes
dating from the 16th
to the 19th century.
Next to the museum
stands the Templo de Santo
Domingo, with its elaborately
gilded Baroque side altars.

Sculpture [
Pedro Coro[

The Palacio de Gobierno, one of the mansions on the Plaza de Armas

🏛 Museo Rafael Coronel

Corner of Abasolo and Matamoros. **(**
(492) 922 81 16. ⏲ *Thu–Tue.* 📷 ▯

Another Coronel collection, this one by Pedro's brother Rafael, is held in the restored ruins of the Ex-Convento de San Francisco. An artist and a lover of folk art, Rafael Coronel amassed 10,000 ritual and dance masks from all over the country. About one-third of them are exhibited alongside a mass of other fine examples of Mexican popular art, pre-Columbian and colonial pottery, and architectural drawings and mural sketches by Diego Rivera, who was Coronel's father-in-law.

Some of the many masks on display in the Museo Rafael Coronel

🏛 Museo Francisco Goitia

Enrique Estrada 102. **(** *(492) 922 02 11.* ⏲ *Tue–Sun.* 📷

Paintings, silkscreens, and sculptures by the Coronel brothers and other Zacatecan artists are exhibited in a Neo-Classical villa. Until 1962 the house was the official residence of state governors. Its formal gardens overlook the Parque Enrique Estrada. This hilly park drops down to the remains of an 18th-century aqueduct and the Quinta Real hotel *(see p301)*, which is built around the city's old bullring.

🚠 Cerro de la Bufa

The hill northeast of the city center has seen blood from many battles. A museum at the summit exhibits items from the 1914 victory won by Francisco "Pancho" Villa *(see p173)*. There are splendid views from the cable car, which stretches 650 m (2,130 ft) from here to the Cerro del Grillo.

🚠 Cerro del Grillo

This hill's main attraction is a tour of three of the seven levels of the legendary Eden

Zacatecas's aqueduct and old bullring, near the Museo Francisco Goitia

silver mine, which includes a ride in a mine train through 600 m (2,000 ft) of tunnel.

🏛 Templo y Museo de Guadalupe

Jardín Juárez Oriente, Guadalupe. **(** *(492) 923 23 86.* ⏲ *daily.* 📷 *Sun free.* ▯

Just 10 km (6 miles) east of the city center lies the small village of Guadalupe, whose imposing Franciscan church and ex-seminary house a museum of colonial religious art second only in importance to that of Tepotzotlán *(see pp140–43)*. The treasures include works by Miguel Cabrera, Rodríguez Juárez, Cristóbal Villalpando, and Juan Correa. Beside the church is the jewel-like Capilla de Nápoles, built in the 19th century and considered to be the paragon of Mexican Neo-Classical expression.

ENVIRONS: About 45 km (28 miles) southwest of Zacatecas lies the historic town of **Jerez**, with its uncrowded streets, quiet squares, and authentic 18th- and 19th-century buildings untouched by restorers.

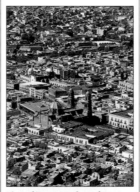

View of Zacatecas, from the summit of the Cerro de la Bufa

Real de Catorce ⓲

San Luis Potosí. 🏘 *1,200.* 🚌
ℹ️ *Carretera Federal 57, (488) 882 50 05.* 🎉 *Feria de San Francisco de Asís (Sep/Oct).*

THE CRUMBLING structures and ghost-town atmosphere of Real de Catorce testify to the rapidly changing fortunes of Mexican silver-mining centers. Hidden high in the mountains of the Sierra Madre Oriental, it is accessible only through a 2.5-km (1.5-mile) tunnel.

In the early 20th century the town boasted a population of 40,000, served by several newspapers, a theater, a grand hotel, and an electric tramway. Then, drastically hit by falling silver prices, its fortunes slumped until only a few families remained to witness the decaying mines and buildings. Its eerie, semi-deserted feel has made it the chosen set for several Mexican cowboy films.

Only the Neo-Classical church, the **Parroquia de San Francisco**, with its reputedly miraculous statue of St. Francis of Assisi and its large collection of votive pictures, was maintained for the sake of the pilgrims who flood the town once a year. Opposite the church is the dilapidated **Casa de Moneda**, a former silver warehouse and mint dating back to the 1860s. The town's former glory can also be seen in the shells of ornate mansions, the ruined bullring, and an octagonal cockfighting ring.

Real de Catorce's fortunes now look set to rise and at least one of the surrounding mines is being tested as a possible new source of precious metals. Ironically, the arrival of modern amenities is reducing the town's touristic appeal.

San Luis Potosí ⑲

San Luis Potosí. 🏛 *670,000*. 🚌 ℹ️
Álvaro Obregón 520, (444) 812 99 39.
🎉 *San Luis Rey de Francia (Aug 25).*

THE MINING WEALTH that the
city of San Luis Potosí
accumulated in the 1600s is
evident in the historic buildings and three main squares
at its core. The most central
square, the **Plaza de Armas**,
is dominated by the cathedral
and the stately **Palacio de
Gobierno**, which was the seat
of Benito Juárez's government
when he denied clemency to
Emperor Maximilian in 1867
(see p53). Behind it stands the
Real Caja, or Royal Treasury,
whose wide staircase enabled
pack animals to reach the
storage chambers above.

The second square is the
Plaza de los Fundadores,
the site of a former Jesuit college and two 17th-century
churches, the **Iglesia de la
Compañía** and the graceful
Capilla de Loreto. On the
eastern side of town is the third
main square, the **Plaza del
Carmen**, on which stand the
church of the same name, the
imposing **Teatro de la Paz**,
and the Museo de la Máscara.

🏛 Museo Nacional de la Máscara
Villerías 2. 📞 *(444) 812 30 25.*
🕐 *Tue–Sun.* ♿ 📷
The walls of a former mansion
are adorned with over 1,000
decorative and ritual masks.
The exhibits come from every
region of Mexico.

**The Capilla de Aranzazú in the
Ex-Convento de San Francisco**

⛪ Templo del Carmen
This Churrigueresque church,
built in the mid-1700s, is by
far the most spectacular religious structure in the city. The
impressive exterior has a three-
tiered main façade, an
ornate tower, and
multi-colored domes.
Even more fabulous
is the interior, not
least for its Baroque
side altars and
Francisco Eduardo
Tresguerras' main
altar. The real high-
light, however, is the
exuberant Altar de
los Siete Príncipes,
which is not actually
an altar but a floor-
to-ceiling interior
façade enclosing the
entrance to a side chapel, the
Camarín de la Virgen. Its white-
stucco surface is dotted with
polychrome statues of angels.

**Detail of Templo de
San Francisco**

🏛 Ex-Convento de San Francisco
Galeana 450. 📞 *(444) 814 35 72.*
🕐 *Tue–Sun.* 📷 *Sun free.* ♿
ground floor only.
The Franciscans, the first
religious order to arrive in
San Luis Potosí, began work
in 1686 on this ambitious
convent and church complex,
which took over a century to
complete. The extensive former convent now contains
the Museo Regional Potosino,
which has colonial and pre-
Columbian exhibits, including
displays on the Huastec
culture of southeastern San
Luis Potosí state.

Upstairs is the splendid
Capilla de Aranzazú, the lavish
private chapel for the former
occupants. A unique Baroque
jewel despite the garish colors
chosen by its restorers, it has
a rare covered atrium and a
carved wooden portal.
Behind the convent,
on the Plaza de San
Francisco, is the
Templo de San
Francisco. Beyond
its classic Baroque
façade lies a richly
furnished main
nave, several side
chapels, and an
original domed
sacristy. The sacristy
and the adjoining
Sala de Profundis
are filled with valu-
able paintings. Also
notable is the church choir,
where there are more paintings and the remains of a
monumental Baroque organ.

ENVIRONS: In the arid hills 27
km (17 miles) to the east lies
the ghost town of **Cerro de
San Pedro**, whose mines were
the source of the city's wealth.
To the southeast, around 45
km (28 miles) from San Luis
Potosí, is **Santa María del Río**,
known for its hand-woven
silk and silk-like *rebozos*, or
shawls. Traditional dyeing,
weaving, and fringe-knotting
can be observed in the Escuela
del Rebozo. Around **Villa de
Reyes**, 57 km (35 miles) south
of San Luis Potosí, former
haciendas show visitors the
architecture of a social system
that engendered, and ended
with, the Revolution *(see p54)*.

Corner of the late 18th-century Baroque Real Caja

Huasteca Potosina ⑳

San Luis Potosí. 🚍 Ciudad Valles.
🛈 Carretera Tamazuchale.

THE SOUTHEASTERN part of San Luis Potosí state is an area of stunning natural beauty known in pre-Columbian times as Tamoanchán, or "Earthly Paradise." It boasts tropical valleys, lush mountains, clear rivers, and majestic waterfalls. The most spectacular cascade is Tamul, which plunges 105 m (344 ft) into a canyon and is up to 300 m (1,000 ft) wide in the rainy season. It is reached by boat from Tanchanchín, southwest of Ciudad Valles.

Of the area's many archaeological sites, the most notable is **El Consuelo**, near Tamuín to the east. It has remnants of a polychrome altar and stepped ceremonial platforms.

Las Pozas ㉑

San Luis Potosí. Off Mex 120, 3 km (2 miles) NW of Xilitla. 🚍 Xilitla then taxi. 📷

HIGH IN THE mountains south of Ciudad Valles, near the spectacularly situated town of Xilitla, is this extraordinary, dreamlike jungle estate created by the British artist, eccentric, and millionaire Edward James. He first used the property to grow orchids and then as a private zoo. Later, with the help of local workers, sometimes numbering up to 150 at a time, he set about producing this architectural fantasy, which took over 30 years to complete. Many of the hundreds of

Flowering, a concrete sculpture by Edward James at Las Pozas

Sculpted hands at Las Pozas

Surrealist metal and concrete sculptures are unfinished or already disintegrating. They are scattered amid thick subtropical vegetation, springs, waterfalls, and pools. Slippery paths weave between the massive structures, which include the *Homage to Max Ernst*, *Avenue of the Snakes*, and *Toadstool Platform*.

Sierra Gorda ㉒

Querétaro. 🚍 Cadereyta, Jalpan.

ONE OF THE largest untamed regions in central Mexico, the semi-arid mountain range of the Sierra Gorda rises northeast of the city of Querétaro *(see pp196–7)* to over 3,000 m (10,000 ft). The lush green of its foothills is interrupted only by the massive monolith **La Peña de Bernal**, which towers 445 m (1,460 ft) above the village of Bernal.

In the mountains beyond **Cadereyta**, with its square of brightly colored churches, are the archaeological sites of **Toluquilla** and **Las Ranas**. These two sites are located on the rugged ridges near San Joaquín, to the east of Mex 120. Both feature fortress-like pre-Columbian ceremonial structures built between the 7th and 11th centuries AD.

Continuing north into the mountains, Mex 120 gets even steeper before descending to **Jalpan**. This town is the site of one of five Franciscan missions founded in the mid-1700s to convert the Indians of these mountains. The missions – the others are in Concá, Tilaco, Tancoyól, and Landa de Matamoros – all have scenic settings, and distinctive façades with strong Indian touches in their profuse mortar decorations.

EDWARD JAMES (1907–84)

The creator of the Las Pozas complex was, according to his friend Salvador Dalí, "crazier than all the Surrealists put together. They pretend, but he is the real thing." Edward Frank Willis James, born into a wealthy English family, was himself a moderately successful poet and artist, but excelled as a patron of the arts. He published books, founded ballet companies, financed large exhibitions, and amassed paintings by Dalí, Picasso, and Magritte, whose social circle he shared. His only marriage, to a Hungarian ballet dancer, ended in a scandalous divorce. In his later years, his private life revolved around the family of his long-time Mexican employee and companion Plutarco Gastelum Esquer, who had helped him create his jungle paradise at Las Pozas. When James died Esquer's children inherited the estate.

Eccentric Edward James relaxing at his Surrealist rain-forest home

Querétaro ㉓

Neptune, on the Jardín Guerrero fountain

THE MODERN SUBURBS of Querétaro hide its central colonial treasures, which UNESCO added to its protected World Heritage List in 1996. The city's location brought it prosperity in New Spain, but from the early 1800s Querétaro fell into decline, a trend interrupted only in 1848, when invading US troops briefly made it Mexico's capital. It was here that the treaty ceding half of Mexican territory to the United States was signed, and here also that Emperor Maximilian (see p53) faced the firing squad.

🏛 Plaza de la Independencia

With its austere colonial fountain, bougainvillea-covered garden, and stately old mansions, this intimate 18th-century square is a corner of Spain transplanted to Mexico. Most of the former residences on the plaza, among them the sumptuous **Casa de Ecala**, now house government offices, including the state congress and court. The only white façade, with plain moldings and sober balconies, is the **Casa de la Corregidora**, which was built in 1700 for Querétaro's royal representatives. Completely restored in 1981, it is now the seat of the state government. A few prison cells have been preserved in its rear courtyard. The bronze statue crowning the square's fountain honors the Marqués de la Villa del Villar, the city's early 18th-century patron.

Façade of a colonial mansion on the Plaza de la Independencia

🏛 Museo Regional

Corregidora Sur 3. 📞 (442) 212 20 31. ☐ Tue–Sun. 🎟 Sun free. 🚫

The state's regional museum is housed in the former convent of San Francisco, a building noted for its cloisters, domes, and stone columns. On the ground floor are the ethnographic, archaeological, and colonial sections. The second floor exhibits weapons, furniture, and photographs that trace Querétaro's pivotal role in Mexican history since the struggle for independence.

Both the convent and its adjoining church, the Templo de San Francisco, were begun by Franciscan missionaries in 1540, and the complex was finished in a blend of styles in the early 1700s. The church has *trompe l'oeil* murals and the city's tallest tower.

The tower of the convent church of San Francisco, Querétaro's tallest landmark

🔒 Templo de Santa Clara and Templo de Santa Rosa

These two 18th-century churches of former nunneries (at some distance apart) rival one another with the exuberance of their Churrigueresque interiors. Each has profusely carved altarpieces that form a floor-to-ceiling tapestry of foliage, shells, cherubs, and clouds. The naves are closed off by double choirs where the nuns once attended mass behind screens of delicately forged iron and gilded lattice. Both interiors are the work of Francisco Martínez Gudiño. Santa Rosa is also notable for its sacristy with life-size statues of Christ and the twelve apostles. A short walk from Santa Clara is the peaceful Jardín Guerrero, with its Fuente de Neptuno (Neptune Fountain).

🏛 Museo de Arte

Allende Sur 14. 📞 (442) 212 23 57. ☐ Tue–Sun. 🎟 Tue free. 🚫

This vast collection of 17th to 19th-century Mexican paintings is displayed alongside temporary art exhibitions and a smattering of contemporary paintings and photographs. They are housed in the 18th-century Ex-Convento de San Agustín, whose church captures the eye with its finely sculpted Plateresque façade and octagonal blue- and white-tiled dome. The real treasure here, however, is the supremely elegant Baroque main cloister, considered the finest of its kind in the Americas. Its richly carved details include caryatids supporting the arches and other symbolic elements.

🔒 Convento de la Santa Cruz

Independencia & Felipe Luna. 📞 (442) 212 02 35. ☐ Tue–Sun. 🎟 🚫

This plain convent has a long history. It started life in 1531 as a hermitage, on the site of the last battle between the Chichimecs and the Spanish. A 450-year-old stone replica of the cross that miraculously appeared in the sky, inducing the Indians to surrender and embrace Christianity, is mounted over the main altar of the small church. By 1683, the hermitage had become the first missionary college in the

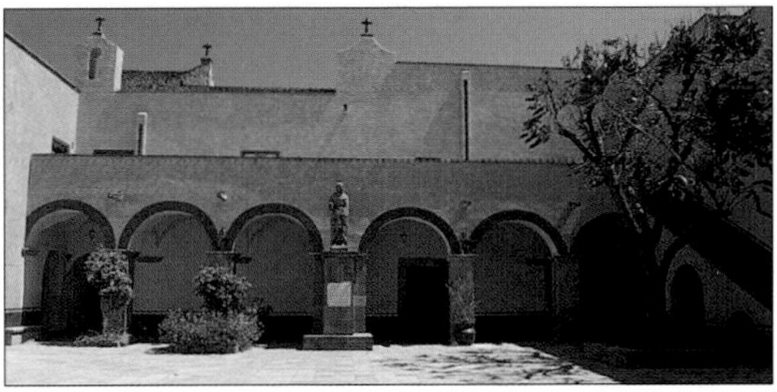

The fortress-like Convento de la Santa Cruz, east of the city center

Americas, and in 1848 the US invaders made the convent their headquarters. A sparsely furnished cell was Emperor Maximilian's prison before he was led to his death in 1867.

Los Arcos

Financed by the Marqués de la Villa del Villar in the 18th century, this is one of the world's largest aqueducts. It has 74 arches up to 23 m (75 ft) high and is 8 km (5 miles) long.

Cerro de las Campanas

The barren hill where Emperor Maximilian was executed with two of his officers on June 19, 1867, is now a tree-filled municipal park. A broad stairway leads to the Neo-Gothic chapel that was donated by the emperor's family to commemorate the renewal of diplomatic relations between Mexico and the Austro-Hungarian Empire in 1900. Inside, three marble slabs mark the spot where the executions took place. The painting on the altar is a copy of Maximilian's wedding gift from his mother. The cross over the altar is made from wood from the frigate that first brought him to Mexico and later returned his body to

Visitors' Checklist

Querétaro. 👥 640,000. 🚌 Prolongación Luis Vega y Monroy 800, (442) 229 01 81. ℹ Luis Pasteur Nte 4, (442) 283 50 00. 🎉 Fundación de Querétaro (Jul 25), Fiestas de Diciembre (Dec).

Europe. Nearby is a small museum with exhibits on the fall of the Second Mexican Empire. The whole site is dominated by a massive statue on the hilltop of the Mexican hero Benito Juárez, Maximilian's nemesis *(see pp52–3)*.

Environs: San Juan del Río, 50 km (31 miles) southeast, is known for its crafts and gemstones. The town's oldest buildings are the hospital and convent of San Juan de Dios, founded in 1661, and the 1690 convent of Santo Domingo.

Around 20 km (12 miles) northeast of San Juan del Río lies the quaint spa town of **Tequisquiapan**. Its cobbled lanes and arcaded main square make it a popular retreat.

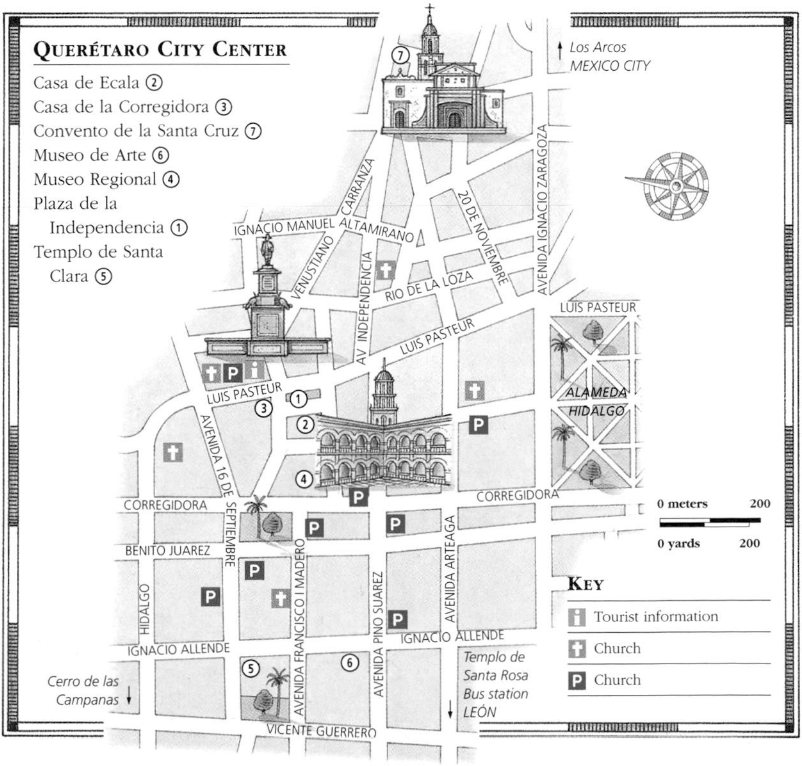
Querétaro City Center
Casa de Ecala 2
Casa de la Corregidora 3
Convento de la Santa Cruz 7
Museo de Arte 6
Museo Regional 4
Plaza de la Independencia 1
Templo de Santa Clara 5
Los Arcos
MEXICO CITY
IGNACIO MANUEL ALTAMIRANO
CARRANZA
VENUSTIANO
20 DE NOVIEMBRE
AVENIDA IGNACIO ZARAGOZA
AV INDEPENDENCIA
RIO DE LA LOZA
LUIS PASTEUR
LUIS PASTEUR
LUIS PASTEUR
ALAMEDA HIDALGO
AVENIDA 16 DE SEPTIEMBRE
CORREGIDORA
CORREGIDORA
BENITO JUAREZ
HIDALGO
AVENIDA FRANCISCO I MADERO
AVENIDA PINO SUAREZ
AVENIDA ARTEAGA
IGNACIO ALLENDE
IGNACIO ALLENDE
VICENTE GUERRERO
Cerro de las Campanas
Templo de Santa Rosa
Bus station
LEÓN
0 meters 200
0 yards 200
Key
Tourist information
Church
Church

Street-by-Street: San Miguel de Allende ㉔

A DELIGHTFUL COLONIAL TOWN, San Miguel de Allende is filled with opulent mansions and handsome churches, all connected by narrow, cobbled streets. Now a popular tourist destination, it was once an important crossroads for mule trains, which carried silver and gold to the capital and returned with European treasures. The town's active cultural life combines traditional charm with the cosmopolitan air of the large non-Mexican population.

Statue of priest at San Felipe Neri

Templo de la Concepción
A huge dome from 1891 towers over the gilded altar of this church.

Escuela de Bellas Artes
This art school, in a former convent, has an unfinished 1940s mural painted by David Alfaro Siqueiros (see p26).

Casa del Mayorazgo de la Canal, the town's most sumptuous mansion, has Neo-Classical and Baroque styling.

Casa Allende, now a historical museum, was the birthplace of Ignacio Allende, a hero of Mexican Independence.

Casa del Inquisidor once housed visiting representatives of the Spanish Inquisition. Built in 1780, the house has fine windows and balconies.

Casa de la Inquisición is thought to have been the prison of the Inquisition.

★ **La Parroquia**
Notable for its fantastic Neo-Gothic exterior, this parish church was remodeled by self-taught local architect Zeferino Gutiérrez in the late 19th century.

KEY

– – – Suggested route

★ Santa Casa de Loreto
Along with the Camarín de la Virgen, this is one of two opulent side chapels of the Oratorio de San Felipe Neri. Its multi-tiered lantern illuminates the lavishly decorated octagonal space within.

VISITORS' CHECKLIST

Guanajuato. 🚶 135,000. 🚌
Calzada de la Estación, (415) 152
22 37. 🛈 Plaza Principal, (4) 152
65 65. 🎭 Sanmiguelada (Sep),
San Miguel Arcángel (early Oct).
Casa Allende 📞 (415) 15 2 24
99. ⏰ Tue–Sun. 🎟 Sun free.

Iglesia de
Santa Ana

★ Oratorio de San Felipe Neri
A series of 33 oil paintings inside this church shows scenes from the life of the Florentine St. Philip Neri. They are attributed to Miguel Cabrera.

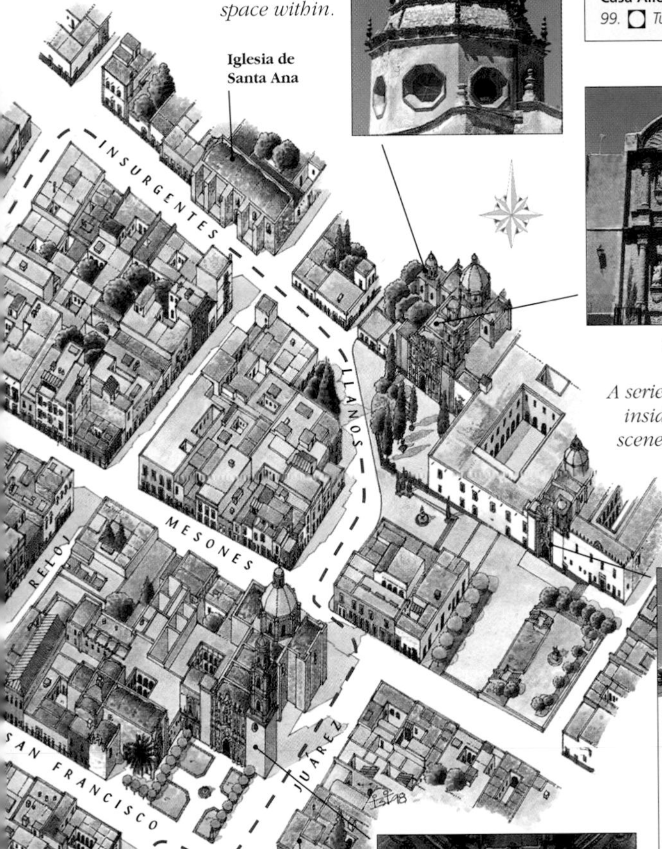

Casa de
las Postas

Casa del Conde
de Casa Loja

Templo de Nuestra Señora de la Salud
This was the chapel for residents of the 18th-century college next door. Its early Churrigueresque entrance beneath a giant shell has strong Indian influences.

STAR SIGHTS

★ Santa Casa de Loreto

★ Oratorio de San Felipe Neri

★ La Parroquia

Templo de San Francisco
The Neo-Classical tower of this 18th-century church contrasts sharply with its two ornate Churrigueresque façades. The decorated ceiling and high windows relieve the solemnity of the interior.

0 meters   75

0 yards   75

Street-by-Street: Guanajuato ㉕

MEXICO'S MOST BEAUTIFUL silver city climbs out of a
rugged ravine and up bald hills that once supplied
a quarter of New Spain's silver output. Mine owners
studded Guanajuato's narrow twisting streets and charming plazas with stately mansions and imposing churches.
A later bonanza added splendid late 19th-century touches,
and modern engineers burrowed an ingenious tunnel
network under the city to help overcome its crazy
geography. The unique result is a center devoid
of traffic lights and neon signs that was made
a UNESCO World Heritage Site in 1988.

**A typical city street
with overhang-
ing balconies**

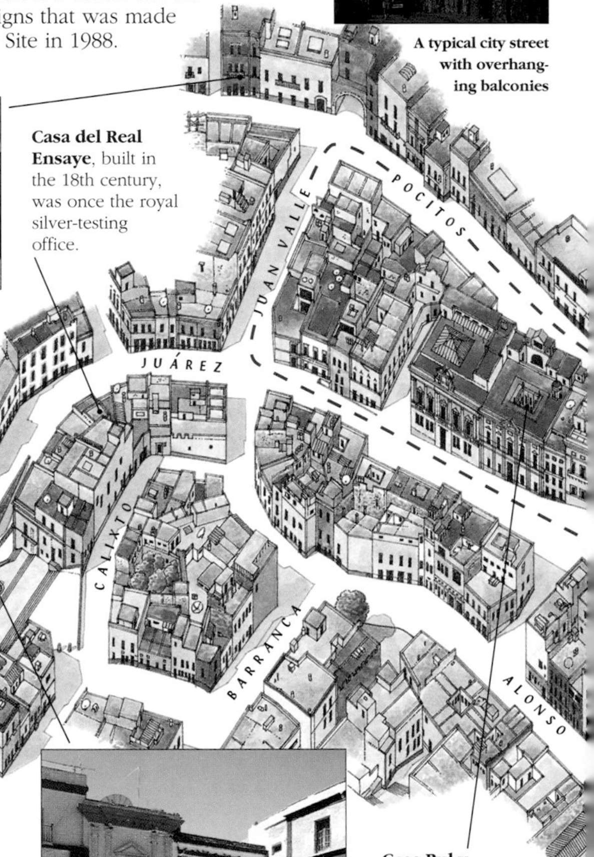

**Casa del Real
Ensaye**, built in
the 18th century,
was once the royal
silver-testing
office.

Casa Diego Rivera
*The house where Rivera
was born in 1886 is now
a museum exhibiting
over 100 samples of
his work, includ-
ing sketches of
his murals
(see p204).*

**Plaza de los
Angeles** is a
popular spot
for students
to gather.

Callejón del Beso (Alley of
the Kiss) is only 68 cm (2 ft)
wide in places. Legend tells of
the tragic death of secret lovers
who were caught exchanging
kisses from opposing balconies.

**Casa Rul y
Valenciana**, a
beautiful late 18th-
century mansion, is
now the courthouse.

Calle Hidalgo
*Converted from a
riverbed in 1965 to
help alleviate traffic
problems, this subter-
ranean street winds
under the city center,
appearing at the sur-
face in a few places.*

STAR SIGHTS

★ **Templo de la
Compañía**

★ **Jardín de la Unión**

★ **Teatro Juárez**

◁ View of Guanajuato from the Pípila monument south of the city center

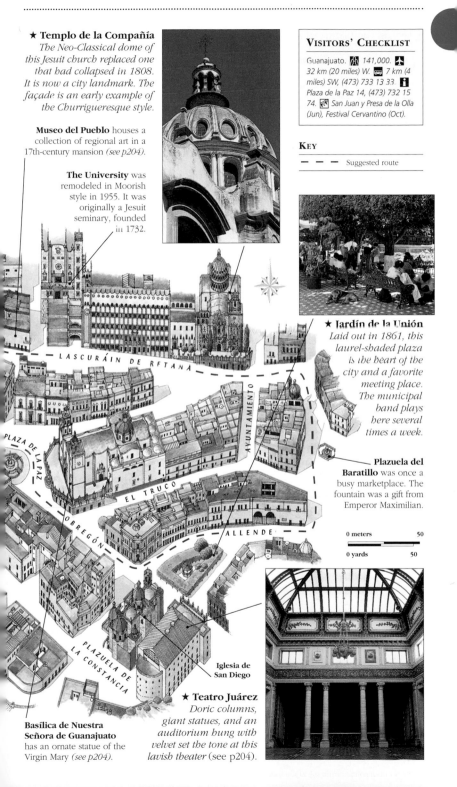

★ **Templo de la Compañía**
The Neo-Classical dome of this Jesuit church replaced one that had collapsed in 1808. It is now a city landmark. The façade is an early example of the Churrigueresque style.

Museo del Pueblo houses a collection of regional art in a 17th-century mansion *(see p204)*.

The University was remodeled in Moorish style in 1955. It was originally a Jesuit seminary, founded in 1732.

KEY

‒ ‒ ‒ Suggested route

★ **Jardín de la Unión**
Laid out in 1861, this laurel-shaded plaza is the heart of the city and a favorite meeting place. The municipal band plays here several times a week.

Plazuela del Baratillo was once a busy marketplace. The fountain was a gift from Emperor Maximilian.

LASCURÁIN DE RETANA

PLAZA DE LA PAZ

EL TRUCO

OBREGÓN

AVUNTAMIENTO

ALLENDE

0 meters   50
0 yards   50

PLAZUELA DE LA CONSTANCIA

Iglesia de San Diego

★ **Teatro Juárez**
Doric columns, giant statues, and an auditorium hung with velvet set the tone at this lavish theater (see p204).

Basílica de Nuestra Señora de Guanajuato has an ornate statue of the Virgin Mary *(see p204)*.

Exploring Guanajuato

MOST OF GUANAJUATO's main sights are located near the center of the city, and one of the pleasures of visiting this colonial gem is strolling around its twisting streets on foot, marveling at the ornate architecture. A range of local buses will take you to sights outside the center, and tours are available from the tourist office.

Madonna statue in the Basílica de Nuestra Señora de Guanajuato

🛐 Basílica de Nuestra Señora de Guanajuato

This 17th-century church facing the Plaza de la Paz contains a bejeweled sculpture of the city's patron saint, the Virgin Mary, on a solid-silver pedestal. The statue was given to the city by Charles I and Philip II of Spain in 1557. Reputed to date from the 7th century, it is considered the oldest piece of Christian art in Mexico. The church interior is especially striking in the evening, when it is lit by Venetian chandeliers.

🎭 Teatro Juárez

Jardín de la Unión. ☎ *(473) 732 01 83.* ○ *Tue–Sun.* 🎫

Statues of the Muses crown the façade of this Neo-Classical theater. Below them a wide stairway flanked by bronze lions leads up to a stately foyer and Moorish-style auditorium. This is the main venue for the Festival Cervantino, the country's top arts festival *(see p32).*

🏛 Museo del Pueblo

Pocitos 7. ☎ *(473) 732 29 90.* ○ *Tue–Sun.* 🎫

The former home of a wealthy mine owner is one of the city's finest buildings. It now exhibits art pieces from pre-Columbian to modern times, concentrating on colonial religious objects.

🏛 Casa Diego Rivera

Pocitos 47. ☎ *(473) 732 11 97.* ○ *Tue–Sun.* 🎫 📷

The house where Diego Rivera *(see p27)* was born is now a museum dedicated to his life and art. His work fills the upstairs rooms, while the ground floor preserves the family living area with its late 19th-century furniture and mementos.

🏛 Alhóndiga de Granaditas

Mendizábal 6. ☎ *(473) 732 11 12.* ○ *Tue–Sun.* 🎫 *Sun free.*

This former granary, built at the end of the 18th century, was the site of the first major rebel victory of the War of Independence. In 1810, revolutionaries burned down the gates and killed most of the government troops barricaded inside. Reminders of the battle are the bullet-scarred walls and the hooks dangling from the building's four top corners, where the heads of four rebellion leaders were later hung.

The huge building is now a regional museum covering art, ethnography, and archaeology. The staircase is decorated with murals depicting the city's history by José Chávez Morado.

Imposing façade of the historic Alhóndiga de Granaditas

🏛 Museo Iconográfico del Quijote

Manuel Doblado 1. ☎ *(473) 732 67 21.* ○ *Tue–Sun.*

Hundreds of art pieces relating to Don Quixote, from postage stamps to huge murals, are displayed here. The unusual collection includes works by Dalí, Picasso, and Daumier.

🎭 La Valenciana

5 km (3 miles) N of city center. ○ *daily.* 🎫

Silver and gold mining began here in the mid-1500s and boomed two centuries later after prospectors struck it rich at a new shaft just to the west. The Bocamina de Valenciana, the original 1557 entrance shaft, is cut 100 m (330 ft) straight down into the rock. Visitors can climb down to half its depth on steep stairs over which miners once hauled up loads of ore-rich rocks on their backs. A small museum at the entrance tells the mine's history.

Pyramid-style walls of La Valenciana mine, backed by the Templo de San Cayetano

🏠 Templo de San Cayetano

Near La Valenciana mine is the most spectacular of the city's churches. Also known as "La Valencianan," it was built between 1765 and 1788 with funds donated by the Count of Valencia, owner of the nearby mine. Its three-tiered pink limestone façade abounds with Churrigueresque pilasters. The Baroque interior has three splendid gold and polychrome altars and a pulpit inlaid with tortoiseshell and ivory.

🏛 Museo de las Momias

Explanada del Panteón. **📞** *(473) 732 06 39.* ⬜ *daily.* 📷 ♿

Southwest of the center is this macabre museum, which owes its popularity to the Mexican obsession with death. In cavernous rooms it exhibits over 100 mummies disinterred from a nearby cemetery where they had mummified naturally.

🏛 Museo Ex-Hacienda de San Gabriel de la Barrera

Marfil, 2.5 km (1.5 miles) SW of city. **📞** *(473) 732 06 19.* ⬜ *daily.* 📷

This restored hacienda was built in the late 17th century as an ore-processing center. It is now a museum displaying European furniture from the 17th to the 19th centuries. The grounds have been converted into 16 gardens, each landscaped in a different style.

ENVIRONS: The small town of **Dolores Hidalgo**, 54 km (34 miles) northeast of the city, is a historic shrine: the battle for independence from Spain began here with Father Miguel Hidalgo issuing his famous *Grito*, or "cry" to arms *(see p49)*, from the parish church.

Elegant garden of the Hacienda de San Gabriel de la Barrera

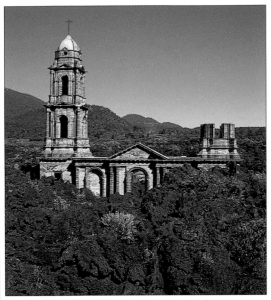

Church half buried by solidified lava from Paricutín volcano

Paricutín ㉖

Michoacán. 30 km (24 miles) NW of Uruapan. 🚌 *Angahuan.*

ONE OF THE youngest volcanoes in the world, Paricutín erupted in February 1943. Amid thunderous explosions, its cone grew to more than 330 m (1,100 ft) within one year. Ash and lava flows buried two villages and, while nobody was killed by the eruptions, more than 4,000 people had to flee their homes. The volcano's activity lasted until 1952, leaving behind a barren cone rising 424 m (1,391 ft) from a sea of black frozen lava. The total elevation above sea level is 2,575 m (8,448 ft).

The *mirador* (lookout) at Angahuan offers a dramatic view of the 25 sq-km (10 sq-mile) lava field and Paricutín behind it. The church tower that can be seen above the lava belongs to the buried village of San Juan Parangaricutiro. For a closer look, walk 3 km (2 miles) or hire a guide and a horse to take you down the steep cliff and through the lava rock formations. The stiff 30-minute climb to the crater rim is rewarded with stunning views of the double crater and surrounding lunar landscape.

The town of **Angahuan** itself has preserved its native character despite the influx of visitors to Paricutín. Most of the people speak Purépecha, the Tarascan language, and the women wear colorful traditional clothing.

Uruapan ㉗

Michoacán. 🏘 *450,000.* ✈ 🚌
ℹ *Juan Ayala 16, (452) 524 71 99.*
🎭 *Coros y Danzas (late Oct).*

MICHOACÁN'S second-biggest city, Uruapan is a busy agricultural center. Nestling against the Sierra de Uruapan, it links the cold upland region *(tierra fría)* to the humid lowlands *(tierra caliente)* that stretch toward the Pacific. Its subtropical climate supports exuberant vegetation, including vast avocado plantations.

The Spanish monk Juan de San Miguel founded the town in 1533 and divided it into nine neighborhoods *(barrios)*, which still preserve their own traditions. He also built **La Huatápera**, a chapel and hospital that now houses a fine museum of Michoacán crafts.

🏛 La Huatapera

Plaza Morelos. **📞** *(452) 524 34 34.*
⬜ *Tue–Sun.*

A Tour Around Lake Pátzcuaro 28

THE ROAD AROUND THIS idyllic lake bedded in rolling hills passes colonial and pre-Columbian architectural gems, and towns with rich craft traditions. Pátzcuaro, Tzintzuntzán, and Quiroga are popular destinations, but the western shore and marshlands to the south see fewer visitors. Yet here the winding road offers spectacular vistas of the lake and rare glimpses of Purépechan (Tarascan) Indian village life.

Quiroga 3
A busy market town, Quiroga sells agricultural and handicraft products from all over Michoacán. Lacquerware, such as wooden bowls and trays painted with bright flowers, is a typical local product.

Tzintzuntzán 2
The *yácatas,* multilevel temple bases, near this town reveal its history as the former Tarascan capital. Also noteworthy are the 16th-century Franciscan convent and the crafts market.

Santa Fé de la Laguna 4
Santa Fe has this 17th-century church, as well as roadside stalls selling the local black pottery.

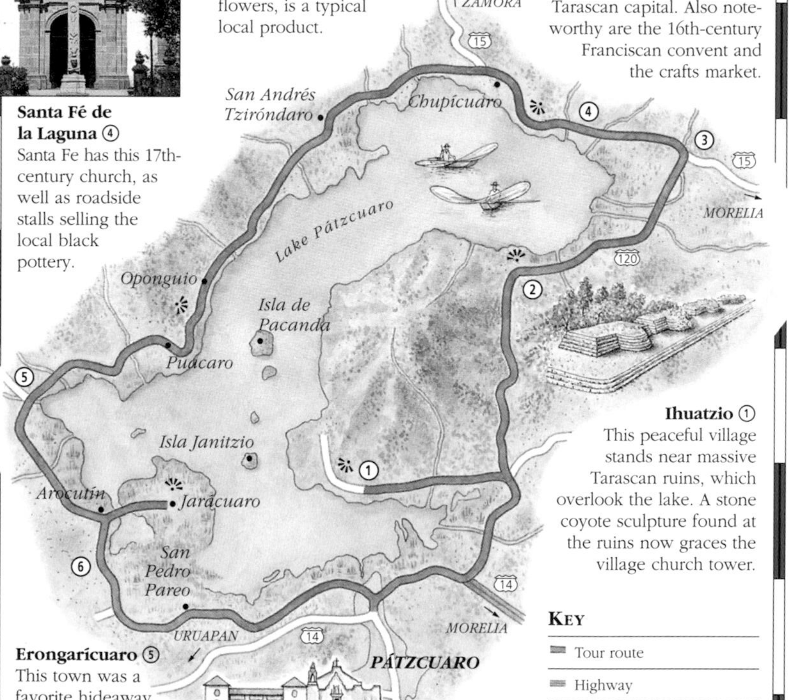
ZAMORA
15
San Andrés Tziróndaro
Chupícuaro
4
3
15
MORELIA
Lake Pátzcuaro
120
Oponguio
2
Isla de Pacanda
Puácaro
5
Isla Janitzio
1
Arocutín
Jarácuaro
6
San Pedro Pareo
14
URUAPAN
14
MORELIA
PÁTZCUARO
120

Ihuatzio 1
This peaceful village stands near massive Tarascan ruins, which overlook the lake. A stone coyote sculpture found at the ruins now graces the village church tower.

Erongarícuaro 5
This town was a favorite hideaway of French Surrealist André Breton.

KEY

- Tour route
- Highway
- Other roads
- Viewpoint

0 kilometers 5
0 miles 3

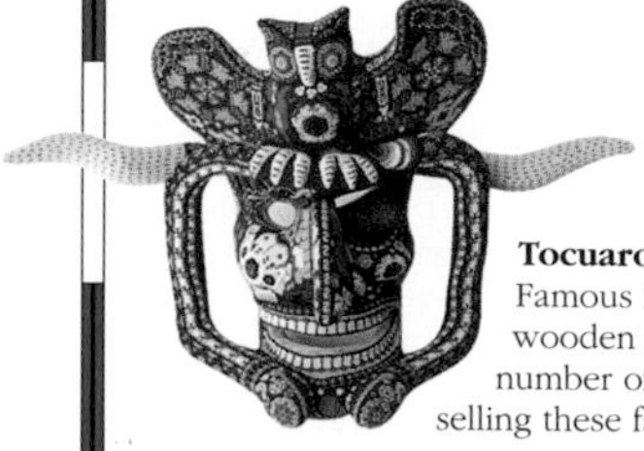

Tocuaro 6
Famous for its prize-winning wooden masks, Tocuaro has a number of unmarked workshops selling these fantastic creations.

TIPS FOR DRIVERS

Tour length: *89 km (55 miles)*
Stopping-off points: *Apart from Pátzcuaro, the best places to eat are a rustic restaurant between Erongarícuaro and Arocutín (see p321) and, for picnics, a small swimming beach near Chupícuaro.*

View of Isla Janitzio, the most important of the six islands on Lake Pátzcuaro

Pátzcuaro ㉙

Michoacán. 🏛 48,000. 🚌
ℹ️ Buenavista 1, (434) 342 12 14.
📅 Año Nuevo Purépecha (late Jan), Day of the Dead (Nov 1–2).

SET AMID the pastures and pine forests on Lake Pátzcuaro's southern shore, this historic town was once an important religious and political center of the Tarascan people. Its colonial splendor owes much to Michoacán's first bishop, Vasco de Quiroga, who temporarily turned it into the civic, religious, and cultural seat of the state.

The **Basílica de Nuestra Señora de la Salud**, an ambitious Vasco de Quiroga project, was to boast five naves and accommodate tens of thousands of people. However, only one nave was completed. Fires and earthquakes ravaged the building over the centuries, and the church was finally finished in a jumble of styles in 1833. Devout Indians flock here to visit the bishop's tomb.

Just to the south is the **Museo de Artes Populares**, a craft museum installed in the 16th-century Colegio de San Nicolás. The museum's collection includes a cabin-like *troje*, with typical Purépecha furnishings, that sits on a former pyramid platform.

The town's other architectural highlights include the Baroque **Templo del Sagrario** and an 18th-century Dominican nunnery. The latter is now the **Casa de los Once Patios**, a crafts center with workshops and stores. Its most attractive section is a small arcaded cloister where a nun and her servants lived.

Huge ash trees shade the quiet, elegant **Plaza Vasco de Quiroga** with its large fountain and statue of the town's benefactor. Many of the colonial mansions that face the square have been converted into shops, restaurants, and

The tranquil courtyard of the Museo de Artes Populares

hotels, but the real commercial hub of the town is the nearby **Plaza Gertrudis Bocanegra**. Named after a local Independence heroine, it gives access to the covered market. On Fridays, the streets toward the Neo-Classical **Santuario de Guadalupe** church (1833) fill with stalls, and pottery is sold in the Plazuela de San Francisco.

ENVIRONS: Tours to the islands on Lake Pátzcuaro leave docks north of town. **Janitzio**, with its monument to Morelos (see p49), is the most popular.

🏛 **Museo de Artes Populares**
Corner of Enseñanza and Alcantarilla.
📞 (434) 342 10 29. 🕐 Tue–Sun.
📷 Sun free. ✔
🏛 **Casa de los Once Patios**
Madrigal de las Altas Torres. 🕐 daily. ✔

The 17th-century Templo del Sagrario in Pátzcuaro

DAY OF THE DEAD

Although Mexicans all over the country commune with the dead on the night of November 1 (see pp34–5), the ceremonies on the island of Janitzio and in the villages around Lake Pátzcuaro are particulary impressive. This is largely because of their deep indigenous roots and unique settings. Throughout the night boats decorated with candles and flowers and laden with chanting people travel between Pátzcuaro docks and the island. The air is filled with wafts of incense and the ringing of bells. In the bustling cemeteries, each grave is covered with private tokens – special foods, photographs, and toys – intended to summon back the dead in celebration.

Wooden skeleton

Street-by-Street: Morelia ③

CAPITAL OF THE STATE of Michoacán, Morelia was founded in the mid-1500s under the name of Valladolid on fertile territory once ruled by Tarascan kings. The first settlers were Spanish nobility and religious orders, who laid out a city of magnificent palaces, convents, and churches, along flagstone avenues and around plazas. The historic center has retained its Spanish character over the centuries; even new buildings sport colonial façades in pink limestone. The city's name was changed in 1828 to honor José María Morelos *(see p49)*, the native son instrumental in leading Mexico toward Independence.

★ Conservatorio de las Rosas
The peaceful courtyard of this former Dominican nunnery is enhanced by the sounds of practicing music students (see p210).

Teatro Ocampo

Templo de las Rosas *(see p210)*

★ Palacio Clavijero
Government offices now surround the courtyard of this former Jesuit college (see p210). The austere Baroque building was named after a historian who taught here in the 1700s.

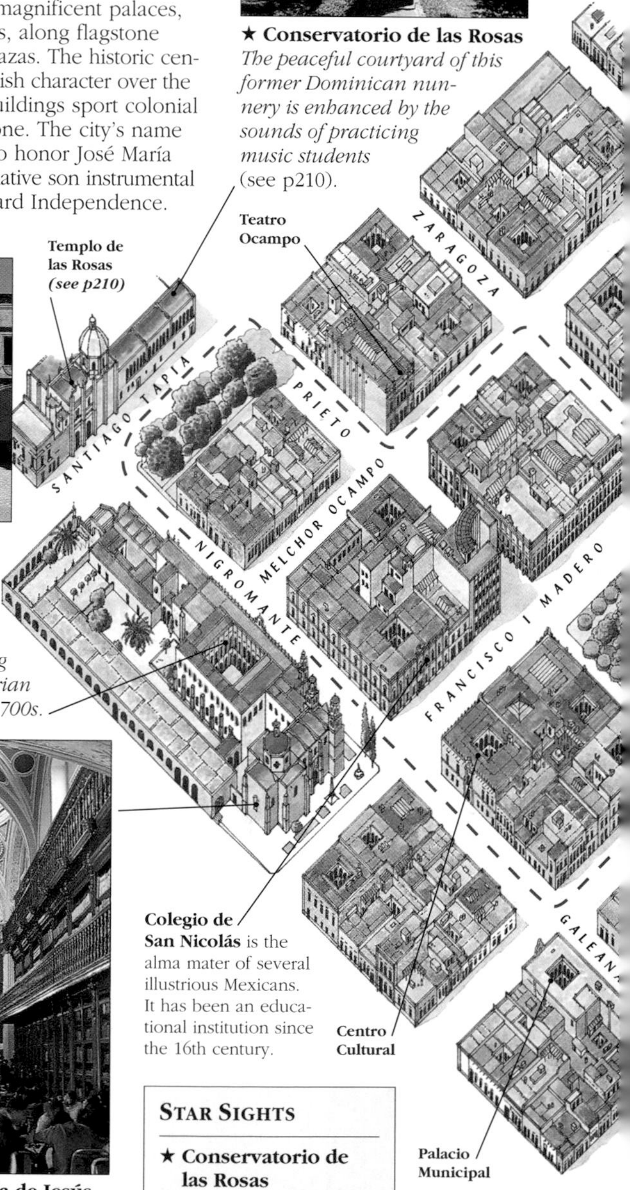

Colegio de San Nicolás is the alma mater of several illustrious Mexicans. It has been an educational institution since the 16th century.

Centro Cultural

Palacio Municipal

Templo de la Compañía de Jesús
This church was built in the 17th century for the adjoining Palacio Clavijero. Since 1930 it has been home to the Public Library.

SANTIAGO TAPIA
ZARAGOZA
PRIETO
NIGROMANTE
MELCHOR OCAMPO
FRANCISCO I MADERO
GALEANA

STAR SIGHTS

★ **Conservatorio de las Rosas**

★ **Palacio Clavijero**

★ **Cathedral**

0 meters	50
0 yards	50

Plaza de Armas was laid out as the center of town in the 16th century The bandstand dates from 1887.

Palacio de Gobierno
This former seminary (see p210) has been the seat of the state government since 1867. Bright murals decorate the upper level

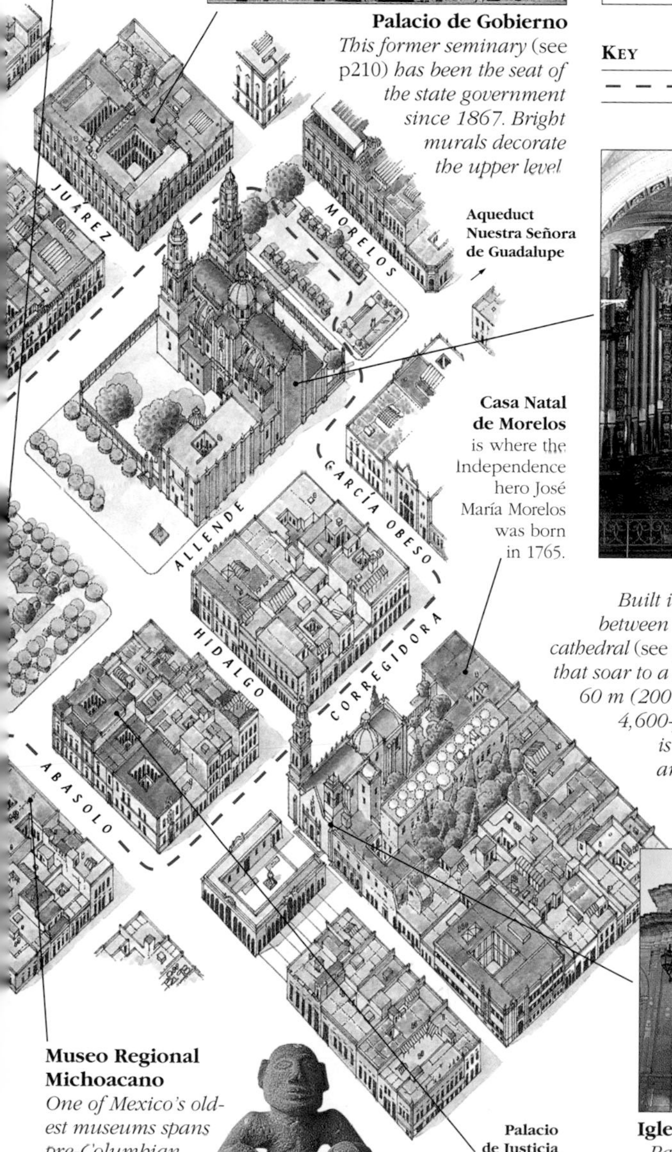

Aqueduct Nuestra Señora de Guadalupe

VISITORS' CHECKLIST

Michoacán. 620,000.
27 km (17 miles) NE.
Libramiento Norte, (443) 334 10 71. Palacio Clavijero, Nigromante 79, (443) 317 23 71. Aniversario de la Fundación de Morelia (May 18).

KEY

– – – Suggested route

Casa Natal de Morelos is where the Independence hero José María Morelos was born in 1765.

★ Cathedral
Built in a mixture of styles between 1660 and 1774, the cathedral (see p210) has two towers that soar to a height of more than 60 m (200 ft). Its monumental 4,600-pipe German organ is the main star of the annual International Organ Festival.

Museo Regional Michoacano
One of Mexico's oldest museums spans pre-Columbian to modern eras (see p210). This figure dates from the Classic Period.

Palacio de Justicia

Iglesia de San Agustín
Part of a 16th-century Augustinian ex-convent, this church has a sober Plateresque façade. It is seen here through the arches of the courtyard in front of it.

JUAREZ
MORELOS
ALLENDE
GARCÍA OBESO
HIDALGO
CORREGIDORA
ABASOLO

Exploring Morelia

STARTING FROM Avenida Francisco I. Madero or the Plaza de Armas, almost all of Morelia's important sights are within short walking distance. The colonial-style streets and captivating Spanish architecture make this a pleasant city to stroll around. A short bus or taxi ride will take you east of the center, to the impressive aqueduct that runs alongside the city park.

🏛 Cathedral
This majestic structure in pink trachyte stone was begun in 1660 but not completed until a century later. The resulting blend of styles – Neo-Classical, Herreresque, and Baroque – can be seen in the twin towers that dominate the surrounding historic city center. Among the remnants of past splendor are the silver baptismal font in a side chapel and the 16th-century corn-paste statue of the Señor de la Sacristía. The statue's gold crown was a gift from Philip II of Spain.

Ornately carved stonework on Morelia's cathedral

🏛 Palacio de Gobierno
Avenida Francisco I. Madero 63.
[(443) 313 07 07. **○** daily.
This colonial edifice opened in 1770 as the Tridentine Seminary, which was attended by several key figures of the Independence *(see p49)* and Reform *(see pp52–3)* movements. It later became the seat of state government. In the 1950s, Alfredo Zalce adorned the staircase and first floor with murals on local themes.

Alfredo Zalce's mural above the grand staircase of the Palacio de Gobierno

🏛 Templo y Conservatorio de las Rosas
Dominican nuns arrived here in 1590, but most of their original buildings were replaced in the 17th and early 18th centuries with the convent and church that now face the Jardín de las Rosas. The Baroque façade of the church has twin portals, a typical feature of nunneries. Other notable features are the unusual gargoyles in the form of crocodiles, and the three gold altars inside. The convent itself was later converted into an orphanage and has housed a music school since 1904.

🏛 Palacio Clavijero
Nigromante 79. **[** (443) 312 80 81. **○** daily.
The grand proportions and Baroque styling of the former Colegio de San Francisco Javier, a 17th-century Jesuit college, are best appreciated from its vast main courtyard. Elegant arcades on

the ground floor contrast with a closed upper cloister where 28 windows with sober moldings replace the arches below. Geometrical patterns in the stone pavement imitate the layout of gardens that once surrounded the octagonal central fountain. The building now houses government offices, including the state tourist information bureau.

🏛 Museo Regional Michoacano
Allende 305. **[** (443) 312 04 07. **○** Tue–Sun. **[**] Sun free. **[**
For more than a century, the Regional Museum has collected objects relating to the state's ecology and history from pre-Columbian to modern times.

About one fifth of its treasures are on public display in the Baroque mansion where Emperor Maximilian *(see p53)* lodged during his visits. Highlights include Indian codices, a rare 16th-century Bible written in three languages, and a celebrated early 18th-century painting entitled *Traslado de las Monjas (The Moving of the Nuns)*. One of the few realistic portrayals of Mexican colonial society, it depicts the 1738 procession of nuns from one convent to another. They are escorted by dignitaries and observed by elegantly dressed ladies, dancing Indians, and black musicians.

🏛 Casa de Artesanías
Fray Juan de San Miguel 129.
[(443) 312 08 48. **○** daily.
The 16th-century Convento de San Buenaventura was restored in the 1970s and is now a showcase for Michoacán's rich craft tradition. The rooms around the arched courtyard contain a selection of items for sale, including pottery, textiles, and lacquerware. In the upstairs rooms visitors can observe artisans at work.

🏛 Aqueduct and Calzada Fray Antonio de San Miguel
Avenida Acueducto.
Water once flowed along this 18th-century aqueduct from a well 8 km (5 miles) away to the city's 30 public fountains and 150 private outlets. The final 1.5-km (1-mile) stretch consists of 253 arches, some

The vividly decorated dome of Santuario de Nuestra Señora de Guadalupe

of which reach a height of 10 m (33 ft). It is especially stunning when lit up at night.

The aqueduct was built by Bishop Fray Antonio de San Miguel, who also created the *calzada* (avenue) that bears his name. This pedestrian esplanade leads from the city end of the aqueduct to the Guadalupe Sanctuary. With its ash trees, Baroque benches, and 18th-century mansions, it recalls a long-gone era.

Las Tarascas fountain, where the aqueduct meets the *calzada*

â Santuario de Nuestra Señora de Guadalupe

This 18th-century church at the far end of Calzada Fray Antonio de San Miguel has a sober Baroque façade but a remarkable interior. Molded clay rosettes and other floral motifs in bright colors and gold cover the walls, ceiling, and dome. These decorations were added in the early 1900s and combine Baroque, Art Nouveau, and folk-art styles.

ENVIRONS: North of Morelia are two wonderfully preserved 16th-century Augustinian monasteries that can be explored on a leisurely day trip. The first is in **Cuitzeo**, a fishing village 34 km (21 miles) from Morelia at the end of a causeway across a vast, shallow lake. The second is in **Yuriria**, an additional 32 km (20 miles) to the north. Both have Indian-influenced Plateresque façades, Gothic vaulting, and elegant cloisters. Fortress-like Yuriria is the larger of the two and was described by a chronicler in the 1620s as "the most superb building imaginable."

El Rosario Monarch Butterfly Sanctuary ㉛

Michoacán. Off Mex 15, 13 km (8 miles) E of Ocampo. 🚌 *Ocampo*. 🔲 *Nov–Mar: daily.* 🎫 🗹

SANTUARIO EL ROSARIO is one of two sanctuaries open to the public in the Monarch Butterfly Biosphere Reserve in the mountains west of Mexico City. The 160-sq-km (60-sq-mile) preserve is the winter home of an estimated 100 million monarch butterflies, which migrate here each year from northern US and Canada. Where monarchs overwinter was a mystery until Canadian zoologist Fred Urquhart found the isolated roosts in the 1970s.

The best time to visit is late February when rising temperatures encourage the insects to search for flowers or begin their journey back north. The hiking route along wooded slopes is well marked but can get very crowded at weekends.

ENVIRONS: The nearby **Sierra Chincua Monarch Butterfly Sanctuary** sees fewer visitors than El Rosario, but is easier to reach and offers horses for its more rustic trails. Guides will accompany visitors on request.

✘ Sierra Chincua Monarch Butterfly Sanctuary
Llano de las Papas, 9 km (6 miles) NE of Angangueo. 🔲 *Nov–Mar: daily.* 🎫

MIGRATION OF THE MONARCH BUTTERFLY

The annual migration of the monarch butterfly (*Danaus plexippus linneo*) begins in the northern parts of North America in early autumn. It is then that a special generation hatches, with a life cycle of up to nine months, four times that of spring and summer butterflies. These autumn-born individuals fly south in groups of several hundred to escape the winter. They cover up to 300 km (190 miles) a day and within a month reach the *oyamel* fir forests

Monarch butterfly

of central Mexico where they spend the winter. In spring they mate and head north again. En route, the females lay about 500 eggs each. Their offspring take up the baton and continue north to arrive in early June. None of the original migrants will survive to return to Mexico the following year.

SOUTHERN MEXICO

CHIAPAS • GUERRERO (SOUTH) • OAXACA

ITH ATTRACTIONS RANGING *from the world-class beach resort of Acapulco to magnificent colonial cities and monumental pre-Columbian sites, Mexico's southern states could be a microcosm of the whole country. The region is also home to many of the country's indigenous communities, whose language, customs, and costume animate rural villages and city markets.*

Southern Mexico's mild climate and fertile soils attracted some of the earliest recorded settlements in Mesoamerica, with the Oaxaca Valley first inhabited in the 7th century BC. Three centuries later, the Zapotecs built their capital at Monte Albán, which dominated the valley for hundreds of years, before giving way to other, smaller cities. Meanwhile, in the east, the Maya were reaching their cultural peak and building the magnificent city of Palenque.

The Spanish Conquest in the 16th century had a massive, and often destructive, impact but resulted in a unique fusion of pre-Columbian and colonial cultures. This is seen in the lives of the local Indians, whose dress, cuisine, fiestas, crafts, and markets rank among the best in the country. Only their languages remained immune, and Spanish is still a minority tongue outside the major towns. This integration has not been achieved without difficulties, however. Long-standing grievances have resulted in rising levels of crime and the emergence of the Zapatista revolutionaries in Chiapas, certain areas of which cannot now be visited.

Geographically, the South is dominated by the mountains of the Sierra Madre del Sur, which make travel difficult but provide spectacular scenery. The Pacific coast is mostly unspoiled. Its sandy beaches are lined with palm trees and pounded constantly by surf.

Peaceful and colorful Plaza Santo Domingo in the attractive colonial city of Oaxaca

◁ A villager beside the vividly painted church in San Juan Chamula, near San Cristóbal de las Casas

Exploring Southern Mexico

THE BEACH RESORTS of Mexico's southern Pacific coast include the world famous Acapulco; the up-and-coming Ixtapa and Zihuatanejo, Puerto Escondido and Huatulco; and the lesser known and more intimate Puerto Angel and Zipolite. The open, unprotected nature of the coast, however, means that the water is usually rough, and strong undertows make swimming unsafe except in sheltered bays.

The interiors of Chiapas and Oaxaca are, by contrast, best known for their colonial towns – such as Oaxaca and San Cristóbal de las Casas – but above all for their pre-Columbian sites. The hilltop Monte Albán and the jungle-shrouded Palenque are both easy to get to and worthy of a long visit. Lesser known but attractive sites include Yagul and Mitla, and the less easily accessible Bonampak (with its splendid murals) and Yaxchilán.

**Tzotzil women and children
in a village in Chiapas**

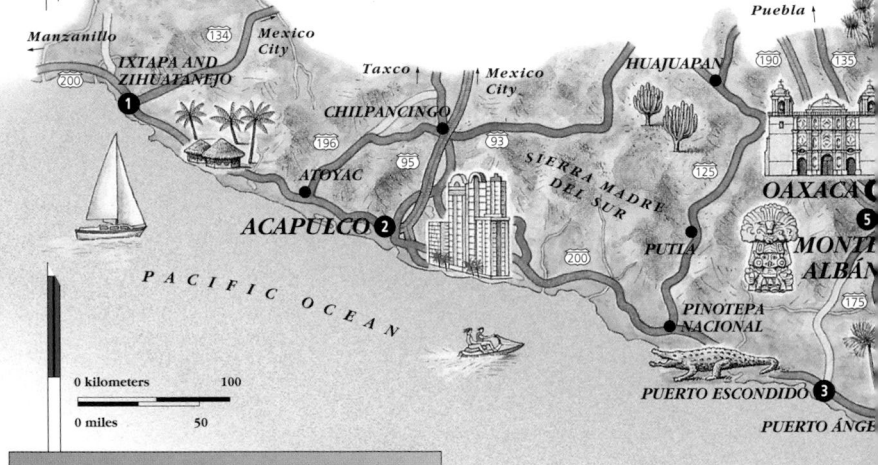

GETTING AROUND

The best way to get around Southern Mexico is by air or long distance bus. Acapulco, Zihuatanejo, Puerto Escondido, and Huatulco have international airports. There are domestic airports at Oaxaca and Tuxtla Gutiérrez. Bus services linking all the major towns and cities are reliable and frequent. For shorter journeys, minibuses *(colectivos)* are a cheap, though often uncomfortable, option. Mountainous terrain, the scarcity of gas stations, and the poor quality of the roads make driving an ordeal. Those who choose to drive are advised to do so only during the day. Access to some parts of Chiapas is restricted because of the Zapatista problem *(see p230).*

**View of Monte Albán
from the south platform**

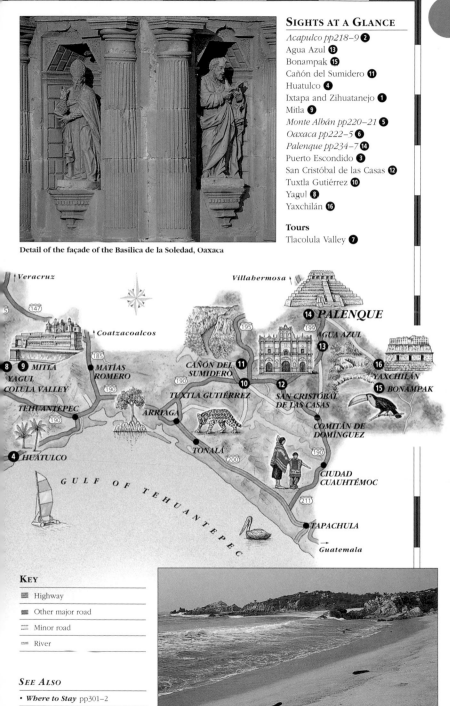

Sights at a Glance

Acapulco pp218–9 **2**
Agua Azul **13**
Bonampak **15**
Cañón del Sumidero **11**
Huatulco **4**
Ixtapa and Zihuatanejo **1**
Mitla **9**
Monte Albán pp220–21 **5**
Oaxaca pp222–5 **6**
Palenque pp234–7 **14**
Puerto Escondido **3**
San Cristóbal de las Casas **12**
Tuxtla Gutiérrez **10**
Yagul **8**
Yaxchilán **16**

Tours
Tlacolula Valley **7**

Detail of the façade of the Basílica de la Soledad, Oaxaca

Key

▬ Highway
▬ Other major road
═ Minor road
═ River

See Also

• **Where to Stay** pp301–2

• **Where to Eat** pp323–5

One of the many deserted beaches on Mexico's southern coast

Ixtapa and Zihuatanejo ❶

Guerrero. 🎭 *1,200.* ✈ *at
Zihuatanejo.* 🚌 ℹ *Boulevard Ixtapa,
(755) 553 19 67.*

IXTAPA AND ZIHUATANEJO are
actually two resorts in one.
Ixtapa, 10 km (6 miles) to the
northwest of its smaller neighbor, is a glitzy modern resort,
full of luxury high-rise hotels. It
is set along an attractive gently
curving 4-km (2.5-mile) beach,
Playa Palmar, which backs
onto a very broad, palm-lined
avenue packed with restaurants, shops, and nightclubs.
  Zihuatanejo, in contrast, is
low-rise and intimate, and still
has the feel of a close fishing
community. Set in a scenic,
sheltered bay, fishermen come
here to sell their daily catch.
  Both Ixtapa and Zihuatanejo
offer world-class deep-sea
fishing, and some of the best

The magnificent beach at Zihuatanejo

scuba diving on Mexico's
Pacific coast. They are also
a good starting point from
which to explore the spectacular, deserted beaches
along the surrounding coast.

Acapulco ❷

See pp218–9.

Puerto Escondido ❸

Oaxaca. 🎭 *15,000.* ✈ 🚌 ℹ *Blvd
Benito Juárez, (954) 582 01 75.*
🏄 *Surfing festival (end of Nov).*

PUERTO ESCONDIDO, literally
the "undiscovered port,"
lived up to its name for centuries. It was finally discovered
by the hippy community in the

The Beaches of Oaxaca

ALTHOUGH BLESSED with some of the country's best
beaches and lagoons, the coast of Oaxaca was untouched by tourism until the 1970s. Since then, limited
development has taken place, but with 480 km (300
miles) of coast and only a couple of significant resorts,
the area still retains a sense of undisturbed charm. The
coast has some remarkable flora and fauna, especially
in the freshwater lagoons west of Puerto Escondido.
The ocean along this stretch of coast is inviting, but
swimming is dangerous
as the undertow can
be very strong. Crime
is also a problem in the
region, particularly
on the beaches and
roads after dark.

*Laguna Manialtepec, "the place
of spring-fed waters," is a natural
lagoon. Encircled by mangroves,
it is home to a wide range of
plant, animal, and bird life. It
also has some beautiful beaches,
accessible by boat.*

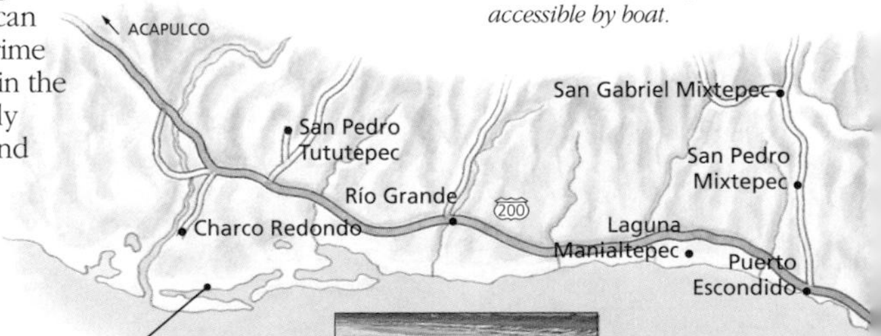

ACAPULCO
San Pedro Tututepec
Río Grande 200
Charco Redondo
San Gabriel Mixtepec
San Pedro Mixtepec
Laguna Manialtepec
Puerto Escondido

**The Parque
Nacional Lagunas
de Chacahua** is an
ecological preserve
with deserted beaches
and a few small fish-
ing communities. A
crocodile sanctuary
can also be visited
on a tour from
Puerto Escondido.

*Puerto Escondido
strikes a happy
medium between
the simplicity of the
smaller resorts on
Oaxaca's coast and
the expensive luxury
of Huatulco. It is
especially popular
with surfers.*

KEY

▬ Major road
═ Minor road
〰 River

1970s and has since become a significant tourist destination. Although showing some signs of the strain of development, it retains much of the fishing village character that originally made it popular.

Playa Marinero, the main beach, is popular with locals and tourists alike. Shaded by palm trees, it faces a small cove dotted with fishing boats and fed by an endless supply of gentle surf. Playa Zicatela is a larger beach to the west and is very popular with surfers, especially in the late summer months when the waves are at their highest.

At the end of November, the town comes alive for an international surfing festival. A popular local fiesta with music and dancing takes place at the same time. Puerto Escondido is also a good base for trips to the nearby freshwater lagoons, such as Laguna Manialtepec.

Huatulco ❹

Oaxaca. 🏛 25,000. ✈ 🚌 ⛴ 🅸 Blvd Benito Juarez, Bahía de Tangolunda, (958) 581 01 76.

Following the success of Cancún (see p279), the Mexican government looked for an equivalent on the Pacific coast. The result was Huatulco, until then virtually unknown except to the local Zapotec people. Based around nine bays and 35 km (22 miles) of beaches, the resort sprang up in the 1980s, and now includes a small international airport, a golf course, and a marina. Beautiful and still largely unspoiled, it has yet to become a major tourist destination.

Boats moored in the Santa Cruz marina in Huatulco

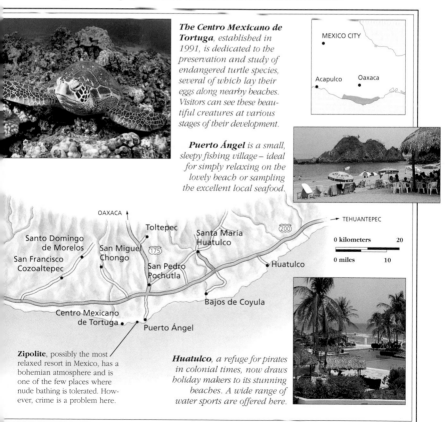

The Centro Mexicano de Tortuga, established in 1991, is dedicated to the preservation and study of endangered turtle species, several of which lay their eggs along nearby beaches. Visitors can see these beautiful creatures at various stages of their development.

Puerto Ángel is a small, sleepy fishing village – ideal for simply relaxing on the lovely beach or sampling the excellent local seafood.

Zipolite, possibly the most relaxed resort in Mexico, has a bohemian atmosphere and is one of the few places where nude bathing is tolerated. However, crime is a problem here.

Huatulco, a refuge for pirates in colonial times, now draws holiday makers to its stunning beaches. A wide range of water sports are offered here.

Acapulco ②

FRINGING ONE of the most beautiful bays on Mexico's Pacific coast, Acalpulco is the country's most famous resort. The Spaniards founded the city in the 16th century, and for the next 300 years it served as the country's main gateway to the Far East. Continued prosperity was guaranteed in the 1940s when the then president, Miguel Alemán, selected Acapulco as Mexico's first tourist resort. Hollywood celebrities such as John Wayne, Errol Flynn, and Elizabeth Taylor arrived shortly afterward, and the high-rise hotels soon followed.

View across Acapulco Bay from the southeast headland

MAP OF ACAPULCO BAY

PIE DE LA CUESTA

Adolfo Ruiz Cortines

TAXCO
MEXICO CITY

Av Constituyentes

Av Cuauhtemoc

Calzada Pie de la Cuesta

Papagayo Park

Playa Condesa

La Costera Miguel Alemán

Playa Hornitos

Playa Hornos

Fuerte de San Diego

Cathedral

Playa Icacos

La Quebrada

Playa Manzanillo

Playa Larga

Playa Honda

ACAPULCO BAY

AIRPORT
PUERTO
MARQUÉS

Playa Caletilla

Playa Caleta

0 kilometers 1

0 miles 1

Playa Roqueta

ISLA LA ROQUETA

KEY

For key see back flap

Exploring Acapulco

Acapulco can be divided into two distinct sections. To the west is the older, historic downtown area, or **Centro**; to the east is the newer "strip," which runs along the 11-km (7-mile) coastal road known as **La Costera Miguel Alemán**. This is lined with hotels, shops, restaurants, and nightclubs. The Centro is home to the

Señor Frog's, a popular restaurant overlooking the bay (see p323)

1930s, Moorish-style **cathedral**, which overlooks the main square, as well as the bullring, the docks, and **La Quebrada**, where the world-renowned cliff divers perform their daily routine. Two blocks east of La Quebrada is a house where artist Diego Rivera (see p27) spent time toward the end of his life. His colorful mosaics adorn his house.

The city boasts magnificent beaches and a worldwide reputation for the high life. It is also a working port and does not escape the environmental implications which that involves. The quality of the bay's water, for example, is not always perfect and drops noticeably in the rainy season (June–October) when litter is washed down from the hills.

Mosaic of Quetzalcoatl by Rivera, on a house near La Quebrada

♣ Fuerte de San Diego

Costera Miguel Alemán. ((744) 482 38 28. ☐ Tue–Sun. 🎫 Sun free. 🅿 Today, one of the few reminders of the city's history is the star-shaped Fuerte de San Diego, an early 17th-century fort that now houses the Museo de Acapulco. The museum details the city's history from pre-Columbian times to Independence, with special emphasis on its importance as a commercial center.

Brightly colored hotels overlooking Playa Icacos

The Beaches
The city's main bay – 7 km (4 miles) wide – is broken up into a number of separate beaches. **Playa Caletilla** and **Playa Caleta** are situated on the peninsula south of the Centro. Smaller and more intimate than the other beaches, they are popular with local families who enjoy the calm, clean waters. Boats can be taken from here for the ten-minute trip to **Isla la Roqueta**, a small offshore island with thatched-roof restaurants, a small zoo, and several beaches.
Playa Honda, **Playa Larga**, and **Playa Manzanillo**, on the northern side of the same peninsula and just south of the main square, were popular

in the 1930s and 40s, but now serve mainly as departure points for charter fishing trips. **Playa Hornos** and **Playa Hornitos** occupy a central position on the bay. They have a family atmosphere but can get busy on the weekends. They also have the advantage of several beachside restaurants and nearby Papagayo Park, which has boating, rides, and other children's activities.
Farther to the east is **Playa Condesa**, the best known and most crowded of all the beaches. It is considered by those in the know to be the resort's "hot-spot" and is a favorite with younger visitors. On the eastern side of the bay, **Playa Icacos** runs from the Presidente Hotel to the naval base and is often less crowded than the other beaches.

ENVIRONS: Pie de la Cuesta, just 25 minutes' drive west of the city, is an attractive, broad, palm-fringed beach, but swimming here can be dangerous because of the powerful currents. The nearby **Laguna de Coyuca** is a large freshwater lake that featured in the early *Tarzan* films, as well as *The African Queen* and *Rambo II*. Fishermen and water-skiers share the lagoon with a wide variety of birds and wildlife. The sunsets here are superb.

Puerto Marqués is a large bay to the east of the city, with a few luxury hotels, food stands on the beach, and safe swimming. Farther to the east is **Playa Revolcadero**, unsafe for swimming due to the strong undertow, but relatively free of crowds and perfect for sunset-watching, surfing, and riding horses (rentals available).

LA QUEBRADA CLIFF DIVERS
The death-defying cliff divers of La Quebrada provide Acapulco's most famous and spectacular attraction. The performance starts with the young men climbing a 38-m (125-ft) cliff on the side of a narrow inlet. On reaching the top, they offer a prayer at a small altar before launching themselves into the shallow waters below. Each dive must coincide with an incoming wave if the diver is to avoid being dashed on the sharp rocks below. The five daily shows, one at 12:45pm and the rest in the evening, can be seen from a viewing platform or from Hotel El Mirador (*see p301*). The last two shows are performed holding flaming torches.

The palm-lined Laguna de Coyuca, west of the city

Monte Albán ❺

SPECTACULARLY SITUATED on a mountain 400 m (1,315 ft) above the Oaxaca Valley, Monte Albán is the greatest of the Zapotec cities. In a triumph of engineering, the mountain top was leveled to allow for the creation of the ceremonial site. Its long history began with the Olmecs *(see p254)* around 500 BC. The city came to dominate the cultural, religious, and economic life of the region.

A skull found on the site

Falling under the influence of Teotihuacán *(see p134–7)* during the height of its power, Monte Albán declined in later years and by AD 800 was largely abandoned. It was subsequently adopted by the Mixtecs, primarily as the site for some magnificent gold-laden burials.

★ **Los Danzantes**
This gallery of carvings shows humans in strange, tortured positions. Once identified as dancers, they are now thought to be prisoners of war.

Mound III

Mound M

The South Platform has stelae at its northeast and northwest corners showing prisoners of war with their arms and legs bound.

Palace

Building P

GRAN PLAZA

Observatory
Thought to have been built as an observatory, or to celebrate victory in battle, this structure has glyphs carved on its walls. These may be the names of conquered tribes.

Altar

Mound II

Buildings G, H, and I, which served as temples, were found to contain several tombs. A tunnel leads from the Palace to Building H, possibly so that dignitaries could appear here as if by magic.

Stela

Ballcourt
A typical ballcourt, this I-shaped structure was used for playing the ceremonial ballgame (see p277). There would originally have been a stone ring at the top of each sloping side to act as a "goal."

The enormous Gran Plaza, aligned on a north-south axis

VISITORS' CHECKLIST

Oaxaca. Off Mex 190, 8 km
(5 miles) W of Oaxaca.
(951) 516 12 15. from
Oaxaca. 8am–6pm daily.
Sun free.

System IV is almost identical to Mound M. Both are well-preserved pyramids that would once have been surmounted by one-room wooden temples.

The Sunken Patio has an altar at its center.

Building B

★ **Tomb 104**
Above the entrance to Tomb 104 is this ceramic urn in the form of a figure seated on a jaguar throne. An image of Cocijo, the Zapotec rain god, is in the center of the headdress. When the tomb was opened in 1937 a vaulted burial chamber containing a single skeleton, surrounded by urns, perfuming pots, and other offerings, was discovered.

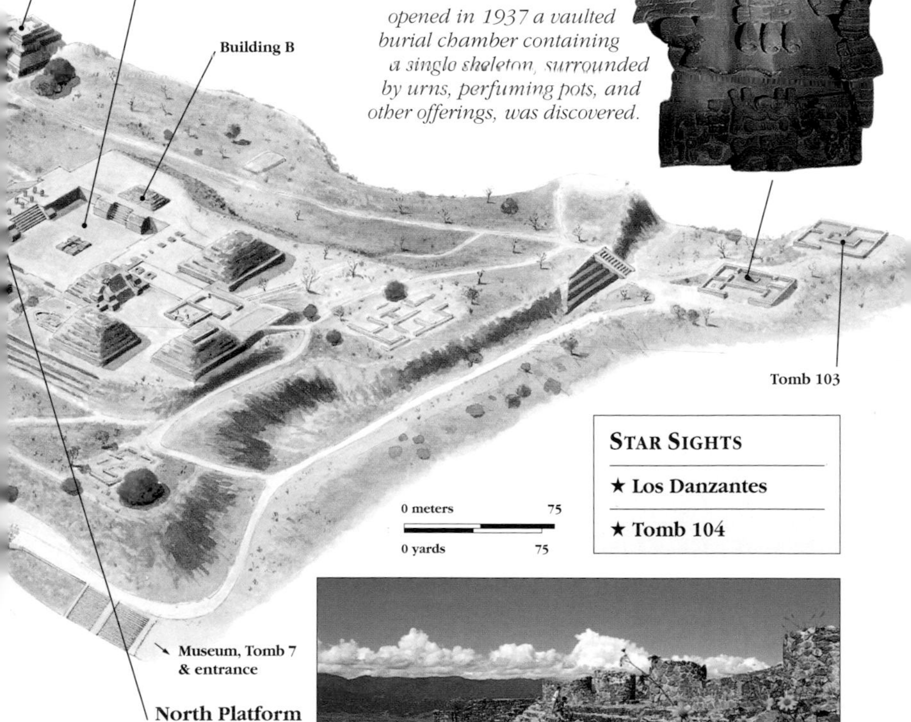

Tomb 103

STAR SIGHTS

★ **Los Danzantes**

★ **Tomb 104**

0 meters 75
0 yards 75

Museum, Tomb 7 & entrance

North Platform
A broad staircase leads up to the North Platform, the largest structure at Monte Albán. At the top of the steps are two rows of broken columns that would once have supported a flat roof.

Oaxaca ❻

Figure on family tree in Iglesia de Santo Domingo

Sᴇᴛ ɪɴ ᴀ ꜰᴇʀᴛɪʟᴇ ᴠᴀʟʟᴇʏ 1,500 m (4,900 ft) up in the mountains of the Sierra Madre del Sur, the city of Oaxaca (pronounced "Wa-harker") is one of the best preserved and most charming of all Mexico's colonial cities. Laid out in 1529, in an area once dominated by the Mixtec and Zapotec cultures, the Spanish settlement quickly became the most important town in the south. Now a major commercial and industrial center, it still manages to retain a certain provincial feel. This is due, in part, to the cultural presence of a large indigenous population.

The main façade of the cathedral, with the Alameda de Léon in front

🔒 Cathedral

The cathedral is on the north side of the *zócalo* but faces the Alameda de León. It was originally constructed in 1553, but a series of earthquakes meant that it had to be rebuilt in 1730, which explains its solid walls and asymmetrical towers. The attractive Baroque façade includes a fine relief of the Assumption of the Virgin Mary above the main door. Inside, the main feature is the splendid bronze altar, which was crafted in Italy.

🏛 Museo de Arte Contemporáneo

Macedonio Alcalá 202. 📞 (951) 514 28 18. ⏰ Wed–Mon. 💲 Sun free. 🖼 🚻

The city's contemporary art museum is housed in a carefully refurbished 16th-century building, called the Casa de Cortés (House of Cortés) after the conquistador who is reputed to have commissioned it. The museum displays works of note by local and international modern artists, including Francisco Toledo and Rodolfo Morales. It is also a popular venue for temporary exhibitions and other cultural events.

🔒 Iglesia de Santo Domingo

Of the many churches in the city, this is the one most likely to take your breath away. Begun in 1572, it was completed over 200 years later at a total cost of over 12 million pesos in gold. Its misleadingly simple façade hides an interior that dazzles with gilded plaster and colored stucco,

Central Oaxaca

The **Plaza de Armas**, or *zócalo*, is the geographical and social center of the city. Closed to traffic, it bustles instead with vendors, students, tourists, and colorfully dressed villagers from outside the city. It is a great place to relax and watch the world go by, especially from the many cafés situated around its perimeter. Just northwest of the *zócalo* is the **Alameda de León**, a lovely square with market stalls that specialize in arts and crafts.

Bᴇɴɪᴛᴏ Jᴜáʀᴇᴢ (1806–72)

A portrait of reformer Benito Juárez by the artist Ángel Bracho

Benito Juárez, one of Mexico's greatest liberal reformers, was born just north of Oaxaca. Of Zapotec Indian parentage, he was orphaned at the age of three, but was educated by priests and went on to become a champion of agricultural reform and Indian rights. He was made president in 1858 and, after defeating the French, personally oversaw the execution of Emperor Maximilian in 1867 (*see p53*). He continued to pursue reform until his death.

Gold ornament in the Centro Cultural Santo Domingo

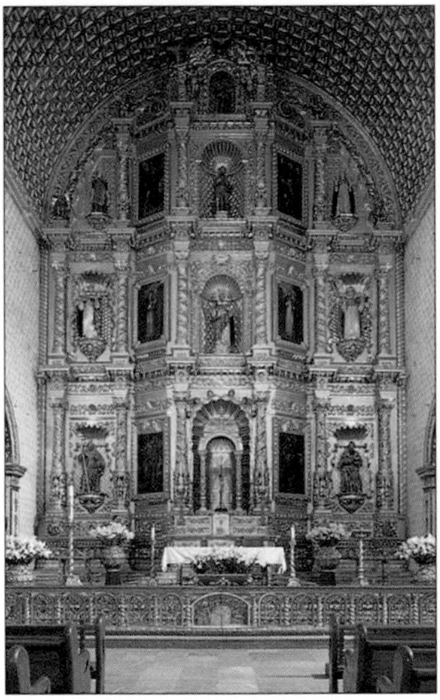

Main altar in the Iglesia de Santo Domingo

in a sublime combination of Gothic, Romanesque, Baroque, and Moorish styles. On the south side is the gilt-covered Capilla del Rosario, where there are numerous paintings of saints and Madonnas in varying sizes. Another highlight is the unusual family tree of St. Dominic, painted on the low ceiling above the main entrance.

🏛 Centro Cultural Santo Domingo

Corner of Alcalá & Gurrión. ☎ *(951) 514 97 34.* 🕐 *Tue–Sun.* 🎟 📷 🛍 ♿

Housed in a former monastery attached to the Iglesia de Santo Domingo, the Centro Cultural Santo Domingo has a museum, a botanical garden, a university library, and a bookstore. The museum is dedicated to pre-Columbian artifacts from the ancient cities of Oaxaca state. On display here are some of the remarkable treasures found at Monte Albán *(see pp220–21)*, in particular the extraordinary cache of Mixtec art and jewelry discovered in Tomb 7. This hoard includes beautifully crafted pieces in alabaster, obsidian, jade, and other precious materials, but is most famous for the objects in gold, regarded as the finest of their kind in the Americas.

🏠 Casa de Juárez

García Vigil 609. ☎ *(951) 516 18 60.* 🕐 *Tue–Sun.* 🎟 *Sun free.*

The house where Benito Juárez lived between 1818 and 1828 now contains a museum devoted to his life and times. Situated around a shady patio, the rooms have been kept almost exactly as they were when Juárez lived here, and provide fascinating insights into the lives of the middle classes in 19th-century Mexico.

Visitors' Checklist

Oaxaca. 👥 *257,000.*
✈ *8 km (5 miles) S.*
🚌 *Calz Niños Héroes 1036, (951) 515 12 14.*
ℹ *Av Independencia 607, (951) 516 01 23.*
🎉 *Guelaguetza (end Jul); Noche de Rábanos (Dec 23).*

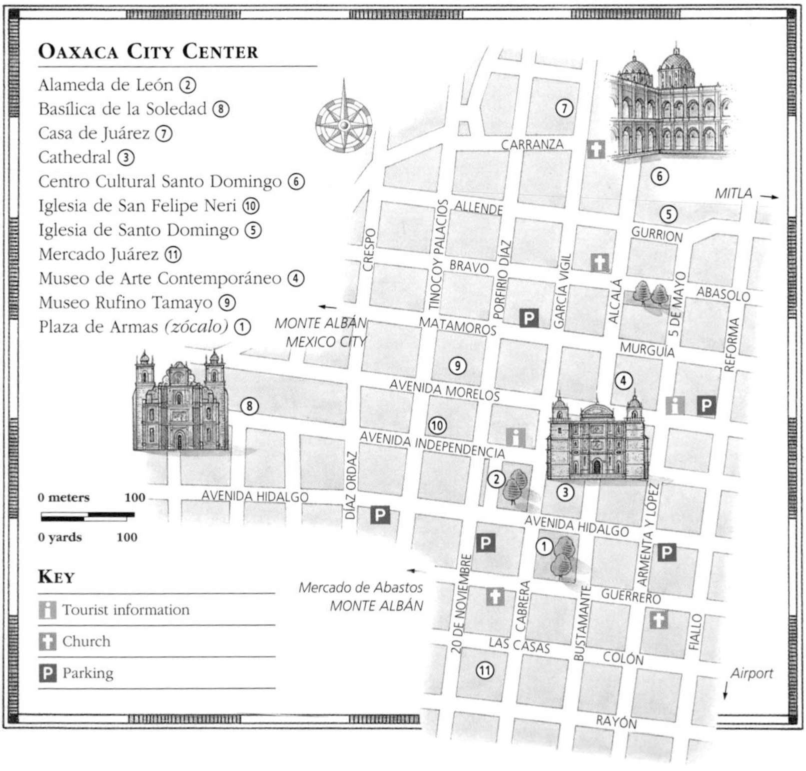

OAXACA CITY CENTER
Alameda de León (2)
Basílica de la Soledad (8)
Casa de Juárez (7)
Cathedral (3)
Centro Cultural Santo Domingo (6)
Iglesia de San Felipe Neri (10)
Iglesia de Santo Domingo (5)
Mercado Juárez (11)
Museo de Arte Contemporáneo (4)
Museo Rufino Tamayo (9)
Plaza de Armas (zócalo) (1)
CARRANZA
MITLA
ALLENDE
GURRION
CRESPO
TINOCOY PALACIOS
BRAVO
PORFIRIO DÍAZ
GARCÍA VIGIL
ALCALÁ
5 DE MAYO
ABASOLO
MONTE ALBÁN
MEXICO CITY
MATAMOROS
MURGUÍA
REFORMA
AVENIDA MORELOS
AVENIDA INDEPENDENCIA
AVENIDA HIDALGO
DÍAZ ORDAZ
ARMENTA Y LÓPEZ
0 meters 100
0 yards 100
KEY
Tourist information
Church
Parking
Mercado de Abastos
MONTE ALBÁN
20 DE NOVIEMBRE
CABRERA
BUSTAMANTE
GUERRERO
LAS CASAS
COLÓN
FIALLO
Airport
RAYÓN

Exploring Oaxaca

OAXACA HAS ITS FAIR SHARE of interesting museums and colonial churches, all within walking distance of the center. However, its real charm lies in the rich blend of cultures on the streets themselves. Zapotec Indians, Mixtecs, and many other groups gather in force on Saturdays – the main trading day at the Mercado de Abastos, the country's biggest Indian market – to sell their traditional crafts. Techniques used to fashion textiles, ceramics, wood, and metal are passed down within families, and can be seen at workshops in villages around the city.

Preclassic female figure from Veracruz, in Museo Rufino Tamayo

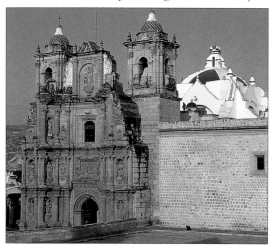

The impressive façade and dome of the Basílica de la Soledad

🛈 Basílica de la Soledad

The Basílica de la Soledad is particularly noted for its 24-m (79-ft) high Baroque façade, which resembles a folding altarpiece, and for its heavily gilded interior. It was built between 1682 and 1690 to house the image of the Virgin of Solitude, Oaxaca's patron saint. This figure can be seen inside, encrusted with 600 diamonds and topped with a 2-kg (4-lb) gold crown. There is a small religious museum attached to the church.

🏛 Museo Rufino Tamayo

Av Morelos 503. 📞 *(951) 516 47 50.* ☐ *Wed–Mon.* 🈲 🎫 *reserve in advance.* 🎫

This beautifully presented museum, housed in a charming 17th-century building, contains a collection of pre-Columbian art once owned by the artist Rufino Tamayo *(see p87)*. It was partly Tamayo's intention in collecting the pieces to stop them from falling into the

hands of illicit artifact traders. He then left them to his native state to make his fellow Mexicans aware of their rich heritage. The fascinating displays are arranged according to aesthetic themes.

🛈 Iglesia de San Felipe Neri

This church also has a façade shaped like an altarpiece, but its highlight is the gilt altarpiece itself, in the Churrigueresque style *(see p25)*. Benito Juárez, Mexico's most celebrated president, was married here.

🛒 Mercado Juárez

Corner of 20 de Noviembre & Las Casas. ☐ *daily.* 🛂

Mercado Juárez was once the city's main market and is still a great place to pick up crafts made in surrounding villages. Traditional clothing, leather goods, and the famous Oaxaca pottery are all sold here.

🛒 Mercado de Abastos

Corner of Periférico and Las Casas. ☐ *daily.* 🛂

Most of the serious trading happens at this huge market, southwest of the center. Crafts such as ceramics, jewelry, and

---

OAXACA'S BLACK AND GREEN POTTERY

Distinctive black or dark green ceramics are seen all around Oaxaca. The black style, from San Bartolo Coyotepec, was popularized by Doña Rosa Real, who mastered and demonstrated the ancient art until her death in 1980. The green pottery, made in Santa María Atzompa, is beautifully decorated. It is best to buy both in the villages themselves.

Potter hard at work at the famous Doña Rosa Pottery in San Bartolo Coyotepec

Green-glazed pot with raised design from Santa María Atzompa

The Virgin of Solitude, draped in a cloak of black velvet, in the Basílica de la Soledad

green-glazed pottery for which the village is famous. **San Antonio Arrazola**, close to Monte Albán *(see pp220–21)*, produces carved wooden figures of animals painted in vivid, multicolored designs.

The former convent at **Cuilapan de Guerrero**, 10 km (6 miles) southwest of the city on Mex 131, was established on the site of a Zapotec pyramid in 1550. It was abandoned two centuries later, but today still retains some impressive architectural features and murals. The roofless chapel has a Renaissance façade, an elegant columned nave, and thick earthquake-proof walls. Vicente Guerrero, hero of the War of Independence *(see p49)*, was imprisoned here before being executed on Valentine's Day 1831. A monument to his memory stands at the convent.

Zaachila, 16 km (10 miles) southwest of Oaxaca on the same road, is the site of the last Zapotec capital. A pyramid and two impressive tombs are open to the public.

San Bartolo Coyotepec, 10 km (6 miles) south of the city, is where the gleaming black pottery (*barro negro brillante*), so common in souvenir shops, is made.

painted wooden animals are sold here, but the real attraction is the chance to take in the noise, heat, smells, and color of one of the most vibrant markets in the country. The buyers and sellers chatter not in Spanish but mostly in the local Zapotec and Mixtec tongues, as they haggle at stalls laid out with the utmost care and attention. The liveliest day is Saturday.

Painted wooden carving

ENVIRONS: The village of **Santa María Atzompa**, 8 km (5 miles) northwest of the city, is home to hundreds of artisans dedicated to making the

(see pp220–21), *(see p49)*

FIESTAS OF SOUTHERN MEXICO

Dancers performing at the Guelaguetza in Oaxaca

Guelaguetza *(last two Mondays of Jul)*, Oaxaca. Dancers from all over the state re-enact Zapotec and Mixtec ceremonies, wearing traditional outfits and feathered headdresses.

Easter Week *(Mar/Apr)*, San Juan Chamula and Zinacantán (Chiapas). Catholic ceremonies combine with pagan rituals in colorful festivals rated among the best in Mexico.

Feria de San Cristóbal *(Jul 25)*, San Cristóbal de las Casas. A torch-lit procession in honor of the town's patron saint finishes at the church of San Cristóbal, which opens its doors to the public only on this day.

Noche de los Rábanos *(Dec 23)*, Oaxaca. On the Night of the Radishes locals compete to carve the vegetables into people, animals, and plants.

The chapel of the former convent at Cuilapan de Guerrero, with the main church in the background

A Tour of the Tlacolula Valley ⓥ

THE AREA AROUND Oaxaca, and in particular the Tlacolula Valley, has been an important cultural and historical center since the 7th century BC. Over 2,500 years of civilization have filled the 50-km (31-mile) valley with diverse attractions reflecting its Olmec, Zapotec, Mixtec, Aztec, and Spanish heritage.

Teotitlán del Valle ④
The oldest town in the Tlacolula Valley, Teotitlán is known for its Zapotec rugs, made with natural dyes. It also has a small museum and some Zapotec ruins.

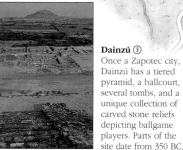

Santa María del Tule ①
Reputed to be over 2,000 years old, the Arbol del Tule in the churchyard here is one of the world's largest trees.

San Jerónimo Tlacochahuaya ②
The 16th-century church in this village was constructed as part of a Dominican monastery. It was decorated by Zapotec artisans and has an ornate bellows organ.

Dainzú ③
Once a Zapotec city, Dainzú has a tiered pyramid, a ballcourt, several tombs, and a unique collection of carved stone reliefs depicting ballgame players. Parts of the site date from 350 BC.

KEY
- 🟫 Tour route
- ▬ Highway
- ═ Other roads
- 🌼 Viewpoint

Yagul ⑧

Oaxaca. Mex 190, 36 km (22 miles) SE of Oaxaca. 🚌 from Oaxaca. 🔘 daily. 📷

THE CITY of Yagul was first inhabited by the Zapotecs in about 500 BC. However, it gained real religious and political influence in the region only after the decline of Monte Albán (see pp220–21), at the end of the 8th century AD, and most of the buildings at the site date from this period. Yagul was subsequently taken over by the Mixtecs and was finally abandoned after the arrival of the Spanish.

Dramatically set on and around a rocky outcrop, the city had a good defensive position. It is divided into two main areas. The lower level, called the **Acropolis**, includes a large ballcourt, more than 30 tombs, and a labyrinthine complex of buildings known as the Palace of the Six Patios. On the summit of the outcrop is the **Fortress**, surrounded by a strong defensive wall and offering superb views.

Zapotec ruins on the lower level of the city of Yagul

Mitla ⑨

Oaxaca. Off Mex 190, 44 km (27 miles) SE of Oaxaca. 🎫 (951) 568 03 16. 🚌 from Oaxaca. 🔘 daily. 📷 Sun free. ⬛ ⬛

AN IMPORTANT Zapotec city-state after the decline of Monte Albán (see pp220–21), Mitla was home to approximately 10,000 people at its height. The city was later occupied by the Mixtecs, who had a significant influence on the architecture and decoration of its buildings. Many of Mitla's temples were destroyed by the Spanish when they invaded, and the stonework was used to build the Iglesia de San Pablo, the Catholic church that dominates the site.

Five main groups of buildings remain, two of which are readily accessible. The **Grupo de las Columnas**, in the east of the site, is a former palace. It consists of three large rooms set around tombs and a courtyard. The palace walls are decorated with the distinctive

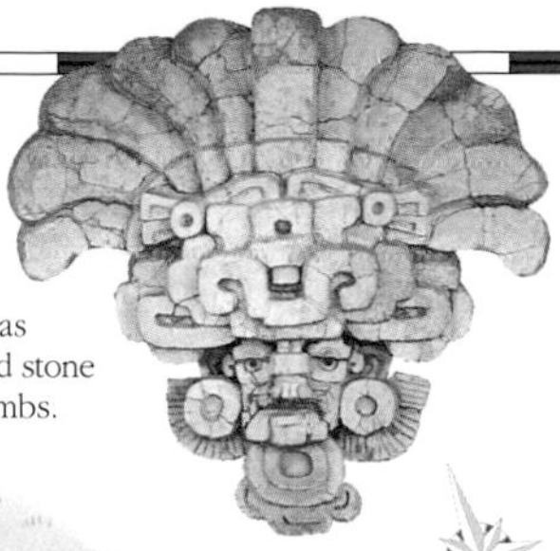

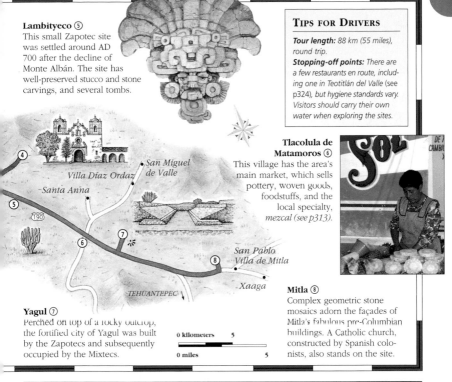

Lambityeco ⑤
This small Zapotec site was settled around AD 700 after the decline of Monte Albán. The site has well-preserved stucco and stone carvings, and several tombs.

Tips for Drivers

Tour length: *88 km (55 miles), round trip.*
Stopping-off points: *There are a few restaurants en route, including one in Teotitlán del Valle (see p324), but hygiene standards vary. Visitors should carry their own water when exploring the sites.*

Tlacolula de Matamoros ⑥
This village has the area's main market, which sells pottery, woven goods, foodstuffs, and the local specialty, *mezcal (see p313).*

Yagul ⑦
Perched on top of a rocky outcrop, the fortified city of Yagul was built by the Zapotecs and subsequently occupied by the Mixtecs.

Mitla ⑧
Complex geometric stone mosaics adorn the façades of Mitla's fabulous pre-Columbian buildings. A Catholic church, constructed by Spanish colonists, also stands on the site.

Mitla's Catholic church, surrounded by pre-Columbian buildings decorated with distinctive geometric mosaics

geometric mosaics that characterize Mitla's buildings. Each frieze is made of up to 100,000 separate pieces of cut stone. One of the rooms, the Salón de las Columnas, houses six monolithic pillars that once supported the roof. To the north is the **Grupo de la Iglesia**, centered around the colonial Catholic church. The pre-Columbian buildings that survived its construction are of similar design to those in the Grupo de las Columnas, but on a smaller scale. They still retain traces of paintwork. Some artifacts from the site are displayed in the **Museo Frisell de Arte Zapoteco Mitla**, in the center of town, which temporarily closed for renovation in 2001.

Museo Frisell de Arte Zapoteco Mitla
Benito Juárez 2. ☎ *(951) 568 01 94.*

The twelve apostles on the bell tower of the cathedral in Tuxla Gutiérrez's main square

Tuxtla Gutiérrez ⑩

Chiapas. 434,000. ✈ 🚌
ℹ️ Boulevard Belisario Domínguez 950, (961) 602 50 74. 🎭 San Sebastián (Jan 15–23), San Marcos (Apr 20–25).

THE CAPITAL of the state of Chiapas, Tuxtla Gutiérrez is a modern, working city, and the major gateway for travelers to the state.

Plaza Cívica, the main square, bustles with life and is regularly used for music and street theater performances. On its south side is the **cathedral**, built at the end of the 16th century and refurbished in a more modern style in the 1980s. Twelve carved wooden figures of the apostles appear from the bell tower as the bells chime out the hour.

To the west, and just south of Avenida Central, is the impressive, if somewhat dilapidated,

A street performer in Plaza Cívica

Monumento a la Bandera (Monument to the Flag), which celebrates the union of Chiapas and Mexico. Farther west on the same street is the Hotel Bonampak (see p302), which has reproductions of the Maya murals at Bonampak (see p232) in its lobby.

The **Museo Regional**, northeast of the center, provides information on the geography and history of Chiapas. Near the museum is the **Jardín Botánico**, which contains a range of plants native to the state, including a selection of beautiful orchids.

On the outskirts of town, in the foothills of the Sierra Madre de Chiapas, is the excellent **Zoológico Miguel Alvarez del Toro**. It was opened in 1980 to help prevent the extinction of the state's indigenous animals. A 1-km (0.5-mile) walk leads through a lush jungle environment in which over 150 species live in their natural habitats.

🏛 **Museo Regional**
Calzada de los Hombres Ilustres.
📞 (961) 613 44 79. 🕐 Tue–Sun.
📷 Sun free. ♿
🐾 **Zoológico Miguel Alvarez del Toro**
Corner of Calzada Cerro Hueco & Libramiento Sur. 📞 (961) 614 47 00.
🕐 daily. 🍴 🚻

The dramatic Cañón del Sumidero, almost 1 km (half a mile) deep

Cañón del Sumidero ⑪

Chiapas. 🚌 Chiapa de Corzo.
🕐 daily. 📷 🚤 by boat from Chiapa de Corzo or Cahuaré.

THE BREATHTAKING Sumidero Canyon forms the heart of a beautiful national park. Legend has it that in the mid-16th century several hundred Indians chose to hurl themselves down its precipitous sides after a defiant last stand, rather than submit to the invading Spanish forces.

Nearly a kilometer (half a mile) deep, and around 14 km (9 miles) in length, the canyon was carved by the Grijalva river over the course of millions of years. This important river stretches from Guatemala to the Gulf of Mexico.

Excellent views of the sheer-sided canyon are available from a series of five lookout points along its western rim. Alternatively, visitors can enjoy a two-hour boat trip along the river. Boats leave from two embarkation points, one at Cahuaré (on the west bank of the Grijalva, on Mex 190), and the other at the docks in Chiapa de Corzo. The trip passes caves and waterfalls. It also provides an opportunity to see a variety of unusual plants, and many animals and birds, including monkeys, crocodiles, iguanas, herons, and kingfishers.

THE ZAPATISTA UPRISING

On January 1 1994, the EZLN (Ejército Zapatista de Liberación Nacional), led by the masked "Subcomandante Marcos," seized the town of San Cristóbal de las Casas. Their aims – taken from those of Emiliano Zapata (see p54) – were a redistribution of power and the state's resources, from the wealthy few to the poor majority. The "Zapatistas," as they

Part of a mural in support of the Zapatista rebels of Chiapas

became known, were forced out of the town by the army and fled into the jungle. Although a ceasefire was agreed in 1995, the land the Zapatistas occupy is still heavily patrolled by government forces. So far, in spite of talks, the two sides have been unable to reconcile their differences.

◁ The flamboyant façade of the cathedral in San Cristóbal de las Casas

San Cristóbal de las Casas ⑫

Chiapas. 🏛 132,000. ✈ 🚌
ℹ Plaza 31 de Marzo, (967) 678 06
60. 🎭 Primavera y Paz (1 week
before Easter), San Cristóbal (Jul 25).

FOUNDED BY THE Spaniards in
1528 and marked by cen-
turies of geographical isolation,
San Cristóbal is still imbued
with an atmosphere of sleepy
colonial charm. However, it has
a long and troubled history of
conflict between the descendants of the Spanish and the
local Indians. It was here that
the Zapatista uprising began in
1994, and there is still a strong
military presence in the town.

Situated at 2,300 m (7,550 ft)
above sea level in the Chiapan
highlands, San Cristóbal has a
refreshingly cool climate. The
town's main square, Plaza 31
de Marzo, is dominated by
the **Palacio Municipal** and
the **cathedral**. The latter was
started in the 16th century,
but construction and alterations
continued until the beginning
of the 19th century. Its lavish
interior contains an elaborate
gold-encrusted pulpit and
several notable altarpieces.

Part of an elaborately gilded altarpiece in the Templo de Santo Domingo

A few blocks to the north is
the 16th-century Dominican
Templo de Santo Domingo,
the most impressive church
in the city. It has an intricate
pink façade, a gilded Baroque
interior with several magnificent altarpieces, and a pulpit
carved from a single piece of
oak. Farther north, on General
Utrilla, is the main market,
where Indians from the surrounding hills come to trade.

The **Na Bolom** museum and
research center, on the east
side of the town, is devoted
to studying and protecting the
indigenous Lacandón Indians
and their rainforest home. It
was founded by a European
couple in the 1950s, and is
credited with having helped to
stop the tribe from dying out.

The **Iglesia de San Cristóbal**
to the west, and the **Iglesia de
Guadalupe** to the east, offer
excellent views over the city
from their hilltop positions.

ENVIRONS: There are several
Indian villages 10 km (6 miles)
or so from San Cristóbal, including **San Juan Chamula**,
which has a beautiful church.
A trip here provides an insight
into the mix of Christian and
pre-Columbian traditions of
the Tzotzil-speaking inhabitants. The village's fiestas and
markets are among the best in
Mexico. Visitors are warned
not to take photos, especially
in religious buildings, as this
may cause serious offense.

Some 84 km (52 miles) to
the southeast of San Cristóbal
is the charming border town
of **Comitán de Domínguez**,
a good base for exploring the
ruins of **Chinkultic**. Among
the numerous mounds here
are several pyramids, a ballcourt, and a number of stelae.
Near Chinkultic are the **Lagos
de Montebello**, a chain of
more than 50 lakes, whose
lovely waters range in color
from light blue to dark green.

🏛 **Na Bolom**
Av Vicente Guerrero 33. ☎ (967)
678 14 18. ◯ daily (tours only, at
11:30am, 4:30pm). 🎥 ♿ 🖥 🚻
🏛 **Chinkultic**
Off Mex 190, 41 km (25 miles) SE of
Comitán de Domínguez. ◯ daily. 🎥

Crowds in front of the church in San Juan Chamula

Agua Azul

Chiapas. Off Mex 199, 125 km (78 miles) NE of San Cristóbal de las Casas. ☷ *from Palenque or San Cristóbal de las Casas.* ☷

A GOOD STOPPING-OFF point en route from San Cristóbal de las Casas to Palenque, the Parque Nacional Agua Azul has some of the most beautiful waterfalls in Mexico. There are over 500 cascades in all, ranging from 3 to 30 m (10–100 ft) in height, together with a series of aquamarine-colored rock pools. It is possible to swim in some of these, which brings welcome relief from the heat and humidity of the lowlands, but do not swim where there are signs warning of dangerous currents. The falls are best visited outside of the rainy season (Jun–Sep), during which the waters become murky.

ENVIRONS: Some 22 km (14 miles) before the road from Agua Azul reaches Palenque is the spectacular, 30-m (100-ft) high waterfall at **Misol-Ha**. Set within the lush surroundings of a tropical rainforest, this is another good place at which to stop for a swim.

Palenque

See pp234–7.

One of the spectacularly beautiful waterfalls at Agua Azul

Bonampak

Chiapas. 153 km (95 miles) SE of Palenque. ☷ *from Palenque.* ☷ *tours from Palenque.* ◯ *Tue–Sun.* ☷

D ISCOVERED IN the 1940s, the Maya site of Bonampak is of ancient origin but reached its apogee under Yahaw Chan Muwan (776–90). The subject of three fine stelae at the site, Yahaw Chan Muwan commissioned Bonampak's remarkable Temple of the Paintings. The walls and vaulted ceilings of the three chambers of this temple are covered with vividly colored murals. These give rich insights into the courtly life of the nobility of Bonampak and the pageantry surrounding Maya warfare. Murals in the two outer rooms (Rooms 1 and 3) show noblemen in fine clothes and elaborate head-dresses. Below them are musicians and dancers, and on the ceiling animals and figures representing constellations of the Maya cosmos.

The two main paintings in the middle room (Room 2) depict a battle, in which Maya warriors are shown defeating their enemy, and the grisly torture of prisoners of war.

As an alternative to making the trip to the site itself, reproductions of the murals can be seen in a hotel in Tuxtla Gutiérrez *(see p230).*

Yaxchilán

Chiapas. 130 km (80 miles) SE of Palenque. ☷ *from Palenque.* ☷ *tours from Palenque.* ◯ *Tue–Sun.* ☷

T HE CITY of Yaxchilán, located 20 m (66 ft) above the Usumacinta River in the heart of the Lacandón rainforest, is one of the most dramatic of all Maya sites. It can only be reached by air or by taking first a bus and then a boat along the river.

Built between AD 350 and 800, it rose to prominence during the 8th century under the command of its most famous kings, "Shield Jaguar," and his son "Bird Jaguar." Yaxchilán is rich in glyphs, stelae, carved lintels, stucco roof combs, and temples. One of the best preserved buildings is Temple 33.

Yaxchilán is in the homeland of the Lacandón Indians *(see p231)*, Mexico's last pagan native people, who live outside Hispanicized society.

Temple 33 at Yaxchilán, with its prominent roof comb

The Art of the Maya

OF ALL MESOAMERICAN civilizations, the Maya produced the most enduring works of art, in the greatest quantity. Maya art is distinguished by its naturalistic approach which makes it more accessible to the modern eye than the art of other ancient Mexican cultures. The Maya used a variety of materials to decorate their buildings and to make sacred and functional objects: stone, wood, ceramics, stucco, shell, jade, and bone. Particularly striking are the Maya's portraits of themselves – as seen especially in the wall paintings of Bonampak and the carved bas-reliefs of Palenque – which give us an understanding of their way of life, methods of warfare, costumes, customs, and beliefs.

Feather plume

Ear flare

Jade bracelet

Glyphs (see pp46–7), often recording royal biographies and events, were carved in stone or modeled in stucco.

Stelae, upright stone slabs placed at ritual sites, usually chronicle the lives of rulers and their victories in war. This one is from Yaxchilán.

Ceramics were used to make delicate sculptures. This figurine, probably of a ruler, was found in a Maya tomb on the island of Jaina off the coast near Campeche (see p260).

Bas-reliefs show the Maya's skill in representing themselves, as seen in this detail from the Tablet of the Slaves in Palenque museum (see p237).

Vases, such as this example depicting a supernatural jaguar, were painted with a mineral slip before firing.

The murals of Bonampak depict scenes of Classic Maya life in vivid colors with an evocative sense of realism. This detail from the battle scene in Room 2 shows a warrior dressed in a jaguar skin seizing an enemy by the hair. Other remarkable frescoes believed to be by Maya artists can be seen at Cacaxtla (see p156).

Palenque ⑭

Detail of glyphs from the Palace courtyard

Palenque is everything that an archaeological site should be: mysterious, solemn, well preserved, and imposing in its beautiful jungle setting. The Maya first settled here as early as 100 BC, and the city reached its apogee between AD 600 and 800, when it served as a regional capital. It fell into a precipitous decline in the early 10th century and was abandoned to the ever-encroaching jungle. Excavations have uncovered ruins emblazoned with fine sculpture and splendid stuccowork.

The Temple of the Foliated Cross is named after a panel showing a cruciform corn plant.

The Temple of the Cross has a striking roof comb, and carvings inside.

Temple XIV
Although badly damaged, this temple has been largely reconstructed. It contains some well-preserved glyphs and carvings, among them this portrait of the ruler Ken Balam II, who is wearing a feathered headdress.

Central Palenque
The site's most important buildings, shown in the illustration, are known as the Principal Group.

Path to Groups B and C, waterfalls, and museum
(see p237)

Ballcourt

Star Features

★ **Temple of the Inscriptions**

★ **The Palace**

North Group
This consists of five temples on a single platform. At the base of the platform is this carving of the god Tlaloc.

The Temple of the Count was for two years in the 1830s the home of an eccentric European nobleman.

Temple of the Sun
One of the best-preserved buildings on the site, this temple on a four-level pyramid is crowned with a prominent roof comb – a massive carved stone slab. Inside are glyphs and stucco friezes, one of which shows the sun.

VISITORS' CHECKLIST

Chiapas. 8 km (5 miles) SW of Palenque town. 🚍 *from Palenque town.* ⏱ *8am–6pm daily.* 🈯 ♿ 🏪 🍽 **Tomb of Pakal** ⏱ *10am–6pm daily.* **Museum** ⏱ *10am–6pm Tue–Sun.* ♿

Water channel

Path to Temple of the Jaguar *(see p237)*

★ **Temple of the Inscriptions**
This pyramid contains the tomb of Pakal, ruler of Palenque (see p236).

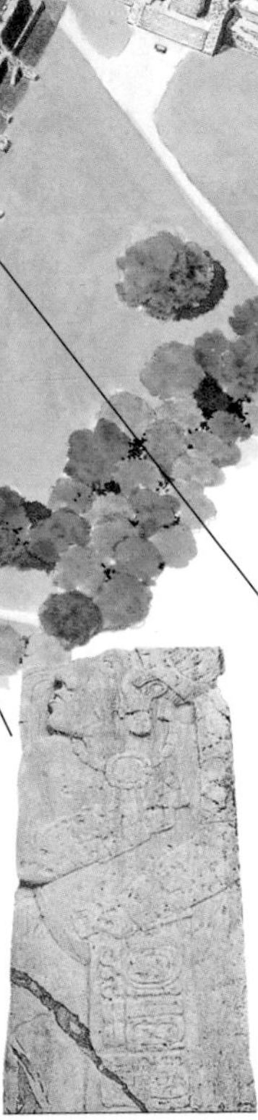

Temple XIII

Temple of the Dying Moon

0 meters   50

0 yards   50

Entrance

Tomb of Alberto Ruz Lhuillier *(see p236)*

★ **The Palace**
Standing on a raised platform, the Palace is a labyrinthine complex of courtyards, corridors, and rooms. It is distinguished by a four-tier tower that probably served as an observatory or lookout post (see p237).

Temple X

Palace carvings
This stone slab carved with a figure is one of nine that can be seen in the courtyard of the palace.

The Temple of the Inscriptions

T HE TALLEST and most imposing building at Palenque
is shown here as a reconstruction, complete with its
roof comb. It was constructed during the 68-year reign
of Pakal (AD 615–83) and subsequently contained his funerary crypt, a fact that was revealed only by the dramatic discovery of his tomb by Alberto Ruz Lhuillier in
1952. Many of the artifacts and pieces of jewelry found
in the tomb are now on display in the Museo Nacional
de Antropología in Mexico City (see pp90–95).

*The entrance to the tomb is
by way of two flights of steep
stone steps that descend 25 m
(82 ft). When the staircase
was discovered in 1949 it was
filled with rubble, which took
three years to remove
before the tomb
could be
explored.*

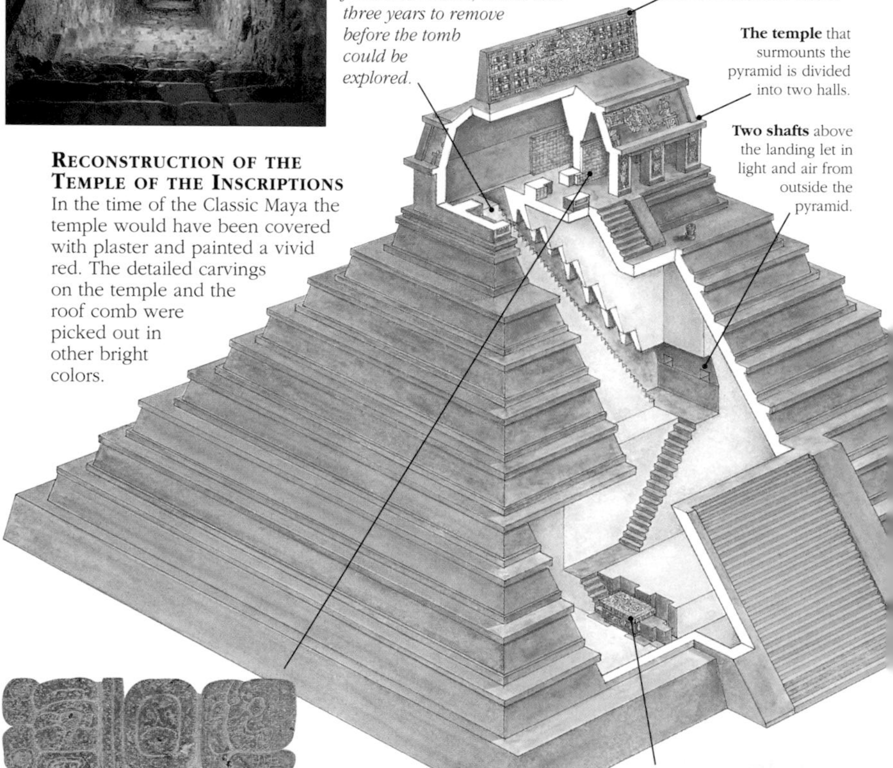

The steep climb of the main staircase at the front of the pyramid

The roof comb would
have been carved with
deities and animal motifs.

The temple that
surmounts the
pyramid is divided
into two halls.

Two shafts above
the landing let in
light and air from
outside the
pyramid.

**RECONSTRUCTION OF THE
TEMPLE OF THE INSCRIPTIONS**
In the time of the Classic Maya the
temple would have been covered
with plaster and painted a vivid
red. The detailed carvings
on the temple and the
roof comb were
picked out in
other bright
colors.

*The inscriptions, which give
the temple its name, can be seen
on the temple walls. There are
617 carved glyphs in total,
arranged on three stone slabs.
To date, they have been only
partially deciphered.*

*The Tomb of Pakal is a chamber
measuring 9 m by 4 m (30 ft by 13 ft),
with a vaulted ceiling almost 7 m
(23 ft) high. Nine stucco figures,
representing dynastic precursors,
adorn the walls. The heavy stone lid
of the sarcophagus is magnificently
decorated with a symbolic scene
of Pakal's resurrection from the
jaws of the underworld.*

Exploring Palenque

THE MOST INTERESTING and best preserved buildings are in the Principal Group (shown on the previous pages). A few lesser-known temples can be reached by easy paths through the jungle. Another path leads from the Principal Group past a series of waterfalls to the site museum.

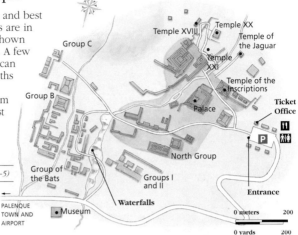

Temple XVIII
Temple XX
Temple of the Jaguar
Group C
Temple XXI
Temple of the Inscriptions
Group B
Palace
Ticket Office
North Group
Group of the Bats
Groups I and II
Entrance
PALENQUE TOWN AND AIRPORT
Museum
Waterfalls

KEY

☐ Principal Group *(see pp234–5)*

0 meters 200
0 yards 200

The Palace

Set on a platform some 100 m by 80 m (328 ft by 262 ft) and 10 m (33 ft) high, the palace complex is the product of many kings. The earliest buildings date to the time of Pakal, but the basal platform conceals earlier phases, some preserved as underground galleries. The palace was the home of the royal family and their immediate entourage. Carvings and stucco decorations can be seen in parts of the building. Particularly interesting are the sculptures of captives in the courtyard *(see p235)*, where visitors could be suitably impressed by the might of the Palenque kings. The Oval Tablet depicts the accession of Pakal, who receives the

Oval Tablet in the Palace

emblems of office from his mother, a short-reigning queen.

Temple of the Jaguar

A short path behind the Temple of the Inscriptions leads to this ruined structure. Its name derives from the image of a king seated on a jaguar throne inside, now destroyed. Unexcavated and overgrown, it gives an idea of what the site must have been like when it was first explored in the late 18th century.

Outlying Temples

Two clearly marked paths that set off from in front of the Temple of the Sun lead to Temples XVIII and XXI, and other isolated buildings that are nearby but hidden by trees.

Temple of the Jaguar, one of many buildings in the jungle

More buildings can be reached by the path from the site to the museum, which passes through Group B and the Group of the Bats. Branches off this path lead to Group C, Group I, and Group II. There are hundreds of similar but less accessible structures at Palenque that are hidden by the surrounding jungle.

The Museum

This modern building on the road between Palenque town and the archaeological site provides an overview of the development of the Maya city. Many artifacts found on the site are on display, including the so-called Tablet of the Slaves *(see p233)*.

The Palace, dominating the center of Palenque

THE GULF COAST

TABASCO • VERACRUZ

THE LUSH, TROPICAL *plains fringing the Gulf of Mexico were once home to three major pre-Columbian cultures – the enigmatic Olmecs, the "mother culture" of ancient Mexican civilization; the Totonacs of Central Veracruz; and the Huastecs. Centuries later, this coast was once again at the fulcrum of Mexican history, when the first Spaniards set out on their historic conquest of the Aztec empire.*

This green and fertile region stretches from Tampico and the Huasteca region in the north, to the steamy, low-lying jungle of the Istmo de Tehuantepec – Mexico's narrow "waist" – in the south. Much of Mexico's sugar cane, tropical fruits, cocoa, and coffee are produced on this coastal plain. Inland temperatures drop as the land rises toward the great heights of the Sierra Madre Oriental and the snow-capped Pico de Orizaba, Mexico's highest mountain at 5,747 m (18,856 ft).

The Olmec civilization arose in the southern part of this area in about 1000 BC. Later, the Maya people used the wide, meandering rivers that criss-cross Tabasco as their trading routes.

Meanwhile, in the north of the region, other indigenous races built great cities, most notably at El Tajín. In 1519, the Spanish conquistador Hernán Cortés disembarked on the coast of Veracruz. He burnt his boats, before going into alliance with the Totonac Indians and setting off to conquer the Aztecs. Throughout the next three centuries, the port of Veracruz shipped endless quantities of gold and silver back to Europe. At the same time, colonial towns like Tlacotalpan grew and prospered. In recent decades, parts of Tabasco and the southern area of Veracruz have been transformed by another economic boom, this time stemming from the exploitation of oil.

A farmer with his crop of sugar cane, one of many plants grown in the humid Gulf Coast region

◁ Palm trees providing welcome shade in the Plaza de Armas, the main square of El Puerto de Veracruz

Exploring the Gulf Coast

THE HUMID GULF COAST REGION has a rich hoard of pre-Columbian treasures. Artifacts from various cultures are preserved in Xalapa, in one of Mexico's best museums; in Villahermosa, meanwhile, an outdoor archaeological park exhibits the monumental art of the Olmec civilization. The ruined city of El Tajín, sacred to the god of thunder, should also not be missed. Other sights in the region include the vibrant port of Veracruz and the charming colonial towns of Tlacotalpan and Coatepec.

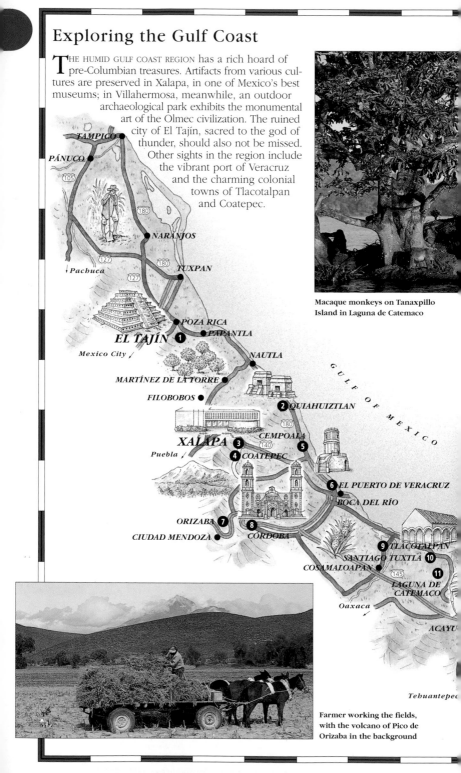

Macaque monkeys on Tanaxpillo Island in Laguna de Catemaco

TAMPICO

PÁNUCO

105

NARANJOS

127

Pachuca

180

TUXPAN

127

POZA RICA

PAPANTLA

EL TAJÍN 1

Mexico City

NAUTLA

MARTÍNEZ DE LA TORRE

FILOBOBOS

QUIAHUIZTLAN 2

GULF OF MEXICO

CEMPOALA

XALAPA 3

140

Puebla

COATEPEC 4

5

EL PUERTO DE VERACRUZ 6

BOCA DEL RÍO

ORIZABA 7

8

TLACOTALPAN 9

CIUDAD MENDOZA

CÓRDOBA

SANTIAGO TUXTLA 10

COSAMALOAPAN

145

11

LAGUNA DE CATEMACO

Oaxaca

ACAYU

Tehuantepec

Farmer working the fields, with the volcano of Pico de Orizaba in the background

SIGHTS AT A GLANCE

Cempoala **5**
Coatepec **4**
Comalcalco **12**
Córdoba **8**
Laguna de Catemaco **11**
Orizaba **7**
El Puerto de Veracruz **6**
Quiahuiztlan **2**
Santiago Tuxtla **10**
El Tajín pp242–3 **1**
Tlacotalpan **9**
Villahermosa **13**
Xalapa pp246–9 **3**

Fishing boats in the harbor of Veracruz

GETTING AROUND

The region has two large airports, at Veracruz and Villahermosa, with Veracruz offering more international destinations. The main towns in the area are linked by highways and regular bus services. However, the northern region is less visited and less well served – the easiest way to get to El Tajín is to fly to the domestic airport at Poza Rica. In the south, Villahermosa is a transportation hub offering road connections with the Yucatán Peninsula *(see pp256–87)* and convenient access to Palenque *(see pp234–7)*.

KEY

▬ Highway
▬ Other major road
▬ Minor road
▬ River

Brightly painted arches
in the unspoiled town
of Tlacotalpan

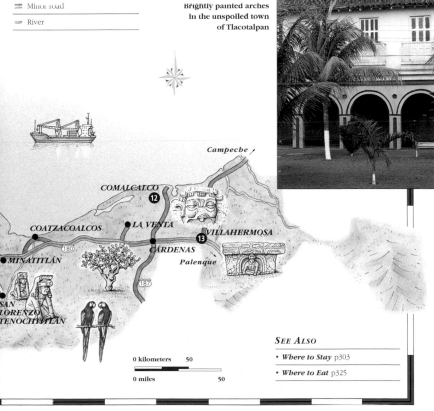

Campeche

COMALCALCO
12

Campeche

COATZACOALCOS
LA VENTA
VILLAHERMOSA
13
CÁRDENAS
MINATITLÁN
Palenque

180

187

SAN
LORENZO
TENOCHTITLÁN

0 kilometers   50

0 miles   50

SEE ALSO

- *Where to Stay* p303
- *Where to Eat* p325

El Tajín ❶

DEVELOPED FROM an earlier settlement, the city of El Tajín was a political and religious center for the Totonac civilization. Many of its buildings date from the early Postclassic period, between AD 900 and 1150. Decorated with relief panels and sculptures, they would have been painted in strong colors such as red, blue, and black. The excavated nucleus of this spectacular ancient city covers about 1 sq km (0.4 sq miles), but the entire urban area once spread over 10 sq km (4 sq miles) and had a population of 25,000.

★ Pyramid of the Niches
Originally crowned by a temple, this pyramid has 365 niches, representing the days of the year. Each niche may have held an offering.

Building 12

Building 10

★ Southern Ballcourt
Six relief panels on the side walls of this ballcourt illustrate rituals of the game (see p277), including the sacrifice of one or more players.

Entrance, visitors' center, museum, and *voladores*

★ Statue of Dios Tajín
This small statue probably represents Tajín, god of thunder and lightning, an important deity to the people of El Tajín.

Plaza del Arroyo
The four pyramids that surround this massive square stand at the cardinal points. They are some of the oldest structures in the city.

Los Voladores

This ancient ritual (see p29) of the Totonac people from the Papantla region takes place daily near the site entrance. The voladores *(fliers) launch themselves from the top of a pole and slowly descend as the ropes around the pole unwind.*

VISITORS' CHECKLIST

Veracruz. Off Mex 180,
12 km (7 miles) SE of Poza
Rica. 🚌 *from Papantla or Poza Rica.* 🕐 *9am–5pm Tue–Sun.*
🎦 🅿 🍴 🛈

El Tajín Chico

Northern Ballcourt

Gran Xicalcoliuhqui

Seen from above, this structure to the north forms an interlocking fretwork. It is thought to be associated with Quetzalcoatl (see p265).

Plaza Oriente and Gran Xicalcoliuhqui

Ballcourt 13/14

0 meters   50

0 yards   50

STAR FEATURES

★ **Pyramid of the Niches**

★ **Southern Ballcourt**

★ **Statue of Dios Tajín**

PLAN OF SITE

The buildings in the lower part of the site were used for ceremonial or religious purposes only.

The Building of the Columns, on the highest part of the site, was the home of the ruler known as 13 Rabbit.

El Tajín Chico, the middle level of the site, was the residential area for the elite ruling class.

Entrance, museum, and *voladores*

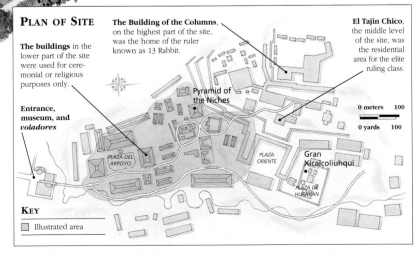

Pyramid of the Niches

PLAZA DEL ARROYO

PLAZA ORIENTE

Gran Xicalcoliuhqui

PLAZA DE HURAKAN

0 meters   100

0 yards   100

KEY

☐ Illustrated area

The steep ascent of the Pyramid of the Niches, which offers stunning views ▷

Small stone tombs in the Totonac cemetery at Quiahuiztlan

Quiahuiztlan ❷

Veracruz. Mex 180, 24 km (15 miles)
N of Cempoala. 🚌 to Cerro de los
Metates then 2-km (1-mile) walk.
🅾 daily. 📷

ONCE INHABITED by 15,000
people, the Totonac city
of Quiahuiztlan was a hilltop
stronghold. It was constructed
in the late Classic period, when
raids by warlike nomads from
the north forced sites like El
Tajín to be abandoned. Despite
originally being ringed by
defensive walls, it was twice
conquered, first by the Toltecs
in the 9th century and then by
the Aztecs in the 13th century.

Today the only part of the
terraced site that can be visited
is the cemetery. Here some 100
tiny tombs were discovered,
each resembling a pre-Columbian temple. Many had human
bones and skulls in burial
chambers in their bases. Small

holes in the backs of the tombs
may have been for relatives to
communicate with the dead.

Across the main road (Mex
180) from Quiahuiztlan is Villa
Rica de la Vera Cruz, the first
Spanish settlement in Mexico,
and now a fishing village.

Xalapa ❸

Veracruz. 🏛 390,000. 🚌
🛈 Torre Animas 5, (228) 841 85 00,
ext. 4330. 🎭 Feria de las Flores (Apr).

THE CAPITAL of Veracruz state,
Xalapa (or Jalapa) is known
for its university and cultural
life, and has the second most
important anthropology museum (see pp248–9) in Mexico.
The city enjoys a beautiful setting: on a clear day there are
splendid views of the 4,250-m
(13,940-ft) Cofre de Perote
peak from Parque Juárez, the
main plaza. To one side of this

square is the Neo-Classical
Palacio de Gobierno, which
has a mural by Mario Orozco
Rivera (1930–98) on its stairs.
Opposite the Palacio is the
18th-century **cathedral**. Uphill
from the city center, brightly
colored houses with sloping
tiled roofs and wrought-iron
balconies line the pretty, cobbled streets around the market.

ENVIRONS: The **Hacienda
Lencero**, originally a 16th-
century inn, was bought by
the controversial General Santa
Anna (see p52) in the 19th
century. It is now a museum,
housing furniture, utensils, and
ornaments from that period.

The remote **Filobobos** consists of two archaeological
sites 4 km (2.5 miles) apart,
which date from AD 700–1200.
Access to the site nearest to
the road, El Cuajilote, is by an
organized rafting trip along the
River Bobos, or via an 8-km
(5-mile) scenic walk. It is worth
the effort of getting there, however, because the Filobobos
ruins are truly spectacular.

🏛 **Palacio de Gobierno**
Calle Enriques. ☎ (228) 841 74 00.
🅾 Mon–Fri. ♿
🏛 **Hacienda Lencero**
10 km (6 miles) E of Xalapa. ☎ (228)
820 02 70. 🅾 Tue–Sun. 📷 🎟 🖵
Filobobos
Off minor road from Tlapacoyan to
Plan de Arroyos, 110 km (68 miles)
NW of Xalapa. 🅾 Tue–Sun. 📷

A charming cobbled street with colorful houses, near the market in Xalapa

Las Chimeneas, named after the hollow columns that line its upper tier

Coatepec ❹

Veracruz. 🏠 *73,000.* 🚌 ℹ️ *Matías Rebolledo 1, (228) 816 09 64.* 📅 *San Jerónimo (Sep 29–30), Feria del Café (Apr 30–May 1).*

A LOVELY TOWN, Coatepec is famous for its coffee, fruit liqueurs, orchids, and seafood restaurants. The town's elegant houses, with tiled roofs and ornate balconies and grilles, were built with the proceeds of the early 20th-century coffee boom. A converted hacienda in the center of the town is now one of Mexico's most charming hotels, the Posada Coatepec *(see p303)*. Near the Posada is the attractive Basílica Menor de Nuestra Señora de Guadalupe.

ENVIRONS: The area around Coatepec has a humid, semi-tropical climate with exuberant vegetation – in some places balls of grass even grow on telephone wires where birds

The Basílica Menor de Nuestra Señora de Guadalupe in Coatepec

have left traces of soil. The quiet colonial town of **Xico**, 9 km (6 miles) south of Coat-epec, is worth a visit, esp-ecially on a Sunday (market day). From Xico, a path leads through coffee and banana plantations to the 40-m (131-ft) high **Texolo Waterfall**.

Cempoala ❺

Veracruz. Mex 180, 44 km (27 miles) N of Veracruz. 🚌 *from Veracruz.* 🔲 *daily.* 📷

S HORTLY AFTER their arrival in Mexico in 1519 *(see p43)*, Cortés and his men sheltered in the Totonac city that stood on the site of modern-day Cempoala (or Zempoala). Like many other cities at the time, it was subjugated by the Aztecs, and the city's gover-nor collaborated with Cortés in return for protection.

The walled archaeological site, which contains the ruins of the Totonac city, adjoins Cempoala town. Around a central plaza, buildings faced with smooth, rounded river stones show strong Aztec in-fluences. Straight ahead from the entrance is the **Templo Mayor**, a 13-tier pyramid topped by a sanctuary, which was originally thatched with palm leaves. Nearby, in **Las Chimeneas** (The Chimneys), so-called because of its hol-low columns, archaeologists found a *chacmool*-like fig-ure *(see p44)*, suggesting the Maya were associated with the site. The east-facing **Gran Pirámide** was a tem-ple dedicated to the sun.

FIESTAS OF THE GULF COAST

Carnival *(Feb/Mar).* Cele-brated in most parts of the Gulf Coast, but particularly in Veracruz, Villahermosa, and Tenosique (Tabasco), Carnival starts with the burning of a huge figure, representing "bad temper," who usually resembles an unpopular politician. There are also floats, parades, and dancing. Tenosique's Carnival is famous for its flour war, the Guerra de Pocho y Blanquitos.

Carnival in Veracruz

Candelaria *(week leading up to Feb 2).* Celebrated throughout Mexico, the Christian festival of Candelaria (Candlemas) is particularly vibrant in the towns of Tlacotalpan and Catemaco. The festival traditionally features numerous street stalls, as well as dancing and music. In Tlacotalpan the local Virgin is taken on a river procession involving hundreds of boats.
Corpus Christi *(May/Jun).* The religious festival of Corpus Christi is especially associated with Papantla. Here the renowned *vol-adores (see p243)* perform their spectacular ancient rite of twirling upside down from a towering pole, with the intention of invoking fertility and honoring the sun.
Feria de Santiago Tuxtla *(Jul 26),* Santiago Tuxtla. In this saint's day celebra-tion, gigantic *mojiganga* dolls are taken around the town. *Danzas de los liseres* (jaguar-mask dances) also take place.

Museo de Antropología de Xalapa

Huastec toy dog on wheels

SECOND ONLY in importance to the anthropology museum in Mexico City, this outstanding collection is displayed in spacious marble halls and open-air patios. It consists of sculptures and artifacts from the Gulf Coast's major pre-Columbian civilizations, found at various sites within the region. The first halls are dedicated to the Olmec civilization (see p254). Central Veracruz and the Totonacs follow, and the final room exhibits the highly stylized sculptures of the Huastec culture.

The Olmec Patio, dominated by El Rey

Olmec Funerary Urn
When it was discovered in Catemaco, this huge terra-cotta urn held the remains of a small child, along with ritual offerings.

GALLERY GUIDE
The exhibits are displayed in a descending series of halls and patios with steps and wheelchair ramps linking each level. Beginning at the main entrance, the items are arranged chronologically. The gardens contain flora representative of different areas of Veracruz state.

El Señor de Las Limas
Found in Las Limas, this greenstone figure (900–400 BC) is thought to be an accession monument. It depicts a lordly figure holding the Werejaguar baby, an important Olmec symbol of divine power.

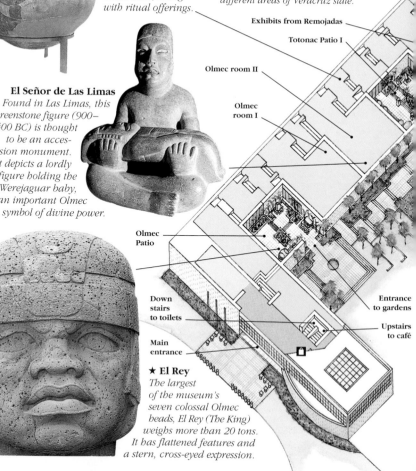

Exhibits from Remojadas

Totonac Patio I

Olmec room II

Olmec room I

Olmec Patio

Down stairs to toilets

Main entrance

Entrance to gardens

Upstairs to café

★ El Rey
The largest of the museum's seven colossal Olmec heads, El Rey (The King) weighs more than 20 tons. It has flattened features and a stern, cross-eyed expression.

Mictlantecuhtli

Representing Mictlantecuhtli, the god of death, this extraordinary skeletal figure (AD 600–900) is made from terra-cotta and painted with tar.

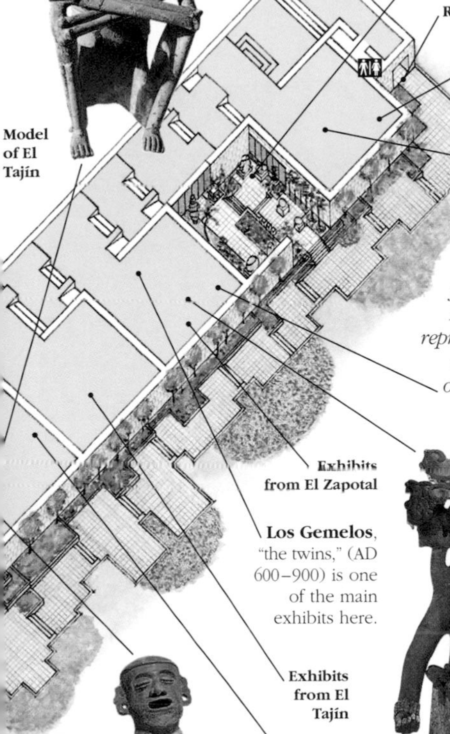

Totonac Patio II

Rear entrance

Huastec room

Model of El Tajín

VISITORS' CHECKLIST

Avenida Xalapa, Xalapa.
(228) 815 09 20. Avila Camacho, Centro and Tesorería.
9am–5pm Tue–Sun (last adm: 4:30pm).

KEY

☐ Permanent collection

☐ Temporary exhibitions

☐ Non-exhibition space

Wheeled dog, a child's toy made by the Huastec culture, is exhibited here.

★ Tlaloc
This expressive terra-cotta figure (AD 600–900) from El Zapotal (see p250) may represent Tlaloc, the rain god of the central highlands, or a warrior or ballplayer.

Exhibits from El Zapotal

Los Gemelos, "the twins," (AD 600–900) is one of the main exhibits here.

Exhibits from El Tajín

Cihuateotl
This life-size figure (AD 600–900) depicts Cihuateotl, a woman deified after dying in childbirth. Her closed eyes and open mouth evoke the screaming faces of women sacrificed in her honor.

Smiling Figure from Veracruz
Characteristic of Central Veracruz culture, these smiling figurines (AD 600–900) may have played a significant part in festive rituals.

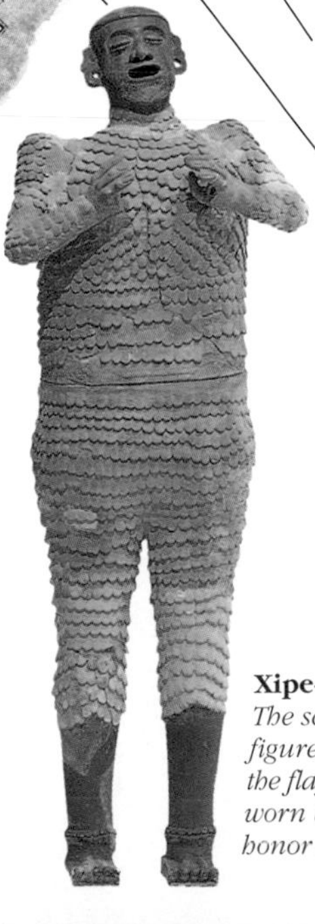

Xipe-Totec
The scaly skin of this terra-cotta figure (AD 1200–1521) represents the flayed skins of human sacrifices worn by priests during rites to honor Xipe-Totec, the god of spring.

STAR EXHIBITS

★ El Rey

★ Tlaloc

El Puerto de Veracruz ❻

Veracruz. 🏙 457,000. ✈ 🚗 🚌
ℹ *Palacio Municipal, (229) 989 88 17.* 🎭 *Carnival (Feb/Mar).*

VERACRUZ IS, more than any-thing else, a place of fun. The life of the city revolves around the Plaza de Armas and the *malecón* (waterfront promenade), an enjoyable place to stroll and watch the ships come and go. The tree-lined Plaza de Armas is flanked by the elegant 17th-century **Palacio Municipal** and the **cathedral**. The dome of the cathedral is covered with Puebla tiles *(see p153)* and crowned with a lantern and a small cross. Opposite the ca-thedral, the **Portales** (arcades) are filled with hotels and cafés. Musicians play here all day and most of the night, and most evenings there is dancing to watch, whether it is a frenetic *zapateo* or a poised, serene *danzón*. The entertainment reaches a peak during the city's famous carnival *(see p247)*.

Situated on the *malecón* is the **Gran Café de la Parroquia** *(see p325)*. This lively, convivial café, opened in 1808, is an institution for locals and visitors alike. Far-ther south is the **Acuario de Veracruz**, said to be the lar-gest and best aquarium in Latin America. Boat trips from the *malecón* run past the Isla de los Sacrificios and around the harbor to the fortress of **San Juan de Ulúa**. Fortified in 1692, it was home to the last Spanish garrison to accept Mexican Independence *(see p49)* and has since seen sev-eral foreign invasions, most recently by the US in 1914. It also became the country's most notorious prison during the

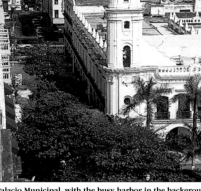

Palacio Municipal, with the busy harbor in the background

porfiriato (see p53). The tiny **Isla de los Sacrificios** was the first place the conquis-tadors landed *(see p43)*, and is named after the remains of human sacrifices they found.

The best of several museums in Veracruz, the **Museo Histórico Naval** is housed in the ex-Naval Academy in the city center. It tells the maritime his-tory of the port. Exhibits include over 300 types of knots, and some intricate models of ships.

In 1880, the fortified wall around Veracruz was torn down leaving only one of the nine original bastions, the **Baluarte de Santiago**. This small fort, built in 1635, now houses a good collection of pre-Columbian gold jewelry.

ENVIRONS: A few kilometers south of the town are the hotel-filled satellite suburbs of **Playa**

Sailors aboard a ship in Veracruz harbor

de Oro and **Mocambo**. The beaches here are cleaner and less crowded than in Veracruz, but still not very appealing. **Boca del Río**, farther along the coast, is famous for its seafood.

In the 1970s, excavations at **El Zapotal**, 75 km (47 miles) south of Veracruz, un-covered hundreds of clay sculptures – offerings to the god of the underworld, Mictlantecuhtli *(see p265)*. Most are in Xalapa's Museo de Antropología *(see pp248–9)*, but the central figure of Mictlantecuhtli, made of un-fired clay, is still at El Zapotal.

🐟 **Acuario de Veracruz**
Boulevard Manuel Avila Camacho.
📞 *(229) 932 79 84.* ⏰ *daily.* 📷 ♿
⚓ **San Juan de Ulúa**
Calle Pedro Sainz de Baranda.
📞 *(229) 938 51 51.* ⏰ *Jul–Aug: daily; Sep–Jun: Tue–Sun.* 📷 *Sun free.* ♿
🏛 **Museo Histórico Naval**
Calle Arista 418. 📞 *(229) 931 40 78.*
⏰ *Tue–Sun.* 🛒 🚻
⚓ **Baluarte de Santiago**
Calle Francisco Canal. 📞 *(229) 931 10 59.* ⏰ *Jul–Aug: daily; Sep–Jun: Tue–Sun.* 📷 *Sun free.*

The 17th-century fortress, San Juan de Ulúa

One of the cafés serving rich local coffee in Córdoba's Portal de Zevallos

Orizaba ❼

Veracruz. 👥 118,000. 🚌
ℹ️ El Palacio de Hierro 🎪 San
Miguel (Sep 29).

HOME TO an Aztec garrison, and then to Spanish soldiers, Orizaba held a strategic position on the trading route between Veracruz and Mexico City in the 15th and 16th centuries. Dominated by the Cerro del Borrego hill, Orizaba today is an industrial city, but it still has some colonial character.

On the corner of the main plaza, Parque Apolinar Castillo, is the 17th-century church **Iglesia de San Miguel**. The **Ex-Palacio Municipal**, also on the plaza, is an ornate Art-Nouveau construction. Built in Belgium in the late 19th century, it was brought over in pieces and reassembled here.

The Neo-Classical **Palacio Municipal**, on Calle Colón, was the base for a workers' education center after the Revolution. It boasts a 1926 mural, *Reconstrucción*, by José Clemente Orozco *(see p27)*.

Orizaba's **Museo de Arte del Estado** has a fine collection of paintings housed in 10 beautifully restored rooms.

ENVIRONS: Pico de Orizaba, Mexico's highest mountain, lies 23 km (14 miles) northwest of Orizaba. A volcano that last erupted in 1546, it is 5,747 m (18,856 ft) high. The Aztecs gave it the name Citlatépetl, "star mountain," for the way moonlight reflects off its snowy summit.

At the other extreme, the **Sierra de Zongolica**, to the south of Orizaba, has some of the world's deepest caves.

🏛️ **Museo de Arte del Estado**
Corner of 4 Oriente & 23 Sur.
📞 (272) 724 32 00. 🕐 Tue–Sun.
🎟️ Sun free. 📷

The Virgen de la Soledad, Córdoba's patron saint

Córdoba ❽

Veracruz. 👥 177,000. 🚌
ℹ️ Palacio Municipal, (271) 717 17 00, ext. 1778. 🎪 Expo Feria (May).

CÓRDOBA IS A BUSY, modern town, although traces of its colonial heritage are still to be found around the central Plaza de Armas. Viceroy Diego Fernández de Córdoba ordered the town's construction in 1618 to protect traders on the route between Veracruz and Mexico City from holdups by a group of escaped black slaves.

Historically, Córdoba's most significant building is the 18th-century **Portal de Zevallos**, an arcade on the north side of the Plaza de Armas. The Treaties of Córdoba, endorsing Mexican Independence, were signed here in 1829. Also on the plaza are the elegant Neo-Classical **Palacio Municipal** and the **Parroquia de la Inmaculada Concepción**. This church houses a lifelike image of the town's patron saint, the Virgen de la Soledad (Virgin of Solitude).

ENVIRONS: West of Córdoba is the **Barranca de Metlac**, a spectacular gorge spanned by four bridges. One of these, a 19th-century railroad bridge, features in several paintings by artist José María Velasco.

Mexico's highest mountain, Pico de Orizaba, towering above the Gulf Coast

Colorful colonnade-fronted houses in the charming town of Tlacotalpan

Tlacotalpan **9**

Veracruz. 🏠 15,000. 🚌 ℹ️ *Palacio Municipal, Plaza Zaragoza, (288) 884 20 50.* 🎭 *Candelaria (Feb 2), San Miguelito (Sep 29).*

EXPLORING this delightful town is like turning the clock back 100 years. Its quiet streets are lined with striking houses fronted by colonnades and painted in a flamboyant range of colors. As the Mexican writer Elena Poniatowska puts it, "when we want to smile, we think of Tlacotalpan."

The town is situated on the banks of the Río Papaloapan ("River of Butterflies"), which is over 300 m (984 ft) wide. Most of the elegant houses, with their Mozarabic-style portals, date from the second half of the 18th century, when large sugar and cotton plantations were established here. Important shipyards were also moved here from Cuba as a direct result of an English blockade of Havana, another Spanish possession, in 1762. During this era, Tlacotalpan was the principal town in southern Veracruz and an important international port, often more in touch with Europe and Cuba than with the rest of Mexico. However, the building of railroad lines left Tlacotalpan without a commercial role. Paradoxically, the same isolation that caused its decline has helped preserve this picturesque town.

Tlacotalpan's most interesting museum is the **Museo Jarocho Salvador Ferrando**. It is named after a local artist, and houses many of his portraits and landscapes, painted in the 19th century. Locally made furniture and crafts from the same period are also on display in the museum.

🏛 Museo Jarocho Salvador Ferrando
Manuel María Alegre 6. ⭕ *daily.*

Santiago Tuxtla **10**

Veracruz. 🏠 54,000. 🚌 🎭 *San Juan (Jun 24), Santiago (Jul 22–7).*

THE TOWN of Santiago Tuxtla is a gateway to the world of the ancient Olmecs *(see p254)*, who lived more than 3,000 years ago. A colossal stone head, typical of the Olmec culture, stands in the middle of the town's main square. The largest of the giant heads found so far, it is 3.4 m (11.2 ft) high and weighs around 50 tons. It is the only one of the heads yet discovered to have closed eyes and lacks the realism of the others.

The **Museo Tuxteco**, on one side of the plaza, has an interesting collection of pieces from nearby sites. They include a head called "El Negro," the legendary powers of which were formerly tapped by local witch doctors. Other exhibits include examples of the Olmec practices of skull deformation and tooth sculpting (probably expressions of beauty and class), another colossal head (this one from San Lorenzo Tenochtitlán), and ceremonial and domestic objects made out of jade and stone.

One pre-Columbian custom that lives on in Santiago Tuxtla is the *danza de los liseres*, in which the dancers don the mask of a jaguar deity. It is performed during fiestas in June and July.

ENVIRONS: A 20-km (12-mile) drive through lush, tropical vegetation, along a potholed road, leads to **Tres Zapotes**. This archaeological site was the center of Olmec culture around 400 BC, after La Venta

Giant Olmec head in the main square of Santiago Tuxtla

THE WITCH DOCTORS OF VERACRUZ

Witch doctors still practice in the state of Veracruz, around San Andrés Tuxtla and Catemaco. Using an assortment of medicinal plants, potions, charms, effigies of saints and devils,

dolls with pins stuck in them, and either black or white magic, they will undertake to cure their clients of diseases, help them find a better job, or resolve their marital problems. The practice is hereditary and can be traced back to a distant pre-Columbian past.

A witch doctor with the tools of his trade

Salto de Eyipantla waterfall, near San Andrés Tuxtla

(see p254) had been abandoned. The site itself is now just a series of mounds, but several of the finds are displayed in the museum in Tres Zapotes village nearby.

San Andrés Tuxtla, 14 km (9 miles) east of Santiago Tuxtla, is a sprawling commercial town famous for its cigars. There are fields of tobacco everywhere, and the roadside is lined with stalls selling the finished products.

A 3-km (2-mile) walk from San Andrés Tuxtla along a dirt track leads to the **Laguna Encantada** (Enchanted Lake), so-named because its water level mysteriously rises in the dry season and falls when it rains. Easier to reach, via a paved road that runs through mountains and fields of sugar cane, papaya, tobacco, and bananas, is the **Salto de Eyipantla**, a 50-m (164-ft) high waterfall. Local children act as guides, accompanying visitors down the 244 steps to the bottom of the falls.

🏛 **Museo Tuxteco**
Parque Juárez. 📞 (294) 947 01 96.
🕐 daily. 🎫 Sun free.

Laguna de Catemaco ⑪

Veracruz. 🚌 🏢 Palacio Municipal, Av Carranza, Catemaco, (294) 943 02 58. 🎉 Candelaria (Feb 2), Carmen (Jul 16).

THIS PICTURESQUE lake lies in the crater of an extinct volcano. Its hot, humid climate suits many birds, including parrots and toucans, and its waters also contain a few crocodiles. Boat trips round the lake leave from the wharf in the town of Catemaco and circle the island of **Tanaxpillo**, which is home to a colony of macaque monkeys. Two ecological parks on the north shore of the lake are accessible by boat or car. The more interesting of these, **Nanciyaga**, is a large swath of tropical rainforest. Visitors to the park can take part in pre-Columbian rituals, such as the *temazcal* (steam bath), or swim in spring-fed pools.

The town of Catemaco itself is dominated by the **Iglesia del Carmen**, a brightly painted church with twin bell towers. The statue of the Virgen del Carmen inside is dripping with jewelry and trinkets left by the many pilgrims who come here.

ENVIRONS: Ten of the 17 great Olmec heads so far discovered were found at **San Lorenzo Tenochtitlán**, 37 km (23 miles) to the southeast of Acayucan. This great Olmec ceremonial center flourished from 1200 BC to 900 BC, when it was destroyed. Most of the objects found here have been removed from the site. However, some of the pieces are on show in three small museums at **Potrero**, **El Azuzul**, and

One of the Divine Twins from San Lorenzo

Tenochtitlán. Exhibits at El Azuzul include the sculpture known as *Los Divinos Gemelos* (The Divine Twins).

🌿 **Nanciyaga**
7 km (4.5 miles) NE of Catemaco. 📞 (294) 943 01 99. 🕐 daily; Thu–Tue Oct–Nov. 🎫 📷 🏠

Boat trip around Tanaxpillo Island, which is inhabited by macaques

Comalcalco ⑫

Tabasco. Off Mex 187, 58 km (36 miles) NW of Villahermosa. 🚌 *from Comalcalco town, Villahermosa, or Cardenas.* ⭘ *Tue–Sun.* 🎟

I N THE LUSH, green, cocoa-producing area northwest of Villahermosa are the Maya ruins of Comalcalco. Dating mainly from the late Classic period of Maya civilization (AD 700–900), the architecture differs quite markedly from that found at Palenque *(see pp234–7)*, which was occupied around the same time. Unlike Palenque, and other Maya sites, Comalcalco has structures built from bricks, held together with oyster-shell mortar. The bricks were sometimes incised with figures and glyphs when wet. Comalcalco's main structures are two pyramids, the Gran Acrópolis and the Acrópolis Este, and the North Plaza. Originally many of the site's structures would have been covered in high-relief stucco carvings. Of those that survive today, the most distinctive is a mask of the god El Señor del Sol, near the base of the Gran Acrópolis.

Mask of El Señor del Sol at the base of the Gran Acrópolis in Comalcalco

Villahermosa ⑬

Tabasco. 🏠 520,000. ✈ 🚌 🛈 *Avenida de los Rios, (993) 316 36 33.* 🎉 *Rio Usumacinta Nautical Marathon (Mar/Apr), Tabasco State Fair (Apr/May).*

N OW THE CAPITAL of the state of Tabasco, Villahermosa was founded in the late 16th century by a community forced to move inland by repeated pirate attacks. Situated on the banks of the Grijalva River, Villahermosa today is a friendly, bustling city. It has two excellent museums, the **Parque-Museo de La Venta** and the **Museo Regional de Antropología Carlos Pellicer**. The latter contains fascinating exhibits from the Olmec, Maya, and other Mesoamerican cultures, including pottery, clay figurines, and jade carvings.

ENVIRONS: Yum-Ká, an ecological park a short drive east of Villahermosa, is named after a mythical Maya dwarf who protects the jungle. Animals, including the endangered ocelot, manatee, and howler monkey, are found in its 100 hectares (247 acres) of natural habitats.

La Venta, 117 km (73 miles) to the west of Villahermosa, is the site of the most important Olmec settlement. Although it can be visited, the principal sculptures are now in the Parque-Museo de La Venta.

🏛 **Museo Regional de Antropología Carlos Pellicer** Av Carlos Pellicer Cámara 511. 📞 *(993) 312 63 44.* ⭘ *Tue–Sun.* 🎟 ♿ 🏋 **Yum-Ká** 16 km (10 miles) E of Villahermosa. 📞 *(993) 356 01 15.* ⭘ *daily.* 🎟 🅿 🚻 ♿

THE OLMECS

Mexico's first notable culture, the Olmec, was established on the hot, humid Gulf Coast by 1200 BC. Often called the *cultura madre* (mother culture) because of their influence on later civilizations, the Olmecs are something of a mystery. Their main sites, at San Lorenzo and La Venta, wielded political, economic, and religious authority over big regions and large numbers of people. The earliest, San Lorenzo *(see p253)*, was systematically destroyed in about 900 BC, although why and by whom is a mystery. About the same time La Venta, farther east, reached the peak of its influence, becoming an important religious and political center and establishing far-flung trade routes. Around the beginning of the first millennium AD Olmec civilization gradually faded into obscurity. Today the most impressive reminders of the ancient culture are the colossal carved stone heads, of which the first to be discovered in modern times was found at Tres Zapotes *(see p252)*. They were fashioned from massive basalt blocks weighing up to 20 tons, which the Olmecs moved large distances, probably using river rafts.

Colossal Olmec head

An ocelot, one of the endangered species in Yum-Ká ecological park

Parque-Museo de La Venta

FOR NEARLY 600 YEARS, from 1000 to 400 BC, the settlement at La Venta was the center of Olmec culture. In the 1950s its treasures were threatened by the discovery of oil nearby. Tabascan poet and anthropologist Carlos Pellicer organized their rescue and had them transported to this outdoor museum on the shore of a lake, the Laguna de las Ilusiones. Its winding jungle paths provide superb settings for 33 pieces, including Olmec heads, *altares* (probably thrones rather than altars), stelae, and mosaics. Part of the park is a wildlife area and there are also some animals housed in the archaeological section.

La Abuela ①
This kneeling old woman holds a vessel as if in offering.

Gran Altar ⑤
The figure under this monument holds a rope binding the two men, probably captives, carved on its sides.

VISITORS' CHECKLIST

Boulevard Adolfo Ruíz Cortínes, Villahermosa. ☎ *(993) 314 16 52.* 🚌 *from Central Camionera or Mercado.* 🕐 *8am–4:00pm daily.* ♿ 📷 ☕ 🛍

KEY

① La Abuela (The Grandmother)
② Jaula de Jaguar (Jaguar's Cage)
③ Personajes con Niños (People with Children)
④ Jaguar Humanizado (Human Jaguar)
⑤ Gran Altar (Great Altar)
⑥ Mosaico del Jaguar (Jaguar Mosaic)
⑦ El Rey (The King)
⑧ Cabeza Colosal 1 (Giant Head 1)
⑨ La Diosa Joven (The Young Goddess)

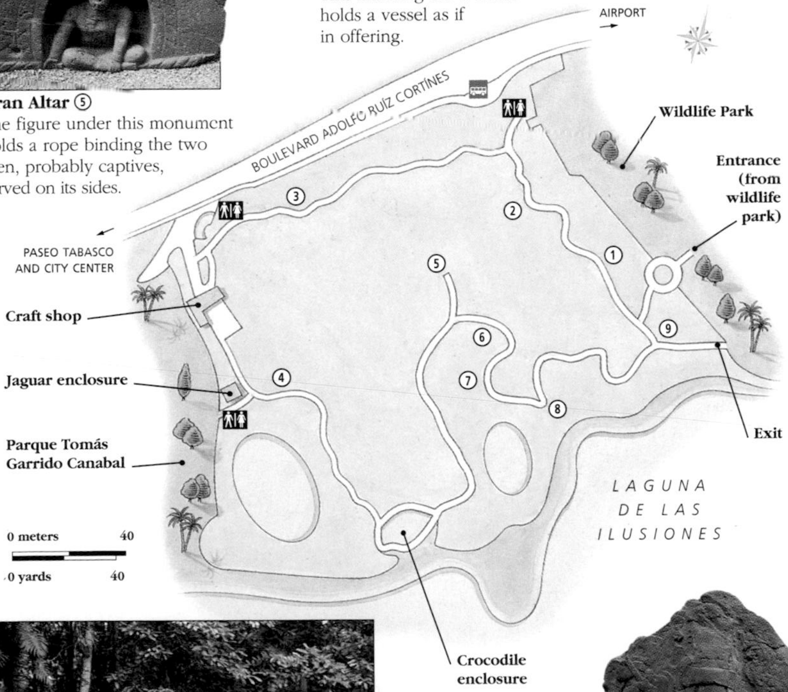
AIRPORT
BOULEVARD ADOLFO RUÍZ CORTÍNES
Wildlife Park
Entrance (from wildlife park)
PASEO TABASCO AND CITY CENTER
Craft shop
Jaguar enclosure
Parque Tomás Garrido Canabal
Exit
LAGUNA DE LAS ILUSIONES
0 meters 40
0 yards 40
Crocodile enclosure

Personajes con Niños ③
Seated in front of this altar, or throne, is an adult figure holding an infant in his arms.

El Rey ⑦
Wearing a tall headdress and carrying a staff across his chest that signifies his power, the figure on this stela was clearly important. He is surrounded by six smaller figures, similarly attired and carrying staves.

THE YUCATÁN PENINSULA

CAMPECHE • QUINTANA ROO • YUCATÁN

THE STUNNING RUINS *of the Yucatán's famous Maya cities and ceremonial sites are reason enough to visit. But the fine white-sand beaches of the Caribbean – often refered to as the "Mayan Riviera" – make the peninsula even more irresistible. Small wonder that for many visitors to Mexico this region is their first or only experience of the country, providing enough to see and do to fill a long vacation.*

When the Spanish first arrived on the Yucatán Peninsula in 1517 they found one of the most remarkable civilizations in the Americas. But the Spanish soldiers, and Franciscan friars who came with them, had scant regard for the Maya's high level of social organization, great knowledge of astronomy, or sophisticated writing system. They swiftly defeated the Maya, colonized their lands, and destroyed most of their historical records. As undisputed rulers of the Yucatán, the Spanish founded Mérida, Campeche, and other colonial cities as bastions in their fight for control of the Caribbean against English, French, and Dutch pirates. In 1847, after Mexico had achieved independence,

civil war erupted on the peninsula between settlers of European origin and the much-exploited descendants of the ancient Maya. This conflict, known as the Caste War, ended in defeat for the Maya, followed by bloody reprisals. The production of henequen and sisal (for rope and fabric making) led to a period of prosperity in the Yucatán in the late 19th and early 20th centuries. Today, oil is the peninsula's main industry, followed by tourism, which centers on the mushrooming resort of Cancún. Away from the coasts, traditional life continues much as it has done for years, in villages where the indigenous Maya live in palm-roofed huts, and preserve their own language, customs, and culture.

Brightly painted colonnade in Izamal, a colonial town in the north of the peninsula

◁ Carvings of the god Chac on the corner of a building at the ancient Maya city of Uxmal

Exploring the Yucatán Peninsula

SOME OF THE FINEST archaeological sites in the Americas are situated on the Yucatán Peninsula. They include the sensational Chichén Itzá and Uxmal, as well as many lesser-known sites such as Cobá, Edzná, Tulum, and Ekbalam. The interior of the peninsula is jungle, some of which is conserved in its natural state, while the Mayan Riviera, on the east coast, has some of Mexico's best beaches. Many people come to the Yucatán to visit the offshore islands of Cozumel and Isla Mujeres and dive or snorkel over the superb coral formations of the Great Mesoamerican Reef, the world's second longest barrier reef. Attractive Spanish colonial architecture can be seen in Campeche, Mérida, Valladolid, and Izamal, and in the Franciscan churches of several towns south of Mérida.

The Ex-Templo de San José in the center of Campeche

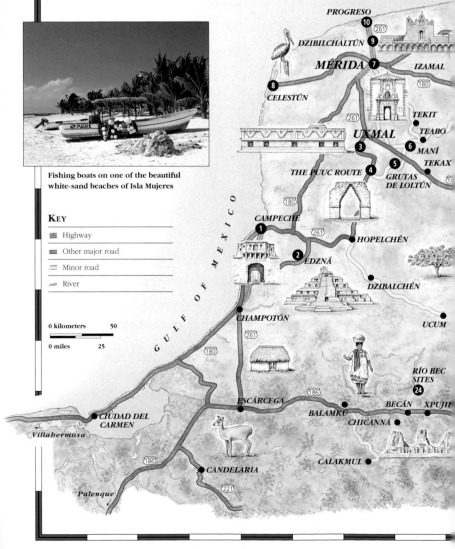

Fishing boats on one of the beautiful white-sand beaches of Isla Mujeres

KEY

▬	Highway
▬	Other major road
═	Minor road
═	River

0 kilometers   50

0 miles   25

PROGRESO
10
261
DZIBILCHALTÚN
9
MÉRIDA
7
IZAMAL
8
180
CELESTÚN
261
TEKIT
TEABO
UXMAL
3
6
MANÍ
THE PUUC ROUTE
5
TEKAX
4
GRUTAS
DE LOLTÚN
180
CAMPECHE
1
261
HOPELCHÉN
2
EDZNÁ
DZIBALCHÉN
CHAMPOTÓN
261
UCUM
180
GULF OF MEXICO
RÍO BEC
SITES
24
ESCÁRCEGA
186
BECÁN   XPUJI
CIUDAD DEL
CARMEN
BALAMKÚ
CHICANNÁ
Villahermosa
186
CANDELARIA
CALAKMUL
221
Palenque

SIGHTS AT A GLANCE

Campeche ❶

Cancún ⓰

Celestún ❽

Chetumal ㉓

Chichén Itzá pp274–6 ⓬

Cobá ⓴

Dzibilchaltún ❾

Edzná ❷

Ekbalam ⓮

Grutas de Loltún ❺

Isla Mujeres ⓱

Izamal ⓫

Maní ❻

Mérida pp270–71 ❼

Progreso ❿

The Puuc Route ❹

Río Bec Sites ㉔

Río Lagartos ⓯

Sian Ka'an Biosphere Reserve ㉒

Tulum ㉑

Uxmal pp262–4 ❸

Valladolid ⓭

Xcaret ⓳

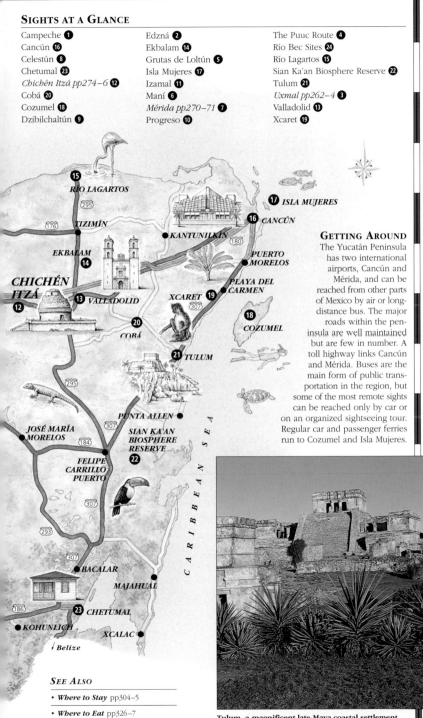

GETTING AROUND

The Yucatán Peninsula has two international airports, Cancún and Mérida, and can be reached from other parts of Mexico by air or long-distance bus. The major roads within the peninsula are well maintained but are few in number. A toll highway links Cancún and Mérida. Buses are the main form of public transportation in the region, but some of the most remote sights can be reached only by car or on an organized sightseeing tour. Regular car and passenger ferries run to Cozumel and Isla Mujeres.

SEE ALSO

• *Where to Stay* pp304–5

• *Where to Eat* pp326–7

Tulum, a magnificent late-Maya coastal settlement

Vivid exteriors of colonial houses in Campeche city center

Campeche ❶

Campeche. 🏛 *217,000.* ✈ 🚌
ℹ *Av Ruiz Cortines, (981) 816 67 67.*
🎭 *Carnival (Feb/Mar), Cristo Negro de San Román (Sep 15–30).*

THE SPANISH settlement of
Campeche was built on
the site of a former Maya
fishing village in about 1540.
In colonial times it was the
most important port on the
Yucatán Peninsula, exporting
large quantities of timber and
roots used to make dyes in
European textile production.

Campeche's prosperity made
it a frequent target for attacks
by English, French, and Dutch
pirates, who harassed ships in
the area, and looted and destroyed the city several times.
The worst attack, in 1663, resulted in the massacre of many
of the city's inhabitants. As a
consequence, thick walls were
built around the town. These

**Tiled doorway of the Ex-Templo
de San José, now a cultural center**

were strengthened by eight
baluartes (bastions), seven of
which have been put to other
uses and can be visited. The
largest of them, in the
middle of the stretch of
wall facing the sea, is
the **Baluarte de la
Soledad**. It is now a
museum displaying
an important collec-
tion of Maya stelae
(see p233), many of
which were found at
the Maya burial ground
on the island of Jaina,
40 km (25 miles) to
the north of Campeche.
The **Baluarte de San-
tiago**, at the northwestern
corner of the walls, has been
transformed into a walled
botanical garden containing
over 200 species of subtropical
plants. On the landward side
of the walls, the **Baluarte de
San Pedro** sells a small selection of regional handicrafts.

Two gateways in the walls –
the **Sea Gate** and the **Land
Gate** – give access to the old

**Jade mask,
in Fuerte de
San Miguel**

part of the city. Between them
runs Calle 59, on which stand
several restored, single-story
colonial houses, painted in
bright blues, pinks, and ochers.
One of the finest buildings is
the **Casa de Teniente del Rey**
(King's Lieutenant's House),
the former residence of the
Spanish king's military representative in the Yucatán.
Transformed into offices, the
house has a splendid courtyard, which can be visited.

The focal point of the old
part of Campeche is the main
square, the **Parque Principal**,
which has elegant arcades
and an elaborate, modern
bandstand. Tours of the city
in open-sided trams start from
here. In the northern corner of
the square is the **cathedral**,
one of the first churches
built on the Yucatán
mainland, although
much of the present
building was con-
structed later, in the
Baroque style. Behind
it, on Calle 10, is the
Mansión Carvajal,
now divided into
government offices.
This building is a
good example of
19th-century Spanish-
Moorish architecture. Another
attractive building in the city
center is the **Ex-Templo de
San José**, a former Jesuit
church, now used as a cultural
center, which has an elaborate
façade of blue and yellow tiles.

Campeche's defenses were
completed by two forts on
hills outside the city, both
of which are now museums.
Situated to the north is the

PANAMA HATS

The town of Becal, between Campeche and Mérida, is renowned for its production of Panama hats. Known locally as
jipis, they received their common name when they became
popular with workers building the Panama canal. The
palm leaves used to make
the hats are split and braided
in caves, where the heat and
humidity make the fibers
more flexible. The finest hats
(finos) have a smooth and
silky feel and can be rolled
up so tightly that they are
able to pass through a man's
wedding ring, and then
regain their former shape.

**Monument to the Panama hat
in the main square of Becal**

The Edificio de los Cinco Pisos (Building of the Five Levels) at Edzná

Fuerte de San José, with exhibits on colonial military history. To the south of the city is the **Fuerte de San Miguel**, begun in 1771 and protected by a moat crossed by a drawbridge. Exhibits inside this fort include distinctive jade masks from Calakmul *(see p287)*, and ceramic figurines from the island of Jaina.

On the way to the Fuerte de San Miguel is the **Iglesia de San Román**, the city's most popular shrine. It is famous for its large black ebony statue of Christ, which is believed to possess miraculous powers.

🏛 **Baluarte de la Soledad**
Calle 8 Circuito Baluartes (seaward side). ◯ *Tue–Sun.* 🖼 *Sun free.*
🏚 **Casa de Teniente del Rey**
Calle 59 No. 38, corner of Calle 14.
📞 *(981) 816 91 11.* ◯ *Mon–Fri.* 🖼
🏛 **Fuerte de San José**
Av Morazán. ◯ *Tue–Sun.* 🖼 *Sun free.*
🏛 **Fuerte de San Miguel**
Av Escénica. ◯ *Tue–Sun.* 🖼 *Sun free.*

Edzná ❷

Campeche. Mex 180 and 186, 60 km (37 miles) SE of Campeche. 🚌 *from Campeche.* ◯ *daily.* 🖼 🎫

A SOPHISTICATED and extensive canal system radiates out from the center of this Maya settlement to the agricultural areas beyond. The canals were primarily used for the transportation of goods, but quite possibly also served a defensive purpose. Edzná may have been founded in around 600 BC, and in its heyday, between AD 600 and 900, it is thought to have had a population of 25,000. The main structure is the Gran Acrópolis, which is dominated by the Edificio de los Cinco Pisos (Building of the Five Levels). Another building of interest is the Templo de los Mascarones (Temple of the Masks), named after its distinctive stucco mask.

Stucco mask on the Templo de los Mascarones, Edzná

FIESTAS OF THE YUCATÁN

Equinoxes *(Mar 21 and Sep 21)*, Chichén Itzá. An optical illusion created by the ancient Maya can be seen when the sun casts a shadow on the north side of El Castillo *(see p276)*, making a "snake" move down the steps behind each of the two stone serpent heads at the base.

The stepped El Castillo pyramid, at Chichén Itzá

Carnival *(Feb/Mar)*. Celebrated in most parts of the Yucatán, but particularly in Campeche. In many villages, a papier-mâché figure of "Juan Carnaval" is paraded through the streets, put in a coffin, and symbolically burned to conclude the festivities.
Cristo de las Ampollas *(Sep 27)*, Mérida. Festivities and processions in honor of "Christ of the Blisters," a wooden statue made in Ichmul and later moved to Mérida cathedral *(see p270)*. The statue is said to have blistered and blackened, but not burned, in a fire at Ichmul's parish church.

Fuerte de San Miguel, once an integral part of Campeche's defenses against naval attack

Uxmal ❸

THE LATE-CLASSIC Maya site of Uxmal ("thrice built") is one of the most complex and harmonious expressions of Puuc architecture *(see p268).* The city's history is uncertain, but most of the buildings date from the 7th–10th centuries AD, when Uxmal dominated the region. The real function of many of the structures is unknown, and they retain the fanciful names given to them by the Spanish. Unlike most Yucatán sites, Uxmal has no cenotes *(see p275),* and water was collected in man-made cisterns *(chultunes),* one of which can be seen near the entrance. The scarcity of water may explain the number of depictions of the rain god Chac on the buildings.

Mask at entrance to the site

View of the Nunnery Quadrangle and Magician's Pyramid from the south

Cemetery Group

Dovecote
Named after its unusual roof comb, this ruined palace faces a rectangular garden and is one of Uxmal's most evocative and peaceful spots.

Great Pyramid
A stairway climbs the 30-m (100-ft) pyramid to a temple decorated with Chac masks and macaws, the latter associated with fire, suggesting it was a temple to the sun.

South Temple

STAR FEATURES

★ Governor's Palace

★ Nunnery Quadrangle

★ Magician's Pyramid

★ Governor's Palace
Regarded as the masterpiece of Puuc architecture, the 9th–10th-century palace is actually three buildings linked by Maya arches. The distinctive hooked noses of the Chac masks stand out against the mosaic frieze that runs the length of the structure.

★ Nunnery Quadrangle
This impressive structure was given its unlikely name because the Spanish thought that the 74 small rooms set around a central courtyard looked like the cells of a nunnery. The stone latticework, ornate masks of Chac, and carved serpents on the walls are remarkable examples of closely fitting mosaic.

VISITORS' CHECKLIST

Yucatán. Mex 261, 78 km
(48 miles) S of Mérida. 🚌 *tours
from Mérida* ⬭ *8am–5pm
daily.* 📷 ✔ 🖬 🛈

Entrance to site

★ Magician's Pyramid
The spectacular pyramid (seen here through an arch in front) is, at 35 m (115 ft), the tallest structure at Uxmal. Begun in the sixth century AD, it was added to over the next 400 years (see p264).

Ballcourt

Jaguar Throne
This throne is carved as a two-headed jaguar, an animal associated with chiefs and kings.

Pyramid of the Old Woman

```
0 meters        100
0 yards         100
```

House of the Turtles
The upper level of this elegant rectangular building is simply decorated with columns and, above them, a frieze of small turtles in procession around the building. Their presence suggests that it might have been dedicated to a water god.

The Magician's Pyramid

TALL, STEEP, and set on an unusual oval base, the Magician's Pyramid is the most striking of Uxmal's monuments. Legend tells that it was built in one night by a dwarf with supernatural powers – the magician – but, in fact, it shows five phases of construction from the 6th–10th centuries AD. At each phase a new temple was built, either on top of or obscuring the previous one. There are thus five temples on the pyramid. Unfortunately, visitors are no longer allowed to climb to the summit, to prevent further erosion.

View of the pyramid showing the west staircase and façades of Temples I and IV

The façade of Temple IV is actually an expressive Chac mask with large rectangular eyes and a curling moustache. Its wide-open, toothed mouth forms the entrance. Temple III is behind Temple IV.

Temple V is part of the final phase of construction – which took place around AD 1000 – and appears to be a small-scale reproduction of the nearby Governor's Palace (*see p262*). It obscures the original roof comb on top of Temples II and III.

Entrance to Temple IV

Chac masks on façade of Temple I

The east staircase provides access to Temple II, which is just a dark room today.

Entrance to Temple I (now blocked)

Temple I was built in the sixth century AD, according to the results of radiocarbon dating, and is now covered by the pyramid. Partially collapsed, it is filled with rubble and cannot be visited.

RECONSTRUCTION OF THE MAGICIAN'S PYRAMID

This shows how the pyramid looked around AD 1000. The surface was probably painted red, with details in blue, yellow, and black. The colors and plaster have now eroded to reveal the limestone beneath.

The west staircase, at the front of the pyramid, is flanked by representations of Chac, the rain god. The staircase is extremely steep and ascends the pyramid at an angle of 60°, meaning that the climb to the summit was very difficult.

The Gods of Ancient Mexico

Xilonen, an
Aztec goddess

A VAST ARRAY of gods and goddesses were worshiped by the civilizations of ancient Mesoamerica (*see pp44–5*). Some of them related to celestial bodies, such as the stars, sun, and moon. Some had calendrical significance. Others held sway over creation, death, and the different aspects of daily life. Frequently gods were passed from one civilization to another, usually changing their names in the process. These deities were feared as much as revered. If they had created the world, and ran it, they could just as easily destroy it. It was therefore essential to appease them as much as possible, often through human sacrifice.

RAIN GODS

Abundant rainfall was vital to farming communities, and rain and lightning gods were venerated in all the civilizations of ancient Mexico.

Tlaloc was the central Mexican god of rain and lightning. He can be recognized by his goggle-like eyes and jaguar teeth, as in this sculpture from Teotihuacán (see pp134–7).

Prominent teeth   Ear ornaments

Staring eyes

Long, blunt, reptilian nose

Chac, the Maya god of rain and lightning, was often represented on buildings. The mask seen here is from a palace at Kabah in the Yucatán (see p268).

QUETZALCOATL

The most famous Mexican god was Quetzalcoatl (called Kukulcan by the Maya). A plumed or feathered serpent, he was a combination of quetzal bird and rattlesnake. The first carvings of him were made by the Olmecs. Subsequent representations of Quetzalcoatl/ Kukulcan can be seen at many ancient sites; this bas-relief is on the Pyramid of the Plumed Serpent at Xochicalco (*see p145*).

CREATOR GODS

Tonacatecuhtli

Mesoamerican societies had differing accounts of creation. According to one myth from central Mexico, Tonacatecuhtli resided in the 13th, or uppermost, heaven with Tonacacihuatl, his consort. From here they sent down souls of children to be born on earth.

THE SUN GOD

This deity was associated with the jaguar in ancient Mexico, an animal that evoked the vigor and power of the rising sun. The Classic and Postclassic Maya venerated Kinich Ahau, the "great sun" or "sun-eyed" lord, seen here as a huge mask at Kohunlich (*see p287*).

Kinich Ahau

GODS OF THE UNDERWORLD

Only those who suffered violent death went directly to one of the heavens. All other mortal souls were condemned to descend the nine levels of the underworld. In Aztec mythology, the soul had to pass through a series of hazards before reaching the deepest of these levels, the dreaded Mictlan, ruled over by Mictlantecuhtli and his consort Mictecacihuatl. The Aztecs depicted their god of death as a frightening skeletal figure, such as this one unearthed at the Templo Mayor in Mexico City (*see pp68–70*).

Mictlantecuhtli, Aztec god of death

Kabah's palace, the Codz Poop, ornamented with hundreds of Chac masks

The Puuc Route ➍

Yucatán. Starts from Mex 261, 20 km (12 miles) SE of Uxmal. 🚌 *tours from Mérida.* **All sites** ◯ *daily.* 🎫 *Sun free.*

FORMING A LOW ridge across the western part of the Yucatán, about 100 km (62 miles) south of Mérida, the Puuc hills provide a welcome relief from the flat monotony of the rest of the peninsula.

Despite a lack of water, they offered a strong defensive position for the ancient Maya people, as well as good soil for cultivating maize, squash, and other vegetables. Several Maya settlements have been discovered in the region. All are believed to have reached their peaks from about AD 600 to AD 900 and they share the striking style of architecture and ornamentation that has become known as the Puuc style. This style is characterized by a façade which has plain walls at the base and detailed stone mosaic masks (often depicting gods) on its upper sections.

Some settlements are linked to each other and to the contemporary site of Uxmal *(see pp262–4)* by *sacbeob,* or "white roads," which were mainly used for ceremonial purposes.

The Puuc Route runs through four Maya sites, starting with **Kabah**. The most important building here is the Codz Poop. The façade of this palace is decorated with more than 250 masks representing the rain god Chac *(see p265),* with his distinctive hooked nose. Kabah was the closest settlement to the important Maya city of Uxmal. A single, undecorated arch straddles the entrance road.

Of all the Puuc sites, **Sayil**, around 10 km (6 miles) south of Kabah, is the one that provides most evidence of how the Maya in this area lived. Around the edge of the site, many of the ordinary dwellings have been excavated, as have the homes of the settlement's ruling elite, located in the central area. It is hard to envisage today, but the excavations suggest that Sayil was once populated by more than 8,000 people, with a similar number living in small, outlying communities surrounding the city. The huge three-tiered palace of Sayil's rulers is a splendid example of the rich Puuc style.

Sayil has no accessible supply of surface water, but several *chultunes,* large man-made cisterns for storing water, have been found at the site.

About 8 km (5 miles) east of Sayil is **Xlapak**. The best-preserved building here is the palace, which has masks of Chac, the rain god, above its entrances. Details such as a frieze of columns stand out on other buildings, but much of this site has yet to be cleared.

The last settlement on the Puuc Route is **Labná**, 5 km (3 miles) to the northeast of Xlapak. Among several spectacular structures here, the Arch is the best known. Originally part of a building between two courtyards, it is adorned

A snake with a human head in its jaws carved on the corner of Labná palace

The magnificent three-tiered palace in Sayil, with its frieze of small columns

◁ Detail of Chac masks adorning the façade of the Codz Poop palace in Kabah

El Mirador (The Observatory) in Labná, crowned by a 4-m (13-ft) crest

with several Chac masks and two representations of thatched Maya huts. Nearby is a structure with a high crest above its façade. Known as El Mirador (The Observatory), it may have been a temple.

At the other end of the site is the main two-story palace, which has a frieze of masks and latticework. On one corner of the palace is a powerful carving of a serpent's head with a human head in its jaws.

Another impressive structure is the Temple of Columns, which has a frieze around it, decorated with small columns.

Grutas de Loltún ❺

Yucatán. Off Mex 180, 20 km (12 miles) SW of Maní. ▦ tours from Mérida. ⭘ daily. ▦ ▦

VISITORS ARE TAKEN on a tour that travels more than 1 km (half a mile) through the Grutas de Loltún, the longest cave system in the Yucatán. The earliest remains discovered here are bison, mammoth, and other animal bones, suggesting that Loltún was inhabited soon after the last Ice Age. The caves contain fascinating wall paintings from various periods of occupation. These include stylized humans and animals, and the superb Warrior of Loltún. However, the caves' most striking features are the stalagmites and stalactites that give them the name Loltún, meaning "stone flowers."

Maní ❻

Yucatán. ▦ 4,700. ▦ ▦ Fiesta tradicional (Aug 20).

FROM THE FOURTH decade of the 16th century, Catholic priests, and in particular Franciscan friars, came from Spain to convert the Maya population of the Yucatán Peninsula. They constructed a network of huge, fortress-like churches and monasteries, often on the sites of earlier Maya temples. The most imposing of these is the **Iglesia de San Miguel Arcángel**, which dominates the town of Maní. It has a vast atrium, an open chapel, and a monastery with 114 cells. It was constructed

Part of the beautiful altarpiece in Maní's Franciscan church

by around 6,000 slaves on ground that was already holy to the Maya – a Maya cenote (natural well) is visible under the front of the church.

ENVIRONS: Other Franciscan churches can be found in the towns all around Maní. Built in 1693–9, the church in **Oxkutzcab**, 10km (6 miles) to the south, has a lovely Baroque altarpiece. The Iglesia de San Pedro Apóstol in **Teabo**, east of Maní, was begun in 1694, and traces of Franciscan murals can still be seen in its powder-blue interior. The road north out of Teabo leads through **Tekit**, which also has a Franciscan church, to **Tecoh**. The church here houses a huge red and blue wooden altarpiece and a beautiful wooden cross with the last hours of Christ's life painted on it.

Between Tekit and Tecoh is **Mayapán**, which became the Maya capital in the north of the peninsula after the fall of Chichén Itzá. Abandoned in the mid-15th century, Mayapán's most remarkable surviving feature is the pyramid of Kukulcan, which is built on nine levels and topped with a temple.

▣ Mayapán
60 km (37 miles) N of Maní.
⭘ daily. ▦

Iglesia de la Candelaria, Tecoh's Franciscan church

Mérida ❼

THE CONQUISTADOR Francisco de Montejo the Younger founded this city in 1542 on the ruins of a large Maya settlement. He named it Mérida because it reminded him of the ruined Roman city of the same name in Spain. An important city during Spanish colonial rule, Mérida rose to prominence again at the turn of the 20th century when it enjoyed an economic boom, based on sales of locally grown sisal for rope-making. In the early 1900s, Mérida was said to have more millionaires per head of population than anywhere else in the world. This prosperity is reflected in its grand mansions, squares, parks, and statues. Modern Mérida is an important manufacturing city, and also a university, business, and cultural center.

The lofty interior of the grand Catedral de San Ildefonso

The Palacio Municipal on the Plaza Grande

Exploring Mérida

As with most Spanish colonial cities, Mérida is built on a grid system based around the main square, the Plaza Grande (also known as the Plaza Mayor or Plaza de la Independencia). In the evenings, and on Sundays, dancing and concerts take place outside the city hall, the **Palacio Municipal**. This building is in a mix of styles and has a notable 1920s clock tower.

The **Casa de Montejo** *(see p22)*, on the south side of the plaza, was built between 1543 and 1549 as the palace of the first Spanish governors. Now a bank, it still has its original portico, with the Montejo family coat of arms and statues of two conquistadors standing triumphantly on the heads of Maya Indians.

Opposite the city hall is the **cathedral**, the oldest in the Americas. It was begun in the early 1560s, and finished in 1598. Three arched doors in the imposing façade lead to a soaring interior with a barreled roof and crisscross arches. There is a huge wooden sculpture of Christ behind the main altar. Another wooden statue, *Cristo de las Ampollas* (Christ of the Blisters, *see p261*), stands in a small chapel on the right. It is a copy of a statue that was brought to Mérida after miraculously surviving a fire. The original, which was later destroyed, is said to have developed blisters, as skin would, instead of burning.

The 19th-century **Palacio de Gobierno**, next to the cathedral, houses the Yucatán state authorities. It is remarkable for the numerous large murals adorning its courtyard, stairs, and first-floor lobby. They were painted in the 1970s by Fernando Castro Pacheco, a local artist, and show his vision of Mexican history from the time of the first Maya to the 19th century.

Just off Calle 60, one of the city's major roads, is **Parque Cepeda Peraza**, a small but bustling square. Visitors can watch the many musicians and street merchants, or relax in one of the open-air cafés. The imposing Jesuit church, the **Templo de la Tercera Orden** (Temple of the Third Order), on the north side of the square, dates from the 17th century. It has a huge entrance and two narrow bell towers. Inside, the gold altar and friezes of biblical scenes are the only decoration.

Mérida prides itself on being the cultural capital of the Yucatán Peninsula, and the **Teatro José Peón Contreras** is one of its main showcases. Built at the turn of the 20th century with money from the sisal trade, it is an extravagant Neo-Classical creation in peach and white, with elaborate chandeliers in its massive foyer.

The small **Iglesia de Santa Lucía**, one of the earliest and most harmonious of the city's churches, is where the local Maya Indians were encouraged to come and worship.

A mural by Fernando Castro Pacheco, in the Palacio de Gobierno

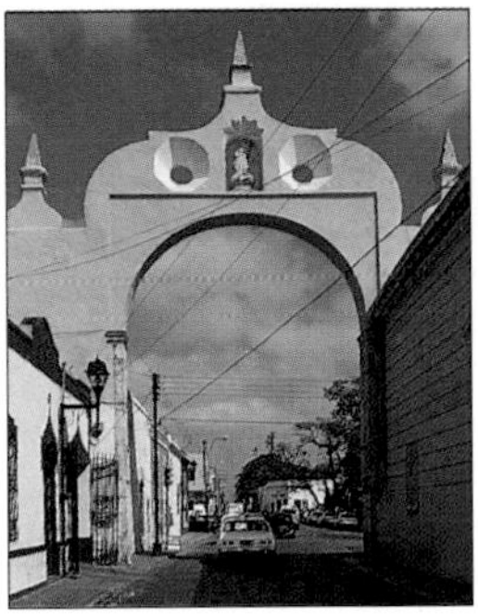

The Arco de San Juan, one of eight city entrances built by the Spanish

To the left of the church, the Parque Santa Lucía is used for dancing and cultural events, and has a lively flea market on Sundays. On its north and west corners are two of the arches built by the Spanish at the original city entrances. A third arch, the **Arco de San Juan**, is situated to the southwest of the Plaza Grande. It is arguably the finest of the eight constructed.

North of Calle 60, the **Paseo Montejo** stretches for several kilometers. It is lined with the elegant town mansions of rich henequen or sisal plantation owners and the private banks that prospered in the late 19th century. Many of the houses were built by Italian architects and are a medley of Neo-Classical elements. One of the finest, the Palacio Cantón, houses the excellent **Museo Regional de Antropología**. Its pre-Columbian exhibits include a jaguar throne from Uxmal *(see pp262–4)*, a *chacmool* from Chichén Itzá *(see pp274–6)*, and many fine examples of funerary offerings.

At the northern end of the Paseo Montejo is the **Altar a la Patria** (Altar to the Fatherland), an elaborate 20th-century work by Colombian sculptor Rómulo Rozo. The striking monument shows historical figures and animal sculptures, and also encloses an eternal flame, a symbol of Mexico's independence.

Environs: Situated a short drive southwest of Mérida, **Hacienda Yaxcopoil**, a mansion surrounded by a henequen plantation, is now a museum providing a view into life on a hacienda *(see pp50–51)*.

Visitors' Checklist

Yucatán. 👥 703,000. ✈ 5 km (3 miles) S. 🚌 Calle 70 No. 555, (999) 924 78 68. [i] Cnr. of Calle 57 & Calle 60 🎉 Cristo de las Ampollas (Sep 27).
[W] www.yuc.gob.mx

🏛 Museo Regional de Antropología Palacio Cantón
Paseo Montejo 485.
☎ *(999) 923 05 57.*
○ *Tue–Sun.* 🎟 *Sun free.* ✋ *in advance.*

🏠 Hacienda Yaxcopoil
Yaxcopoil, 35 km (22 miles) SW of Mérida.
☎ *(999) 927 26 06.*
○ *daily.* 🎟 ✋ 🔒

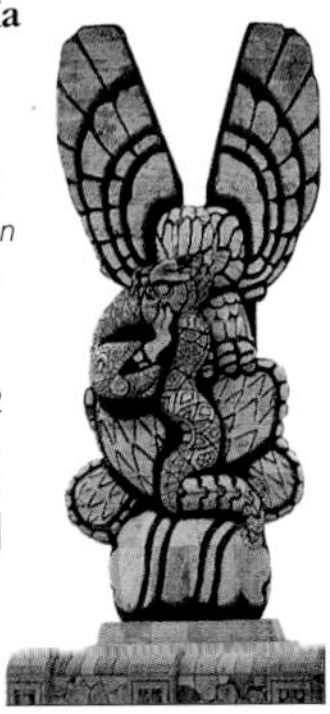

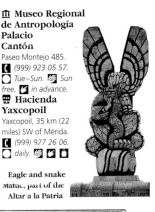

Eagle and snake statue, part of the Altar a la Patria

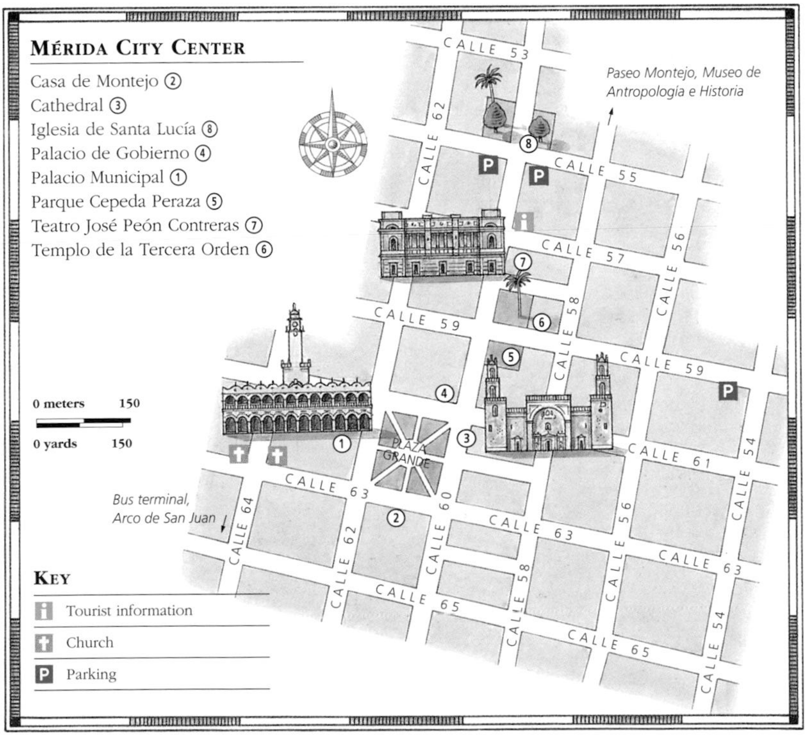

Mérida City Center
Casa de Montejo ②
Cathedral ③
Iglesia de Santa Lucía ⑧
Palacio de Gobierno ④
Palacio Municipal ①
Parque Cepeda Peraza ⑤
Teatro José Peón Contreras ⑦
Templo de la Tercera Orden ⑥
Paseo Montejo, Museo de Antropología e Historia
Calle 53
Calle 55
Calle 57
Calle 59
Calle 61
Calle 63
Calle 65
Calle 54
Calle 56
Calle 58
Calle 60
Calle 62
Calle 64
Plaza Grande
Bus terminal, Arco de San Juan
0 meters 150
0 yards 150
Key
Tourist information
Church
Parking

Celestún **8**

Yucatán. 🏠 6,000. 🚌

THE SMALL fishing village of Celestún is situated on a spit of land almost entirely separated from the mainland. Several kilometers of palm-fringed beaches line the coast to the west of the village, but it is the flamingos on the estuary to the east that attract most of the visitors. Boats can be hired to get closer to the birds, which include pelicans and various waders, as well as flamingos, but many of the boats go too near, disturbing the birds' feeding and repeatedly forcing them to fly. Ask your guide to keep the boat at a distance from the birds so you can see their natural behavior.

Pink flamingos in the estuary

Other excursions on small launches are available, depending on weather conditions, including visits to the *bosque petrificado*, a forest of petrified wood. This surreal, desolate place, on the Isla de Pájaros to the south of Celestún, was created by prolonged salinization.

Dzibilchaltún **9**

Yucatán. Off Mex 261, 15 km (9 miles) N of Mérida. 🚌 *from Mérida*. 🔲 *daily.* 🖼️ 📷

LITERALLY THE "place with writing on flat stones," Dzibilchaltún was one of the most important centers in pre-Columbian Yucatán, and one of the earliest to be built. However, it was explored only in the 1940s, making it one of the latest to be rediscovered.

The site is arranged concentrically. A *sacbe*, or "white road," leads from the central plaza to the impressive Temple of the Seven Dolls. This building is named after the tiny clay dolls found buried in front of its altar. Several of the dolls have deformities, and are thought to be associated with rituals. They are displayed in

The cenote at Dzibilchaltún, a good place for a refreshing swim

the ultra-modern and extremely well laid-out museum. Other notable exhibits include the stelae and sculptures in the gardens leading up to the museum, ceramic figures, wooden altarpieces from the colonial era, and an attractive display on the pirates who plagued the seas around the Yucatán coast in the 16th and 17th centuries. Interactive screens and audio-visual commentaries provide information about the ancient Maya world view, the Maya today, and the history of the henequen industry.

The remains of a Franciscan chapel built of Maya masonry, probably at the end of the 16th century, are also worth seeing. This open chapel, where the monks preached to the local Indians, is still standing.

Dzibilchaltún's cenote, a natural turquoise pool more than 40 m (130 ft) deep, is a refreshing place for a swim after visiting the other sights. Many artifacts have been recovered from its depths.

The Temple of the Seven Dolls in Dzibilchaltún

Progreso **10**

Yucatán. 🏠 48,700. 🚌 ℹ️ *Calle 80 No. 176, (969) 935 01 04.*

SITUATED ON the north Yucatán coast, Progreso was once an important port. With the construction of the railroad linking the port to Mérida in the 1880s, it experienced a boom that is hard to imagine now as one approaches the relaxed, low-lying town past mangrove swamps. Attempts to turn Progreso into an international resort have so far been unsuccessful, but the town still comes alive on weekends and during the holiday season when many of Mérida's citizens flock here.

Progreso has probably the longest stone pier in the world, often bustling with people. Near its landward end is an attractive 19th-century lighthouse. On the town front, by the narrow sandy beach, are many good seafood restaurants.

Progreso's stone pier, thought to be the longest in the world

Izamal's imposing Convento de San Antonio de Padua, built by Franciscan monks from Spain

Izamal ⑪

Yucatán. 🏙 23,000. 🚌 🎭 Cristo de Sitilpeth (Oct 18), Virgen de la Inmaculada (Dec 7–8).

ONCE AS IMPORTANT a site as Chichén Itzá, Izamal is believed to have been founded around AD 300. The original village grew into an influential city-state and, by AD 800, it was governing the surrounding region. Modern Izamal is a fascinating combination of Maya remains and Spanish colonial buildings. There are around 20 Classic Maya structures still standing. Chief among these is the pyramid K'inich K'ak' Mo', named after the ruler "Great-Sun Fire Macaw." It is one of the largest pyramids in the Yucatán.

The importance of Izamal had declined by the time the Spanish arrived in the mid-16th century, but it retained enough religious influence for the Franciscan monks to construct the spectacular Convento de San Antonio de Padua here. They demolished a Maya temple and built the church on its massive platform base, giving it an elevated position. The huge atrium is surrounded by open cloisters, and contains some early Franciscan frescoes.

The church acquired even more importance when Bishop Diego de Landa installed in it a statue of the Virgen de la Inmaculada, which he had brought from Guatemala. This was immediately attributed with miraculous powers by the local Maya population, and in 1949 the Virgin was adopted as the patron saint of the Yucatán. A small museum in the church commemorates the visit of Pope John Paul II to Izamal in 1993, the International Year of Indigenous People, when he pledged the Catholic Church's support for the Maya Indians.

Adjacent to the church are two attractive arcaded squares. Here, and in the surrounding streets of low Spanish colonial houses, the majority of the buildings' façades are painted a glowing ocher color. This led to Izamal being nicknamed La Ciudad Amarilla, literally "The Yellow City."

The massive Maya pyramid, K'inich K'ak' Mo', in Izamal

HAMMOCKS

Brightly colored hammocks are a common sight in the markets of Campeche, Mérida and Izamal. Probably introduced to Mexico by Spanish colonists from the Caribbean, they are now used for sleeping by many Mexicans in the Yucatán region. The hammocks are traditionally made from twine produced from henequen, a type of fibrous agave plant that can be seen growing all over the Yucatán Peninsula (though modern hammocks tend to be made from cotton or silk). The leaves are cut from the spiky plants, shredded into long fibers, and then dried. The fibers can be dyed and braided, or woven into twine or rope. Other products made from henequen include mats and bags.

Traditional hammocks for sale in Mérida

Chichén Itzá ⑫

Carved figure, Temple of the Warriors

ᴅESPITE BEING the best preserved Maya site on the peninsula, Chichén Itzá confounds the archaeologists. The date of first settlement in the older, southern part of the site is uncertain, but the northern section was built during a renaissance in the 11th century AD. Similarities with Tula *(see p144)*, and myths that tell how exiled Toltec god-king Quetzalcoatl (Kukulcan) settled at Chichén Itzá, suggest that the renaissance was due to a Toltec invasion. However, other theories hold that Tula was influenced by the Maya, not vice versa. In its heyday as a commercial, religious, and military center, which lasted until about the 13th century, Chichén Itzá supported over 35,000 people.

★ Ballcourt
At 168 m (550 ft) in length, this is the largest ballcourt in Mesoamerica. Still in place are the two engraved rings that the ball had to pass through (see p277).

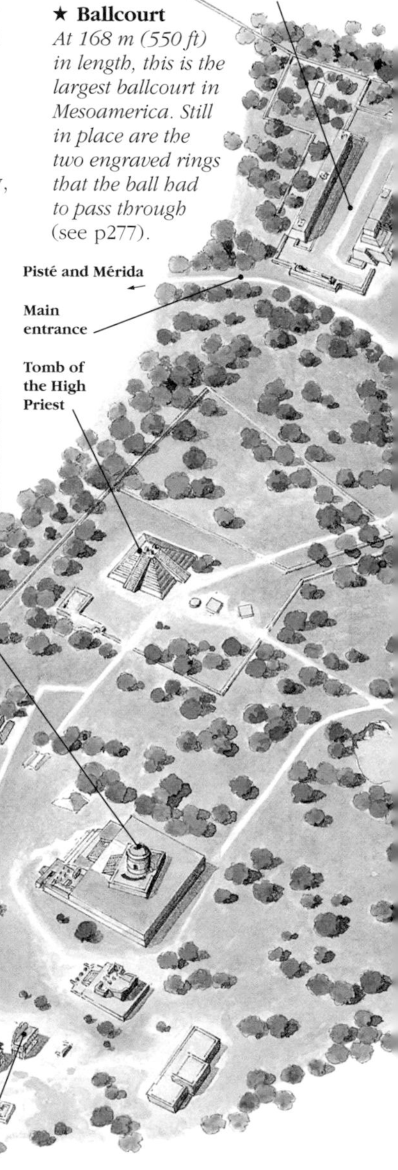

Pisté and Mérida

Main entrance

Tomb of the High Priest

★ Observatory
Also called El Caracol (The Snail) for its spiral staircase, this building was an astronomical observatory (see p47). The various slits in the walls correspond to the positions of certain celestial bodies on key dates in the Maya calendar.

Nunnery
So named because its small rooms reminded the Spaniards of nuns' cells, this large structure, built in three stages, was probably a palace. The façade of the east annex (seen here) has particularly beautiful stone fretwork and carvings.

Chichén Viejo

The Church, or Iglesia, is decorated with fretwork, masks of the rain god Chac, and the *bacabs* – four animals who, in Maya myth, held up the sky.

| 0 meters | | 150 |
| 0 yards | | 150 |

The Tzompantli is a low platform whose perimeter is carved with grinning skulls. Archaeologists believe that it was used to display the heads of victims of human sacrifice, practiced during Chichén Itzá's late period.

Sacred Cenote
A sacbe (Maya road) leads to this huge natural well, thought to have been revered as the home of rain god Chac, and used for human sacrifice.

Platform of the Jaguars and Eagles

★ **El Castillo**
Built on top of an older structure that can also be visited, this 24-m (79-ft) high pyramid (see p276) was dedicated to Kukulcan, the Maya representation of the god Quetzalcoatl. Its height and striking geometric design dominate the whole site.

The Group of a Thousand Columns, made up of carved stone colonnades on two sides of a huge plaza, may have been used as a market.

Entrance

↓ **Valladolid and Cancún**

STAR FEATURES

★ **Ballcourt**

★ **Observatory**

★ **El Castillo**

Temple of the Warriors
Set on a small pyramid, this temple is decorated with sculptures of the rain god Chac and the plumed serpent Kukulcan. A chacmool (see p44), and two columns carved to represent snakes, guard the entrance.

El Castillo

THE MOST AWE-INSPIRING structure at
Chichén Itzá is the pyramid known as
El Castillo (The Castle), built around AD
800. It has a perfect astronomical design:
four staircases face the cardinal points,
various features correspond to aspects of
the Maya calendar *(see pp46–7)*, and, twice
yearly at sunrise, a fascinating optical illusion occurs on the north staircase *(see
p261)*. The climb to the top is rewarded
by a breathtaking view. It is also possible
to scale an older pyramid inside the structure, but this is not for the claustrophobic.

**View of El Castillo from beside the Platform
of the Jaguars and Eagles**

RECONSTRUCTION OF EL CASTILLO

This shows how the pyramid
would have looked on comple-
tion. It was originally covered in
plaster and painted a vivid red.

**Temple entrance, divided
by snake-shaped columns**

Temple of Kukulcán

The 52 panels on each of the pyramid's faces represent the number of
years in the Maya sacred cycle.

The nine stepped levels
on each side of the pyramid
are divided by the staircase
into 18 terraces, which
symbolize the 18 months
of the Maya calendar.

The temple at the top of the
inner pyramid contains a
chacmool (see p44) and
a beautiful, bright-red
throne carved as a
jaguar and encrust-
ed with jade.

**North
staircase**

**Entrance to
inner pyramid**

**Inner
pyramid**

Two serpents' heads at the foot
of the north staircase are thought
to represent the god Kukulcán, the
Maya Quetzalcóatl. At the two yearly
equinoxes, the play of light and shadow on the staircase makes them
appear to crawl up the pyramid.

The west staircase, like
the other three, is made
up of 91 steps. So the four
staircases, together with
the temple platform at the
top, make a total of 365
steps, the number of days
in the year. The staircase
rises at 45°, and a chain
is provided to help visitors
negotiate the steep incline,
which is particularly
difficult on the descent.

The Ballgame

MORE THAN A SPORT or a form of entertainment, the ballgame that was played throughout Mesoamerica had some kind of ritual significance. Two teams would compete against each other to manipulate a large rubber ball through a stone ring set high on the wall at the side of the court. It is thought that the losers of the

Maya figurine of a ball player

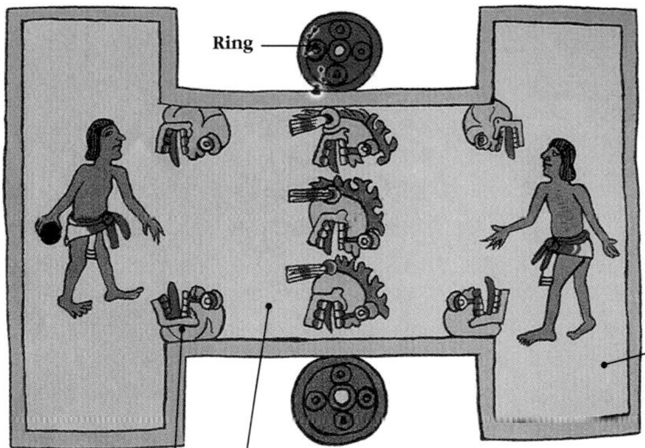

game were subsequently put to death. Ballcourts have been found at all the main pre-Columbian sites, the largest being at Chichén Itzá. The cities of Cantona *(see p157)* and El Tajín *(see pp242–3)* each had a great number of ballcourts. A version of the game, called *hulama*, is still played today by Indians in the state of Sinaloa *(see p178)*.

THE BALLCOURT
Although there were probably several versions of the game, it was always played on an I-shaped court, as seen in this Aztec codex illustration. Ballcourts varied in size, but early examples were usually aligned north-south, and later ones east-west.

Ring

Outer court

Stone markers are thought to have been part of the normal system of scoring.

The aisle or central court had steeply sloping sides.

A heavy rubber ball, about as big as a man's head but shown here in exaggerated size, was used to play the game.

The ballgame player wore substantial body protection, as seen in this decoration on a Maya vessel. The ball had to be kept off the ground using only knees, elbows, or hips, never the hands or feet.

Arm protector

Padded hip protector

The ballcourt ring was a tiny "goal" that the ball had to pass through. This was just one way of scoring and would have been a rare event, as it clearly took a prodigious feat to achieve.

THE FATE OF THE LOSERS
The losers were often sacrificed after the game, but this was considered an honorable way to die. This carved panel, one of six that decorate the South Ballcourt at El Tajín, shows two victors killing one of the losing team with an obsidian knife, while a third player looks on from the right. A savage looking death god descends from the skyband at the top of the panel to receive the human offering.

Valladolid

Yucatán. 🏛 57,000. 🚌 ℹ️ *Palacio Municipal, Calle 40 No. 200, (985) 856 20 63, ext. 211.* 🎭 *Candelaria (Feb 2).*

LYING ALMOST EXACTLY halfway between Mérida and Cancún, Valladolid is the third largest city on the Yucatán Peninsula. It was founded by the Spaniards on an earlier Maya settlement known as Zaci, and quickly became an important religious center. It was here in 1552, that the Franciscans built the Yucatán's first ecclesiastical buildings, the **Iglesia de San Bernardino de Siena** and the adjoining **Ex-Convento de Sisal**. These have recently been restored, revealing original frescoes behind two side altars in the church. Also restored are the small Spanish colonial houses on Calle 41-A, the street from the town center to the church.

The *zócalo* (main square) is the focal point, and often the liveliest part, of this quiet and attractive city. Maya women sell *huipiles* (embroidered blouses) around its perimeter, and in the northeast corner small, inexpensive restaurants serve tasty local dishes and fruit juices late into the night. Overlooking the square is the **cathedral**, with its elegant

The intricately painted high altar of the Iglesia de San Bernardino de Siena, Valladolid

façade, and the colonial hotel **El Mesón del Marqués** *(see p305).* Also on the square is the **Palacio Municipal** (City Hall). In the first-floor hallway are painted panels showing the history of the town from Maya times, and portraits of military leaders from Valladolid who helped initiate the Revolution *(see p54).*

A little farther out from the main square, the churches of **Santa Ana** (four blocks east) and **Santa Lucía** (six blocks north), are fine examples of stark Franciscan architecture. These churches were originally used by Maya converts, and are still the most popular in the town.

ENVIRONS: West of town is the **Cenote de Dzitnup**, a natural well, apparently unearthed by a pig in the 1950s. Visitors can climb down the steep steps to the underground pool, where a hole in the roof and electric lighting illuminate the dramatic setting. You can also swim here among the fish in the blue water.

West, near Chichén Itzá, are the **Grutas de Balamkanché**, huge caves discovered in 1959. Maya artifacts found here suggest that this was

Hanging stalactites and clear, turquoise water in the Cenote de Dzitnup

a place of worship as early as 300 BC, dedicated to the rain god Chac. Guides point out some of the Maya objects still in situ, which include miniature corn-grinding stones, and decorated incense burners. There is a small museum on site.

🏛 **Cenote de Dzitnup**
7 km (4 miles) W of Valladolid.
🚪 *daily.* 💰

🏛 **Grutas de Balamkanché**
Off Mex 180, 35 km (22 miles) W of Valladolid.
🚪 *daily.* 💰

Statue on the main square in Valladolid

Ekbalam ⓮

Yucatán. Off Mex 295, 25 km (16 miles) N of Valladolid. 🚌 *Temozón then taxi.* 🚪 *daily.* 💰 *Sun free.*

ONLY RECENTLY excavated, Ekbalam ("Black Jaguar") was an important Maya city and religious center and dates predominantly from AD 700–1000. It is relatively compact, and has an unusual double perimeter wall for fortification. The main entrance is through a fine Maya arch, but the real highlight is the Tower – a massive tiered pyramid, 30 m (98 ft) high, which visitors can climb. On each of the pyramid's tiers, there are pits sunken into the structure that are thought to be *chultunes* (Maya cisterns). From gaps in the surrounding walls at the cardinal points, Maya processional roads, or *sacbeob (see p285)*, radiate out to a distance of over 1.5 km (1 mile).

Río Lagartos ⑮

Yucatán. Mex 295, 104 km (65 miles)
N of Valladolid. 🚌 *from Valladolid
and Mérida.* ⬜ *daily.*

THE NATURE PRESERVE of Río
Lagartos, occupying brackish lagoons on the north coast
of the peninsula, is a bird-
watcher's paradise. It is home
to over 260 species, including
the huge colonies of pink
flamingos that breed here in
the summer. Between April
and June, the flamingos' nests
are protected, but at other
times of the year, boat trips to
see the elegant birds can be
arranged in Río Lagartos village. Occasionally, snakes
and turtles can also be seen.

Thatched shelters on Playa Marlín, near the Sheraton Hotel in Cancún

The safe waters of Playa Langosta, Cancún

Cancún ⑯

Quintana Roo. 🏠 *419,000.* ✈ 🚌
🚌 🏢 ℹ *Calle Pecari 23, (998) 881 90
00.* 🎭 *Festival of Jazz (May), Cultural
and Caribbean Festival (Nov).*
🌐 www.groo.gob.mx

BEFORE 1970, Cancún was
little more than a sandy
island and a fishing village of
barely 100 inhabitants. The
government decided to turn it
into a new resort, and in the
late 1960s building began in
earnest. Since then the population has soared to hundreds
of thousands, and over two
million (mainly non-Mexican)
visitors flock here every year
to enjoy the white-
sand beaches and
perfect weather.
   There are, in
fact, two Cancúns.
The downtown
area, on the main
land, has very few
hotels and no
beaches, while the
Cancún that most
visitors see has
plenty of both. The latter,
known as **Isla Cancún** or the
zona hotelera (hotel zone), is
a narrow, 23-km (14-mile) L-
shaped island connected to
the mainland by two bridges.
   Although many of the hotels
appear to command private
stretches of sand, all beaches
in Mexico are public and can
be enjoyed by anybody. The
ones in front of the Hyatt
Cancún and Sheraton hotels
are particularly beautiful.

If the resort beach scene and
constant presence of hotel
staff do not appeal, however,
head for the equally attractive
"public" beaches. **Playa Linda**,
Playa Langosta, and **Playa
Tortugas**, on the northern
arm of the island, offer relaxed
swimming in the calm Bahía
Mujeres, while bigger waves
and fine views can be found
at **Playa Chac-Mool, Playa
Marlín**, and **Playa Ballenas**,
which face the open sea on the
eastern side. The protected
Laguna Nichupté, between
Isla Cancún and the mainland,
is perfect for watersports.
   Toward the southern end of
the island is the small Maya
site of **El Rey** (The King),
occupied from AD 1200 until
the Conquest. Here, a low
pyramid and two plazas provide a quiet, cultural retreat
from the beachfront action.
   Some ferries for Isla Mujeres
(see p281) leave from a dock
near Playa Linda, but the
majority depart from Puerto
Juárez or Punta Sam, both
just to the north of Cancún.

The pyramid and other ruins of El Rey, echoed by one of Cancún's many hotels in the background

The Mayan Riviera

THE DEVELOPMENT of Cancún *(see p279)*, and other smaller resorts, has brought profound changes to the Yucatán's east coast. Now known as the Mayan Riviera, it is a major tourist destination, and it is easy to see why. As well as idyllic sandy beaches and warm waters, the coast has the second longest coral reef in the world, providing ideal conditions for snorkeling and diving.

A dolphin, one of the animals that visitors can see at Xcaret *(see p284)*

Playa del Carmen is the second biggest resort on the coast after Cancún. The town has a relaxed atmosphere and Quinta Avenida, the main street, is lined with small shops, coffee bars, and traditional restaurants. Ferries to Cozumel leave from a pier close to the lively central square.

Akumal is an uncrowded resort based around what was once a coconut plantation. Its beautiful beach is a breeding ground for green turtles, and migrating whale sharks can sometimes be spotted swimming past in December and January. In the past decade, the sheltered bay has increasingly attracted wind-surfers, divers, and snorkelers.

VALLADOLID

0 kilometers   20

0 miles   10

VALLADOLID ←

Xel-Ha nature preserve is a series of interconnecting lagoons set among spectac-ular rocks and caves. A huge variety of tropical fish swim in its beautifully clear waters. For years it was government-run and rather neglected, but it is now franchised to the same company that oper-ates Xcaret. It has taken on a new lease of life, offering superb snorkeling and diving.

Xcaret *(see p284)* is a combination of zoo, beach resort, archaeological area, and theme park.

Playa de Carmer

Pamul

LAGUNA EL CONTINENTE

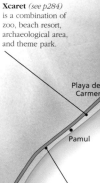

Akumal

Puerto Aventuras is a purpose-built resort with a range of facilities, in-cluding an 18-hole golf course and a marina. It is popular for reef diving.

Tulum Playa, *the most easy-going resort along the coast, is essentially a rapidly growing strip of beach huts and a handful of restaurants, bor-dering a magnificent sandy beach. Nearby is the late-Maya site of Tulum (see pp284–5).*

COBÁ

307

Xel-Ha

Tulum

Tulum Playa

CHETUMAL

***Puerto Morelos** is the least developed place on the riviera, a small, laid-back resort built around a fishing village. There is excellent snorkeling and diving on the reef just offshore.*

Isla Mujeres, situated close to the coral reef, is popular with divers.

Cancún is huge, attracting more visitors than any other resort in Mexico.

Cozumel *(see p282)* is one of the world's top diving sites.

KEY

For key to map see back flap

A flotilla of small tour boats moored in the harbor on Isla Mujeres

Isla Mujeres ⑰

Quintana Roo. 🚢 *passenger ferry from Puerto Juárez, car ferry from Punta Sam.* 🛈 *Avenida Rueda Medina 130, (998) 877 03 07.*

THIS SMALL ISLAND is just 1 km (half a mile) wide by 8 km (5 miles) long. Its name, meaning "The Island of Women," probably derives from Maya female statuettes found here and destroyed by the Spanish. It has developed considerably since first becoming popular in the 1960s, but there are few high-rise buildings, and its small town is still relatively quiet, especially in the evening when the day trippers from Cancún have left.

A lifeguard's lookout on Playa Los Cocos

The best way to explore the island is on a bike or scooter. Its middle part is taken up by a brackish lagoon and an airstrip for small planes from the mainland. Also in the island's center is the ruined **Mundaca Hacienda**, said to have been built by the pirate Fermín Mundaca to try to win the love of an island beauty.

Playa Los Cocos, located just to the north of the island's only town, has clean white sand and warm shallow water.

At Isla Mujeres' rather rugged southern tip are the **Garrafón National Park**, and **Playa de Garrafón**. The exciting diving afforded by the coral reef just offshore here is one of the main reasons for visiting the island. The snorkeling is also spectacular, but the beach gets very crowded in the middle of the day. Nearby are the ruins of what is said to be an old Maya lighthouse, as well as a more modern one.

ENVIRONS: A popular day trip from Isla Mujeres is to **Isla Contoy**, a tiny island 30 km (19 miles) away, off the northern tip of the Yucatán Peninsula. It is located at the northernmost part of the barrier reef, where the waters of the Caribbean Sea and Gulf of Mexico meet. The mingling currents create ideal conditions for plankton – food for the many fish, which in turn support an abundant bird life. Over 50 species of birds, including large flocks of egrets, pelicans, frigate birds, and flamingos, nest on the island, which is now a protected nature preserve.

An intricate bas-relief carving on the entrance arch of the Mundaca Hacienda

Cozumel ⑱

Quintana Roo. ✈ 🚢 *car ferry from Puerto Morelos, passenger ferry from Playa del Carmen.*

SITUATED OFF the east coast of the Yucatán Peninsula, Cozumel is Mexico's largest island, 14 km (9 miles) wide by 50 km (31 miles) long.

The Maya called the island Cuzamil, the "place of the swallows." It was an important center for the cult of Ixchel, goddess of fertility, pregnancy, and childbirth, and traces of Maya occupation can be found in several parts of the island. The ruins of two of the main settlements are at **El Cedral** and **San Gervasio**. Both are overgrown, but visiting them provides an opportunity to see some of Cozumel's varied birdlife in the jungle habitat that characterizes the interior of the island. San Gervasio, the larger site, has several restored buildings. **El Caracol** in the south of the island, is an isolated Maya shrine that is thought to have been used as a landmark for navigation.

Moored boats at the pier in San Miguel de Cozumel

A pelican, one of many birds seen on Cozumel

The Spaniards also came to Cozumel. The first Mass in Mexico was said here in 1518, and Hernán Cortés, warmly received by the local inhabitants, planned his conquest of mainland Mexico from the island. Today, Cozumel is a tourist resort, and one of the world's foremost diving locations. Ferries from the mainland arrive at the pier in **San Miguel de Cozumel**, the island's only town. Near the dock are many tourist shops and restaurants, but a few blocks away, the town is quieter with a more traditional feel. The pretty **Iglesia de San Miguel Arcángel**, the town's only church, stands on the main square. Three blocks north of this square is the **Museo de la Isla**, which gives a good overview of the island's history.

Cozumel is ringed by stunning beaches, many of which are accessible only in a four-wheel drive vehicle. Those on the eastern, windward side are beautiful, but the sea here is dangerous, with heavy waves and a strong undertow. Safe swimming beaches are on Cozumel's sheltered western side. The best diving sites are here too, particularly around the **Colombia**, **Palancar**, **San Francisco**, and **Santa Rosa** reefs. Also on the west coast is **Chankanaab Park**, with hundreds of varieties of tropical plants. Next to the park is a shallow lagoon that is ideal for snorkeling.

🏛 **Museo de la Isla**
Cnr of Av Rafael Melgar & Calle 6 Norte. 📞 *(987) 872 14 34.* 🕐 *daily.* 🌐 *Sun free.* 📷 🚻

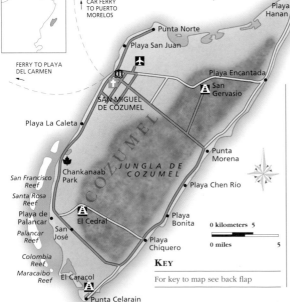

The Iglesia de San Miguel Arcángel in Cozumel's only town

Map labels:
CAR FERRY TO PUERTO MORELOS
FERRY TO PLAYA DEL CARMEN
Punta Molas
Playa Hanan
Punta Norte
Playa San Juan
Playa Encantada
San Gervasio
SAN MIGUEL DE COZUMEL
Playa La Caleta
Punta Morena
JUNGLA DE COZUMEL
San Francisco Reef
Chankanaab Park
Playa Chen Rio
Santa Rosa Reef
Playa de Palancar
El Cedral
San José
Playa Bonita
Palancar Reef
Colombia Reef
Maracaibo Reef
El Caracol
Playa Chiquero
Punta Celarain
COZUMEL

0 kilometers 5
0 miles 5

KEY
For key to map see back flap

Diving in the Mexican Caribbean

THE GREAT Mesoamerican Reef System stretches for more than 1,000 km (620 miles) down the eastern coast of Yucatán to Belize, Guatemala, and Honduras. Home to an amazing variety of sea creatures, the crystal waters along the Yucatán coast are ideal for snorkeling and skindiving. There are diving sites

Snorkeling in the clear tropical waters around Cozumel

on the reefs to suit every ability, from beginner to professional, the best known places being off the island of Cozumel. Equipment can be bought or rented from the many diving schools found on the coast. These also offer diving training, and lead groups of more experienced divers to explore the reef.

Blue chromis are a common midwater sight in Cozumel.

Blue-striped grunts, often seen in schools, shelter on the reef by day and feed by night.

A tiger grouper can change color to blend in with a coral reef or a rocky bottom.

Flamingo tongue
Unlike most snails, this mollusk species extends its mantle over its shell as camouflage. It feeds and reproduces on soft corals.

Sea rods, a soft coral, have skeletal spicules, or spikes, in their skin instead of internal skeletons.

Sea fans, which are often brilliantly colored, are a very delicate and brittle type of coral.

Fire coral is named after its stinging, poisonous cells.

Tube sponges can grow up to 2 m (7 ft) high. Their size depends on age, food supply, and environmental conditions.

Massive corals are the main basis of a reef. They grow only 3 mm (1/10 inch) a year, but can reach over 10 m (33 ft) in diameter.

YUCATÁN CORAL GARDEN
The dramatic underwater landscape boasts abundant and colorful coral gardens, whose nooks and crannies teem with marine creatures in search of food and shelter.

Splendid toadfish
Active only at night, the pointed barbels and striped head of the splendid toadfish may give away its daytime hideaway.

Hawksbill turtle
These increasingly rare turtles nest along Cozumel's eastern coast. An endangered species, they are protected by law.

Basket star
Capable of reaching a diameter of up to 1 m (3 ft), basket stars can sometimes be seen when feeding at night.

Xcaret ⑲

Quintana Roo. Mex 307, 7 km (4 miles)
S of Playa del Carmen. 📞 (998) 883
31 43. 🚌 from Cancún and Playa del
Carmen. 🕐 daily. 🎫 🖼 🛈

Beaches fringing a lagoon in Xcaret theme park

THIS LARGE, well-planned
"eco-archaeological" theme
park is a combination of zoo,
activity center, and beach resort. It is built around the
ruins of Polé, an important
Postclassic Maya coastal settlement. A highlight for many
visitors is a chance to float
down the clear waters of the
two naturally
illuminated
subterranean
rivers that
cross the park.
Another popular
activity is to swim
with dolphins in a
saltwater pool. The
park's animal collection also
includes bats, butterflies, and
turtles, as well as pumas and
jaguars, which are
kept on two Big
Cat Islands. Other
attractions are a re-
created Maya
village and, at
night, a sound-
and-light show
about the Maya.

**Puma, on one of
Xcaret's Big Cat Islands**

Cobá ⑳

Quintana Roo. 47 km (29 miles) NW
of Tulum. 🚌 from Valladolid and
Cancún. 🕐 8am–5pm daily. 🎫

BUILT AROUND a group of
lakes, Cobá is one of the
most interesting archaeo-
logical sites in the Yucatán
Peninsula. The city flourished
from about AD 300 to AD

Tulum ㉑

SPECTACULARLY POSITIONED on a cliff overlooking the
Caribbean, Tulum is a late-Maya site that was at
its height from around AD 1200 until the arrival of the
Spanish. The name, which means "enclosure" or "wall,"
is probably modern. It is thought that the site was originally called Zama, or "dawn," reflecting its location
on the east coast, and the west-east alignment of its
buildings. Its inhabitants traded with Cozumel, Isla
Mujeres, Guatemala, and central Mexico.

The House of the Cenote *is so
named because it stands above
a cenote, a subterranean well.*

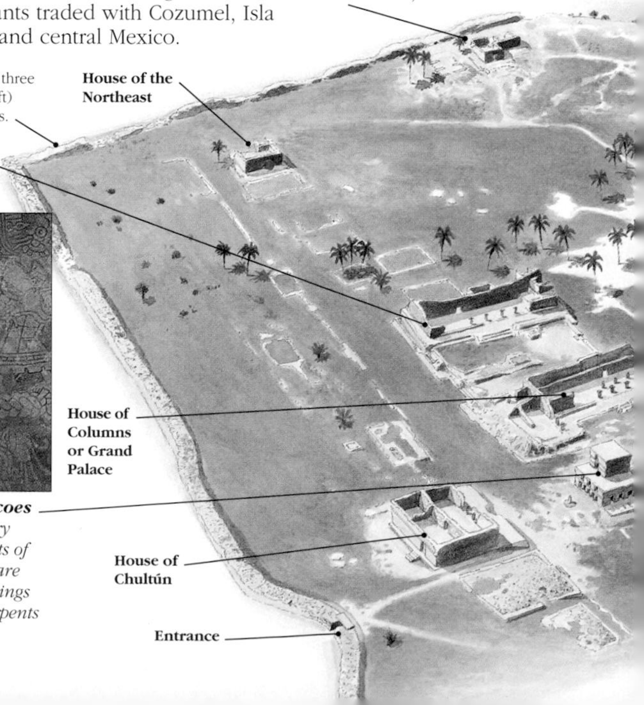

A perimeter wall runs along three
sides of the site. It is 5 m (16 ft)
thick and pierced by five gates.

**House of the
Northeast**

**House of the Halach
Uinic, or Overlord**

**House of
Columns
or Grand
Palace**

The Temple of the Frescoes
*was used as an observatory
for tracking the movements of
the sun. Its interior walls are
richly adorned with paintings
in which supernatural serpents
are a common motif.*

**House of
Chultún**

Entrance

1000, and stood at the center of a network of *sacbeob* (meaning "white roads"): straight processional routes paved with limestone that connected Maya buildings or settlements to each other. More of these roads have been found here than at any other location.

Up to 40,000 people are thought to have lived at this enormous site, thanks to the local abundance of water. However, only a small proportion of its area has been excavated so far. Much of it is still shrouded in jungle.

There are three principal clusters of buildings to visit. Be prepared for long walks along the trails between them. Close to the entrance of the site is the **Cobá Group**. The main building in this group is a pyramid known as La Iglesia

The ballcourt, part of the extensive ruins of Cobá

(the Church), because local people regard it as a shrine. Nearby is a ballcourt *(see p277)*. A trail beginning on the other side of Lago Macanxoc leads to the **Macanxoc Group**, where a collection of stelae carved by the Maya as historical records can be seen.

About 1.5 km (1 mile) to the north is the **Nohoch Mul Group**. Standing at 42 m (138 ft), Nohoch Mul is the highest pyramid in the Yucatán. It's a hard climb to the temple at the top, but once reached, there is an incomparable view of the lakes and jungle below.

The Temple of the Descending God has a carving over its door showing a swooping or falling figure. Similar carvings, of what is thought to be a deity associated with the setting sun, can be seen on El Castillo and in several other buildings on the site.

VISITORS' CHECKLIST

Quintana Roo. Mex 307, 128 km (80 miles) S of Cancún. from Cancún. 8am–5pm daily.

Temple of the Wind

The temple that crowns El Castillo has three niches above the doorway. A beautiful sculpture of the descending god remains in the central niche.

Temple of the Initial Series

El Castillo, on its spectacular clifftop vantage point

To Temple of the Sea

El Castillo (The Castle) is the largest and most prominent building on the site, and as such would have served as a landmark for seafarers. Its wide external staircase leads up to a late-Postclassic temple.

Ceremonial platform

Sian Ka'an Biosphere Reserve ㉒

Quintana Roo. 🚐 tours from Cancún or Tulum. 🏢 Amigos de Sian Ka'an, Crepúsculo 18, (998) 848 21 36.

COMPRISING OVER 4,500 sq km (1,700 sq miles) of low jungle and marshlands, and 110 km (69 miles) of coral reef, Sian Ka'an has a range of natural habitats that makes it one of the most important conservation areas in Mexico. It is run by a government agency and is not primarily geared towards tourism. Indeed, the poor roads within the preserve deter all but the most intrepid. However, the Amigos de Sian Ka'an (Friends of Sian Ka'an), run night tours for visitors, which focus on the croco-

The rare Jabirú stork, Sian Ka'an

diles that inhabit the mangrove swamps. Lucky visitors may also see the flocks of local and migrating birds in the marshlands around Boca Paila, in the northern part of the preserve, including the rare Jabirú stork, or the elusive turtles and manatees that live in the waters off the coast.

Punta Allen, south of Boca Paila but still within the preserve, is a small fishing village. Lobsters, the main source of income here, are still caught using old Maya methods.

The Maya site of Kohunlich, near Chetumal

Chetumal ㉓

Quintana Roo. 🏔 115,000. ✈ 🚌 🏢 Calzada del Centenario 622, (983) 835 08 60.

FOUNDED ON THE estuary of the Río Hondo in 1898, Chetumal is now the capital of Quintana Roo state. It is situated near the frontier with Belize, and is a typical border town. There is a large naval base and a duty-free zone, with stores selling cut-rate luxury items from all over the world. Visitors from Belize and Guatemala come here for shopping, giving the city an exciting atmosphere. Most of the original wooden and tin-roofed buildings were destroyed in a hurricane in the 1950s, and the

State emblem of Quintana Roo

town has been rebuilt around wide avenues, some of which still end in undergrowth. Chetumal's spacious **Museo de la Cultura Maya** explores the Maya world, including astronomy, daily life, and Maya codices. Many of the exhibits are replicas, but there are good explanatory panels and interactive screens.

ENVIRONS: Situated 40 km (25 miles) northwest of Chetumal, is the village of **Bacalar**. There is a natural pool here, over 60 m (200 ft) deep. Named **Cenote Azul** for its vivid blue color, it is perfect for a swim. Nearby **Laguna de Siete Colores**, overlooked by the Spanish fort in Bacalar, is also popular. West along Mex 186, farmed fields give way to

A pleasure boat plying the clear, blue waters of the Laguna de Siete Colores, near Chetumal

jungle, the setting for the Maya site of **Kohunlich** and its Temple of Masks. Dedicated to the Maya sun god, the steps of this 6th-century pyramid are flanked with masks facing the setting sun. About 29 km (18 miles) north of Kohunlich lie the attractive, if rather unremarkable, ruins of **Dzibanché**.

🏛 **Museo de la Cultura Maya**
Cnr of Av Héroes and Cristobal Colón.
📞 *(983) 832 68 38.* ⏰ *Tue–Sun.*
🎟 *Sun free.* 📷 ♿
🅰 **Kohunlich & Dzibanché**
⏰ *daily.* 📷

Río Bec Sites ㉔

Campeche. Mex 186, 120 km
(75 miles) W of Chetumal. 🚌 *Xpujil.*
All sites ⏰ *daily.* 📷

A GROUP OF stylistically similar Maya sites, situated in the lowlands west of Chetumal, are known collectively as the Río Bec sites. Many are hidden by jungle, but three of them, Xpujil, Becán, and Chicanná, are near enough to the main road (Mex 186) to be accessible to the casual visitor. These three can be visited on a day-trip from Chetumal, or en route to the city from Villahermosa *(see p254)* or Palenque *(see pp234–7)*.

The area may have been occupied from at least 550 BC, but the Río Bec style, which the sites share, was dominant between AD 600 and 900. The style is characterized by elongated platforms and buildings, flanked by slender towers with rounded corners. These towers are "fake" temple-pyramids – the steps are too steep to be used, and the structures seem to have no inner chamber and no special function apart from decoration. Representations of Itzamná, the creation god responsible for life and death, are the main ornamentation.

Coming from Chetumal, the first site is **Xpujil**, just across the border in the state of Campeche, and clearly visible from the road. Here, 17 building groups surround a central square, but the most remarkable structure is the main temple, whose three towers rise over 15 m (50 ft) from a

Structure X at Becán, its decorative stonework just visible at the top

low platform. These pointed towers, which are a classic example of Río Bec architecture, soar enigmatically above the surrounding jungle.

Just 6 km (4 miles) farther west, a track north of the main road leads to **Becán**. The site dates from around 550 BC, and is thought to have been the principal Maya center in the Río Bec region. The substantial number of nonlocal artifacts found during excavations suggests it was an important trading center linking the two sides of the peninsula. Unusually, the main buildings here were surrounded by a trench or moat (now dry) that is up to 5 m (16 ft) deep and 16 m (52 ft) wide, and about 2 km (1 mile) in circumference.

Various Río Bec towers can be seen here, but Becán is also noted for the unusual rooms found inside Structure VIII. These chambers had no

means of light or ventilation and may have been used for religious rituals that required darkness and isolation.

Chicanná, 3 km (2 miles) farther west, and south of the main road, has the most extraordinary architecture of the three sites. Its name means "house of the serpent's mouth," which refers to Structure II, whose façade is a snake's head formed by an intricate mosaic of stone. This striking zoomorphic shape represents the god Itzamná, while the snake's mouth forms the doorway. Structure XX, set apart from the main plaza, is a two-level building that echoes the design of Structure II. Its sides are decorated with masks of Chac, the rain god *(see p265)*.

ENVIRONS: Near the village of Conhuás, 60 km (37 miles) west of Xpujil, a minor road branches to the south and, after another 60 km, reaches **Calakmul**, one of the most important Maya cities in the Classic period. The 50 m (165-ft) high pyramid here is the largest in Mexico. Around a hundred stelae remain on site, but the jade masks found in the tombs are now on display in Campeche *(see p260)*.

Just west of Conhuás is the site of **Balamkú**, discovered by chance in 1990. Its most striking feature is a 17-m (55-ft) long stucco frieze on the building known as the House of the Four Kings. The frieze is thought to represent the relationship between Maya royalty and the cosmos.

The three Río Bec towers rising above the principal temple at Xpujil

TRAVELERS'
NEEDS

WHERE TO STAY 290-305
WHERE TO EAT 306-327
SHOPPING IN MEXICO 328-333

WHERE TO STAY

THE CONSTANT increase in numbers of visitors to Mexico has been matched by a growth in the variety of accommodations available. Apart from hotels, there are guest houses, apartments, hostels, campgrounds, and even hammocks for rent. The hotels themselves range from budget motels to world-class luxury resorts in extraordinary settings. Room prices vary greatly, depending on region of the country,

**Maids in a hotel
in Querétaro**

location of the hotel, season, prestige, and services provided. Visitors should be aware that inexpensive establishments may not conform to the standards they might expect in the US or Europe. The hotel listings *(see pp292–305)* describe some of the best hotels around Mexico in every style and price category, from modern chain hotels to small, typical, family-run lodgings and stunningly converted colonial haciendas.

**Main entrance to El Gran Hotel
in Mérida *(see p305)***

HOTEL GRADING

ROOM PRICES are regulated by the state, and hotels are classified into categories ranging from one to five star, plus a special category and a Grand Tourism category. Private bathrooms with showers, linen change, and daily room cleaning are provided in all hotels from one star upward. At the other extreme, Grand Tourism hotels are very luxurious and usually offer a gym, a nightclub, and a gourmet restaurant. Special category hotels are ones that have been designated historic monuments. They are not classified by their facilities, nor given a star rating.

CHAIN HOTELS

MEXICO HAS a number of hotel chains, with varying services and prices. **Fiesta Americana** and **Presidente Intercontinental** are two

local chains that offer reliable service, while **Camino Real** and **Quinta Real** have luxurious rooms. International chains, such as **Sheraton**, **Westin**, and **Marriott**, are also represented, and two good mid-range options are **Calinda** and **Howard Johnson**.

HISTORIC BUILDINGS

MEXICO HAS plenty of old convents, mansions, and haciendas *(see pp50–51)* that have been converted into extraordinary hotels. Many have been declared national monuments and feature original furniture and decor. Those housed in haciendas often have spacious gardens and modern amenities. However, some hotels in convents and mansions are not permitted to alter their structure in order to provide modern facilities.

BUDGET ACCOMMODATIONS

THERE ARE many inexpensive hotels in towns and villages across Mexico, but ask to have a look before you commit to staying anywhere as the standards can vary hugely. The so-called *casas de huéspedes*, family-run guest houses, are one of the best forms of budget accommodations.

Camping is also very popular. Beaches in Mexico are public property; it is perfectly acceptable to camp on them. There are also numerous campgrounds scattered around the country, particularly in Baja California, on the Pacific coast, and on the Yucatán Peninsula. In the south, *cabañas* (beachside cabins) and hammocks, which can be rented and hung almost anywhere, offer a low-cost way to spend the night.

Reservoir at the Hacienda San Miguel Regla, near Huasca *(see p294)*

◁ **Ornate interior of La Casa de la Marquesa in Querétaro *(see p300)***

Tranquil garden at Cuernavaca's Las Mañanitas hotel *(see p294)*

Booking and Paying

IT IS ADVISABLE to book rooms in advance if you are traveling during high season. This includes July and August, and the days around Christmas, Easter, and other public holidays *(see p31)*. Mexico has a number of hotel booking services, among them **Operadora Sidektur**, **Utell International**, and **Corresponsales de Hoteles**, which provide lists of available quality lodgings all around the country.

Otherwise, it is safest to book through a travel agent or by telephone or fax because the postal service can be unreliable. If a deposit is required you can pay by credit card and ask for a confirmation. In some hotels you may be asked to sign a blank credit card slip on arrival. Travelers' checks are accepted in most hotels, and many will change or accept foreign currency, but not always at the best rate. Some budget hotels are cash only.

Most hotels have set prices that may vary according to season, facilities, and type of room. Hotels that depend on business travelers often have reduced rates for long stays and weekends. The normal 15% IVA tax is supplemented with a 2% lodging tax. These are not always included in the advertised rate. It is customary to tip bellhops and chambermaids US$1–2. Checkout time is normally around noon.

Efficiency Apartments

BUDGET-PRICED, comfortable apartments with well-equipped kitchens are available for rent all over the country. Some rental agencies, such as **Condo Corner**, **Olinalá**, and **GEA Holidays**, have properties in a range of locations. Others which concentrate on one resort include **Cozumel Vacation Rentals**, **Se Renta Luxury Villas** (Acapulco), **Ocean Club Los Cabos** (San José del Cabo), and **Rent 'n Vallarta** (Puerto Vallarta). At the beach resorts there are also luxury houses and apartment hotels with hotel-standard services. Rates vary according to location and season.

Youth Hostels

MOST OF the country's youth hostels are attached to sports centers and have clean, single-sex dormitories. Many are run by the **Instituto Mexicano de la Juventud**, but private hostels also exist. **Mundo Joven** is the representative of Youth Hosteling International in Mexico and will make reservations for hostels all over the country.

Villas with *palapa* (palm-thatched) roofs near Careyes *(see p186)*

DIRECTORY

CHAIN HOTELS

Calinda
📞 50 80 08 70.
FAX 52 07 03 99.

Camino Real
📞 52 27 72 00.
FAX 52 50 69 35.
@ reservas@crmexico.com.mx

Fiesta Americana
📞 53 26 69 00.
FAX 53 26 67 02.

Howard Johnson
📞 55 31 40 07.
FAX 55 31 98 22.

Marriott
📞 52 07 10 16.
FAX 55 11 15 81.

Presidente Intercontinental
📞 53 27 77 77.
FAX 53 27 77 87.

Quinta Real
📞 55 20 93 00.
FAX 55 40 13 00.

Sheraton
📞 52 08 15 35.
FAX 52 42 40 84.

Westin
📞 52 27 05 55.
FAX 52 27 05 15.

HOTEL BOOKING SERVICES

Corresponsales de Hoteles
📞 55 21 47 68.
FAX 55 18 45 82.

Operadora Sidektur
📞 & FAX 56 24 24 24.
🌐 www.misvacaciones.com.mx

Utell International
📞 53 87 96 00.
FAX 52 80 79 11.

EFFICIENCY APARTMENT RENTALS

Condo Corner
📞 (314) 822 2781 (US).
FAX (314) 569 0552 (US).

Cozumel Vacation Rentals
📞 & FAX (987) 2 17 74.

GEA Holidays
📞 & FAX 55 53 10 05.
🌐 www.autodromo.com.mx

Olinalá
📞 52 11 47 14.
FAX 52 11 87 01.

Ocean Club Cabos
📞 (624) 142 11 32.
FAX (624) 142 11 76.

Rent 'n Vallarta
📞 (322) 22 04 77.
FAX (322) 22 17 03.

Se Renta Luxury Villas (Acapulco)
📞 (744) 484 10 60.
FAX (744) 484 12 29.

YOUTH HOSTELS

Instituto Mexicano de la Juventud
📞 57 05 60 72.

Mundo Joven
Insurgentes Sur 1510, Mexico City. 📞 56 61 32 33.

Choosing a Hotel

MOST OF THE HOTELS in this guide have been included because of the excellence of their service and facilities. Where a town or city has no hotel of outstanding quality, however, we suggest somewhere to stay which at least offers the best value available. For details of restaurants in Mexico, see pages 314–27.

	NUMBER OF ROOMS	CREDIT CARDS ACCEPTED	PRIVATE PARKING	SWIMMING POOL	RESTAURANT

MEXICO CITY

HISTORIC CENTER: *Capitol* Map 2 D2. $$$
República de Uruguay 12. 🗍 55 18 17 50. FAX 55 21 11 49. @ reserv@hotelcapitol.com.mx
Near the Palacio de Bellas Artes, this is one of the oldest hotels in the city. Its restaurant serves Spanish specialties. 📺 ♿

| 75 | ● | | | ■ |

HISTORIC CENTER: *Catedral* Map 2 E1. $$$
Donceles 95. 🗍 55 18 52 32. FAX 55 12 43 44. @ hcatedra@infosel.net.mx
This modern and inexpensive hotel is extraordinarily well situated close to the Templo Mayor. It has comfortable rooms and a rooftop terrace. 📺

| 116 | ● | ■ | | ■ |

HISTORIC CENTER: *Gillow* Map 2 E2. $$$
Isabel la Católica 17. 🗍 55 18 14 40. FAX 55 12 20 78. @ hgillow@prodigy.net.mx
Located next to the Iglesia de la Profesa, between the Zócalo and the Alameda, this former monk's house built in 1875 has been converted into a modern hotel, with comfortable rooms surrounding a courtyard. 📺 ♿

| 103 | ● | | | ■ |

HISTORIC CENTER: *Metropol* Map 2 C2. $$$
Luis Moya 39. 🗍 55 21 49 01. FAX 55 12 12 73. @ metropol@mail.internet.com.mx
A pianist plays nightly in the lobby bar of this hotel located close to the Alameda. Mexican and Spanish food are served in the restaurant. 📺 ♿

| 156 | ● | ■ | | ■ |

HISTORIC CENTER: *Best Western Hotel de Cortés* Map 2 C1. $$$$
Avenida Hidalgo 85. 🗍 55 18 21 81. FAX 55 12 18 63.
@ reservaciones@hoteldecortes.com.mx This, the oldest hotel in the Americas, is particularly notable for its red, carved *tezontle* façade. 📺 ♿

| 29 | ● | | | ■ |

HISTORIC CENTER: *Gran Hotel* Map 2 E2. $$$$
Avenida 16 de Septiembre No. 52. 🗍 & FAX 10 83 77 00. 🖿 www.granhotel.com.
Decorated in Art Nouveau style, this hotel has an Italian domed stained-glass ceiling *(see p60)* and a rooftop restaurant overlooking the Zócalo. 🗎 📺

| 122 | ● | ■ | | ■ |

HISTORIC CENTER: *Best Western Majestic* Map 2 E2. $$$$
Avda Francisco I. Madero 73. 🗍 55 21 86 00. FAX 55 12 62 62. @ majestic@supernet.com.mx
Occupying an unrivaled position in the heart of the city, this hotel offers a magnificent view of the Zócalo from its rooftop restaurant-terrace. 📺 ♿

| 85 | ● | | | ■ |

REFORMA & CHAPULTEPEC: *Casa González* Map 1 E3. $$
Río Sena 69. 🗍 55 14 33 02. FAX 55 11 07 02. @ j_ortiz_moore@hotmail.com
Just in front of the British Embassy are these two Porfirian-style mansions, joined together and converted into a guesthouse, with simple rooms.

| 22 | | | | ■ |

REFORMA & CHAPULTEPEC: *Hotel Park Villa* Map 2 F2. $$$
Gómez Pedraza 68. 🗍 55 15 52 45. FAX 55 15 45 14. @ reservaciones@hotelparkvilla.com.mx
Near Parque de Chapultepec, this unpretentious two-story colonial-style hotel offers spacious and comfortable rooms. 📺 ♿

| 45 | | ■ | | ■ |

REFORMA & CHAPULTEPEC: *Casa Blanca* Map 2 A1. $$$$
Lafragua 7. 🗍 57 05 13 00. FAX 57 05 41 97. @ hotel@hotel-casablanca.com.mx
Close to the Monumento a la Revolución, this colorful hotel has a beautiful view from its terrace, and a rooftop swimming pool. 🗎 📺 ♿

| 269 | ● | ■ | ● | ■ |

REFORMA & CHAPULTEPEC: *Emporio* Map 2 F2. $$$$
Paseo de la Reforma 124. 🗍 55 66 77 66. FAX 57 03 14 24.
@ reservaciones@hotelesemporio.com
Every room has a Jacuzzi in this hotel, which has Neo-Classical decor. Parking is two blocks away, but valet parking is available. 🗎 📺 ♿

| 145 | ● | ■ | | ■ |

REFORMA & CHAPULTEPEC: *María Cristina* Map 1 E2. $$$
Río Lerma 31. 🗍 57 03 18 44. FAX 55 66 91 94. 🖿 www.hotelmariacristina.com.mx
Located near the American Embassy, this quiet, colonial-style hotel has bright, sunny rooms surrounding a central patio. 📺

| 150 | ● | ■ | | ■ |

Price categories for a standard double room per night in the tourist season, including tax and service:
$ under US$25
$$ US$25–40
$$$ US$40–80
$$$$ US$80–140
$$$$$ over US$140

CREDIT CARDS ACCEPTED
One or more of the following credit cards are accepted: American Express, Diners Club, MasterCard, or VISA.

PRIVATE PARKING
The hotel has its own parking lot or parking spaces. These may not be on the same premises and are not necessarily locked.

SWIMMING POOL
The pool is outdoors unless otherwise stated in the text.

RESTAURANT
This is not necessarily recommended, although particularly good hotel restaurants are also listed in the restaurant section.

Hotel	Number of Rooms	Credit Cards Accepted	Private Parking	Swimming Pool	Restaurant
REFORMA & CHAPULTEPEC: *Polanco* Map 1 E3. $$$$ Edgar Allan Poe 8, Polanco. ☎ & [FAX] 52 80 80 82. This inexpensive hotel is close to the French Embassy. It has clean rooms with mahogany furniture, and a very good Italian restaurant. [TV]	77	●	■		■
REFORMA & CHAPULTEPEC: *Calinda Geneve* Map 1 E3. $$$$ Londres 130, Zona Rosa. ☎ 50 80 08 00. [FAX] 50 80 08 33. [@] calindageneve@hotmail.com A well-kept establishment with an attractive lobby, a spa, and a popular glass-canopied restaurant run by Sanborn's *(see p328)*. [TV] ♿	270	●			■
REFORMA & CHAPULTEPEC: *Sevilla Palace* Map 2 A2. $$$$ Paseo de la Reforma 105. ☎ 57 05 28 00. [FAX] 57 03 15 21. [@] reserva@sevillapalace.com.mx The Sevilla Palace is modern, and suitable for both business travelers and tourists. Take a ride in the glass elevator to the rooftop swimming pool and Jacuzzi, with their panoramic views of the city. ▤ [TV] ♿	403	●	■	●	■
REFORMA & CHAPULTEPEC: *Camino Real* Map 1 B3. $$$$$ Mariano Escobedo 700. ☎ 52 63 88 88. [FAX] 52 63 88 98. [@] reservas@caminoreal.com.mx This is one of the most eloquent expressions of modern Mexican architecture. Rufino Tamayo's mural, *Man Facing Eternity*, is at the entrance of this luxurious hotel. Rooms are elegant and contemporary in style. ▤ [TV] ♿	709	●	■	●	■
REFORMA & CHAPULTEPEC: *Casa Vieja* Map 1 E3. $$$$$ Eugenio Sue 45, Polanco. ☎ 52 82 00 67. [FAX] 52 81 37 80. [W] www.casavieja.com This is one of the most exclusive hotels in the country. Its ten suites are artistically decorated, giving a taste of Mexican Baroque splendor. ▤ [TV]	10	●	■		■
REFORMA & CHAPULTEPEC: *Imperial Reforma* Map 2 A2. $$$$$ Paseo de la Reforma 64. ☎ 57 05 49 11. [FAX] 57 03 31 22. [@] imperial@internet.com.mx Built in 1904, the Imperial is considered a historic monument. Its interior has been adapted to satisfy the needs of a modern hotel. ▤ [TV] ♿	65	●	■		■
REFORMA & CHAPULTEPEC: *Melia México Reforma* Map 2 B1. $$$$$ Reforma 1. ☎ 51 28 50 00. [FAX] 51 28 50 50. [@] reservas@melia-mexico.com.mx A vast lobby with a high atrium is the attraction of this modern hotel. It offers quiet rooms, business facilities, a gym, and three restaurants. ▤ [TV] ♿	490	●	■	●	■
REFORMA & CHAPULTEPEC: *Four Seasons* Map 1 C4. $$$$$ Paseo de la Reforma 500. ☎ 52 30 18 18. [FAX] 52 30 18 08. [@] mex.reservations@fourseasons.com This hacienda-style building surrounds a flower-filled courtyard with a fountain. There is an excellent restaurant, a gym, a spa, and elegant and luxurious rooms with high ceilings. ▤ [TV] ♿	240	●	■	●	■
REFORMA & CHAPULTEPEC: *María Isabel Sheraton* Map 1 D3. $$$$$ Reforma 325. ☎ 52 42 55 55. [FAX] 52 07 06 84. A deluxe hotel facing the Monumento a la Independencia with top-class facilities, including a health center, two tennis courts, a sauna, three good restaurants, a *mariachi* nightclub, and spacious rooms. ▤ [TV] ♿	756	●	■	●	■
REFORMA & CHAPULTEPEC: *Marquis Reforma* Map 1 C4. $$$$$ Paseo de la Reforma 465. ☎ 52 29 12 00. [FAX] 52 29 12 12. [@] divetos@marquisreformahl.com An attractively decorated Art Deco hotel with an atmosphere of beauty and creativity. It has a gym and a spa. ▤ [TV] ♿	208	●	■		■
REFORMA & CHAPULTEPEC: *JW Marriott* Map 1 E3. $$$$$ Andrés Bello 29, Polanco. ☎ 30 03 00 00. [FAX] 59 99 00 01. There are more than 1,500 Marriott hotels in the world but only seven have the JW nomination for fine service. This is one of them. ▤ [TV] ♿	311	●	■	●	■
REFORMA & CHAPULTEPEC: *Nikko* Map 1 E3. $$$$$ Campos Elíseos 204, Polanco. ☎ 52 83 87 00. [FAX] 52 80 91 91. [@] nikkosal@nikko.com.mx This Japanese hotel is the tallest in the city. The public areas are decorated with paintings and sculptures by various artists. ▤ [TV] ♿	744	●	■	●	■

For key to symbols see back flap

Price categories for a standard double room per night in the tourist season, including tax and service:

$ under US$25
$$ US$25–40
$$$ US$40–80
$$$$ US$80–140
$$$$$ over US$140

CREDIT CARDS ACCEPTED
One or more of the following credit cards are accepted: American Express, Diners Club, MasterCard, or VISA.

PRIVATE PARKING
The hotel has its own parking lot or parking spaces. These may not be on the same premises and are not necessarily locked.

SWIMMING POOL
The pool is outdoors unless otherwise stated in the text.

RESTAURANT
This is not necessarily recommended, although particularly good hotel restaurants are also listed in the restaurant section.

	NUMBER OF ROOMS	CREDIT CARDS ACCEPTED	PRIVATE PARKING	SWIMMING POOL	RESTAURANT
REFORMA & CHAPULTEPEC: *Presidente Intercontinental* Map 1 E3. $$$$$ Campos Elíseos 218, Polanco. 53 27 77 00. FAX 53 27 77 30. www.interconti.com Catering to business travelers, this hotel has various restaurants, a lobby bar with live music, and modern rooms.	659	•	■		
FARTHER AFIELD: *La Casona* Map 1 D5. $$$$$ Durango 280, Roma. 52 86 30 01. FAX 52 11 08 71. casona@data.net.mx This charming hotel, housed in a renovated old mansion, has a gym with sauna and steam bath, and rooms furnished with antiques.	29	•	■		■
FARTHER AFIELD: *Marriott Aeropuerto* $$$$$ Puerto México 80. 30 03 00 33. FAX 30 03 00 34. mexicoarso@dsi.com.mx Located beside Mexico City's International Airport, this modern hotel offers a health club, a 24-hour business center, and well-equipped rooms.	600	•	■		■
FARTHER AFIELD: *Royal Pedregal* $$$$$ Periférico Sur 4363, Jardines de la Montaña. 54 49 40 00. FAX 56 45 79 64. www.hotelesroyal.com.mx Decorated in Mexican style, and with sculptures, this modern hotel is popular with business travelers. It has a spa, and a good restaurant.	340	•	■	•	■

AROUND MEXICO CITY

	NUMBER OF ROOMS	CREDIT CARDS ACCEPTED	PRIVATE PARKING	SWIMMING POOL	RESTAURANT
CHOLULA: *Villas Arqueológicas* $$$ Zona Arqueológica. (222) 247 19 60. FAX (222) 247 15 08. www.clubmed.com At the foot of the pyramid, with a great view of the temple, this Club Med hotel has a good restaurant serving French and Mexican dishes.	44	•	■	•	■
COCOYOC: *Hacienda Cocoyoc* $$$$ Mex 95, 32 km (20 miles) E of town. (735) 356 22 11. FAX (735) 356 12 12. hcocoyoc@prodigy.net.mx A former 17th-century hacienda, converted into a splendid hotel with a golf course, tennis courts, a gym, and stables.	287	•	■	•	■
CUERNAVACA: *Hacienda de Cortés* $$$$$ Plaza Kennedy 90, Atlacomulco, Jiutepec. (777) 315 88 44. FAX (777) 315 00 35. ventas@haciendadecortes.com A tastefully restored 16th-century hacienda built by Hernán Cortés. It has large gardens and attractive rooms.	23	•	■	•	■
CUERNAVACA: *Hostería Las Quintas* $$$$$ Avenida Díaz Ordaz 9. (777) 318 39 49. FAX (777) 318 38 95. lasquintas@hlasquintas.com A family-run hotel with extensive gardens, a collection of bonsai trees, a pond with colorful fish, Jacuzzis, and a spa with a sauna.	86	•	■	•	■
CUERNAVACA: *Las Mañanitas* $$$$$ Ricardo Linares 107. (777) 314 14 66. FAX (777) 318 36 72. reservaciones@lasmananitas.com.mx An elegant establishment with fireplaces and terraces in most rooms. The restaurant is excellent *(see p317).*	22	•		•	■
CUERNAVACA: *Rancho Cuernavaca* $$$$$ Callejón del Arrastradero 1, Chamilpa. (777) 313 39 62. FAX (777) 313 78 28. eventos@ranchocuernavaca.com.mx Built on an old ranch in Dutch and Mexican colonial styles, this luxurious complex has a chapel, stables, and gardens.	15	•	■	•	
HUASCA: *Hacienda San Miguel Regla* $$$$ Huasca de Ocampo. (771) 792 01 02. FAX (771) 792 00 54. payger@prodigy.net.mx A beautiful, 17th-century hacienda surrounded by gardens and lakes. It has a private chapel, aqueducts, boats, and rooms with fireplaces.	95	•	■	•	■
PACHUCA: *Fiesta Inn* $$$$ Mex 130, Venta Prieta. (771) 711 30 11. FAX (771) 711 43 96. www.fiestainnpachuca.com Next to the Club de Golf Campestre, this hotel is a classic example of Mexican architecture, with pastel-colored interiors, and pleasant, verdant gardens.	114	•	■		■

PUEBLA: *Colonial* $$ 69
Calle 4 Sur No. 105. ☎ *(222) 246 46 12.* FAX *(222) 246 08 18.* @ *colonial@giga.com*
A former 18th-century Jesuit seminary that has been converted into a
charming hotel. The large rooms have tiled floors and balconies. TV

PUEBLA: *Royalty* $$$ 45
Portal Hidalgo 8. ☎ *(222) 242 47 40.* FAX *(222) 242 47 43.* W *www.hotelr.com*
Set in a 19th-century building, in the heart of the old city *(see p151)*,
this hotel has a popular restaurant, and an antique elevator. TV 🔧

PUEBLA: *Holiday Inn Centro Histórico* $$$$ 78
Avenida 2 Oriente No. 211. ☎ *(222) 223 66 00.* FAX *(222) 242 11 76.*
Two blocks from the *zócalo*, this hotel is housed in an 1894 Porfirian-
style building. It has a fine lobby and a stained glass ceiling. ▤ TV 🔧

PUEBLA: *Real Mesón del Ángel* $$$$$ 192
Avenida Hermanos Serdán 807. ☎ *(222) 223 83 00.* FAX *(222) 223 83 01.*
@ *reservaciones@gruporeal.com.mx*
This former hacienda has three different lodging areas, well-kept gardens,
a business center, a tennis court, and a choice of restaurants. ▤ TV 🔧

PUEBLA: *Posada San Pedro* $$$$ 80
Avda 2 Oriente 202. ☎ *(222) 246 50 77.* FAX *(222) 246 53 76.* @ *reservaciones.hpsp*
@seccionamanilla.com.mx A colonial hotel situated one block from the *zócalo*.
The rooms are carpeted, with modern furniture and large bathrooms. ▤ TV 🔧

PUEBLA: *Camino Real* $$$$$ 83
Avda 7 Poniente No. 105. ☎ *(222) 229 09 10.* FAX *(222) 232 92 51.*
The converted 16th-century convent of La Inmaculada Concepción has
former nuns' cells transformed into beautiful bedrooms with tiled floors,
original frescoes, and some antiques. It has four lovely courtyards. TV 🔧

PUEBLA: *Mesón Sacristía* $$$$$ 15
Callejón de los Sapos No. 304. ☎ *(222) 232 45 13.* FAX *(222) 42 35 54.*
W *mesones-sacrista.com*
Situated in the center of town, this 18th-century mansion has been
converted into an exclusive hotel and fine gourmet restaurant *(see p317)*.
It is decorated with antiques, many of which are for sale. TV

TAXCO: *Los Arcos* $$ 21
Juan Ruíz de Alarcón 4. ☎ *(762) 622 18 36.* FAX *(762) 622 79 82.*
@ *losarcoshotel@hotmail.com* Housed in a former 17th-century monastery, this is
a cheerful hotel with a pretty courtyard, tiled floors, and colonial-style furniture.

TAXCO: *Agua Escondida* $$$ 50
Plaza Borda 4. ☎ *(762) 622 07 26.* FAX *(762) 622 13 06.* @ *hotelaguaesc@prodigy.net.mx*
Located in the heart of town, this rambling old building has a
large rooftop swimming pool, and terraces with great views. TV

TAXCO: *Victoria* $$$ 63
Carlos J. Nibbi 5. ☎ *(762) 622 02 10.* FAX *(762) 622 00 10.*
This peaceful, hilltop hotel, built in the 1940s, has a wonderful view of
the city. The rooms have some original furniture and decorations.

TAXCO: *Posada de la Misión* $$$$$ 125
Cerro de la Misión 32. ☎ *(762) 622 00 63.* FAX *(762) 622 21 98.*
@ *hpmreserva@posada.mision.com* On a hilltop next to the highway, this colonial-
style hotel has a good terrace restaurant with a panoramic view of Taxco. TV 🔧

TEOTIHUACÁN: *Villas Arqueológicas* $$$ 39
Zona Arqueológica, San Juan Teotihuacán. ☎ *(594) 956 09 09.* FAX *(594) 956 02 44.*
W *www.teotihuacaninfo.com*
Located in the south of the archaeological area, this hacienda-style hotel
belongs to Club Med. The rustic rooms look onto a courtyard. ▤ TV 🔧

TEPOZTLÁN: *Posada el Tepozteco* $$$$$ 20
Paraíso 3, Barrio de San Miguel. ☎ *(739) 395 00 10.* FAX *(739) 395 03 23.*
@ *tepozhot@prodigy.net.mx* This colonial-style hotel has panoramic views and
lovely gardens. Each room, decorated with watercolors, has its own terrace. TV 🔧

TEQUESQUITENGO: *Hacienda Vista Hermosa* $$$$$ 105
Mex 95, 7 km (4 miles) S. ☎ *(734) 345 53 61.* FAX *(734) 345 53 60.*
@ *tourbymexico@infosel.net.mx* Founded in 1529 by Hernán Cortés, this former
hacienda has good facilities including a large swimming pool and stables. 🔧

For key to symbols see back flap

Price categories for a standard double room per night in the tourist season, including tax and service: Ⓢ under US$25 ⓈⓈ US$25–40 ⓈⓈⓈ US$40–80 ⓈⓈⓈⓈ US$80–140 ⓈⓈⓈⓈⓈ over US$140	**CREDIT CARDS ACCEPTED** One or more of the following credit cards are accepted: American Express, Diners Club, MasterCard, or VISA. **PRIVATE PARKING** The hotel has its own parking lot or parking spaces. These may not be on the same premises and are not necessarily locked. **SWIMMING POOL** The pool is outdoors unless otherwise stated in the text. **RESTAURANT** This is not necessarily recommended, although particularly good hotel restaurants are also listed in the restaurant section.	**NUMBER OF ROOMS**	**CREDIT CARDS ACCEPTED**	**PRIVATE PARKING**	**SWIMMING POOL**	**RESTAURANT**

TLAXCALA: *Calinda and Spa Tlaxcala* ⓈⓈⓈⓈ Carretera Tlaxcala–Apizaco, 10 km (6 miles) N. [C] (246) 461 00 00. FAX (246) 461 01 78. [W] www.hotelescalinda.com.mx This former hacienda has gardens, a spa and tennis courts. ▤ TV ♿	102	●	■	●	■
TLAXCALA: *Posada San Francisco* ⓈⓈⓈⓈ Pl de la Constitución 17. [C] (246) 462 60 22. FAX (246) 462 68 18. [@] posadasanfrancisco@yahoo.com This 19th-century mansion, with two lovely courtyards and fountains, and a gray stone façade, has been declared a national monument. ▤ TV	68	●	■	●	■
TOLUCA: *Colonial* ⓈⓈⓈ Avenida Hidalgo Oriente 103. [C] (722) 215 97 00. FAX (722) 214 70 66. Simple and inexpensive, the Colonial is the oldest hotel in town and is located two blocks from the *zócalo*. Each room has a balcony. TV ♿	30	●			■
TULA: *Sharon* ⓈⓈⓈ Callejón de la Cruz 1, Panzacola. [C] & FAX (773) 732 35 00. This seven-story modern hotel, opposite the town hall and not far from the archaeological area, is popular with business travelers. TV	120	●	■		■
VALLE DE BRAVO: *Avándaro Golf & Spa Resort* ⓈⓈⓈⓈⓈ Vega del Río, Fraccionamiento Avándaro. [C] (726) 266 02 00. FAX (726) 266 03 70. [W] www.grupoavandaro.com.mx Located in the Sierra Madre mountains, this resort hotel has tennis courts, a spa, and rooms with fireplaces overlooking an 18-hole golf course. TV	79	●	■	●	■
NORTHERN MEXICO					
BAHÍA DE LOS ANGELES: *Las Hamacas* ⓈⓈⓈ Bahía de los Angeles. [C] & FAX (200) 124 91 02. [@] hotellashamacas@hotmail.com This family-run hotel is on the outskirts of the city, but enjoys great ocean views. Excursions to visit nearby cave paintings can be arranged. ▤ ♿	10	●	■		
BATOPILAS: *Margaritas Hacienda* ⓈⓈ Santo Domingo. [C] (635) 456 00 45. FAX (635) 456 02 45. [W] www.coppercanyon-mexico.com This inexpensive, ex-hacienda colonial-style hotel is a relaxing place to stay right next to the river just outside town. All rooms have a bath tub.	10	●	■		■
CABO SAN LUCAS: *Siesta Suites Hotel* ⓈⓈⓈ Emiliano Zapata, between Guerrero and Hidalgo. [C] & FAX (624) 143 27 73. [@] siesta@cabonet.net.mx Close to the beach and the marina is this four-story modern hotel comprising suites with fully equipped kitchens. ▤ TV	19	●	■		
CABO SAN LUCAS: *The Bungalows Breakfast Inn* ⓈⓈⓈⓈ Antiguo Lienzo Charro. [C] (624) 143 05 85. FAX (624) 143 50 35. [W] www.cabobungalows.com Decorated with terra-cotta tiles, carved stone fountains, and plenty of plants, this is a cozy, relaxing bungalow hideaway. ▤ TV ♿	16	●	■	●	
CABO SAN LUCAS: *Twin Dolphin* ⓈⓈⓈⓈⓈ Mex 1, 11 km (7 miles) E. [C] (624) 145 81 90. FAX (624) 145 81 96. [@] twindolphin@ twindolphin.com On a quiet cove overlooking the Sea of Cortés, this small hotel offers luxurious accommodations and exceptional amenities. ▤ TV ♿	50	●	■	●	■
CHIHUAHUA: *San Francisco* ⓈⓈⓈⓈ Victoria 409. [C] (614) 416 75 50. FAX (614) 415 35 38. [W] www.hotelsanfrancisco.com.mx This comfortable hotel in the city center is decorated in a blend of modern and period styles. The rooftop terrace has panoramic views. ▤ TV ♿	131	●	■	●	■
CIUDAD CUAUHTÉMOC: *Motel Tarahumara Inn* ⓈⓈⓈ Allende 373. [C] & FAX (625) 581 19 19. [W] www.tarahumarainn.com Situated three blocks from the bus station, this hotel is decorated in a Mexican Indian style. Its rooms have carved wooden beds. ▤ TV ♿	65	●	■		■

CREEL: *Motel Cascada Inn* ☒ www.motelcascadainn.com $$$ | 33
Avenida López Mateos 49. ☎ (635) 456 02 53. FAX (635) 456 01 51.
This two-story motel, surrounded by apple trees, has a heated pool and a disco. Excursions to nearby places of interest can be organized. TV ♿

EL DIVISADERO: *Divisadero Barrancas* $$$$ | 50
Av Mirador 4516, Residencial Campestre. ☎ (614) 415 11 99. FAX (614) 415 65 75.
@ hoteldivisadero@infosel.net.mx Some rooms in this small hotel have views of the Copper Canyon *(see p176).* ♿

DURANGO: *Gobernador* $$$$ | 99
Avenida 20 de Noviembre No. 257 Oriente. ☎ (618) 813 19 19. FAX (618) 811 14 22.
@ hgreservaciones@infosel.net.mx This colonial-style hotel in a converted prison has balconied rooms. Arrangements can be made for hunting. ☰ TV ♿

ENSENADA: *Baja Inn Hotel Cortés* ☒ www.bajainn.com $$$$ | 82
Avenida López Mateos 1089. ☎ (646) 178 23 07. FAX (646) 178 39 04.
This colonial-style hotel has a basketball court, a gym, and small carpeted rooms with balconies. It also has a very good Italian restaurant. ☰ TV ♿

ENSENADA: *Estero Beach Hotel & Resort* ☒ www.hotelesterobeach.com $$$$ | 112
Playas del Estero, Ejido Chapultepec. ☎ (646) 176 62 25. FAX (646) 176 69 25.
Situated next to an estuary, this hotel is decorated in a Maya style. It has three tennis courts, watersports facilities, and rooms with terraces. TV ♿

GUERRERO NEGRO: *Cabañas Don Miguelito* $$$ | 16
Blvd Emiliano Zapata, Fundo Legal. ☎ & FAX (615) 157 01 00. ☒ www.malarrimo.com
This *cabaña*-style hotel is part of the Malarrimo complex, where whale watching tours are available between January and March *(see p164).* TV ♿

HERMOSILLO: *Araiza Inn* $$$$ | 156
Blvd Eusebio Kino 353. ☎ (662) 210 27 17. FAX (662) 210 45 41. ☒ araizainn.com.mx
A modern, American-style hotel, centering around a swimming pool. There are pleasant gardens, and a tennis court. ☰ TV ♿

HIDALGO DEL PARRAL: *Hotel Acosta* $ | 26
Agustín Barbachano 3. ☎ (627) 522 02 21. FAX (627) 522 06 57.
Run by a friendly family, this simple, bargain hotel has a terrace with a great panoramic view of the Plaza de Armas and the city. ☰ ♿

LORETO: *Oasis Loreto* ☒ www.hoteloasis.com $$$$ | 39
Corner of López Mateos & Baja California. ☎ (613) 501 12. FAX (613) 507 95.
This beachfront rustic hotel, surrounded by date palms, is decorated with fishing memorabilia. It offers beautiful views of the sunrise. ☰ ♿

MAZATLÁN: *Costa de Oro Beach Hotel* @ info@costaoro.com $$$$ | 290
Calzada Camarón Sábalo, Zona Dorada. ☎ (669) 913 58 88. FAX (669) 914 42 09.
A popular beachfront hotel in modern colonial style, with a tennis court and gardens, and panoramic views of the ocean. ☰ TV ♿

MONTERREY: *Crowne Plaza* $$$$ | 403
Avda Constitución 300 Or. ☎ (81) 8319 60 60. FAX (81) 8344 30 07. ☒ www.hotelesmilenium.com
This modern, 18-story hotel, two blocks from the Macro Plaza, has a lobby bar, a business center, and a tennis court. ☰ TV ♿

MULEGÉ: *Serenidad* $$$ | 49
El Cacheno. ☎ (615) 153 05 30. FAX (615) 153 03 11. ☒ www.hotelserenidad.com
Near the estuary, this peaceful, one-story *cabaña*-style hotel offers fishing and sports facilities, bicycles, and rooms with fireplaces and porches. ☰ ♿

NUEVO CASAS GRANDES: *Motel Piñon* $$ | 50
Avenida Benito Juárez 605. ☎ & FAX (636) 694 0166.
This hotel is 10 km (6 miles) from the Paquimé ruins, near the town's cathedral. Artifacts from the archaeological site are on display inside. ☰ TV ♿

LA PAZ: *La Perla* $$$$ | 110
Malecón Álvaro Obregón 1570. ☎ (612) 122 08 21. FAX (612) 125 53 63.
@ reservaciones@hotelperlabaja.com
This three-story hotel is the oldest in the city. ☰ TV ♿

LA PAZ: *Los Arcos* $$$$ | 130
Avenida Álvaro Obregón 498. ☎ (612) 122 27 44. FAX (612) 125 43 13. ☒ www.losarcos.com
Overlooking the bay, this colonial-style hotel has carpeted rooms with balconies, and 52 bungalows with thatched roofs and fireplaces. ☰ TV ♿

For key to symbols see back flap

Price categories for a standard double room per night in the tourist season, including tax and service: $ under US$25 $$ US$25–40 $$$ US$40–80 $$$$ US$80–140 $$$$$ over US$140	**CREDIT CARDS ACCEPTED** One or more of the following credit cards are accepted: American Express, Diners Club, MasterCard, or VISA. **PRIVATE PARKING** The hotel has its own parking lot or parking spaces. These may not be on the same premises and are not necessarily locked. **SWIMMING POOL** The pool is outdoors unless otherwise stated in the text. **RESTAURANT** This is not necessarily recommended, although particularly good hotel restaurants are also listed in the restaurant section.				

Hotel	NUMBER OF ROOMS	CREDIT CARDS ACCEPTED	PRIVATE PARKING	SWIMMING POOL	RESTAURANT
SALTILLO: *Camino Real* $$$$$ Blvd los Fundadores 2000. ((844) 430 00 00. FAX (844) 438 00 09. @ slw@caminoreal.com A colonial-style, modern motel with a putting green, a gym, a tennis court, and comfortable rooms with spacious marble bathrooms. ▤ TV ♿	164	●	■	●	■
SAN IGNACIO: *La Pinta* $$$ San Ignacio. (& FAX 01800 02 63 605. Situated on the main road as you enter town, and surrounded by palms, this colonial-style hotel has a courtyard and arched corridors. ▤ TV	28	●			■
SAN JOSÉ DEL CABO: *El Delfín Blanco* W www.eldelfinblanco.net $$$ Calle Delfines, Pueblo la Playa. ((624) 142 12 12. FAX (624) 142 11 99. Close to the lighthouse, these small and modern palm-thatched *cabañas* overlooking the water are run as a hotel by a Mexican-Swedish couple. ▤	5	●			
SAN JOSÉ DEL CABO: *Tropicana Inn* $$$$ Boulevard Mijares 30. ((624) 142 09 07. FAX (624) 142 15 90. W www.tropicanacabo.com Each room is decorated with hand-painted tiles and rustic furniture in this colonial-style hotel with a cobblestone courtyard and fountains. ▤ TV	40	●			■
SAN JOSÉ DEL CABO: *Westin Regina Resort* $$$$$ Mex 1, 22.5 km (14 miles) SE. ((624) 142 90 00. FAX (624) 142 90 11. @ reservations.01087@westin.com Every deluxe room in this Mexican-style, oceanfront resort hotel boasts a balcony with breathtaking views. There are seven swimming pools. ▤ TV ♿	295	●	■	●	■
SANTA ROSALÍA: *El Morro* $$$ Mex 1 Sur, 1.5 km (1 mile) S. (& FAX (615) 152 23 90. This colonial hotel is perched on a cliff, giving beautiful views. It has large gardens and a Mexican-French restaurant. ▤ TV ♿	39		■	●	■
TIJUANA: *El Conquistador* $$$ Boulevard Agua Caliente 10750. ((664) 681 79 55. FAX (664) 686 22 51. A colonial-style hotel, close to the racetrack. It has a Jacuzzi, gardens, a sauna, and spacious rooms with Louis XV furniture. ▤ TV ♿	105	●	■	●	■
THE COLONIAL HEARTLAND					
AGUASCALIENTES: *Quinta Real* $$$$$ Avda Aguascalientes Sur 601. ((449) 978 58 18. FAX (449) 978 56 16. @ reser-ags@quinta-real.com Located close to the Descubre science museum (*see p191*), this colonial-style hotel is built of stone and decorated with antiques. The luxurious, carpeted rooms have marble bathrooms. ▤ TV ♿	85	●	■		■
ANGANGUEO: *Don Bruno* $$$ Morelos 92, El Rescate. (& FAX (715) 156 00 26. Close to the Iglesia de la Inmaculada Concepción is this picturesque colonial hotel. The carpeted rooms all have fireplaces.	29	●	■		■
COLIMA: *Los Candiles* $$$ Boulevard Camino Real 399. ((312) 312 32 12. FAX (312) 313 17 07. W www.loscandiles.com Located at the entrance to the city, this simple, casual hotel is decorated with chandeliers and rustic wooden furniture. ▤ TV ♿	75	●	■	●	■
COSTA CAREYES: *The Careyes* $$$$$ Mex 200. ((315) 351 00 00. FAX (315) 351 01 00. W www.luxurycollection.com The activities at this marvelous beachfront hotel include horseback riding and midnight turtle-watching during the nesting season. ▤ TV	48	●	■	●	■
GUADALAJARA: *La Rotonda* $$$ Liceo 130. (& FAX (33) 3614 10 17. @ hotelesucasa@yahoo.com A former 19th-century convent and hospital makes a pleasant setting for La Rotonda. It is located one-and-a-half blocks from the cathedral. ▤ TV	32	●	■		■

GUADALAJARA: *Misión Carlton* $$$$ Avenida Niños Héroes 125. ☎ *(33) 3614 72 72.* [FAX] *(33) 3613 55 39.* @ *rvas@prodigy.net.mx* Located a few blocks from the *zócalo*, this modern 20-story hotel has large, well-furnished rooms with fine views. [≡] [TV] ♿	193	●	■	●	■
GUADALAJARA: *Quinta Real* $$$$$ Avda México 2727, Monraz. ☎ *(33) 3669 06 00.* [FAX] *(33) 3669 06 01.* @ *reserv-gdl@quintareal.com.mx* This elegant colonial-style hotel has beautiful gardens, and rooms individually decorated with antiques. [≡] [TV] ♿	76	●	■	●	■
GUANAJUATO: *Posada Santa Fé* $$$$ Jardín Unión 12. ☎ *(473) 732 00 84.* [FAX] *(473) 732 46 53.* @ *santafe@redes.int.com.mx* With an unrivaled location, this 19th-century mansion has been declared a national monument. It is the oldest, most popular hotel in the city. [TV]	50	●	■		■
GUANAJUATO: *Castillo de Santa Cecilia* $$$$ Mex 110, 1km (half a mile) NW. ☎ & [FAX] *(473) 732 04 85.* @ *castillstacecilia@yahoo.com.mx* Incorporating the original walls of an old hacienda, the design of this hotel resembles a medieval castle. The rooms have canopied beds. [TV]	90	●	■	●	■
GUANAJUATO: *Howard Johnson Parador San Javier* $$$$ Pl Aldama 92, San Javier. ☎ *(473) 732 06 26.* [FAX] *(473) 732 31 14.* @ *hpsjgto@redes.int.com.mx* This hotel is in a former silver-mining hacienda, surrounding lovely gardens. It has well-furnished rooms. [TV] ♿	113	●	■	●	■
GUANAJUATO: *La Casa de los Espíritus Alegres* $$$$$ Ex-Hacienda de Trinidad 1, Marfil. ☎ & [FAX] *(473) 733 10 13.* @ *casaspirit@aol.com* Rooms in this former 18th-century hacienda have a variety of fireplaces, balconies, terraces, and patios. Each one is decorated with Mexican folk art. Breakfast overlooking the garden is included.	8		■		
HUASTECA POTOSINA: *Posada el Castillo* $$$ Ocampo 105, Xilitla. ☎ *(489) 365 00 38.* [FAX] *(489) 365 00 55.* @ *info@junglegossip.com* This hillside hotel is part of the surreal estate of artist Edward James *(see p195)*. It is a whimsical blend of Mexican, English, and Moorish styles, and has a large living-dining room and a well-stocked library.	8		■	●	
LAGUNA DE CHAPALA: *Nueva Posada* $$$ Donato Guerra 9, Ajijic. ☎ *(376) 766 14 14.* [FAX] *(376) 766 13 44.* @ *nuevaposada@laguna.com.mx* Facing Lake Chapala, this attractive colonial-style hotel, decorated with antiques, offers spacious suites and beautiful gardens. [≡] [TV] ♿	19	●	■	●	■
MORELIA: *Soledad* $$$ Ignacio Zaragoza 90. ☎ *(443) 312 18 88.* [FAX] *(443) 312 21 11.* @ *hsoledad@hsoledad.com* One block from the cathedral, this 18th-century colonial hotel has two lovely courtyards, and rooms with lofty ceilings. [TV] ♿	58	●	■		■
MORELIA: *Virrey de Mendoza* $$$$ Portal Matamoros 16. ☎ *(443) 312 49 40.* [FAX] *(443) 312 67 19.* @ *hvirrey@prodigy.net.mx* This 17th-century colonial house has been converted into a tasteful hotel, with antiques, chandeliers, and wooden floors. [TV] ♿	55	●	■		■
MORELIA: *Villa Montaña* $$$$$ Patzimba 201, Vista Bella. ☎ *(443) 314 02 31.* [FAX] *(443) 315 14 23.* @ *hotel@villamontana.com.mx* Set on the Santa María ridge, overlooking the city, is this small, luxury hotel. Its rooms feature fireplaces and wood beams, and are furnished with antiques. [TV] ♿	38	●	■	●	■
PARICUTÍN: *Centro Turístico de Angahuan* $ Centro Turístico de Angahuan, Camino al Paricutín. ☎ & [FAX] *(452) 523 39 34.* Close to the Paricutín volcano, these rustic cabins have fireplaces and wonderful terrace views of the lava fields and the volcano *(see p205)*.	9		■		■
PÁTZCUARO: *Posada la Basílica* $$$$ Arciga 6. ☎ *(434) 342 11 08.* [FAX] *(434) 342 06 59.* @ *hotelpb@hotmail.com* This colonial hotel stands opposite the church. It has a lovely courtyard, large rooms with fireplaces and antique furniture, and a terrace with a panoramic view of the city, the mountains, and the lake. [TV]	12	●	■		■
PUERTO VALLARTA: *Rosita* $$$ Paseo Díaz Ordáz 901. ☎ *(322) 223 20 00.* [FAX] *(322) 223 43 93.* @ *ventas@hotelrosita.com* At one end of the *malecón* is the oldest hotel in Puerto Vallarta, built in 1948. Most of the rooms have an ocean view and a balcony. [≡] ♿	115	●		●	■

For key to symbols see back flap

	Number of Rooms	**Credit Cards Accepted**	**Private Parking**	**Swimming Pool**	**Restaurant**
Price categories for a standard double room per night in the tourist season, including tax and service: Ⓢ under US$25 ⓈⓈ US$25–40 ⓈⓈⓈ US$40–80 ⓈⓈⓈⓈ US$80–140 ⓈⓈⓈⓈⓈ over US$140 / **CREDIT CARDS ACCEPTED** One or more of the following credit cards are accepted: American Express, Diners Club, MasterCard, or VISA. / **PRIVATE PARKING** The hotel has its own parking lot or parking spaces. These may not be on the same premises and are not necessarily locked. / **SWIMMING POOL** The pool is outdoors unless otherwise stated in the text. / **RESTAURANT** This is not necessarily recommended, although particularly good hotel restaurants are also listed in the restaurant section.					
PUERTO VALLARTA: *Bugambilias Sheraton* ⓈⓈⓈⓈⓈ Francisco Medina Ascencio 999. **(** *(322) 226 04 04.* **FAX** *(322) 222 05 00.* **W** *www.sheratonvallarta.com* A luxurious, beachside hotel with two swimming pools, ample gardens, a gym, a spa, and four tennis courts. ▤ 📺 ♿	960	●	▨	●	▨
QUERÉTARO: *La Casa de la Marquesa* ⓈⓈⓈⓈⓈ Madero 41. **(** *(442) 212 00 92.* **FAX** *(442) 212 00 98.* **W** *www.lacasadelamarquesa.com* Housed in an 18th-century Baroque mansion in front of the Iglesia de Santa Clara, this spectacular and well-maintained hotel has a lovely courtyard, antique furniture, and a private chapel. ▤ 📺	25	●	▨		
REAL DE CATORCE: *El Mesón de la Abundancia* ⓈⓈⓈ Lanzagorta 11. **(** *(488) 887 50 44.* **FAX** *(488) 887 50 45.* **@** *hotelabundancia@hotmail.com* This rustic family-run hotel, built in the former 19th-century treasury, has kept its original doors, keys, and furniture.	11	●			▨
SAN BLAS: *Garza Canela* ⓈⓈⓈⓈ Paredes 106 Sur. **(** & **FAX** *(323) 285 01 12.* **W** *www.garzacanela.com* Close to the beach is this pleasant, modern hotel set in large gardens. It has a handicraft boutique, and a good restaurant *(see p322).* ▤ 📺 ♿	45	●	▨	●	▨
SAN JUAN DEL RÍO: *Fiesta Americana Hacienda Galindo* ⓈⓈⓈⓈⓈ Carretera San Juan del Río–Amealco, 5 km (3 miles) S. **(** *(427) 271 82 00.* **FAX** *(427) 275 09 99.* This former 16th-century hacienda features a collection of altarpieces. Rooms have balconies. Outside are gardens, tennis courts, and stables. ▤ 📺 ♿	168	●	▨	●	▨
SAN LUIS POTOSÍ: *Westin San Luis Potosí* ⓈⓈⓈⓈⓈ Avenida Real de Lomas 1000, Lomas IV Sección. **(** *(444) 825 01 25.* **FAX** *(444) 825 02 00.* **W** *www.westinslp.com.mx* Elegance and formal service are hallmarks of this luxurious, colonial-style hotel. The rooms have high-vaulted ceilings and antique furniture. ▤ 📺 ♿	123	●	▨	●	▨
SAN MIGUEL DE ALLENDE: *Casa Luna* ⓈⓈⓈⓈ Pila Seca 11. **(** & **FAX** *(415) 152 11 17.* **@** *casaluna@unisono.net.mx* A restored, 17th-century colonial house with thick walls, high ceilings, and a courtyard with a fountain. The rooms have fireplaces and antiques.	9	●			
SAN MIGUEL DE ALLENDE: *La Casa de Liza en el Parque* ⓈⓈⓈⓈⓈ Bajada del Chorro 7, El Chorro. **(** *(415) 152 03 52.* **FAX** *(415) 152 61 44.* **@** *casaliza@unisono.net.mx* These guesthouses, situated in the gardens of a 17th-century hacienda, have been tastefully restored and decorated with antiques and altarpieces. 📺	7	●	▨	●	
SAN MIGUEL DE ALLENDE: *Casa de Sierra Nevada* ⓈⓈⓈⓈⓈ Hospicio 35. **(** & **FAX** *(415) 152 70 40.* **@** *sierranevada@prodigy.net.mx* The small but luxurious Sierra Nevada is made up of several adjoining 16th-century mansions. Most of the rooms have patios. ▤ 📺	33	●	▨	●	▨
SIERRA GORDA: *Misión Concá* ⓈⓈⓈⓈ El Salitrillo, Mex 69. **(** *01800 029 42 40.* **FAX** *01800 029 42 41.* **W** *www.hotelesmision.com.mx* This is an 18th-century hacienda where most of the rooms have balconies overlooking the extensive grounds crisscrossed by streams.	75	●	▨	●	▨
TLAQUEPAQUE: *La Villa del Ensueño* ⓈⓈⓈⓈ Florida 305. **(** *(33) 3635 87 92.* **FAX** *(33) 3659 61 52.* **@** *ensueno1@prodigy.net.mx* A 17th-century, colonial-style bed-and-breakfast with flower-filled patios, fountains, and statues. The rooms are tastefully decorated.	18	●	▨	●	▨
URUAPAN: *Mansión del Cupatitzio* ⓈⓈⓈⓈ Parque Nacional. **(** *(452) 523 21 00.* **FAX** *(452) 524 67 72.* **@** *reservaciones@mansioncupatitzio.com* The service is friendly at this flower-decked hotel situated at the edge of the Cupatitzio National Park. 📺 ♿	57	●	▨	●	▨

ZACATECAS: *Hostal del Vasco* $$$
Avenida Velazco 1. ☎ & [FAX] *(492) 922 04 28.* @ *lelijo3@prodigy.net.mx*
This hotel is housed in a 17th-century, colonial mansion with a covered courtyard filled with flowers. Most of the rooms have balconies. ▤ [TV] ♿

18	●	■		

ZACATECAS: *Mesón de Jobito* $$$$$
Jardín Juárez 143. ☎ *(492) 924 17 22.* [FAX] *(492) 924 35 00.* @ *hmjobito@loginet.com.mx*
This small, intimate, and engaging hotel is housed in a two-story 19th-century dwelling. Rooms are tastefully decorated and furnished. ▤ [TV]

31	●			■

ZACATECAS: *Quinta Real* $$$$$
Avenida Rayón 434. ☎ *(492) 922 91 04.* [FAX] *(492) 922 84 40.* @ *reserv-zac@quinta-real.com*
At the foot of the aqueduct, this unique hotel was built on the site of the old bullring. It has an outdoor restaurant, La Plaza, and large and luxurious rooms with bathtubs or Jacuzzis. ▤ [TV] ♿

49	●	■		■

ZITÁCUARO: *Rancho San Cayetano* @ *ranchosancayetano@hotmail.com* $$$
Mex 51, 2.5 km (1.5 miles) S. ☎ *(715) 153 19 26.* [FAX] *(715) 153 78 79.*
This rustic country inn has well-kept gardens filled with fruit trees, a restaurant with a fireplace *(see p323)*, and spacious rooms. ♿

12	●	■	●	■

SOUTHERN MEXICO

ACAPULCO: *Malibú* @ *acamal@delta.acabtu.com.mx* $$$$$
Costera Miguel Alemán 20. ☎ *(744) 484 10 70.* [FAX] *(744) 484 09 94.*
A waterfront hotel with a family atmosphere, in two circular buildings. The octagonal rooms have terraces and refrigerators. ▤ [TV] ♿

80	●		●	■

ACAPULCO: *El Mirador* $$$$
Plazoleta La Quebrada 74. ☎ *(744) 483 11 55.* [FAX] *(744) 482 45 64.*
[W] *www.hotelelmiradoracapulco.com.mx* Ask for a room with a balcony for a view of the ocean and of the famous cliff divers at La Quebrada *(see p219)*. ▤ [TV]

133	●	■	●	■

ACAPULCO: *Las Brisas* [W] *www.brisas.com.mx* $$$$$
Ctra Escénica Clemente Mejía 5255. ☎ *(744) 469 69 00.* [FAX] *(744) 446 53 28*
Ideal for honeymooners, this exclusive pink-and-white estate on a hillside offers terraced *casitas* with views of the ocean. It has private and shared swimming pools where fresh flowers are scattered daily. ▤

263	●	■	●	■

ACAPULCO: *Hyatt* $$$$$
Costera Miguel Alemán 1, Icacos. ☎ *(744) 469 12 34.* [FAX] *(744) 484 30 87.*
[W] *www.hyattacapulco.com.mx*
A modern, beachside hotel with great ocean views. ▤ [TV] ♿

640	●	■	●	■

HUATULCO: *Barceló Huatulco Beach Resort* $$$$$
Paseo Benito Juárez. ☎ *(958) 581 00 55.* [FAX] *(958) 581 01 13.* [W] *www.barcelo.com*
This modern, six-story beachfront hotel has three restaurants, four tennis courts, and a fitness center with steam bath and sauna. The rooms have balconies, and are decorated in contemporary Mexican style. ▤ [TV] ♿

347	●	■	●	■

IXTAPA: *Radisson Resort* $$$$$
Boulevard Ixtapa 5-A. ☎ *(755) 553 00 03.* [FAX] *(755) 553 15 55.* [W] *www.radisson.com*
Situated next to the golf course, this modern hotel has spacious rooms with pastel walls and balconies overlooking the sea. ▤ [TV] ♿

275	●	■	●	■

OAXACA: *Las Golondrinas* $$
Corner of Tinoco & Palacios 411. ☎ *(951) 514 32 98.* @ *lasgolon@prodigy.net.mx*
This picturesque Oaxacan house has rooms with tiled floors surrounding interior patios filled with bougainvillea, roses, and banana trees.

24				

OAXACA: *Calesa Real* $$$$
García Vigil 306. ☎ *(951) 516 55 44.* [FAX] *(951) 516 72 32.* @ *cale7310@prodigy.net.mx*
This colonial hotel has spacious rooms. The terrace and restaurant overlook the swimming pool in the pleasant courtyard. [TV] ♿

78	●	■	●	■

OAXACA: *Hostal de la Noria* $$$$$
Avenida Hidalgo 918. ☎ *(951) 514 78 28.* [FAX] *(951) 516 39 92.* [W] *www.lanoria.com.mx*
Two blocks from the main plaza, this hotel is decorated in Oaxacan style. It has a courtyard restaurant and rooms with high ceilings. ▤ [TV]

50	●	■	●	■

OAXACA: *Victoria* [W] *www.hotelvictoriaoax.com.mx* $$$$
Lomas del Fortín 1, Mex 150. ☎ *(951) 515 26 33.* [FAX] *(951) 515 24 11.*
Surrounded by landscaped gardens, the Victoria offers one of the best views of the city. The rooms are furnished in a modern style. ▤ [TV]

150	●	■	●	■

For key to symbols see back flap

Price categories for a standard double room per night in the tourist season, including tax and service:

- $ under US$25
- $$ US$25–40
- $$$ US$40–80
- $$$$ US$80–140
- $$$$$ over US$140

CREDIT CARDS ACCEPTED
One or more of the following credit cards are accepted: American Express, Diners Club, MasterCard, or VISA.

PRIVATE PARKING
The hotel has its own parking lot or parking spaces. These may not be on the same premises and are not necessarily locked.

SWIMMING POOL
The pool is outdoors unless otherwise stated in the text.

RESTAURANT
This is not necessarily recommended, although particularly good hotel restaurants are also listed in the restaurant section.

Hotel		Number of Rooms	Credit Cards Accepted	Private Parking	Swimming Pool	Restaurant
OAXACA: *Camino Real* — $$$$$ 5 de Mayo No. 300. (951) 516 06 11. FAX (951) 516 07 32. @ oax@caminoreal.com Occupying a 16th-century, former convent, this luxury hotel has beautiful courtyards and exceptionally comfortable rooms. 目 TV 占		91	●		●	■
PALENQUE: *Hotel Palenque* @ hpalenque@dtcmexico.com — $$$ Avenida 5 de Mayo No. 15. (916) 345 01 88. FAX (916) 345 00 39. Located next to the church, Palenque is the oldest hotel in town. The rooms have Maya-style decoration and overlook a central courtyard. 目 占		35	●	■		■
PALENQUE: *Ciudad Real* — $$$$ Pakalna, Mex 199. (916) 345 13 15. FAX (916) 345 13 43. @ reserve@ciudadreal.com.mx Ten km (6 miles) from the ruins (see p234–7), this pleasant hotel has a restaurant and cozy rooms surrounding a large pool. 目 TV 占		72	●	■	●	■
PUERTO ANGEL: *La Buena Vista* — $$ Calle de la Buena Compañía. & FAX (958) 584 31 04. @ adriangc@prodigy.net.mx Every room in this plant-filled hotel, located on a hillside, has a mosquito screen, fan, balcony, and hammock, and is spotlessly clean.		23		■		
PUERTO ESCONDIDO: *Flor de María* — $$$ Playa Marinero. (954) 582 05 36. FAX (954) 582 26 17. @ pajope@hotmail.com This Mediterranean-style hotel has a good restaurant, and tiled rooms artistically decorated by the owner with murals and *trompe l'oeil*.		24	●		●	■
PUERTO ESCONDIDO: *Santa Fé* W www.hotelsantafe.com.mx — $$$$$ C del Morro, Marinero. (954) 582 01 70. FAX (954) 582 02 60. This colonial-style hotel has eight bungalows with kitchens, and well-designed rooms with terraces. An excellent restaurant offers vegetarian and seafood specialties, and there are two courtyard swimming pools. 目 TV 占		59	●	■	●	■
SAN CRISTÓBAL DE LAS CASAS: *Ciudad Real Centro Histórico* — $$$ Plaza 31 de Marzo 10. (967) 678 04 64 FAX (967) 678 57 40. @ reserve@ciudadreal.com.mx A Neo-Classical hotel centrally located on the south side of the main square, with a traditional restaurant in a covered courtyard. TV		31	●	■		■
SAN CRISTÓBAL DE LAS CASAS: *Mansión de los Angeles* — $$$ Francisco I. Madero 17. & FAX (967) 678 43 71. @ hotelangeles@prodigy.net.mx This three-story hotel, half a block from the *zócalo*, has vaulted ceilings, and carpeted rooms, with rustic furniture facing the lovely courtyard. TV		20	●	■		■
SAN CRISTÓBAL DE LAS CASAS: *Santa Clara* — $$$ Insurgentes 1, corner of Plaza Central. (967) 678 11 40. FAX (967) 678 11 40. @ hotelstaclara@hotmail.com This colonial hotel was once the 16th-century hacienda of Don Diego de Masariegos and is conveniently located in the old heart of the city. TV		38	●	■		■
TUXTLA GUTIÉRREZ: *Bonampak* — $$$ Blvd Belisario Domínguez 180, Colonia Moctezuma. (961) 602 59 25. FAX (961) 602 59 14. This large, comfortable hotel features a reproduction of the murals of Bonampak (see p232). There is also a tropical garden. 目 TV 占		70	●	■	●	■
ZIHUATANEJO: *La Casa que Canta* — $$$$$ Camino Escénico a Playa la Ropa. (755) 555 70 30. FAX (755) 554 79 00. @ lacasaquecanta@prodigy.net.mx This luxurious hideaway, perched on a cliffside, is considered by some as the most beautiful hotel in the country. The rooms have gorgeous views. 目		24	●	■	●	■
ZIHUATANEJO: *Villa del Sol* — $$$$$ Playa la Ropa. (755) 554 32 39. FAX (755) 554 27 58. @ hotel@villasol.com.mx This small but deluxe beachfront hotel set among lush gardens and waterfalls offers superb facilities. Reserve well in advance. 目 TV		70	●	■	●	■

THE GULF COAST

CATEMACO: *La Finca* $$$$ 57
Laguna de Catemaco, Carretera 180. [& FAX *(294) 943 03 22.* @ *lafinca@lafinca.com.mx*
The rooms in this modern hotel have terraces overlooking the gardens and
the lake. There is a pool with a waterfall, Jacuzzi, and water slide. ▤ TV &

CHACHALACAS: *Chachalacas* $$$$ 96
Playa de Chachalacas. [& FAX *(296) 962 52 36.*
Eight km (five miles) from the Cempoala ruins, this beachfront hotel has
two swimming pools, a water slide, and a basketball court. ▤ TV &

COATEPEC: *Posada Coatepec* @ *poscoa@prodigy.net.mx* $$$$ 23
Hidalgo 9, corner of Aldama. [*(228) 816 06 70.* FAX *(228) 816 00 40.*
Situated near the *zócalo*, this exquisitely converted colonial mansion is
now a beautiful hotel with courtyards, original painted friezes, and tiled
rooms decorated with antiques. TV &

CÓRDOBA: *Real Villa Florida* @ *vflorida@ver1.telmex.net.mx* $$$ 81
Avenida 1 No. 3002. [*(271) 716 33 33.* FAX *(271) 716 33 36.*
A modern hotel with delightful gardens and well decorated rooms,
some of which have private swimming pools or Jacuzzis. ▤ TV

ORIZABA: *Fiesta Cascada* @ *fcascada@prodigy.net.mx* $$$ 51
Mex 150, 3 km (2 miles) N. [*(272) 724 15 96.* FAX *(272) 724 55 99.*
Right beside the waterfall of Cascada del Elefante, this colonial-style hotel
has large gardens, a tennis court, and a swimming pool. TV

PAPANTLA: *Provincia Express* $$$ 20
Juan Enríquez 103. [*(784) 842 16 45.* FAX *(784) 842 42 14.*
@ *hotprovi@prodigy.net.mx* Some of the large bedrooms in this hotel have
small balconies overlooking the main square. ▤ TV

SANTIAGO TUXTLA: *Castellanos* $$ 53
Calle Comonfort, corner of 5 de Mayo [& FAX *(294) 947 04 00.*
This modern hotel, set in a circular building on the north side of the
zócalo, has spacious and clean rooms with fine views. ▤ TV &

TLACOTALPAN: *Doña Lala* $$$ 36
Carranza 11. [& FAX *(288) 884 25 80.*
This 19th-century family-run hotel, opposite the Papaloapan River, used
to be a casino. It has a good restaurant (*see p325*) and comfortable
rooms, 20 of which have balconies and traditional furniture. ▤ TV

VERACRUZ: *Mocambo* $$$$ 103
Calzada Ruíz Cortines 4000, Boca del Río. [*(229) 922 02 00.* FAX *(229) 922 02 12.*
W *www.hotelmocambo.com.mx*
The Mocambo was built in the 1930s with Art Deco and Moorish influences.
It has swimming pools, a sauna and Jacuzzi, and tennis courts. ▤ TV &

VERACRUZ: *Colonial* $$$ 185
Lerdo 117. [*(229) 932 01 93.* FAX *(229) 932 24 65.* @ *hcolonial@infosel.net.mx*
Right on the Plaza de Armas, this colonial hotel has bright rooms, an
indoor pool, and a beautiful view from the top-floor bar. ▤ TV &

VILLAHERMOSA: *Best Western Maya Tabasco* $$$$$ 154
Avenida Ruíz Cortines 907. [*(993) 312 11 11.* FAX *(993) 312 10 97.*
This modern hotel caters mainly to business travelers. It has tropical
gardens, and carpeted rooms decorated with rustic furniture. ▤ TV &

VILLAHERMOSA: *Cencali* $$$$ 120
Cnr of Juárez & Paseo Tabasco. [& FAX *(993) 315 19 99.* @ *cencali@cencali.com.mx*
Next to the Laguna de las Ilusiones, this hacienda-style hotel has
gardens and comfortable rooms with balconies. ▤ TV &

XALAPA: *María Victoria* $$$ 114
Zaragoza 6. [& FAX *(228) 818 66 56.* @ *mariavic@gorsa.net.mx*
This six-story hotel behind the Palacio de Gobierno has a colonial façade,
small, carpeted rooms, and a restaurant-bar with live music. ▤ TV

XALAPA: *Mesón del Alférez* @ *mesonalferez@hotmail.com* $$$ 28
Corner of Zaragoza & Sebastián Camacho. [*(228) 818 63 51.* FAX *(228) 812 47 03.*
Built in the 18th century, this is the former house of the Spanish Viceroy's
representative. The rooms have their original doors. TV &

For key to symbols see back flap

Price categories for a standard double room per night in the tourist season, including tax and service:

Ⓢ under US$25
ⓈⓈ US$25–40
ⓈⓈⓈ US$40–80
ⓈⓈⓈⓈ US$80–140
ⓈⓈⓈⓈⓈ over US$140

CREDIT CARDS ACCEPTED
One or more of the following credit cards are accepted: American Express, Diners Club, MasterCard, or VISA.

PRIVATE PARKING
The hotel has its own parking lot or parking spaces. These may not be on the same premises and are not necessarily locked.

SWIMMING POOL
The pool is outdoors unless otherwise stated in the text.

RESTAURANT
This is not necessarily recommended, although particularly good hotel restaurants are also listed in the restaurant section.

THE YUCATÁN PENINSULA

	NUMBER OF ROOMS	CREDIT CARDS ACCEPTED	PRIVATE PARKING	SWIMMING POOL	RESTAURANT
AKUMAL: *Club Akumal Caribe (Villas Maya Club)* ⓈⓈⓈ Mex 307, 104 km (65 miles) S of Cancún. ☎ (984) 875 90 12. FAX (984) 875 90 15. @ clubakumal@aol.com Beachfront bungalows with comfortable furniture, pretty tiled floors, and well-equipped kitchens. Diving and watersports are available. ▤ ♿	61	●	▥	●	▥
BACALAR: *Rancho Encantado* ⓦ www.encantado.com ⓈⓈⓈⓈ Carretera Bacalar–Carrillo Puerto, 3 km (1.5 miles) N. ☎ & FAX (983) 831 00 37. These lakeside *casitas* are decorated with folk art, Zapotec rugs, murals, and mahogany furniture. Prices include breakfast and dinner. ♿	13	●	▥	●	
CAMPECHE: *Baluartes* ⓈⓈⓈ Avenida 16 de Septiembre 128. ☎ (981) 816 39 11. FAX (981) 816 24 10. ⓦ www.baluartes.com.mx One block from the *zócalo*, this colonial-style hotel has a beautiful façade and modern interiors where every room has a view. ▤ TV ♿	104	●	▥	●	▥
CANCÚN: *Hilton Cancún Golf and Beach Resort* ⓈⓈⓈⓈ Retorno Lacandones, 17 km (10.5 miles) S. ☎ (998) 881 80 00. FAX (998) 881 80 80. ⓦ www.hiltoncancun.com This resort has a pyramid construction and a 18-hole golf course. ▤ TV ♿	426	●	▥	●	▥
CANCÚN: *Camino Real* @ cun@caminoreal.com ⓈⓈⓈⓈ Blvd Kukulcán, Punta Cancún. ☎ (998) 848 70 00. FAX (998) 848 70 01. This peaceful hotel, in a spectacular setting, has Mexican architecture, a private saltwater lagoon with sea turtles, and a private beach. ▤ TV ♿	381	●	▥	●	▥
CANCÚN: *Casa Turquesa* ⓈⓈⓈⓈ Boulevard Kukulcán, 13.5 km (8.5 miles) S. ☎ (998) 885 29 24. FAX (998) 885 29 22. @ Info@casaturquesa.com This elegant, Mexican-style mansion, decorated with a wonderful collection of Latin American art, has spacious suites with private balconies. ▤ TV ♿	37	●	▥	●	▥
CANCÚN: *Krystal Cancún* ⓈⓈⓈⓈ Boulevard Kukulcán, 9 km (5.5 miles) S. ☎ (998) 883 11 33. FAX (998) 883 17 90. ⓦ www.nh.hoteles.com Superbly located in Punta Cancún, this modern luxury hotel, decorated in marble and wood, has four good restaurants, and a popular disco. ▤ TV ♿	325	●	▥	●	▥
CANCÚN: *Melia Cancún Beach & Spa Resort* ⓈⓈⓈⓈ Boulevard Kukulcán 16.5 km (10 miles) S. ☎ (998) 881 11 00. FAX (998) 881 17 40. @ reservas.melia.cancun@solmelia.com This luxurious resort with glass pyramids has a large plant-filled atrium, a fitness center, watersports facilities, and tennis courts. ▤ TV ♿	800	●	▥	●	▥
CANCÚN: *Ritz-Carlton* ⓈⓈⓈⓈ Retorno del Rey 36, Zona Hotelera. ☎ (998) 881 08 08. FAX (998) 881 07 72. @ emartinez@rc-cancun.com.mx This elegant hotel has a fitness center with sauna and steam baths, and sumptuous rooms, all with balconies overlooking the Caribbean. ▤ TV ♿	365	●	▥	●	▥
CHETUMAL: *Holiday Inn Puerta Maya* @ hotel@holidayinnmaya.com.mx ⓈⓈⓈ Avenida Héroes 171-A. ☎ (983) 835 04 00. FAX (983) 832 16 07. This modern hotel with Maya decor has a courtesy service providing transportation to and from the airport. Tours to Belize can be arranged. ▤ TV ♿	85	●	▥	●	▥
CHICHÉN ITZÁ: *Villas Arqueológicas* ⓈⓈⓈ Mex 180, SE of archaeological site. ☎ (985) 856 60 00. FAX (985) 856 60 08. ⓦ www.clubmedvillas.com A Club Med hotel built around a courtyard with a swimming pool shaded by colorful flame trees. It has small but comfortable rooms, tennis courts, a library, and a good restaurant (*see p326*). ▤ ♿	40	●	▥	●	▥

COBÁ: *Villas Arqueológicas* $$$ 43
Carretera a Valladolid, 42 km (26 miles) S of Tulúm. 📞 & FAX *(985) 858 15 27.*
Just an eight-minute walk from the Cobá ruins *(see p284–5)* is this
lakeside Club Med hotel with beautiful gardens, a tennis court, and
rooms built around a courtyard containing a swimming pool. 🟦 &

COZUMEL: *Meliá Cozumel* $$$$$ 212
Ctra Costera Norte. 📞 *(987) 872 04 11.* FAX *(987) 872 15 99.*
@ *reservas.paradisus.cozumel@solmelia.com*
This all-inclusive first-class hotel is surrounded by gardens, and offers
horseback riding, kayaking and windsurfing, cycling, and a gym. 🟦 📺

COZUMEL: *Playa Azul* $$$$$ 50
Carretera a San Juan, 4km (3 miles) N. 📞 *(987) 872 00 33.* FAX *(987) 872 01 10.*
@ *playazul@playa-azul.com*
At the north end of the island of Cozumel, this family-run hotel features a
restaurant with a waterfront terrace. The beach is a short walk away. 🟦 &

ISLA MUJERES: *D'Gomar* $$$ 19
Avenida Rueda Medina 150. 📞 & FAX *(998) 877 05 41.*
A inexpensive hotel facing the ferry pier. The rooms have rattan
furniture and huge windows to let in the breeze. 🟦 &

MÉRIDA: *El Gran Hotel* $$$ 32
Calle 60 No. 496. 📞 *(999) 923 69 63.* FAX *(999) 924 76 22.* @ *granh@sureste.com*
This picturesque hotel, opposite the Iglesia de San Ildefonso, was built
in 1901. The carpeted rooms have high ceilings and balconies. 🟦 📺

MÉRIDA: *Los Aluxes* $$$$ 155
Calle 60 No. 444. 📞 *(999) 924 21 99.* FAX *(999) 923 38 58.* @ *aluxes@pibil.finred.com.mx*
Close to the popular Parque Santa Lucía, this modern colonial-style hotel has
mural paintings of pre-Columbian culture, and a botanical garden. 🟦 📺 &

MÉRIDA: *Casa del Balam* $$$$ 52
Calle 60 No. 488. 📞 *(999) 924 88 44.* FAX *(999) 924 50 11.* @ *balamhtl@finred.com.mx*
This charming, colonial-style hotel with carved stone arches, marble floors,
and a beautiful 18th-century courtyard, is decorated with antiques. 🟦 📺 &

PLAYA DEL CARMEN: *Continental Plaza* @ *info@mtmcorp.com* $$$$$ 185
Fraccionamiento Playacar, Mex 307. 📞 *(984) 873 01 00.* FAX *(984) 873 01 05.*
A Mediterranean-style, beachfront hotel close to the ferry pier, decorated
with pre-Columbian items found during its construction. 🟦 📺 &

PUERTO AVENTURAS: *Oasis Puerto Aventuras* $$$$$ 296
Mex 307, 90 km (56 miles) S of Cancún. 📞 *(984) 873 50 50.* FAX *(984) 873 50 51.*
@ *dirpuerto@oasishotels.com.mx* This all-inclusive resort offers the use of bicycles,
a gym, a tennis court, diving facilities, a supermarket, and a disco. 🟦 📺

PUNTA ALLEN: *Cuzan Guest House* $$$$ 12
Mex 307, 50 km (31 miles) S of Cancún. 📞 & FAX *(983) 834 02 92.*
w *www.flyfishmx.com*
Rustic seafront *cabañas* surrounded by palm trees, each with a porch for
hanging hammocks. There are six boats for snorkeling and fishing.

PUNTA BETE: *La Posada del Capitán Lafitte* $$$$$ 62
Mex 307, 62 km (39 miles) S of Cancún. 📞 *(984) 873 02 14.* FAX *(984) 873 02 12.*
@ *lafitte@qroo1.telmex.net.mx*
Each of these peaceful bungalows has a porch with a hammock
overlooking the Caribbean. Breakfast and dinner are included. 🟦 &

RÍO BEC: *Chicanná Ecovillage Resort* $$$$ 32
Mex 186, 144 km (90 miles) E of Campeche. 📞 *(981) 816 22 33.* FAX *(981) 811 16 18.*
w *www.hoteldelmar.com.mx*
These cottages, with Polynesian-style architecture and nicely furnished
rooms, are close to the Río Bec archaeological sites *(see p287)*.

TULÚM: *Acuario & Cabañas Cristina's* @ *hotel_acuario@yahoo.com.mx* $$$ 32
Mex 307, 127 km (79 miles) S of Cancún. 📞 & FAX *(984) 871 21 94.*
This two-story family-run hotel is within walking distance of the ruins. 🟦 📺

VALLADOLID: *El Mesón del Marqués* $$$ 72
Calle 39 No. 203. 📞 *(985) 856 20 73.* FAX *(985) 856 22 80.* @ *h_marques@chichen.com.mx*
Located opposite the cathedral, this colonial hotel has a 17th-century
courtyard and a restaurant *(see p327)* with a fountain at its center. 🟦 📺

For key to symbols see back flap

WHERE TO EAT

MEXICAN CUISINE is considered by many to be one of the world's richest and most creative. Chiefly a mix of Spanish and pre-Columbian elements, it has been influenced more recently by other European and Asian flavors. Dishes originating from all corners of the country are served in a wide variety of restaurants. Visitors will find authentic Mexican cuisine different from the "Tex-Mex" Mexican food they may be used to at home. For one thing, it is not necessarily as spicy. However, those who prefer it still milder can order their meals without chili (*sin chile*). In the big cities there are a good number of French and Italian restaurants, as well as other international options, such as Japanese sushi, Argentinian steaks, and Chinese chop suey. Vegetarian restaurants are rare, but many ordinary Mexican dishes, especially *antojitos (see p310)*, are meat-free.

Waitress with bread and pastries

Outdoor café at Parque Cepeda Peraza in Mérida *(see p270)*

TYPICAL RESTAURANTS AND BARS

THE CHEAPEST PLACES to eat good Mexican food are the small, family-run *fondas* where fixed-price menus (*menú del día* or *comida corrida*) are served at lunch time. These are generally four-course meals followed by coffee or tea.

The most common restaurants are the popular *taquerías*, small places serving tacos at a few tables around a cooking area, where the tortilla-makers can often be seen in action. Cantinas *(see p116)* are rowdy establishments where heavy drinking is common, and women will not generally feel very comfortable. They can be differentiated from other, more elegant bars, by their Wild West-style swing doors.

The big cities also have a good selection of cafés, which generally serve light snacks rather than three course meals.

CHAIN RESTAURANTS

ALL THE PRINCIPAL US fast-food chains are conspicuous in Mexico, including McDonald's, Burger King, KFC, and Pizza Hut. These days, however, there are also a number of good homegrown chains. One of the most famous is VIPS, which offers great breakfasts and international dishes like steaks and burgers. These are true fast-food restaurants – customers are not encouraged to linger. Carlos and Charlie's and Señor Frog's serve similar food to VIPS, but have a more relaxed, party atmosphere.

Those who fancy some shopping with their meal should try one of the many branches of Sanborn's where CDs, books, magazines, and videos are sold alongside the restaurant. The specialties here are the *enchiladas (see p310)*.

Other chains are more typically Mexican. Taco Inn serves tasty and original tacos, as well as a good range of vegetarian options. El Fogoncito sells *tacos al carbon (see p311)*. Potzolcalli specializes in *pozole (see p311)* and *tostadas (see p310)*, while Pollos Río offers a selection of grilled chicken dishes.

One of the Sanborn's chain, in the Casa de los Azulejos *(see p314)*

FOOD HYGIENE

IN WELL-VISITED areas of Mexico, health standards are reasonably good, but it is still worth taking precautions. Drink only purified water, canned or bottled carbonated drinks, beer, wine, spirits, or hot drinks made from boiled water. Bottled water is available in restaurants, hotels, drugstores, and supermarkets. In restaurants and bars, order drinks without ice (*sin hielo*). Diners should avoid salads and uncooked vegetables in all but the best restaurants

A rustic roadside café near Laguna de Chapala *(see p190)*

Interior of the charming Café Tacuba *(see p314)*, in the historic heart of Mexico City

and remember to peel all fruit. It is also best to steer well clear of unpasteurized milk and undercooked shellfish, meat, or fish. Open-air markets and street food stalls should be treated with caution.

EATING HOURS

THE STREETS are always full of food vendors because Mexicans will eat at any time of day. They often have two breakfasts *(desayunos)*. The first, eaten at home, is a light meal of fruit or pastries with milky coffee. A more substantial breakfast, or *almuerzo*, may follow between 10 and 11am and is usually available in restaurants until lunchtime. It may consist of spicy eggs with tortillas, or even a steak.

From about 1:30pm restaurants are ready to provide lunch *(comida)*, traditionally the main meal of the day. Mexicans take two or three hours for lunch, so restaurants are busy until 4 or 5pm.

Between 6 and 8pm is the *merienda*, a time for snacks, or *antojitos (see p310)*, and coffee, tea, or alcoholic drinks. A normal Mexican dinner *(cena)* at home is a light meal served between 8 and 10pm. However, restaurants will also serve more substantial dinners.

Although many restaurants are open all year round, some close for various public holidays *(see p31)*.

ENTERTAINMENT

MEXICANS LIKE their meals accompanied by music, and many restaurants have live acts performing at least once a week. The music ranges from classical piano to local styles such as festive *mariachi (see p28)*, with dancers in colorful costumes, *jarocho* songs from Veracruz, and Mexican-style country music known as *música ranchera*.

PRICES AND PAYING

FIXED-PRICE MENUS such as *comida corrida* normally offer better value than the à la carte equivalent. Prices shown on menus do not include the mandatory 15 percent tax (IVA), but this will automatically be added to your bill. Service charge is not included, and the level of tip is left to diners' discretion. It is usual to tip around 15 percent if you have had good service. You are not obliged to leave anything if the service has been poor.

Credit cards can be used in many restaurants in the larger cities, but in smaller places cash will definitely be necessary. If in doubt, check before ordering. VISA is the most widely accepted card, followed by MasterCard and American Express; few places take Diners Club. Travelers' checks are usually accepted but often at a poor rate of exchange.

WHEELCHAIR ACCESS

HARDLY ANY restaurants in Mexico make any special provision for wheelchair users. The staff in most restaurants will do their best to be helpful, but access is frequently difficult and restaurants with a lavatory that can accommodate a wheelchair are nonexistent.

Tortilla-maker at a traditional restaurant in Oaxaca *(see pp222–5)*

CHILDREN

MEXICANS AS a rule love children and most restaurants welcome them, especially family-run places. Few provide high chairs, however, and there is often little room for maneuvering strollers. Child portions are not usually available, but you can always ask for a spare plate and share a dish between two.

SMOKING

SMOKING IS VERY POPULAR in Mexico, and it is common for people to light up between, or even during, courses. Recently passed laws levying fines for smoking in public places are rarely enforced, and there are few nonsmoking areas in restaurants.

Diners at a thatch-roofed beachside restaurant in Puerto Ángel *(see p217)*

What to Eat in Mexico

MEXICAN FOOD blends the influences of the Old and New Worlds. Many common ingredients (such as tomatoes, chilies, turkey, vanilla, chocolate, and corn) were consumed in pre-Columbian times, whereas others (dairy foods, beef, chicken, wheat, onions, and garlic) were introduced by the Spanish and French. The staples of the north are beans, dried meat, chilies, and wheat-flour tortillas. Less meat is eaten in the south, where food is served with corn tortillas and spicy sauces.

Chili peppers

Huevos rancheros, *fried eggs on fried tortilla, smothered in tomato sauce, make an appetizing breakfast or lunch.*

Orejas

Glaseado

Cuerno (croissant)

Bizcochos *(sweet cakes and cookies) are often eaten for breakfast. Other types include* chilindrinas *and* campechanas.

Tamales *are steamed corn-dough dumplings with meat and chili sauce, wrapped in corn husks or banana leaves.*

Chilaquiles *is a popular breakfast dish of tortilla chips in tomato sauce garnished with raw onions and cheese.*

Wheat tortillas

Corn tortillas

Tortillas, *flat wheat or corn pancakes, are a Mexican staple. They are used to roll, dip, scoop, and mop up other foods. Corn tortillas come in various colors.*

Tacos *are warmed or fried tortillas filled with cooked meats, usually topped with guacamole, cream, and sauce.*

Beans, *the main source of fiber and protein in the Mexican diet, are often served refried (refritos) to concentrate the flavor.*

Salsa de chipotle

Salsa mexicana   **Salsa de tomate verde**   **Salsa de jitomate**   **Pickled chilies**

SALSAS

Wherever you eat in Mexico *salsas* (sauces) will be put on the table to enhance the flavor of the dishes. The most common are *salsa cruda* (chopped raw vegetables); *salsa de tomate verde* (green tomatillos, cilantro, and chilies); *salsa de jitomate* (cooked tomato sauce); pickled chilies; and *salsa de chipotle* (smoked jalapeño chilies in a tomato sauce).

Mole poblano, *Mexico's national dish, originated in Puebla (see pp150–53). Cooked turkey meat is covered in a rich dark sauce made with chilies, spices, nuts, and a little bitter chocolate. The same sauce is used for other dishes.*

Ensalada de nopalitos *is made with tender prickly pear leaves, garnished with onions and crumbled white cheese.*

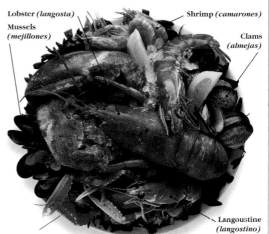

Lobster *(langosta)*
Mussels *(mejillones)*
Shrimp *(camarones)*
Clams *(almejas)*
Langoustine *(langostino)*

Seafood, *abundant, fresh, and delicious, is often served a la plancha (grilled) or al mojo de ajo (with garlic). Varieties include lobster, langoustine (a kind of small lobster), mussels, shrimp, and clams. Eating raw shellfish should be avoided.*

Arroz a la Mexicana, *the main Mexican rice dish, is made tasty and colorful with the addition of peas, carrots, and tomatoes.*

Pescado a la Veracruzana *is a popular and tasty way of preparing red snapper in a tomato, olive, and caper sauce.*

Pollo al pibil, *a Yucatecan specialty, is chicken colored red with* achiote *seasoning (see p311) and steamed in an oven.*

Crepas de cuitlacoche *(huitlacoche) are savory crepes filled with a cooked corn fungus that tastes like mushrooms.*

TROPICAL FRUITS
A huge variety of exotic fruits is grown in Mexico. A plate of mixed fresh fruit can make a wholesome breakfast, a good dessert, or a snack at any time of the day.

Pomegranate kernels
Walnut sauce
Ground meat and almond stuffing
Green chilies

Chiles en nogada *is called the "Independence dish" as its colors are those of the Mexican flag. Green chilies, stuffed with ground meat and almonds, are covered in walnut sauce, and garnished with pomegranate kernels.*

Flan *(crème caramel) is the most popular Mexican dessert. It is found on almost all menus.*

Papaya

Naseberry or sapodilla *(chico zapote)*

Watermelon *(sandía)*

Sweet sop or custard apple *(chirimoya)*

Prickly pear *(tuna)*

Antojitos

MEXICAN APPETIZERS are called *antojitos* and are
similar to Spanish *tapas.* The name derives from
antojo, "a craving" or "whim," and *antojitos* are literally "what you fancy." An *antojito* can be anything from
decoratively presented fruit to a substantial savory dish.
These tasty little snacks are enjoyed everywhere in
Mexico – in homes, bars, restaurants, markets, parks,
and streets – at any time, day or night. An *antojito* can
be ordered as an aperitif with drinks (when it is called
a *botana*) or, in a restaurant, served as a first course.

Tostadas *is an attractive dish
of crispy fried tortillas topped
with refried beans, chicken,
salad, guacamole, soured
cream, or crumbled cheese.*

Scallions
(spring
onions)

Chopped tomato

Totopos

Avocado

Cilantro
(coriander)

Guacamole con totopos *(mashed avocado dip with tortilla chips)
is possibly the most popular Mexican dish. Guacamole is also served
as a filling for tortillas and as a garnish to many main courses.*

Sopes *are miniature fried
corn-dough bowls filled with
beans and sauce, and topped
with cheese. Every region has
its own variety of garnishes.*

Quesadillas *are fried or
grilled corn or wheat tortillas
filled with cheese. Order your
preferred choice from a range
of other fillings.*

Enchiladas, *fried, filled,
rolled tortillas covered in a
sauce, can have a variety of
fillings such as cheese and
onion or chicken.*

Tacos de rajas poblanas *are
soft corn or wheat-flour tortillas
filled with wedges of stewed
chili and slices of onion in a
tomato sauce.*

Enfrijoladas *are lightly fried
tortillas which are folded and
then smothered in a smooth
sauce made with beans. A
variety of toppings is added.*

Empanaditas, *puff pastry
turnovers filled with meat or
tuna fish, may have been introduced to Mexico by miners
from Cornwall, England.*

Tortas compuestas, *tasty
sandwiches made with small
French-style loaves called*
bolillos *or* teleras, *come with
a choice of fillings.*

Reading the Menu

GENERAL VOCABULARY likely to be useful when eating out is given in the *Phrase Book* on pages 381–4. The list below gives the main items and ingredients you will probably see on a Mexican menu, in alphabetical order. Not all regional variations of dishes are listed here. Some dishes commonly thought to be Mexican – burritos, fajitas, taco shells, and nachos – were, in fact, invented in the United States.

Street market in San Cristóbal de las Casas (see p231)

achiote red paste made from annatto seeds.

adobo a light version of *mole* sauce.

albóndigas meatballs.

annatto small, dark red seed used by the Maya Indians to color and flavor food.

ate thick fruit jelly, typically made of quince or guava, often served with cheese.

atún tuna fish. Note that *tuna* is a fruit (see p309).

barbacoa lamb cooked in a pit.

buñuelos a sweet made with crispy, fried wheat pancakes

cajeta de Celaya fudge sauce made with goat's milk.

Varieties of dried chilies

caldo largo soup made with fish and seafood.

carne a la Tampiqueña thin strips of beef, grilled.

carnitas a dish of marinated fried pork.

cecina semi-dried salted meat in thin slices.

ceviche cocktail of raw fish marinated in lime and mixed with onions, chilies, garlic, and tomatoes.

chalupas boat-shaped, fried corn tortillas garnished with sauce, lettuce, and onions.

chicharrón pork scratchings.

chiles rellenos chilies stuffed with cheese or ground meat, battered, fried, and covered in tomato sauce.

chongos milky dessert of curds in syrup and cinnamon.

chorizo spicy pork sausage.

churros sugary fried batter sticks usually served with hot chocolate.

cochinita pibil Maya dish of suckling pig cooked in a *pib*, an oven in the ground.

cuitlacoche (or *huitlacoche*) fungus growing on corncobs.

dulce de calabaza stewed pumpkin in a syrup made with cinnamon.

enchiladas suizas corn tortillas filled with chicken, covered in sauce and garnished with melted cheese and cream.

energético fruit salad with muesli and yogurt. Served for breakfast.

entomatada soft tortilla in a tomato sauce.

epazote aromatic herb used to flavor beans, soups, and other dishes.

flor de calabaza pumpkin flower.

frijoles beans. Often eaten refried (see p308) or freshly cooked as *frijoles de olla*.

gorditas thick tortillas stuffed with cheese.

horno (al) baked.

huevos a la mexicana scrambled eggs with tomatoes, chilies, and onions.

huevos motuleños tortilla topped with ham, fried eggs, and a sauce made with cheese, peas, and tomato.

huevos revueltos scrambled eggs.

jícama a raw vegetable similar to a turnip. It is salted and sprinkled with lime and cayenne pepper.

Ate, served with cheese

machaca sundried shredded beef from the state of Nuevo León.

mole means "sauce" in Nahuatl. All *moles* are made in a similar way using chilies, nuts, and spices. Green, red and yellow *moles* are usually served with pork or chicken.

moros con cristianos a nutritious rice dish made with black beans and garnished with fried plantain.

nopal the fleshy leaf of the prickly pear (paddle cactus).

panucho a Yucatecan dish of layered tortillas stuffed with beans.

pescado al mojo de ajo fish fillet smothered in a white, garlic sauce.

pipián pumpkin-seed sauce.

plátano macho frito fried plantain. Goes well with rice.

pollo verde almendrado chicken in green tomatillo and almond sauce.

pozole pork and corn soup.

puntas de filete quartered beef fillet ends.

queso fresco a white cheese that is crumbled over some cooked dishes.

rajas chili strips and onion slices in tomato sauce.

sopa soup. Varieties include *de aguacate* (avocado), *de fideo* (chicken broth with noodles), and *de lima* (chicken stock flavored with lemon).

tacos al carbón soft corn tortillas wrapped around cooked meats.

tamales corn dumplings or fish or meat wrapped in corn husks or banana leaves and steamed (see p308).

tomatillo a berry related to the Cape gooseberry (*Physalis*), which is used for flavoring sauces.

Veracruzana (a la) fish cooked with tomatoes and onions (see p309).

What to Drink in Mexico

MEXICO OFFERS A WIDE variety of drinks, both alcoholic and nonalcoholic, but choose carefully if you don't want health problems. Never drink tap water, whatever anyone tells you; always buy bottled water from a supermarket or reputable shop. It is wise to avoid fruit juices, milkshakes, and other drinks sold at market and street stalls or in bars of dubious cleanliness. Soft drinks in bottles, cartons, and cans are all safe.

BEER

BEER *(CERVEZA)* WAS introduced to Mexico by German immigrant miners. Much of the beer drunk is lager *(cerveza rubia)*, but there are also several good dark beers *(cerveza oscura)* available. Popular brands are Corona, Negra Modelo, and XX Dos Equis. *Michelada* is a refreshing drink made with beer and lime juice, and served with salt on the rim of the glass.

Light and dark Mexican beers

Cantina La Guadalupana in Mexico City *(see p104)*

OTHER ALCOHOLIC DRINKS

MANY OTHER DRINKS are served in Mexican bars and restaurants, especially *kahlúa,* (a coffee liqueur flavored with vanilla), *ron* (rum), and *rompope,* an eggnog made in Puebla, often offered to children or the elderly. *Aguardiente* is a fiery spirit, not for the faint hearted. Standard international cocktails include piña colada, a refreshing blend of pineapple juice, rum, and coconut, and daiquiri, made with rum, lime juice, and sugar.

Kahlúa   ***Rompope***

HOT DRINKS

COFFEE IS generally medium-strength filter coffee *(café americano)* which can be served with milk. For a strong, authentic Mexican coffee order *café de olla,* sweetened and flavored with cinnamon. Black coffee is *café negro, tinto,* or *solo.* Tea is not widely drunk but herb teas, such as camomile *(manzanilla),* mint *(hierbabuena),* and lemon grass *(té limón),* are available. *Atole* is a nutritious drink of corn meal and milk, flavored with chocolate or fruits. Hot chocolate *(chocolate caliente),* made with vanilla or cinnamon, is also popular.

WINES

ALTHOUGH MEXICO is the oldest wine producer in the Americas, Mexicans are not big wine drinkers. The principal vineyards are in the Valle de Guadalupe near Ensenada *(see p162),* where the pioneer Bodega Santo Tomás is based, as is Monte Xanic. Other Baja California producers include Pinson and Cetto. Wine is also made in Querétaro (by Cavas de San Juan and Domecq) and Zacatecas (by Pinson). Imported wine is available too.

White wine by Domecq

COLD DRINKS AND FRUIT JUICES

THERE ARE PLENTY of soft drinks available, but in a restaurant or bar always make sure you drink from a bottle that has been opened in front of you. Water can be ordered still *(sin gas)* or fizzy *(con gas).* Canned fizzy drinks are called *refrescos.* All the international varieties are available. A selection of freshly prepared fruit juices is also available, but try to choose those made with fruits that need to be peeled. Made like lemonade, *naranjada* is a refreshing orange juice drink. *Agua de Jamaica* is made from a hibiscus flower steeped in hot water.

Agua de Jamaica   **Orange juice**

Atole   ***Café de olla***

Hot chocolate

Tequila and Mezcal

Tequila and mezcal are both internationally known Mexican aperitifs, distilled from the sap of different species of the agave plant. Tequila is to mezcal as Cognac is to brandy – a refined, connoisseur's drink. Both are made from similar ingredients by a similar process, but tequila can be produced only in a strictly defined region that centers on the town of

Statue in Tequila

Tequila near Guadalajara *(see p187)*. Both drinks are distantly derived from pulque, a low-alcohol, fermented beverage made from another species of agave, which was drunk by the people of ancient Mexico. If you stay any length of time in Mexico you will almost certainly be offered at least one glass of mezcal or tequila.

Pulque was first made as early as 200 BC. It was used by priests as a way of inducing a religious trance and given to sacrificial victims to ease their passage into the next world. Pulque, which is never bottled, is an acquired taste.

Buying Tequila and Mezcal

The best tequila is made from 100 percent blue agave: this is stated on the label to prove that sugar has not been added. Tequila comes in three varieties. *Blanco* (white) is unaged, clear, and colorless. *Reposado* and *añejo* are tequilas which have been aged in oak barrels (for up to a year and three years respectively), turning them an amber color. *Mezcal con gusano* is made near Oaxaca. A caterpillar is placed in the bottle to prove that the mezcal is high enough in alcohol to preserve it.

**Mezcal
con gusano**

**Tequila
reposado**

How Tequila is Made

Tequila is made by fermenting the sap of the agave and distilling the resultant mixture twice before bottling.

Stage one The agave (Agave tequilana weber) is harvested after 8–10 years, before it flowers. The leaves are removed, leaving a compact heart or piña *(literally "pineapple").*

Stage two The piñas *are steamed in an oven and crushed to release their sap, the raw material for tequila.*

Stage three Yeast is added to the sap. After a period of fermentation the liquid is distilled twice to purify it. The tequila is then either bottled or aged in oak vats.

How to Drink Tequila

Tequila is usually served with lime and salt or as a *vampiro* with a tomato and orange chaser called a *sangrita. Tequila blanco* is often mixed with other drinks to make cocktails like tequila sunrise (with grenadine and orange juice), and margarita, made with lime juice and triple sec and served with salt around the rim of the glass.

**Tequila with
lime and salt**

Choosing a Restaurant

THE RESTAURANTS in this guide have been selected, as far as possible, for their atmosphere and the excellence of their food. In some parts of Mexico, however, there are no restaurants worth a visit in their own right. In such cases we suggest somewhere to eat which at least offers good value. For details of chain restaurants see p308.

MEXICO CITY

Restaurant	Price	Credit Cards Accepted	Outdoor Tables	Vegetarian Dishes	Live Entertainment
HISTORIC CENTER: *La Casa de los Azulejos – Sanborn's.* **Map** 4 D2. Francisco Madero 4. ☎ *55 12 13 31.* [FAX] *55 18 66 76.* This historic 16th-century mansion, covered in glazed tiles, houses the first and finest restaurant in the Sanborn's chain. Enjoy *enchiladas suizas (see p311)*, invented here, in the attractive courtyard. ▤ ♿ ◯ *B, L, D.*	$$	●	■	●	
HISTORIC CENTER: *Casino Español.* **Map** 4 D5. Isabel la Católica 31. ☎ *55 21 88 94.* [FAX] *55 18 55 57.* Sample the excellent lunch cuisine in this atmospheric venue. Specialties include *zarzuela de mariscos* – seafood in an almond sauce. ▤ ♿ ◯ *L.*	$$	●			
HISTORIC CENTER: *México Viejo.* **Map** 4 E1. Tacuba 87. ☎ *55 10 37 48.* [FAX] *55 21 15 85.* Facing the cathedral, México Viejo is decorated with old photos. Try Suprema Moctezuma, a chicken dish with *cuitlacoche (see p311).* ♿ ◯ *B, L, D.* ● *Sun D.*	$$	●		●	
HISTORIC CENTER: *La Terraza.* **Map** 4 E2. Francisco Madero 73–7. ☎ *55 21 86 00.* [FAX] *55 12 62 62.* Savor the fish au gratin served on a cactus leaf in this restaurant on the seventh floor of the Hotel Majestic. There is a wonderful view of the Zócalo. ◯ *B, L, D.*	$$	●	■		■
HISTORIC CENTER: *Bar La Ópera.* **Map** 4 D1. 5 de Mayo No. 14. ☎ *55 12 89 59.* [FAX] *55 18 35 14.* Guests here can have a drink and eat paella in surroundings in which Mexico's pre-Revolutionary aristocracy would have felt at home. ♿ ◯ *L, D.* ● *Sun D.*	$$$	●			■
HISTORIC CENTER: *Café Tacuba.* **Map** 4 D1. Tacuba 28. ☎ *55 21 20 48.* [FAX] *55 10 88 55.* Founded in 1912, in a 17th-century house, this traditional restaurant has a varied menu, including enchiladas with spinach and long green chilies. ▤ ♿ ◯ *B ,L, D.*	$$$	●		●	■
HISTORIC CENTER: *Los Girasoles.* **Map** 4 D1. Xicoténcatl 1. ☎ *55 10 32 81.* [FAX] *55 10 06 30.* The view of the palaces on the Plaza Manuel Tolsá, the Mediterranean decor, and the haute cuisine recipes (such as chicken breast in three fruit juices) are all part of the appeal of Los Girasoles. ▤ ◯ *L, D.*	$$$	●	■	●	
HISTORIC CENTER: *Hostería Santo Domingo.* **Map** 4 E1. Belisario Domínguez 72. ☎ *55 10 14 34.* [FAX] *57 82 18 47.* Established in 1860, Hostería Santo Domingo claims to be the oldest restaurant in Mexico. *Chiles en nogada (see p309)* is served year round. ♿ ◯ *B, L, D.*	$$$	●		●	■
HISTORIC CENTER: *Danubio.* **Map** 4 D2. Uruguay 3. ☎ *55 12 09 12.* [FAX] *55 21 09 76.* In 1936 two Basques created this restaurant, which today offers over 100 dishes. The haddock fillet stuffed with seafood is delicious. ♿ ◯ *L, D.*	$$$$	●			
HISTORIC CENTER: *Cicero Centenario.* **Map** 4 E1. República de Cuba 79. ☎ *55 12 15 10.* [FAX] *55 18 44 47.* Old and eclectic, this curious establishment is a living museum. Tasting its repertoire of old Mexican recipes is an adventure. ▤ ♿ ◯ *L, D.* ● *Sun D.*	$$$$$	●		●	■
REFORMA & CHAPULTEPEC: *Tako's Takos* Corner of Ariosto & Campos Elíseos, Polanco. ☎ *52 80 89 48.* [FAX] *52 80 55 65.* Close to Parque Polanco, this restaurant makes common dishes seem elegant. Don't miss the *niño envuelto* (fried cheese stuffed with meat). ♿ ◯ *L, D.*	$	●	■	●	
REFORMA & CHAPULTEPEC: *El Farolito* Newton 130, Polanco. ☎ *55 45 34 51.* [FAX] *55 45 53 01.* There is a family atmosphere and a huge variety of tacos on offer here. A large sculpture of a *charro* eating tacos presides over the entrance. ▤ ♿ ◯ *B, L, D.*	$$	●	■	●	

Price categories are for a three-course meal for one, with a glass of house wine, including tax and service:

$ under US$10
$$ US$10–15
$$$ US$15–20
$$$$ US$20–25
$$$$$ over US$25

CREDIT CARDS ACCEPTED
One or more of the following credit cards are accepted: American Express, Diners Club, MasterCard, VISA.

OUTDOOR TABLES
Facilities for eating outdoors, on a terrace or in a garden or court-yard, often with a good view.

VEGETARIAN DISHES
Meat- and fish-free main courses are usually available, but vegan (dairy- and egg-free) dishes are not necessarily on the menu.

LIVE ENTERTAINMENT
Musicians or other live entertainers perform at some or all mealtimes.

	CREDIT CARDS ACCEPTED	OUTDOOR TABLES	VEGETARIAN DISHES	LIVE ENTERTAINMENT
REFORMA & CHAPULTEPEC: *Casa Portuguesa.* **Map** 1 A2. $$ Emilio Castelar 121-K, Polanco. & FAX 52 81 00 75. This small restaurant offers Portuguese cuisine. Try one of the six codfish specials, accompanied by green wine or port. B, L, D. *Easter, Sat, Sun D, Mon.*	●	■		
REFORMA & CHAPULTEPEC: *Otro Lugar de la Mancha* $$$ Esopo 11, Chapultepec los Morales. 52 80 48 26. FAX 52 80 48 34. Inspired by the novel *Don Quixote*, this restaurant has an attached bookstore. You can read while enjoying shrimp in mango sauce. B, L, D.	●	■	●	
REFORMA & CHAPULTEPEC: *Los Almendros* $$$$ Campos Eliseos 164, Polanco. 55 31 66 46. FAX 52 03 46 43. Delicious *tikinxic* fish in *achiote (see p311)* and *xnipec* (white pepper) sauce is one of the treats available at Los Almendros, one of the best restaurants serving Yucatecan cuisine in the city. B, L, D.	●		●	■
REFORMA & CHAPULTEPEC: *La Bottiglia* $$$$ Edgar Allan Poe 8, Polanco. 52 80 06 09. FAX 52 80 95 31. This pleasantly rustic Italian restaurant offers specialties such as spinach and ricotta ravioli served in a four cheese sauce. B, L, D. *Sun D.*	●		●	
REFORMA & CHAPULTEPEC: *El Rincón Argentino* $$$$ Presidente Masarik 177, Polanco. 52 54 87 75. FAX 55 31 88 77. The huge steaks here are large enough for two people. Superb desserts include *Aconcagua* (ice cream with cookies, meringue, and orange liqueur). L, D.	●		●	
REFORMA & CHAPULTEPEC: *Troita.* **Map** 1 A2. $$$$ Sudermann 336, Chapultepec los Morales. 55 45 93 00. FAX 55 31 52 11. Mediterranean cuisine is offered at this attractive restaurant. Dishes include *trucha rellena* (fish in a vegetable sauce). B, L, D. *Mon, Tue, Sun D.*	●	■	●	
REFORMA & CHAPULTEPEC: *Villa María* $$$$ Homero 704, Polanco. 52 50 69 32. FAX 52 03 03 06. With an exceptional blend of tradition and good taste, Villa María offers creative dishes including fish in tamarind sauce. L, D.	●	■		■
REFORMA & CHAPULTEPEC: *Hacienda de los Morales* $$$$$ Avenida Vásquez de Mella 525, Del Bosque. 50 96 30 54. FAX 50 96 30 56. This magnificent old hacienda is surrounded by beautiful courtyards, gardens, and a chapel. It offers superb international and Mexican food, and more than 480 different tequilas. Jacket and tie required. L, D.	●	■	●	■
REFORMA & CHAPULTEPEC: *Les Moustaches.* **Map** 2 E3. $$$$$ Río Sena 88, Cuauhtémoc. 55 33 33 90. FAX 52 07 71 49. With delectable French cuisine and an excellent wine list, Les Moustaches is widely considered to be one of the best restaurants in Mexico. The duck in green olive sauce is particularly good. Jacket and tie required. L, D. *Sun.*	●	■	●	■
COYOACÁN: *Las Lupitas* $ Jardín de Santa Catarina 4. & FAX 55 54 33 53. Situated in a lovely corner of Coyoacán, this small cozy restaurant offers excellent northern Mexican dishes. Try the *atole* (corn porridge). B, L, D.	●		●	
COYOACÁN: *El Jolgorio* $$ Higuera 22. 56 58 83 39. FAX 659 74 59. Discover what the enterprising owner of El Jolgorio calls the "world's culinary crafts." Dishes on the menu include the delicious *Bagna Caôda* (mushroom fondue) from Tuscany. B, L, D. *Mon & Tue D, Sat B.*	●		●	■
COYOACÁN: *Los Danzantes* $$$$ Plaza Jardín Centenario 12. 56 58 64 51. FAX 55 54 28 96. Guests are welcomed with a glass of mezcal at this restaurant serving contemporary Oaxacan cuisine. The decor has a pre-Columbian style. L, D, Sat & Sun B.	●	■	●	■

Price categories are for a three-course meal for one, with a glass of house wine, including tax and service:

$ under US$10
$$ US$10–15
$$$ US$15–20
$$$$ US$20–25
$$$$$ over US$25

CREDIT CARDS ACCEPTED
One or more of the following credit cards are accepted: American Express, Diners Club, MasterCard, VISA.

OUTDOOR TABLES
Facilities for eating outdoors, on a terrace or in a garden or courtyard, often with a good view.

VEGETARIAN DISHES
Meat- and fish-free main courses are usually available, but vegan (dairy- and egg-free) dishes are not necessarily on the menu.

LIVE ENTERTAINMENT
Musicians or other live entertainers perform at some or all mealtimes.

	Credit Cards Accepted	Outdoor Tables	Vegetarian Dishes	Live Entertainment
SAN ANGEL: *Fonda San Angel* $$ Plaza San Jacinto 3. **(** 55 50 16 41. FAX 55 50 17 21. Popular with intellectuals, this restaurant occupies an 18th-century house just off the historic Plaza San Jacinto. There are more than 100 excellent Mexican dishes on the traditional menu. **&** ○ *B, L, D.*	●	■	●	
SAN ANGEL: *Vivace* $$$ Avenida de la Paz 57. **(** 56 16 57 80. Situated in Del Carmen Square, Vivace offers Italian food and a good wine selection. Menu highlights include three-cheese *fetuccine* and spagetti with salmon. 目 **&** ○ *L, D.*	●	■		
SAN ANGEL: *San Angel Inn* $$$$$ Diego Rivera 50. **(** 56 16 22 22. FAX 56 16 09 73. Guests in this luxurious restaurant, formerly a Carmelite monastery *(see p101)*, can enjoy delicious dishes such as roast duckling with blackberry sauce. Jacket and tie required. **&** ○ *L, D.*	●	■	●	■
FARTHER AFIELD (CONDESA): *Garufa* $$$ Michoacán 93. **(** 52 86 82 95. FAX 52 86 26 72. One of many restaurants with a bohemian ambience, Garufa serves Argentinian and Italian cuisine. Try the *manigotti alla pomarolla* (eggplant rolls stuffed with ricotta cheese and tomato sauce). 目 **&** ○ *B, L, D.* ● *Mon B.*	●	■	●	■
FARTHER AFIELD (CONDESA): *El Principio* $$$ Montes de Oca 17. **(** 52 86 06 57. FAX 52 11 86 16. Dumain, a renowned French chef, once said: "The greatness and soul of the kitchen lies in its simplicity." El Principio clearly follows this philosophy with great Mediterranean dishes like *filete negro* (beef sautéed in black butter). **&** ○ *L, D.*	●	■		■
FARTHER AFIELD (CONDESA): *Spezia* $$$$$ Amsterdam 241. **(** 55 64 13 67. FAX 55 64 13 67. This is an excellent restaurant for those who want to sample Central European cuisine. The mouthwatering menu includes baked duckling stuffed with apple and red cabbage. **&** ○ *L, D.* ● *Sun D.*	●	■		
FARTHER AFIELD (ROMA): *La Tecla.* **Map** 2 E5. $$ Durango 186-A. **(** & FAX 55 25 49 20. Facing the Plaza de las Cibeles, this small restaurant serves innovative Mexican food. Large green chilies stuffed with crab are a specialty. ○ *L, D.* ● *Sun D.*	●			
FARTHER AFIELD (ROMA): *Ixchel.* **Map** 2 E5. $$$ Medellín 65. **(** 52 08 40 55. FAX 55 25 07 30. Located in an old Porfirian house, close to Plaza de las Cibeles, this restaurant offers dishes such as tuna fillet in vinegar sauce. 目 ○ *L, D.* ● *Sun.*	●	■	●	
FARTHER AFIELD (ROMA): *El Discreto Encanto de Comer.* **Map** 2 F4. $$$$ Orizaba 76. **(** 55 11 38 60. FAX 55 11 15 50. Situated near Plaza Río de Janeiro, in a 19th-century house, this restaurant offers French and Mexican haute cuisine. Sea bass in tangerine sauce is the specialty, and there is a good wine list. ○ *L, D.* ● *Sun, Mon & Tue D.*	●			■
FARTHER AFIELD (TLALPAN): *Enrique* $$$ Insurgentes Sur 4061. **(** 55 73 99 88. FAX 55 73 64 59. Mexican dances and mariachis are played every day in this cheerful restaurant. The menu includes *mixiote de carnero*, lamb wrapped in thin parchment and cooked in a traditional earth oven. 目 ○ *L, D.*	●	■	●	■
FARTHER AFIELD (TLALPAN): *Antigua Hacienda de Tlalpan* $$$$$ Calzada de Tlalpan 4619. **(** 56 55 73 15. FAX 55 73 33 95. This restaurant has attractive gardens where swans and peacocks roam *(see p112)*. The chicken breast stuffed with salt-cured ham and cream cheese, and covered with peach sauce, is delicious. 目 **&** ○ *L, D.* ● *Sun D.*	●	■	●	■

AROUND MEXICO CITY

CHOLULA: *El Portón* Ⓢ
Avenida Hidalgo 302. ☎ *(222) 247 02 73.*
El Portón offers traditional family cooking, including specialties like *lengua a la Veracruzana* (beef tongue with olives in tomato sauce). 🔲 ⬜ *B, L.* ⬤ *Nov 2.*

CHOLULA: *Los Jarrones* ⓈⓈ
Portal Guerrero 7. ☎ *(222) 247 10 98.*
Facing the Convento de San Gabriel, this rustic restaurant has an eclectic menu that includes *parrillada* (a selection of broiled meats). 🔲 ⬜ *B, L, D.*

CUERNAVACA: *Los Arcos* Ⓢ
Jardín de los Héroes 4. ☎ *(777) 312 15 10.*
The historic Plaza de Armas acts as a dramatic backdrop to this popular restaurant. Try the *cecina de Yecapixtla* (salted steak with guacamole). 🔲 ⬜ *B, L, D.*

CUERNAVACA: *La Trattoria Marco Polo* ⓈⓈ
Hidalgo 30. ☎ *(777) 312 34 84.* FAX *(777) 318 09 02.*
With a magnificent view of the cathedral, this excellent Italian restaurant offers dishes such as *pollo della casa* – chicken stuffed with spinach, egg, ham, and mozzarella. A very good selection of Italian wines is also available. ⬜ *L, D.*

CUERNAVACA: *Las Mañanitas* ⓈⓈⓈⓈⓈ
Ricardo Linares 107. ☎ *(777) 314 14 66.* FAX *(777) 318 36 72.*
Las Mañanitas is one of the best restaurants in Mexico, with tables overlooking the garden where peacocks and African cranes wander freely. The specialties include goose liver tamale and calf brains in black butter. 🔲 ⬜ *L, D.*

METEPEC: *Finca de Adobe* ⓈⓈⓈ
Leona Vicario 763 Poniente, La Purísima. ☎ *(777) 270 25 94.* FAX *(777) 270 25 95.*
This rustic restaurant offers typical Mexican food. Try the *pipián verde* (mole with ground pumpkin and sesame and chili seeds). 🔲 ⬜ *B, L, D.*

PACHUCA: *Alex Steak* ⓈⓈⓈⓈ
Glorieta Revolución 102. ☎ & FAX *(771) 713 00 56.*
This prestigious restaurant is, as its name suggests, particularly known for its steaks, which are enormous and superbly prepared. 🔲 ⬜ *L, D.*

PACHUQUILLA: *Don Horacio* ⓈⓈ
Avenida Hidalgo 24. ☎ & FAX *(771) 716 05 25.*
In this town near Pachuca, Don Horacio serves tasty local fare such as *mixiote de carnero* (lamb wrapped in parchment) and *paste* (pork turnover). ⬜ *B, L.*

PUEBLA: *La Vaca Negra* Ⓢ
Avenida Reforma 106. ☎ *(222) 246 20 51.*
This Mexican fast-food restaurant has a mixed menu of marrow-bone soup, brain soup, and tacos. ▤ 🔲 ⬜ *B, L, D.*

PUEBLA: *1800* ⓈⓈⓈ
Paseo de San Francisco No. 402. ☎ *(222) 297 67 65.*
Situated in the historic center, this rustic venue serves regional food like *pipián* (pumpkin seed sauce) and *mole poblano (see p308).* 🔲 ⬜ *B, L, D.* ⬤ *Sun.*

PUEBLA: *Fonda de Santa Clara* ⓈⓈⓈ
Avenida 3 Poniente No. 920. ☎ *(222) 242 26 59.* FAX *(222) 232 05 03.*
In this traditional restaurant guests can sample *tinga poblana* (seasoned pork with smoked chilies) and tripe tacos. 🔲 ⬜ *B, L, D.*

PUEBLA: *La Guadalupana* ⓈⓈⓈ
Avenida 5 Oriente No. 605, Los Sapos. ☎ *(222) 242 48 86.* FAX *(222) 232 18 51.*
Specialties here include beef fillet in tomato sauce. Many dishes are served in a *molcajete* (a traditional bowl made from volcanic stone). 🔲 ⬜ *B, L, D.*

PUEBLA: *Mesón Sacristía* ⓈⓈⓈⓈ
Calle 6 Sur No. 304. ☎ *(222) 242 35 54.* FAX *(222) 232 45 13.*
Try the *mole*, accompanied by a *cazuela sacristía* cocktail (gin, vodka, tequila, and fruit juices), in the tastefully decorated old courtyard. 🔲 ⬜ *L, D.* ⬤ *Sun D.*

PUEBLA: *Bodegas del Molino* ⓈⓈⓈⓈⓈ
Molino de San José del Puente, Puente de México. ☎ *(222) 249 03 99.* FAX *(222) 249 97 49.*
A historic 16th-century mill and fort houses this prestigious restaurant where *huachinango a la sal* (salted red snapper) is one of the special dishes. The wine cellar contains more than 7,000 bottles. 🔲 ⬜ *L, D.* ⬤ *Mon, Sun D.*

For key to symbols see back flap

	Price categories are for a three-course meal for one, with a glass of house wine, including tax and service: $ under US$10 $$ US$10–15 $$$ US$15–20 $$$$ US$20–25 $$$$$ over US$25	CREDIT CARDS ACCEPTED One or more of the following credit cards are accepted. American Express, Diners Club, MasterCard, VISA. OUTDOOR TABLES Facilities for eating outdoors, on a terrace or in a garden or courtyard, often with a good view. VEGETARIAN DISHES Meat- and fish-free main courses are usually available, but vegan (dairy- and egg-free) dishes are not necessarily on the menu. LIVE ENTERTAINMENT Musicians or other live entertainers perform at some or all mealtimes.	CREDIT CARDS ACCEPTED	OUTDOOR TABLES	VEGETARIAN DISHES	LIVE ENTERTAINMENT

TAXCO: *El Adobe* $$
Plazuela de San Juan 13. **C** *(762) 622 14 16.* FAX *(762) 622 16 83.*
If you want a memorable experience, try *Don Pancho* (steak with *jumiles* – seasonal edible beetles), available from November to January only. ☐ *B, L, D.*

	●	■	●	■

TAXCO: *Bar Paco* $$
Plaza Borda 12. **C** & FAX *(762) 622 00 64.*
Established in 1937, Bar Paco is set across the square from the Iglesia de Santa Prisca. Savor the parsley cheese with sesame seeds and scallions. ☐ *L, D.*

	●	■	●	■

TAXCO: *Del Angel Inn* $$
Celso Muñoz 4. **C** *(762) 622 55 25.* FAX *(762) 622 33 18.*
Lovely views can be enjoyed from two terraces here. The regional dishes include baked beef with ham, cheese, tomato, onion, and *epazote (see p311).* ☐ *B, L, D.*

	●	■	●	

TAXCO: *La Parroquia* $$
Plazuela de los Gallos 2. **C** *(762) 622 30 96.*
The tasty baked chicken with cheese, chili, and *epazote* served at La Parroquia is complemented by an attractive view of the Iglesia de Santa Prisca. ☐ *B, L, D.*

	●	■	●	■

TAXCO: *Señor Costillas* $$$
Plaza Borda 1. **C** & FAX *(762) 622 32 15.*
The party atmosphere is helped along by free "muppets" (tequila with grapefruit soda) in the evenings. Barbecued ribs and chicken are the specialties. ☐ *L, D.*

	●	■		

TEOTIHUACÁN: *La Gruta* $$$
Zona Arqueológica 1, Puerta 5. **C** *(594) 956 01 27.* FAX *(594) 956 01 04.*
This peculiar restaurant, situated in a cave, has been open every single day since 1929. The chicken breast stuffed with squash blossoms and *xoconoxtle* (sour prickly pear fruit) in mushroom and tequila sauce is delightful. ☐ *L, D.*

	●	■	●	■

TEPOTZOTLÁN: *Los Virreyes* $$
Plaza Virreinal 32. **C** *5 876 02 35.* FAX *5 876 43 11.*
The menu at this rustic establishment includes *cabrito* (young goat served with french fries). ☐ *B, L, D.*

	●	■	●	

TEPOZTLÁN: *Los Colorines* $$
Avenida del Tepozteco 13, La Santísima. **C** *(739) 395 01 98.*
This popular Mexican restaurant has tiled tables and pink walls inlaid with pottery. Try the *huazontle* (a leafy plant) in tomato sauce. ☐ *B, L, D.* ● *Tue D.*

		■	●	

TEPOZTLÁN: *El Ciruelo* $$$
Zaragoza 17. **C** *(739) 395 12 03.* FAX *(739) 395 10 37.*
Eat in the courtyard here to enjoy a fabulous view of Cerro Tepozteco *(see p148).* Dishes include coriander soup with almonds and chicken breast stuffed with *cuitlacoche (see p311)* in a goat's cheese sauce. ☐ *L, D.* ● *Tue–Thu, Sun D.*

	●	■	●	■

TLAXCALA: *Mi Viejo Café* $
Plaza Xicoténcatl 7. **C** & FAX *(246) 462 22 75.*
Situated down the hill from the Convento de San Francisco, this regional restaurant serves dishes such as *tizatlán* (bean soup) and *pollo Tocatlán* – chicken wrapped in a *mixiote* leaf, with tomato, cheese, and *epazote.* ☐ *B, L, D.*

	●	■	●	■

TLAXCALA: *Los Portales* $$
Plaza de la Constitución 8. **C** & FAX *(246) 462 54 19.*
The specialties here include *tlaxcalteca* soup, and grilled beef fillet covered with *cuitlacoche* sauce and cheese. ☒ ☐ *B, L, D. Fri & Sat until 3am.*

	●	■		■

TOLUCA: *La Cabaña Suiza* $$$$$
Carretera México–Toluca km 63, Paseo Tollocan. **C** *(722) 216 33 63.* FAX *(722) 216 17 70.*
Among the specialties in this Swiss restaurant are pigs' feet, frogs' legs, and meat fondue. Children will enjoy looking at the ponies and llamas that live in the gardens outside. ☒ ☐ *B, L, D.* ● *Sun D.*

	●		●	■

TULA: *Los Fresnitos* $$$$ Carretera Tula–Refinería km 4.5, El Llano. 🍴 *(773) 732 18 42.* FAX *(773) 732 26 68.* Among the 50 or so dishes served here are unusual items such as *escamoles* (ant eggs) and *chinicuiles* (red agave worms). 🍴 ◯ *B, L, D.*	•			•	■
VALLE DE BRAVO: *Da Ciro* $$$ Vergel 201. 🍴 *(726) 262 01 22.* FAX *(726) 262 14 28.* Da Ciro's Italian dishes are baked in a Neapolitan oven, giving them a distinctive flavor. There is a good choice of meats, fish, and pizzas. 🍴 ◯ *L, D.* ● *Mon–Thu.*	•	■		•	

NORTHERN MEXICO					
CABO SAN LUCAS: *Pancho's* $$$$$ Corner of Hidalgo & Zapata. 🍴 *(624) 143 09 73.* FAX *(624) 143 50 95.* This restaurant is dedicated to the bandit-turned-revolutionary Pancho Villa *(see p173)*. Grilled shrimp wrapped in bacon, fish in mango sauce, and over 350 tequilas are offered. ◯ *B, L, D.*	•	■		•	■
CHIHUAHUA: *Gerónimo* $ Aldama 1001. 🍴 *(614) 415 50 83.* FAX *(614) 416 46 20.* An inexpensive daily buffet of Mexican food is offered here. Dishes include tripe stew. ▤ 🍴 ◯ *B, I, D. Fri & Sat 24 hrs.*	•				■
CIUDAD CUAUHTÉMOC: *Tarahumara Inn* $$ Allende 373. 🍴 & FAX *(625) 581 19 19.* Classic regional cooking is served here. The specialty is *filete Barba* (grilled steak with slices of chili, refried beans, and *nachos*). ▤ 🍴 ◯ *B, L, D.*	•				
CREEL: *La Cabaña* $ Avenida López Mateos 36. 🍴 *(635) 456 00 68.* Enjoy the excellent fried chicken and other meats in this cozy, friendly restaurant decorated with Tarahumaran Indian handicrafts. 🍴 ◯ *B, L, D.*				•	
DURANGO: *La Fogata* $$$$ Avenida Cuauhtemoc 200. 🍴 *(618) 817 03 47.* Paintings of Durango adorn the walls of this popular lunch restaurant near the cathedral. The Mexican cuisine is from the North of the country ▤ ◯ *L.*	•	■			
ENSENADA: *El Charro* $$ Avenida López 475. 🍴 *(646) 178 38 81.* *Pollo al pastor* (roast chicken with *adobo* – a savory paste of chili, herbs, spices, tomato, and vinegar) is the specialty in this rustic establishment. 🍴 ◯ *L, D.*				•	
ENSENADA: *Las Cazuelas* $$$$ Agustín San Gines No. 46. 🍴 *(646) 176 10 44.* Specializing in *cazuelas* – casserole dishes – this Mexican restaurant near the beach has superb views through its large stained-glass windows. ▤ 🍴 ◯ *B, L, D.*	•				■
GUERRERO NEGRO: *Malarrimo* $$$$ Boulevard Emiliano Zapata. 🍴 *(615) 157 02 50.* FAX *(615) 157 01 00.* Decorated with nautical memorabilia and thousands of bottles, Malarrimo offers tasty seafood including lobster, white sea bass, and giant scallops. 🍴 ◯ *B, L, D.*		■			
HERMOSILLO: *Viva Sonora* $$ San Pedro el Saucito, 15 km (9 miles) NE of town. 🍴 *(662) 237 02 00.* FAX *(662) 237 02 01.* This country restaurant has an enchanting rural setting. Its menu includes good regional dishes such as *machaca* (dried, salted, and shredded beef), *pozole de trigo* (wheat broth), and melted cheese soup. ▤ 🍴 ◯ *L.* ● *Mon.*	•	■		■	
HIDALGO DEL PARRAL: *Turista* $ Plazuela Independencia 14. 🍴 & FAX *(627) 523 40 24.* Typical Mexican cooking is served in this simple and inexpensive restaurant where *alambre* (beef kabob) is the specialty. 🍴 ◯ *B, L, D.* ● *Sun D.*					
LORETO: *El Nido* $ Avenida Salvatierra 154. 🍴 *(613) 135 00 27.* FAX *(613) 135 02 84.* In this cowboy-style restaurant the delicious Sonora steaks are cooked using *mesquite* firewood, which gives the dishes a distinctive flavor. ▤ 🍴 ◯ *L, D.*		■		•	■
MAZATLÁN: *Los Arcos* $$ Avenida Camarón Sábalo. 🍴 *(669) 913 95 77.* FAX *(669) 914 09 99.* This colonial-style restaurant has an interesting menu, with the emphasis on seafood. Dishes include *pescado Culichi* (baked sea bass with chilies, cream, and cheese) and *taco gobernador* (with shrimp and cheese). ▤ 🍴 ◯ *L, D.*	•				■

For key to symbols see back flap

	CREDIT CARDS ACCEPTED	OUTDOOR TABLES	VEGETARIAN DISHES	LIVE ENTERTAINMENT

Price categories are for a three-course meal for one, with a glass of house wine, including tax and service:

$ under US$10
$$ US$10–15
$$$ US$15–20
$$$$ US$20–25
$$$$$ over US$25

CREDIT CARDS ACCEPTED
One or more of the following credit cards are accepted: American Express, Diners Club, MasterCard, VISA.

OUTDOOR TABLES
Facilities for eating outdoors, on a terrace or in a garden or courtyard, often with a good view.

VEGETARIAN DISHES
Meat- and fish-free main courses are usually available, but vegan (dairy- and egg-free) dishes are not necessarily on the menu.

LIVE ENTERTAINMENT
Musicians or other live entertainers perform at some or all mealtimes.

MULEGÉ: *Los Equipales* $$ ■ ● ■
Moctezuma. (615) 153 03 30. FAX (615) 153 01 90.
A wide variety of seafood and Sonora meat dishes is served here, all prepared from first-class ingredients. Enjoy them on the lovely terrace. ◯ *B, L, D.*

NUEVOS CASAS GRANDES: *México Español* $ ●
Avenida Benito Juárez 605. (636) 694 18 35. FAX (636) 694 17 05.
Situated 8 km (5 miles) from Paquimé *(see p170)*, México Español serves Mexican and Spanish food, including excellent paella. 🍴 ♿ ◯ *B, L, D.* ● *Sun D.*

LA PAZ: *La Terraza* $$$ ● ■
Álvaro Obregón 1570. (612) 122 08 21. FAX (612) 125 53 63.
Located in Hotel La Perla *(see page 297)*, this restaurant specializing in Mexican food offers diners delightful sea views. ♿ ◯ *B, L, D.*

SALTILLO: *El Tapanco* $$$$$ ● ■ ■
Allende Sur 225. (844) 414 00 43. FAX (844) 412 75 25.
Quiet, cozy, and very traditional, this establishment is located in an 18th-century house. It serves tasty food like shrimp with pine nuts. ♿ ◯ *L, D.* ● *Sun D.*

SAN JOSÉ DEL CABO: *Damiana* $$$ ● ■
Boulevard Mijares 8. (624) 142 04 99. FAX (624) 142 14 70.
A pleasant old hacienda, Damiana has a patio shaded by a bougainvillea. The abalone in garlic and *guajillo* (mild chili) sauce is exquisite. 🍴 ◯ *L, D.*

SAN JOSÉ DEL CABO: *Tropicana Bar & Grill* $$$$$ ● ■
Boulevard Mijares 30. (624) 142 15 80.
Inside the Tropicana hotel, this busy family restaurant serves seafood and live lobster as well as typical Mexican fare. 🍴 ♿ ◯ *B, L, D.*

SANTA ROSALÍA: *El Muelle* $$$ ■ ●
Cnr of Constitución y Plaza. (615) 152 09 31.
Set right on the corner of the main square, near the cathedral, this restaurant offers a tempting selection of dishes, including steak and seafood. Sit on the large outdoor terrace amid the palm trees. 🍴 ◯ *B, L, D.*

TIJUANA: *Cien Años* $$$$ ● ● ■
José María Velasco 1407, Río Tijuana. (664) 634 30 39. FAX (664) 634 37 94.
If you want something different, try one of the unusual options, such as manta ray burritos, served here. There are also excellent steaks. 🍴 ♿ ◯ *L, D.*

THE COLONIAL HEARTLAND

AGUASCALIENTES: *Capriccio* $$$ ● ■ ■
Avenida Universidad 219. (449) 914 99 76. FAX (4) 918 37 59.
International food is on offer here, including fondues and steaks as specialties. The impressive interior has monumental stairs and a high roof. ◯ *D.* ● *Sun; Apr.*

AJIJIC: *La Nueva Posada* $$ ● ■ ●
Donato Guerra 9. (376) 766 14 44. FAX (376) 766 20 49.
There is a superb view of the lake (Laguna de Chapala) from the terrace and garden tables at La Nueva Posada. The trout with almonds is delicious. ♿ ◯ *B, L, D.*

ANGANGUEO: *La Margarita* $
Morelos 83. (715) 156 01 49.
This rustic restaurant offers home-style cooking with dishes like pork loin and *pechuga al pastor* – chicken breast in *adobo (see p311).* ◯ *B, L, D.*

COLIMA: *Ah Que Nanishe* $$ ● ■ ● ■
5 de Mayo No. 267. (312) 314 21 97.
Oaxacan cuisine and various other regional dishes are served at Ah Que Nanishe, which is Zapotecan for "how tasty." Specialties include *tlayuda* (a platter-size tortilla with meat) and bananas filled with ground meat and cheese. ♿ ◯ *L, D.*

GUADALAJARA: *Trattoria Pomodoro*　　　　　　($)
Avenida Niños Héroes 3051, Jardines del Bosque. 【 (33) 3122 18 17. FAX (33) 3647 40 95.
Located close to Plaza del Sol, this excellent Italian restaurant offers a wide
variety of pastas, meat dishes, and seafood. 目 & ☐ *L, D.*

GUADALAJARA: *La Chata*　　　　　　($)($)
Avenida Ramón Corona 126. 【 (33) 3613 05 88. FAX (33) 3614 36 82.
Decorated with Tonalá handicrafts, this is a popular restaurant. *Jaliscience* – fried
chicken with an enchilada and a *sope (see p310)* – is the specialty. & ☐ *B, L, D.*

GUADALAJARA: *Tanto Monta*　　　　　　($)($)($)
Colón 383. 【 & FAX (33) 3614 42 78.
Tanto Monta has 15th-century-style decor and offers dishes such as *arroz
negro* (paella with squid ink). Flamenco is played on Friday. 目 & ☐ *L, D.* ● *Mon.*

GUADALAJARA: *La Fonda de San Miguel*　　　($)($)($)($)
Donato Guerra 25. 【 (33) 3613 08 09. FAX (33) 3613 07 93.
This charming restaurant in a converted convent offers nouvelle cuisine,
Mexican-style, to the accompaniment of live music every day. & ☐ *L, D.*

GUANAJUATO: *Las Piñatas Che Café*　　　　　($)
Alonso 34. 【 & FAX (473) 732 97 59.
A 17th-century building houses this Mexican and Mediterranean restaurant.
Tuna with capers, celery, and parsley is the specialty. ☐ *L, D.* ● *Sun.*

GUANAJUATO: *Restaurante Bar El Tapatio*　　　　($)
Lascuráin de Retana 20. 【 (473) 732 32 91.
Situated opposite the Universidad de Guanajuato, this colonial-style restaurant
has rustic decor and wooden beams. It is a popular eatery serving simple, tasty
dishes such as enchiladas and *pozole (see p311).* ☐ *B, L, D.* ● *Sun D.*

GUANAJUATO: *La Hacienda de Marfil*　　　　($)($)($)
Arcos de Guadalupe 3, Marfil, 4 km (2.5 miles) SW of town. 【 (473) 733 11 48. FAX
(473) 733 08 36. Surrounded by a wonderful garden, this small, exclusive restaurant
in an 18th-century hacienda blends French and Mexican cuisines in interesting
dishes such as *la fondue tequileña* (cheese and tequila fondue). & ☐ *L.* ● *Mon.*

GUANAJUATO: *Casa del Conde de la Valenciana*　($)($)($)($)
Valenciana, 5 km (3 miles) N of town. 【 & FAX (473) 732 25 50.
A short but well-chosen menu is offered at this restaurant, which is located in
the 18th-century former home of the Count of Valenciana. The beef in peanut
sauce and pork loin in dried-plum sauce are delicious. & ☐ *L.* ● *Sun.*

MORELIA: *Las Viandas de San José*　　　　　($)($)
Álvaro Obregón 263. 【 (443) 312 37 28.
Situated in a lovely colonial house, this restaurant serves Michoacán specialties,
including *corundas* and *uchepos* (regional corn tamales, *see p308*). & ☐ *B, L.*

MORELIA: *Fonda las Mercedes*　　　　　　($)($)
León Guzmán 47. 【 (443) 312 61 13. FAX (443) 313 32 22.
This restaurant in a 17th-century house is decorated with colorful masks. Try the
Sábana Mercedes (steak in garlic and sweet pepper sauce). ☐ *L, D.* ● *Sun D.*

MORELIA: *San Miguelito*　　　　　　($)($)($)($)
Corner of Avenida Camelinas & Beethoven. 【 (443) 324 44 11. FAX (443) 324 23 00.
Antiques – some for sale – adorn this restaurant. Dishes include *medallones San
Miguelito* (beef medallions in *salsa de chilpotle, see p308*). & ☐ *L, D.* ● *Sun D.*

MORELIA: *Las Trojes*　　　　　　($)($)($)
Juan Sebastián Bach 51, La Loma. 【 (443) 324 32 83. FAX (443) 314 73 44.
Housed in an old *troje* (large log cabin) with a tropical garden, and featuring a
local artist's paintings, this restaurant specializes in seafood. & ☐ *L, D.* ● *Sun D.*

PÁTZCUARO: *Campestre Alemán*　　　　　($)($)
Arocutín, 14 km (9 miles) W of town. 【 (434) 344 00 06. FAX (434) 344 02 99.
This charming country restaurant, surrounded by ponds where visitors can
fish, provides a peaceful setting for guests to enjoy the German cuisine. Savor
the smoked trout soup and the trout stuffed with salt-cured ham. & ☐ *L.*

PÁTZCUARO: *El Primer Piso*　　　　　　($)($)($)
Plaza Vasco de Quiroga 29. 【 (434) 342 01 22.
Occupying a restored 16th-century house, with balconies overlooking a charming plaza, El Primer Piso has many interesting dishes on its menu, including *pollo
bindú* (curried chicken breast with yogurt, nuts, fruit, and rice). ☐ *L, D.* ● *Tue.*

For key to symbols see back flap

<table>
<tr><td colspan="4">

Price categories are for a three-course meal for one, with a glass of house wine, including tax and service:

$ under US$10
$$ US$10–15
$$$ US$15–20
$$$$ US$20–25
$$$$$ over US$25

</td></tr>
</table>

CREDIT CARDS ACCEPTED
One or more of the following credit cards are accepted: American Express, Diners Club, MasterCard, VISA.

OUTDOOR TABLES
Facilities for eating outdoors, on a terrace or in a garden or courtyard, often with a good view.

VEGETARIAN DISHES
Meat- and fish-free main courses are usually available, but vegan (dairy- and egg-free) dishes are not necessarily on the menu.

LIVE ENTERTAINMENT
Musicians or other live entertainers perform at some or all mealtimes.

	CREDIT CARDS ACCEPTED	OUTDOOR TABLES	VEGETARIAN DISHES	LIVE ENTERTAINMENT
PUERTO VALLARTA: *Las Palomas* $$$ Paseo Díaz Ordaz 610. ☏ *(322) 222 36 75.* FAX *(322) 223 05 54.* Renowned for its magnificent view of the ocean, Las Palomas offers tasty dishes such as *chilaquiles* (chicken served with tortillas, onions, cheese, chili sauce, and sour cream). ○ *B, L, D.*	●	■	●	■
PUERTO VALLARTA: *La Dolce Vita* $$$$$ Paseo Draz Ordaz 674. ☏ *(322) 222 38 52.* FAX *(322) 222 38 52.* The delightful terrace at this restaurant gives excellent views of the bay. The cosmopolitan food includes antipasto, fresh pasta, lemon shrimps, pizza, and tiramisu. ○ *L, D.* ● *Sun D; last week Sep.*	●	■		■
QUERÉTARO: *Nicos* $$ Boulevard Bernardo Quintana 506, Arboledas. ☏ *(442) 212 66 17.* FAX *(442) 212 21 33.* Mexican haute cuisine, including strong-tasting goat's cheeses, is served under the vaulted brick ceilings of Nicos. ▤ ⅋ ○ *B, L, D.*	●		●	■
REAL DE CATORCE: *El Mesón de la Abundancia* $ Lanzagorta 11. ☏ *(488) 887 50 44.* This rustic restaurant in a hotel *(see p300)*, serves Mexican, Swiss, and Italian dishes, such as homemade *fettuccine al pesto* with garlic bread. ⅋ ○ *B, L, D.*	●	■	●	
SAN BLAS: *El Delfín* $$$ Paredes 106 Sur. ☏ *(323) 285 01 12.* FAX *(323) 285 03 08.* Diners come to the Hotel Garza Canela's restaurant from as far afield as Puerto Vallarta. The saffron shrimp broth, salmon and lobster salad, and shrimp patties in coriander vinegar are delicious. ▤ ⅋ ○ *B, L, D.*	●	■	●	
SAN LUIS POTOSÍ: *Fonda Orizatlán* $$ Pascual M. Hernández 240. ☏ *(444) 814 67 86.* Rustic and colorful, this restaurant is decorated with old photographs. It offers Huastecan-style cooking, with tamales as the specialty. ⅋ ○ *B, L, D.* ● *Sun D.*	●	■	■	■
SAN MIGUEL DE ALLENDE: *Mama Mia* $$$ Umarán 8. ☏ *(415) 152 20 63.* FAX *(415) 152 36 79.* Set in a pleasant courtyard, Mama Mia offers dishes such as *pescado Mama Mia* (fish with mushrooms, bacon, cheese, and spring onions). ⅋ ○ *B, L, D.*	●	■	■	■
SAN MIGUEL DE ALLENDE: *El Rincón Español* $$$ Correo 29. ☏ *(415) 152 29 84.* This small, cozy restaurant is decorated with Cubist paintings. The superb Spanish-influenced menu includes paella and baked lamb. ○ *L, D.*	●		●	■
SAN MIGUEL DE ALLENDE: *Bugambilia* $$$$ Hidalgo 42. ☏ *(415) 152 01 27.* FAX *(415) 152 43 82.* Located in a beautiful, typically Mexican courtyard, Bugambilia offers regional dishes such as *pacholes* (ground meat with special spices). ⅋ ○ *L, D.*	●	■		■
TLAQUEPAQUE: *El Abajeño* $$$ Francisco I. Madero 80. ☏ *(33) 3635 90 15.* FAX *(333) 3657 09 08.* Tasty lamb steaks served with bacon, mushrooms, and tortillas are on offer here – the only restaurant in Tlaquepaque with parking. ⅋ ○ *B, L, D.*	●	■		■
URUAPAN: *La Mansión* $$$$ Corner of Rodilla del Diablo & Parque Nacional. ☏ *(452) 523 21 00.* FAX *(452) 524 67 72.* A delightful, flower-filled restaurant, La Mansión overlooks the source of the Río Cupatitzio. *Trucha tarasca* (trout in nut sauce) is the specialty. ⅋ ○ *B, L, D.*	●	■	●	■
ZACATECAS: *El Pueblito* $ Avenida Hidalgo 403. ☏ & FAX *(492) 924 38 18.* Decorated with a small-scale reproductions of buildings in nearby Sombrerete, El Pueblito specializes in regional food. Try the *reliquia Zacatecana* (steak served with pasta soup and beans). ○ *L, D.* ● *Tue.*	●		●	■

ZACATECAS: *Cenaduría los Dorados de Villa* ⓈⓈ
Plazuela de García 1314. █ &. FAX *(492) 922 57 22.*
The decor in this family-run restaurant evokes the era of the Revolution.
Pozole (see p311) is among the traditional dishes served. █ ▢ *L, D.*

ZITÁCUARO: *Rancho San Cayetano* ⓈⓈⓈ
Mex 51, 2.5km (1.5 miles) S. █ *(715) 153 19 26.* FAX *(715) 153 19 26.*
At this friendly restaurant the menu varies according to what fresh produce
is available in its own garden. The French-Mexican cuisine is delightful, and
there is an excellent wine list. █ ▢ *B, L, D.*

SOUTHERN MEXICO

ACAPULCO: *El Zorrito* ⓈⓈ
Corner of Costera Miguel Alemán & Antón de Alaminos. █ *(744) 485 79 14.*
Open 23 hours a day, this small, typical Mexican restaurant offers tacos and
many varieties of *antojitos (see p310).* █ ▢ *L, D.*

ACAPULCO: *El Campanario* ⓈⓈⓈⓈⓈ
Calle Paraíso, Fraccionamiento Condesa. █ *(744) 484 88 31.* FAX *(744) 484 03 58.*
This colonial-style restaurant has a magnificent view from its lovely terrace.
There is a good set menu available and the restaurant's specialty is beef fillet
with shrimp medallions. █ ▢ *D.*

ACAPULCO: *Señor Frog's* ⓈⓈⓈⓈ
Carretera Escénica 28, Fraccionamiento El Guitarrón. █ *(744) 446 57 34.* FAX *(744) 446
57 65.* "If the music is too loud, you are too old" is one of many sayings on the
walls of Señor Frog's – and it accurately sums up the atmosphere here. There is a
superb view to enjoy while dancing or eating barbecued chicken or beef. ▢ *L, D.*

ACAPULCO: *Madeiras* ⓈⓈⓈⓈⓈ
Carretera Escénica 33, Fraccionamiento El Guitarrón. █ *(744) 446 57 23.*
The Madeiras is beautifully furnished and has a lovely view. Its generous set
menu includes gourmet Mexican dishes such as pork loin stuffed with a light
corn paste and *cuitlacoche (see p311),* all baked in a banana leaf. █ ▢ *D.*

ACAPULCO: *El Olvido* ⓈⓈⓈⓈⓈ
Plaza Marbella, Costera Miguel Alemán. █ *(744) 481 02 03.* FAX *(744) 481 02 56.*
The menu at this restaurant offers French haute cuisine with a Mexican touch,
such as sautéed shrimp in smoked chili and hollandaise sauce. █ ▢ *D.*

HUATULCO: *El Sabor de Oaxaca* ⓈⓈ
Guamúchil 206. █ *(958) 587 00 60.*
A cozy restaurant at the Hotel Las Palmas, El Sabor de Oaxaca serves a good
range of authentic Oaxacan dishes. █ ▢ *B, L, D.*

IXTAPA: *Los Mandiles* ⓈⓈ
Corner of Andador Punta Carrizo & Isla de a pie. █ *(755) 553 03 79.* FAX *(755) 553 17 20.*
This restaurant-cum-disco has a festive atmosphere. It serves interesting dishes,
such as beef with *nopales* (paddle-cactus leaves), and a strong but tasty drink
called *mandil* (made from rum, vodka, gin, and passion fruit juice). █ ▢ *L, D.*

OAXACA: *El Asador Vasco* ⓈⓈ
Portal de Flores 10-A. █ *(951) 514 47 55.* FAX *(951) 514 47 62.*
Eleven arched balconies look out onto the *zócalo* at this rustic restaurant,
which offers tasty Oaxacan and Basque dishes. ▢ *L, D.*

OAXACA: *La Casa de la Abuela* ⓈⓈ
Avenida Hidalgo 616. █ & FAX *(951) 516 35 44.*
Overlooking the Alameda and the *zócalo,* this restaurant is decorated with
sculptures of saints. It offers typical Mexican dishes such as *tasajo* (thin pieces
of dried beef) and chilies stuffed with *picadillo* (ground meat). ▢ *L, D.*

OAXACA: *El Naranjo* ⓈⓈⓈ
Valerio Trujano 203. █ *(951) 514 18 78.*
Occupying a renovated 18th-century building, El Naranjo offers contemporary
Oaxacan cuisine such as stuffed chilies. A different kind of *mole (see p311)* is
served every day of the week. █ ▢ *L, D.*

OAXACA: *Los Pacos Santo Domingo* ⓈⓈ
Constitución 104. █ & FAX *(951) 516 17 04.*
Set around two old courtyards, Los Pacos is considered by many to be among
the region's best restaurants. Guests can try authentic local dishes, including seven
types of *mole (see p311),* and Los Pacos' own mezcal *(see p313).* ▢ *B, L, D.*

	Price categories / legend	CREDIT CARDS ACCEPTED	OUTDOOR TABLES	VEGETARIAN DISHES	LIVE ENTERTAINMENT

Price categories are for a three-course meal for one, with a glass of house wine, including tax and service:

$ under US$10
$$ US$10–15
$$$ US$15–20
$$$$ US$20–25
$$$$$ over US$25

CREDIT CARDS ACCEPTED
One or more of the following credit cards are accepted: American Express, Diners Club, MasterCard, VISA.

OUTDOOR TABLES
Facilities for eating outdoors, on a terrace or in a garden or courtyard, often with a good view.

VEGETARIAN DISHES
Meat- and fish-free main courses are usually available, but vegan (dairy- and egg-free) dishes are not necessarily on the menu.

LIVE ENTERTAINMENT
Musicians or other live entertainers perform at some or all mealtimes.

Restaurant	Price	Credit Cards	Outdoor Tables	Vegetarian	Live Entertainment
OAXACA: *Terranova* Portal Benito Juarez 116. ℂ & FAX *(951) 514 05 33.* There is a great atmosphere here, with live music every day from 8–11pm. The food is good too, including steaks as well as regional food. ♿ ⬜ *B, L, D.*	$$$	●	■	●	■
PALENQUE: *Maya* Corner of Independencia & Hidalgo. ℂ *(916) 345 00 42.* FAX *(916) 345 10 96.* Opened in 1958, the Maya is a simple and unpretentious restaurant located on the main square of Palenque town. The dishes offered include *carne a la Tampiqueña (see p311)* and succulent sea bass in garlic. ♿ ⬜ *L, D.*	$	●		●	■
PALENQUE: *La Selva* Carretera Palenque–Ruinas km 0.5. ℂ *(916) 345 03 63.* FAX *(916) 345 00 46.* Surrounded by a tropical garden, La Selva occupies an attractive thatched building. The appetizing menu includes *filete jacaranda* (beef fillet with ham, cheese, and brandy flambé) and squid with capers and olives. ⬜ *L, D.*	$$$	●	■		■
PUERTO ÁNGEL: *Villa Florencia* Avenida Virgilio Uribe. ℂ & FAX *(958) 584 30 44.* Situated near the pier at the center of the village, this Italian restaurant offers tasty meals and has a view of the sea from its terrace. ♿ ⬜ *B, L, D.*	$	●	■	●	
PUERTO ESCONDIDO: *Junto al Mar* Avenida Pérez Gazga 600. ℂ & FAX *(954) 582 12 72.* Located on the beach, this restaurant is the oldest in the port and serves fresh fish and shellfish, including shrimp kabob (kebab). ♿ ⬜ *B, L, D.*	$$$	●	■		
SAN CRISTÓBAL DE LAS CASAS: *Madre Tierra* Avenida Insurgentes 19. ℂ & FAX *(967) 678 42 97.* This vegetarian restaurant, situated just in front of the Iglesia de San Francisco, offers delicious dishes such as mushroom lasagna. ⬜ *B, L, D.*	$		■	●	
SAN CRISTÓBAL DE LAS CASAS: *Tuluc* Avenida Insurgentes 5. ℂ & FAX *(967) 678 20 90.* Inexpensive international food is offered here. Try the *filete Tuluc* (beef wrapped around spinach, bacon, and cheese, and served with fried potatoes). ♿ ⬜ *B, L, D.*	$				
SAN CRISTÓBAL DE LAS CASAS: *El Fogón de Jovel* Avenida 16 de Septiembre No. 11. ℂ *(967) 678 11 53.* FAX *(967) 678 31 45.* In this old colonial house decorated with orchids, the waiters proudly wear their ethnic costumes while serving Chiapanecan dishes such as *asado buvul* (beef fillet with melted cheese and mashed potatoes). ⬜ *L, D.*	$$			●	■
SAN CRISTÓBAL DE LAS CASAS: *La Margarita* Real de Guadalupe 34-A. ℂ *(967) 678 09 57.* FAX *(967) 678 78 32.* This cheerful colonial restaurant offers dishes such as *parrillada* (grilled beef, smoked pork, chicken breast, sausage, and cheese, all on one plate). ⬜ *L, D.*	$$				■
TEOTITLÁN DEL VALLE: *Tlamanalli* Avenida Juárez 39. ℂ & FAX *(951) 524 40 06.* Named after an ancient god of food, this restaurant is run by four Zapotec sisters who serve authentic and homemade Zapotec cuisine. The menu changes frequently, but the staff will happily explain any dish. ⬜ *L.* ● *Mon.*	$$$$			●	
TUXTLA GUTIÉRREZ: *Las Pichanchas* Avenida Central Oriente 837. ℂ *(961) 612 53 51.* FAX *(961) 611 12 67.* Guests at Las Pichanchas can enjoy Chiapanecan dishes such as *chipilín soup*, made from corn, cheese, sour cream, and the native *chipilín* herb. ♿ ⬜ *L, D.*	$	●	■	●	■
TUXTLA GUTIÉRREZ: *Cafetería Bonampak* Boulevard Belisario Domínguez 180. ℂ *(961) 602 59 25.* FAX *(961) 602 59 14.* Regional specialties, such as *cochito chiapaneco* (baked, marinated pork), are served at the Hotel Bonampak's modern restaurant. ▤ ♿ ⬜ *B, L, D.*	$$	●		●	

ZIHUATANEJO: *La Sirena Gorda* Paseo del Pescador 20-A. ☎ & [FAX] *(755) 554 74 64.* This small restaurant, which has a casual, comfortable atmosphere, is known for such exotic recipes as blackened red snapper. ♿ ◻ *B, L, D.* ● *Wed.*	$$		■		
ZIHUATANEJO: *La Gaviota* Playa la Ropa. ☎ & [FAX] *(755) 554 38 16.* Situated right on the beach, La Gaviota serves fresh seafood. The fish stuffed with shrimp in almond sauce is delicious. ♿ ◻ *L, D.*	$$$$	●	■		

THE GULF COAST

COATEPEC: *Casa Bonilla* Cuauhtémoc 20. ☎ *(228) 816 03 74.* [FAX] *(228) 816 00 09.* This popular colonial-style restaurant offers more than 60 fish and shellfish dishes including the tasty sea bass in *acuyo* (an aromatic leaf). ♿ ◻ *B, L.*	$	●	■		■
CÓRDOBA: *El Cordobés* Avenida 1 No. 111. ☎ & [FAX] *(271) 712 30 15.* *El Cordobés* (fried beef fillet in eel broth) is the specialty at this picturesque restaurant, which is located in the Portal de Zevallos. ♿ ◻ *B, L, D.*	$	●	■		
LAGUNA DE CATEMACO: *Canimao* Km 2 Carretera Asontecamapan. ☎ *(942) 943 00 42.* Located inside the Playa Azul hotel, this relaxed restaurant has a lovely view of the lake. There is national and regional food on offer, including "monkey meat" – actually smoked pork – which is delicious. ♿ ◻ *B, L, D.*	$$	●	■		
ORIZABA: *Romanchú* 7 Poniente No. 208. ☎ & [FAX] *(272) 725 25 85.* This popular establishment offers a selection of seafood and meat dishes. *Langostinos Romanchú* (crayfish in garlic) is a favorite. ♿ ◻ *B, L, D.*	$	●		●	
PAPANTLA: *Sorrento* Enriquez 105b. ☎ *(784) 842 00 67.* Sorrento serves Mexican food and is just one block from the main square in front of a large mural depicting Totonacás culture. Fixed-rate menu. ◻ *B, L, D.*	$				
SANTIAGO TUXTLA: *Los Faisanes* Corner of Comonfort & 5 de Mayo. ☎ *(294) 947 04 00.* [FAX] *(294) 947 03 32.* This pleasant restaurant, at the Hotel Castellanos, offers a good choice of seafood and meat dishes, including beef fillet with onions and mushrooms. ♿ ◻ *B, L, D.*	$$				
TLACOTALPAN: *Doña Lala* Carranza 11. ☎ & [FAX] *(288) 884 25 80.* Regional dishes such as *arroz a la tumbada* (rice with mixed seafood) are served in this restaurant in the 19th-century hotel Posada Doña Lala. ▤ ◻ *B, L, D.*	$$$	●	■	●	
VERACRUZ: *Gran Café de la Parroquia* Gómez Farías 34. ☎ *(229) 932 18 55.* [FAX] *(229) 932 89 23.* This establishment is one of the oldest and best-known restaurants in Mexico. Customers traditionally bang their glasses with a spoon to call for cups of the famous coffee. Try the *pescado a la Veracruzana (see p309).* ▤ ♿ ◻ *B, L, D.*	$$	●	■		■
VERACRUZ: *Villa Rica Mocambo* Calzada Mocambo 527, Boca del Río. ☎ & [FAX] *(229) 922 21 13.* A thatched-roof restaurant, Villa Rica Mocambo is situated in a beautiful tropical setting. The *caracol al ajillo* (sea snail in garlic) is superb. ▤ ♿ ◻ *L, D.*	$$$	●	■		■
VILLAHERMOSA: *Los Tulipanes* Conjunto Cicom. ☎ & [FAX] *(993) 312 92 17.* Right beside the University and the Museo Carlos Pellicer, Los Tulipanes has huge windows and a good-sized terrace. There is a mixture of regional dishes, including seafood, shrimps, and soup. ▤ ♿ ◻ *B, L.*	$$$	●	■		■
XALAPA: *Churrería del Recuerdo* Victoria 158. ☎ & [FAX] *(228) 818 16 78.* This lovely *churrería* serves *churros (see p311)*, *horchata* (a melon-seed drink), and fruit *atole (see p312)*, as well as typical Mexican dinners. ◻ *D.*	$			●	
XALAPA: *La Casona del Beaterio* Zaragoza 20. ☎ & [FAX] *(228) 818 21 19.* Relax on the patio and enjoy the Mexican and Spanish cooking served here. Try the thinly sliced beef with ham, pineapple, and cheese. ♿ ◻ *B, L, D.*	$$	●	■	●	■

For key to symbols see back flap

Price categories are for a three-course meal for one, with a glass of house wine, including tax and service:

ⓢ under US$10
ⓢⓢ US$10–15
ⓢⓢⓢ US$15–20
ⓢⓢⓢⓢ US$20–25
ⓢⓢⓢⓢⓢ over US$25

CREDIT CARDS ACCEPTED
One or more of the following credit cards are accepted: American Express, Diners Club, MasterCard, VISA.

OUTDOOR TABLES
Facilities for eating outdoors, on a terrace or in a garden or courtyard, often with a good view.

VEGETARIAN DISHES
Meat- and fish-free main courses are usually available, but vegan (dairy- and egg-free) dishes are not necessarily on the menu.

LIVE ENTERTAINMENT
Musicians or other live entertainers perform at some or all mealtimes.

THE YUCATÁN PENINSULA

	CREDIT CARDS ACCEPTED	OUTDOOR TABLES	VEGETARIAN DISHES	LIVE ENTERTAINMENT
AKUMAL: *La Buena Vida* ⓢⓢⓢ Carretera Cancún–Chetumal km 104. 📞 *(984) 875 90 61.* FAX *(984) 875 90 58.* This popular and casual beachfront restaurant offers favorites such as shrimp tacos and steak. 🔧 ⃝ *L, D.*	●	■		
CAMPECHE: *Marganzo* ⓢⓢ Calle 8 No. 262. 📞 *(981) 811 38 98.* FAX *(981) 816 25 30.* Housed in one of the oldest buildings in the city, this colonial restaurant is known for its *pan de cazón* (tacos filled with beans and dogfish). 📋 🔧 ⃝ *B, L, D.*	●	■		■
CANCÚN: *María Bonita* ⓢⓢⓢⓢ Punta Cancún. 📞 *(998) 848 70 00 ext. 7960.* FAX *(998) 848 70 06.* This restaurant is divided into different areas, each with its own atmosphere. Dishes include chicken breast filled with shrimp and cheese. 📋 🔧 ⃝ *D, Sun L, D.*	●		●	■
CANCÚN: *La Dolce Vita* ⓢⓢⓢⓢⓢ Boulevard Kukulcán km 14.5, Zona Hotelera. 📞 *(998) 885 01 50.* FAX *(998) 884 04 61.* Delicious Italian food, including lobster and shrimp medallions, is served on a terrace overlooking the lagoon. There is an excellent wine list. 📋 🔧 ⃝ *L, D.*	●	■	●	■
CANCÚN: *La Habichuela* ⓢⓢⓢⓢⓢ Margaritas 25. 📞 *(998) 884 31 58.* FAX *(998) 884 09 40.* Guests can dine under the stars in the garden of this restaurant and try exotic dishes such as *cocobichuela* (curried shrimp and lobster with rice, fresh coconut, and grilled pineapple and banana). 📋 🔧 ⃝ *L, D.*	●	■	●	
CANCÚN: *La Hacienda del Mortero* ⓢⓢⓢⓢⓢ Boulevard Kukulcán, Zona Hotelera. 📞 *(998) 883 11 33 ext. 746.* FAX *(998) 883 17 90.* This restaurant is a copy of a hacienda in Durango. The house specialty is parrillada (a plate of grilled beef, smoked pork, chicken, and cheese). 📋 ⃝ *D.*	●	■	●	■
CANCÚN: *La Joya* ⓢⓢⓢⓢⓢ Boulevard Kukulcán km 9.5, Zona Hotelera. 📞 *(998) 881 3200 ext. 4200.* FAX *(998) 881 32 83.* The Coral Beach Hotel's restaurant, La Joya is one of the city's most elegant and expensive places to eat. It offers Mexican and international haute cuisine. 📋 ⃝ *D.*	●		●	■
CHETUMAL: *Nah Balam* ⓢⓢ Avenida Héroes 171-A. 📞 *(983) 835 04 00 ext. 153.* FAX *(983) 832 16 07.* Enjoy tasty international and regional dishes and good service at this modern, comfortable restaurant in the Holiday Inn. 📋 🔧 ⃝ *B, L, D.*	●	■	●	
CHETUMAL: *Sergio's Pizzas* ⓢⓢⓢ Avenida Álvaro Obregón 182. 📞 & FAX *(983) 832 08 82.* Besides a good selection of pizzas and pasta, Sergio's offers steak dishes such as *arrachera Tampiqueña* (beef fillet with beans and guacamole). 📋 🔧 ⃝ *B, L, D.*	●		●	
CHICHÉN ITZÁ: *Villas Arqueológicas* ⓢⓢ Mex 180, SE of site. 📞 *(985) 856 60 00.* FAX *(985) 856 60 08.* Situated adjacent to the archaeological site, this hotel restaurant serves French food, plus local dishes such as *pollo al pibil (see p309).* 📋 🔧 ⃝ *B, L, D.*	●	■	●	
COZUMEL: *La Choza* ⓢⓢ Adolfo Rosado Salas 200. 📞 *(987) 872 09 58.* FAX *(987) 872 34 17.* This popular family-run establishment serves typical Mexican homemade dishes such as *relleno negro* (chicken in a sauce of blackened chilies). 🔧 ⃝ *B, L, D.*	●	■	●	
COZUMEL: *Pepe's Grill* ⓢⓢⓢⓢⓢ Corner of Avenida Rafael Melgar & Rosado Salas. 📞 *(987) 872 58 66.* FAX *(987) 872 13 86.* Sample the delicious grilled steaks and fish and excellent wines, while enjoying the beautiful view from the second floor of this waterfront restaurant. 📋 ⃝ *D.*	●			■

ISLA MUJERES: *Pizza Rolandi's* $$ — ● ■ ● ·
Avenida Hidalgo 110. ☎ *(998) 877 04 30.* [FAX] *(998) 877 04 29.*
Rolandi's serves superb pizzas, baked in a wood-burning oven, and a wide variety of meat and fish dishes. ◯ *L, D.*

MÉRIDA: *Los Almendros* $$$ — ● · · ■
Calle 50 A No. 493. ☎ *(999) 928 54 59.* [FAX] *(999) 923 81 35.*
Well known for its traditional home-style Yucatecan cuisine, this popular and inexpensive restaurant serves tasty dishes such as *poc-chuc* (grilled pork with marinated and blackened tomatoes) and lime soup. ▤ ♿ ◯ *L, D.*

MÉRIDA: *Hacienda Teya* $$ — ● ■ · ■
Mex 180, 12.5 km (7.5 miles) E of town. ☎ *(999) 988 08 00.* [FAX] *(999) 988 08 02.*
This stunning 17th-century hacienda, surrounded by gardens and impeccably restored, now houses an elegant restaurant and hotel. The chef will delight you with traditional Yucatecan dishes. ▤ ♿ ◯ *L.*

MÉRIDA: *Pórtico del Peregrino* $$$ — ● ■ · ·
Calle 57 No. 501. ☎ & [FAX] *(999) 928 61 63.*
This centrally located restaurant serves good international food. The house specialty – *zarzuela* (a seafood platter) – is delicious. ▤ ♿ ◯ *L, D.*

MÉRIDA: *El Tucho* $$$ — ● · · ■
Calle 60 No. 482. ☎ *(999) 924 23 23.*
Situated close to the Iglesia Santa Lucía, this restaurant offers good Mexican regional cooking. The dishes on the menu include *papadzules* (corn tortillas stuffed with hard-boiled eggs). ♿ ◯ *L.*

MÉRIDA: *Pancho's* $$$ — ● ■ ● ■
Calle 59 No. 509. ☎ *(999) 923 09 42.* [FAX] *(999) 927 04 34.*
The waiters wear cartridge belts and huge hats in this cheerful restaurant. Try the *camarón al tequila* (shrimp flambéed with tequila and white wine). ♿ ◯ *D.*

PLAYA DEL CARMEN: *Señor Frog's* $$ — ● ■ ● ■
Centro Comercial Plaza Marina. ☎ & [FAX] *(984) 873 09 30.*
Señor Frog's is located next to the ferry dock. Guests here can try tasty flambé dishes such as bull shot (beef with laurel leaves in vodka) and have a good time dancing to the live music. ♿ ◯ *B, L, D.*

PLAYA DEL CARMEN: *La Parrilla* $$$ — ● ■ ● ■
Corner of 8 Norte & Quinta Avenida. ☎ & [FAX] *(984) 873 06 87.*
Situated on the attractive Plaza Rincón del Sol, this popular restaurant is decorated with big Mexican hats. It offers grilled meats and lobster. ♿ ◯ *L, D.*

PROGRESO: *Le Saint Bonnet* $$$$ — ● ■ · ■
Calle 19 No. 150-D. ☎ & [FAX] *(969) 935 22 99.*
This thatched-roof restaurant, situated next to Progreso's pier, offers French cuisine, including shrimp cooked in sparkling wine. ♿ ◯ *B, L, D.*

PUERTO MORELOS: *Los Pelícanos* $$$$ — ● ■ · ·
Avenida Rafael E. Melgar 2. ☎ & [FAX] *(998) 871 00 14.*
Fish dominates the menu at this rustic restaurant beside the pier. Guests can enjoy dishes like *platón pelícanos* (a platter of seafood) on the terrace. ♿ ◯ *B, L, D.*

TULUM: *Ambrosio's 24 Horas* $ — ● ■ · ·
Jupiter 2. ☎ *(984) 871 21 78.* [FAX] *(984) 871 24 08.*
The specialty at this 24-hour, family-run restaurant is *filete Ambrosio's* (beef fillet stuffed with cheese, ham, and olives). ♿ ◯ *B, L, D.*

TULUM: *Garibaldi* $$$ — ● ■ ● ■
Centro Comercial. ☎ *(984) 871 21 76.* [FAX] *(984) 871 20 52.*
Situated very close to the archaeological site, this popular restaurant has an extensive menu of meat, seafood, and regional dishes. ♿ ◯ *B, L.*

UXMAL: *Villas Arqueológicas* $$$ — ● ■ ● ■
Mex 261, E of site. ☎ *(997) 974 60 20.* [FAX] *(997) 976 20 40.*
Located just outside Uxmal archaeological site, this hotel restaurant is operated by Club Med. It serves Mexican and international cuisine, such as chicken in lemon sauce and grouper fish *a la Veracruzana* *(see p309)*. ▤ ♿ ◯ *B, L, D.*

VALLADOLID: *El Mesón del Marqués* $ — ● ■ ● ·
Calle 39 No. 203. ☎ *(985) 856 20 73.* [FAX] *(985) 856 22 80.*
This colonial restaurant offers traditional Yucatecan dishes such as *lomito Valladolid* (pork loin in tomato sauce) and pickled chicken. ▤ ◯ *B, L, D.*

SHOPPING IN MEXICO

Basket seller taking his wares to market

FOR MANY PEOPLE, shopping is one of the highlights of a trip to Mexico. Some enjoy the upscale boutiques or jewelry stores in big-city malls or beach resorts. (For shopping in Mexico City, see pp114–5.) Others prefer the excitement of a colorful, bustling street market piled high with unfamiliar fruits and vegetables, or of finding an isolated roadside stall selling beautiful earthenware pots or bright, handwoven rugs.

Bartering is not appropriate everywhere. At craft stalls in tourist resorts, a certain amount of haggling is usually acceptable and even expected, but in most shops, prices are fixed. You can ask *¿Cuánto es lo menos?* (What is your best price?) but when buying from craftsmen, bear in mind that their profit is usually already pitifully low. Larger stores will ship your purchases home for you; it is illegal to export archaeological artifacts.

Roadside stall selling colorful souvenirs including rugs and bags

OPENING HOURS

SHOPS GENERALLY open from 9am through 7 or 8pm, Monday through Saturday. Bakeries and corner shops may open earlier, at 8am, and some stay open until 10pm. Boutiques and craft shops usually open at 10am. Sunday shopping is possible at supermarkets and in tourist areas.

Large American-style shopping malls have sprouted all over Mexico's cities in recent years. They open on Sundays, but some close on Mondays.

Outside Mexico City, most shops close for lunch between 2 and 4pm. Department stores and supermarkets everywhere stay open over lunchtime. Street markets usually pack up at about 2 or 3pm.

PAYING

CASH AND MAJOR credit cards (VISA, MasterCard, and, to a lesser extent, American Express and Diner's Club) are acceptable forms of payment in most Mexican shops. Prices generally include 15 percent IVA (sales tax, or VAT). Credit card payments are usually subject to a small surcharge. All but the most touristy markets accept only cash.

GENERAL STORES

GLITZY DEPARTMENT stores, modern malls, and expensive, trendy boutiques are the norm in certain parts of the capital and in a handful of cities and resorts around the country. In most big cities, there is at least one Sanborn's *(see p114)*, which has a good

The bustling market in Tepoztlán, a lively jumble of people and products

selection of books, magazines, maps, gifts, chocolates, and toiletries. For everyday shopping, supermarkets like Aurrera or Comercial Mexicana are huge and well stocked with many familiar brand names.

Away from modern shopping centers, ordinary life in Mexico still revolves around the market and traditional shops in the surrounding streets: the *panadería* (bakery), *tienda de abarrotes* (grocery store), and *ferretería* (hardware store).

SPECIALTY SHOPS

LEÓN, GUADALAJARA, and Monterrey are all known for their fine-quality leatherware. Shoes, with designs ranging from trendy to classical, are particularly good value, and are sold in shops and markets all over the country. Belts and bags are also an excellent buy. The sturdy, rubber-soled *huarache* sandals are best bought in Guadalajara's *(see pp188–9)* San Juan de Dios market. In Jalisco, craftsmen also make *equipales*, the typically Mexican, rustic leather and wood armchairs.

Mexico is the world leader in silver production, and prices are well below those of Europe or the US. Silversmiths in Taxco *(see pp146–7)*, Guanajuato *(see pp202–4)*, and Zacatecas *(see pp192–3)* create modern designs, as well as those inspired by pre-Columbian jewelry. A 925 stamp will ensure that the silver is good quality. Alpaca, which is on sale all over Mexico, is a nickel alloy and contains no silver at all. Opals, jadeite, lapis lazuli, obsidian, onyx, and many other semiprecious stones, are relatively inexpensive to purchase.

CLOTHING

CASUAL CLOTHING is available in all major tourist resorts and big cities. Imported designer labels, such as Gucci and Hermès, can be found in a few select boutiques and department stores. Less expensive clothes are on sale in smaller shops and markets everywhere. Any designer clothes and accessories that are for sale on cheap market stalls are almost certain to be fakes.

Villages in the south and southeast of Mexico are the best places to buy traditional, hand-embroidered Indian costumes. The more commercial designs – often using synthetic fabrics – are sold in craft shops everywhere.

Hats and scarves on a souvenir stall in a street market

REGIONAL PRODUCTS

THE VARIETY OF crafts available in Mexico is vast (see pp330–31). Every region has its specialties, and it is more interesting – and usually cheaper – to buy artesanías in the region where they are made. For an overview of what is available, most regional capitals have a Casa de las Artesanías, which houses exhibitions and

Typical tourist shops in the resort of Playa del Carmen

sales of local craftwork. The most outstanding artesanías are found in those areas which have a significant Indian population, such as the states of Oaxaca, Puebla, Chiapas, Guerrero, Michoacán, and Nayarit.

FOOD AND DRINK

FRESH AND DRIED chilies, spices, and pastes for preparing mole and other Mexican dishes are best bought from market stalls. Although not quite as good, mole is also found in jars or packages at supermarkets. Similarly, there are several varieties of chili bottled and in cans, which are more easily packed.

The best añejo tequilas (see p313) are made in Jalisco, and good brands, like Herradura or Centenario, can be bought at supermarkets and vinaterías (liquor stores) all over Mexico. Avoid non-labeled tequila, which may be contaminated with methanol. Mezcal, less widely sold, is best bought in its native Oaxaca.

Handmade sweets and candies are a specialty of central Mexico's colonial towns. Sweet-toothed visitors will want to try cajeta from Celaya, chongos from Zamora, camote from Puebla, and cocada envinada from Guadalajara. These, and more, can be found in Mexico City's Dulcería de Celaya (see p114).

MARKETS

EVERY TOWN IN Mexico has at least one market. There is often a permanent indoor market, as well as a once-weekly street market, or tianguis, which is usually held in or around the main square. In large cities, each neighborhood has its mercado sobre ruedas (street market) on a different day of the week. These markets are a colorful array of fresh fruit, vegetables, fish and meat, and piles of herbs, spices, and chilies. Clothes, trinkets, and household items are also for sale. Prices are generally cheaper here than in supermarkets.

Markets are transformed at fiesta time. At Easter in Mexico City, there is an abundance of red papier mâché diablos (devils). Just before the Days of the Dead (see pp34–5), stalls overflow with sugar skulls and dancing skeletons. And at Christmas, the usual decorations rub shoulders with typically Mexican nativity figures.

Vivid array of chilies, legumes (pulses), and spices for sale in a Mexican market

Folk Art of Mexico

CRAFTS IN MEXICO are an essential part of daily and ceremonial life, with techniques passed down from generation to generation. Contemporary folk art results from the fusion of Old and New World traits. After the Conquest, the impact of Spanish technology was widely felt. While some native arts such as feather working were lost, others were gained. Mission schools taught European skills, and Spanish methods for treating leather were introduced, together with treadle-loom weaving and the glazing of ceramics. Today, traditional methods and designs co-exist with recent innovations, producing a wide range of high-quality crafts for sale *(see pp332–3).*

Ceremonial beaded gourd

Spanish galleons, displaying the sign of the cross, brought Christianity to Mexico.

Religious festivals marked out the pre-Columbian year. Despite efforts by Spanish missionaries to ban the dance of the *voladores*, it is still performed today *(see p29).*

The art of pottery goes back thousands of years in Mexico, and in other parts of the New World. Many ancient techniques are still in use today.

Pot making still utilises traditional methods. Tzeltal women, for instance, work without a wheel in Amatenango del Valle, Chiapas. Tubes of clay are coiled and pressed down with the fingers. The surfaces are burnished and decorated before being fired.

This weaver is using a backstrap loom. Textile skills in Tzotzil and other indigenous communities, are used primarily to make clothing. As in pre-Conquest times, weavers rely on techniques such as brocading to pattern cloth on the loom.

Corn (or maize) originated in the Americas, and formed part of the staple diet of Mesoamerican civilizations *(see p45).* Then, as now, it was ground on a *metate* (grinding stone).

Silversmiths have practiced their art for many centuries in Mexico. After the Conquest, some processes like "lost wax casting" disappeared, but modern jewelers retain enormous skill. The above pieces were sand-cast.

Bark paper
(amate) is still made in the Otomí village of San Pablito (Puebla), using an ancient, pre-Columbian method. Popular with collectors, the cut-out figures represent supernatural forces. They are used by Otomí shamans during rituals to encourage the growth of crops and to cure the sick.

THE MEETING OF TWO WORLDS

Metepec, outside Toluca, is famous for its exuberant pottery. Brightly painted "Trees of Life" are inspired by history, nature, and the Bible. The one pictured here, by Tiburcio Soteno, shows Spanish conquistadors discovering Aztec civilization in 1519.

Markets *have always been good sources of local craft items. The vendors, who are often the makers, may travel long distances to sell their wares.*

The Aztec calendar alluded to on the Sun Stone *(see p95)* combined a solar calendar of 365 days and a sacred calendar of 260 days, leading to cycles of 52 years *(see p47).*

Human sacrifices took place in Aztec temples. The victims, regarded as the gods' messengers, had their hearts cut out on the sacrificial stone.

This papier-mâché dragon **(alebrije)** *is by Felipe Linares. European paper, introduced after the Conquest, is used in Mexico City and Celaya (west of Querétaro) to make fantastical papier-mâché figures of all shapes and kinds.*

Tenochtitlán *(see p94)* was founded when the Aztecs entered the Valley of Mexico and saw the promised sign of an eagle on a prickly pear *(see p43).*

Glazed ceramics *are decorative as well as functional. The pottery must be fired twice, and enclosed kilns have generally replaced pre-Columbian firing methods. The glaze is often transparent, but yellow, black, and green are used too.*

Embroidery was practiced in Mexico before the Conquest, but was given new impetus under Spanish rule. The blouse, here embroidered with flowers, was a garment introduced from Spain.

Tinsmiths *are particularly prominent in Oaxaca City. The craftsmen use shears to cut through thin and flexible sheets of tin. Lanterns and decorative figures can be plain, or painted with bright, industrial colors.*

Buying Mexican Crafts

MEXICAN FOLK ART has a unique vitality. Good craft items are sold in street markets, as well as in shops and galleries. Work can also be bought directly from the makers. Craftspeople of various trades can be found in many villages and small towns by making inquiries on arrival. Although it is advisable to negotiate a fair price when buying crafts, purchasers should take into consideration the rising cost of materials, as well as the skill and time invested by the maker. Many folk artists now sign their work, aware that it is highly valued by an increasing number of museums and private collectors.

Tin-glazed earthenware dish
from Guanajuato

CERAMICS

Mexican ceramists practice a vast range of ancient and modern techniques. In Oaxaca, traditional firing methods produce pottery with a black, metallic lustre. Green glazes are popular in Michoacán. Puebla City is famous for its tin-glazed earthenware, and brightly-painted toys are produced in many places.

Painted pottery mermaid   Pottery bandstand

Ceramic
Adam and Eve

Cockerel made of wire
and papier-mâché

Jointed papier-
mâché doll

PAPIER-MÂCHÉ

Papier-mâché is used to create decorative figures and toys for seasonal festivities. Masks are made all year round, skeletons and skulls for the Days of the Dead *(see pp34–5).*

Human and animal masks for children

WOODEN TOYS AND CARVINGS

Inexpensive wooden toys are made in several states, including Michoacán, Guerrero, and Guanajuato. In the villages of Oaxaca, carved, painted figures and dance masks can fetch high prices.

Fragile items
When transporting craft objects, any hollows should be padded out, and projecting features wrapped in paper.

Toy truck and passengers

Wooden tiger with sequin eyes

Lacquer-coated wooden lizard from Guerrero

TEXTILES

In some states, traditional garments such as sashes, shawls, wrap-around skirts, and *huipiles* (tunics) are woven on a backstrap loom from hand-spun wool or cotton. Treadle-loomed blankets and rugs are made in Oaxaca. Embroidered blouses can be found in many regions. The Huichol specialize in netted beadwork.

Woven cloth, patterned on the loom

Otomí cloth with embroidery

Caring for textiles
Textiles should always be washed by hand in cold water. Even under these conditions, colors may run, so it is advisable to test-wash a small corner first.

Huichol netted beadwork bag

Nahua embroidered blouse

METALWORK AND JEWELRY

Copper is worked only in Michoacán. It is hammered while red hot to form jugs, platters, and candlesticks. Taxco is world famous for its silverwork. In the Yucatán, gold- and silversmiths specialize in delicate earrings and necklaces.

Cockerel

Bull

Tin decorations
In Oaxaca City, the tinsmiths work from sheets of tin. The shapes are cut out and painted with translucent colors to form lamps, boxes, and shimmering figures. In central regions of Mexico, elegant candlesticks and Baroque mirror-frames are made from unpainted tin.

Mexican bird

Armadillo

Oaxacan woman

Silver earrings from Puebla

OTHER CRAFTS

In Mexico, there is hardly a substance that is not made to serve a functional, decorative, or ceremonial purpose. Fine and unusual work is done using sugar, bone, horn, vanilla, and gum. Pictures are often painted on tree-bark paper.

Lacquered gourd

Basketry
Beautiful yet sturdy, baskets are made in several regions of Mexico, including Oaxaca and Guerrero. Makers use palm, willow, cane, wheat-straw, and agave fibers.

Lacquered box

Lacquer work
Gourds and wooden items such as trays and boxes are given a hard, glossy coat. Archaeological remnants show that lacquer working dates from pre-Columbian times.

SURVIVAL
GUIDE

PRACTICAL INFORMATION 336-347
TRAVEL INFORMATION 348-357

PRACTICAL INFORMATION

Mexico is gradually acquiring a modern tourist infrastructure and is now an easier country to travel around, although tourist facilities in more remote areas may be limited. There are national tourist offices in all large cities; in smaller towns, visitors can obtain information on hotels, restaurants, attractions, and activities

Mexican Ministry of Tourism logo

in the area from the *palacio municipal* (town hall). Be prepared to slow down your pace of life in Mexico: everything takes a little longer. This may be desirable when you are relaxing on the beach, but it can become frustrating if you are up against bureaucracy when traveling. Patience and a philosophical outlook are definitely a help.

WHEN TO GO

THE BEST TIME to visit inland sites is from February to June, before the rainy season begins *(see pp36–7)*. In Chiapas, Tabasco, and Veracruz, the rains are diluvial, but in most areas the rains are only a refreshing daily downpour.

November is ideal for the beach: the climate is fresh, and prices are lower than the mid-December high season. Mexicans also visit the coast during July, August, and on *puentes (see pp30–33)*. On the Caribbean coast, September and October may bring hurricanes. The smog in Mexico City is worst during the winter, from December to February.

VISAS AND PASSPORTS

CITIZENS OF North America, Australasia, Great Britain, and all Western European countries do not require visas

to enter Mexico as tourists, but if going more than 30 km (19 miles) past the border, they must obtain a *Forma Migratoria de Turista* (FMT). The free form is available at borders, airports, ports, and at Mexican embassies or tourist offices.

To obtain the FMT, issued for 180 days, visitors need a passport valid for six months from the date of travel, a return or onward ticket, and proof of finances. US and Canadian citizens need only show proof of citizenship and, for Canadians, a birth certificate. Visitors are required to carry their FMT at all times.

Mexican customs alcohol allowance

Unaccompanied travelers under 18 need a consent form signed by both parents. (British minors only need an FMT.) Non-tourist visitors need to

obtain a visa, and all visitors should check requirements before travelling.

CUSTOMS INFORMATION

VISITORS OVER 18 have a duty-free allowance of 3 liters of wine, beer, or spirits, and 400 cigarettes or 50 cigars. All visitors are allowed one video camera and one still camera, with up to 12 rolls of film. People using APS cameras are advised to bring film with them as the system is not known in all areas of Mexico.

Anyone driving beyond Baja California or the 20-km (12-mile) border zone, will need a vehicle permit *(permiso de importación temporal de vehículos)* from customs, or the Registro Federal de Vehículos *(see p355)*.

Archaeological artifacts may not be taken out of Mexico; the penalties for doing so are harsh. Good, certified reproductions are quite acceptable.

LANGUAGE

THE OFFICIAL language of Mexico is Spanish, spoken by almost everyone. In the big tourist towns many locals will speak some English, but for anyone traveling off the beaten track, a smattering of Spanish is a great advantage.

The 57 indigenous groups in Mexico each have their own language. In remote villages some people speak little Spanish, although there are usually a few bilingual locals.

Mexico City on a rare smog-free day, from the Torre Latinoamericana

◁ **A carnival parade in Huejotzingo, near Puebla**

SOCIAL CUSTOMS

COURTESY IS appreciated in Mexico. On greeting, it is usual to shake hands or kiss on one cheek. When addressing people, use their relevant title *(señor, señora, señorita)*, or professional title according to their university degree, such as *Licenciado (Lic.)* for arts or law graduates.

Road sign to a local museum

Attire is casual, except when visiting churches. Observe signs that forbid photography. Some indigenous people also do not like to be photographed, so ask first to avoid any confrontation.

Mexican *machismo* is world famous but generally harmless, although lone women should avoid isolated areas *(see p340)*.

Entrance tickets to a range of tourist attractions

TOURIST INFORMATION

THE SECTUR (Secretaría de Turismo) offices in Mexico City, state capitals, and main tourist centers provide maps (of variable quality), and information on where to stay and what to see in their area. In smaller towns, visit the town hall for information.

A SECTUR tourist office, providing local information and advice

OPENING HOURS

MOST OF MEXICO'S museums and archaeological sites are governed by the state-run INAH (Instituto Nacional de Antropología e Historia) and art galleries are under the care of the INBA (Instituto Nacional de Bellas Artes). Admission is generally charged, but children go half-price, and Sundays are free to all. Opening times are 9am to 5pm, Tuesdays to Sundays.

DISABLED TRAVELERS

MOST AIRPORTS, and good hotels and restaurants, have wheelchair ramps and adapted toilets. Elsewhere, Mexico does not have good disabled facilities, though the situation is improving in cities.

TIME

THERE ARE four time zones in Mexico. Most of the country is six hours behind Greenwich Mean Time (GMT). Quintana Roo is five hours behind; Baja California Sur, Nayarit, Sinaloa, Sonora, and Chihuahua seven hours; and Baja California Norte eight hours behind.

ELECTRICITY

ELECTRICAL CURRENT – 110 volts, 60 cycles – is the same in Mexico as in the US and Canada. Three-prong, polarized and European two-pin plugs will need adaptors.

CONVERSION CHART

US to metric
1 inch = 2.54 centimeters
1 foot = 30 centimeters
1 mile = 1.6 kilometers
1 ounce = 28 grams
1 pound = 454 grams
1 pint = 0.6 liter
1 gallon = 3.79 liters

Metric to US
1 millimeter = 0.04 inch
1 centimeter = 0.4 inch
1 meter = 3 feet 3 inches
1 kilometer = 0.6 mile
1 gram = 0.04 ounce
1 kilogram = 2.2 pounds
1 liter = 2.1 pints

Health Precautions

Sunhat

WHEREVER YOU PLAN to travel within Mexico, it is wise to pack a small medical kit of essentials before leaving home, including plasters, bandages, tape, gauze, and tweezers. Antiseptic ointment can prevent infection of minor wounds, and insect repellent is essential. Bring supplies of any prescribed medication with you, and solutions for contact lenses if you wear them. The sun's rays are very strong in Mexico, so pack sunscreen with a protection factor of 15-plus, as well as a sunhat. Water purification tablets are a good idea for those traveling off the beaten track.

Mexican ambulance

VACCINATIONS AND INSURANCE

NO SPECIFIC vaccinations are required to enter Mexico, except for travelers coming from a country where yellow fever is present, in which case an inoculation document is required. But it is worth observing a few precautions, depending on the region.

Malaria is found in some rural parts of Mexico, particularly in the south, and antimalarial medication is recommended for these areas. More for comfort than necessity, visitors to the Pacific and Gulf coasts are also advised to use repellent against mosquitoes. Travelers to remote regions should be immunized against diphtheria, hepatitis A and B, and typhoid, and make sure their polio and tetanus vaccinations are up to date.

Travel insurance is essential; public health care is not always adequate, and private treatment can be expensive.

MEDICAL TREATMENT

THERE ARE THREE types of hospital in Mexico. Social Security (IMSS) hospitals are restricted to Mexican residents, and ISSSTE hospitals and

clinics are for civil servants and university workers only. Everyone else, including visitors, must either pay for private treatment or rely on the local, and generally overcrowded, Centro de Salud (Civil Hospital) run by the state, or the Cruz Roja (Red Cross). The level of care is variable in all types of hospital. In major centers such as Mexico City, Monterrey, and Guadalajara, public hospitals are fairly well equipped, but in more remote towns they often lack basic requirements. Equally, the large private hospitals in big cities, such as the

Sign for a Cruz Roja hospital

ABC Hospital in Mexico City, are often very good, but the smaller, private clinics are sometimes poorly equipped.

Hotels usually have a list of reliable doctors (English-speaking if necessary), as will your relevant embassy, or the nearest local tourist office.

IN AN EMERGENCY

IN CASE OF emergency, the Red Cross has an ambulance service in most major cities and tourist centers. If you are in a remote area, it may be quicker to take a taxi to the nearest hospital. If you are not covered by medical insurance, go to the emergency room (*Emergencias*) of any state hospital.

SECTUR, the Mexican Ministry of Tourism, has a 24-hour telephone hotline. Although this is primarily for immediate assistance, it can also provide general, non-emergency health guidance.

PHARMACIES

MEXICO HAS a fairly tolerant attitude to medication. Many drugs that are not available, or have been banned, in the USA, Canada, or Europe can be bought in Mexico, often without a prescription. Prices for all drugs are high, except for social security patients who receive basic drugs free of charge. Packets of oral rehydration salts are provided free at health centers for people suffering from diarrhea.

A busy pharmacy in the center of Mexico City

Tourists wearing hats in the sun

MINOR HAZARDS

VISITORS TO archaeological sites often have to walk long distances with little or no shade. Sunscreen, hats, and bottled water are strongly recommended for these excursions, as well as for the beach and other exposed places. It is also a good idea to carry bottled water and oral rehydration salts when traveling in tropical regions.

Coral cuts and jellyfish stings should be bathed in vinegar, then dabbed with antiseptic ointment. If the wound becomes infected, seek the advice of a doctor.

Some people are affected by the combination of high altitude and severe air pollution when they first arrive in Mexico City, and may experience dizziness, nosebleeds, breathlessness, or fatigue. While acclimatizing, it is best to avoid excessive exercise and alcohol. The elderly, and anyone with anemia, hypertension, or respiratory or cardiac problems, should consult their doctor before traveling to Mexico City.

STOMACH UPSETS

BY FOLLOWING a few rules, there is a good chance you will avoid diarrhea, or "Moctezuma's revenge" as the local version is often called. Never drink water straight from the tap, and when ordering cold drinks at local establishments, ask for them without ice (*sin hielo*). Most hotels provide purified water (*agua de garrafón*), and bottled water is readily available. Otherwise, boil water for 20 minutes or disinfect it with drops (*gotas*) bought at any supermarket or pharmacy.

Foods to be particularly wary of are lettuce, strawberries, and all raw, unpeeled fruits or vegetables; these need to be washed and disinfected prior to consumption. Raw fish, which is the main ingredient of *ceviche (see p311)*, is also risky because it can carry waterborne diseases such as cholera.

Exercise discretion, especially at street food stalls (*tacos al pastor* are notorious), but with a little care there is no need to spend your vacation eating in fast-food outlets.

INSECTS

THE MAJORITY OF visitors to Mexico are unlikely to come across any dangerous creatures, and it is rare for tourists to become seriously ill as a result of an insect bite.

Scorpions are common in Mexico. Black or dark brown ones are quite harmless, but the light yellow ones, found in hot, dry places, will need an antidote (free from any Centro de Salud). Tarantulas look more intimidating than they are; far worse is the *capulina*, or black widow spider, found in western Mexico. Always check shoes and shake out clothing before putting them on, especially in more rural areas.

Insect repellent and a mosquito coil for protection against bites

SERIOUS DISEASES

DISEASES SUCH as typhoid, malaria, hepatitis, and yellow fever can be protected against by immunization. Standard food and water precautions are the best forms of protection against cholera.

Common parasitic infections include tapeworm as well as giardiasis, which is acquired by drinking contaminated water. It can cause chronic diarrhea, abdominal cramps, fatigue, nausea, nausea, loss

of appetite, and weight loss. A prescribed treatment with the drug metronidazole is usually very successful in curing the infection.

Dengue fever is a viral illness spread by mosquitoes for which there is no vaccination. The best protection is to use plenty of insect repellent, cover up well when outside (particularly at night, but also in the daytime), and sleep under mosquito nets. The onset of dengue is sudden, with fever, headache, joint pains, nausea, vomiting, and a rash. Although not usually serious, it may last up to 10 days and full recovery can take up to 4 weeks. In the case of all serious illnesses, see a physician as soon as you can.

PUBLIC TOILETS

PUBLIC TOILETS ARE few and far between in Mexico, and those that do exist (in gas stations, markets, cafés, and bus and train terminals, for example) are often badly equipped and unhygienic. In larger cities it is best to make for a Sanborn's (*see p114*), or another large department store, restaurant, or supermarket, as they provide better facilities.

Toilets at airports and major tourist centers vary from good to adequate. Elsewhere it is always advisable to carry a roll of toilet paper and a bar of soap.

Toilet sign

Personal Security

CRIME IS ON THE INCREASE in Mexico, and although most visitors do not encounter problems, it is important to be aware of dangers and take appropriate precautions. Pickpockets are common in cities, and rife in the capital. Leave valuables in a hotel safe and keep cash in a moneybelt under your clothing. If traveling by car, avoid driving at night, park in hotel parking lots, and never leave possessions visible inside the car. Avoid isolated routes or beaches, where attacks can sometimes occur.

Auxiliary police officers guarding a store

POLICE FORCES

AS A GENERAL RULE it is best to avoid all police in Mexico; they are rarely helpful and can make difficult situations worse. (The federal traffic police and the tourist police are exceptions; the former will assist you if you get stuck on the highway, and the latter usually speak some English and can be useful if you need help or directions.) However, should you find yourself in contact with the police during your stay, it is useful to recognize the various divisions.

Most visitors are likely to come into contact with three or four types of police officer. From time to time the uniforms worn by Mexico's police forces change, and colors vary from region to region. The traffic police (*Policía de Tránsito*) direct traffic and impose fines for traffic offenses. In Mexico City they are nicknamed *tamarindos* (tamarinds) because of their dark brown uniforms.

The auxiliary police *(Policía Auxiliar)*, dressed in dark blue, are an important force in the capital. They provide backup to the traffic police, and work as security guards in shops, restaurants, and metro stations. The bank and industry police *(Policía Bancaria e Industrial)*, who also wear blue-colored uniforms, work on contract to banks and businesses.

Mexico City traffic police   **Baja California traffic police**

Outside the cities, the federal traffic police (*Policía Federal de Caminos*), patrol the highways in black and white cars. A few states have a tourist police force (*Policía Turística*) to assist visitors to Mexico.

Other forces include the mounted police, riot police, and, most notoriously, the *Policía Judicial Federal* (PJF). These *judiciales*, as they are called, work for the Federal Chief Prosecutor, and deal with crimes such as homicide and drug pushing. They wear plain clothes, have a sinister reputation, and are best avoided.

DEALING WITH THE MEXICAN POLICE

IF YOU FIND yourself in any trouble while in Mexico, it is more advisable to contact your embassy than the police.

However, should you come into contact with the police, the first rule is to stay as calm and polite as possible. If you get stopped and booked by the traffic police (a common occurrence with the *Policía de Tránsito*, especially in the capital), first try explaining that you are a tourist. If that does not impress them, they may ask you to pay an unofficial fine, which many people pay. Officers' wages are very low in Mexico, and these *mordidas* (literally "bites") are generally considered a supplement to their income. The *mordidas* are also negotiable and usually cost less than the official fine (*infracción*). To make a complaint against any police officer, take a note of his or her name, badge, and patrol car number.

WOMEN TRAVELERS

ANY WOMAN WHO travels alone in Mexico is likely to get a stream of uninvited compliments. This is usually no more than a verbal game, but if it becomes too persistent, a firm *déjeme en paz* (leave me be) should work. This *machismo* can be a help at times, as men will come to your aid. Women should avoid going to isolated beaches or rural areas, or wandering through lonely streets at night. Nude or topless bathing is not generally acceptable.

Policía Federal de Caminos police car

Fire engine ready for action

STREET HAZARDS

PEDESTRIANS DO NOT have the right of way in Mexico. Whether walking or driving, it is important to keep your eyes wide open at all times. Be prepared for uneven road surfaces and sidewalks, or even unexpected gaping holes in the middle of a busy street.

Be sure to look both ways when crossing one-way streets in Mexico City, as on some of them the buses are allowed to travel in both directions. Be careful at junctions too – traffic signals and signs are not always obeyed by drivers.

Green and white VW taxi in Mexico City, to be avoided if possible

MEXICO CITY TAXIS

AS A RESULT OF increasing incidences of robbery and assaults on passengers in taxis, visitors to Mexico City are officially advised against flagging down taxis in the street. When in need of a cab, it is best to telephone for a radio taxi *(sitio)*. As an additional precaution, you can ask

the telephone dispatcher for the driver's name and the cab's license plate number. Visitors arriving at the international airport in Mexico City should take only airport taxis, which are yellow, with an airport symbol on the door. For these you must pre-pay the fare at one of the special booths inside the airport.

LOST AND STOLEN PROPERTY

THERE IS LITTLE point in reporting lost or stolen property to the Mexican police unless you need to file an official report *(levantar un acta)* for insurance purposes. You will need to do this at the nearest police station *(delegación)*, usually within 24 hours of the robbery. Lost passports and travelers' checks should be reported to your embassy and to the issuing bank, respectively.

NATURAL DISASTERS

IN MEXICO, as in all countries with a variable, tropical climate and landscape, natural disasters do occur, but they are by no means a regular threat. In the event of an earthquake, try to remain calm and move away immediately from electricity poles, wires, or any high structure that could fall on you. Do not attempt to use elevators. If you are in a building, the best place to stand is in a doorway, but never under the stairs. Most injuries in earthquakes are caused by broken glass, so keep shoes and a flashlight near your bed at night. If you are unlucky enough to be on the

DIRECTORY

EMERGENCY NUMBERS

Tourist Security
52 50 01 23.

Ambulance
065.

Police
060; 5242 51 00.

Stolen Property
061.

Fire Department and Earthquake Advice
56 83 11 42.

MEXICO CITY TAXIS

Super Sitio 160
52 71 91 46 (24 hours).

Sitio 210
55 95 60 03 (24 hours).

Sitio 252
52 71 25 60 (24 hours).

Servitaxis
55 16 60 20 (24 hours).

Caribbean coast when a hurricane hits and are unable to leave the area, stay in your hotel, shut all windows tightly, and stand as far away from them as you possibly can.

Since December 1994, the Popocatépetl volcano has registered seismic activity *(see p149)*. The authorities have restricted access to the area, and have closed parks and hiking trails on the mountain's slopes. Similar restrictions are in place on Colima's Volcán de Fuego *(see p187)*. If you plan to hike in the vicinity, be alert to posted warnings, and contact your embassy or SECTUR (Secretaría de Turismo) for the latest information.

Fire and earthquake safety instructions

Banking and Currency

THE UNIT OF CURRENCY in Mexico is the peso, but US dollars are widely accepted in tourist areas, and most large hotels, shops, and restaurants accept the major credit cards. Only in smaller places will you find difficulties without pesos. Bring cash or traveler's checks in US dollars; other foreign currencies are not readily exchanged in all banks. There are no restrictions on the import or export of peso notes and coins.

Standard cash dispensing machine

BANKS AND BUREAUX DE CHANGE

THE TWO LARGEST banks are **BBVA Bancomer** and **Banamex**, but a growing number of foreign banks also operate branches in Mexico. Opening hours are normally from 9am to 5pm, weekdays only, although in the capital and other large cities, many stay open until 7pm, and are open on Saturdays until 2pm. Ask at your hotel for opening times of the nearest branches.

Mexican bank's logo

Remember, however, that many branches do not change foreign currency or traveler's checks after 2pm, so aim to go in the morning. Bureaux de change (casas de cambio) are open longer hours than banks, and offer a quicker service and better exchange rates, particularly compared to hotels and shops. The main international airports have at least one casa de cambio – useful for changing a small amount for taxis or buses.

TRAVELER'S CHECKS AND CREDIT CARDS

TRAVELER'S CHECKS drawn in US dollars are the safest way of carrying money. They can be changed at casas de cambio, and at most banks. When cashing the checks you will be asked to show your passport or another form of identification. Fees are not charged, but the exchange rate is likely to be lower for checks than for cash. Keep the receipt and a record of the serial numbers separate from the checks, in case they are lost or stolen. The credit cards most widely accepted are Master-Card, VISA and, to a lesser extent, American Express. Cash dispensing machines (cajero automático) are common in Mexico's big cities. As a precaution against theft, draw money from the machines only during business hours, and then in populated areas like main streets, banks, or shopping malls.

Changing money at a casa de cambio

DIRECTORY

BANKS

BBVA Bancomer
Bolívar 38,
Mexico City.
(56 21 34 34.

Banamex
Isabela Católica 44,
Mexico City.
(52 25 30 00.

LOST CARDS AND TRAVELER'S CHECKS

American Express
(53 26 26 66.

MasterCard (Access)
(001 800 307 7309 (toll free).

VISA
(001 800 84 72 911 (toll free).

TIPPING AND TAXES

IN MEXICO, tips are generally unofficial, but appreciated. In restaurants, tip between 10 and 15 percent of the total bill. If paying by credit card, fill in the tip box (propina) on the payment slip with the amount you wish to give – if you leave the box blank some unscrupulous staff may fill it in with a far greater amount. Taxi drivers do not expect to be tipped unless they have carried your luggage or provided some other extra service. Porters, on the other hand, especially those at airports or large hotels, expect a gratuity.

It is everyday practice to give small change to people who help you in any way, such as chambermaids or gas station attendants. Most of these workers earn a minimal wage so tips are an essential part of their income. Parking attendants and the children who help in supermarkets are unpaid, and survive on tips.

Prices usually include the 15 percent sales tax, or VAT, (Impuesto al Valor Agregado, or IVA), but sometimes a price is given as más IVA (plus sales tax) which means that 15 percent will be added to the bill.

CURRENCY

THE MEXICAN PESO is divided into 100 centavos. On January 1, 1993, three zeros were knocked off the peso so that 1,000 pesos became 1 Nuevo Peso (N$1). The word *nuevo* (new) has now been dropped, and the currency is again referred to as simply the peso ($1). Nuevos pesos are no longer legal tender.

The peso's symbol, $, is easily confused with that of the US dollar. To solve this problem, prices are often printed with the letters MN after them, meaning *moneda nacional* (national currency). Always carry small amounts of cash around in both coins and small denomination bills, for tips and minor purchases. Shops, taxis, and buses are often unable to give change for larger denomination notes.

Coins
There are four peso coins, in denominations of $1, $2, $5, $10, and $20. All peso coins are silver and gold, and increase in size according to their value. Centavo coins are in denominations of 5¢, 10¢, 20¢, and 50¢. The denominations are clearly marked on the front.

Bank Notes
Mexican bank notes are issued in five denominations: $20, $50, $100, $200, and $500.

10 pesos

5 pesos

1 peso

50 centavos

20 centavos

10 centavos

20 pesos

50 pesos

100 pesos

200 pesos

Communications

Mexican post office logo

THE TELEPHONE is the most popular means of communication in Mexico, largely because the postal service is so slow and unreliable – letters can take weeks, even months to reach their destination. Public telephones are easy to find and, in most cases, take phonecards. If mailing a letter, mail boxes are mostly yellow, although in Mexico City and tourist resorts, the new ones, marked *Buzón Expresso*, are bright red. For entertainment, Mexico has nine television channels and two national radio stations. English-language visitors can catch up on events by reading the *Mexico City Times* and *The News*.

TELEPHONE NUMBERS

THE COUNTRY CODE for calling Mexico is 52, followed by an area code. These area codes are currently one or two digits, followed by numbers of seven, six, or five digits. All area codes are in the process of changing. Two- and three-digit codes become one-digit, the last numbers of the code being incorporated into the main number. In Monterrey and Guadalajara, the one-digit codes are being added to the local number, to give eight digits and no code. The one-digit code has already been dropped in Mexico City.

Logo of the Mexican telephone company Telmex

USING A PUBLIC TELEPHONE

1 Lift the receiver, and wait for the dial tone. The display will indicate that you should insert your phonecard (*inserte su tarjeta*) in the slot to the right of the receiver.

2 Once the phonecard is inserted, the current value of the card will be indicated on the digital display.

3 Key in the number you want to dial. As you dial, the number you are calling will appear on the display. You will also be able to see how much money is left on the phonecard.

4 When your call is finished, replace the receiver. At the end of the call the phonecard will automatically re-emerge. If the card runs out mid-call you will be cut off and have to start the call again.

Phonecards in various designs and denominations

PUBLIC TELEPHONES

LOCAL CALLS, which cost a small amount, can be made from call boxes in the street, and from coin-operated phones in stores or restaurants displaying a telephone sign.

The blue LADATEL telephones, run by Teléfonos de México (TELMEX), take LADATEL phonecards, which are available in denominations of 30 or 50 pesos from most newsstands and stores. A few public phones can also be used with credit cards, or with US and UK phonecards, accessed by dialing the appropriate code. With TELMEX, long-distance calls are cheapest at weekends, and after 8pm on weekdays. A 50-pesos LADATEL phonecard is the best one to use when making a transatlantic call.

If there is no working LADATEL phone available, most towns and some villages have a *caseta de larga distancia*. These commercially-run telephone booths charge higher rates than public phones but are cheaper than phoning from a hotel. It is a good idea to ask how much the call will cost beforehand.

Mexicans generally answer the telephone by saying "*¿Bueno?*" and then waiting for you to identify yourself.

DIALING CODES

- For operator/directory service, dial 040.
- To make a collect (reverse-charge) call, dial 020 (national) or 090 (international), ask for *llamada por cobrar*, and give the number you wish to call.
- For long-distance calls within Mexico, dial 01 followed by the area code and the number.
- For international calls, dial 00 followed by the country code, then the area code and number. Country codes are: Australia 61; Ireland 353; New Zealand 64; South Africa 27; UK 44; USA and Canada 1.

Mexican stamps decorated with themes of the country, including culture and wildlife

MAIL SERVICES

SENDING (and receiving) parcels by regular mail service in Mexico is not recommended. Registering both letters and parcels improves the odds against pilfering. However, the safest way to send anything abroad is through one of the international courier services.

The main post offices (*oficinas de correos*) open from 8am to 8pm on weekdays, and from 8am to 3pm on Saturdays. Smaller post offices usually have shorter opening hours. Stamps for postcards can usually be purchased from the larger hotels.

A mail holding service is available at most main post offices. *Poste restante* letters should be addressed to the *Lista de Correos*, followed by the name of the town and state. You will need to show ID when collecting letters.

American Express also provides a free holding service for their customers. You can have your mail sent directly to one of their offices, from where you can then collect it.

Mail box

MEXICAN ADDRESSES

MEXICAN ADDRESSES list the house number after the name of the street. In some cases, the street number is followed by a hyphen and then the number or letter of the apartment. The next line of the address may indicate the name of the *Fraccionamiento (Fracc.)* if the house is on an estate. The *colonia (col.)* refers to the neighborhood or area within the city. Include the *Código Postal* (zip code) if you can.

RADIO AND TELEVISION

NOT ALL OF MEXICO's nine television channels can be seen across the whole country, and some regions broadcast local programs at certain times of the day. Seven of the channels are private. Channels 11 and 22, which broadcast films and programs of cultural and scientific interest, are run by the state.

The largest television company is Televisa; Cablevisión and MVS are the two principal cable television companies.

Foreign programs are generally dubbed into Spanish, but movies are occasionally shown in their original language with Spanish subtitles. Most hotels provide cable television, with programs in both Spanish and English.

Satellite TV is often available at the more upscale hotels throughout the country.

Almost every city in Mexico has a local radio station, and some, particularly in the more touristy areas, play English-language songs and have daily slots for English programs. In northern areas it is possible to pick up US radio stations.

NEWSPAPERS AND MAGAZINES

THE *Mexico City Times* and *The News*, both published in the capital, cover mostly Mexican and US news, and have listings pages for cultural activities in Mexico City. (For Spanish-speaking visitors, the listings in *Tiempo Libre*, published on Thursdays by *La Jornada* newspaper, and *¿dónde?* are more complete.) Outside Mexico City, English-language newspapers are published in areas with English-speaking communities, such as Guadalajara and San Miguel de Allende.

The *International Herald Tribune* and *New York Times* are usually on newsstands the day after publication. News magazines such as *Time* and *Newsweek* are also available.

The widely read national broadsheet newspapers are *Reforma*, *El Universal*, *La Jornada*, and *Excelsior*. The tabloids, such as *La Prensa*, have a far larger readership.

INTERNET AND FAX

AN E-MAIL ADDRESS is a good way of keeping in touch while traveling. Cybercafés, where you can pick up e-mail and surf the internet, are on the increase in Mexico's cities and tourist areas. Hourly rates are usually very reasonable.

Public fax machines are also widely available in large towns and cities. Look out for a sign saying *Fax Público*.

Sending mail at a Mexican post office counter

Spectator Sports

MEXICANS ARE SPORTS MAD. Mexico is the only country to have hosted soccer's World Cup twice, and it is the home of the World Boxing Council – one of that sport's most important governing bodies. There are three daily sports newspapers in Mexico City alone, and television provides saturation coverage. Every Mexican soccer league game is shown live, and baseball is broadcast live on radio. Most major sports events take place at venues in Mexico City *(see p117)*.

The masked wrestlers of *lucha libre*

WRESTLING

THIS MUCH-LOVED national sport, known as *lucha libre*, attracts aficionados from all levels of society, both young and old. There are two main places to see it: Arena México on Friday nights, and at the Toreo de Cuatro Caminos on Sundays. The wrestlers are theatrically costumed and often represent organizations or causes, such as Superbarrio, who champions the disenfranchised of Mexico. Spectators in the front row risk being injured by falling wrestlers.

BOXING

BOXING MATCHES are staged every weekend in Mexico City. To catch a fight, go to the Arena Coliseo on a Saturday night, an unglamorous hall where many of Mexico's past and current champions cut their teeth. There are usually at least four bouts, one of which is often a Mexican title fight.

CHARRERIA

THE ONLY SPORT that can be considered uniquely Mexican is *charreria (see p74)*. The elaborately dressed *charros* (horsemen) perform a variety of disciplines comparable to rodeo riders. The sport consists of ten tests, all of which take place in a ring similar to that used in bullfighting. Charros can be seen in the Rancho del Charro in Mexico City, but this is more of a rural event celebrated in the central and northern parts of the country. Music is an essential part of a *charreria* event, with mariachi musicians providing the entertainment.

SOCCER

SOCCER IS A national passion in Mexico. There are two tournaments a year: the Winter Tournament that runs from July through December, and the Summer Tournament that starts in January and ends in May. The biggest teams are America and Cruz Azul (from Mexico City), and Guadalajara, which is famous for signing only Mexican players. The best place to see the matches live is at the Estadio Azteca, the only stadium ever to have hosted two World Cup Finals. To join the victory celebrations after international matches, go to the Angel of Independence *(p84)*, where hordes of fans wave flags and blow whistles.

BULLFIGHTING

THE MAIN bullfighting season *(temporada grande)* runs from November through April. Mexico attracts top toreros to pit their wits against these heavy beasts. Mexico City's bullring *(see p110)* is the largest in the world and is the place both to see and be seen. Politicians, film stars, millionaire businessmen, soap opera stars, and many other Mexican celebrities can regularly be spotted in the ring's VIP seats. The bullfights begin there at 4pm every Sunday afternoon.

Ticket for a bullfight in Mexico City

BASEBALL

BASEBALL IS ALSO a popular sport in Mexico, principally in the south and north of the country. There are two leagues, the Mexican Baseball League, and the Pacific League. The big matches in Mexico often sell out, particularly the play-off finals in August. The two main clubs in the capital, the Tigres and the Diablos Rojos, both play their matches in the Foro Sol, on Magdalena Michuca. It is not necessary to reserve tickets; just pay at the gate.

***Charro* riders in high-speed action**

Outdoor Activities

THE MANY DIVERSE landscapes of Mexico create the ideal conditions for a range of outdoor pursuits. Many hotels have their own sporting facilities, or will advise on what there is to do locally. Tuesday's edition of the *Reforma* newspaper lists a variety of adventure activities available. Tourist information offices, in Mexico or abroad, can help locate the best areas for a particular sport.

WATERSPORTS

HOTELS IN MOST of Mexico's beach resorts will arrange for scuba or snorkeling trips in local waters. Alternatively, independent companies offering the same kind of trips can be found along any built-up waterfront. Shop around, and be sure to ask for as many details as possible before signing up. The best place to snorkel or scuba dive is at Cozumel, off the Yucatán coast *(see pp282–3)*.

Water skis, jetskis, and small launches can also be rented at all major tourist resorts. Other water-based activities include parasailing, and riding on the "banana" – a yellow inflatable pulled by a speed boat. Surfing is very popular on the Pacific coast. Puerto Escondido is a surfing mecca, and surfers also gather on the beaches of Baja California *(see pp162–9)*.

One of the big booms in Mexico in recent years has been in freshwater adventure vacation travel. There are a host of companies offering trips for such activities as white-water rafting, kayaking, and canoeing, particularly in the states of San Luis Potosi and Veracruz. Accommodations on these trips vary from comfortable hotels to more basic riverside campsites.

Horseback riding in Mexico

HORSEBACK RIDING

SEVERAL STABLES rent out horses by the hour in the area around Mexico City. Most of these clubs give lessons, and some provide guides to take you on preplanned treks. At the quieter vacation resorts, such as Pie de la Cuesta to the north of Acapulco, children rent out horses by the hour for visitors to ride along the beach.

HIKING AND CLIMBING

MEXICO HAS an array of spectacular mountain areas. The two ranges of the Sierra Madre, running through north and central Mexico, provide good trekking routes. There are also some great places for climbing in Mexico

State, easily accessible from the city. But not all mountain areas welcome visitors, and it is essential to check that the area is safe before you set off.

Some remote parts of the country are used to grow illegal harvests of marijuana and heroin poppies. Others are the refuge of guerrillas, or used as training grounds for soldiers, and civilians can be in danger in such places. Yet more areas are governed by indigenous peoples *(see pp20–21)*, and it is advisable to seek written permission from the tribal elders before entering their territory.

GOLF

MOST BIG COASTAL resorts have at least one golf course, and places such as Acapulco, Cancún, and Puerto Vallarta have several. Many are owned by hotel chains, offering guests a discount per round of golf. However, nonguests can usually get a game by phoning in advance. There are over 70 courses to choose from across the country.

Golfers in Cancún

FISHING

GOOD FISHING can be found at many Mexican vacation resorts. Large hotels may organize their own fishing trips, but independent operators can always be found running similar services. The most common saltwater fish are tuna, swordfish, sea bass, and snook. Mazatlán is home to Mexico's biggest sport fishing fleet.

The fishing season starts in October and ends in May. Although mostly saltwater fishing is available on the coast, there are freshwater lagoons in Acapulco, Campeche, Mazatlán, and Tampico. Freshwater fishing is available in many inland states.

White-water rafting, an exhilarating pastime

TRAVEL INFORMATION

MEXICO IS A huge country, and although internal travel is not always as fast as visitors might hope, the transport system is increasingly easy to use. There are airports within reach of all the major cities. Flights from the USA and around the world arrive at more than a dozen international airports, and domestic flights offer an alternative to land travel. Privatization of the railroad system

Mexicana airplane waiting to depart

has eliminated train travel, since most passenger services have been cut. However, there is an extensive bus network reaching even tiny villages. Driving offers the most flexibility in terms of speed and accessibility, but it can be hair-raising, and road conditions are not always good. Ferries connect the mainland with Baja California and the Caribbean islands of Cozumel and Isla Mujeres.

ARRIVING BY AIR

MEXICO CITY's Aeropuerto Benito Juárez is the key arrival point for international flights into Mexico. There are scheduled flights here from over 20 US cities. As well as to the capital, travelers can fly direct from numerous cities in the USA to Acapulco, Cancún, Cozumel, Guadalajara, Guaymas, Huatulco, Loreto, La Paz, Manzanillo, Mazatlán, Puerto Vallarta, San José del Cabo, Veracruz, and Zihuatanejo. Flying times from New York and Los Angeles to Mexico City are five-and-a-half and three-and-a-half hours respectively. **Air Canada** flies daily from Toronto to Mexico City in just under five hours.

From Europe, some international airlines still fly via the USA, although **AeroMéxico**, **British Airways**, **Iberia**, **Air France**, **Northwest/KLM**,

Arrivals area of Aeropuerto Benito Juárez in Mexico City

and **Lufthansa** operate direct flights, cutting travel time considerably. British Airways (BA) operates four direct flights from London to Mexico City each week, with a flying time of 12 hours. There is also a weekly BA scheduled flight to Cancún. Air France and AeroMéxico fly direct from Paris; Northwest/KLM from Amsterdam; Lufthansa from Frankfurt; and Iberia and AeroMéxico from Madrid (a flight time of just over 11 hours). Some chartered flights

travel direct from Europe to the major beach resorts. Visitors transferring in Mexico City must claim their baggage before boarding their onward domestic flight.

There are no direct flights from New Zealand or Australia, but you can transfer in Los Angeles to a connecting flight. The total flying time from Sydney to Mexico City, via LA, is sixteen-and-a-half hours.

Central and South American airlines **Aviateca** and **Varig** run flights into Mexico City. **Mexicana** and **AeroMéxico** also offer connections between Central and South American cities and Mexico City.

AIRPORTS

THERE ARE 60 airports in Mexico. Of these, 15 operate international flights for tourists. Another 30 are classified as "international,"

AIRPORT	🛈 INFORMATION	DISTANCE TO TOWN OR RESORT	AVERAGE TIME BY ROAD FROM AIRPORT
Mexico City	55 71 36 00	Zócalo 15 km (9 miles)	45 minutes
Acapulco	(744) 466 94 29	Downtown 30 km (19 miles)	30 minutes
Cancún	(998) 848 72 00	Cancún City 20 km (12 miles)	30 minutes
Cozumel	(987) 872 04 85	Cozumel town 6 km (4 miles)	5 minutes
Guadalajara	(33) 3688 51 20	Downtown 16 km (10 miles)	20 minutes
La Paz	(612) 124 63 36	Downtown 14 km (9 miles)	10 minutes
Puerto Vallarta	(322) 221 12 98	Calle Madero 7 km (4 miles)	10 minutes
Tijuana	(664) 607 82 00	Downtown 7 km (4 miles)	15 minutes
Veracruz	(229) 934 90 08	Downtown 18 km (11 miles)	15 minutes

Modern interior of Mexico City's international airport

but are either towns on the US border, or operate only one or two flights to foreign destinations. The other 15 airports are for domestic flights only *(see pp350–51)*.

PACKAGE DEALS AND ORGANIZED TOURS

AIR FARES can vary greatly from one travel agent to another, and also from season to season. Christmas, summer, and to a lesser extent, Easter, tend to be the most expensive times. Fixed-date returns are always cheaper than open returns, though less flexible. It is also worth noting that international air tickets are expensive to buy in Mexico.

Packages for main resorts are available at travel agencies worldwide and are becoming increasingly popular. These inclusive vacations tend to be cheaper than independent travel. The most popular package destinations are Cancún,

Mexican airport sign

Acapulco, Baja California Sur, Huatulco, Puerto Vallarta, and Ixtapa and Zihuatanejo.

There are also companies, both in Mexico and abroad, that organize inclusive tours (*viaje todo pagado* or VTP) to sites or regions of particular interest, such as the Copper Canyon, the Maya ruins of the Yucatán, and the Colonial Heartland. Popular special interest vacations include mountain climbing, horseback riding, scuba diving, whitewater rafting, and bird-watching.

ARRIVING BY LAND FROM THE USA

VISITORS ARE free to enter Mexico's border zone (including the Baja California peninsula and the Sonora Free Trade Zone) without passing through immigration control. If you wish to travel past the free zone, you must obtain an FMT tourist card or visa *(see p336)*. There are bus services into Mexico from some US border towns, but most people arriving by bus or train prefer to cross the border on foot, and pick up one of the cheaper Mexican buses.

Vehicle entry into Mexico is strictly regulated, and drivers bringing their cars across the border need to obtain

The border crossing between Mexico and the USA, which is strictly controlled at all times

a *permiso de importación temporal* (temporary import permit), as well as separate car insurance *(see p355)*.

ARRIVING BY LAND FROM CENTRAL AMERICA

THERE ARE THREE border crossings from Guatemala into Chiapas, and one from Belize into Quintana Roo. The official immigration procedure is the same as when entering from the USA, although it is invariably less efficient. Visitors traveling south of the border must hand in their tourist card. On returning to Mexico, a new FMT card will be issued.

DIRECTORY

AEROMÉXICO

(51 33 40 00.
(001 800 02 14 000 (toll free).

MEXICANA

(54 48 09 90.

OTHER AIRLINES

Air Canada
(91 38 02 80.

Air France
(21 22 82 00.

British Airways
(53 87 03 10.

Iberia
(51 30 30 30.

Northwest/KLM
(52 79 53 90.

Lufthansa
(52 30 00 00.

CENTRAL AND SOUTH AMERICAN AIRLINES

Aviateca
(52 11 66 40.

Varig
(52 80 91 92.

Domestic Flights

IN A COUNTRY the size of Mexico, internal flights can sometimes offer a convenient alternative to long bus trips or traveling by car, especially for those people on a tight schedule. Costs, however, are considerably higher than long-distance bus travel, so it is not an option for visitors on a budget. The domestic airline network is extensive, with AeroMéxico and Mexicana providing the majority of services, although there are not necessarily direct routes between all of the country's 60 airports. Travelers will find that many internal flights involve a brief stopover in Mexico City.

Poster advertising Aerocaribe and Aerocozumel domestic airlines

Restaurant in the departure lounge at Monterrey airport

DOMESTIC AIRLINES

PASSENGERS ARRIVING at Mexico City airport from international, long-haul destinations can connect with scheduled domestic flights. These flights travel direct from the capital to all Mexico's big cities and vacation resorts, although their published timetables are not always 100 percent reliable.

Most internal flights are operated by the two largest airlines, **AeroMéxico** and **Mexicana**. Between them, they reach most national, as well as many international *(see p348)*, destinations. From Mexico City airport, there are frequent daily flights to all the regional capitals. They also both serve the main tourist centers, including Acapulco, Cancún, and Zihuatanejo.

Mexico has a number of regional airlines. **Aero California** operates domestic flights to and from cities in northern and central Mexico, as well as flights to cities in the USA. **Aero California Vacations**, based in La Paz, offers package vacations and tours in northern and central Mexico. **Aviacsa** serves the southeast, as well as Mexico City, Guadalajara, Monterrey, and Tijuana. It also operates flights to Las Vegas and Houston in the United States.

Aeromar operates in central Mexico, and has its own terminal at Aeropuerto Benito Juárez in Mexico City. There are two subsidiaries of Mexicana: **Aerocozumel** serves the southern regions of Mexico; and **Aerocaribe** runs flights to the Caribbean. **Aerolitoral**, which is part of AeroMéxico, flies to various destinations in northern Mexico, as well as flights to Tuscon, Arizona.

RESERVATIONS AND CHECKING IN

STANDARD FARES FOR domestic flights are usually at least double the equivalent trip by bus, but special deals are often available so it is worth shopping around. Reservations should be made as far in advance as possible, especially at the peak seasons of Christmas and Easter, and during the summer. Tickets can be reserved by telephone or in person at the airline reservation and ticket office, or through a travel agent.

Aerial view of the runway at Cozumel airport, served by both international and domestic flights

A small airport departure tax, payable either in US dollars or pesos, is levied on all flights in Mexico. Check your travel details carefully, however, as this tax may already have been included in the price of your ticket.

The baggage allowance for domestic flights is usually 25 kilos (55 pounds). Arrive for check in at least one hour before takeoff for domestic flights, and up to one-and-a-half hours before takeoff for all international flights. Most airlines operate a no smoking policy on flights of less than 90 minutes.

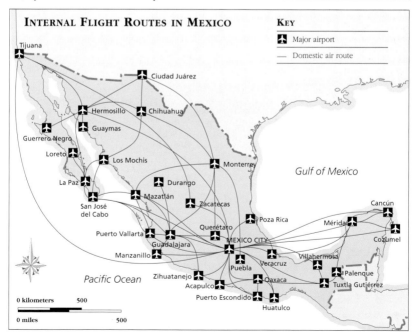

A small, domestic plane at Palenque airport

CONCESSIONARY FARES

INFANTS UNDER two years old travel free on domestic flights, provided they do not have a seat of their own. Children over two, but under 12, pay 67 percent of the full fare, and are entitled to a seat and standard baggage allowance.

Certain airlines, including Aerolitoral, also offer discounts of 50 percent for students and senior citizens (aged 65 years or over) but they must be able to produce the appropriate identification or proof of age.

THE MEXIPASS

AEROMÉXICO AND Mexicana offer a reduced fare (the Mexipass) for any foreign visitor to Mexico who intends to make several domestic flights. This multi-flight airpass is available for domestic flights on these two airlines (which includes most flights with Aerocaribe). It has to be bought before traveling to Mexico, and is issued in conjunction with an international airline ticket. The cost of the airpass is calculated according to five designated zones (A, B, C, D, or E) within the country. Each passenger must purchase a minimum of two coupons, to be used within 90 days. Conditions of travel vary from one year to the next. Check with a travel agent for the latest, up-to-date details.

DIRECTORY

AEROMÉXICO

📞 51 33 40 00.
📞 01 800 02 14 050 (toll free).

MEXICANA

📞 54 48 09 90.

OTHER DOMESTIC AIRLINES

Aero California
📞 52 07 83 08.

Aerocaribe
📞 55 36 90 46

Aerolitoral
📞 51 33 40 00.

Aeromar
📞 51 33 11 11.

Aviacsa
📞 57 16 90 04.

Líneas Aereas Azteca
📞 57 16 89 89.

VACATIONS AND TOURS

Aero California vacations
📞 52 07 83 08.

INTERNAL FLIGHT ROUTES IN MEXICO

KEY

✈ Major airport

— Domestic air route

Tijuana
Ciudad Juárez
Hermosillo
Chihuahua
Guaymas
Guerrero Negro
Loreto
Los Mochis
Monterrey
La Paz
Durango
San José del Cabo
Mazatlán
Zacatecas
Puerto Vallarta
Querétaro
Poza Rica
Cancún
Mérida
Guadalajara
MEXICO CITY
Cozumel
Manzanillo
Puebla
Veracruz
Villahermosa
Zihuatanejo
Oaxaca
Palenque
Acapulco
Tuxtla Gutiérrez
Puerto Escondido
Huatulco

Gulf of Mexico

Pacific Ocean

0 kilometers   500

0 miles   500

Traveling by Bus and Train

SINCE PRIVATIZATION OF THE COUNTRY'S extensive rail network and the shut-down of passenger train services,
buses are the best and most economical way of traveling
around the regions of Mexico on public transportation.
Although second-class buses can provide a bone-rattling
experience, the luxury services are extremely comfortable
and compete favorably with domestic airlines.

A long-distance luxury bus for direct intercity services

BUSES AND TERMINALS

MEXICO'S numerous private
bus companies can make
bus terminals busy, and at
first confusing, places. It is
worth making a little effort to
understand the way in which
these companies operate.

There are three types of
intercity bus *(camión)*, offering luxury, first class, or second
class services. In some towns
there are separate bus terminals for first and second class.

Traditionally, the Central
Camionera or Terminal de
Autobuses was located downtown, but increased traffic
volume has meant that in most
large towns, bus terminals have
been moved to the outskirts.

Mexico City has four bus
terminals, providing regular
services to all the main cities
in the country *(see Directory
opposite)*. Generally, buses to
the north of Mexico leave from
Terminal del Norte, to southern regions from **Terminal
del Sur**, to western Mexico
from **Terminal Poniente**,
and to the cities of the Gulf
Coast and Yucatán Peninsula

from **Terminal Oriente TAPO**.
For long-distance travel it is
advisable to book in advance,
especially at Christmas or
Easter. Timetables, fares, and
routes are posted at bus
terminals. Information and advance bookings for some
companies are also
available from travel
agents, and many
large companies
have their own
booking offices in
town centers.
Tickets are usually
refundable if canceled
at least three hours
before departure. Some
buses give student discounts
to travelers who can show an
International Student Identification Card (ISIC).

LUXURY AND FIRST CLASS BUSES

FOR LONG-DISTANCE travel,
luxury or first-class buses
are recommended. These services are more reliable, more
comfortable, safer, and less
likely to break down. The
buses have a controlled speed
of 95 km/h (60 mph)
and use mainly toll
roads, which are
not so common a
target for highway
robbers. On shorter
trips, between small
towns or villages,
the more basic, less
reliable second-class
buses may be the
only option avail-
able to travelers.

One of Mexico City's main bus terminals

Top-of-the-range luxury *(de
lujo)* buses offer direct intercity
services, with air-conditioning,
fully reclining seats, hostesses,
refreshments, video screens,
and on-board toilets. First-class
(primera) buses are air-conditioned, with semi-reclining
seats. Some have a video, hot
or cold drinks, and a toilet.

Each company identifies its
de lujo service with names
such as Plus, ETN, Diamante,
Uno, Ejecutivo, or Elite. Fares
are between 30 and 50 percent
more than first-class tickets.
Services marked *directo* or *sin
escalas* (nonstop) will be fas-
ter than those that make stops.

In resort areas, numerous
excursions, on air-conditioned
buses with qualified guides,
can be booked at your hotel.

TRAINS

ALTHOUGH MOST of Mexico's
original train lines still
exist, passenger services have
dwindled as a result of
privatization,
coupled with
improvements in
the road network.
The rails today are
the preserve of
freight services.
The only first-class
(primera plus) pass-
enger train that still

Copper Canyon
railroad logo

runs is the scenic **Chihuahua-
al-Pacífico Railroad**, through
the Cañón del Cobre (Copper
Canyon) region *(see pp176–7)*.
This train service departs daily
from Los Mochis, on the
Pacific coast, at 6am, and
from Chihuahua, in the center
of the country, at 7am.

The colorful Chihuahua-al-Pacífico
Railroad first-class passenger train

Boarding an island passenger ferry destined for Playa del Carmen

Considered one of the world's great railroad journeys, it covers 670 km (415 miles) and takes a relaxing 13 hours, traversing some of Mexico's most spectacular landscapes. Because this service is very popular, it is essential to book tickets in advance. There are both first- and second-class coaches. Children under 12 pay a reduced adult fare, and children under 5 travel free.

Ticket office for ferries from the Caribbean coast to Cozumel island

FERRIES

Passenger and car ferries leaving from Santa Rosalía and La Paz connect the Baja California peninsula to Guaymas, Topolobampo, and Mazatlán on the Pacific mainland. Two standards of cabin are offered – a *turista*, with bunkbeds and a washbasin, or a more expensive *especial*, which has an entire suite of rooms.

On the Caribbean coast, ferries leave from Puerto Morelos (car ferry) and Playa del Carmen (passenger only) to the island of Cozumel (*see p282*). Ferries from Puerto Juárez (passenger only) and Punta Sam (car ferry), both north of

Cancún, travel to Isla Mujeres (*see p281*). Another, more expensive ferry leaves for Isla Mujeres from Playa Linda, in Cancún, four times every day.

LOCAL TRANSPORTATION

The local bus, also known as a *camión*, is the cheapest and easiest way to get around the provincial towns of Mexico. Buy your ticket on the bus. Supplementing this service are *colectivos* – vans or minibuses that follow fixed routes but charge a flat rate, regardless of distance.

Taxis can be summoned by phone in most towns, or by flagging one down in the street. In Mexico City, however, it is always safer to call for a radio taxi (*see p341*).

A convenient and commonly used alternative to renting a car is to hire a driver and vehicle, or a taxi, by the hour or day. This can be arranged by one of a number of rental companies, by your hotel, or through a travel agent. The price for the car and driver will vary according to the area.

A line of blue taxis waiting to be called into service

DIRECTORY

BUS TERMINALS IN MEXICO CITY

Norte
Eje Central Lázaro Cárdenas 4907.
Ⓜ *Autobuses del Norte.*
🅒 *55 87 15 52.*
Destinations: *Acapulco, Huatulco, Colima, Cuernavaca, Chihuahua, Durango, Guadalajara, Guanajuato, Hermosillo, Ixtapa and Zihuatanejo, León, Mazatlán, Mexicali, Monterrey, Morelia, Pátzcuaro, Poza Rica, Puerto Escondido, Puerto Vallarta, Querétaro, Saltillo, San Luis Potosí, San Miguel de Allende, Taxco, Tepic, Tijuana, Uruapan, Zacatecas.*

Oriente TAPO
Calz Ignacio Zaragoza 200.
Ⓜ *San Lázaro.*
🅒 *57 62 54 14.*
Destinations: *Campeche, Cancún, Chiapas, Mérida, Oaxaca, Puebla, Tlaxcala, Veracruz, Xalapa.*

Poniente
Sur 122, corner of Río Tacubaya.
Ⓜ *Observatorio.*
🅒 *52 71 45 19.*
Destinations: *Aguascalientes, Colima, Guanajuato, León, Manzanillo, Morelia, Puerto Vallarta, Querétaro, San Juan de los Lagos, San Luis Potosí, San Miguel de Allende, Toluca, Uruapan.*

Sur
Av Taxqueña 1320.
Ⓜ *Taxqueña.*
🅒 *56 89 97 45.*
Destinations: *Acapulco, Cuernavaca, Ixtapa and Zihuatanejo, Oaxaca, Puebla, Taxco, Tepoztlán.*

TRAIN SERVICES

Ferrocarril Mexicano Railroad
Corner of Mendez & 24, Chihuahua.
🅒 *(614) 439 72 11.*

Prolongación Bienestar, Los Mochis.
🅒 *(668) 824 11 67.*

Driving in Mexico

Street signs

TRAVELING AROUND BY CAR at your own pace is the most practical and flexible way to explore Mexico (the only exception being Mexico City). Driving is generally safe, but motorists need to take some precautions. Robberies do occur, and it is advisable not to drive at night and to avoid overnight street parking. In Mexico city, drive with the doors locked and the windows rolled up. Try to plan your trip in advance, take a good road map, and know where your stops are likely to be. Hitchhiking is not recommended.

Lonely highway in the Sierre Madre Occidental, Northern Mexico

RULES OF THE ROAD

MEXICANS DRIVE on the right-hand side of the road, and distances are measured in kilometers rather than miles. Most traffic regulations and warnings are represented by internationally recognized symbols and signs, but some signs are unique to Mexico.

Parking, which can often be a problem in the big cities, is permitted where you see a sign with a black E (for *estaciona-miento*) in a red circle. The same E with a diagonal line through it means no parking. A white E on a blue background indicates a parking lot. The wearing of seat belts is compulsory. Normal speed limits are 40 km/h (25 mph) in built-up areas, 70 km/h (45 mph) in rural areas and 110 km/h (68 mph) on freeways. Traffic must come to a complete stop at *Alto* (halt) signs.

Slow down when approaching villages, where there are often speed bumps *(topes)*. These can be very high, and are not always marked, so you may hit them without warning.

Take extreme care at rail crossings, both in cities and in the open country, as there is often no system to warn that a train is coming, and accidents do sometimes occur.

Avoid driving at night when, apart from the risk of robbery, animals roam freely. Potholes are often unmarked, and it is harder in the dark to spot any obstacles on the road (which could be anything from an old tire to a dead animal).

Rows of rush hour traffic on the busy roads of Mexico City

ROAD CLASSIFICATION

THERE ARE THREE main kinds of highway in Mexico: four-lane *super carreteras*, ordinary *cuota* (toll) roads, and *libre* (free) roads.

The *super carreteras*, most of which are less than 10 years old, are expensive but fast. The cost of the tolls is much higher than the ordinary *cuota* roads and, as a result, there is much less traffic, no trucks, and few buses. Service stations on the superhighways are few and far between, so fill up your gas tank before using these roads.

Cuota highways range from fast, four-lane roads, to those that are little better than *libres*. Tolls are charged according to distance and the number of axles on the vehicle. If there is a choice of toll payment booth, opt for the lane marked *autos*. On *cuotas*, drivers are insured against accident or breakdown.

Two-lane *libre* (free) roads are often very busy with local traffic, trucks, and second-class buses, so they are not the ideal choice for long-distance, intercity travel. For shorter trips, however, they provide a quiet and scenic alternative to the main roads. In very remote areas, some *libre* roads may not be well surfaced, and can be prone to robbery, especially at night.

MEXICAN ROAD SIGNS

Speed bumps

End of surfaced road

Highway number

Public convenience

Medical assistance

Car parking available

MAPS

A SELECTION OF reliable city, regional, and national road maps are published by PEMEX (Petróleos Mexicanos, the state gasoline monopoly), and by the publishing company Guía Roji. These maps can be bought at bookstores, supermarkets, branches of Sanborn's *(see p114)*, newsstands, and some gas stations. SECTUR offices can provide free maps. The American Automobile Association (AAA) also publishes a map of Mexico, which is available to AAA members.

A selection of recommended road maps, available all over Mexico

PERMITS AND INSURANCE

R EGULATIONS FOR bringing cars into Mexico are very strict. To obtain a *permiso de importación temporal* (temporary import permit), a motorist needs an authorized immigration form (FMT) or visa. The vehicle registration certificate, or document of legal possession, must then be presented at the *Módulo de Control Vehicular*, at a border post.

You will also need a valid driver's license (US, Canadian, British, Australian, and New Zealand licenses are all valid) and a credit card (VISA, MasterCard, or American Express), in the same name as the car registration papers. Those without a credit card must pay a bond, or make a substantial cash deposit. Drivers are charged a small fee for the issue of a six-month, multiple-entry permit.

US car insurance does not cover driving south of the border, so separate coverage must be arranged. Insurance is sold in most cities and towns on both sides of the border.

One of the many PEMEX gas stations found across the country

FUEL AND GAS STATIONS

P EMEX FRANCHISES all gas stations in Mexico, so fuel is the same price throughout the country, bar the US border where it is cheaper. Priced by the liter, *Gasolina* is unleaded. It is graded either *Magna Sin* (standard) or *Extra* (premium). Leaded *(Nova)* fuel is scarce.

Gas stations are plentiful in towns but are less common in some rural areas. To be on the safe side, always set out with a full tank, and when it reaches the halfway mark, refill as soon as you can. In some regions it is possible to drive for 100 km (62 miles) without seeing a gas station. Fuel prices are higher than they are in the US, but lower than in Europe. Gas stations are usually open 7am–10pm and are not self-service. The attendant asks *¿cuánto?* (how much?), to which you reply *lleno por favor* (fill the tank please), or specify an amount.

ACCIDENTS AND SAFETY

I N THE EVENT of an accident, do not abandon your vehicle. The insurance companies should be informed immediately, and a claim must be filed before you leave the country. If anyone has been hurt in the accident, you may be detained by the police until fault can be established. If nobody is hurt, it is best to resolve the situation without involving the police at all *(see p340)*.

The Angeles Verdes (Green Angels) are a fleet of pickup trucks which patrol major tourist routes, helping motorists in difficulties. The service

is provided free of charge by Mexico's Ministry of Tourism (SECTUR). The mechanics, who speak English and can also administer first aid, charge only for spare parts or fuel, although tips are appreciated.

CAR, BICYCLE, AND MOTORBIKE RENTAL

C AR RENTAL IS expensive in Mexico. International car rental companies, such as Hertz, Budget, and National, have offices in all main airports, and in the center of large towns, but local companies may offer the cheapest deals.

When pre-booking, make sure the price incorporates the 15 percent tax, and full insurance. It is important that the insurance includes theft and collision damage waiver. Some policies provide only nominal coverage, and additional insurance cover may be necessary.

The most economical vehicles, such as VW Beetles, may not be available to customers pre-booking from abroad. To rent a car in Mexico you must be 21 or over (25 for some agencies) and have held a valid driver's license for at least one year. Rental must be paid for with a major credit card. Companies often require customers to sign a blank credit card slip, which is then torn up when the car is returned intact.

Bicycles, mopeds, and motorbikes can be rented in resorts – tourist offices can provide information. Before setting out, make sure that the vehicle is in good condition and that your insurance cover is adequate. Also check that your personal travel insurance covers motorbike accidents.

Traveling by moped

Getting Around Mexico City

An old-fashioned trolleybus

Traffic congestion in Mexico City is appalling, and driving is not practical. Walking is the easiest way to negotiate certain areas in the center or south of the city, but elsewhere distances are so vast that some form of transport is necessary. Trolleybuses still run on a few routes, but more regular services are provided by an extensive bus and subway system. In the south, an electric train connects the subway at Taxqueña to Embarcadero in Xochimilco. Taxis are inexpensive, and *peseros* (collective taxis) are cheaper. Traffic is worst during rush hours (6:30–9am and 4–7pm).

Green and white VW street taxi

Crowd in front of the Basílica de Guadalupe *(see p108)*

WALKING

Walking is a great way to explore the heart of Mexico City's historic center, as well as areas like San Ángel, Coyoacán, and the Zona Rosa. Avoid too much walking or sightseeing, however, until you are accustomed to the altitude and pollution *(see pp338–9)*. To escape the noise of the traffic and the heat of the sun, find a shady square with a café.

Some central streets are pedestrianized, but those on foot generally take second place to vehicles. Do not assume that a car will automatically stop at a pedestrian crossing. Keep to busy, well-lit streets at night and always avoid underpasses, as robbers tend to lurk there *(see pp340–41)*. Carry valuables in a money belt and hold your camera in front of you.

BUSES AND PESEROS

Buses are cheap but overcrowded, especially during rush hour. They run from 5am to midnight. Fares are paid to the driver on entering the bus. Free route maps are available at tourist offices, and routes are identified by destination rather than number. A west to east route connects Chapultepec Park with the Zócalo, along Reforma and past the Alameda. North to south, buses run along Avenida Insurgentes. The crowded *peseros* (sedans, vans, or minibuses) use the same routes and charge a flat rate.

TAXIS

Mexican taxis are good value by US or European standards, and for intensive sightseeing it is possible to hire one by the hour. It is now considered unsafe to flag down one of the city's typical green and white VW taxis. Fortunately, there are plenty of *sitios* (radio taxis) available, which are slightly more expensive, but much safer. Tariffs for any taxi go up by 10 percent after 10pm. From the airport it is essential to take a pre-paid, official taxi *(see p341)*. *Turismo* sedans, with hooded meters and English-

Airport taxi receipt

speaking drivers, are usually parked outside big hotels. They are more expensive for short trips but can also be hired out by the hour. Check with the hotel that the driver is known to be genuine before getting in.

DRIVING

Driving in Mexico City can be a nerve-racking experience and is best avoided if possible. If you do decide to drive, or are passing through the city, keep calm and take nothing for granted. A green traffic light does not necessarily mean the road is clear. Check in your mirror before stopping at an amber light, as the car behind may not think you are going to stop. Car theft is rife, so remove or hide all possessions and be sure your hotel has safe night-parking.

Signs on the city's freeways are erratic at best. If it is hard to get on them it is even more difficult to know where to exit. There are two main ring roads: an inner one, *El Circuito Interior*, and an outer one, the *Anillo Periférico*. A third freeway, *Viaducto Miguel Alemán*, cuts across from west to east *(see map on p119)*. Invest in a good map, such as the *Guía Roji* guide.

To reduce pollution, cars are banned from use in the city between 5am and 10pm, one day a week. The day depends on the last digit of the number plate: 5 and 6 on Mondays; 7 and 8 on Tuesdays; 3 and 4 on Wednesdays; 1 and 2 on Thursdays; 9 and 0 on Fridays. New models, with Mexico City number plates and the required paperwork and stickers, are exempt.

THE METRO

THE SUBWAY SYSTEM in Mexico City is one of the cheapest, cleanest, and busiest in the world. Each day, the modern trains transport millions of people along the 160-kilometer (100-mile) network. Lines are represented by numbers and colors; stations are identified by their name and a pictographic representation. On the front of each train is the name of the last station on that line. Metro maps are not

Metro ticket, valid for one journey

always available. There is usually one on the wall at each station and inside the trains themselves, but none on the platforms.

Metro tickets *(boletos)* are bought at booths in all stations, singly or in strips of five. Buying in bulk saves standing in line but is no cheaper. Tickets must be validated in the machine at the entrance to the platforms. Each flat-rate ticket is valid for one trip, including transfers to other metro lines.

At peak times during the day, the metro can be unbearably crowded. Any person carrying large or bulky luggage may not be allowed on the metro at all during busy times. There are,

Sign outside Copilco station

Mexico City Metro symbol

however, speical carriages designated for women and children only during the rush hours.

Some of the central subway stations are worth visiting in their own right, even if you do not plan to use the metro to travel around the city. The Zócalo station has interesting models of the city center, before and after the Spanish conquest. Inside Pino Suárez station there is a small Aztec pyramid, discovered during construction of the subway. Replicas of archaeological pieces are displayed at Bellas Artes station; and contemporary art exhibitions are often organized at Copilco station.

USEFUL MEXICO CITY METRO ROUTES

Of the ten intersecting lines, represented by different colors, most visitors will only use sections of lines 1, 2, and 3. The electric train from Taxqueña is shown as a dotted line.

General Index

Page numbers in **bold** refer to main entries

A

ABC (American British Cowdray) Hospital 339
Acapulco **218–19**
  airport 348
  climate 37
  hotels 301
  map 218
  restaurants 323
Accidents
  driving in Mexico 355
Addresses **345**
Adobe buildings
  Paquimé 170
Adoration of the Kings (Rodríguez Juárez) 64
Adventure sports **347**
Aerdinias Argentinas 349
Aero California 351
Aero California Vacations 351
Aerolitoral 351
Aeromar 351
AeroMéxico 349, 351
Aeropuerto Benito Juárez (Mexico City) 348
Agua Azul **232**
Aguascalientes **191**
  fiestas 185
  hotels 298
  restaurants 320
Aguascalientes (state) 181
Agustín I, Emperor *see* Iturbide, Agustín de
Air Canada 349
Air France 349
Air travel **348–51**
  domestic flights **350–51**
Airports **348–9**
  taxis 341
Ajijíc 190
  restaurants 320
Akumal
  hotels 304
  Mayan Riviera 280
  restaurants 326
Alameda Central (Mexico City)
  Street-by-Street map 78–9
Alameda de León (Oaxaca) 222
Alamos **175**
Alcohol
  Tequila and Mezcal **313**
  What to Drink in Mexico **312**
Alemán, Miguel 55, 218
Alhóndiga de Granaditas (Guanajuato) **204**
Allende, Ignacio 198
Altitude, health problems 339
Alvarado, Pedro de 102
Alvarado family 173
Ambulances 339

American Express 342
American Revolution (1776) 49
Angahuan 205
Angangueo
  hotels 298
  restaurants 320
Angel of Independence (Mexico City) 84
Anthropology
  Museo de Antropología (Xalapa) **248–9**
  Museo Nacional de Antropología (Mexico City) **90–95**
Antiguo Colegio de San Ildefonso (Mexico City) **71**
Antiques
  shopping in Mexico City **114**, 115
Antojitos (appetizers) **310**
Aquariums
  Acuario de Veracruz (El Puerto de Veracruz) 250
  Acuario Mazatlán (Mazatlán) 178
  see also Zoos
Aqueduct (Morelia) **210–11**
Aragón, Luis 172
Archaeological sites
  Balamku 287
  Cacaxtla **156**
  Calakmul 287
  La Campana 187
  Cantona **157**
  El Castillo (Chichén Itzá) **276**
  Cempoala 247
  Cerro de la Estrella 112
  Chichén Itzá **274–6**
  Cholula 149
  Cobá **284–5**
  Comalcalco 254
  El Consuelo 195
  Dzibilchaltún 272
  Ekbalam 278
  Filobobos 246
  Grutas de Loltún 269
  Izamal 273
  Kohunlich 286, 287
  Malinalco **145**
  Mitla 226–7
  Monte Albán **220–21**
  Palenque **234–7**
  Paquimé 170
  Pirámide de Cuicuilco **112**
  Puuc Route 268–9
  La Quemada 191
  El Rey 279
  Río Bec sites **287**
  San Lorenzo
  Tenochtitlán 253
  Santiago Tuxtla 252
  El Tajín **242–3**
  Teotihuacán **134–7**

Archaeological sites (cont.)
  Tres Zapotes 252–3
  Tula **144**
  Tulum **284–5**
  Uxmal **262–4**
  Xochicalco **145**
  Xochitécatl 156
  Yagul 226
  El Zapotal 250
Architecture **22–5**
  church architecture **24–5**
  haciendas **50–51**
  Maya 46
Los Arcos (Querétaro) **197**
Area telephone codes 344
Arena Coliseo (Mexico City) 117
Arena México (Mexico City) 117
Art
  The Art of the Maya **233**
  Folk Art of Mexico **330–31**
  Muralists **26–7**
  shopping in Mexico City **114**, 115
  see also Museums and galleries
Assumption of the Virgin (Rodríguez Juárez) 64
Astronomy, Maya 47
Asúnsolo, Ignacio 98
Asúnsolo, María 75
La Audiencia 186
Auditorio Blas Galindo (Mexico City) 117
Auditorio Nacional (Mexico City) 117
Augustinians
  Convento de Actopan **139**
  San Agustín Acolman 138
Australian Embassy 337
Autumn in Mexico **32**
Avenida Francisco Sosa (Mexico City) **102**
  Street-by-Street map 104
  A Walk from San Ángel to Coyoacán 99
Avenida Insurgentes Sur (Mexico City) **110**
Avenue of the Dead (Teotihuacán) 134
Aviacsa 351
Aviateca 349
Aztecs **42–3**
  ballcourts 277
  Cempoala 247
  gods 265
  human sacrifices 44
  The Lake City of Tenochtitlán 94
  Malinalco 145
  Mexcaltitán 184
  Museo Nacional de Antropología (Mexico City) 91, 92, **94–5**

Aztecs (cont.)
  Palacio Nacional mural 66, 67
  pyramids 44
  Quiahuiztlan 246
  Sun Stone **95**
  Templo Mayor (Mexico City) **68–70**
  Teotihuacán 134
  Xochimilco **112–13**
Azulejos (tiles)
  Casa de los Azulejos (Mexico City) **75**
El Azuzul 253

B

Bacalar 286
  hotels 304
Bacon, Francis 87
Bahía Concepción 168
Bahía de los Angeles **163**
  hotels 296
Bahía de Navidad 186
Baja California 128, 159
  Ancient Cave Paintings of Baja California **165**
  Transpeninsular Highway **163**
  Whale-watching in Guerrero Negro **164**
Baja Mil Off Road Race 32
Balamku 287
Ballgame and ballcourts 44, **277**
  Cantona **157**
  Chichén Itzá 274
  Monte Albán 220
  Sinaloa 178
  El Tajín 242
Banamex 342
Bank notes 343
Banking **342–3**
Bar Bertha (Taxco)
  Street-by-Street map 146
Bar La Ópera (Mexico City) 314
  Street-by-Street map 79
Bar León (Mexico City) 117
Bardot, Brigitte 101
Bark paper
  Folk Art of Mexico 330
Baroque architecture 22, 24–25
Barra de Navidad 186
Barragán, Luis 23
Barranca del Cobre see Copper Canyon
Barranca de Metlac 251
Barrio del Artista (Puebla) Street-by-Street map 151
Bars **116**, 117
  cantinas **116**, 117
Baseball **346**
Basílica de Guadalupe (Mexico City) **108**

Basílica de Nuestra Señora de Guanajuato (Guanajuato) **204**
  Street-by-Street map 203
Basílica de Ocotlán 156, **157**
Basílica de la Soledad (Oaxaca) 214, 224
Basílica de Zapopan (Guadalajara) 189
Batopilas **175**, 176
  hotels 296
Battle of Puebla (Puebla) 139
Bazar del Sábado (Mexico City) 115
BBVA Bancomer 342
Beaches
  Acapulco 219
  Cabo San Lucas 169
  Cancún 279
  Costalegre 186
  Cozumel 282
  Ensenada 162
  Manzanillo 186
  Mayan Riviera **280–81**
  Mazatlán 178
  Oaxaca **216–17**
  San Blas 184
  San José del Cabo 169
Becal
  Panama hats 260
Becán 287
Beer
  What to Drink in Mexico 312
Bello, Mariano 152
Beloff, Angelina 113
Biblioteca Central (Mexico City) 111
Biblioteca Palafoxiana (Puebla)
  Street-by-Street map 151
Bicycles, rental 355
Biosphere Reserve, Sian Ka'an **286**
Birds
  Celestún 272
  Landscape and Wildlife of Mexico **18–19**
  Museo de las Aves de México (Saltillo) 179
  Río Lagartos 279
  see also Wildlife
Bisbee International Marlin Fishing Tournament (Cabo San Lucas) 32
Boari, Adamo 80
Boats
  ferries **353**
  Museo Histórico Naval (El Puerto de Veracruz) 250
Boca del Río 250
Bocanegra, Gertrudis 207
Bolsa de Valores (Mexico City) 84
Bolsón de Mapimí 173

Bonampak **232**
  Maya murals 46
Bookstores
  Mexico City 114, 115
Borda, José (Joseph) de la
  Iglesia de Santa Prisca (Taxco) 147
  Jardín Borda (Cuernavaca) 148
  Taxco 146
Borda family 146
Border, Mexico-US **162**, 349
Bosque de Chapultepec (Mexico City) 58, **88–9**
  see also Paseo de la Reforma and Bosque de Chapultepec
Bourbon dynasty 49
Bowie, David 62
Boxing **346**
Bracho, Ángel
  Portrait of Benito Juárez 222
Bravo, Guillermo 178
Breton, André 206
Las Brisas 186
British Airways 349
Bucerías 185
La Bufadora 162
Bullfighting 32, **346**
Bureaux de change 342
Buses
  local transportation **353**
  luxury and first class buses **352**
  in Mexico City 356
  terminals **352**, 353
Butterflies
  Migration of the Monarch Butterfly **211**
  El Rosario Monarch Butterfly Sanctuary **211**
  Sierra Chincua Monarch Butterfly Sanctuary 211
  see also Wildlife

C

El Caballito 75, **85**
Cabo San Lucas **169**
  festivals 32
  hotels 296
  Lovers' Beach 160
  restaurants 319
Cabrera, Miguel
  Iglesia de San Francisco Javier 142
  Museo Nacional del Virreinato 141
  Oratorio de San Felipe Neri (San Miguel de Allende) 199
  Templo y Museo de Guadalupe (Zacatecas) 193
Cacaxtla **156**
Cactuses of Northern Mexico **171**

Cadereyta 195
Calakmul 287
Calendar, Maya 46–7
Calinda 291
Calle Hidalgo (Guanajuato)
   Street-by-Street map
   202
Callejón del Beso
   (Guanajuato)
   Street-by-Street map 202
Calles, Plutarco Elías 55, 66
Calzada Fray Antonio de San
   Miguel (Morelia) **210–11**
Camino Real 291
La Campana 187
Campeche 257, 258, **260–61**
   hotels 304
   restaurants 326
Campeche (state) 257
Canada
   Embassy 337
   SECTUR office 337
Cancún **279**
   airport 348
   hotels 304
   Mayan Riviera 281
   restaurants 326
Candelaria
   Fiestas of the Gulf Coast
   33, 247
Candy stores
   Mexico City **114**, 115
Cañón del Cobre (Copper
   Canyon) 128, **176–7**,
   map 176–7
Cañón del Sumidero **230**
Cantinas **116**, 117, 306
Cantona **157**
Canyons 19
Capilla de San Antonio
   Panzacola (Mexico
   City) **101**
El Caracol 282
Cárdenas, Lázaro 55, 89
Careyes 186
Caribbean
   Diving in the Mexican
   Caribbean **283**
Carlota, Empress 112
El Carmen (Mexico City)
   Museo del Carmen
   100
   A Walk from San Ángel to
   Coyoacán 98
Carnival 28, 33
   Fiestas of the Yucatán
   Peninsula 261
   Gulf Coast 247
   Northern Mexico 163
Carranza, Venustiano 54–5
Carrillo, Dr. Alvaro 101
Carrington, Leonora 73, 88
Cars
   accidents and safety 355
   customs information 336
   driving in Mexico **354–5**

Cars (cont.)
   driving in Mexico City 356
   fuel and gas stations 355
   hiring drivers 353
   permits and insurance 355
   rental 355
   road classification 354
   rules of the road 354
   see also Tours by car
Casa del Alfeñique
   (Puebla) **152**
   Street-by-Street map 150
Casa Allende (San Miguel
   de Allende)
   Street-by-Street map 198
Casa Alvarado (Mexico
   City) 102
Casa de los Amigos 291
Casa de Artesanías
   (Morelia) **210**
Casa de los Azulejos
   (Mexico City) **75**
   Street-by-Street map 79
Casa Borda (Taxco)
   Street-by-Street map 146
Casa de Cortés (Mexico City)
   Street-by-Street map 104
Casa de los Cuatro Pueblos
   (Tepic) 184
Casa de Diego Ordaz
   (Mexico City)
   Street-by-Street map 104
Casa Diego Rivera
   (Guanajuato) **204**
   Street-by-Street map 202
Casa de Figueroa (Taxco)
   Street-by-Street map 146
La Casa del Fumador
   (Mexico City) 115
Casa Gilardi 23
La Casa del Habano
   (Mexico City) 115
Casa Humboldt (Taxco)
   Street-by-Street map 147
Casa de la Inquisición (San
   Miguel de Allende)
   Street-by-Street map 198
Casa del Inquisidor (San
   Miguel de Allende)
   Street-by-Street map 198
Casa de Juárez
   (Oaxaca) 223
Casa Lamm (Mexico City) 115
Casa de la Malinche
   (Mexico City)
   Street-by-Street map 105
Casa del Mayorazgo de la
   Canal (San Miguel de
   Allende)
   Street-by-Street map 198
Casa de los Muñecos (Puebla)
   architecture 22
   Street-by-Street map 150
Casa/Museo Leon Trotsky
   (Mexico City) **103**
Casa Natal de Morelos

(Morelia)
   Street-by-Street map 209
Casa Portuguesa 317
Casa del Real Ensaye
   (Guanajuato)
   Street-by-Street map 202
Casa del Risco (Mexico
   City) 100
Casa Rul y Valenciana
   (Guanajuato)
   Street-by-Street map 202
Cascada de Basaséachic 174
Cascada Cusárare 174
El Castillo (Chichén Itzá)
   261, **276**
Castillo de Chapultepec
   (Mexico City), 49, **88–9**
Castro, Veronica 86
Castro Lenero, Alberto 88
Castro Pacheco, Fernando 270
Catedral Metropolitana
   (Mexico City) 59, **64–5**
   Street-by-Street map 62
Catemaco 253
   hotels 303
Cathedrals
   Acapulco 218
   Aguascalientes 191
   Campeche 260
   Catedral Metropolitana
   (Mexico City) 59, **64–5**
   Chihuahua 172
   Cuernavaca 148
   Durango 178
   Guadalajara **188**
   Hermosillo 170
   Mazatlán 178
   Mérida 270
   Morelia 209, **210**
   Oaxaca 222
   Puebla 151, **152**
   El Puerto de Veracruz 250
   Saltillo 179
   San Cristóbal de las
   Casas 231
   San Juan de los Lagos
   190–91
   Tlaxcala 156
   Tuxtla Gutiérrez 230
   Valladolid 278
   Xalapa 246
   Zacatecas 192
Catholic Church 15, 21
   Virgin of Guadalupe **109**
La Catrina (Posada) **35**, 81
Caudillos 52
Cave paintings
   Ancient Cave Paintings of
   Baja California **165**
   Cueva de las Flechas 165
   Cueva Pintada 165
   Cueva del Ratón 165
Caves
   Grutas de Balamkanché 278
   Grutas de García 179
   Grutas de Loltún **269**

Caves (cont.)
  Sierra de Zongolica 251
El Cedral 282
Celestún **272**
Cempoala **247**
Cenote Azul 286
Cenote de Dzitnup 278
Central America
  map 11
Centro Artesanal de
  Buenavista (Mexico
  City) 115
Centro Cultural Mexiquense
  (Toluca) 145
Centro Cultural Telmex
  (Mexico City) 116
Centro Mexicano de Tortuga
  Beaches of Oaxaca 217
Ceramics
  buying 332
  Folk Art of Mexico 330, 331
  Oaxaca's pottery **224**
  Paquimé 170
  Talavera pottery **153**
Cerro de la Bufa
  (Zacatecas) **193**
Cerro de las Campanas
  (Querétaro) **197**
Cerro de la Estrella 112
Cerro del Grillo
  (Zacatecas) **193**
Cerro de Guadalupe
  (Puebla) **153**
Cerro de San Pedro 194
Cervantes, Miguel
  Festival Internacional
  Cervantino 32
Chac 265
Chachalacas
  hotels 303
Chacmool 44, 68
Chain hotels **290**, 291
Chain restaurants 306
Chalma 145
Chalma Pilgrimages
  (Chalma) 139
Chankanaab Park 282
Chapala 190
Chapultepec, Bosque de
  (Mexico City) see Paseo de
  la Reforma and Bosque
  de Chapultepec
Chapultepec, Castillo de
  (Mexico City) see Castillo
  de Chapultepec
Chapultepec Zoo (Mexico
  City) 117
Charles III, King of Spain
  49, 86
Charles IV, King of Spain 75
Charles V, Emperor (Charles I,
  King of Spain)
  Basílica de Nuestra Señora
  de Guanajuato
  (Guanajuato) 204
  statue of 79

Charrería **74**, 346
  Museo de la Charrería
  (Mexico City) **74**
Charros (Mexican cowboys) 74
Chávez Morado, José 204
Chetumal **286–7**
  hotels 304
  restaurants 326
Chiapas 213
  rebellion 55
  Zapatista National
  Liberation Army 17,
  213, 230
Chicanná 287
Chichén Itzá 42, 129,
  274–6
  El Castillo **276**
  equinoxes 261
  hotels 304
  Observatory 47, 274
  restaurants 326
El Chico 138
Chihuahua 159, **172**
  climate 36
  hotels 296
  restaurants 319
Chihuahua-al-Pacífico
  Railroad **176**, 353
Chihuahuan Desert 159
Children
  air travel 351
  entertainment 117
  in restaurants 307
Las Chimeneas
  (Cempoala) 247
Chinampas (floating gardens)
  112–13
Chinkultic 231
Cholula **149**
  hotels 294
  restaurants 317
Christmas 33
Chupaderos 178, 179
Churches in Mexico City
  architecture **24–5**
  Basílica de Guadalupe **108**
  Capilla de San Antonio
  Panzacola 99, **101**
  Iglesia de la Conchita 105
  Iglesia de San Francisco 75
  Iglesia de San Jacinto
  98, 100
  Iglesia de San Juan
  Bautista 105
  Iglesia de San Juan de
  Dios 78
  Iglesia de Santa
  Catarina 99
  Iglesia de la Santísima
  Trinidad 73
  San Hipólito 85
  San Sebastián
  Chimalistac 99
  Santo Domingo 72–3
  Templo de la Enseñanza
  62, **72**

Churches in Mexico City
(cont.)
  Templo de Santiago 108–9
  see also Cathedrals and
  individual towns and
  cities
Cigar shops
  Mexico City 115
Cinco de Mayo 31
Ciudad Cuauhtémoc **172–3**
  hotels 296
  restaurants 319
Ciudad de los Deportes
  (Mexico City) 110
Civil wars 54
Clausell, Joaquín 74
Cliff divers
  La Quebrada 218, **219**
Climate **36–7**
  when to go 336
Climbing **347**
Clothes
  Panama hats **260**
  shops 329
Clubs **116**, 117
Coahuila 159
Coasts 19
Coatepec **247**
  hotels 303
  restaurants 325
Coavarrubias, Luis 95
Cobá **284–5**
  hotels 305
Cocoyoc
  hotels 294
Coffee
  What to Drink in
  Mexico 312
Coins 343
Cola de Caballo 179
Colegio de San Nicolas
  (Morelia)
  Street-by-Street map 208
Colima **187**
  hotels 298
  restaurants 320
Colima (state) 181
Colombia reef 282
Colomilla 186
Colonial architecture 22
Colonial Heartland **180–211**
  fiestas **185**
  Guadalajara 188–9
  Guanajuato 202–5
  hotels 298–301
  map 182–3
  Morelia 208–11
  Querétaro 196–7
  restaurants 320–23
  San Miguel de Allende:
  Street-by-Street map
  198–9
  A Tour Around Lake
  Pátzcuaro 206
Coloniart (Mexico City) 115
Columba, St. 138

Comalcalco **254**
Comitán de Domínguez
  231
Communications **344–5**
Conchero dancers 29
Condesa
  restaurants 316
Condo Corner 291
The Conquest of Mexico
  (O'Gorman) 43
Conquistadors 39, **43**, **48**
Conservatorio de las Rosas
  (Morelia)
  Street-by-Street map 208
El Consuelo 195
Contreras, Jesús F. 74
Convento de Actopan **139**
Convento del Carmen
  (Mexico City) **100**
Convento de la Merced
  (Mexico City) 109
Convento de la Santa Cruz
  (Querétaro) 15, **196–7**
Conversion chart **337**
Copper Canyon 128, **176–7**
  map 176–7
Coral cuts
  first aid 339
Coral reefs
  Diving in the Mexican
  Caribbean **283**
Corbeteña 185
Córdoba 251
  hotels 303
  restaurants 325
Córdoba, Treaties of
  (1829) **251**
Córdoba, Viceroy Diego
  Fernández de 251
Coronel, Pedro 193
Coronel, Rafael 193
Corpus Christi 247
Correa, Juan
  Iglesia de San Bernardino
  (Xochimilco) 113
  Santo Domingo (Mexico
  City) 73
  Templo y Museo de
  Guadalupe (Zacatecas) 193
Corresponsales de
  Hoteles 291
Cortés, Hernán 43, 156
  Cempoala 247
  Cholula 149
  Coyoacán (Mexico City)
  97, 104
  Cozumel 282
  Cuernavaca 148
  kills Cuauhtémoc 109
  Palacio Nacional (Mexico
  City) 66, 67
  La Paz 169
  and Teotihuacán 137
Costalegre **186**
Costa Careyes
  hotels 298

La Costera Miguel Alemán
  (Acapulco) 218
Courier services 345
Coyoacán (Mexico City)
  map 58
  restaurants 315
  A Walk from San Ángel to
  Coyoacán **98–9**
  see also San Ángel and
  Coyoacán
Coyolxauhqui
  Templo Mayor (Mexico
  City) 68–70
Cozumel **282**
  airport 348, 351
  fiestas 33
  hotels 305
  map 282
  Mayan Riviera 281
  restaurants 326
Cozumel Vacation
  Rentals 291
Crafts
  buying **332–3**
  Days of the Dead **35**
  Folk Art of Mexico **330–31**
  Indigenous peoples of
  Mexico 20–21
  shops **114**, 115, 329
The Creation (Rivera) 71
Creator gods 265
Credit cards **342**
  in hotels 291
  in restaurants 307
  in shops 328
Creel **174**, 177
  hotels 296
  restaurants 319
Creel, Enrique 174
Crime **340–41**
  driving in Mexico 354
Cristo de las Ampollas
  (Mérida) 261
Croix, Carlos Francisco de 78
Cuauhtémoc 109
Cuauhtémoc, Emperor 67
Cuautla 148
Cuernavaca **148**
  hotels 294
  restaurants 317
Cueva de las Flechas 165
Cueva Pintada 165
Cueva del Ratón 165
Cuevas, Bertha 73
Cuevas, José A.
  Lotería Nacional (Mexico
  City) 23, 85
Cuevas, José Luis
  The Giantess 73
  Museo José Luis Cuevas
  (Mexico City) **73**
Cuicuilco *see* Pirámide de
  Cuicuilco
Cuilapan de Guerrero 225
Cuiteco 176
Cuitzeo 211

Cumbres de Majalca National
  Park 172
Cunningham, Oswaldo
  Barra 191
Currency **343**
Customs and excise **336**
Cuyutlán **186–7**
Cuyutlán Lagoon 186
Cybercafés 345

D

Dainzú
  A Tour of the Tlacolula
  Valley 226
  Museo Iconográfico del
  Quijote (Guanajuato) 204
Dance
  Mexico City **116**, 117
  Music and Dance **28–9**
Danish Hostel 291
Daumier, Honoré 204
Day of the Holy
  Innocents 33
Days of the Dead 17, 32,
  34–5
  in the Colonial
  Heartland 185
  Janitzio and Lake
  Pátzcuaro **207**
Dengue fever 339
Department stores 328
  Mexico City 115
Descubre (Aguascalientes) 191
Deserts 18
Día de la Armada 31
Día de la Bandera 31
Día de la Constitución 31
Día de la Marina
  (Guaymas) 163
Día de la Raza 31, 32
Día de la Revolución 31, 32
Día de Santa Cecilia 32
Día del Trabajo 31
Día de la Virgen de
  Guadalupe 31, 33
Diana Cazadora
  (Olaguibel) 84
Diarrhea 339
Díaz, Porfirio **53**
  Mexican Revolution 54, 152
  Monumento a la Revolución
  (Mexico City) 85, 86
  Palacio Nacional
  mural 66
  Pancho Villa and 173
Diego, Juan 108, 109
Disabled travelers **337**
  in restaurants 307
Discounts, air travel 351
Diseases **339**
  vaccinations **338**
Diving 347
  Diving in the Mexican
  Caribbean **283**
El Divisadero 174, 176
  hotels 297

Doctors 338
Dolores Hidalgo 205
Domingo, Placido 86
Dominicans
    San Ignacio 165
    San Jerónimo
    Tlacochahuaya 226
    Templo y Conservatorio de
    las Rosas (Morelia) 210
    ¿donde? 345
*Dream of a Sunday Afternoon
    in the Alameda Central*
    (Rivera) **26–7**, 81
Drinks *see* Food and drink
Driving in Mexico **354–5**
Dulcería de Celaya (Mexico
    City) 115
Durango 159, **178**
    fiestas 163
    Hollywood in Mexico **179**
    hotels 297
    restaurants 319
Duty free allowances 336
Dzibanche 287
Dzibilchaltún 272

E

E-mail **345**
Early Colonial architecture 22
Earthquakes 341
Easter Week 30
    in the Colonial Heartland 185
    Fiestas of Northern
    Mexico 163
    Fiestas of Southern
    Mexico 225
Echave, Manuel de 111
Ecological parks
    Yum-Ká 254
Efficiency apartment
    rentals 291
Edzná 44, **261**
Eiffel, Gustave 168
Ekbalam **278**
Electricity 337
Embassies 337
Embroidery
    Folk Art of Mexico 331
Emergencies 339
    medical 338
    phone numbers 341
Ensenada 162–3
    fiestas 32, 163
    hotels 297
    restaurants 319
La Enseñanza (Mexico City)
    see Templo de la Enseñanza
Entertainment
    Mexico City 116–17
    Music and Dance 28–9
    in restaurants 307
Epiphany 33
Equinoxes (Chichén Itzá) 261
Erongarícuaro
    A Tour Around Lake
    Pátzcuaro 206

Escuela de Bellas Artes
    (San Miguel de Allende)
    Street-by-Street map 198
Espallargues, Pere 86
Espinazo del Diablo 178
Estación de Ferrocarriles
    Buenavista 353
Estadio Azteca
    (Mexico City) 117
Etiquette **337**
Ex-Convento de San Agustín
    (Zacatecas) **192**
Ex-Convento de San Francisco
    (San Luis Potosí) **194**
Ex-Convento de San Miguel
    Arcángel 139
*The Execution of Emperor
    Maximilian* (Manet) 53
EZLN 17
    Zapatista uprising 55, 213,
    230, 231

F

The Family (Orozco) 27
Fax machines **345**
Feast of the Assumption 31
La Feria (Mexico City) 117
Feria Artesanal del Mundo
    Maya (Mérida) 33
Feria de San Cristóbal (San
    Cristóbal de las Casas) 225
Feria de San Marcos
    (Aguascalientes) 185
Feria de Santiago Tuxtla 247
Ferrando, Jarocho Salvador
    Museo Jarocho Salvador
    Ferrando (Tlacotalpan) 252
Ferries **353**
Festival Internacional
    Cervantino 32
Festivals *see* Fiestas
Fiesta Americana 291
Fiesta de Año Nuevo
    (Ihuatzio) 185
Fiesta de las Flores
    (Nogales) 163
Fiesta de los Tiznados
    (Tepoztlán) 139
Fiesta de la Virgen de la
    Caridad (Huamantla) 139
Fiestas **30–33**
    around Mexico City **139**
    Colonial Heartland **185**
    Days of the Dead **34–5**, **207**
    Gulf Coast **247**
    Northern Mexico **163**
    Southern Mexico **225**
    Yucatán Peninsula **261**
Film 15–16
    Hollywood in Mexico **179**
Filobobos 246
Fire department 341
Fish
    Diving in the Mexican
    Caribbean **283**
    fishing **347**

Flag Day 33
La Flor de L1s (Mexico City)
    115
Flowers
    San Ángel flower market
    (Mexico City) 101
Flynn, Errol 218
Folk Art of Mexico **330–31**
Fonart (Mexico City) 115
Food and drink
    Antojitos 310
    hygiene 306
    Indigenous Peoples of
    Mexico 21
    Mesoamerican 45
    Reading the Menu **311**
    shops 329
    Tequila and Mezcal **313**
    What to Drink in Mexico
    312–13
    What to Eat in Mexico
    308–9
    see also Restaurants
Food poisoning 339
Forests, tropical 19
Forma Migratoria de Turista
    (FMT) 336
Foro Sol (Mexico City) 117
Franciscans
    Dzibilchaltún 272
    Ex-Convento de San
    Francisco (San Luis
    Potosí) **194**
    Izamal 273
    Maní 269
    Museo Regional
    (Querétaro) 196
    Palacio Nacional mural 67
    Valladolid 278
Fruit juices
    What to Drink in
    Mexico 312
Fuel and gas stations 355
Fuente de Tláloc (Mexico
    City) 88
Fuente de la Zona Lacustre
    (Mexico City)
    Street-by-Street map 62
Fuentes, Carlos 15
Fuerte de San Diego
    (Acapulco) 218

G

Galería Misrachi
    (Mexico City) 115
Galería de Historia (Museo
    del Caracol, Mexico
    City) 89
Galería Kin (Mexico City) 115
Galería OMR (Mexico
    City) 115
Galleries *see* Museums and
    galleries
Gamboa, Federico 98
Gardens *see* Parks and
    gardens

Garrafón National Park 281
Garza de León, Aldegundo 179
Gas stations 355
Gastelum, Plutarco 195
GEA Holidays 291
General stores 328
Gerzso, Gunther 101
The Giantess (Cuevas) 73
Giardiasis 339
Glyphs, Maya **46–7**
Gods of Ancient Mexico **265**
Golf **347**
Gómez Marín, Manuel 175
Gonzalez de León,
　Teodore 87
Goya, Francisco de 86, 192
Gran Hotel (Mexico City) 61
Grijalva river 230, 254
El Grito 17, 32, 205
Grutas de Balamkanché 278
Grutas de García 179
Grutas de Loltún **269**
Guadalajara 128, 183, **188–9**
　airport 348
　architecture 23
　climate 36
　hotels 298–9
　map 189
　restaurants 321
La Guadalupana (Mexico
　City) 104, 117
Guadalupe Hidalgo,
　Treaty of (1848) 52
Guanajuato **202–5**
　Easter Week 185
　hotels 299
　restaurants 321
　Street-by-Street map 202–3
Guanajuato (state) 181
Guaymas
　fiestas 163
Guelaguetza (Oaxaca)
　31, 225
Guerrero (state) 213
Guerrero, Vicente 225
Guerrero Negro **164**
　hotels 297
　restaurants 319
　Whale-watching in Guerrero
　　Negro **164**
Gulf Coast **239–55**
　Fiestas of the Gulf
　　Coast **247**
　hotels 303
　map 240–41
　Museo Nacional de
　　Antropología (Mexico
　　City) 93
　restaurants 325–6
Gutiérrez, Zeferino 198

H

Hacienda Lencero 246
Hacienda Yaxcopoil 270
Haciendas **50–51**
Las Hadas 186

Hammocks **273**
Hats, Panama **260**
Health **338–9**
Hemiciclo a Juárez
　(Mexico City)
　Street-by-Street map 78
Hepatitis 339
Hermosillo **170**
　hotels 297
　restaurants 319
Hernández, Desiderio 156
Hidalgo, Father Miguel 15
　Chihuahua 172
　El Grito (call for
　　independence) 17, 32, 205
　independence movement 49
　Palacio de Gobierno
　　(Guadalajara) 188
Hidalgo del Parral 159, **173**
　hotels 297
　restaurants 319
Highways 354
Hiking **347**
Historic Center (Mexico City)
　61–81
　Alameda Central: Street-by-
　　Street map 78–9
　Catedral Metropolitana
　　64–5
　hotels 292
　map 61
　Palacio Nacional **66–7**
　restaurants 314
　Templo Mayor **68–70**
　Zócalo: Street-by-Street
　　map 62–3
History **39–55**
Hitchhiking 354
Hogarth, William 192
Holidays, public 31
Hollywood in Mexico **179**
Horses
　charrería **74**, **346**
　Lienzo Charro (Mexico
　　City) 31
　Museo de la Charrería
　　(Mexico City) **74**
　riding **347**
Hospitals 338, 339
Hotels **290–305**
　Around Mexico City
　　294–6
　booking and paying 291
　budget accommodations 290
　chain hotels **290**, 291
　Colonial Heartland
　　298–301
　grading 290
　Gulf Coast 303
　historic buildings 290
　Mexico City 292–4
　Northern Mexico 296–8
　Southern Mexico 301–2
　tipping 342
　Yucatán Peninsula 304–5
Howard Johnson 291

Huamantla 157
　fiestas 159
Huasca **139**
　hotels 294
Huasteca Potosina **195**
　hotels 299
Huastecs
　Museo Nacional de
　　Antropología (Mexico
　　City) 93
Huatulco (Bahías de) **217**
　Beaches of Oaxaca 217
　hotels 301
　restaurants 323
Huerta, Victoriano 54
Huichol Indians 20, **184**
　yarn paintings 20–21
Huitzilopochtli 69, 70
Humboldt, Baron von 147
Hurricanes 341
Hussong family 162
Huston, John 179
Hygiene, food 306–7

I

Iberia 349
Iglesia de la Compañía
　(Puebla) 132
Iglesia de la Conchita
　(Mexico City)
　Street-by-Street map 105
Iglesia de San Agustín
　(Morelia)
　Street-by-Street
　map 209
Iglesia de Santa Catarina
　(Mexico City)
　A Walk from San Ángel
　to Coyoacán 99
Iglesia de Santo Domingo
　(Oaxaca) 222–3
Iglesia de Santo Domingo
　(Puebla) **153**
Iglesia de San Felipe Neri
　(Oaxaca) 224
Iglesia de San Francisco
　Javier **142–3**
Iglesia de San Jacinto
　(Mexico City) 100
　A Walk from San Ángel to
　　Coyoacán 98
Iglesia de San Juan Bautista
　(Mexico City)
　Street-by-Street map 105
Iglesia de San Juan de Dios
　(Mexico City)
　Street-by-Street map 78
Iglesia de Santa Prisca
　(Taxco) **24–5**
　Street-by-Street map 146
Ihuatzio
　fiestas 185
　A Tour Around Lake
　　Pátzcuaro 206
Independence Day 17, 31, 32
Independence movement 49

Indigenous peoples of
Mexico **20–21**
Huichol Indians **184**
Tarahumara Indians **174**
Inquisition 48
Palacio de la Antigua
Escuela de Medicina
(Mexico City) 73
Palacio Nacional mural 66
San Miguel de
Allende 198
Insects **339**
Institutional Revolutionary
Party (PRI) 16–17
Instituto Cultural Cabañas
(Guadalajara) **188–9**
Instituto Mexicano de la
Juventud 291
Instituto Nacional de Bellas
Artes (Mexico City) 117
Insurance
driving in Mexico 355
health **338**
International Silver Fair 32
Internet **345**
Isla de los Alacranes 190
Isla Contoy 281
Isla Espíritu Santo 169
Isla Janitzio 207
Isla de la Piedra 178
Days of the Dead 34, 185
Isla Mujeres 258, **281**
fiestas 31
hotels 305
Mayan Riviera 281
restaurants 327
Isla Navidad 186
Isla Río Cuale 185
Isla la Roqueta 219
Iturbide, Agustín
Mexican independence 52
Museo de las Intervenciones
(Mexico City) 111
Palacio de Iturbide 79
IVA tax 342
in hotels 291
in restaurants 307
in shops 328
Ixtapa **216**
hotels 301
restaurants 323
Ixtolinque 105
Izamal 257, **273**
architecture 24
Iztaccíhuatl **149**

J
Jalapa *see* Xalapa
Jalisco 181
Jalpan 195
James, Edward **195**
Janitzio *see* Isla Janitzio
Jardín de la Bombilla
(Mexico City)
A Walk from San Ángel to
Coyoacán 98

Jardín Botánico (Mexico
City) 111
Jardín Botánico (Tuxtla
Gutiérrez) 230
Jardín Centenario
(Mexico City)
Street-by-Street map 104
A Walk from San Ángel to
Coyoacán 99
Jardín de Libertad
(Colima) 187
Jardín de la Unión
(Guanajuato)
Street-by-Street map 203
Jazz (Rodriguez) **99**, 102
Jellyfish stings 339
Jerez 193
Jesuits
Antiguo Colegio de San
Ildefonso (Mexico City) 71
Casa de las Artesanías
(Creel) 174
expulsion 49
Misión Nuestra Señora de
Loreto (Loreto) 168
Mulegé 168
Museo Nacional del
Virreinato 140–43
San Ignacio 165
Satevó Church 177
Jewelry
buying 333
Jimenez, Francisco 85
John Paul II, Pope 273
Juana Inés de la Cruz,
Sor 48
Juárez, Benito **222**
Casa de Juárez
(Oaxaca) 223
Iglesia de San Felipe Neri
(Oaxaca) 224
Museo de las Intervenciones
(Mexico City) 111
Museo Nacional de Historia
(Mexico City) 89
Natalicio de Benito Juárez
30, 31
Palacio Nacional mural 67
portrait of 222
La Reforma 52–3
San Luis Potosí 194
statue of 197
Juárez, José 81
Juárez, Luis 111
Juárez, Rodriguez 193
Jueves Santo 31

K
Kabah 268
Kahlo, Frida 15, 81, **102**
Museo de Arte Moderno
(Mexico City) 88
Museo Dolores Olmedo
Patiño (Xochimilco) 113
Museo Estudio Diego Rivera
(Mexico City) 100–101

Kahlo, Frida (cont.)
Museo Frida Kahlo (Mexico
City) **103**
Museo Robert Brady
(Cuernavaca) 148
San Ángel and Coyoacán
(Mexico City) 97
Secretaría de Educación
Pública mural (Mexico
City) 72
Ken Balam II 234
Kinich Ahau 265
Kissinger, Henry 101
KLM 349
Kohunlich 286, 287

L
Labná 268–9
Labor Day 31
Laboratorio Arte Alameda 81
Lacandón Indians 20
Yaxchilán 232
Lacandón rainforest 232
Lago Arareco 174
Lagos de Montebello 231
Lagos de Moreno **191**
Laguna de Catemaco 240, **253**
restaurants 325
Laguna de Chapala **190**
hotels 299
Laguna de Coyuca 219
Laguna Encantada 253
Laguna Manialtepec
Beaches of Oaxaca 216
Laguna Nichupté 279
Laguna de Siete Colores 286
Lagunas de Zempoala Park 148
Lambityeco
A Tour of the Tlacolula
Valley 227
Landa, Bishop Diego de 273
Landscape and Wildlife of
Mexico **18–19**
Language **336**
Latin American music **116–17**
Lawrence, D.H. 190
Leal, Fernando 71
Leather shops 328
Lenin 103
Libraries
Biblioteca Central (Mexico
City) 111
Biblioteca Palafoxiana
(Puebla) 151
Museo Pedro Coronel
(Zacatecas) 192
Templo de la Compañia de
Jesus (Morelia) 208
Librería Gandhi (Mexico City)
114–5
Lienzo Charro (Mexico City) 31
Liverpool (Mexico City) 115
Llosa, Mario Vargas 16
Local transportation **353**
López de Arteaga,
Sebastián 81

López de Herrera, Alonso 73
Loreto **168**
  hotels 297
  restaurants 319
Lost property **341**
  cards and traveler's
  checks 342
Lotería Nacional (Mexico
  City) 23, 85
Lourdes, Guillermo de 178
Lovers' Beach 160
Lucha libre **346**
Lufthansa 349

M

Madero, Francisco I.
  Museo Nacional de Historia
  (Mexico City) 89
  Palacio Nacional mural 66
  Revolution 54
Madrid, Miguel de la 102
Magazines **345**
Magician's Pyramid
  (Uxmal) **264**
Magritte, René 195
Malaria 338
Malinalco **145**
"La Malinche" 156
  Casa de la Malinche
  (Mexico City) 105
  Coyoacán (Mexico City) 104
  Parroquia de San José
  (Tlaxcala) 156
Mama Rumba (Mexico
  City) 117
*Man, Controller of the
  Universe* (Rivera) 80
Manet, Édouard
  *The Execution of Emperor
  Maximilian* 53
Maní **269**
Manzanillo **186**
Mapimí Biosphere Reserve 173
Maps
  Acapulco 218
  Beaches of Oaxaca **216–17**
  Cantona 157
  Climate of Mexico **36–7**
  Colonial Heartland 182–3
  Copper Canyon 176–7
  Cozumel 282
  driving in Mexico 355
  Guadalajara 189
  Guanajuato 202–3
  Gulf Coast 240–41
  Indigenous peoples of
  Mexico 21
  internal flight routes 351
  Maya 46
  Mayan Riviera **280–81**
  Mérida 271
  Mesoamerica **44–5**
  Mexico 10–11, 128–9
  Mexico City 8–9
  Mexico City: The Alameda
  Central 78–9

Maps (cont.)
  Mexico City: Bosque de
  Chapultepec 88–9
  Mexico City: Coyoacán
  104–5
  Mexico City: Farther
  Afield 107
  Mexico City: Greater
  Mexico City 10
  Mexico City: Historic
  Center 61
  Mexico City: Paseo de la
  Reforma 84–5
  Mexico City: Paseo de la
  Reforma and Bosque de
  Chapultepec 83
  Mexico City: San Ángel
  and Coyoacán 58, 97
  Mexico City: A Walk
  from San Ángel to
  Coyoacán **98–9**
  Mexico City: Zócalo 62–3
  Mexico City Metro 357
  Morelia 208–9
  North, Central, and South
  America 11
  Northern Mexico 160–61
  Oaxaca 223
  Palenque 237
  Parque-Museo de la Venta
  (Villahermosa) **255**
  Puebla 150–51
  Querétaro 197
  San Miguel de Allende
  198–9
  Southern Mexico 214–15
  El Tajín 243
  Taxco 146–7
  A Tour Around Lake
  Pátzcuaro 206
  A Tour of the Tlacolula
  Valley 226–7
  Yucatán Peninsula 258–9
Mariachi music 16, **28**
  Mexico City **116–17**
  Plaza Garibaldi (Mexico
  City) 109
Las Marietas 185
Mariscal, Federico 80
Markets **329**
  Bazar del Sábado (Mexico
  City) 115
  Mercado de Abastos
  (Oaxaca) 224–5
  Mercado de la Ciudadela
  (Mexico City) 115
  Mercado Juárez (Oaxaca) 224
  Mercado de La Merced
  (Mexico City) **109**, 115
  Mercado de Sonora (Mexico
  City) 115
  Mexico City 115
  opening hours 328
  San Ángel flower market
  (Mexico City) 101
  Taxco 146

Marriot 291
Martinez de Hoyos,
  Oliverio 86
Martinez Gudiño,
  Francisco 196
Masks, traditional **29**
MasterCard 342
Matachén, Bay of 184
Maximilian, Emperor 15,
  53, 194
  Castillo de Chapultepec
  (Mexico City) 88
  execution **53**, 196, 197, 222
  Jardín Bordan
  (Cuernavaca) 148
  Morelia 210
  Museo de las Intervenciones
  (Mexico City) 111
  Museo Nacional de Historia
  (Mexico City) 89
  Paseo de la Reforma
  (Mexico City) 83, 84
  Plazuela del Baratillo
  (Guanajuato) 203
  rebellions 112
Maya 20, **46–7**
  The Art of the Maya **233**
  ballgame 277
  Bonampak **232**
  Calakmul 287
  calendar 46–7
  El Castillo (Chichén
  Itzá) **276**
  Chichén Itzá **274–6**
  Classic era **40–41**
  Cobá 284–5
  Comalcalco 254
  Cozumel 282
  Dzibilchaltún 272
  Edzná 261
  Ekbalam 278
  glyphs **46–7**
  gods 265
  Izamal 273
  Kohunlich 286, 287
  Museo Nacional de
  Antropología (Mexico
  City) 90, 93
  Palenque **234–7**
  Puuc Route 268–9
  pyramids 44
  El Rey 279
  Río Bec sites **287**
  Tulum **284–5**
  Uxmal **262–4**
  Xcaret 284
  Yaxchilán **232**
Mayan Riviera **280–81**
  map 280–81
Mayapán 42, 269
Mayer, Franz
  Museo Franz Mayer
  (Mexico City) **81**
Mazatlán **178**
  hotels 297
  restaurants 319

Medicine
  medical treatment 338
  Museum of Medicine of
    the National University
    (Mexico City) 73
Melaque 186
Mennonites
  Ciudad Cuauhtémoc 172–3
Menus, reading 311
Mercader, Ramon 103
Mercado de Abastos
  (Oaxaca) 224–5
Mercado de la Ciudadela
  (Mexico City) 115
Mercado de La Merced
  (Mexico City) 109, 115
Mercado de Sonora
  (Mexico City) 115
Mercado Juárez (Oaxaca) 224
La Merced (Mexico City) see
  Mercado de La Merced
Mérida 270–71
  climate 37
  fiestas 33, 261
  hotels 305
  map 271
  restaurants 327
Mesoamerica 44–5
Mesoamerican Reef
  System 283
Metalwork
  buying 333
  see also Silver
Metepec 145
  restaurants 317
Metro, Mexico City 357
Mexcaltitán 184
Mexican-American War
  (1846–48) 52
Mexican Revolution 16, 39,
  53, 54
  Monumento a la Revolución
    (Mexico City) 86
  Museo Regional de la
    Revolución Mexicana
    (Puebla) 150, 152
Mexican Society of
  Cartoonists 71
Mexicana 351
Mexico
  map 128–9
Mexico City 57–125
  airport 348
  Alameda Central: Street-by-
    Street map 78–9
  Around Mexico City 130–57
  bus terminals 353
  climate 37
  Coyoacán: Street-by-Street
    map 104–5
  entertainment 116–17
  fiestas 31
  Farther Afield 107–13
  Historic Center 61–81
  hotels 292–4
  maps 10, 58–9

Mexico City (cont.)
  Paseo de la Reforma and
    Bosque de Chapultepec
    83–95
  restaurants 314–16
  San Ángel and Coyoacán
    97–105
  shopping 114–15
  taxis 341
  travel 356–7
  A Walk from San Ángel to
    Coyoacán 98–9
  Zócalo: Street-by-Street
    map 62–3
Mexico-US border 162, 349
Mexipass 351
Mezcal 313
Mezcala 190
Michoacán 181, 208
Mictlantecuhtli 70, 265
Migrants 17
Military Museum (Mexico
  City) see Museo del Ejército
  y Fuerza Aérea
Mineral del Monte 138–9
Miró, Joan 87
Mismaloya 185
Misol-Ha 232
Mitla 226–7
  architecture 24
  history 41
  A Tour of the Tlacolula
    Valley 227
Mixtecs
  Mitla 226–7
  Monte Albán 220
  Yagul 226, 227
Mocambo 250
Moctezuma II 43, 66
Modern architecture 23
Monarch butterflies
  Migration of the Monarch
    Butterfly 211
  El Rosario Monarch
    Butterfly Sanctuary 211
  Sierra Chincua Monarch
    Butterfly Sanctuary 211
Monasteries
  architecture 24
  Convento de Actopan 139
  Convento de San Gabriel
    (Cholula) 149
  Museo Convento del
    Carmen (Mexico City) 100
  San Agustín Acolman 138
Money 342–3
Monte Albán 13, 214, 220–21
  wall paintings 41
Monte de Piedad (Mexico
  City) 115
Montejo the Younger,
  Francisco de 270
Monterrey 179
  hotels 297
Montoya de la Cruz,
  Francisco 178

Monumento a Álvaro
  Obregón (Mexico City) 98
Monumento a Cuauhtémoc
  (Mexico City) 85
Monumento a la
  Independencia (Mexico
  City) 84
Monumento a los Niños
  Héroes (Mexico City) 89
Monumento a la Revolución
  (Mexico City) 59, 85, 86
Morales, Rodolfo 222
Morelia 208–11
  hotels 299
  restaurants 321
  Street-by-Street map 208–9
Morelos, José María 15
  Casa Natal de Morelos
    (Morelia) 209
  independence movement 49
  Morelia 208
  portrait 49
  Tlalpan 112
Moreno, Mario 86
Moreno, Saulo 35
El Morro 185
Mosquitoes 338, 339
Mother's Day 14, 31
Motorbikes, rental 355
Mountaineering 347
Mountains 19
Mujeres, Isla see Isla Mujeres
Mulegé 168
  architecture 24
  hotels 297
  restaurants 320
Mundaca, Fermin 281
Mundaca Hacienda 281
Mundo Joven 291
Muralists 26–7
  Antiguo Colegio de San
    Ildefonso (Mexico City) 71
  Casa de los Azulejos
    (Mexico City) 75
  Cuernavaca 148
  Escuela de Bellas Artes (San
    Miguel de Allende) 198
  Ex-Convento Dominico
    de la Natividad
    (Tepoztlán) 148
  Instituto Cultural Cabañas
    (Guadalajara) 189
  Museo Mural Diego Rivera
    (Mexico City) 81
  Museo Nacional de Historia
    (Mexico City) 89
  Palacio de Bellas Artes
    (Mexico City) 80
  Palacio de Cortés
    (Cuernavaca) 148
  Palacio de Gobierno
    (Guadalajara) 188
  Palacio de Gobierno
    (Morelia) 210
  Palacio Nacional
    (Mexico City) 66–7

Polyforum Siqueiros (Mexico City) 110
Sala de Arte Siqueiros (Mexico City) **87**, 89
San Juan de los Lagos 191
Secretaría de Educación Pública (Mexico City) 72
Taller Siqueiros (Cuernavaca) 148
Teatro de los Insurgentes (Mexico City) 110
Teotihuacán 135
Universidad Nacional Autonoma de Mexico (Mexico City) 111
Murals, pre-Columbian
Bonampak 232, 233
Cacaxtla 156
Maya 46
Quetzalpapalotl Palace Complex (Teotihuacán) 136
Murillo, Bartolomé Esteban 188
Murillo, Genaro 80
Museums and galleries (general)
admission charges 337
opening hours 337
Museums and galleries (individual)
Baluarte de la Soledad (Campeche) 260
Casa del Alfeñique (Puebla) 150, **152**
Casa Allende (San Miguel de Allende) 198
Casa de las Artesanías (Creel) 174
Casa de los Cuatro Pueblos (Tepic) 184
Casa de Juárez (Oaxaca) 223
Casa/Museo Leon Trotsky (Mexico City) **103**
Casa de Teniente del Rey (Campeche) 260
Cave Museum (San Ignacio) 165
Centro Cultural Mexiquense (Toluca) 145
Centro Cultural Santo Domingo (Oaxaca) 223
Centro Cultural Tijuana (Tijuana) 162
Cerro de la Bufa (Zacatecas) **193**
Convento de San Gabriel (Cholula) 149
Descubre (Aguascalientes) 191
Ex-Convento de San Miguel Arcángel 139
Fototeca Nacional (Pachuca) 138
Fuerte de San José (Campeche) 261

Museums and galleries (cont.)
Fuerte de San Miguel (Campeche) 261
Galería de Historia (Museo del Caracol, Mexico City) 89
La Huatápera (Uruapan) 205
Instituto Cultural Cabañas (Guadalajara) **188–9**
Laboratorio Arte Alameda 81
Monumento a la Revolución (Mexico City) 86
Museo de Acapulco (Acapulco) 218
Museo Amparo (Puebla) **152**
Museo del Anahuacalli 34–5, **111**
Museo de Antropología (Xalapa) **248–9**
Museo de Arte (Querétaro) **196**
Museo de Arte de Carrillo-Gil (Mexico City) **101**
Museo de Arte Contemporáneo (MARCO, Monterrey) 179
Museo de Arte Contemporáneo (Oaxaca) 222
Museo de Arte del Estado (Orizabo) 251
Museo de Arte Moderno (Aguascalientes) 191
Museo de Arte Moderno (Mexico City) **88**, 89
Museo de Arte Prehispánico (Tepoztlán) 148
Museo de Artes Populares (Pátzcuaro) 207
Museo de Artes y Tradiciones Populares (Tlaxcala) 157
Museo de la Caricatura (Mexico City) **71**
Museo de las Aves de México (Saltillo) 179
Museo de Bellas Artes (Toluca) 144
Museo Bello (Puebla) 23, **152**
Museo de Cera (Mexico City) **86**
Museo de la Caricatura (Mexico City) 62, 71
Museo de la Charrería (Mexico City) **74**
Museo de la Ciudad de México (Mexico City) **74**
Museo del Carmen (Mexico City) **100**
Museo Costumbrista (Alamos) 175
Museo de la Cultura Maya (Chetumal) 286, 287
Museo de las Culturas de Occidente (Colima) 187

Museums and galleries (cont.)
Museo Dolores Olmedo Patiño (Xochimilco) **113**
Museo del Ejército y Fuerza Aérea (Mexico City) **74**
Museo Estudio Diego Rivera (Mexico City) **100–101**
Museo Ex-Hacienda de San Gabriel de la Barrera (Guanajuato) **205**
Museo de Fotografía (Pachuca) 138
Museo Francisco Goitia (Zacatecas) **193**
Museo Francisco Villa (Hidalgo del Parral) 173
Museo Franz Mayer (Mexico City) 78, **81**
Museo Frida Kahlo (Mexico City) **103**
Museo Frissell de Arte Zapoteco Mitla (Mitla) 227
Museo Guillermo Spratling (Taxco) 147
Museo Histórico Minero (Santa Rosalía) 168
Museo Histórico Naval (El Puerto de Veracruz) 250
Museo Iconográfico del Quijote (Guanajuato) **204**
Museo de las Intervenciones (Mexico City) **110–11**
Museo de la Isla (Cozumel) 282
Museo Jarocho Salvador Ferrando (Tlacotalpan) 252
Museo José Guadalupe Posada (Aguascalientes) 191
Museo José Luis Cuevas (Mexico City) **73**
Museo de la Máscara (San Luis Potosí) 194
Museo de Mineralogía (Pachuca) 138
Museo de Minería (Pachuca) 138
Museo de las Misiones (Loreto) 168
Museo de las Momias (Guanajuato) **205**
Museo Mulegé (Mulegé) 168
Museo Mural Diego Rivera (Mexico City) **81**
Museo Nacional de la Acuarela (Mexico City) 99, **102**
Museo Nacional de Antropología (Mexico City) 58, **90–95**
Museo Nacional de Arte (Mexico City) **75**, 79
Museo Nacional de las Culturas (Mexico City) 63
Museo Nacional de la Estampa (Mexico City) 78, **80**

Museums and galleries (cont.)
Museo Nacional de Historia
(Mexico City) 89
Museo Nacional de San
Carlos (Mexico City) **86**
Museo Nacional del
Virreinato (Tepotzotlán)
140–43
"Papalote" Museo del Niño
(Mexico City) 88
Museo del Orígen
(Mexcaltitlán) 184
Museo Pedro Coronel
(Zacatecas) **192**
Museo de la Platería
Antonio Pineda (Taxco) 146
Museo del Pueblo
(Guanajuato) 203, **204**
Museo Rafael Coronel
(Zacatecas) **193**
Museo Regional
(Chihuahua) 172
Museo Regional
(Querétaro) **196**
Museo Regional (Tlaxcala)
156–7
Museo Regional (Tuxtla
Gutiérrez) 230
Museo Regional
Cuauhnáhuac
(Cuernavaca) 148
Museo Regional de
Antropología (La Paz) 169
Museo Regional de
Antropología Carlos Pellicer
(Villahermosa) 254
Museo Regional de
Antropología e Historia
(Mérida) 270
Museo Regional de la
Cerámica (Tlaquepaque)
190
Museo Regional de
Guadalajara (Guadalajara)
188
Museo Regional Michoacano
(Morelia) 209, **210**
Museo Regional de Nayarit
(Tepic) 184
Museo Regional Potosino
(San Luis Potosí) 194
Museo Regional de la
Revolución Mexicana
(Puebla) 150, **152**
Museo Histórico de la
Revolución (Chihuahua) 172
Museo Ripley (Mexico City)
86–7
Museo Robert Brady
(Cuernavaca) 148
Museo Rufino Tamayo
(Mexico City) **87**, 89
Museo Rufino Tamayo
(Oaxaca) 224
Museo de la Sal (Cuyutlán)
186, 187

Museums and galleries (cont.)
Museo de Santa Mónica
(Puebla) **153**
Museo de Santa Rosa
(Puebla) **153**
Museo de Sonora (Sonora)
170
Musco Tuxteco (Santiago
Tuxtla) 252
Museo Universitaria de
Artes Populares (Colima) 187
Museo Universitario
(Mexico City) 111
Museo Universitario de
Arqueología (Manzanillo) 186
Museum of Medicine of the
National University
(Mexico City) 73
Na Bolom (San Cristóbal
de las Casas) 231
Palacio de Cortés
(Cuernavaca) 148
Palacio de Gobierno
(Guadalajara) **188**
Palacio de Gobierno
(Sonora) 170
Palenque 237
Parque-Museo de la Venta
(Villahermosa) 254, **255**
Pinacoteca Virreinal
(Mexico City) 81
Planetario (Monterrey) 179
Sala de Arte Siqueiros
(Mexico City) 89
Taller Siqueiros
(Cuernavaca) 148
Templo Mayor (Mexico
City) **68–70**
Templo y Museo de
Guadalupe (Zacatecas) **193**
Teotihuacán 137
Villa del Oeste
(Durango) 178
Music
classical music **116**, 117
Latin American music
116–17
mariachi music 16, **116–17**
Music and Dance **28–9**
in restaurants 307
rock music **116**, 117

N
Nacional Monte de Piedad
(Mexico City)
Street-by-Street map 62
Nahua Indians 131
Nanciyaga 253
Napoleon I, Emperor 49
Napoleon III, Emperor 53
Natalicio de Benito Juárez
30, 31
National Anthropology
Museum (Mexico City) see
Museo Nacional de
Antropología

National parks
Agua Azul 232
Cañón del Sumidero **230**
El Chico 138
Constitución de 1857 162
Cumbres de Majalca
National Park 172
Garrafón National Park 281
Lagunas de Chacahua 216
Las Cumbres de
Monterrey 179
San Pedro Mártir 163
Natural disasters **341**
Nature preserves
Rio Lagartos 279
Sian Ka'an Biosphere
Reserve **286**
Xel-Ha 280
Navidad 31
Navy Day 31
Nayarit 181
Neo-Classical architecture 23
El Nevado de Colima 187
Nevado de Toluca 145
Newspapers 344, **345**
Mexico City **114**, 115
Nicholson, Jack 179
Night of the Radishes
(Oaxaca) 33, 225
Niños Héroes 52
El Nivel (Mexico City) 117
Nixon, Richard 101
Noche Buena 31
Noche Triste (1520) 43
Nogales (fiestas) 163
Norte bus terminal
(Mexico City) 353
North American Free Trade
Agreement (NAFTA) 17, 55
Northern Mexico **159–79**
Cactuses of Northern
Mexico **171**
Copper Canyon (Cañón
del Cobre) **176–7**
Fiestas **163**
hotels 296–8
map 160–61
restaurants 319–20
Northwest/KLM 349
Nuestra Señora del Refugio
(Durango) 163
Nuevo Casas Grandes
hotels 297
restaurants 320
Nuevo León 159
Numbers, Maya 47

O
Oaxaca 129, 213, **222–5**
fiestas 31, 33, 225
hotels 301–2
map 223
Museo Nacional de
Antropología (Mexico
City) 93
restaurants 323–4

Oaxaca (state) 213
  Beaches of Oaxaca **216–17**
  Oaxaca's black and green
  pottery **224**
Obregón, General Álvaro
  54–5
  Ciudad Cuauhtémoc 172
  monument to 98
  Palacio Nacional mural 66
  Pancho Villa and 173
O'Gorman, Juan
  Biblioteca Central
  (Mexico City) 111
  Castillo de Chapultepec
  murals 49, 53
  The Conquest of Mexico 43
  Museo del Anahuacalli 111
  Museo Estudio Diego Rivera
  (Mexico City) 100
Los Ojitos 177
El Ojo de Talamantes 173
Olaguibel, Juan Fernando
  Diana Cazadora 84
Olinalá 291
Olmecs **40**, **254**
  gods 265
  Monte Albán 220
  Museo Nacional de
  Antropología (Mexico
  City) 90, 93
  Parque-Museo de la Venta
  (Villahermosa) **255**
  San Lorenzo Tenochtitlán 253
  Santiago Tuxtla 252
Olmedo, Dolores 113
Olympic Games (1968) 55
Omniscience (Orozco) 27
Opening hours **337**
  restaurants 307
  shops 328
Opera 116
Operadora Sidektur 291
Oratorio de San Felipe Neri
  (San Miguel de Allende)
  Street-by-Street map 199
Ordaz, Diego de
  Casa de Diego Ordaz
  (Mexico City) 104
Oriente Tapo bus terminal
  (Mexico City) 353
Orizaba **251**
  hotels 303
  restaurants 325
Orizaba, Counts of 75
Orozco, José Clemente 15
  Antiguo Colegio de San
  Ildefonso (Mexico City) 71
  Casa de los Azulejos
  (Mexico City) **75**
  The Family 27
  Instituto Cultural Cabañas
  (Guadalajara) 189
  Mexican Muralists 27
  Museo de Arte de Carrillo-
  Gil (Mexico City) 101
  Museo de Arte Moderno

Orozco, José Clemente (cont.)
  (Mexico City) 88
  Museo Nacional de Arte
  (Mexico City) 75
  Omniscience 27
  Palacio de Bellas Artes
  (Mexico City) 80
  Palacio de Gobierno
  (Guadalajara) 188
  Reconstrucción 251
Ortiz, Emilio 88
Oscar Román (Mexico
  City) 115
Otomí Indians 131
Oxkutzcab 269

P

Paalen, Wolfgang 101
Pachuca **138**
  hotels 294
  restaurants 317
Pachuquilla
  restaurants 317
Pagelson, Heriberto 111
Paintings *see* Art; Museums
  and galleries
Pakal, King of Palenque 40, 41
  Temple of the Inscriptions
  (Palenque) 235, **236**
Palace of Atetelco
  (Teotihuacán) 137
Palace of Tepantitla
  (Teotihuacán) 137
Palace of Tetitla (Teotihuacán)
  137
Palace of Yayahuala
  (Teotihuacán) 137
Palace of Zacuala
  (Teotihuacán) 137
Palacio de la Antigua Escuela
  de Medicina (Mexico City) 73
Palacio de Bellas Artes
  (Mexico City) 59, **80**, 117
  Street-by-Street map 78
Palacio Clavijero (Morelia) **210**
  Street-by-Street map 208
Palacio de Cortés
  (Cuernavaca) 148
Palacio de Gobierno
  (Guadalajara) **188**
Palacio de Gobierno
  (Morelia) **210**
  Street-by-Street map 209
El Palacio de Hierro (Mexico
  City) 115
Palacio de Iturbide
  (Mexico City)
  architecture 22
  Street-by-Street map 79
Palacio de la Minería
  (Mexico City)
  Street-by-Street map 79
Palacio Nacional (Mexico
  City) **66–7**
  Diego Rivera murals 39, **66–7**
  Street-by-Street map 63

Palacio Postal (Mexico City)
  Street-by-Street map 53, 78
Palacios, Irma 88
Palafox, Juan de, Bishop
  of Puebla 152
Palancar 282
Palenque 129, **234–7**
  history 40
  hotels 302
  map 237
  restaurants 324
  Temple of the Inscriptions
  236–7
PAN (Partido de Acción
  Nacional) 16, **55**, 175
Panama hats **260**
Papaloapan River 252
Papántla
  hotels 303
  restaurants 325
Papier-mâché
  buying 332
Paquimé **170**
Paricutín **205**
  hotels 299
Parking 354
Parks and gardens
  Alameda Central
  (Mexico City) 78
  Baluarte de Santiago
  (Campeche) 260
  Bosque de Chapultepec
  (Mexico City) 58, **88–9**
  Cerro de Guadalupe
  (Puebla) **153**
  Chankanaab Park 282
  Cosmo Vitral Jardín
  Botánico (Toluca) 144
  Jardín de la Bombilla
  (Mexico City) 98
  Jardín Borda (Cuernavaca)
  148
  Jardín Botánico
  (Mexico City) 111
  Jardín Botánico (Tuxtla
  Gutiérrez) 230
  Jardín Centenario
  (Mexico City) 99, 104
  Jardín de Libertad
  (Colima) 187
  Jardín de la Unión
  (Guanajuato) 203
  Lagunas de Zempoala
  Park 148
  Museo Dolores Olmedo
  Patiño (Xochimilco) 113
  Museo Ex-Hacienda de San
  Gabriel de la Barrera
  (Guanajuato) 205
  Museo Francisco Goitia
  (Zacatecas) 193
  Museo Nacional del
  Virreinato 140
  Nanciyaga 253
El Parnaso (Mexico
  City) 115

Parque-Museo de la Venta
  (Villahermosa) 254, **255**
Parque Nacional Agua Azul 232
Parque Nacional Constitución
  de 1857 162
Parque Nacional las Cumbres
  de Monterrey 179
Parque Nacional Lagunas
  de Chacahua
  Beaches of Oaxaca 216
Parque Nacional San Pedro
  Mártir 163
Parral see Hidalgo del Parral
La Parroquia (San Miguel
  de Allende)
  Street-by-Street map 198
Partido Nacional
  Revolucionario (PNR) 54, 55
Paseo de la Reforma and
  Bosque de Chapultepec
  (Mexico City) **83–95**
  Bosque de Chapultepec
  88–9
  hotels 292–4
  map 83
  Museo Nacional de
  Antropología **90–95**
  Paseo de la Reforma **84–5**
  restaurants 314–15
Paso de Cortés 149
Passion plays 30
Passports **336**
Patria Independencia 31, 32
Patriots and Parricides
  (Siqueiros) 26, 72
Pátzcuaro **207**
  fiestas 185
  hotels 299
  restaurants 321
Pátzcuaro, Lake 207
  A Tour Around Lake
  Pátzcuaro **206**
La Paz **169**
  airport 348
  Carnival 163
  hotels 297
  restaurants 320
Paz, Octavio 15, 30, 35
Pedestrians 341
Pellicer, Carlos 148, 255
The People for the University,
  The University for the People
  (Siqueiros) 26
Peredo, Rocio 105
Permits
  driving in Mexico 355
Personal security **340–41**
Peseros
  Mexico City 356
Peyote cactus 184
Pharmacies **338**
Philip II of Spain 204, 210
Philip IV, King of Spain 156
Phonecards 344
Photography
  duty free allowances 336

Photography (cont.)
  etiquette 337
  Museo de Fotografía
  (Pachuca) 138
Picasso, Pablo 195
  Museo Iconográfico del
  Quijote (Guanajuato) 204
  Museo Rufino Tamayo
  (Mexico City) 87
Pickpockets 340
Pico de Orizaba 239, 240, 251
Pie de la Cuesta 219
Piña Mora, Aarón 172
Pinacoteca Virreinal
  (Mexico City) **81**
Pinocelly, Salvador 80
Pirámide de Cuicuilco **112**
Plants
  Cactuses of Northern
  Mexico **171**
  San Ángel flower market
  (Mexico City) 101
Playa Azul 186
Playa Ballenas (Cancún) 279
Playa Caleta (Acapulco) 219
Playa Caletilla (Acapulco) 219
Playa Chac-Mool (Cancún) 279
Playa los Cocos (Isla
  Mujeres) 281
Playa Condesa
  (Acapulco) 219
Playa de Garrafón 281
Playa de los Muertos 185
Playa de Oro (El Puerto de
  Veracruz) 250
Playa del Carmen
  hotels 305
  Mayan Riviera 280
  restaurants 327
Playa Estero (Ensenada) 162
Playa El Faro (Ensenada) 162
Playa Honda (Acapulco) 219
Playa Hornitos (Acapulco) 219
Playa Hornos (Acapulco) 219
Playa Icacos (Acapulco) 219
Playa Langosta (Cancún) 279
Playa Larga (Acapulco) 219
Playa Linda (Cancún) 279
Playa Manzanillo
  (Acapulco) 219
Playa Marlin (Cancún) 279
Playa El Médano 169
Playa Miramar 186
Playa Revolcadero
  (Acapulco) 219
Playa Tortugas (Cancún) 279
Plaza 23 de Mayo (Mexico
  City) see Plaza de Santo
  Domingo
Plaza del Ángel (Mexico
  City) 115
Plaza de los Angeles
  (Guanajuato)
  Street-by-Street map 202
Plaza de Armas (Morelia)
  Street-by-Street map 209

Plaza de Armas
  (Oaxaca) 222
Plaza Borda (Taxco)
  Street-by-Street map 146
Plaza de la Conchita
  (Mexico City)
  Street-by-Street map 105
Plaza Federico Gamboa
  (Mexico City)
  A Walk from San Ángel to
  Coyoacán 98–9
Plaza Garibaldi (Mexico
  City) **109**
Plaza Hidalgo (Mexico City)
  Street-by-Street map 104
Plaza de la Independencia
  (Querétaro) **196**
Plaza Mayor **22**
Plaza México (Mexico
  City) 110
Plaza Monumental de Toros
  México (Mexico City) 117
Plaza de las Tres Culturas
  (Mexico City) **108–9**
Plaza Santa Catarina
  (Mexico City)
  A Walk from San Ángel to
  Coyoacán 99
Plaza de Santo Domingo
  (Mexico City) **72–3**
Plaza de San Jacinto (Mexico
  City) **100**
  A Walk from San Ángel to
  Coyoacán 98
Plazuela del Baratillo
  (Guanajuato)
  Street-by-Street map 203
Polé 284
Police 339, **340**
  emergency numbers 341
  lost and stolen
  property 341
Politics **16–17**
Polyforum Siqueiros
  (Mexico City) 110
Poniatowska, Elena 252
Poniente bus terminal
  (Mexico City) 353
Popocatépetl **149**, 341
A Popular History of Mexico
  (Rivera) 27
Porfirian architecture 23
Porfiriato 53
Posada, José Guadalupe 53
  La Catrina **35**, 81
  Museo de la Caricatura
  (Mexico City) 71
  Museo José Guadalupe
  Posada (Aguascalientes) 191
  Museo Nacional de la
  Estampa (Mexico City) 80
  portrait of 35
Posadas 33
Las Posas **195**
Postage stamps 345
Postal services **345**

Poste restante 345
Potrero 253
Pottery
  buying 332
  Folk Art of Mexico 330, 331
  Oaxaca's black and green
    pottery **224**
  Paquimé 170
  Talavera pottery **153**
Las Pozas 195
Presidente 291
Presidential Address 32
Prieto, Alejandro 110
Prismas Basálticos 139
Progreso **272**
  restaurants 327
Public holidays 31
Public toilets **339**
Puebla **150–53**
  fiestas 139
  hotels 295
  restaurants 317
  Street-by-Street map
    150–51
Puebla, Battle of (1862)
  31, 139
Pueblo la Playa 169
Puerto Ángel
  Beaches of Oaxaca 217
  hotels 302
  restaurants 324
Puerto Aventuras
  hotels 305
  Mayan Riviera 280
Puerto Escondido **216–17**
  Beaches of Oaxaca 216
  festivals 32
  hotels 302
  restaurants 324
Puerto Escondido
  International Surf
  Tournament 32
Puerto Marqués 219
Puerto Morelos
  Mayan Riviera 281
  restaurants 327
Puerto Vallarta **185**
  airport 348
  hotels 299–300
  restaurants 322
El Puerto de Veracruz 239, **250**
Pulque 313
Punta Allen 286
  hotels 305
Punta Bete
  hotels 305
Punta Mita 185
Puuc architecture
  Uxmal 262
Puuc Route **268–9**
Pyramids
  Templo Mayor 70
  Calakmul 287
  El Castillo (Chichén Itzá)
    261, 275, **276**
  Cempoala 247

Pyramids (cont.)
  Cholula 149
  Cobá 285
  Edificio de los Cinco Pisos
    (Edzná) 261
  Ekbalam 278
  Izamal 273
  Kohunlich 287
  Magician's Pyramid
    (Uxmal) **264**
  Mayapán 269
  Mesoamerican 44
  Palenque 234–5
  Pirámide de Cuicuilco **112**
  Pyramid of the Moon
    (Teotihuacán) 135
  Pyramid of the Sun
    (Teotihuacán) 132, 135, **137**
  El Rey 279
  El Tajín **242–3**
  Temple of the Inscriptions
    (Palenque) **236**
  Tula 144
  Uxmal 262–3
  Xochicalco 145

Q
La Quebrada cliff divers
  218, **219**
El Quelite 178
La Quemada **191**
Querétaro 15, 196–7
  hotels 300
  map 197
  restaurants 322
Querétaro (state) 181
Quetzal dancers 28
Quetzalcoatl 42
  Chichén Itzá 274
  The Gods of Ancient
    Mexico 265
Quetzalpapalotl Palace
  Complex (Teotihuacán)
  135, **136**
Quiahuiztlan **246**
Quinn, Anthony 179
Quinta Real 291
Quintana Roo 257, 286
Quiroga
  A Tour Around Lake
    Pátzcuaro 206
Quiroga, Vasco de 207

R
Radio 344, **345**
Radio taxis 341
Railroads see Trains
Rain gods 265
Rainfall 36–7
Las Ranas 195
Rancho del Charro
  (Mexico City) 117
Real, Doña Rosa 224
Real de Catorce **193**
  hotels 300
  restaurants 322

Real del Monte see Mineral
  del Monte
Recohuata 174
Red Cross 338
La Reforma 53
  Paseo de la Reforma
    (Mexico City) **84–5**
Reforma & Chapultepec
  (Mexico City) see Paseo de
  la Reforma and Bosque
  de Chapultepec
Religion 15
  Gods of Ancient Mexico **265**
Rental
  car, bicycle, and
    motorbike 355
Rent'n Vallarta 291
Restaurants **306–27**
  Around Mexico City 317–19
  chain restaurants 306
  children in 307
  Colonial Heartland 320–23
  eating hours 307
  entertainment 307
  food hygiene 306–7
  Gulf Coast 325–6
  Mexico City 314–16
  Northern Mexico 319–20
  prices and paying 307
  Reading the Menu **311**
  smoking in 307
  Southern Mexico 323–5
  tipping 342
  typical restaurants and
    bars 306
  wheelchair access 307
  Yucatán Peninsula 326–7
  see also Food and drink
Reto al Tepozteco
  (Tepoztlán) 139
Revolution Day 31, 32
El Rey 279
Riding **347**
Río Bec sites **287**
  hotels 305
Río Lagartos **279**
Ripley museum (Mexico
  City) **87**
Rivera, Diego 15
  Acapulco 218
  Casa Diego Rivera
    (Guanajuato) 202, **204**
  The Creation 71
  Days of the Dead 34–5
  *Dream of a Sunday
    Afternoon in the Alameda
    Central* **26–7**, 81
  and Frida Kahlo 102
  Fuente de Tláloc
    (Mexico City) 88
  *Man, Controller of the
    Universe* 80
  murals 27, 48, 54
  Museo de Arte de Carrillo-
    Gil (Mexico City) 101
  Museo de Arte Moderno

Rivera, Diego (cont.)
(Mexico City) 88
Museo del Anahuacalli 111
Museo Dolores Olmedo
Patiño (Xochimilco) **113**
Museo Estudio Diego Rivera
(Mexico City) **100–101**
Museo Frida Kahlo 103
Museo Mural Diego Rivera
(Mexico City) **81**
Museo Nacional de Arte
(Mexico City) 75
Museo Rafael Coronel
(Zacatecas) 193
Palacio de Cortés
(Cuernavaca) 148
Palacio Nacional murals
39, 63, **66–7**
*A Popular History of
Mexico* 27
San Ángel and Coyoacán
(Mexico City) 97
Secretaría de Educación
Pública murals 72
Teatro de los Insurgentes
(Mexico City) 110
Universidad Nacional
Autónoma de Mexico
(Mexico City) 111
Rivera, Mario Orozco 246
Rivera, Ruth 111
Road classification 354
Road signs 354
Rock music **116**, 117
Rockefeller, John D. 80
Rocky Desert 163
Rodin, Auguste 86
Rodriguez, Angel Mauro
Jazz **99**, 102
Rodriguez, Manuel
("Manolete") 110
Rodríguez Juárez, Juan
Adoration of the Kings 64
Assumption of the Virgin 64
Roma
restaurants 316
Roman Catholic Church 15, 21
Virgin of Guadalupe **109**
Romero de Terreros,
Pedro 138
El Rosario Monarch Butterfly
Sanctuary **211**
Rothko, Mark 87
Rozo, Romulo 270
Rubens, Peter Paul 191
Rural architecture 23
rural Baroque architecture 25
Ruz Lhuillier, Alberto 236

S
Safety
driving in Mexico 354
mountainous areas 347
natural disasters **341**
personal security **340–41**
St. Isidore's Day 31

Sala de Arte Siqueiros
(Mexico City) **87**, 89
Sala Nezahualtcóyotl
(Mexico City) 117
Sala Ollin Yoliztli
(Mexico City) 117
Salinas de Gortari, Carlos
16, 55
Salón México (Mexico
City) 117
Salón Tropicana (Mexico
City) 117
Salt
Guerrero Negro 164
Museo de la Sal (Cuyutlán)
186, 187
Saltillo 179
hotels 298
restaurants 320
Salto de Eyipantla 253
San Agustín Acolman 24, **138**
San Andrés Tuxtla 253
San Ángel and Coyoacán
(Mexico City) 58, **97–105**
map 97
restaurants 316
Street-by-Street map 104–5
A Walk from San Ángel to
Coyoacán **98–9**
San Ángel flower market
(Mexico City) 101
San Antonio Arrazola 225
San Antonio Panzacola
(Mexico City)
A Walk from San Ángel to
Coyoacán 99
San Bartolo Coyotepec 225
San Blas **184**
hotels 300
restaurants 322
San Cristóbal de las Casas
214, **231**
architecture 22
fiestas 225
hotels 302
market 14
restaurants 324
Zapatista uprising 55,
230, 231
San Francisco 282
San Francisco Acatepec
25, 149
San Gervasio 282
San Hipólito (Mexico City) 85
San Ignacio **165**
hotels 298
San Jerónimo Tlacochahuaya
A Tour of the Tlacolula
Valley 226
San José del Cabo **169**
hotels 298
restaurants 320
San Juan Chamula 213, **231**
fiestas 225
San Juan Cosalá 190
San Juan de los Lagos **190–91**

San Juan del Río 197
hotels 300
San Juan de Ulúa (El Puerto
de Veracruz) 250
San Lorenzo Tenochtitlán 253
Olmecs 40, 254
San Luis Potosí **194**
hotels 300
restaurants 322
San Luis Potosí (state) 181
San Miguel, Fray Antonio
de 211
San Miguel, Juan de 205
San Miguel de Aguayo,
Marqués de 100
San Miguel de Allende **198–9**
Easter Week 185
hotels 300
restaurants 322
Street by Street map
198–9
San Miguel de Cozumel 282
San Miguel Regla
(Huasca) 139
San Sebastián Chimalistac
(Mexico City)
A Walk from San Ángel to
Coyoacán 99
Sanborn's (Mexico City) 115
Santa Ana Chiauhtempan 157
Santa Anna, General Antonio
López de 52
Hacienda Lencero 246
Tlalpan 112
Palacio Nacional mural 67
Santa Casa de Loreto (San
Miguel de Allende)
Street-by-Street map 199
Santa Cruz, Alonso de 39
Santa Eulalia 172
Santa Fe de la Laguna
A Tour Around Lake
Pátzcuaro 206
Santa María Atzompa 225
Santa María del Oro 184
Santa María Regla (Huasca) 139
Santa María del Río 194
Santa María Tonantzintla 149
Santa María del Tule
A Tour of the Tlacolula
Valley 226
Santa Prisca (Taxco)
Street-by-Street map 147
Santa Rosa 282
Santa Rosalía **168**
hotels 298
restaurants 320
Santacília, Carlos Obregón
Monumento a la Revolución
(Mexico City) 86
Santiago de Calimaya,
Counts of 74
Santiago Tuxtla **252–3**
fiestas 247
hotels 303
restaurants 325

Santuario de Nuestra Señora
de Guadalupe (Morelia)
181, **211**
Satevó 175, 177
Sayil 268
Scorpions 339
Se Renta Luxury Villas
(Acapulco) 291
Sea Side Vacations 291
Secretaría de Educación
Pública (Mexico City) **72**
SECTUR (Secretaría de
Turismo) offices 337
Serdán, Aquiles 152
Shamans 21
Shepherd, Alexander 175
Sheraton 291
Shoe shops 328
Shopping **328–33**
buying crafts **332–3**
clothing 329
Folk Art of Mexico **330–31**
food and drink 329
general stores 328
markets 329
Mexico City **114–15**
opening hours 328
paying 328
regional products 329
specialty shops 328–9
Sian Ka'an Biosphere
Reserve **286**
Sierra Chincua Monarch
Butterfly Sanctuary 211
Sierra Gorda **195**
hotels 300
Sierra Madre 159, 185, 347
Sierra Madre Occidental 176
Sierra de San Francisco
164, 165
Sierra Tarahumara 159, 173
Sierra de Zongolica 251
Silva, Federico 109
Silver
Alamos 175
Batopilas 175
Cerro del Grillo
(Zacatecas) 193
Folk Art of Mexico 330
Guanajuato 202
International Silver Fair 32
Museo de la Platería
Antonio Pineda (Taxco) 146
Real de Catorce 193
shops 328–9
La Valenciana
(Guanajuato) **204**
Sinaloa 159, 178
Siqueiros, David Alfaro
Antiguo Colegio de San
Ildefonso (Mexico City) 71
The Assassination of
Trotsky 103
Cuauhtémoc Against
the Myth 109
Escuela de Bellas Artes

Siqueiros, David Alfaro (cont.)
(San Miguel de Allende) 198
murals 15, 26
Museo de Arte de Carrillo-
Gil (Mexico City) 101
Museo de Arte Moderno
(Mexico City) 88
Museo Nacional de Arte
(Mexico City) 75
Museo Nacional de Historia
(Mexico City) 89
Palacio de Bellas Artes
(Mexico City) 80
Patriots and Parricides 26, 72
The People for the University,
The University for the
People 26
Polyforum Siqueiros
(Mexico City) 110
Sala de Arte Siqueiros
(Mexico City) **87**, 89
Taller Siqueiros
(Cuernavaca) 148
Universidad Nacional
Autónoma de Mexico
(Mexico City) 111
Smoking
in restaurants 307
Soccer **346**
Social customs **337**
Sol a Sol Regatta (Isla
Mujeres) 31
Sonora 159
Sonoran Desert 159
South America
map 11
Southern Mexico **213–37**
Acapulco **218–19**
The Art of the Maya **233**
Beaches of Oaxaca
216–17
Fiestas 225
hotels 301–2
map 214–15
Monte Albán **220–21**
Oaxaca **222–5**
Palenque **234–7**
restaurants 323–5
A Tour of the Tlacolula
Valley **226–7**
Spanish conquistadors 39,
43, 48
Spanish Inquisition 48
Spanish language 336,
381–4
Specialty shops 328–9
Spider bites 339
Sports 16
outdoor activities **347**
spectator sports 117,
346
Spratling, William 146
Museo Guillermo Spratling
(Taxco) 147
Museo de la Platería Antonio
Pineda (Taxco) 146

Spring in Mexico **30–31**
Stalin, Joseph 87, 103
Statues in Mexico City
El Caballito (The Little
Horse) 75, **85**
Charles V 79
Diana Cazadora 84
Monumento a la
Independencia 84
Stomach upsets **339**
Street hazards **341**
Students
air travel 351
Summer in Mexico **31**
Sun God 265
Sun Stone **95**
Sunshine 36–7
Sur bus terminal (Mexico
City) 353
Surfing 347
Puerto Escondido
International Surf
Tournament (Puerto
Escondido) 32
Tecate Mexicali Surf Festival
(Ensenada) 32
Swimming 347
Diving in the Mexican
Caribbean 283

T
Tabasco 239
El Tajín 129, **242–3**
map 243
South Ballcourt 277
Talavera pottery **153**
Taller Uriarte (Puebla) **153**
Tamaulipas 159
Tamayo, Olga 87
Tamayo, Rufino 15
Museo de Arte
Contemporáneo
(Oaxaca) 222
Museo de Arte Moderno
(Mexico City) 88
Museo Robert Brady
(Cuernavaca) 148
Museo Rufino Tamayo
(Mexico City) **87**, 89
Museo Rufino Tamayo
(Oaxaca) 224
Palacio de Bellas Artes
(Mexico City) 80
Tamul 195
Tanaxpillo 240, 253
Taquerías (restaurants) 306
Tarahumara Indians **174**
Casa de las Artesanías
(Creel) 174
Copper Canyon 176
Easter Week 30
The Indigenous Peoples
of Mexico 20
Tarascans
Museo Nacional de Antro-
pología (Mexico City) 93

Tarascans (cont.)
Palacio Nacional mural 67
Pátzcuaro 207
Tarímbaro 185
Taxco 130, **146–7**
hotels 295
restaurants 318
Street-by-Street map 146–7
Taxes 342
in hotels 291
in restaurants 307
in shops 328
Taxis 353
Mexico City **341**, 356
tipping 342
Taylor, Elizabeth 218
Teabo 269
Teatro de la Danza
(Mexico City) 117
Teatro Degollado
(Guadalajara) **188**
Teatro Hidalgo (Mexico
City) 117
Teatro de los Insurgentes
(Mexico City) 110, 117
Teatro Juárez (Guanajuato)
23, **204**
Street-by-Street map 203
Teatro Raúl Flores Canelo
(Mexico City) 117
Tecate Mexicali Surf Festival
(Ensenada) 32
Tecoh 269
Tekit 269
Telephones **344**
Television 344, **345**
Temperatures 36–7
Temple of the Inscriptions
(Palenque) **236**
Temple of the Jaguar
(Palenque) 237
Temple of Quetzalcoatl
(Teotihuacán) 134
Templo del Carmen (San Luis
Potosí) **194**
Templo de la Compañía
(Guanajuato)
Street-by-Street map 203
Templo de la Compañía de
Jesús (Morelia)
Street-by-Street map 208
Templo de la Concepción
(San Miguel de Allende)
Street-by-Street map 198
Templo y Conservatorio de
las Rosas (Morelia) **210**
Templo de la Enseñanza
(Mexico City) **72**
Street-by-Street map 62
Templo Mayor (Mexico City)
59, **68–70**
The Building of 70
floorplan 68–9
Street-by-Street map 63
Templo y Museo de
Guadalupe (Zacatecas) **193**

Templo de Nuestra Señora
de la Salud (San Miguel
de Allende)
Street-by-Street map 199
Templo de San Cayetano
(Guanajuato) **205**
Templo de San Cristóbal
(Puebla)
Street-by-Street map 150
Templo de San Francisco
(San Miguel de Allende)
Street-by-Street map 199
Templo de Santa Clara
(Querétaro) **196**
Templo de Santa Rosa
(Querétaro) **196**
Templo de Santiago
(Mexico City) 108–9
Tenampa (Mexico City) 117
Tenochtitlán 253
history 39, 43
The Lake City of
Tenochtitlán **94**
Palacio Nacional mural 67
Teocalli 68
Teotenango 145
Teotihuacán 129, 131,
134–7
history 41
hotels 295
Museo Nacional de
Antropología (Mexico City)
92
pyramids 137
Quetzalpapalotl Palace
Complex **136**
restaurants 318
The Unearthing of
Teotihuacán 137
Teotitlán del Valle
A Tour of the Tlacolula
Valley 226
restaurants 324
Tepic **184**
Tepotzotlán
Museo National del
Virreinato **140–43**
restaurants 318
Tepoztécatl 148
Tepoztlán 133, 148
fiestas 139
hotels 295
restaurants 318
Tequesquitengo
hotels 295
Tequila (drink) **313**
Tequila (place) **187**
Tequisquiapan 197
Texas
Mexican-American War
(1846–48) 52
Texolo Waterfall 247
Textiles
Folk Art of Mexico 330
buying 333
Theater **116**, 117

Theft 340, 341
Ticketmaster (Mexico City) 117
Tickets
for entertainment **116**, 117
Metro (Mexico City) 357
Tiffany Studios 80
Tiger dancers 29
Tijuana **162**
airport 348
hotels 298
restaurants 320
Time zones **337**
Tinsmiths
Folk Art of Mexico 331
Tipping 342
in restaurants 307
Tizatlán 157
Tizoc 95
Tlacolula de Matamoros
A Tour of the Tlacolula
Valley 227
Tlacolula Valley
A Tour of the Tlacolula
Valley 226–7
Tlacotalpan 241, **252**
hotels 303
restaurants 325
Tlaloc 70, 265
Tlalpan **112**
restaurants 316
Tlaquepaque **190**
hotels 300
restaurants 322
Tlatelolco
Plaza de las Tres Culturas
(Mexico City) 108
Tlaxcala **156–7**
Carnival 28
hotels 296
Palacio Nacional
mural 66
restaurants 318
Tocuaro
A Tour Around Lake
Pátzcuaro 206
Toilets, public **339**
Toledo, Francisco 88, 222
Toll roads 354
Tolsá, Manuel
El Caballito (The
Little Horse) 75
Instituto Cultural Cabañas
(Guadalajara) 188
Puebla Cathedral 151, 152
Toltecs **42**
Chichén Itzá 274
Museo Nacional de
Antropología (Mexico
City) 92–3
Quiahuiztlan 246
Tula **144**
Toluca **144–5**
hotels 296
restaurants 318
Toluquilla 195
Tonacatecuhtli 265

Topiltzín, King 144
Toreo de Cuatro Caminos
   (Mexico City) 117
Torre Latinoamericana
   (Mexico City) **75**
   Street-by-Street map 79
Totonacs
   Museo Nacional de
   Antropología (Mexico
   City) 93
   Quiahuiztlan 246
   El Tajín **242–3**
Tourist information **337**
Tourist police 341
Tours by car
   Lake Pátzcuaro **206**
   Tlacolula Valley 226–7
La Tovara 184
Trains **352–3**
   Chihuahua-Al-Pacífico
   Railroad **176**
Transpeninsular Highway
   163
Travel **348–57**
   air **348–51**
   Around Mexico City 133
   buses **352**, **353**
   Colonial Heartland 183
   driving in Mexico **354–5**
   ferries **353**
   Gulf Coast 241
   Mexico City **356–7**
   Northern Mexico 161
   Southern Mexico 214
   taxis 353
   trains **352–3**
   Yucatán Peninsula 259
Traveler's checks **342**
   in hotels 291
   in restaurants 307
Tres Zapotes 252–3
   Olmecs 254
Tresguerras, Francisco
   Eduardo 194
Trique peoples 20
Tropical forests 19
Trotsky, León 87
   The Assassination of
   Trotsky 54, **103**
   Casa/Museo León Trotsky
   (Mexico City) **103**
   and Frida Kahlo 102
   San Ángel and Coyoacán
   (Mexico City) 97
Tula **144**
   hotels 296
   restaurants 319
   Toltecs 42
Tulum 259, **284–5**
   hotels 305
   restaurants 327
Tulúm Playa
   Mayan Riviera 280
Turtles
   Centro Mexicano de
   Tortuga 217

Tuxtla Gutiérrez **230**
   hotels 302
   restaurants 324
Tzintzuntzán
   Easter Week 185
   A Tour Around Lake
   Pátzcuaro 206
Tzotzil Maya peoples 20

U
UNESCO 196, 202
United Kingdom
   Embassy 337
   SECTUR office 337
United States of America
   Embassy 337
   Mexican-American War
   (1846–48) 52
   Mexico-US border **162**, 349
   SECTUR office 337
Universidad Nacional
   Autónoma de Mexico
   (UNAM, Mexico City) **111**
University (Guanajuato)
   Street-by-Street map 203
Uruapan **205**
   hotels 300
   restaurants 322
Usumacinta river 13, 232
Utell International 291
Uxmal 257, **262–4**
   Magician's Pyramid **264**
   restaurants 327

V
Vaccinations **338**
Valenciana, Count of 205
La Valenciana (Guanajuato)
   204
Valladolid **278**
   hotels 305
   restaurants 327
Valle de Bravo **144**
   hotels 296
   restaurants 319
Valle de los Hongos 174, 177
Valley of Mexico 13
Varig 349
Vázquez, Pedro Ramírez 90
VAT see IVA tax
Velasco, José María 75, 251
Velasco, Luis de 78
Vendimia Wine Festival
   (Ensenada) 163
La Venta 254
   Olmecs 254
   Parque-Museo de la Venta
   (Villahermosa) 254, **255**
   airport 348
   climate 37
   hotels 303
   El Puerto de Veracruz
   241, **250**
   restaurants 325
Veracruz (state) 239
   Witch Doctors **252**

Viernes Santo 31
Villa, Francisco (Pancho)
   173
   assassination 54
   Bar La Opera (Mexico
   City) 79
   Cerro de la Bufa
   (Zacatecas) 193
   Chihuahua 172
   civil war 54
   Hidalgo del Parral 173
   Monumento a la Revolución
   (Mexico City) 86
Villa Calmecac 291
Villa del Oeste 178
Villa de Reyes 194
Villahermosa **254**
   hotels 303
   restaurants 325
Villalpando, Cristóbal de
   El Carmen (Mexico City)
   98, 100
   Iglesia de San Bernardino
   (Xochimilco) 113
   Puebla Cathedral 152
   Templo y Museo de
   Guadalupe (Zacatecas) 193
Villar del Villa, Marqués
   del 197
Virgin of Guadalupe 15,
   48, **109**
   Basílica de Guadalupe
   (Mexico City) **108**
   Día de la Virgen de
   Guadalupe 33
VISA 342
Visas **336**
Vizcaíno Biosphere Preserve
   164–5
Voladores **29**
   El Tajín 243
Volcanoes
   climbing 347
   Paricutín **205**
   Popocatépetl and
   Iztaccíhuatl **149**
   safety 341
   Volcán de Fuego 187

W
Wade, Robert 102
Walking
   hiking **347**
   in Mexico City 356
   A Walk from San Ángel
   to Coyoacán (Mexico City)
   98–9
Walsh, Janet 102
War of the Castes
   (1840–46) 52
War of the Reform (1858–61)
   52, 53
Waterfalls
   Cascada de Basaséachic
   174
   Cascada Cusárare 174

Waterfalls (cont.)
 Cola de Caballo 179
 Misol-Ha 232
 Parque Nacional Agua
  Azul 232
 Salto de Eyipantla 253
 Tamul 195
 Texolo Waterfall 247
Watersports **347**
Wax Museum (Mexico City)
 see Museo de Cera
Wayne, John 179, 218
Weather **36–7**
 when to go 336
Weaving 330
Westin 291
Wetlands 18
Whales
 Vizcaíno Biosphere
  Preserve 164
 Whale-watching in Guerrero
  Negro **164**
Wheelchair access *see*
 Disabled travelers
White-water rafting 347
Wildlife
 Cañón del Sumidero 230
 Celestún 272
 Centro Mexicano de
  Tortuga 217
 Diving in the Mexican
  Caribbean **283**
 Isla Contoy 281
 Landscape and Wildlife of
  Mexico **18–19**
 Mapimí Biosphere
  Reserve 173
 Migration of the Monarch
  Butterfly **211**
 Parque Nacional
  Constitución de 1857 162
 Parque Nacional Lagunas de
  Chacahua 216
 Río Lagartos 279
 El Rosario Monarch
  Butterfly Sanctuary **211**
 Sierra Chincua Monarch
  Butterfly Sanctuary 211
 Vizcaíno Biosphere
  Preserve **164–5**
 Whale-watching in Guerrero
  Negro **164**
 Xcaret 284
 Yum-Ká 254
 see also Aquariums; Zoos

Wines
 Vendimia Wine Festival
  (Ensenada) 163
 What to Drink in
  Mexico 312
Winter in Mexico **33**
Witch doctors of
 Veracruz **252**
Wooden toys and carvings
 buying 332
World Trade Center
 (Mexico City) 110
World War II 54
Wrestling **346**
Writing
 Maya glyphs **46–7**

X
Xalapa (Jalapa) **246**
 hotels 303
 Museo de Antropología
  (Xalapa) **248–9**
 restaurants 325
Xcaret **284**
 Mayan Riviera 280
Xel-Ha
 Mayan Riviera 280
Xico 247
Xlapak 268
Xochicalco **145**
Xochimilco 107, **112–13**
Xochitécatl 156
Ypujil 287

Y
Yagul **226**
 A Tour of the Tlacolula
  Valley 227
Yahaw Chan Muwan
 232
Yaqui Indians 20
Yaxchilán **232**
Youth hostels **291**
Yucatán Peninsula
 257–87
 Chichén Itzá **274–6**
 Fiestas of the Yucatán
  Peninsula **261**
 hotels 304–5
 map 258–9
 Mérida **270–71**
 restaurants 326–7
 Uxmal **262–4**
Yum-Ká 254
Yuriria 211

Z
Zaachila 225
Zabludovsky, Abraham 87
Zacatecas **192–3**
 history 48
 hotels 301
 restaurants 322–3
Zacatecas (state) 181
Zalce, Alfredo 210
Zapata, Emiliano 81
 grave of 148
 Mexican Revolution 54
 Museo de Cera (Mexico
  City) 86
 Palacio Nacional mural 67
 portrait of 54
 Zapatista uprising 230
Zapatista National Liberation
 Army (EZLN) 17
 Zapatista uprising 55,
  230, 231
El Zapotal 250
Zapotecs
 crafts 45
 Cuilapan de Guerrero 225
 Dainzú 226
 Lambityeco 227
 Mitla 226–7
 Monte Albán **220–21**
 Teotitlán del Valle 226
 Yagul 226, 227
Zaragoza, General Ignacio 153
Zedillo, Ernesto 16
Zihuatanejo **216**
 hotels 302
 restaurants 325
Zinacantán
 fiestas 225
Zipolite
 Beaches of Oaxaca 217
Zitácuaro
 hotels 301
 restaurants 323
Zócalo (Mexico City)
 Street-by-Street map 62–3
Zona Rosa (Mexico City) 85
"Zone of Silence" 173
Zoos
 Chapultepec Zoo
  (Mexico City) 117
 Zoológico Miguel Alvarez
  del Toro (Tuxtla
  Gutiérrez) 230
 see also Aquariums;
  Wildlife

Acknowledgments

DORLING KINDERSLEY would like to thank the following people whose contributions and assistance have made the preparation of this book possible.

CONTRIBUTORS AND CONSULTANTS
ANTONIO BENAVIDES has worked as an archaeologist in the Yucatán Peninsula since 1974. He has written several books on the Maya and the colonial history of the Yucatán.

NICK CAISTOR, a specialist on Latin American literature, is a writer, translator, and broadcaster. He works for the BBC World Service.
MARIA DOULTON is a freelance writer who has been involved with Mexico for many years.
PETRA FISCHER is a writer and television producer working in Mexico. German born, she has spent much of her life in Mexico.
EDUARDO GLEASON, a former tour guide, is a writer and researcher based in Mexico City.
PHIL GUNSON is a journalist and naturalist. He is the former Latin America correspondent for *The Guardian* newspaper.
ALAN KNIGHT is Professor of Latin American history at St Anthony's College, Oxford.
FELICITY LAUGHTON, a freelance writer, has lived and worked in Mexico for many years.
SIMON MARTIN is an epigrapher at the Institute of Archaeology, University College London, and specializes in ancient Maya inscriptions.
RICHARD NICHOLS is half-Mexican and has had a life-long connection with Mexico. He is a former businessman turned writer.
LOURDES NICHOLS, an authority on Mexican cuisine, is the author of *The Complete Mexican Cookbook*. Born in Mexico, she now divides her time between Mexico and England.
CHLOË SAYER has written numerous books about Mexico, worked on television documentaries about the country, and made ethnographic collections in Mexico for the British Museum.

ADDITIONAL CONTRIBUTORS
Andrew Downie, David Maitland, Rosa Rodríguez.

PROOFREADER
Stewart J Wild.

INDEXER
Hilary Bird.

EDITORIAL AND DESIGN ASSISTANCE
Tessa Bindloss, Sam Borland, Stephanie Driver, Joy Fitzsimmons, Emily Hatchwell, Carolyn Hewitson, Elly King, Francesca Machiavelli, Sue Metcalfe-Megginson, Rebecca Milner, Naomi Peck, Zoë Ross.

PHOTOGRAPHERS
Demetrio Carrasco, Linda Whitwam, Peter Wilson, Francesca Yorke

ADDITIONAL PHOTOGRAPHY
Eva Gleason, Clive Streeter.

ILLUSTRATORS
Gary Cross, Richard Draper, Isidoro González-Adalid Cabezas (Acanto Arquitectura y Urbanismo S.L.), Paul Guest, Stephen Guapay, Claire Littlejohn, John Woodcock

ADDITIONAL ILLUSTRATIONS
José Luis de Andrés de Colsa, Javier Gómez Morata (Acanto Arquitectura y Urbanismo S.L.).

FOR DORLING KINDERSLEY
Fay Franklin, Louise Bostock Lang, Annette Jacobs, Vivien Crump, Gillian Allan, Douglas Amrine, Marie Ingledew, David Proffit

SPECIAL ASSISTANCE
Arq. Humberto Aguirre; Emilia Almazán; Margarita Arriaga; Juan Francisco Becerra Ferreiro; Patricia Becerra Ramírez (Posada Coatepec); Sergio Berrera; Lic. Marco Beteta; Giorgio Brignone; Rosa Bugdud; Fernando Bustamante (Antropólogo); Libby Cabeldu; Canning House (London); Lic. Laura Castro; Santiago Chávez; Josefina Cipriano; Ana Compean; María Eugenia Cruz Terrazas (INEGI); Greg Custer; Jane Custer; Mary Lou Dabdoub; Avery Danziger; Lenore Danziger; Areli Díaz (Instituto Nacional de Antropología, Mexico); Lucía Díaz Cholico; Fernando Díaz de León; Lic. Roberto Durón Carrillo; Peter McGregor Eadie; Ana María Espinoza; Ludwig Estrada; José Falguera; Lic. Lincoln Fontanills (Secretaría de Turismo, Mexico); Elena Nichols Gantous; Robert Graham; Ma. del Carmen Guerrero Esquivel; Lic. José Luis Hernández (Secretaría de Turismo del Estado de Puebla); Ing. Guillermo Hidalgo Trujillo; Ariane Homayunfar; Jorge Huft; Instituto Nacional Indigenista (Nayarit); Carlos Jiménez; Lourdes Jiménez Coronel; Ursula Jones; Eric Jordan; La Mexicana Quality Foods Ltd; Marcela Leos (Mexican Embassy to the UK); Kevin Leuzinger (Cozumel Fan Club); Sol Levin Rojo (Instituto Nacional de Antropología, Mexico); Oscar López; Carlos Lozano de la Torre; Alan Luce; Arq. Alfredo Lugo; Berta Maldonado; Gabriel Martínez; Manuel Mata; Cathy Matos (Mexican Tours); Fabián Medina; Enrique Mendoza; Meteorological Office; Mexico Ministry of Tourism, London; Ivalu Mireles Esparza; Silvia Niembro (Antropóloga, Museo de Antropología de Xalapa); María Novaro; Diego de la O Peralta; Magdalena Ordóz Estrada; Dolores Ortuño Araiza; Margarita Pedraza; Ma. Irma del Peral; Ma. del Pilar Córdoba; Margaret Popper; Petra Puente; Bertha Alicia Ramírez; José Rangel Navarro; Jesus Rodríguez Morales; Anita Romero de Andrade; Celia Romero Piñón; Elena de la

Rosa; Idalia Rubio; Paulina Rubio; Carlos Salgado; Alejandro Sánchez Galván; Alejandro Santes García (Antropólogo); Marta Santos; David Saucedo; Gloria Soledad González; Lisette Span; Pablo Span; Turismo del Estado de Aguascalientes (Dirección); Turismo del Estado de Colima (Secretaría); Turismo del Estado de Guanajuato (Secretaría); Turismo del Estado de Hidalgo (Dirección General); Turismo del Estado de Jalisco (Secretaría); Turismo del Estado de Michoacan (Secretaría); Turismo del Estado de Nayarit (Secretaría); Turismo del Estado de Querétaro (Secretaría); Turismo del Estado de San Luis Postosí (Dirección General); Turismo del Estado de Veracruz-Llave (Dirección); Turismo del Estado de Zacatecas (Dirección); Juan Carlos Valencia; Gilberto Miguel Vázquez; Josefina Vázquez; Luis Antonio Villa; Jesús Villafaña; Helen Westwood; John Wiseman.

SPECIAL PHOTOGRAPHY
© INAH, Cambridge Museum of Archaeology and Anthropology, Philip Dowell, Neil Mersh, Stephen Whitehorne, Jerry Young, Michel Zabé.

MEXICO'S CULTURAL HERITAGE
All archaeological and historical sites form part of the Cultural Heritage of Mexico, which is protected by the Instituto Nacional de Antropología e Historia (INAH), Mexico. The reproduction, by whatever means, of any images in this book which form part of the Cultural Heritage of Mexico, is subject to the Mexican federal laws pertaining to monuments and artistic, historical, and archaeological sites, and the Mexican federal law of copyright. Reproduction of these images must be previously approved by INAH.

PHOTOGRAPHY PERMISSIONS
The Publisher would like to thank all the cathedrals, churches, museums, restaurants, hotels, shops, galleries, and others sights, too numerous to thank individually, for their co-operation and contribution to this publication.

PICTURE CREDITS
Key: t=top; tl=top left; tlc=top left centre; tc=top centre; trc=top right centre; tr=top right; cla=centre left above; ca=centre above; cra=centre right above; cl=centre left; c=centre; cr=centre right; clb=centre left below; cb=centre below; crb=centre right below; bl=bottom left; b=bottom; br=bottom right; bcl=bottom centre left; bc=bottom centre; bcr=bottom centre right; (d)=detail. Every effort has been made to trace the copyright holders. Dorling Kindersley apologizes for any unintentional omissions and would be pleased, in such cases, to add an acknowledgment in future editions.

Some of the following photographs form part of the Cultural Heritage of Mexico, which is protected by the Instituto Nacional de Antropología e Historia, Mexico.

Works of art have been reproduced with the permission of the following copyright holders: Museo Mural Diego Rivera *Dream of a Sunday Afternoon in Alameda Central* Diego Rivera (1947–48) © DACS, 1999 26–27, 81b; Teatro de los Insurgentes *A Popular History of Mexico* Diego Rivera (1953) 27tl © DACS, 1999; Palacio Nacional *The Zapotec Civilization* Diego Rivera (1942) © DACS, 1999 27tr; Casa de los Azulejos *Omniscience* José Clemente Orozco (1925) © DACS, 1999 27cb; Palacio de Cortés *The History of Cuernavaca y Morelos – The Enslavement of the Indian* Diego Rivera (1929–30) © DACS, 1999 48c, 148ca(d); Palacio Nacional *The History of Mexico* Diego Rivera (1929–35) © DACS, 1999 66–20, 67, 66b(d), 67t(d), 67br(d); Palacio Nacional *Arrival of Cortés* Diego Rivera © DACS, 1999 67ca; Palacio Nacional *The Tarascans* Diego Rivera © DACS, 1999 67c; Bolivar Amphitheatre Antiguo Colegio de San Idelfonso *Creation* Diego Rivera © DACS, 1999 71t; Palacio de Bellas Artes *Man at the Crossroads* Diego Rivera (1934) © DACS, 1999 80b; Palacio del Gobierno *Miguel Hidalgo* José Clemente Orozco © DACS, 1999 188b; Ex-Aduana de Santo Domingo (west wall) *Patriots and Parricides* David Alfaro Siqueiros (1945) © Instituto Nacional de Bellas Artes (INBA) – Sala de Arte Público Siqueiros 26ca, 72b; National Autonomous University of Mexico *The People for the University. The University for the People* Relief mosaic David Alfaro Siqueiros (1952–56) © Instituto Nacional de Bellas Artes (INBA) – Sala de Arte Público Siqueiros 26b.

The publisher would like to thank the following individuals, companies, and picture libraries for their kind permission to reproduce their photographs in this publication:
PABLO DE AGUINACO, Mexico: 15b, 21c, 31c, 31b, 32c, 34b, 34–35, 35t, 139c, 165ca, 225b; A.P. Giberstein 165ca, 247c; Carlos Puga 170cb, 179cb, 227b, 347b; AKG PHOTO, London: 48t; Erich Lessing 53t; ARDEA LONDON LTD: Piers Cavendish 19br; Wardene Weisser 19br. BANCO NACIONAL DE MEXICO SA: Fomento Cultural 43t; JOHN BRUNTON: 28t, 29cla, 218b, 219b, 255bl.

MICHAEL CALDERWOOD: 12, 216tl; DEMETRIO CARRASCO: 340bl, 341t, 341ca, 342t, 342c, 354b; BRUCE COLLEMAN COLLECTION: John Cancalosi 19bc; Michael Fogden 18tl; Jeff Foott Productions 18bl; S. Nielsen 18crb; Pacific Stock 217cl; John Shaw 18c.

MICHAEL DIGGIN: 33c, 92tr, 92c, 276br.

TOR EIGELAND: 20cb; EMBAJADA DE MEXICO, London: 29br.

LUIS FELIX © 1979: 195b; ROBERT FRIED PHOTOGRAPHY: 18br.

EVA MARIA GLEASON, Mexico: 64tl, 64tr, 64bl, 64br, 65b, 141t, 141b, 142t, 142ca, 142b, 143ca, 143b, 337b, 338ca, 338c, 339b, 340d, 341cb, 341b, 344d, 344ca, 344cb, 345c, 345b, 348d, 348c, 349c, 352t, 352bl, 355t, 357t; ANDREAS GROSS, Germany: 34tr, 171t, 261cra.

ROBERT HARDING PICTURE LIBRARY: Robert Freck/Odyssey 51ca, 51c; DAVE G. HAUSER: 164cr, 171c, 219c, 221b; John Elkins 128t; Susan Kaye Mosaic in Dolores Olmeda's house Diego Rivera © DACS, 1999 26tr, 218crb, 247b; HUTCHISON LIBRARY: 218t, 232b.

FOTOTECA DEL INAH FONDO CASASOLA: 50t, 50b; INDEX, Barcelona: 39b, 49b; Mithra *El Feudalismo Porfirista* Juan O'Gorman 53c.

JUSTIN KERR: 277crb.

DAVID LAVENDER: 29ca, 29cra, 34tl, 35cra, 35crb, 330–331, 330t, 330bl, 331br, 331bl, 331ca, all 332 except bl, all 333.

ENRICO MARTINO: 16t, 17c, 22c, 30c, 30b, 32t, 163c, 175t, 177b, 262ca; MEXICANA AIRLINES: 350t; JOSE LUIS MORENO: 283bl, 283bc.

JUAN NEGRIN: 20–21; NHPA: John Shaw 211b.

G. DAGLI ORTI: 46t, 233cra, 233cr; OXFORD SCIENTIFIC FILMS: N. Mitchel 246t.

PLANET EARTH PICTURES: Mary Clay 19crb; Beth Davidow 19cb; Brian Kenney 19clb; Ken Lucas 18clb; John Lythgoe 171cr, 216c; Claus Meyer 286ca; Nancy Sefton 19tr, 283cl; Doug White 19tl.

REX FEATURES: 55c, 349b; Sipa Press/L. Rieder 55b.

CHLOE SAYER: 14c, 20cla, 20b, 22cr, 22cra, 25b, 28bl, 28br, 29t, 29crb, 35bl, 330ca, 330br;

SEXTO SOL, Mexico: 18cra, 20t, 176t; EDN 34ca; Adalberto Rios Szalay 13t, 33b, 52c, 117t, 170t, 170b, 171bl, 179t, 184t, 225tr, 244–245, 349t, 350c, 350b; Adalberto Rios Lanz 32b; A.M.G. 16c, 346t; Ernesto Rios Lanz 18cla, 171cra; Bob Schalkwijk 21br, 27b, *La Familia* José Clemente Orozco (1926) © DACS, 1999 27b, 49t, *Padre Hidalgo* O'Gorman, 49c, *The Death of the Capitalist* Diego Rivera © DACS, 1999 54t, 95c; SIQUEIROS ARCHIVE: *Tropical America* and *Study Drawing for Tropical America* David Alfaro Siqueiros (1932) © Instituto Nacional de Bellas Artes (INBA) – Sala de Arte Público Siqueiros 26cl, 26clb; SOUTH AMERICAN PICTURES: Tony Morrison 221t; Chris Sharp 41t, 243t; HERI STIERLING: 47b, 233bc.

TERRAQUA: 283cr, 283br; TONY STONE IMAGES: 236t, Richard During 219t.

MIREILLE VAUTIER: 9 (inset), 14t, 20c, 21bl, 24tr, 29tl, 29b, 30t, 31t, 33t, 34cl, 35cla, 35c, 38, 40c, 42bl, 42br, 43c *The Conquest* O'Gorman 44t, 44b, 45tr, 51t, 52b, 54c, 54b, 55t, 57 (inset), *Daily Life in Tenochtitlán – The Market in Tlatelolco* Diego Rivera © DACS, 1999 63c; *Battle between the Aztecs and Tlaxcaltecs* Xochitiotzin 66c; *Daily Life in Tenochtitlán – The Market in Tlatelolco* Diego Rivera © DACS, 1999 67bl; 92tl, 93cb, 94b, 118t, 127 (inset), 162t, 162b, 185c, 235ca, 264b, 265clb, 277ca, 289 (inset), 329cla, 335 (inset), 346b.

WERNER FORMEN ARCHIVE: Museo Nacional de Antropología, Mexico 44ca; ELIZABETH WHITING ASSOCIATES: 23br, 50c; PETER WILSON: 16b, 126–127.

ALEJANDRO ZENTENO: 187b, 248c, 249t, 277b, 277b.

Front endpaper: All special photography.

JACKET Front - JAMES DAVIS TRAVEL PHOTOGRAPHY: main image; DK PICTURE LIBRARY: Linda Whitman c, bl; Peter Wilson bc. Back - DK PICTURE LIBRARY: Linda Whitman t br. Spine - JAMES DAVIS TRAVEL PHOTOGRAPHY.

All other images © Dorling Kindersley. For further information see: www.dkimages.com

DORLING KINDERSLEY SPECIAL EDITIONS

Dorling Kindersley books can be purchased in bulk quantities at discounted prices for use in promotions or as premiums. We are also able to offer special editions and personalized jackets, corporate imprints, and excerpts from all of our books, tailored specifically to meet your own needs.

To find out more, please contact: (in the United Kingdom) – Sarah.Burgess@dk.com or SPECIAL SALES, DORLING KINDERSLEY LIMITED, 80 STRAND, LONDON WC2R 0RL;

(in the United States) – SPECIAL MARKETS DEPARTMENT, DK PUBLISHING, INC., 375 HUDSON STREET, NEW YORK, NEW YORK 10014.

Phrase Book

MEXICAN SPANISH IS essentially the same as the Castilian spoken in Spain, although there are some differences in vocabulary and pronunciation.

The most noticeable are the use of *ustedes* (the plural version of "you") in both informal and formal situations, and the pronunciation of the soft "c" and the letter "z" as "s" rather than "th."

Mexicans use *carro* (instead of *coche*) for a car, and often call buses, as well as trucks, *camiones*. Words of indigenous origin are common. A word for market used only in Mexico is *tianguis*, for example, although *mercado* is also employed. Mexicans tend to be fairly formal, and it is good manners to use *usted* (rather than *tú*) for "you," unless you know the person well. Always say *buenos días* or *buenas tardes* when boarding a taxi, and address both taxi drivers and waiters as *señor*.

If you wish to decline goods from street vendors, a polite shake of the head and a *muchas gracias* will usually suffice. Adding *muy amable*, literally "very kind," will help to take the edge off the refusal. A term to be handled with care is *madre* (mother), as much bad language in Mexico is based on variants of this word. When referring to someone's mother, use *tu mama* (your mom), or the formal version *su señora madre*, just to be safe.

In an Emergency

Help!	¡Socorro!	soh-**koh**-roh
Stop!	¡Pare!	pah-reh
Call a doctor!	¡Llame a un médico!	yah-meh ah oon meh-dee-koh
Call an ambulance!	¡Llame una ambulancia!	yah-meh ah oonah ahm-boo-lahn-see-ah
Call the fire department!	¡Llame a los bomberos!	yah-meh ah lohs bohm-**beh**-rohs
Where is the nearest telephone?	¿Dónde está el teléfono más cercano?	dohn-deh ehs-tah ehl teh-leh-foh-noh mahs sehr-**kah**-noh
Where is the nearest hospital?	¿Dónde está el hospital más cercano?	dohn-deh ehs-tah ehl ohs-pee-tahl mahs sehr-**kah**-noh
policeman	el policía	ehl poh-lee-**see**-ah
Could you help me?	¿Me podría ayudar?	meh poh-**dree**-yah ah-yoo-dah
I've/we've been mugged	Me/nos asaltaron	meh/nohs ah-sahl-**tahr**-ohn
They stole my ...	Me robaron el/la...	meh roh-**bahr**-ohn ehl/lah

Communication Essentials

Yes	Sí	see
No	No	noh
Please	Por favor	pohr fah-**vohr**
Thank you	Gracias	**grah**-see-ahs
Excuse me	Perdone	pehr-doh-neh
Hello	Hola	oh-lah
Good morning	Buenos días	bweh-nohs dee-ahs
Good afternoon (from noon)	Buenas tardes	**bweh**-nahs tahr-dehs
Good night	Buenas noches	**bweh**-nahs noh-chehs
Bye (casual)	Chau	chau
Goodbye	Adiós	ah-dee-**ohs**
See you later	Hasta luego	ah-stah loo-**weh**-goh
Morning	La mañana	lah mah-**nyah**-nah
Afternoon/ early evening	La tarde	lah **tahr**-deh
Night	La noche	lah noh-cheh
Yesterday	Ayer	ah-**yehr**
Today	Hoy	oy
Tomorrow	Mañana	mah-**nyah**-nah
Here	Aquí	ah-**kee**
There	Allí	ah-**yee**
What?	¿Qué?	keh
When?	¿Cuándo?	kwahn-doh
Why?	¿Por qué?	pohr-**keh**
Where?	¿Dónde?	dohn-deh
How are you?	¿Cómo está usted?	koh-moh ehs-**tah** oos-tehd
Very well, thank you	Muy bien, gracias	mwee bee-**ehn grah**-see-ahs
Pleased to meet you	Mucho gusto	moo-choh goo-stoh
See you soon	Hasta pronto	ahs-tah **prohn**-toh
I'm sorry	Lo siento	loh see-**ehn**-toh

Useful Phrases

That's fine	Está bien	ehs-tah bee-**ehn**
Great/fantastic!	¡Qué bien!	keh bee-ehn
Where is/are ...?	¿Dónde está/están ...?	dohn-deh ehs-tah/ehs-tahn
How far is it to ...?	¿Cuántos metros/ kilómetros hay de aquí a ...?	**kwahn**-tohs meh-trohs/kee-loh-meh-trohs eye deh ah-**kee** ah
Which way is it to ...?	¿Por dónde se va a ...?	pohr **dohn**-deh seh vah ah
Do you speak English?	¿Habla inglés?	ah-blah een-**glehs**
I don't understand	No comprendo	noh kohm-**prehn**-doh
Could you speak more slowly, please?	¿Puede hablar más despacio, por favor?	pweh-deh ah-**blahr** mahs dehs-**pah**-see-oh pohr fah-**vohr**
I want	Quiero	kee-**yehr**-oh
I would like	Quisiera/ Me gustaría	kee-see-**yehr**-ah meh goo-stah-**ree**-ah
We want	Queremos	keh **reh** mohs
Do you have change (for 50 pesos)?	¿Tiene cambio (de cincuenta pesos)?	tee-**eh**-neh **kahm**-bee-yoh deh seen-**kwehn**-tah peh-sohs
(It's) very kind of you	Muy amable	mwee ah-**mah**-bleh
There is/there are	Hay	eye
Do you have/is there/are there?	¿Hay?	eye
Is there any water?	¿Hay agua?	eye ah-gwah
It's broken	Está roto/a	ehs-**tah** roh-toh/tah
Is it far/near?	¿Está lejos/cerca?	ehs-**tah leh**-hohs/**sehr**-kah
Take care/be careful!	¡Ten cuidado!	tehn koo-ee-**dah**-doh
We are late	Estamos atrasados	ehs-**tah**-mohs ah-trah-**sah**-dohs
We are early	Estamos adelantados	ehs-**tah**-mohs ah-deh-lahn-**tah**-dohs
OK, all right	De acuerdo	deh ah-**kwehr**-doh
Yes, of course	Claro que sí	**klah**-roh keh see
Of course!/with pleasure	¡Cómo no!/con mucho gusto	koh-moh noh/ kohn moo-choh goo-stoh
Let's go	Vámonos	**vah**-moh-nohs

Useful Words

big	grande	**grahn**-deh
small	pequeño/a	peh-keh-nyoh/nyah
hot	caliente	kah-lee-**ehn**-teh
cold	frío/a	free-oh/ah
good	bueno/a	**bweh**-noh/nah
bad	malo/a	**mah**-loh/lah
enough	suficiente	soo-fee-see-**ehn**-teh
well	bien	bee-**ehn**
open	abierto/a	ah bee **ehr**-toh/tah
closed	cerrado/a	sehr-**rah**-doh/dah
full	lleno/a	**yeh**-noh/nah

English	Spanish	Pronunciation
empty	vacío/a	vah-see-oh/ah
left	izquierda	ees-key-ehr-dah
right	derecha	deh-reh-chah
(keep) straight ahead	(siga) derecho	(see-gah) deh-reh-choh
near	cerca	sehr-kah
far	lejos	leh-hohs
up	arriba	ah-ree-bah
down	abajo	ah-bah-hoh
early	temprano	tehm-prah-noh
late	tarde	tahr-deh
now/very soon	ahora/ahorita	ah-ohr-ah/ah-ohr-ee-tah
more	más	mahs
less	menos	meh-nohs
very	muy	mwee
a little	(un) poco	oon poh-koh
very little	muy poco	mwee poh-koh
(much) more	(mucho) más	(moo-choh) mahs
too much	demasiado	deh-mah-see-ah-doh
too late	demasiado tarde	deh-mah-see-ah-doh tahr-deh
farther on/ahead	más adelante	mahs ah-deh-lahn-teh
farther back	más atras	mahs ah-trahs
opposite	frente a	frehn-teh ah
below/above	abajo/arriba	ah-bah-hoh/ah-ree-bah
first, second, third	primero/a segundo/a tercero/a	prec-meh-roh/ah seh-goon-doh/ah tehr-sehr-oh/ah
floor (of a building)	el piso	ehl pee-soh
ground floor	la planta baja	lah plahn-tah bah-hah
entrance	entrada	ehn-trah-dah
exit	salida	sah-lee-dah
elevator	el ascensor	ehl ah-sehn-sohr
toilets	baños/servicios sanitarios	bah-nyohs/sehr-vee-see-yohs sah-nee-tah-ree-ohs
women's	de damas	deh dah-mahs
men's	de caballeros	deh kah-bah-yeh-rohs
sanitary napkins	toallas sanitarias/ higiénicas	toh-ah-yahs sah-nee-tah-ree-yahs/hee-hyeh-nee-kahs
tampons	tampones	tahm-poh-nehs
condoms	condones	kohn-doh-nehs
toilet paper	papel higiénico	pah-pehl hee-hyen-ee-koh
(non-)smoking area	área de (no) fumar	ah-ree-ah deh (noh) foo-mahr
camera	la cámara	lah kah-mah-rah
(a roll of) film	(un rollo de) película	(oon roh-yoh deh) peh-lee-koo-lah
batteries	las pilas	lahs pee-lahs
passport	el pasaporte	ehl pah-sah-pohr-teh
visa	el visado	ehl vee-sah-doh

Health

I feel ill	Me siento mal	meh see-ehn-toh mahl
I have a headache	Me duele la cabeza	meh doo-eh-leh lah kah-beh-sah
I have a stomach-ache	Me duele el estómago	meh doo-eh-leh ehl ehs-toh-mah-goh
I need to rest	Necesito descansar	neh-seh-see-toh dehs-kahn-sahr
The child is/the children are sick	El niño está/los niños están enfermo(s)	ehl nee-nyoh ehs-tah/lohs nee-nyos ehs-tahn ehn-fehr-moh(s)
We need a doctor	Necesitamos un médico	neh-seh-see-tah-mohs oon meh-dee-koh
thermometer	el termómetro	ehl tehr-moh-meh-troh
drug store	la farmacia	lah fahr-mah-see-ah
medicine	la medicina/ el remédio	lah meh-dee-see-nah/ehl reh-meh-dee-oh

English	Spanish	Pronunciation
pills	las pastillas/ píldoras	lahs pahs-tee-yahs/ lahs peel-doh-rahs

Post Offices and Banks

Where can I change money?	¿Dónde puedo cambiar dinero?	dohn-deh pweh-doh kahm-bee-ahr dee-neh-roh
What is the dollar rate?	¿A cómo está el dolar?	ah koh-moh ehs-tah ehl doh-lahr
How much is the postage to...?	¿Cuánto cuesta enviar una carta a...?	kwahn-toh kweh-stah ehn-vee-yahr oo-nah kahr-tah ah
and for a postcard?	¿y una postal?	ee oo-nah pohs-tahl
I need stamps	Necesito estampillas	neh-seh-see-toh ehs-tahm-pee-yahs
cashier	cajero	kah-heh-roh
ATM	cajero automático	kah-heh-roh ahw-toh-mah-tee-koh
withdraw money	sacar dinero	sah-kahr dee-neh-roh

Shopping

How much does this cost?	¿Cuánto cuesta esto?	kwahn-toh kwehs-tah ehs-toh
I would like ...	Me gustaría ...	meh goos-tah-ree-ah
Do you have?	¿Tienen?	tee-yeh-nehn
I'm just looking, thank you	Sólo estoy mirando, gracias	soh-loh ehs-toy mee-rahn-doh grah-see-ahs
What time do you open?	¿A qué hora abren?	ah keh oh-rah ah-brehn
What time do you close?	¿A qué hora cierran?	ah keh oh-rah see-ehr-rahn
Do you take credit cards/ traveler's checks?	¿Aceptan tarjetas de crédito/ cheques de viajero?	ahk-sehp-tahn tahr-heh-tahs deh kreh-dee-toh/ cheh-kehs deh vee-ah-heh-roh
I am looking for...	Estoy buscando...	ehs-toy boos-kahn-doh
Is that your best price?	¿Es su mejor precio?	ehs soo meh-hohr preh-see-oh
discount	un descuento	oon dehs-koo-ehn-toh
clothes	la ropa	lah roh-pah
this one	éste	ehs-teh
that one	ése	eh-seh
expensive	caro	kahr-oh
cheap	barato	bah-rah-toh
size, clothes	talla	tah-yah
size, shoes	número	noo-mehr-oh
white	blanco	blahn-koh
black	negro	neh-groh
red	rojo	roh-hoh
yellow	amarillo	ah-mah-ree-yoh
green	verde	vehr-deh
blue	azul	ah-sool
antique store	la tienda de antigüedades	lah tee-ehn-dah deh ahn-tee-gweh-dah-dehs
bakery	la panadería	lah pah-nah-deh-ree-ah
bank	el banco	ehl bahn-koh
bookstore	la librería	lah lee-breh-ree-ah
butcher's	la carnicería	lah kahr-nee-seh-ree-ah
cake store	la pastelería	lah pahs-teh-leh-ree-ah
department store	la tienda de departamentos	lah tee-ehn-dah deh deh-pahr-tah-mehn-tohs
fish store	la pescadería	lah pehs-kah-deh-ree-ah
greengrocer's	la frutería	lah froo-teh-ree-ah
grocer's	la tienda de abarrotes	lah tee-yehn-dah deh ah-bah-roh-tehs
hairdresser's	la peluquería	lah peh-loo-keh-ree-ah

jeweler's	la joyería	lah hoh-yeh-ree-yah
market	el tianguis/ mercado	ehl tee-ahn-goo-ees/mehr-kah-doh
newsstand	el kiosko de prensa	ehl kee-ohs-koh deh prehn-sah
post office	la oficina de correos	lah oh-fee-see-nah deh kohr-reh-ohs
shoe store	la zapatería	lah sah-pah-teh-ree-ah
supermarket	el supermercado	ehl soo-pehr-mehr-kah-doh
travel agency	la agencia de viajes	lah ah-hehn-see-ah deh vee-ah-hehs

Sightseeing

art gallery	el museo de arte	ehl moo-seh-oh deh ahr-teh
beach	la playa	lah plah-yah
cathedral	la catedral	lah kah-teh-drahl
church	la iglesia/ la basílica	lah ee-gleh-see-ah/ lah bah-see-lee-kah
garden	el jardín	ehl hahr-deen
library	la biblioteca	lah bee-blee-oh-teh-kah
museum	el museo	ehl moo-seh-oh
pyramid	la pirámide	lah pee-rah-meed
ruins	las ruinas	lahs roo-ee-nahs
tourist information office	la oficina de turismo	lah oh-fee-see-nah deh too-rees moh
town hall	el palacio municipal	ehl pah-lah-see-oh moo-nee-see-pahl
closed for holidays	cerrado por vacaciones	sehr-rah-doh pohr vah-kah-see-oh-nehs
ticket	la entrada	lah ehn-trah-dah
how much is the entrance fee?	¿Cuánto vale la entrada?	kwahn-toh vah-leh lah ehn-trah-dah
guide (person)	el/la guía	ehl/lah gee-ah
guide (book)	la guía	lah gee-ah
guided tour	una visita guiada	oo-nah vee-see-tah gee-ah-dah
map	el mapa	ehl mah-pah
city map	el plano de la ciudad	ehl plah-noh deh lah see-oo-dahd

Transportation

When does the... leave?	¿A qué hora sale el. . .?	ah keh oh-rah sah-leh ehl
Where is the bus stop?	¿Dónde está la parada de buses?	dohn-deh ehs-tah lah pah-rah-dah deh boo-sehs
Is there a bus/train to...?	¿Hay un camion/ tren a. . .?	eye oon kah-mee-ohn/trehn ah
the next bus/train	el próximo camion/tren	ehl prohx-ee-moh kah-mee-ohn/trehn
bus station	el central camionera/ de autobuses	ehl sehn-trahl kah-mee-ohn-ehr-ah/deh aw-toh-boo-sehs
train station	la estación de trenes	lah ehs-tah-see-ohn deh treh-nehs
subway/metro	el metro	ehl meh-troh
platform	el andén	ehl ahn-dehn
ticket office	la taquilla	lah tah-kee-yah
round-trip ticket	un boleto de ida y vuelta	oon boh-leh-toh deh ee-dah ee voo-ehl-tah
one-way ticket	un boleto de ida solamente	oon boh-leh-toh deh ee-dah sol-lah-mehn-teh
airport	el aeropuerto	ehl ah-ehr-oh-poo-ehr-toh
customs	la aduana	lah ah-doo-ah-nah
departure lounge	sala de embarque	sah-lah deh ehm-bahr-keh

boarding pass	pase de abordar	pah-seh deh ah-bohr-dahr
taxi stand/rank	sitio de taxis	see-tee-oh deh tahk-sees
car rental	renta de automóviles	rehn-tah deh aw-toh-moh-vee-lehs
motorcycle	la moto(cicleta)	lah moh-toh(see-kleh-tah)
mileage	el kilometraje	ehl kee-loh-meh-trah-he
bicycle	la bicicleta	lah bee-see-kleh-tah
daily/weekly rate	la tarifa diaria/ semanal	lah tah-ree-fah dee-ah-ree-ah/ seh-mah-nahl
insurance	los seguros	lohs seh-goo-rohs
gas station	la gasolinera	lah gah-soh-leen ehr-ah
garage	el taller de mecánica	ehl tah-yehr deh meh-kahn-ee-kah
I have a flat tire	Se me ponchó la llanta	seh meh pohn-shoh lah yahn-tah

Staying in a Hotel

Do you have a vacant room?	¿Tienen una habitación libre?	tee-eh-nehn oo-nah ah-bee-tah-see-ohn lee-breh
double room	habitación doble	ah-bee-tah-see-ohn doh-bleh
with a double bed	con cama matrimonial	kohn kah-mah mah-tree-moh-nee-ahl
twin room	habitación con dos camas	ah-bee-tah-see-ohn kohn dohs kah-mahs
single room	habitación sencilla	ah-bee-tah-see-ohn sehn-see-yah
room with a bath	habitación con baño	ah-bee-tah-see-ohn kohn bah-nyoh
shower	la ducha	lah doo-chah
Do you have a room with a view (of the sea)?	¿Hay alguna habitación con vista (al mar)?	eye ahl-goo-nah ah-bee-tah-see-ohn kohn vees-tah (ahl mahr)
I have a reservation	Tengo una habitación reservada	tehn-goh oo-nah ah-bee-tah-see-ohn reh-sehr-vah-dah
The . . . is not working	No funciona el/la. . .	noh foon-see-oh-nah ehl/lah
I need a wake-up call at . . . o'clock	Necesito que me despierten a las . . .	neh-seh-see-toh keh meh dehs-pee-ehr-tehn ah lahs
Where is the dining-room/bar?	¿Dónde está el restaurante/ el bar?	dohn-deh ehs-tah ehl rehs-toh-rahn-teh/ehl bahr
hot/cold water	agua caliente/ fría	ah-goo-ah kah-lee-ehn-teh/ free-ah
soap	el jabón	ehl hah-bohn
towel	la toalla	lah toh-ah-yah
key	la llave	lah yah-veh

Eating Out

Have you got a table for . . .	¿Tienen mesa para . . .?	tee-eh-nehn meh-sah pah-rah
I want to reserve a table	Quiero reservar una mesa	kee-eh-roh reh-sehr-vahr oo-nah meh-sah
The bill, please	La cuenta, por favor	lah kwehn-tah pohr fah-vohr
I am a vegetarian	Soy vegetariano/a	soy veh-heh-tah-ree ah no/na
waiter/waitress	mesero/a	meh-seh-roh/rah
menu	la carta	lah kahr-tah
fixed-price menu	menú del día/comida corrida	meh-noo dehl dee-ah/koh-mee-dah koh-ree-dah
wine list	la carta de vinos	lah kahr-tah deh vee-nohs
glass	un vaso	oon vah-soh

bottle	una botella	oo-nah boh-**teh**-yah
knife	un cuchillo	oon koo-**chee**-yoh
fork	un tenedor	oon teh-neh-**dohr**
spoon	una cuchara	oo-nah koo-**chah**-rah
breakfast	el desayuno	ehl deh-sah-**yoo**-noh
lunch	la comida	lah koh-**mee**-dah
dinner	la cena	lah **seh**-nah
main course	el plato fuerte	ehl **plah**-toh foo-**ehr**-teh
starters	las entradas	lahs ehn-**trah**-das
dish of the day	el plato del día	ehl **plah**-toh dehl **dee**-ah
rare	termino rojo	**tehr**-mee-noh **roh**-hoh
medium	termino medio	**tehr**-mee-noh **meh**-dee-oh
well done	bien cocido	bee-**ehn** koh-**see**-doh
Could you heat it up for me?	¿Me lo podría calentar?	meh loh pohd-**ree**-ah kah-lehn-**tahr**
chair	la silla	lah **see**-yah
napkin	la servilleta	lah sehr-vee-**yeh**-tah
tip	la propina	lah proh-**pee**-nah
Is service included?	¿El servicio está incluido?	ehl sehr-**vee**-see-oh ehs-**tah** een-kloo-**ee**-doh
Do you have a light?	¿Tiene fuego?	tee-**eh**-nee foo-**eh**-goh
ashtray	cenicero	seh-nee-**seh**-roh
cigarettes	los cigarros	lohs see-**gah**-rohs

Menu Decoder *(see also pp308–13)*

el aceite	ah-**see**-eh-teh	oil
las aceitunas	ah-seh-**toon**-ahs	olives
el agua mineral	**ah**-gwa mee-neh-**rahl**	mineral water
sin gas/con gas	seen gas/kohn gas	still/sparkling
el ajo	**ah**-hoh	garlic
el arroz	ahr-**rohs**	rice
el azúcar	ah-**soo**-kahr	sugar
la banana	bah-**nah**-nah	banana
una bebida	beh-**bee**-dah	drink
el café	kah-**feh**	coffee
la carne	**kahr**-neh	meat
la cebolla	seh-**boh**-yah	onion
la cerveza	sehr-**veh**-sah	beer
el cerdo	**sehr**-doh	pork
el chocolate	choh-koh-**lah**-teh	chocolate
la ensalada	ehn-sah-**lah**-dah	salad
la fruta	**froo**-tah	fruit
el helado	eh-**lah**-doh	ice cream
el huevo	oo-**eh**-voh	egg
el jugo	ehl **hoo**-goh	juice
la langosta	lahn-**gohs**-tah	lobster
la leche	**leh**-cheh	milk
la mantequilla	mahn-teh-**kee**-yah	butter
la manzana	mahn-**sah**-nah	apple
los mariscos	mah-**rees**-kohs	seafood
la naranja	nah-**rahn**-hah	orange
el pan	**pahn**	bread
las papas	**pah**-pahs	potatoes
las papas a la francesa	**pah**-pahs ah lah frahn-**seh**-sah	French fries
las papas fritas	**pah**-pahs **free**-tahs	potato chips
el pastel	pahs-**tehl**	cake
el pescado	pehs-**kah**-doh	fish
picante	pee-**kahn**-teh	spicy
la pimienta	pee-mee-**yehn**-tah	pepper
el pollo	**poh**-yoh	chicken
el postre	**pohs**-treh	dessert
el queso	**keh**-soh	cheese
el refresco	rch-**frehs**-koh	soft drink/soda
la sal	**sahl**	salt
la salsa	**sahl**-sah	sauce
la sopa	**soh**-pah	soup
el té	teh	herb tea (usually camomile)
el té negro	teh neh-groh	tea
la torta	**tohr**-tah	sandwich
las tostadas	tohs-**tah**-dahs	toast
el vinagre	vee-**nah**-greh	vinegar
el vino blanco	**vee**-noh **blahn**-koh	white wine
el vino tinto	**vee**-noh teen-toh	red wine

Numbers

0	cero	**seh**-roh
1	uno	**oo**-noh
2	dos	dohs
3	tres	trehs
4	cuatro	**kwa**-troh
5	cinco	**seen**-koh
6	seis	says
7	siete	**see**-eh-teh
8	ocho	**oh**-choh
9	nueve	**nweh**-veh
10	diez	dee-**ehs**
11	once	**ohn**-seh
12	doce	**doh**-seh
13	trece	**treh**-seh
14	catorce	kah-**tohr**-seh
15	quince	**keen**-seh
16	dieciséis	dee-eh-see-**seh**-ees
17	diecisiete	dee-eh-see-see-**eh**-teh
18	dieciocho	dee-eh-see-**oh**-choh
19	diecinueve	dee-eh-see-**nweh**-veh
20	veinte	**veh**-een-teh
21	veintiuno	veh-een-tee-**oo**-noh
22	veintidós	veh-een-tee-**dohs**
30	treinta	**treh**-een-tah
31	treinta y uno	treh-een-tah ee **oo**-noh
40	cuarenta	kwah-**rehn**-tah
50	cincuenta	seen-**kwehn**-tah
60	sesenta	seh-**sehn**-tah
70	setenta	seh-**tehn**-tah
80	ochenta	oh-**chehn**-tah
90	noventa	noh-**vehn**-tah
100	cien	see-**ehn**
101	ciento uno	see-**ehn**-toh **oo**-noh
102	ciento dos	see-**ehn**-toh dohs
200	doscientos	dohs-see-**ehn**- tohs
500	quinientos	khee-nee-**ehn**-tohs
700	setecientos	seh-teh-see-**ehn**-tohs
900	novecientos	noh-veh-see-**ehn**-tohs
1,000	mil	meel
1,001	mil uno	meel **oo**-noh

Time

one minute	un minuto	oon mee-**noo**-toh
one hour	una hora	oo-nah **oh**-rah
half an hour	media hora	**meh**-dee-ah **oh**-rah
half past one	la una y media	lah oo-nah ee **meh**-dee-ah
quarter past one	la una y cuarto	lah oo-nah ee **kwahr**-toh
ten past one	la una y diez	lah oo-nah ee dee **ehs**
quarter to two	un cuarto para las dos	oon **kwahr**-toh pah-rah lahs **dohs**
ten to two	diez para las dos	dee-**ehs** pah-rah lahs **dohs**
Monday	lunes	**loo**-nehs
Tuesday	martes	**mahr**-tehs
Wednesday	miércoles	mee-**ehr**-koh-lehs
Thursday	jueves	hoo-**weh**-vehs
Friday	viernes	vee-**ehr**-nehs
Saturday	sábado	**sah**-bah-doh
Sunday	domingo	doh-**meen**-goh
January	enero	eh-**neh**-roh
February	febrero	feh-**breh**-roh
March	marzo	**mahr**-soh
April	abril	ah-**breel**
May	mayo	**mah**-yoh
June	junio	**hoo**-nee-oh
July	julio	**hoo**-lee-oh
August	agosto	ah-**gohs**-toh
September	septiembre	sehp-tee-**ehm**-breh
October	octubre	ohk-**too**-breh
November	noviembre	noh-vee-**ehm**-breh
December	diciembre	dee-see-**ehm**-breh
Two days ago	Hace dos días	**hah**-seh dohs dee-ahs
In two day's time	En dos días	ehn dohs dee-ahs
May 1	El primero de mayo	ehl pree-**meh**-roh deh **mah**-yoh

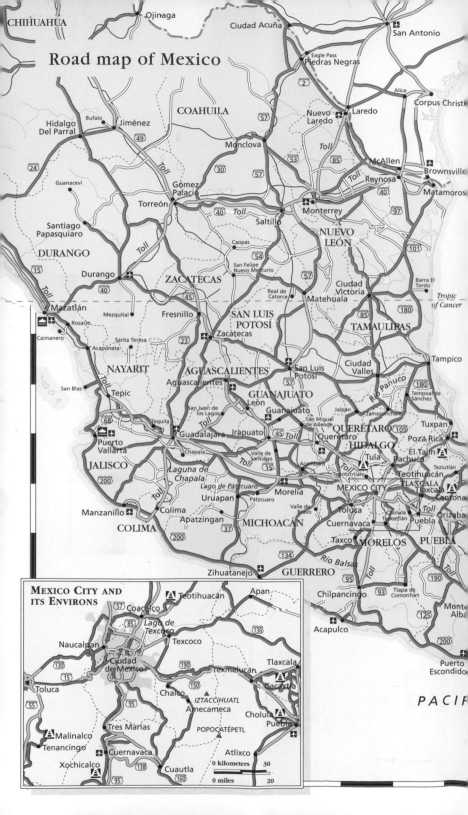